Marketing Research

MEANING, MEASUREMENT, AND METHOD

Donald S. Tull
Del I. Hawkins

University of Oregon

RESEARCH

Meaning,
Measurement,
and Method

A TEXT WITH CASES

Macmillan Publishing Co., Inc.

New York

COLLIER MACMILLAN PUBLISHERS

London

To Marge, Susan, David, and Brooks
and Lu-Nita, Jim, Cheri, and Sheila

Copyright © 1976, Macmillan Publishing Co., Inc.

Printed in the United States of America

Macmillan Publishing Co., Inc.
866 Third Avenue, New York, New York 10022

Collier Macmillan Canada, Ltd.

Library of Congress Cataloging in Publication Data
Tull, Donald S
  Marketing research.

  Includes bibliographies and indexes.
  1. Marketing research. I. Hawkins, Del I.,
joint author. II. Title.
HF5415.2.T83   658.8'35   75–17570
ISBN 0–02–421740–9

Printing: 3 4 5 6 7 8   Year: 7 8 9 0 1 2

Preface

This is an introductory text in marketing research. As such, it is primarily concerned with *decisional* research rather than *basic* research. Decisional research is done to provide information for a pending decision. Basic research is done primarily to advance the level of scientific knowledge.

A "good" decisional research project results in helping to make the best decision that can be made at the least cost of making it. A "good" basic research project results in the best estimate that can be made or the best hypothesis test that can be run. These differing objectives result in differing ways of deriving *meaning,* applying *methods,* and making *measurements* in the two types of research.

This book is concerned with the doing of "good" decisional research, specifically "good" marketing research. The competently conducted marketing research project provides information to help identify, structure, and solve a marketing problem. The information it provides will have *meaning* to the manager who is to use it so that it will be relevant to his perception of the problem and will have the required level of accuracy.

It will have been obtained by using the *methods* and making the *measurements* appropriate for the problem. The project will have been designed in such a way that the information will be *worth more than it costs* to obtain and will be provided at the *time* it is needed.

As those who have some acquaintance with decisional research projects are aware, meeting these requirements is not easy. The problems of proper design and sound implementation in basic research are serious ones; they are compounded in decisional research by the insistent constraints of time and of the economics of information acquisition.

In this text we have attempted to deal with these problems as clearly and directly as possible. Our continuing concern has been the illustration of the concepts and techniques discussed by the use of actual examples. Students, whether they are users or doers of research, are better motivated and taught when they can see how a concept is applied or learn how a technique is used in actual situations.

Regardless of the degree of clarity and directness we may have achieved in this book, our task was made much easier by the many people who helped us. Susan Beyerlein and Francis Pickett typed the original drafts of the manuscript with patience and competence. Mary Beth Corrigan typed the revised drafts with what she asserts was little patience but nonetheless with care.

Gerald Albaum of the University of Oregon, Gary Ford of the University of Maryland, and Donald Morrison of Columbia University read and made many suggestions for improving the manuscript.

Many individuals and firms contributed cases or materials for use in cases and examples. A special debt is owed those students who utilized earlier versions of the manuscript and whose comments have helped shape this version.

We are indebted to all, but they are to be absolved from any errors of omission or commission that remain.

Eugene, Oregon

D. S. T.
D. I. H.

Contents

13. Analysis of Data: Data Reduction   477

14. Analysis of Data: Statistical Techniques   507

15. Demand Analysis   552

16. Forecasting   608

List of Cases

Marketing Research and Decision Making

Effective marketing decisions are based on sound information; this is true whether the decision is by a consumer on which brand and model to buy or by a marketer on the number and characteristics of the models to be offered. These judgments can be no better than the information on which they are based.

Consider some of the decisions that had to be made concerning the introduction of the SX 70 Camera, a pocket-sized camera developed by the Polaroid Company that takes conventional sized, self-processing pictures in color:

Should the camera be introduced?

Should there be more than one model? If so, what different features should each model have?

Should the profit from the new model(s) be derived primarily from the camera, the film, or both?

What should the suggested retail prices be for the camera and the film?

What discounts should be given to dealers?

Through what channels should the camera be marketed? Should different channels be used for the film?

What should the advertising budget be for the introductory period?

To what media and in what amounts should the advertising budget be allocated?

What warrantee should be made?

In each of these decisions it was necessary to predict what people outside the company—consumers, retailers, competitors—would do in response to each alternative being considered. This is a distinguishing characteristic of marketing decisions; information to help predict the behavioral response of those affected by the decision being made is always necessary when a marketing problem is involved.

The acquisition of information for making decisions about the marketing of products and services is our principal concern in this book. We are concerned with both the *economics* and the *methodology* of acquiring information for solving marketing problems.

In this chapter the nature and interrelationships of managing, decision making, and research in marketing are examined. The chapter begins with a discussion of the *role of marketing research* in marketing management. The nature of *decision making* is examined and the steps involved are discussed in the context of an actual problem situation. The relationship of *marketing research and marketing information systems* is then considered. The chapter concludes with a discussion of the *organization of the research function*.

Role of Research in Marketing Management

Management is usually defined in terms of the functions performed; management *is* what management *does*. A widely accepted listing of management functions includes *planning, organizing, staffing, directing,* and *controlling.*[1]

Decision making, although not the only activity involved in the performance of any one of these activities, is basic to all of them. Decision making underlies and permeates the management process at every level. This interrelationship is so pervasive that we use the terms *managing* and *decision making* as if they were synonymous.[2] *Marketing management,* then, *is the process of making decisions with respect to marketing problems.*

---

[1] See, for example, H. Koontz and C. O'Donnell, *Principles of Management,* 5th ed. (New York: McGraw-Hill Book Company, 1972), 46.

[2] H. A. Simon, *The New Science of Management Decision* (New York: Harper & Row, Publishers, Inc., 1960) uses this same approach to defining management.

Marketing research has an advisory role in marketing management. It is used to acquire and analyze information and to make recommendations to management as to how marketing problems should be solved. An appropriate definition of *marketing research,* therefore, is that it *is a formalized means of obtaining information to be used in making marketing decisions.* This statement effectively summarizes the role of marketing research in marketing management.

Information and Decision Making

The decision-making process in marketing is essentially the same as it is in any other area of human affairs. The management of the Polaroid Company had to go through the same general steps in deciding to develop and introduce the SX 70 Camera, as did Congress in voting the latest tax increase or the Metropolitan Museum of Art in deciding to hold an exhibition of the paintings of Vincent van Gogh. A decision by a customer to buy the SX 70 after it was introduced also required the same general sequence of steps, although they were probably carried out in a less formal manner. In each case it was necessary for those involved in making the decision to: (1) *establish objectives,* (2) *measure performance to determine when objectives were not being met* (and thus identify problems), (3) *select the problem to solve,* (4) *develop alternatives,* (5) *choose the best alternative,* and (6) *implement the solution.* These steps, which are illustrated in Figure 1–1, can be summarized under the headings of *problem identification, problem selection,* and *problem solution.*

Problem Identification Research

Problems are identified when (1) objectives are established and (2) a measurement of performance indicates that the objectives are not being met. Situations in which actual market share is less than the targeted share, sales are below the level forecast, or expenses are over the amount budgeted are all examples of performance being below the objective. For example, a long-range forecast of sales may have led to the development of the SX 70 by indicating that the level of Polaroid's sales would be less than desired unless the company developed and successfully introduced new products during the period covered by the forecast.

Marketing research, if it is used properly, is involved in both the setting of objectives and the measuring of performance. The basic objectives that fall within the responsibility of the marketing department are attaining a

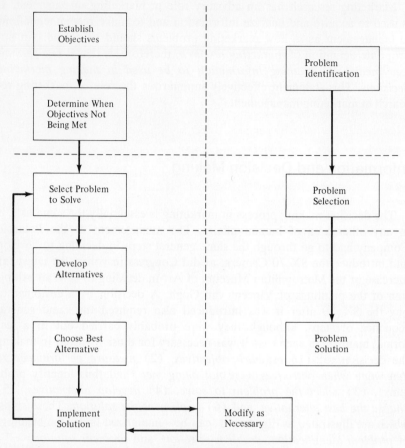

Figure 1–1   Steps in the decision-making process.

specified *share of the market* while controlling expenditures so as not to exceed a *marketing budget*. Other objectives may be used by the firm that are partially dependent upon these objectives; level of sales and net profit are two prominent examples.

Neither the market share that marketing is expected to produce nor the budget allocated for producing that share can be specified on other than an arbitrary basis unless information is available on the markets served by the company and its competitors. Boyd and Britt have listed the following types of information as being necessary to establish sales objectives:

1. *the generic wants/needs the firm wishes to satisfy;*
2. *the competing products or services, both present and potential, for these same uses;*
3. *the segments of the market that exist both presently and potentially;*
4. *the target segments of the firm;*

5. *an estimate of the size of each of these target market segments;*
6. *an estimate of the share of sales by segment that the firm can capture over a stated period of time at a given expenditure for promotion and distribution.*[3]

The other half of the problem identification process is the measurement of performance. A set of specific objectives for market share in each of several market segments is of no real value unless the actual market share in each segment can be ascertained. Marketing research is needed to determine industry sales by segment (and sometimes for sales of the firm by segment as well) so that market share can be determined.

Table 1–1 Problem Identification Research Conducted by Companies

Type of Research	Per Cent of Companies Doing	Per Cent Done by Marketing Research Department	Per Cent Done by Other Departments	Per Cent Done by Outside Firms
Market Potential	68	60*	8*	6*
Market Share	67	58	9	5
Market Characteristics	68	61	6	6
Sales Analysis	65	46	23	2
Short-range Forecasting	63	45	23	1
Long-range Forecasting	61	43	22	2
Studies of Business Trends	61	46	16	3

* The total of the percentages "done by market research department," "done by other departments," "done by outside firm" is greater than "per cent of companies doing" because some firms have studies done by both inside departments and outside firms.
Source: D. W. Twedt, *A Survey of Marketing Research* (Chicago: American Marketing Association, 1973), 41.

The extent to which companies with marketing research departments conduct problem identification research is indicated by Table 1–1. Over two-thirds of all companies conduct studies of *market potential* and *market characteristics* to help identify opportunities and set objectives; about 60 per cent of all companies have these studies conducted by their marketing research departments. About two-thirds of all companies also have *market share* studies and *sales analyses* conducted; the percentage of companies in which these studies are performed by the marketing research department is 61 and 45 per cent, respectively. (Accounting departments and outside accounting firms are frequently used sources for sales analyses.) About

[3] Adapted from H. W. Boyd, Jr., and S. H. Britt, "Making Marketing Research More Effective by Using the Administrative Process," *Journal of Marketing Research,* **2** (February 1965), 13–19.

60 per cent of the companies are engaged in short-term and long-term forecasting, and in studies of business trends. About 45 per cent of all companies have such studies performed by their marketing research departments.

The discussion of the role of marketing research in identifying problems would be incomplete without reference to a recent, but important, development in this area. An increasing number of companies are doing research in the area of "corporate responsibility." About one company in four has conducted studies in such areas as "consumer right to know," ecological impact, legal constraints of advertising and promotion, and social values and policies. Although many of these studies are done by legal departments and some are done by outside firms, about 10 per cent of all companies have such studies done by their marketing research departments.[4]

Problem Selection

The usual situation facing the management of a company is that there is a backlog of problems that need attention. Since too many problems have been identified to solve at once, priorities must be assigned. Continuing decisions must be made about which problems should receive attention now and which should be set aside for later consideration.

Two considerations are important in assigning these priorities. The first is the *estimated cost of delay*. A decision concerning the opening of a new sales office may be put aside temporarily in order to give attention to a potential price change and an increase in the promotional budget, for example, if the estimated cost of delaying the pricing and promotional budget decisions is greater than that for the sales office.

A second consideration is the *expected value of additional information*. Decisions should be delayed so that additional information can be obtained in those cases where the expected value of additional information is greater than the estimated cost of acquiring the information. The cost of acquisition of information must include the costs of delay as well. If it is expected that it will cost the firm X dollars to delay a decision while additional information is being obtained and Y dollars to obtain this information, the total cost relevant to the decision of whether or not to get the information is $X + Y$ dollars.

The question of the value of additional information is, of course, central to the question of whether or not a marketing research project should be conducted. This question is examined in detail in Chapter 3.

---

[4] D. W. Twedt, *A Survey of Marketing Research* (Chicago: American Marketing Association, 1973), 41.

Problem Solution

In order for there to be a problem, there must be at least *two or more actions that could be taken and doubt as to which is the best one to take.* If there is only one possible action, it is obvious that no decision is needed. Similarly, if there are several possible solutions but there is no doubt as to which is the best, no decision is required. Problem solution, then, consists of two separable steps: (1) *developing alternatives to meet objectives,* and (2) *evaluating these alternatives in terms of the objective(s).*

Developing Alternatives to Meet Objectives. The development of alternatives is the aspect of decision making that, if done well, requires invention and innovation. The creativity of the problem solver is called upon to suggest possible solutions that have not been tried before. The need to change and revitalize an ailing product line, for example, requires both a sound understanding of the situation and an open, inventive approach to its solution if a comprehensive set of viable alternatives is to be developed.

It is apparent that the development of alternatives is a highly important part of decision making. The solution can be no better than the best of the alternatives being considered. Even the worst of a superior set of alternatives can be better than the best of an inferior set.

Experience suggests, and the available evidence tends to confirm, that marketing research has generally performed well in the area of developing alternatives that had not previously been considered. After examining some 300 applications of research in a large number of companies, one investigator has concluded that:

Research focuses attention on possible actions that probably would not have been recognized in the absence of research. . . . The very discipline of objective recording of data forces people to look at things they would never have looked at otherwise and to question assumptions that would not otherwise have been challenged. . . .[5]

Evaluating Alternatives in Terms of the Objectives. Reference was made earlier to the recent trend toward having marketing research departments conduct studies in the area of the social responsibilities of the corporation. Although this is a development that is to be encouraged, marketing research is still used primarily to help solve problems that are concerned with the profitability of the firm. An economic choice among alternatives is based upon some form of measurement of the net cash flows that each alternative is expected to generate. This measurement may be expressed in many ways: *anticipated profit, return on investment, internal rate of return,*

[5] H. V. Roberts, "The Role of Research in Marketing Management," *The Journal of Marketing,* **22** (July 1957), 29.

and *discounted cash flow* are some commonly used forms of measuring the economic consequences of alternatives.

Perhaps the simplest and most direct of these measurements is *discounted cash flow*. It is a measurement of the present value of the cash flows anticipated over the planning period if the alternative being evaluated is accepted. Defined more technically, *cash flow* is the sum of the present values of the forecast cash flows for each period in the future considered in evaluating the alternative.

As an illustration, suppose a publisher is considering putting out a new edition of a successful textbook this year instead of waiting until next year as had originally been scheduled. A forecast of revenues and expenditures for each year of a five-year planning period might yield the following net cash flow estimates:

	Net Cash Flows	
Year	*New Edition This Year*	*New Edition Next Year*
1	<$ 20,000>	$ 25,000
2	35,000	<20,000>
3	50,000	35,000
4	35,000	50,000
5	25,000	35,000
Total	$125,000	$125,000

< > denotes outlays greater than receipts.

Which alternative should be chosen?

It is not immediately obvious which alternative is better. A discounted cash flow analysis at, say, a 15 per cent annual rate, however, yields the following results:

	New Edition This Year		*New Edition Next Year*	
Year	*Net Cash Flows*	*Discounted Cash Flows*	*Net Cash Flows*	*Discounted Cash Flows*
1	<$ 20,000>	<$17,400>	$ 25,000	$21,750
2	35,000	26,460	<20,000>	<15,120>
3	50,000	32,900	35,000	23,030
4	35,000	20,020	50,000	28,600
5	25,000	12,425	35,000	17,395
Totals	$125,000	$74,405	$125,000	$75,655

Given that five years is the appropriate planning period (the average length of time between revisions of successful textbooks is approximately five years), and 15 per cent is the discount rate that should be used, we see that putting out the new edition next year gives a higher discounted cash flow than if it were published this year. From an economic standpoint then, publishing it next year is the better of the two alternatives.

Discounted cash flow is often referred to as *payoff* and that practice is followed here. The formula for calculating the payoff of an alternative is

$$\text{discounted cash flow} = \frac{R_1 - O_1}{1 + r} + \frac{R_2 - O_2}{(1 + r)^2} \cdots + \frac{R_n - O_n}{(1 + r)^n}$$

$$= \sum_{t=1}^{n} \frac{(R_t - O_t)}{(1 + r)^t}$$

where

R_t = revenues during period t
O_t = outlays during period t
r = the discount rate.

The discount rate r will ordinarily be equal to the return on capital that the firm can obtain, on the average, from other uses. If the publishing company has a backlog of books to be published on which a return of 20 per cent is expected, for example, r should be set at .20 rather than .15.[6]

A table of present values that eliminates much of the tedium of calculating payoffs is given in Appendix C.

Extent of Problem-Solving Research Conducted. Problems in marketing are related to choosing the right *products* and the appropriate levels of *price* and *promotion,* and selecting and maintaining the right *distribution channels.* Table 1–2 provides an indication of the extent to which problem-solving research is conducted by companies, marketing research departments, other departments, and outside firms.

Marketing Research and Marketing Information Systems

The discussion of the role of marketing research thus far has concentrated on research as consisting of individual projects. Research can also be conducted on a continuing basis as a part of a *marketing information system* (MIS).

An example is a system of collecting and using information for pricing that was developed by a large food chain.[7] The company carries between

---

[6] For a more complete discussion of the question of what discount rate should be used see J. C. Van Horne, *Financial Management and Policy* (Englewood Cliffs, N.J.: Prentice-Hall, Inc., 1971), 65–70.

[7] Reported in J. Cardwell, "Marketing and Management Science: A Marriage on the Rocks?," *Marketing Insights* (January 20, 1969), 12–17.

Table 1–2   Research for Solving Marketing Problems

	Per Cent of Com- panies Doing	Per Cent Done by Marketing Research Depart- ment	Per Cent Done by Other Depart- ments	Per Cent Done by Outside Firms
Product Research				
Competitive product studies	64	52*	11*	6*
New product acceptance and potential	63	51	9	8
Testing of existing products	57	35	20	7
Product mix studies	51	36	16	2
Packaging research	44	23	17	9
Pricing Research	56	33	25	2
Promotion Research				
Studies of ad effectiveness	49	26	7	21
Media research	44	16	10	21
Promotional studies of premiums, coupons, sampling, deals, etc.	39	25	13	6
Copy research	37	17	6	18
Distribution Research				
Distribution channel studies	48	30	19	3
Plant and warehouse location	47	18	28	3

* The total of the percentages "done by market research department," "done by other departments," "done by outside firm" is greater than "per cent of companies doing" because some firms have studies done by both inside departments and outside firms.
Source: D. W. Twedt, *A Survey of Marketing Research* (Chicago: American Marketing Association, 1973), 41.

6,500 and 7,000 items, and it found that supplier cost changes and competitor price changes were so frequent that a weekly review of its own prices was necessary if it were to remain competitive and still be profitable. It was clear that a system would have to be developed for obtaining and processing the large amounts of information needed for reviewing prices and making changes where necessary.

A listing was made of the cost and demand factors bearing on price including manufacturer's cost, handling and selling costs, competitor prices, and movement of the product. A set of rules was then developed for setting prices in each product category. An example is "Nationally branded canned peas must generate a gross profit of 25 per cent, provided the resulting retail price does not exceed the average price of the three competitors with the lowest prices." A set of exception criteria were also developed to ensure that the pricing rules would not result in changes in price beyond an acceptable range. An example of one such criterion is "single out for judgmental review items on which the computed price reduced movement by 5 per cent or more during the previous period."

Information on competitors' prices is collected each week (by shoppers hired by the company) and fed into the computer. Changes in supplier costs and movement of each product during the prior week are also computerized. The computer generates a set of suggested prices and exceptions for review by buyers and those responsible for pricing. New prices are set and the cycle is repeated the next week.

This system deals with pricing and has not yet been extended to provide information for decisions on what products to carry, how much and in what media to advertise, where to locate supermarkets, and other marketing problems. Much has been written about the desirability of an overall marketing information system as an orderly means of *collecting, storing, analyzing,* and *providing information on call* to marketing managers.[8] The actual development and use of such systems has been limited to a relatively small percentage of the larger companies. A survey in 1972 of the *Fortune* 500 companies resulted in 193 responses of which 75 reported that their company had an operational MIS, 74 indicated that such a system was under development, and 44 stated that development of an MIS had not begun.[9]

Marketing research and marketing information systems are closely interrelated and complementary. Marketing research is a necessary part of the development of an MIS with respect to (1) the *specification of the information required* (if the food chain system were extended to include advertising, for example, it would be necessary to specify what information was needed to decide the size of the advertising budget, its allocation among media, and how effective the advertising program is), (2) the *determination of the relationship of the variables involved* (how does readership of an advertisement relate to sales, over what range is this relationship reasonably linear, and so on) and (3) *the collection of the data required* (what was the average readership of last month's Thursday advertisements, how much of a differential increase was there in sales of advertised versus unadvertised items, and so on).

---

[8] See for example, P. Kotler, "A Decision for the Firm's Marketing Nerve Center," *Business Horizons* (Fall 1966), 63–74; D. B. Montgomery and G. L. Urban, "Marketing Information Systems: An Emerging View," *Journal of Marketing Research* (May 1970), 226–234; R. H. Brien and J. E. Stafford, "Marketing Information Systems: A New Direction for Marketing Research," *Journal of Marketing* (July 1970), 19–23; K. K. Cox and B. M. Enis, *The Marketing Research Process* (Pacific Palisades, Calif.: Goodyear Publishing Company, Inc., 1972), Chaps. 1 and 14; and R. R. Andrus, *Marketing Information: Concepts and Perspectives* (Abo, Sweden: Abo Swedish University, School of Economics, 1974).

[9] L. E. Boone and D. L. Kurtz, "Marketing Information Systems: Current Status in American Marketing," in F. C. Allvine, ed., *Marketing in Motion/Relevance in Marketing* (Chicago: American Marketing Association, 1972), 163–167.

Individual marketing research projects are also required after the MIS is developed. A system cannot be designed to be omniscient and, even if it were, would undoubtedly be too expensive to make it worthwhile to keep it in operation. Marketing research projects are needed both to complement and to extend the information provided by the MIS.

Organization of the Marketing Research Function

The location of the marketing research function in the organization and the extent to which it is staffed varies from firm to firm. Some firms do all of their own research whereas others depend heavily upon their advertising agency, marketing research firms, and independent consultants. Some companies have only a single marketing research department that is responsible for all research projects conducted, whereas others have decentralized the research responsibilities such that sales and distribution cost analyses are conducted by the accounting department, advertising research by the advertising department, forecasting by the staff of the chief executive, and the remaining areas requiring research (studies of market potential, market share, market characteristics, salesmen's effectiveness, sales quotas, distribution channel effectiveness, location of plants and distribution facilities, price policies and their effects on sales, and so on) are the responsibility of the marketing research department. There is no one optimum method of organization: the best organization for a particular company depends upon its needs and the way it has organized the marketing and other functions of the firm.

Source of Research—Make or Buy?

As indicated by Tables 1–1 and 1–2, it is not unusual for companies to have marketing research studies conducted by outside firms. Many firms do research on a contract or fee basis, including all major advertising agencies, marketing research firms, and management consulting firms, as well as independent consultants, university bureaus of business and economic research, and some trade associations.

Firms that use outside research services for a substantial proportion of their research are generally large manufacturers of consumer convenience goods. Here the need for continuing information from consumer panels, and inventory and other data obtained from store panels, is substantial and the cost to the individual company of doing such research itself would be prohibitive. These companies tend to market relatively large numbers of new products that require specialized kinds of marketing research such as market tests, consumer surveys, and laboratory experiments. A considerable amount of research on advertising is the usual rule for such companies as well. This research is often done by the company's advertising agency.

There are advantages both to doing research with company personnel and to having it done by an outside firm. The advantages of doing it "in house" are (1) greater familiarity with the company and background of the problem, (2) more contact and control while the research is being done, and (3) retention of the experience within the firm when the project is completed. The advantages of using an outside firm include (1) the ability to provide specialists (behavioral scientists, statisticians, specialists in particular kinds of research projects such as market tests, and so on) that the company may not be able to afford to have on its own staff, (2) an opportunity for greater objectivity as an outsider, and, in some instances, (3) substantial savings in the cost of doing the research.

Reporting Level of Marketing Research

Every manager of a staff activity would like to report to the chief executive of the organization. This may reflect vanity and a desire for status in some cases, but far more than that is involved. If the staff activity is consistently to be successful in getting timely consideration and acceptance of its recommendations, it must report to a line executive at a level that can ensure that action is taken when warranted.

As indicated by Table 1–3, marketing research managers report to first or second tier management almost without exception. By far the majority of the marketing research managers at both the corporate and division levels report to the senior marketing executive.

The Marketing Research Manager's Job

The specific tasks assigned the marketing research manager range from purchasing marketing research studies from outside research firms to developing and operating a complex marketing information system. The specific assignment varies with the role that research plays within each firm and the "style" of the management. Although these factors make it impossible to provide a generalized job description for a marketing research manager, a reasonably representative job description is provided here.

Table 1–3   Reporting Level of Marketing Research Managers

| | MR Function at | |
| | Corporate Level | Division Level |
MR Manager Reports to:	Per Cent	Per Cent
Top Management (Chairman, President, Executive Vice-President at corporate level, Group V.P., Division V.P. at division level)	14	23
Other General Management (Senior V.P., V.P. Research and Development, V.P. Research, et al.)	11	3
Marketing or Sales Management (V.P. Marketing, Director of Marketing, Sales Manager, Sales Director, V.P. Sales, Marketing Manager, et al.)	64	61
General Planning or Development (V.P. Advertising, V.P. Communications, Advertising Manager or Director, et al.)	6	6
Advertising or Communications (V.P. Advertising, V.P. Communications, Advertising Manager or Director, et al.)	3	3
Product Management (V.P. Product Planning, Product Planning Manager, Director of New Product and Market Management, et al.)	2	4
	100	100
	172	100

Source: L. W. Forman and E. L. Bailey, *The Role and Organization of Marketing Research* (New York: The Conference Board, 1969). Reprinted by permission of The Conference Board.

Position Description for Marketing Research Manager—A Fabricating Company

I. *Position Title:* Marketing Research Manager

II. *Position Summary:*
Is in charge of Marketing Research and the purposes of the function are to be the information and control center of marketing and sales and to assure that factual marketing advice and counsel are available to the Corporate and Division executives.

III. *Reports To:* Director of Marketing

IV. *Positions Reporting to Title Position:* Department Personnel.

V. *Position Duties:*

   A. *Planning*

     He will plan and recommend to the Director of Marketing:

     1. *Long- and short-range studies,* plans, procedures, policies, and controls which will promote marketing effectiveness in the attainment of the Corporate and Divisional objectives and goals in a manner which shall continuously enhance the growth and reputation of the Corporation.

     2. *Prepare and submit annual budget* and revisions thereof for his department to the Director of Marketing for approval.

     3. *Marketing Studies and Research* (quantitative and qualitative) for use in all marketing functions, including, but not limited to, evaluation of:

       a. Size and location of markets.

       b. Attitude, preference, and needs regarding company products, service, or policies.

       c. Sales and distribution methods, channels, and territories.

       d. Price indices, price trends, and product pricing.

       e. Sales and advertising programs.

       f. Present products, product line extensions, and new products.

       g. Products and markets of possible acquisitions and mergers.

     4. *Studies of current conditions,* trends, and forecasts of industry activity and position, including:

       a. Industry sales—total, by product, by geographical area, by type of outlet, by competitor.

       b. Company competitive position in (share of markets).

       c. Short- and long-range forecasts of company sales by product by area.

   B. *Organization*

     As a Department Manager, he will staff and administer his department in accord with established management personnel policies for the optimum benefit of the Corporation with the minimum number of capable and qualified personnel required to assist him in discharging his service and analytical functions.

     Responsibilities

     1. As a staff member of management reporting to the Director of Marketing, the Marketing Research Manager will assist the Corporate Executives, Marketing Staff, and Operating Management to obtain optimum sales volume at least cost by:

       a. Aiding in the formulation of overall marketing objectives, policies, plans, and budgets.

       b. Undertaking market research studies (defining problems, programming, budgeting, scheduling, securing facts, analyzing and recommending solutions), as directed, in the areas of product line improvements and extensions, new products, new merchandise items, and proposed acquisitions and mergers.

       c. Establish and maintain continuous evaluation of the marketing effectiveness of the Divisions from analysis of control data and make timely recommendations to the Director of Marketing concerning recommended changes or improvements.

d. Acting in advisory capacity to the Director of Marketing and other Corporate Executives in matters pertaining to Marketing Research, thus facilitating the formulation of policy and the determination of Management decisions.

e. Providing Marketing Research services (conducting, assisting, advising, counseling, and recommending) as directed, to the Corporate Executives, Marketing Staff, and the Operating Divisions.

f. Conducting analyses, as directed, of effectiveness, economy, and efficiency of all phases of marketing performance (reviewing, finding, appraising, recommending, and reporting).

g. Developing integrated data, systems, procedures, and controls to promote the interchange of useful information in the attainment of Corporate and Divisional marketing objectives.

h. Providing economic and business research, studies of performance, and forecasts; and interpreting these in the performance, plans, or programs of the Corporation and the Divisions.

i. Proposing creative, imaginative, and strategically aggressive plans and policies to maintain the Corporation leadership in desired markets.

j. Assuring the Corporation leadership in the Marketing Research function through the planning, organizing, controlling, and coordinating of the Marketing Research Department, as well as integrating it harmoniously as a component in the Corporation's overall organization.

k. Evaluating, or recommending, as required, and coordinating the use of outside marketing services or assisting the Corporation and Divisions in arranging for and using such services.

l. Being continuously acquainted with the sales programs and programs of the respective operating Divisions in order to assist in:

    (1) Developing their sales programs and interpreting their significance in terms of overall Corporate and Division plans and policies.

    (2) Analyses of competitive market and product developments which might offer expanding or new sales opportunities or which might have an adverse effect on present markets and sales.

    (3) Conducting or arranging for marketing studies within the Divisions or for Corporate product lines.

    (4) Planning, establishment and maintenance of customer potentials, call budgeting, sales goals or quotas, sales territory alignment and performance evaluation.

m. Maintain adequate controls to insure effective and efficient utilization of Corporate resources assigned to him and to insure timely completion of his assigned tasks.

n. Provide the Director of Marketing with a monthly activity report on accomplishments, conditions, problems, trends, plans, ideas and recommendations for his Department.

VI. *Authority:*

As a staff member of management, the Marketing Research Manager will exercise no direct authority over Divisional operations.

Within the limits of the approved programs, budgets, Corporate policies, and control procedures, the Marketing Research Manager is responsible for and has delegated authority in all matters pertaining to Marketing Research, and direct authority in the operation of the Marketing Research Department.

VII. *Standards for Measuring Performance:*
The Marketing Research Manager is accountable for the fulfillment of responsibilities and relationships described herein. The primary measurements of satisfactory performance are as follows:
A. The quality, quantity, timeliness and continuity of guidance and assistance rendered to the Operating Divisions.
B. The soundness of the policies and procedures recommended to the Director of Marketing.
C. The quality and timeliness of suggestions given to the Corporate Office Executives.
D. The extent to which the services of his Department are requested by those in a position to benefit the Corporation thereby.
E. The cordiality of relations which exist between the Marketing Research Department and other areas, both within and without the Corporation.
F. The example of good management, high morale, personal conduct and effective teamwork evidenced by the Manager and his staff in their contacts with members of the Corporation and others.*

The research manager needs to have both training and experience as a researcher and knowledge of the industry in which his company is a part. He needs to be *management oriented:* able to understand the problems with which management is faced, analyze them to determine what information is needed to help solve them, and devise means of obtaining such information in a timely and economic way.

Although a good marketing research manager can be an invaluable aid to management, he cannot do some things. He cannot and should not make decisions for the executive to whom he reports; he *recommends* but does not *decide*. The functions of his department are to help set the objectives, identify problems, find alternative solutions, and reduce the level of uncertainty about what will happen if each alternative were to be adopted. The information that he provides can never be complete, however, just as the predictions that he makes can never be made with certainty. If the research manager has done his job properly, the uncertainty will have been reduced.

The Research Analyst's Job

Just as it was difficult to generalize about the responsibilities of the marketing research manager because of variation between companies, the

Source: L. W. Forman and E. L. Bailey, *The Role and Organization of Marketing Research* (New York: The Conference Board, 1969), 48–51. Reprinted by permission of the Conference Board.

differences in size and organization of marketing research departments result in a wide range of assignments for research analysts. The analyst in the two- or three-person department will, of necessity, become a research generalist. At one time or another he will very likely work on studies involving all of the company's products and each of the major marketing problem areas (products, pricing, advertising, and distribution). An analyst in a large department, on the other hand, may be assigned to work on research projects dealing with only one product line or studies involving only one major problem area (advertising, for example). If he has a research specialty, such as training as a behavioral scientist or as a statistician, he may even be assigned to work only on those aspects of projects requiring his particular type of expertise.

People may choose to become research analysts for several reasons. The job is interesting and challenging for someone with an analytical turn of mind. The analyst is confronted with a continuing set of problems, each one new and none of them easy. It is an opportunity to obtain exposure to and experience in helping to solve problems being dealt with by the top management of the company. The position pays well initially and the pay increases for the first few years keep pace in most companies with those in other areas of marketing. Finally, for those who are interested in staying in research, a job as an analyst provides an obvious avenue for progressing through the research hierarchy and becoming a research manager.

For someone who wants to become a marketing or general management executive, two or three years of experience as a research analyst early in his career may be a sound investment. This period will afford the individual a view of and an opportunity to participate in the management process that he could not get in any other way at that stage of his career. It also gives one an understanding of the research process that will help him make more efficient use of research when he becomes a line executive. Someone with a management objective is well advised to limit his stay in a research department to no more than three years, however. After that time, the value of such experience will very likely be less than that of taking a line position in marketing or another department.

Summary

The role of marketing research in marketing management is to provide information to aid in making decisions. Marketing research should help in the entire decision-making process, beginning with the providing of information to help set realistic objectives. It should be involved in problem identification and the formulation as well as the choice among alternative solutions for the problem. In identifying problems, the marketing research department will typically be responsible for studies on *market potential, market share, market characteristics, sales analysis,* and *short-range* and *long-range forecasting.* Research to help solve problems involves *product research*—new product research, research on competitive products, product characteristics, product line research, packaging studies; *advertising research*—copy research, media studies, studies of advertising effectiveness; *personal selling research*—establishing sales territories, establishing sales quotas, salesmen effectiveness; *distribution research*—plant and warehouse location studies, distribution cost analysis, dealer relations, and effectiveness of channels of distribution; and *pricing research*—price policies and their effect on sales volume, discounts, and shipping cost policies.

Marketing information systems (MIS) to provide an orderly and continuing means of *collecting, storing, analyzing,* and *providing* information on call to marketing managers are now in the early stages of development and use. Marketing research is needed to help develop the MIS, and individual research projects are required to complement and extend the information provided by the system once it is in use.

The marketing research manager typically reports to the first or second level of management, with the most common organizational arrangement being reporting to the chief marketing executive. Most companies use outside research firms as well as their own research departments to supply their research needs.

Questions and Problems

1.1. Does the role of marketing research include a responsibility for providing information on ethical questions? Explain.

1.2. Should the marketing research department only provide information to help in decision making or should it also recommend courses of action? Explain.

1.3. Many companies in the food and drug sundries field subscribe to one or more syndicated research services. One of these services provides data that is obtained from a panel of families on a regular basis on purchases of each brand in the product class by package size, price, type of store at which purchased, frequency of purchase, demographic characteristics of the purchasing family, and other characteristics.
Would you expect these data to be useful for: (a) Identifying problems? (b) Solving problems?
Explain.

1.4. Can a parallel be drawn between an accounting system in providing information on costs of products and a marketing information system on providing information on demand for products? Explain.

1.5. A company that produces and markets a well-known soft drink is considering developing a marketing information system. The marketing research department has done an exploratory study that indicates it will cost approximately $1 million to develop and $250,000 per year to operate and maintain. (a) What factors should the management consider in making the decision about adding the MIS? (b) How could information be obtained on each?

1.6. An equipment manufacturer is considering spending $1 million on research and development of an electric antiskid device for truck brakes. The company estimates that the device will take four years to develop and will have a product life of five years beyond development. Estimates of net cash flow for each of the next nine years are as follows:

Year	Net Cash Flow	Year	Net Cash Flow
1	<$300,000>	5	$1,000,000
2	< 500,000>	6	1,000,000
3	< 500,000>	7	700,000
4	< 200,000>	8	500,000
		9	200,000

Should research and development be authorized? Explain.

1.7. A company is considering adding a warehousing facility in an area in which sales have been increasing. It estimates that the warehouse would take one year to build, would cost $2 million, and would save $200,000 in shipping costs each year after it was built for the next 20 years. Assume the building is worth $1 million at the end of the 21st year. Should the facility be built? Explain.

1.8. Prepare an argument that the marketing research manager for a bicycle manufacturer should report to (a) the president of the company, (b) the marketing manager of the company.

Selected Bibliography

BARNARD, CHESTER I. *The Functions of the Executive.* Cambridge, Mass.: Harvard University Press, 1947. One of the few books written by an executive in which a systematic analysis of the management process is attempted and the only one of which we are aware in which it is successful.

BOYD, HARPER W., JR., and STEUART HENDERSON BRITT. "Making Marketing Research More Effective by Using the Administrative Process." *Journal of Marketing Research,* **11** (February 1965) 15–19. A literate and sound appraisal of the role of marketing research in the management of marketing.

CHURCHMAN, C. WEST. *Theory of Experimental Inference.* New York: Macmillan Publishing Co., Inc., 1948. This is an invaluable book for the reader who is interested in a review of writings on methods of inquiry.

LUCE, R. DUNCAN, and HOWARD RAIFFA. *Games and Decisions.* New York: John Wiley & Sons, Inc., 1957. A book that is aging somewhat now but contains a well-written section on decision making under uncertainty.

MACK, RUTH P. *Planning on Uncertainty*. New York: Wiley-Interscience, 1971. A very good exposition and critique of decision making using probabilistic decision models.

SIMON, HERBERT A. *The New Science of Management Decision*. New York: Harper & Row, Publishers, Inc., 1960. An excellent review of the decision-making process and the generic kinds of decisions that must be made in organizations.

SORENSON, THEODORE C. *Decision Making in the White House*. New York: Columbia University Press, 1963. A small book that is based on a series of lectures given at Columbia University while the author was still a special counselor to President Kennedy. An interesting and informative recounting of the process of decision making at the presidential level.

Case 1–1

Dubow Sporting Goods

Dubow Sporting Goods produces two primary product lines—golf products and inflated sporting goods. The former accounts for approximately 75 per cent of the firm's $4 million annual sales. Both the inflated goods and the golf equipment are sold primarily as private brands. The products sold under the firm's own brand name, Dubow, are generally considered "promotional" type goods. That is, both the inflated goods and golf equipment sold under the Dubow name are generally relatively low priced and are often featured as a loss leader or promoted item by retail outlets.

The golf equipment line includes golf clubs, golf balls, and putting trainers. Dubow markets approximately 20 brands of golf clubs, 25 putters, 6 wedges, 5 models of King Putt Practice Putters, and 14 brands of golf balls. This does not include the various private brands that Dubow supplies.

The firm maintains this rather large number of brand names, despite the fact that the differences between several of them are minor and the price is identical, in order to achieve greater distribution in a town or area. Dubow believes that this is important since it allows several retailers in a town to each have an "exclusive" brand within that town. Dubow has also experienced trouble in dropping a brand name once it has achieved distribution since retailers dislike the possibility of obsolete stock and customers like to be able to replace damaged clubs or expand basic sets.

Until recently, the firm made no attempt to identify these various brands with Dubow Sporting Goods at the consumer level. Now, however, the Dubow brand name is being stamped on the sole of some of the "top of the line" golf clubs.

Dubow, like other manufacturers of golf clubs, prepares a "new line" each year. That is, different materials, different designs, and different items are added each year. Dubow frequently incorporates these changes in a new brand name. In other cases, it incorporates the changes within existing brands. Dubow relies on its sales representatives for many of the new product ideas that the firm introduces each year.

The firm's line of inflated sports equipment is composed of basketballs, footballs, volley balls, soccer balls, and tether balls as well as sets of these balls containing kicking tees, basketball goals, volley ball nets, and tether ball poles. Unlike the golf equipment line, all of the inflated goods marketed directly by Dubow are under the Dubow brand name. However, a substantial portion of the total sales volume from inflated goods comes from private brands. In addition to direct sales and private brands, Dubow also produces directly for "packagers"—firms that combine various pieces of equipment into a package such as a volley ball and badminton set. The sales pattern for inflated goods is fairly stable throughout the year, with slight increases prior to Christmas and during the spring season.

The firm's golf equipment and inflated goods are both relatively low priced lines. The golf equipment is the highest priced of the "low priced" lines, although this reflects costs and quality factors more than a deliberate pricing policy. Although it is relatively high priced as compared to the other low priced brands, Dubow's golf equipment is priced well below the major brands. For example, Dubow sells its seven-piece starter set of golf clubs for $22.75 compared to a major brand's set that costs $30.00. Despite the price difference between the Dubow and the major brand and the fact (according to Dubow executives) that the Dubow set is as good or better than the major brand, the major brand set heavily outsells Dubow's.

Dubow relies solely on sales representatives to sell both its golf products and inflated goods to retailers throughout the country. The only house account maintained by the firm is Sears. Within the industry as a whole, the distribution pattern is mixed with some firms, particularly the larger ones, using their own sales force, some only sales representatives, and some a combination of both. The typical sales representative will carry four to six complementary lines. Although Dubow would prefer that its account be the basic one for their sales representatives, Dubow is frequently unable to secure adequate coverage of an area on this basis and, in fact, has rather weak distribution in a number of areas because of a lack of good sales representatives who are willing to carry the line. Dubow pays its sales representatives a 5 per cent commission plus a bonus when a certain level of sales is reached.

Although the ultimate goal of the firm is to have a company sales force, Dubow executives estimate that nonhouse account sales will have to triple before the firm can support its own sales force. As an intermediate step, the firm hopes to establish several regional sales managers to work directly with the sales representatives in each region.

An area of distribution in which Dubow is just becoming active is premium redemptions. Dubow executives believe that the volume of premium business in both golf equipment and inflated goods is almost as great as that sold through regular sporting goods outlets. In fact, Dubow executives believe that only a very small share of this business would allow them to double sales. For example, it recently began supplying basketball and goal sets to a small regional stamp company at a rate of approximately 250 per week. However, the premium business is not a simple one. The stamp companies and the larger firms who are experienced with premiums make detailed projections far in advance. For example, Dubow is considering an opportunity to distribute certain items of its golf line through a major premium company. However, in order to secure this business it will have to guarantee the price of the equipment for 18 months. This poses a difficult cost projection problem. At the other extreme, many manufacturers that are inexperienced with premium offers will suddenly find themselves needing large quantities of golf balls or inflated goods on short notice. Dubow often picks up this type of business by producing for other manufacturers.

The firm's advertising program has been primarily trade oriented. It has used an advertising agency to place its approximately $15,000 space purchases. The bulk of the advertising goes into full page advertisements in *Sporting Goods Dealer,* in which Dubow has had an advertisement in every issue since it began advertising. The remainder of the advertising budget is spread among such publications as *Selling Sporting Goods, Sporting Goods Business,* and *Sporting Goods Merchandiser.*

The firm also spends a considerable sum on the preparation and distribution of its catalogs. The golf equipment catalog is 16 full-color, glossy, magazine-size pages. Approximately 14,000 copies of this catalog are distributed as an insert (inside the front cover) in the *Sporting Goods Dealer,* with another 6,000 copies going out through direct mail or trade shows. The cost of preparing and distributing this catalog is approximately $12,000 per year. The inflated goods catalog is four pages in two colors—light and dark brown. Approximately 5,000 copies of this catalog are distributed by direct mail and through the sales representatives. The total cost of preparation and distribution of this catalog is $1,500 per year.

Dubow's first "major" consumer advertising campaign was for its new "Chi Chi Rodriguez *Aristocrat"* golf ball in late 1969. In this campaign, it placed ads in *Golf Digest, Sports Illustrated,* and *Golf.* However, the major purpose of the advertisement was as much to influence the sales representatives and dealers as the public. A flier reproducing the advertisement and stressing the fact that the product was nationally advertised was sent to a large number of current and potential sales representatives and dealers.

Dubow's major form of sales promotion is participation in various trade shows. It currently participates in the New York Sporting Goods Fair, the Chicago Sporting Goods Show, and the West Coast Sporting Goods Show. Participation in these shows is a rather expensive matter, with exhibition space alone costing approximately $1,200 for each show.

Whereas Dubow hopes to vastly increase sales during the next few years, it also wants to reduce its reliance on private brands. Thus, its goal is to maintain private brand sales at their current level while greatly expanding the sales of its own brands. It hopes to accomplish this with increased emphasis on the Dubow name for its higher quality goods, new products, expanded distribution, and increased consumer promotion on a local or regional level.

1. What role should marketing research play in the day-to-day operations of a firm such as Dubow Sporting Goods?

2. How could marketing research help Dubow achieve its goal of increased sales of its own brand name?

3. How much should a firm such as Dubow spend on marketing research each year?

Case 1–2
Hiram Walker Cordials

The terms *cordial* and *liqueur,* while referring to technically distinct products, are generally used interchangeably to refer to "sweet, flavored liquors."

For a number of years, Hiram Walker, de Kuyper, and Leroux were the major producers of cordials and smaller competitors had not been able to penetrate the market except in limited regions or with one specialized product. Within the past ten years, however, a number of producers have been able to gain market acceptance by altering products and engaging in extensive promotional efforts. One approach has been to reduce the primary bottle size from a 25.6 ounce fifth to a 24 ounce three-fourths quart and to use the savings for increased promotion. Another approach has been to produce cordials at less than the customary proof, which results in a substantial tax reduction. These savings can then be divided between a lower price and increased promotion. Strategies such as these have greatly increased the level of competition in the cordial market.

Hiram Walker-Gooderham & Worts Limited is a Canadian company. It is the second largest liquor company in the world and is divided into a number of different marketing and production companies. The firm produces and markets a complete line of distilled products and limits its activities to the manufacture and sale of distilled spirits and directly related activities. These related activities involve such by-products as dry ice derived from the carbon dioxide produced in the distilling process, dried grains for cattle feed, vitamins derived from dried grains, as well as such activities as the operation of glass bottle plants used to ensure a continuous flow of bottles and of grain elevators to aid in the buying and selling of grain.

The firm added cordials to its growing number of product lines in the 1930s. However, until after World War II, it produced only a few basic cordials such as Creme de Menthe and Creme de Cacao. In the late 1940s, it added a line of flavored brandies. Then in 1964 it began to add a number of specialty items such as Creme de Banana, Creme de Cassis, and Creme de Noyaux. Today the cordial line consists of over 25 items.

The firm is constantly searching for new products or flavors. A recent addition to its cordial line was Chocolate Mint. The rationale behind the development of this product was the demonstrated popularity of these two flavors in various candies and desserts, both singularly and in combination. However, even with what Hiram Walker executives believed was a taste favorite, over two years were needed to devise a method of blending the flavors so that they would not separate when bottled. After the product development department had perfected this process, it sent several versions of the product to company headquarters for testing. The product was then taste-tested by the firm's division managers. Their reactions were recorded and sent to the product development people, who revised the product in response to the comments. The revised product was subjected to a taste-test by the same division managers who agreed that this version would sell and provided sales estimates for the first year. The product was so successful that the initial production was sold out and, despite the fact that numerous areas were out of the product for a period of time, the first year's sales were approximately two and a half times the projected level.

Hiram Walker executives believe that the market for their cordial line is composed of individuals with above-average income and education. This would be consistent with the overall industry pattern. In addition, the consumption of cordials is highly concentrated in urban areas. William Buesching, national manager of the cordial division, states that the average consumer of cordials begins experimenting with cordials at the age of 26 or 27 after several years of marriage. The primary motivation behind the first purchase of a cordial is to experiment or acquire a greater degree of variety. This motivation often holds for subsequent purchases of new types of cordials. In addition to the desire for variety and new and pleasant taste sensations, the status associated with serving cordials, either as drinks or when used in desserts or cooking, plays a definite role in motivating consumers to purchase cordials.

The per capita consumption of cordials varies widely throughout the country. Part of this variation may be explained by the relative concentration of consumers with the characteristics described previously. Legal regulations and the social atmosphere of the area also influence consumption. In addition to variations in the per capita consumption, the types of cordial sold also vary by geographic regions. For example, Peppermint Schnapps is very popular in Kansas, whereas the West accounts for most of the sales of Triple Sec, used in the *Margarita Cocktail.* The long-term popularity of drinks such as the *Grasshopper* and *Alexander* have helped maintain the popularity of Creme de Cacao and Creme de Menthe. On the other hand, a recent rapid increase in the sales of Sloe Gin was traced to a fad with younger consumers mixing Sloe Gin and Coca Cola.

Buesching rates packaging as one of the most critical areas that the firm faces. Since most producers have approximately 25 types of cordials, a package store carrying 4 lines would have over 100 packages in each bottle size. Unless the consumer knows the exact type and brand he wants, he is likely to select from among those bottles that attract his attention. Thus, for new products or new purchasers of an established flavor, the package often "sells" the first purchase whereas the product itself must "sell" the repeat purchases.

As an indication of the importance attached to packaging, the firm's new cordial, Chocolate Mint, is packaged in a bottle styled after the old keystone bottle and glazed twice with a ceramic finish. Although it is an extremely attractive package, it costs almost three times as much as the approximately $.07 a "regular" bottle would cost.

In addition to the bottle design, the labels that are attached to the bottles receive considerable attention by company executives. The labels on the front of the bottles must attract attention, name the product, and meet certain legal requirements. In addition, labels are frequently applied to the back of the products primarily to provide recipes for using the product. These recipes must be short and utilize ingredients that the individual is likely to have readily available if they are to increase consumption of the product.

The firm's cordials, like all liquor products, are sold to retail outlets through wholesale liquor distributors since federal regulations preclude any producer from selling directly to retail outlets. In states where the liquor stores are state-owned, the producer may deal directly with the state, but not with the individual stores. For a number of years Hiram Walker has attempted to maintain a complete line of liquor products to offer to its distributors. Thus, the salesmen handle a complete range of liquor products in addition to the cordials.

Hiram Walker is divided into seven divisions—eastern, southeastern, southwestern, central, north central, western, and control states (the state performs the wholesaler function). Each division is headed by a division manager who reports directly to the president. The division manager is responsible for the marketing of all Hiram Walker products in his territory, including sales forecasting, sales planning, advertising, merchandising, sales training, public relations, and so on. Working under each division manager are a number of district managers, and, in states with only one distributor, state managers. The duties of these managers are similar to those of the division managers but on a smaller scale.

All aspects of the liquor industry are closely supervised and regulated by a host of federal, state, and local governmental bodies. The fact that these regulations come from a variety of sources frequently complicates the operations of the industry. This problem is especially apparent in the area of pricing. Each state has the ability to control the pricing practices of the liquor distributors operating within its boundaries. The result is that the liquor manufacturer faces a vast array of pricing regulations.

As an overall philosophy, Hiram Walker does not like to compete in any liquor group on the basis of price. Thus, most Hiram Walker product lines are priced at or above the industry average. A few products, such as vodka, which are produced mainly as a service to their distributors, are marketed on a price basis. However, the cordial line is priced well above the industry average.

Hiram Walker has its own advertising department, which, in cooperation with the company executives and the appropriate brand manager, suggest specific guidelines to the various advertising agencies for the creation of advertisements for Hiram Walker products. For the cordial line, the advertisements are aimed at young married couples and emphasize the *use* of the various cordials. Thus, the advertisements provide recipes for desserts, drinks, and dishes and emphasize their usage in successful entertaining. Although a number of cordials, such as Peppermint Schnapps, are often consumed straight, the advertising does not show that type of utilization. Instead, the advertisements attempt to create a "glamorous, prestigious, high-status image for cordials—one that upgrades the product and the consumer." Advertising is relied on to perform the critical task of creating general interest in cordials and triggering the first purchase of a given type of cordial. Once the bottle is in the home, it is believed that the consumer will find ways to use it through advertised recipes, recipe booklets, recipes on the label, and experimentation.

The firm places a large share of its cordial advertising in *Time* and

Gourmet, with some advertisements also appearing in *U.S. News and World Report* and *Newsweek.* All of the cordial advertisements are full color, full page advertisements. Hiram Walker spends an estimated $425,-000 per year on magazine advertising for cordials but unlike some competitors does not engage in extensive newspaper advertising.

Hiram Walker provides the retailer with numerous merchandising aids, all of which are closely coordinated with the firm's current advertising campaign. This portion of the firm's selling effort is so important that it has a group of individuals, called merchandisers, working under the district and state managers, whose primary duty is to set up displays and aid the retailers with seasonal promotions. In many areas, the firm also uses outside merchandising services especially during the holiday seasons.

Successful merchandising aids such as counter or floor displays, brochures, recipe books, and the like must attract the consumers' attention to the product and aid in making the first sale. These devices have assumed an increasing importance as the competition for the cordial market has grown. Hiram Walker has found that unless it can convince its own sales force and merchandisers of the value of each merchandising aid, they in turn are not able to convince their wholesalers and retailers to use them. Hiram Walker expends a great deal of effort in this area and believes that its merchandising aids for its cordials are the best in the industry.

1. What role should marketing research play in the daily operations of the cordial division of Hiram Walker?

2. The Chocolate Mint cordial was not taste-tested among consumers. Part of the rationale for using the firm's division managers rather than a sample of consumers was: "Our division managers make their living selling these products. They know a lot more about what will sell than some unconcerned consumer." Comment.

3. If the cordial division believes that it needs research for a new product introduction, should it "make or buy?"

4. How should a research department fit into a multidivision firm such as Hiram Walker?

Case 1–3
VSM Computers

The management of Bradford Electronics, a large electronics engineering company specializing in research and development of miniaturized electrical circuitry, was considering the commercial possibilities of a desk-top sized computer. The company had had a number of contracts that involved the design of circuitry for computer subsystems. Drawing on this experience, one of the engineers, Richard Loewe, suggested to the management that a miniaturized computer could be designed and built that would have the storage and computational capacity of computers then on the market that were several times its size. He stated that he believed such a computer might have a good commercial potential.

The management was sufficiently interested in the possibility of producing and marketing such a computer to authorize an engineering feasibility study. Loewe and another engineer were assigned to the project. They worked out a preliminary design of the logical circuitry and made size and cost estimates. They reported that a VSM (Very SMall) computer could be designed with a central processing unit with outside dimensions of no more than 30 inches by 20 inches by 12 inches that would have storage and computational capacities equivalent to the IBM 1620 (and other computers of that class). They estimated that it could be built for about $9,000 per copy. This would allow it to be sold for about $20,000 and to have a monthly lease price in the $450–550 range. It would take about two and one-half years to complete the design and prepare the engineering drawings for production, according to their estimates, and the cost of this research and development would be about $400,000.

The marketing research analyst for the company, Tom Rich, was asked to prepare a forecast of the number of VSM units that would be sold and leased and to estimate the profits (or losses) that the company might expect if it decided to commercialize the computer. He made yearly forecasts of sales and leases based on estimated shares of the forecast total number of computers with comparable capabilities that would be on the market. Three forecasts were prepared for each year for six years following introduction: an "optimistic" forecast that assumed a 25 per cent share of the market for that general class of computers, a "most probable" forecast that assumed a 20 per cent market share, and a "pessimistic" forecast that was based on a 15 per cent market share. The number of service contracts for each level of sales was also forecast. The costs of developing, manufacturing, marketing, and servicing were estimated for each year for each forecast level. Finally, with the help of an accountant, Rich developed a set of *pro forma* accounting statements for the "optimistic," "most probable," and "pessimistic" forecasts.

The *pro forma* statements are given as follows. What action should the Bradford management take?

Table 1 VSM Computer—Pessimistic Balance Sheet

Assets	Year 1	Year 2	Year 3	Year 4	Year 5	Year 6	Year 7	Year 8	Year 9
Current Assets									
Accounts Receivable				$ 49,000	$ 162,000	$ 327,000	$ 498,000	$ 673,000	$ 897,000
Inventory									
Computers			$ 250,000	$ 601,000	$ 675,000	$ 720,000	700,000	$ 690,000	$ 190,000
Spares			100,000	207,000	283,000	278,000	219,000	153,000	87,000
Total Inventory			$ 350,000	$ 808,000	$ 958,000	$ 998,000	$ 919,000	$ 843,000	$ 277,000
Total Current Assets			$ 350,000	$ 857,000	$ 1,120,000	$ 1,325,000	$ 1,417,000	$1,516,000	$1,174,000
Fixtures & Equipment (Net)			$ 76,000	$ 122,000	$ 113,000	$ 108,000	$ 105,000	$ 65,000	$ 44,000
Leased Computers (Net)				$ 536,000	$ 1,262,000	$ 1,798,000	$ 2,175,000	$2,345,000	$2,485,000
Deferred Charges		$ 65,000	$ 50,000	$ 30,000	$ 10,000	—	—	—	—
Total Assets	—	$ 65,000	$ 476,000	$1,545,000	$ 2,505,000	$ 3,231,000	$ 3,697,000	$3,926,000	$3,703,000
Liabilities									
Current Liabilities	$ 45,000		$ 10,000	$ 30,000	$ 40,000	$ 45,000	$ 50,000	$ 50,000	$ 35,000
Royalties & Indemnities			—	$ 8,000	$ 35,000	$ 91,000	$ 176,000	$ 291,000	$ 446,000
Net Corporate Investment									
Corporate Investment		$ 430,000	$1,070,000	$2,482,000	$ 3,842,000	$ 4,728,000	$ 4,848,000	$4,071,000	$2,144,000
Accumulated Profit (Loss)	(45,000)	(365,000)	$ (604,000)	$ (975,000)	$(1,412,000)	$(1,633,000)	$(1,377,000)	$ (486,000)	$1,078,000
Net Corporate Investment	—	$ 65,000	$ 466,000	$1,507,000	$ 2,430,000	$ 3,045,000	$ 3,471,000	$3,585,000	$3,222,000
Total Liabilities	—	$ 65,000	$ 476,000	$1,545,000	$ 2,505,000	$ 3,231,000	$ 3,697,000	$3,926,000	$3,703,000

Table 2 VSM Computer—Pessimistic Income Statement

	Year 1	Year 2	Year 3	Year 4	Year 5	Year 6	Year 7	Year 8	Year 9
Revenue									
Equipment Sales				$ 100,000	$ 236,000	$ 336,000	$ 286,000	$ 168,000	$ 100,000
Lease Rentals				158,000	679,000	1,516,000	2,527,000	3,602,000	4,691,000
Service				33,000	78,000	110,000	148,000	197,000	225,000
Total Revenue				$ 291,000	$ 993,000	$1,962,000	$2,961,000	$3,967,000	$5,016,000
Returns and Allowances				6,000	19,000	39,000	60,000	81,000	108,000
Net Revenue				$ 285,000	$ 974,000	$1,923,000	$2,901,000	$3,886,000	$4,908,000
Cost of Revenue									
Equipment Sales				$ 67,000	$ 154,000	$ 178,000	$ 138,000	$ 74,000	$ 38,000
Lease Rentals				161,000	575,000	1,060,000	1,485,000	1,839,000	2,122,000
Service				17,000	39,000	56,000	75,000	100,000	114,000
Total Cost of Revenue				$ 245,000	$ 768,000	$1,294,000	$1,698,000	$2,013,000	$2,274,000
Gross Profit (Loss)				$ 40,000	$ 206,000	$ 629,000	$1,203,000	$1,873,000	$2,634,000
Selling, G&A Expenses									
Selling Expenses			$ 184,000	$ 315,000	$ 502,000	$ 672,000	$ 741,000	$ 754,000	$ 838,000
G&A Expenses			20,000	88,000	114,000	122,000	121,000	113,000	77,000
Total Selling, G&A Expenses			$ 204,000	$ 403,000	$ 616,000	$ 794,000	$ 862,000	$ 867,000	$ 915,000
Operating Profit (Loss)			$(204,000)	$(363,000)	$(410,000)	$ (165,000)	$ 341,000	$1,006,000	$1,719,000
Other Income Deductions									
Royalties & Indemnities	$ —	$ —	$ —	$ 8,000	$ 27,000	$ 56,000	$ 85,000	$ 115,000	$ 155,000
Research & Development	45,000	320,000	35,000	—					—
Total Income Deductions	$ 45,000	$ 320,000	$ 35,000	$ 8,000	$ 27,000	$ 56,000	$ 85,000	$ 115,000	$ 155,000
Net Income (Loss)	$(45,000)	$(320,000)	$(239,000)	$(371,000)	$(437,000)	$ (221,000)	$ 256,000	$ 891,000	$1,564,000

Table 3 VSM Computer—Most Probable Balance Sheet

Assets	Year 1	Year 2	Year 3	Year 4	Year 5	Year 6	Year 7	Year 8	Year 9
Current Assets									
Accounts Receivable				$ 60,000	$ 210,000	$ 405,000	$ 580,000	$ 775,000	$ 995,000
Inventory									
Computers			$ 200,000	$ 607,000	$ 734,000	$ 814,000	$ 784,000	$ 785,000	$ (1,000)
Spares			100,000	207,000	255,000	237,000	196,000	163,000	141,000
Total Inventory			$ 300,000	$ 814,000	$ 989,000	$ 1,051,000	$ 980,000	$ 948,000	$ 140,000
Total Current Assets			$ 300,000	$ 874,000	$ 1,199,000	$ 1,456,000	$ 1,560,000	$1,723,000	$1,135,000
Fixtures & Equipment (Net)			$ 56,000	$ 82,000	$ 53,000	$ 28,000	$ 15,000	$ (16,000)	$ (36,000)
Leased Computers (Net)				$ 579,000	$ 1,532,000	$ 2,011,000	$ 2,432,000	$2,843,000	$3,408,000
Deferred Charges		$ 65,000	$ 50,000	$ 30,000	$ 10,000	—	—	—	—
Total Assets	—	$ 65,000	$ 406,000	$1,565,000	$ 2,794,000	$ 3,495,000	$ 4,007,000	$4,550,000	$4,507,000

Liabilities	Year 1	Year 2	Year 3	Year 4	Year 5	Year 6	Year 7	Year 8	Year 9
Current Liabilities			$ 10,000	$ 40,000	$ 55,000	$ 55,000	$ 55,000	$ 65,000	$ 55,000
Reserve for Royalties and Indemnities			—	$ 10,000	$ 44,000	$ 111,000	$ 208,000	$ 340,000	$ 512,000
Net Corporate Investment									
Corporate Investment	$ 45,000	$ 430,000	$ 954,000	$2,446,000	$ 4,134,000	$ 4,815,000	$ 4,770,000	$4,080,000	$2,065,000
Accumulated Profit (Loss)	(45,000)	(365,000)	(558,000)	(931,000)	(1,439,000)	(1,486,000)	(1,026,000)	65,000	1,875,000
Net Corporate Investment	—	$ 65,000	$ 396,000	$1,515,000	$ 2,695,000	$ 3,329,000	$ 3,744,000	$4,145,000	$3,940,000
Total Liabilities	—	$ 65,000	$ 406,000	$1,565,000	$ 2,794,000	$ 3,495,000	$ 4,007,000	$4,550,000	$4,507,000

Table 4 VSM Computer—Most Probable Income Statement

	Year 1	Year 2	Year 3	Year 4	Year 5	Year 6	Year 7	Year 8	Year 9
Revenue									
Equipment Sales				$ 150,000	$ 386,000	$ 554,000	$ 504,000	$ 386,000	$ 218,000
Lease Rentals				182,000	861,000	1,872,000	3,016,000	4,368,000	5,963,000
Service				40,000	95,000	145,000	195,000	220,000	235,000
Total Revenue				$ 372,000	$1,342,000	$2,571,000	$3,715,000	$4,974,000	$6,416,000
Returns and Allowances				7,000	25,000	48,000	70,000	93,000	119,000
Net Revenue				$ 365,000	$1,317,000	$2,523,000	$3,645,000	$4,881,000	$6,297,000
Cost of Revenue									
Equipment Sales				$ 95,000	$ 233,000	$ 277,000	$ 231,000	$ 161,000	$ 90,000
Lease Rentals				176,000	680,000	1,228,000	1,664,000	2,123,000	2,643,000
Service				20,000	49,000	75,000	102,000	116,000	124,000
Total Cost of Revenue				$ 291,000	$ 962,000	$1,580,000	$1,997,000	$2,400,000	$2,857,000
Gross Profit (Loss)				$ 74,000	$ 355,000	$ 943,000	$1,648,000	$2,481,000	$3,440,000
Selling, G&A Expenses									
Selling Expense			$ 134,000	$ 329,000	$ 671,000	$ 771,000	$ 932,000	$1,076,000	$1,302,000
G&A Expense			24,000	108,000	158,000	152,000	159,000	182,000	156,000
Total Selling, G&A Expenses			$ 158,000	$ 437,000	$ 829,000	$ 923,000	$1,091,000	$1,258,000	$1,458,000
Operating Profit (Loss)			$(158,000)	$(363,000)	$ (474,000)	$ 20,000	$ 557,000	$1,223,000	$1,982,000
Other Income Deductions									
Royalties and Indemnities	—	—	—	$ 10,000	$ 34,000	$ 67,000	$ 97,000	$ 132,000	$ 172,000
Research & Development	45,000	320,000	35,000	—	—	—	—	—	—
Total Income Deductions	$ 45,000	$ 320,000	$ 35,000	$ 10,000	$ 34,000	$ 67,000	$ 97,000	$ 132,000	$ 172,000
Net Income (Loss)	$(45,000)	$(320,000)	$(193,000)	$(373,000)	$ (508,000)	$ (47,000)	$ 460,000	$1,091,000	$1,810,000

Table 5 VSM Computer—Optimistic Balance Sheet

Assets	Year 1	Year 2	Year 3	Year 4	Year 5	Year 6	Year 7	Year 8	Year 9
Current Assets									
Accounts Receivable				$ 125,000	$ 348,000	$ 606,000	$ 811,000	$1,062,000	$1,404,000
Inventory									
Computers			$ 500,000	$ 908,000	$ 985,000	$ 960,000	$1,190,000	$1,190,000	$ 95,000
Spares			100,000	171,000	166,000	132,000	113,000	156,000	123,000
Total Inventory			$ 600,000	$1,079,000	$1,151,000	$1,092,000	$1,303,000	$1,346,000	$ 218,000
Total Current Assets			$ 600,000	$1,204,000	$1,499,000	$1,698,000	$2,114,000	$2,408,000	$1,622,000
Fixtures & Equipment (Net)		$ 65,000	$ 16,000	$ 86,000	$ 128,000	$ 129,000	$ 130,000	$ 115,000	$ 72,000
Leased Computers (Net)				$1,058,000	$1,988,000	$2,419,000	$2,834,000	$3,479,000	$4,471,000
Deferred Charges			$ 50,000	$ 30,000	$ 10,000	—	—	—	—
Total Assets	—	$ 65,000	$ 666,000	$2,378,000	$3,625,000	$4,246,000	$5,078,000	$6,002,000	$6,165,000
Liabilities									
Current Liabilities	$ 45,000		$ 17,000	$ 57,000	$ 63,000	$ 63,000	$ 74,000	$ 85,000	$ 75,000
Royalties & Indemnities				$ 18,000	$ 70,000	$ 162,000	$ 286,000	$ 450,000	$ 670,000
Net Corporate Investment									
Corporate Investment		$ 430,000	$1,266,000	$ 3,502,000	$ 5,128,000	$ 5,439,000	$5,415,000	$4,757,000	$2,510,000
Accumulated Profit (Loss)	$(45,000)	$(365,000)	$ (617,000)	$(1,199,000)	$(1,636,000)	$(1,418,000)	$ (697,000)	$ 710,000	$2,910,000
Net Corporate Investment	—	$ 65,000	$ 649,000	$ 2,303,000	$ 3,492,000	$ 4,021,000	$4,718,000	$5,467,000	$5,420,000
Total Liabilities	—	$ 65,000	$ 666,000	$ 2,378,000	$ 3,625,000	$ 4,246,000	$5,078,000	$6,002,000	$6,165,000

Table 6 VSM Computer—Optimistic Income Statement

	Year 1	Year 2	Year 3	Year 4	Year 5	Year 6	Year 7	Year 8	Year 9
Revenue									
Equipment Sales				$ 335,000	$ 670,000	$ 960,000	$ 840,000	$ 620,000	$ 505,000
Lease Rentals				331,000	1,232,000	2,369,000	3,664,000	5,307,000	7,455,000
Service				85,000	185,000	310,000	360,000	445,000	465,000
Total Revenue				$ 751,000	$2,087,000	$3,639,000	$4,864,000	$6,372,000	$8,425,000
Returns and Allowances				$ 15,000	$ 42,000	$ 73,000	$ 97,000	$ 127,000	$ 169,000
Net Revenue				$ 736,000	$2,045,000	$3,566,000	$4,767,000	$6,245,000	$8,256,000
Cost of Revenue									
Equipment Sales				$ 217,000	$ 378,000	$ 466,000	$ 375,000	$ 209,000	$ 171,000
Lease Rentals				322,000	993,000	1,562,000	2,035,000	2,626,000	3,427,000
Service				43,000	95,000	159,000	187,000	231,000	243,000
Total Cost of Revenue				$ 582,000	$1,466,000	$2,187,000	$2,597,000	$3,066,000	$3,841,000
Gross Profit (Loss)				$ 154,000	$ 579,000	$1,379,000	$2,170,000	$3,179,000	$4,415,000
Selling, G&A Expenses									
Selling Expense			$ 169,000	$ 553,000	$ 782,000	$ 896,000	$1,113,000	$1,373,000	$1,785,000
G&A Expense			48,000	165,000	182,000	174,000	212,000	235,000	209,000
Total Selling, G&A Expense			$ 217,000	$ 718,000	$ 964,000	$1,070,000	$1,325,000	$1,608,000	$1,994,000
Operating Profit (Loss)			$(217,000)	$(564,000)	$ (385,000)	$ 309,000	$ 845,000	$1,571,000	$2,421,000
Other Income Deductions									
Royalties and Indemnities	$ —	$ —	$ —	$ 18,000	$ 52,000	$ 91,000	$ 124,000	$ 164,000	$ 221,000
Research and Development	45,000	320,000	35,000	—	—	—	—	—	—
Total Income Deductions	$ 45,000	$ 320,000	$ 35,000	$ 18,000	$ 52,000	$ 91,000	$ 124,000	$ 164,000	$ 221,000
Net Income (Loss)	$(45,000)	$(320,000)	$(252,000)	$(582,000)	$ (437,000)	$ 218,000	$ 721,000	$1,407,000	$2,200,000

Meaning and Research

In this chapter we are concerned with two kinds of research, *basic research* and *decisional research. Basic research* is research that is conducted to extend the boundaries of knowledge. It is done for the purpose of making *the best possible estimate or conducting the best possible hypothesis test on the parameter or issue in question.* And it is done to help reach a conclusion rather than to help make a decision.[1] In contrast, *decisional research* is done for the purpose that its name implies—to help make *the best possible decision.*

An example of the two kinds of research applied to the same general problem is estimates of the price elasticity of gasoline. A study of the demand for gasoline made by Houthakker and Taylor[2] was conducted as basic research with no immediate application of the findings in mind. The

[1] J. W. Tukey, "Conclusions versus Decisions," *Technometrics,* **2** (November 1960), 423–433.

[2] H. S. Houthakker and L. D. Taylor, *Consumer Demand in the United States, 1929–1970* (Cambridge, Mass.: Harvard University Press, 1966), 116.

Federal Energy Office, on the other hand, in 1973 commissioned a study of gasoline price elasticity with a very pressing application waiting for the findings: the need to choose between higher gasoline prices (to result from increased taxes on crude oil) and coupon rationing of gasoline as a means of dealing with shortages.

It is not unusual to read the statement that "marketing research consists of scientific method applied to marketing problems." This can be taken to imply that, given the same general problems and time and cost constraints, the optimal design for both basic and decisional research projects is the same. This usually is not the case. The reasons for the differences become evident as we discuss the two types of research.

In a decisional research context, a research design is the specification of procedures for acquiring the information to structure and/or solve a problem. As such, a research design is concerned with *meaning, method,* and *measurement* in information acquisition, where *meaning* is derived from an evaluation of *relevance* and *accuracy* of information, *method* is the selection of a set of rules of evidence and the specification of how they are to be applied in obtaining information, and *measurement* is the operational process of acquiring and analyzing information. We are primarily concerned with *meaning* in research information in this chapter.

In order for information to be meaningful in a decisional situation, it must be *relevant* to the problem being considered. Relevancy is determined by the *problem situation model* and the *choice criterion model* of the person(s) making the decision. These two types of models are discussed in the first part of the chapter.

Information must also have the required level of *accuracy* if it is to be useful for decision making. *Accuracy* is judged on the basis of the *rules of evidence* held by those concerned with the research findings. Applicable rules of evidence of basic and decisional research studies are discussed in the latter part of the chapter.

Relevance of Information for Decision Making

Problem Situation Models

Meaning is derived from rules of evidence for evaluating relevance and accuracy of information. For example, a forecast by the weatherman that there will be eight inches of new, powdery snow in the mountains this weekend will have meaning if we are considering going skiing and are inclined to believe weather forecasts.

In order for information to be relevant, it must relate to the problem situation model held by the recipient of the information. A *problem situation model* may be defined as a conceptual way of relating a desired outcome with the variables that affect that outcome. The forecast of several inches of new powder on the slopes is relevant to the skier because he knows from past experience that this is one of the necessary elements for good skiing conditions. That is, his personal model of what is required for good skiing includes new snow that is dry and not too granular. In a research context, relevancy is determined by a model of the problem situation as well.

A problem situation model may take many forms, ranging from a set of informal, implicit opinions and beliefs that the holder may not be able to verbalize completely to complex and elaborately formulated models that are expressed in mathematical form. A marketing executive might respond to a question about a proposed price increase, for example, by making a statement such as, "I think if we increase the price our dollar sales will remain about the same, if our competitors don't increase their prices, and I don't think they will." A similar view might be expressed by the graph of the demand relationship shown in Figure 2–1 for the range of contemplated price changes.

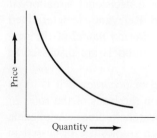

Figure 2–1 Price-quantity relationship with revenues constant.

Or, the relationship might be expressed as the equation,

$$\log k = \log q + n \log p$$

where

   k = a constant level of revenue
   q = quantity of units sold
   n = a positive number numerically equal to the elasticity of demand, and
   p = price,

all for that range of prices that is relevant. Regardless of whether it is implicit or explicit, informal or formal, qualitative or quantitative, any representation of outcome and the variables affecting that outcome comprise a model of the situation.

An Example of a Problem Situation Model

A problem situation model of some sort is necessary for conducting research as well as for making decisions. The researcher must understand the problem well enough to determine what the relevant variables are before he can decide what kinds of information are needed to help solve it. *The researcher also needs to know the problem situation model held by the manager.* The research information developed will only have meaning for the manager as it relates to the model of the problem that he holds. The manager's model also is often a valuable source of suggestions for research hypotheses to be tested and/or estimates that need to be made.

An illustration of a problem situation model and its role in the research process is provided by the experience of a chain of convenience markets. A few years ago the management of the chain, headquartered in a major city in the Southeast, decided to expand the chain's operations by entering the Miami market area. Sites were bought, and a large number of stores were built and opened in a short period of time. After three years of operation, more than one-half of the stores were still operating at a loss and the overall operation was highly unprofitable. A consultant was called in to review the situation and to advise the management as to what actions should be taken.

Conversations with the management indicated that it held a well-formulated model of what was required to produce a profitable store. This model had been developed from successful operations in other market areas and included the following elements:

1. *High store traffic* is generated by carrying convenience items (food, tobacco, beverages), being located at major arterial intersections, staying open long hours, building neighborhood customer loyalty, and advertising on radio during rush hours and in newspapers.
2. *High gross operating revenues* per store are generated by charging prices 10 to 15 per cent higher than supermarkets, making purchases in volume, and having high sales volume.
3. *Low operating expenses* are the result of carrying only fast turning items in inventory, keeping personnel at a minimum, operating in standardized, low maintenance cost buildings, and having a profit-sharing plan with store managers.
4. *A satisfactory contribution of store operating profits to corporate general expenditures and profit is the result of high gross operating revenues and low operating expenses.*

The model is shown schematically in Figure 2–2.

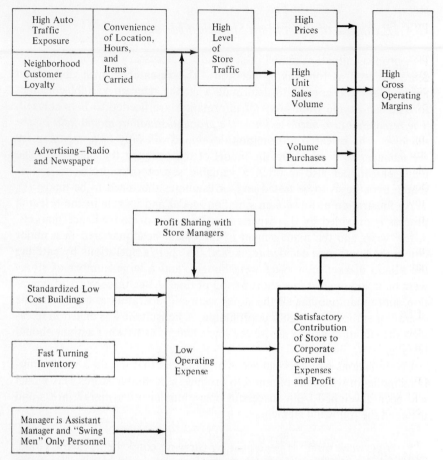

Figure 2–2 Schematic model of controllable factors in operation of convenience market.

After discussing the problem with the management, observing the operations of three of the stores, talking with other convenience store operators in the city, and doing a search of secondary data sources, the consultant's model of the problem situation was as follows:

1. *Factors affecting store traffic.* Management is probably correct that carrying convenience items, staying open long hours, and building neighborhood customer loyalty help generate store traffic. However, it is not clear that a large proportion of the store's customers arrive by automobile and there does not seem to be a large buildup of store traffic during the rush hours. It may be that location at major intersections and advertising on radio during peak automobile traffic hours are not contributing much to

store traffic. Other stores located in the vicinity that carry the same items probably reduce store traffic.

2. *Gross operating revenues.* The policy of charging prices 10 to 15 per cent higher than supermarkets may or may not contribute to higher gross operating revenues, depending upon the price elasticity of demand for convenience items. The problem may lie in the average sale per customer being too low rather than there not being enough customers in the store.

3. *Operating expenses.* The management policies of carrying fast turning items in inventory, keeping personnel at a minimum, operating in standardized, low maintenance cost buildings, and having a profit-sharing plan with store managers all seem to be effective in keeping operating expenses down. The arrangement of the stores contributes to shoplifting, however, and this may be more of an addition to operating expenses than management realizes.

4. *Store operating profits (or loss).* It appears that the problem of the unprofitable stores is in not generating enough gross revenue rather than having operating expenses that are too high.

The subsequent research conducted by the consultant revealed a number of factors contributing to the problem. A comparison of the operations of profitable versus unprofitable stores in the chain revealed that management's belief that location at the intersection of major arterials and radio advertising during peak traffic hours would generate a high amount of drive-in store traffic was wrong. About two-thirds of the customers of the typical market in the chain came from within a five-block radius and 85 per cent came from a one-mile radius of the market. There was even a negative factor associated with being located at an intersection of a heavily trafficked street; mothers were reluctant to send younger children to the market to buy items when they had to cross busy streets. Recognition of radio advertising themes was low among drive-in customers.

Stores with the highest average number of customers per day were located in neighborhoods that had a relatively high proportion of apartments occupied by families in which the age of the head was between 20 and 40. One or more supermarkets located within a half-mile radius of the convenience market substantially reduced sales volume. Customers reported that they realized that prices in the convenience market were higher than in the supermarkets but, in general, they believed that this was offset by the ease of buying at the convenience market they patronized.

The major problem was that average sales per customer were too low. From secondary data, it was found that the national average sale per customer for a convenience market was $1.32 whereas for stores of this chain it was $1.06. An increase of $.26 per customer was found to be enough to make the average store in the chain profitable with the store traffic it had. Among other recommendations, the consultant suggested an immediate program to train store personnel in checkout selling (suggesting items related to those brought to the checkout stand by the shopper) and an increase of point-of-purchase displays in the stores.

Choice Criterion Models

Managements, like individuals, acquire recognizable characteristics that distinguish them from others. One company in an industry may be known as a cautious, conservative organization that is soundly managed but that has neither the flair nor the interest for industry leadership or innovation. Another company in the same industry may have a forward-looking, risk-taking image with a long series of striking successes—and not a few impressive failures—to support the image. The way in which a management deals with risk involves a *choice criterion* model. The model used has an important effect on both the decisions made and the relevancy of the information used to help make them.

An example is provided by a supermarket chain headquartered on the West Coast. The responsibilities of the marketing research department include the evaluation of potential sites on which to build new units. A classification system has been developed that has four categories of market areas: a Class A market area has "very high potential," a Class B area has "high potential," a Class C area has "average potential," and a Class D area has "limited potential." One of three sizes of stores is built depending upon the evaluation of the market area in which the site is located. A Class I store is the standard size and the one that is built most often, a Class II store is about 20 per cent larger, and a Class III store is still

Table 2–1 Conditional Payoff Estimates for Supermarket Site Selection Problem ($000)

	Market Area			
Alternatives	*Class A (very high potential)*	*Class B (high potential)*	*Class C (average potential)*	*Class D (limited potential)*
A–1 Build Class I Store (Standard)	$250	$200	$100	$ 0
A–2 Build Class II Store (Large)	400	300	0	<100>
A–3 Build Class III Store (Variety Market)	600	400	0	<200>
A–4 Do not build store	0	0	0	0

larger to accommodate a variety department as well as a grocery section.

Operating experience has provided the company with payoff estimates for the eight-year planning period used by the company for the various sized stores built on sites located in each class of market area. These estimates are similar to the ones shown in Table 2–1.

Suppose that a site evaluation has just been made and the analyst has reported that the area "appears to be either Class B or Class C. There is little chance of its being either Class A or D." What size store should be built?

The answer to this question is dependent upon the way one wants to deal with the risk of misclassification of market area. Several choice criteria models have been developed that set forth decision rules for choosing among alternatives under uncertainty. The *maximin,* the *maximax,* the *minimax regret,* the *average monetary value (AMV),* and the *expected monetary value (EMV)* choice criterion models are used to provide such decision rules. The choice among these rules has a substantial effect on the use of marketing research.

A discussion of these decision rules follows.

The Maximin Rule

The maximin rule requires that one should always act in such a way as to *maxi*mize the *min*imum payoff. That is, the action should be chosen whose worst possible outcome is better than (or at least no worse than) the worst possible outcome of any other action.[3]

When applied to the supermarket site problem, one quickly sees that the appropriate action is to build a standard sized (Class I) store. Reference to Table 2–1 shows that the worst possible consequence of that action is to break even if the site turns out to be located in a Class D market area. If either a Class II or Class III store is built on the mistaken assumption that the market area is Class C or higher, a loss will be incurred.

The use of the maximin rule implies a high aversion to risk of out-of-pocket loss. In effect, the assumption that underlies its use is that the worst that *can* happen *will* happen. The rule is applied as if this worst possible outcome were certain to happen and the only sensible action to take is to minimize its effects. Although the *probability of incurring an out-of-pocket cost is greatly reduced, the probability of incurring an opportunity cost is substantially increased.*

If the management of the supermarket chain were actually using such a rule, it would build only Class I stores. Building Class II or Class III stores could result in a loss and would thus not be acceptable alternatives.

---

[3] See R. D. Luce and H. Raiffa, *Games and Decisions* (New York: John Wiley & Sons, Inc., 1957), chap. 13 for a discussion of this and the rules that follow.

By so doing, however, the possibility of added returns from building larger stores under favorable market conditions would be foregone.

The use of a maximin rule has a substantial effect on the kind of information required by management and thus on the nature of any marketing research conducted to provide it. The only information required for each alternative being considered when using a maximin rule is an estimate of the *payoff for the least favorable market condition.* Neither estimates of payoffs for more favorable conditions nor assessments of the probabilities of each market condition being the actual one are needed for making a decision using this rule.

An example is a market test of a new bowling ball conducted by Brunswick a few years ago. The company chose to test market its new ball in New Jersey, the most highly competitive area for bowling equipment in this country. The reasoning given for choosing this market area for the test was "if it survives there it will survive anyplace." Note from the conditional payoff table (Table 2–2) for the introduction that only one estimate was being sought—the estimate of the payoff that would result from the least favorable market condition.

Table 2–2   Conditional Payoff Table for Introduction of Bowling Ball

	Market Condition					
	Very Favorable		Favorable		Unfavorable	
	Prob-ability	Payoff	Prob-ability	Payoff	Prob-ability	Payoff
Introduce	—	—	—	—	—	Estimate Sought
Do Not In-troduce	—	0	—	0	—	0

The Maximax Rule

The *maximax* rule reflects an entirely different view of risk than the *maximin* rule. It suggests that the firm should choose that action that *maxi*mizes the *maxi*mum gain. The maximaxer wants to run the lowest possible risk of incurring an opportunity cost. To do so he must greatly increase the probability of undergoing an outlay cost.

Reference to Table 2–1 permits the determination of which size of store should be built by the supermarket chain if the management is using a maximax rule. The highest payoff is obtained by building a Class III store in a Class A market area. So long as there is some possibility of the site's being in a Class A market area, the maximax rule would require that the Class III store be built.

The use of the maximax rule also has a substantial effect on the kind of information required by management. The only information needed is the *estimate of payoff for the most favorable market condition.* Neither estimates of payoffs for less favorable market conditions nor assessments of probabilities of each market condition's being the actual one are needed for making a decision using this rule.

An example of a research project that is consistent with the use of a maximax rule is a poll commissioned by President Johnson in early 1968. The poll was taken for the purpose of providing added information to help him decide whether he should run for re-election in that year. The sampling area used was Tennessee, a border state that has consistently elected Democratic candidates since the Civil War. The reasoning for selecting the state of Tennessee for the poll may well have been, "If I run and can't carry Tennessee, I can't win the election."

The Minimax Regret Rule

L. J. Savage[4] has proposed a rule that emphasizes *mini*mizing the maximum regret that could result from the decision; it is known as the *minimax regret* rule. His rule requires that the payoffs be transformed into opportunity losses and that the maximin rule then be applied. An opportunity loss, as the name implies, is the loss that results from not having chosen a better alternative; an opportunity for greater gain is lost if an inferior action is taken.

The opportunity loss for each action is conditional upon the state of the market. We can convert Table 2–1 to a conditional opportunity loss table by subtracting the highest payoff under each market condition from all other payoffs under that same condition. Thus, for Class A market areas the largest potential payoff is for a Class III store and is estimated to be $600,000. If that alternative is chosen and the site turns out to be in a Class A market area, there will be no opportunity loss. The conditional opportunity loss is zero, and no regret will result from having made that decision. Building any other size of store will necessarily involve opportunity loss and, thus, regret. If a Class II store is built in a Class A market area, the payoff is estimated to be only $400,000, or $200,000 less than if a Class I store is built.

The values for the conditional opportunity losses shown in Table 2–3 were arrived at in this way. Once the conditional opportunity losses are determined, the minimax regret rule is applied by (1) determining the maximum opportunity loss (potential maximum regret) for each alterna-

[4] L. J. Savage, "The Theory of Statistical Decision," *Journal of the American Statistical Association,* **46** (March 1951), 56–57.

Table 2–3 Conditional Opportunity Loss Table for a Supermarket Site Selection
Problem ($000)

	Market Area			
	Class A (very high potential)	Class B (high potential)	Class C (average potential)	Class D (limited potential)
A–1. Build Class I store	$350	$200	$ 0	$ 0
A–2. Build Class II store	200	100	100	100
A–3. Build Class III store	0	0	100	200
A–4. Do not build store	600	400	100	0

tive and (2) finding the minimum for these maximum losses. From Table
2–3 we can see that the maximum opportunity loss is $350,000 for build-
ing a Class I store and $200,000 for building Class II and Class III
stores. Using the minimax regret rule, then, one would choose to build
either a Class II or Class III store but not a Class I store.

Again, the use of the minimax regret rule affects the kind of information required by management in order to make a decision. In this case
estimates of payoffs for each alternative under each market condition are
required. No assessments of the probabilities of each market condition's
being the true one are needed, however. If this rule had been used by the
bowling equipment company, it would have had to develop estimates of
payoffs under favorable market conditions as well as under unfavorable
ones. If these estimates were to be developed directly from market test
results, it would have been necessary for Brunswick to have conducted
the market test of the new bowling ball in an area (or areas) where there
was less competition and conditions were otherwise more favorable.

The Average Monetary Value (AMV) Rule

In some situations it might be argued that there is no basis for expecting
that one market condition is more likely to be the actual one than another.
In such a case it is reasonable to argue that the alternative with the highest *average* payoff should be selected.

The application of such a rule in the supermarket problem would result
in a Class III store being built. As shown in Table 2–4, the average payoff
for that size store is $200,000 compared to $150,000 for a Class II store
and $137,500 for a Class I store.

Expected Monetary Value (EMV) Rule

The expected monetary value (EMV) rule requires that a probability
be assigned to the occurrence of each market condition and that an

Table 2–4   Estimated and Average Conditional Payoffs for Supermarket Site Selection Problem ($000)

	Market Area				
Alternative	Class A (very high potential)	Class B (high potential)	Class C (average potential)	Class D (limited potential)	Average monetary value (AMV)
A–1. Build Class I store	$250	$200	$100	$ 0	$137,500
A–2. Build Class II store	400	300	0	<100>*	150,000
A–3. Build Class III store	600	400	0	<200>	200,000
A–4. Do not build store	0	0	0	0	0

* <   > denotes loss.

expected monetary value be calculated for each alternative. The expected monetary value for an alternative is the sum of the payoffs for that alternative under each market condition weighted by the probability of the market condition occurring. The alternative that has the highest expected monetary value is chosen.

In the supermarket site problem it will be recalled that the analyst who made the (hypothetical) site evaluation reported that "the market area appears to be Class B or Class C. There is little chance of it being either Class A or Class D." Suppose he were to express his judgment about the probability of each class being the correct classification of the market area as a numerical value. He might have concluded that there was a probability of about .40 for each of the Class B and Class C designations and of .10 for each of the Class A and Class D designations that they were the correct classifications of the market area in which the site was located. These judgments would then have been expressed as *personal probabilities* and are reflected in Table 2–5.

The *EMV* for an alternative was earlier defined as the sum of the payoffs for that payoff under each market condition weighted by the probability of the market condition occurring. Thus, for the alternative of building a Class I store (alternative I)

$$EMV = .10(\$250,000) + .40(\$200,000) + .40(\$100,000) + .10(\$0)$$
$$= \$25,000 + \$80,000 + \$40,000 + 0$$
$$= \$145,000$$

The *EMVs* for all of the remaining alternatives being considered are shown in Table 2–5. It may be seen that the *EMV* for building a Class III store (alternative 3) is the highest at $200,000. If the EMV rule were used, therefore, this action should be selected.

Table 2-5 Estimated Payoffs and Probabilities of Market Area Potentials for Supermarket Site Selection Problem ($000)*

| | Market Area | | | | | | | | |
| | Class A (Very High Potential) | | Class B (High Potential) | | Class C (Average Potential) | | Class D (Limited Potential) | | Expected Monetary Value |
Alternative	Prob-ability	Payoff	Prob-ability	Payoff	Prob-ability	Payoff	Prob-ability	Payoff	
A–1. Build Class I store	.1	$250	.4	$200	.4	$100	.1	$ 0	$145
A–2. Build Class II store	.1	400	.4	300	.4	0	.1	<100>	150
A–3. Build Class III store	.1	600	.4	400	.4	0	.1	<200>	200
A–4. Do not build store	.1	0	.4	0	.4	0	.1	0	0

* < > denotes loss.

The use of personal probabilities and the application of the EMV rule in determining the expected value of information to be provided by a research project being considered are discussed in Chapter 3.

Results of Application of Decision Rules in Decision on Supermarket Size

The results of applying the various decision rules to the problem of deciding which size supermarket to build are as follows:

Rule	Decision
Maximin	Class I store
Maximax	Class III store
Minimax Regret	Class II or Class III store
Average Monetary Value (AMV)	Class III store
Expected Monetary Value (EMV)	Class III store

The different decisions are the result of the different preferences with respect to risk that are reflected in the rules. No one rule can be said to be "better" than another except as it relates to the risk preferences of the user.

Monetary Values and Utilities

Finding a valid average (mean) or expected value of a set of payoffs requires that the unit of measurement is constant over the full range of the data. A valid measurement of the mean height of a group of people cannot be obtained, for example, if each person is measured with an elastic rule that measures in inches but stretches increasingly disproportionate amounts as it is extended.

Something similar to this may occur when conditional payoffs are averaged or when their expected value is found. Although the payoffs are each measured using the same dollar unit, the *utility* represented by equal dollar amounts may vary depending upon the size of the payoff. To a small company, for example, the possibility of a loss of $50,000 on a prospective venture may represent a much greater loss of utility than a profit of $50,000 would represent in gain. Both may represent a greater change in utility than that resulting from an increase in profit from, say $50,000 to $100,000. In all instances, however, the same $50,000 increment (or decrement) in dollar amounts is involved.

The usual practice when using an average or expected monetary value rule is *not* to adjust the payoffs for differences in utilities. The implicit assumption that we make in the examples and illustrations in this book is that such adjustment is not required,[5] although it may be needed in some situations. Procedures are available and can be used to make the adjustment of payoffs when required.[6]

Use of Choice Criterion Models. The foregoing discussion was not meant to imply that in the typical situation a management systematically examines choice criterion models and decides which one it will use in making decisions. The managements of some companies have done so but the available evidence suggests that they represent a small minority of all companies.[7]

Although the type of rule that management is inclined to use may not be well defined, it is important for the researcher to become as familiar as possible with the risk preferences of the persons to whom his findings and recommendations will be directed. As we have already seen, these risk preferences can have a considerable effect on the kind of information desired and, therefore, on the research conducted. Had the management of Brunswick been using a different decision rule, the market test that was run would almost certainly have been in a different market area. Had President Johnson been using a rule similar to the one Brunswick used, the poll to determine voter preferences would not have been taken using only a sample of a favorable electorate.

The importance of knowing the type of decision rule(s) that management uses extends to considerations other than the type of information required. A researcher who is making recommendations based upon one implicit decision rule to a management using a different rule is almost certain to lose effectiveness. As was demonstrated in the supermarket site evaluation problem, the choice of alternatives may turn on the decision rule used. It will often be possible, and it may well be desirable, to condition recommendations upon relevant decision rules when there is reason to believe that more than one rule will be (or should be) considered.

As was stated at the beginning of the chapter, in order for information to be meaningful in a decisional situation, it must be both *relevant* and *accurate*. We now need to consider the accuracy of information.

---

[5] Such adjustment is not required as long as the decision maker's utility function is linear with respect to money. For a discussion see P. E. Green and D. S. Tull, *Research for Marketing Decisions,* 3rd ed. (Englewood-Cliffs, N.J.: Prentice-Hall, Inc., 1974), 33–36.

[6] See W. J. Baumol, *Economic Theory and Operations Analysis,* 2nd ed. (Englewood-Cliffs, N.J.: Prentice-Hall, Inc., 1965), for a discussion of this procedure. For descriptions of applications of the procedure to actual problems see P. E. Green, "Risk Attitudes and Chemical Investment Decisions," *Chemical Engineering Progress* (January 1963), and J. D. Barnes, *A Strategic Competitive Bidding Approach to Pricing Decisions for Petroleum Industry Drilling Contractors,* unpublished doctoral dissertation, University of Oregon, 1972.

[7] R. V. Brown, "Do Managers Find Decision Theory Useful?" *Harvard Business Review* (May–June 1970), 78–89.

Accuracy of Information

The accuracy of a measurement is inversely related to the amount of total error present. If a compilation of industry sales for the year showed a total of $11 million and actual sales were only $10 million, we could say that there was a 10 per cent error, or that the amount arrived at by the compilation was 90 per cent accurate.

The total error in a measurement includes both systematic errors (bias) and variable errors. The total error concept is an important one in research. The various sources of error and strategies for dealing with error in research are discussed in Chapter 4.

If we always knew the actual value being measured we would have no trouble determining the amount of error present in a recorded value. We almost never know the true value, however, because if we did we would not have needed to try and measure it in the first place. It is, therefore, necessary to try and assess by other means the amount of error that *may* be present in the research. *Rules of evidence* are used for this purpose.

Rules of evidence of some sort are necessary for all formal investigatory proceedings. A trial in a court of law, for example, is a formal investigation to determine guilt or innocence and the degree thereof. Rules concerning the admissibility and the weight to be given various types of evidence—such as "hearsay," "direct," and "circumstantial"—have been developed and are carefully observed in the course of the trial. The phrase "audited in conformity with generally accepted accounting principles" that appears on financial statements prepared by accounting firms is indicative of a set of rules of evidence that are commonly accepted in the accounting profession.

Rules of Evidence in Basic Research

The rules of evidence that are the operational ones in evaluating research information are those subscribed to by the "client" of the research. The "client" of the basic research project is the scientific community to which it is reported. This group normally will not have commissioned the research; nor, as a group if not individuals, will it be affected personally by the outcome. The investigator may or may not be known to the majority of those to whom the results are to be reported.

As a result of the impersonal nature of the researcher-"client" relationship, evaluation of basic research studies is necessarily based on the procedures used in the study rather than the competence of the investigator. One of the fundamental procedures in basic research is the *hypothesis test*.

Testing of Hypotheses

Suppose a basic research study were to be carried out to determine the differences, if any, between "blue-collar" and "white-collar" families in the readership of daily newspapers. Several estimates of blue-collar and white-collar readership characteristics are to be made and a number of hypotheses are to be tested.

In a study using the accepted procedures of scientific method, several steps are involved in conducting a hypothesis test. They are:

Step 1. formulate a hypothesis about the problem of interest;
Step 2. make a prediction based on the hypothesis;
Step 3. devise a test of the prediction;
Step 4. conduct the test;
Step 5. analyze to determine if test results are significant.

In the newspaper study, for example, one might hypothesize that there is no difference between blue-collar and white-collar families with respect to the proportion subscribing to newspapers (*step 1*). A prediction based upon this hypothesis would be that, in a survey of blue-collar and white-collar families, there would be no significant difference in the proportions of the respondents who subscribe to one or more daily newspapers (*step 2*). A survey could then be designed to test this prediction (*step 3*). It would involve taking a sample of blue-collar and a sample of white-collar families and determining whether or not they subscribe to at least one daily newspaper and if the sample proportions differ significantly. The survey could then be conducted (*step 4*) and the resulting data analyzed to determine if there were in fact differences beyond those that could reasonably be laid to sampling variation—if the findings are significant (*step 5*).

Suppose a random sample of 100 blue-collar and 100 white-collar families were taken and the number of subscribers to one or more daily newspapers determined for each. Further suppose the number of blue-collar subscribers turns out to be 50 and the number of white-collar subscribers is 60. What should the researcher conclude about the difference in the proportion of subscribers?

The basic researcher will answer this question by running a *test of significance*. He will recognize that certainly some, and perhaps all, of the difference in the proportion of blue-collar and white-collar families who are subscribers could be a result of sampling variation alone. He will run the test of significance to determine if it is reasonable to conclude that all of the difference in the two values could be the result of sampling variation.

Suppose in this case the researcher is willing to allow a probability of only .05 (a level commonly used in basic research) that the difference in proportions subscribing was a result of sampling variation. By a process described more fully later (Chapter 14), he can calculate that the probability of the observed difference in sample proportions resulting from sampling variation alone is .101. Since this is greater than the allowable probability of .05, the conclusion is drawn that the results are insignificant —the hypothesis of "no difference" cannot be rejected. The importance of the significance level can be seen by the fact that a probability of .049 will result in the hypothesis of no difference being rejected whereas a probability of .051 will not permit it to be rejected.

Rules of Evidence for Hypothesis Tests

The generally accepted rules of evidence for the testing of hypotheses in basic research investigations are stated as follows (and shown in Table 2–6).

Table 2–6 Rules of Evidence for Hypothesis Tests in Basic Research

Stage of Investigation	Rules of Evidence
Develop hypothesis	(1) Prior probability of truth of hypothesis is ignored.
Make prediction	(2) Predictions must involve only evidence that is accessible to other investigators. (3) The evidence to be used for the test must be prespecified.
Devise test	(4) Test must be conducted by prespecified method. (5) Criteria for rejection of hypothesis must be prespecified.
Conduct test	(6) Procedures must be public. (7) Procedures must be investigator independent. (8) Test must be replicable. (9) Test must be designed to obtain unbiased estimates.

Table 2–6 (*Continued*)

Stage of Investigation	Rules of Evidence
Analyze to determine if test results are "significant"	(10) Analysis conducted using applicable methods of inferential statistics with no inferences based on investigator judgment. (11) Estimation of unmeasured errors based upon judgment of the investigator not permitted. (12) Unmeasured errors ignored.

1. *Prior probability of truth of hypothesis is ignored.* Whether or not the investigator believes that blue-collar and white-collar families do subscribe to daily newspapers in the same proportions is irrelevant to the test.
2. *Predictions must involve evidence that is accessible to other investigators.* Advancements in knowledge cannot rely upon the unverified observations or judgments of a single person.
3. *The evidence to be used for the test must be prespecified.* The evidentiary basis for the test cannot be changed once the test is underway. This requirement prevents changes that would tend to favor rejecting or failing to reject the hypothesis being made by the investigator to affect the outcome of the test.
4. *The procedures for testing the hypothesis must be prespecified.* The basic procedures involved in the hypothesis test cannot be adjusted to conform to the evidence obtained after the test is begun.
5. *The criteria for the rejection of the hypothesis must be prespecified.* One cannot conduct the test and then decide on either the criteria or the level of significance of the evidence necessary for rejection.

   In the readership study, for example, a significance level should be prespecified. A significance level is the probability set that the outcome observed is not the result of sampling variation alone. Regardless of where it is originally set (.10, .05, or .01, for example), it should not be changed to either a higher or lower level after the test has been run.
6. *The test procedures must be publicly available.* Potential verification by another investigator requires full disclosure of test procedures.
7. *The test procedures must be investigator independent.* Accessibility of evidence to more than one investigator requires tests that do not depend upon any one investigator to conduct.
8. *The test should be replicable.* Although there are rare but necessary exceptions to this rule (one might want to test readership concern-

ing some sensational event, for example), when possible the test must be designed to be replicable.

9. *The test must be designed to obtain estimates that are as free of bias as possible.* Although tests can sometimes be made using data that are known to be biased in a given direction, unbiased data are to be obtained if possible.

    One result of this requirement that is of particular importance is that *random samples* must be used. Nonrandom samples may have bias as well as sampling variation reflected in the measurements made from it; random samples have only sampling variation.

10. *The analysis is conducted using applicable methods of interferential statistics with no inferences based on investigator judgment.* The need to preserve investigator independence in the test removes the possibility of using investigator judgment in the analysis of data.

11. *Estimation of unmeasured errors by judgments of the investigator is not permitted.* Although *sampling* error and some nonsampling errors (errors of measurement, nonresponse, inadequate sampling frame, and others) that are unmeasured may be known to be present in the study, the preservation of investigator-free procedures does not allow estimation of the errors through the exercise of judgment.

    Although it may be known that the nonrespondents in the newspaper readership study differ from the respondents (higher proportion of working wives and lower proportion of preschool age children so that it is less likely that someone will be home during the day, for example) and that some of these differences will affect readership of newspapers, estimation of their effects using investigator judgment is not permitted.

12. *Unmeasured errors are ignored.* Since unmeasured errors cannot be estimated, ignoring them is the only remaining possibility.

Rules of Evidence in Decisional Research

As in basic research, it is the client for the decisional research project who is the final determinant of the admissible rules of evidence. The client of a decisional research project is the person (or persons) who will use the information developed by the project for making a pending decision. The managing editor of a newspaper might authorize a readership study of blue-collar and white-collar families, for example, to assist him in making decisions concerning editorial policy for the paper. The information sought might be the same as that in the basic research study described earlier but the purpose of obtaining it would be entirely different.

The steps involved in decisional research projects are similar to, but not identical with, those described earlier for hypotheses tests in basic research. Decisional research is concerned with helping to identify and solve problems. As such, it necessarily involves the development and evaluation of alternatives.

The steps involved in a decisional research project designed to help solve a problem are as follows:

Step 1. develop alternative solutions for the problem;
Step 2. describe possible outcomes if each alternative is adopted;
Step 3. devise means of predicting actual outcomes;
Step 4. make the measurements necessary for the predictions;
Step 5. analyze the results.

Although the procedural steps are similar, depending upon the client and the nature of the decision to be made, the rules of evidence for a decisional research project may differ in important respects from those for basic research. The several reasons for such possible differences include considerations of (1) *cost versus value of information,* (2) *direct association of client and investigator,* (3) *limited need for replication,* (4) *differences in measurement requirements,* and (5) *the need to know probability level rather than whether or not results are significant.*

1. *Cost versus value of information.* If research projects were costless and required no time to conduct, the decisional research client would always choose to have research done rather than to make the decision without it. Further, he would choose research procedures that were investigator independent and called for objective measures of potential error.

As the financial sponsor of the research as well as the user of it, however, he knows that for many decisions research information will not be worth its cost. He also understands that at some point in some research projects reliance upon investigator judgment instead of more costly procedures that are investigator independent may result in a better informational buy. The same reasoning applies to the estimation of the errors in the information by the analyst instead of attempting to measure them; the value added to the information by the objective measurement of the errors may not be worth the additional cost that such measurement involves.

An important difference that one often finds in the designs of decisional and basic research projects is the kind and size of sample that is taken. A random sample should be taken in the basic research project since judgmental estimates of error (sampling or others) are not permitted. Nonrandom samples are often taken in decisional research because judgmental errors of estimates *are* accepted and a random sample may not be considered to be worth the additional cost.

A method of determining the expected value of research information was developed in the late 1950s as a part of *Bayesian* statistics. This is discussed in detail in Chapter 3.

2. *Direct association of client and researcher.* The decisional research client has an added means of assessing research information that is often not available to those involved in basic research. He will typically have been closely associated with the project from its inception, in many cases even to the point of having chosen the principal researcher(s) involved. He will have had an opportunity to assess both the general competency of the researchers and the manner in which the project was conducted. At the time the report is presented to him he will be able to ask any questions concerning procedures or analysis or findings. The need for objective measurement of error and for investigator independent procedures, in this situation, is therefore less.

3. *Limited need for replication.* There is rarely a need for replication in decisional research projects. The same general types of marketing mix decisions (product, price, promotion, and distribution) continue to be made but the circumstances are always different. Including features in the design that incur added costs solely to permit replication is seldom worthwhile in decisional research.

4. *Differences in measurement requirements.* The people to whom the results of basic research projects are reported are interested in the researcher's having obtained the best possible measurement. The decisional research client may not be interested in an error free measurement for two reasons.

First, as we saw earlier in this chapter, a *biased* measurement is sometimes preferred to an unbiased one. (The word *bias* is used here to mean the result of "collection of evidence in such a way that one alternative answer to a research question is favored."[8] This was the case in both the poll commissioned by President Johnson (a favorable state was chosen as the polling area and thus an upward bias produced in the estimate of those who would vote for him) and the market test of the new Brunswick bowling ball (an unfavorable market test area was chosen with a resultant downward bias in the results of the market test). These resulted from the use of decision rules that were close approximations of the *maximax* and *maximin* decision rules.

Second, added precision in measurements can sometimes be meaningless in a decisional context. It makes no difference whether losses produced by shoplifting in a department store are running at a rate of 4 per cent or 5 per cent of sales, for example, if both rates are unacceptable and the same actions will be taken regardless of which is the correct figure.

5. *Need to know probability level rather than whether or not results are significant.* Rather than being done as a basic research project, suppose that the readership study described earlier were being done for a newspaper to help decide where promotional efforts should be concen-

[8] C. Selltiz, et al., *Research Methods in Social Relations,* rev. ed. (New York: Holt, Rinehart, and Winston, Inc., 1959), 501.

trated in a promotional drive. For this purpose, the researcher and the manager will not be interested in significance as such but in the *probability* that the subscription proportions differ among blue-collar and white-collar families, so long as some form of expected value decision rule is being used.

Recall that the probability of the difference in sample subscription proportions was calculated to be .101. If the findings assumed previously are applicable to the newspaper for which the study is being done, there is a probability of $1.000 - .101 = .899$ that the proportion of blue-collar families actually subscribing is less than that for white-collar families. This information should be reported to the manager.

Summary

This chapter was concerned with *meaning* in research information. *Meaning* was defined as being derived from an evaluation of relevance and accuracy in research information.

Two kinds of research were identified: *basic* research and *decisional* research. The distinction between them is the purpose for which they were conducted. *Basic research* is done to add to the existing store of knowledge in a field whereas *decisional research* is conducted to provide information to help make a pending decision.

Relevancy of information is derived from the *problem situation model* and the *choice criterion model* of the person(s) involved in the decision. A *problem situation model* is the way we conceptualize the relationship of the outcome desired from solving the problem with the variables that affect that outcome. Information is *relevant* when it leads to an alternative being considered or helping to predict what will happen if an alternative course of action is adopted.

A *choice criterion model* is concerned with how one chooses among alternatives in an uncertain situation. A decision rule is associated with each model. The *maximin, minimax regret, average monetary value,* and *expected monetary value* rules are the more commonly known decision rules. Each of these rules was described and its effects on the research conducted to help make a decision when it was used was discussed.

An assessment of the *accuracy* of information provided by research comes from *rules of evidence*. The rules of evidence of hypothesis tests in basic research were examined and the differences with the rules for decisional research were described. The rules of evidence for hypothesis tests are properly designed to ensure that the findings are independent of the person doing the investigation and that the study can be replicated. Advancements in scientific knowledge cannot rest on the unverified observations of a single investigator.

The rules of evidence applicable to decisional research differ for a number of reasons. The cost versus the value of the information to be obtained from alternative designs must be considered. The close working relationship between researcher and manager allows for greater use of investigator judgment than is the case in basic research. There is seldom any need for replication and so design features installed for this purpose can be eliminated. There may be differences in measurement requirements between the two types of research as well. Depending upon the problem situation and decision rule being used, relatively gross measurements may be entirely adequate and measurements containing biasing elements may be preferred. Finally, significance tests are not the usual interest of the manager; rather, he is interested in the probability that a specified outcome will occur.

Questions and Problems

2.1. (a) Develop a problem situation model that is applicable to the decision by a brewery as to whether it should market a premium brand of beer in biodegradable plastic cans. (b) Indicate how this problem situation model relates to a consumer use test to be run by the research department in which beer in the plastic containers is to be provided consumers over a period of time and consumer reaction obtained.

2.2. Develop a problem situation model for a decision concerning whether or not to increase the advertising budget for next year by 5 per cent that is: (a) verbal in form, (b) graphic in form, (c) a mathematical equation.

2.3. Identify each of the following situations by the decision rule that is being used. Explain why you believe your answer to be the correct one.
(a) A milling firm in Minneapolis buys 100,000 bushels of No. 2 Hard Winter Wheat to make into flour. It will take about two months before the flour is milled and has been sold. Not wishing to speculate on price changes of wheat during this period, and knowing that the price of wheat and flour move very closely together, the firm *sells* 100,000 bushels of No. 2 Hard Winter Wheat on the futures market at the same time it bought the wheat to mill. Two months later the firm *sells* the flour and *buys* 100,000 bushels of No. 2 Hard Winter Wheat back on the futures market. (This is known as a hedging operation.) What decision rule was the firm using? Explain.
(b) The president of a major tire manufacturing firm asks for two sales forecasts; an optimistic one and a pessimistic one. He averages them for his own use but gives the pessimistic one to the financial planning and the optimistic one to the marketing department for market planning. What decision rule is he using when he averages the forecasts for his own use? Explain.
(c) What decision rule is the president of the tire manufacturing firm using when he gives the finance department the pessimistic forecast to use for financial planning? Explain.
(d) A marine underwriting company has recently provided policies to protect tanker owners against damages arising from oil polluting

beaches after collisions. The company determined that there is a .04 chance per year of collision involving one or more tankers that is serious enough and close enough to land to incur damages. It estimates that damages from a collision will average about $500,000 and has set the premium per year at (.04 × $500,000) plus $25,000, or $45,000 per year. What decision rule is the company using (basically)? Explain.

(e) What decision rule are the tanker owners using who take out this policy? Explain.

(f) A well-known football coach explains his reasoning for making only sparing use of the forward pass by saying, "When you pass, only three things can happen and two of them are bad." What decision rule does he appear to be using? Explain.

2.4. What "rules of evidence" should be applied in evaluating each of the following informational inputs?

(a) A pre-election poll of voters to determine the probable outcome of a senatorial race.

(b) An opinion of a consultant called in to advise on which action should be taken in a marketing problem.

(c) The results of a preference test of a chocolate drink as compared with three competitive chocolate drinks.

(d) The recalling by a marketing executive about to make a decision on a price reduction that every time prices had been cut in the past two years every competitor had followed within one week.

(e) The conclusion that average fixed costs do not affect marginal revenues and, therefore, do not need to be known in a pricing procedure in which price is set at the point where estimated marginal cost equals marginal revenue.

(f) The reaction of the advertising manager that a proposed new campaign does not "feel right."

2.5. What rules of evidence would you apply to each of the following situations?

(a) A study published in the *Journal of Marketing Research** of the physicians use of commercial and scientific sources of information to learn about new ethical drugs.

(b) A study by the research department of a pharmaceutical house (of which you are vice president of marketing) conducted to determine the use by physicians of commercial and scientific sources of information to learn about new ethical drugs.

2.6. What rules of evidence would you apply to each of the following situations?

(a) A pre-election poll of voters to determine the probable outcome of a senatorial race that is taken so that the results may be published as a part of a syndicated newspaper column written by the pollster.

(b) A pre-election poll commissioned by the incumbent in the senatorial race taken to determine his standing among the electorate and for use for fund raising if the results are favorable.

---

* See R. A. Bauer and L. H. Wortzel, "Doctors Choice: The Physician and His Sources of Information about Drugs," *Journal of Marketing Research,* **III** (February 1966), 40–47, as an example.

Selected Bibliography

ACKOFF, RUSSELL, L., and FRED E. EMORY. *On Purposeful Systems.* Chicago: Aldine Publishing Company, 1972. A thoughtful enquiry into human behavior viewed as a system for accomplishing desired ends. Part II presents an especially useful view of how problem situation models are formed and choices are made.

DIEŞING, PAUL. "Objectivism versus Subjectivism in the Social Sciences." *Philosophy of Science,* **33** (March–June, 1966), 124–133. An outstanding review article on the debate over investigator independence in basic research.

HELMER, OLAF, and NICHOLAS RESCHER. "On the Epistemology of the Inexact Sciences." *Management Science,* **6,** no. 1 (October 1959), 25–52. An excellent review article on the methods of enquiry in the behavioral sciences.

KUHN, THOMAS S. *The Structure of Scientific Revolutions.* Chicago: The University of Chicago Press, 1962. This book documents the close relationship between underlying model and research by a series of examples drawn from the physical sciences. It is a book that should be read by every serious student of research, whether in the physical or the behavioral sciences.

Case 2–1

Fashion Tree Shops: Location Analysis

The largest and most profitable of the four stores in the Fashion Tree chain was located in the downtown shopping area of a small city. The store had been in the same location for a number of years and had built a good reputation and an established clientele. Only high quality brands of women's clothing were carried. The chain was owned by four partners, each of whom managed one of the stores.

A shopping center was soon to be constructed across the river from the downtown area in an easily accessible location. It was to be called the Valley River Center and was to be a large-scale project underwritten by a national chain of department stores. One of the stores was to occupy a central position in an air-conditioned shopping mall. The center was planned to have an amount of floor space just about equal to that already existing in the downtown shopping area. It was, therefore, apparent that there would be an excess of retail space in the area.

The management of Fashion Tree had to make an early decision about whether to open a store in the new shopping center. The most desirable space locations in the center were being leased rapidly. The decision was made more difficult by the terms of the lease; a long-term commitment was required and the cost per square foot was relatively high. A hedging strategy of opening a store in the shopping center while maintaining the one in the downtown area was, therefore, not as attractive as it might otherwise have been.

An added source of uncertainty was the urban renewal program then taking place in the central area. A central pedestrian shopping mall with the replacement or renovation of older buildings was already underway. Overhead parking facilities conveniently located were also to be built.

The management of the company was considering several alternatives. They could:

1. keep the downtown store and not open a store in the shopping center,
2. keep the downtown store and open a second store in the shopping center,
3. sell the downtown store and open a store in the center, or
4. sell the downtown store and not open a store in the center.

In an attempt to get some better basis for predicting the effect of the center, Sarah Gilligan, one of the partners and the manager of the store in the city where the center was being built, visited a number of cities in which a major shopping center had recently been built. She also visited several cities where downtown pedestrian malls had been built. She talked to developers and clothing store operators in both the shopping centers and central shopping areas.

During the course of this trip she talked with the owner of a store in a central shopping area who had opened a small shop in a suburban shopping center. Instead of carrying a large inventory at both locations, he had been experimenting with using closed circuit color television to display items from the inventory in the downtown store. He had not had the closed circuit television installed very long and, although he was encouraged by the results thus far, it was too early to judge whether this practice was going to be successful over the long run. It had resulted in a reduction of lease and inventory costs. It did not, however, give a customer the opportunity to feel or to try on those items displayed to her but it did encourage her to visit the downtown store after she saw an item of interest.

Ms. Gilligan believed that this approach warranted consideration by Fashion Tree and proposed the alternative of:

5. keeping the downtown store and opening a small shop in the Valley River Center that would carry only limited inventory with closed circuit color television being used to display other items from the main store.

Another partner suggested a modification of this alternative, which would involve:

6. selling the downtown store, opening a full-sized store in the center, and then opening a small shop downtown that would carry limited inventory and rely on closed circuit television to display other items.

An evaluation of these alternatives was made in terms of net profit to the company over the next three years (the length of lease required). The evaluation was made for each of three possible market conditions:

1. the downtown shopping area would remain the primary shopping area of the city,
2. the shopping center would become the primary shopping area,
3. the downtown area and shopping center would each obtain approximately one-half of the area's clothing sales.

The net profit estimates were as shown in Table 1.

Table 1   Estimated Conditional Net Profits for Fashion Tree for Three-Year Period (000 dollars)

	Market Condition		
Alternatives	*1—Downtown Area Dominant*	*2—Shopping Center Dominant*	*3—Neither Dominant*
1. Retain downtown store only	$400	<$200>*	$150
2. Keep downtown store plus open store in center	125	125	125
3. Sell downtown store and open store in center	<200>	500	100
4. Sell downtown store and do not open store in center	0	0	0
5. Keep downtown store plus open small store in center	450	<150>	175
6. Sell downtown store, open store in center, plus open small store in downtown area	<150>	450	100

* <   > denotes loss

There was considerable uncertainty as to which alternative to choose. If it were certain that the downtown area were going to remain the dominant shopping area, the clear choice among the alternatives would have been to keep the downtown store and open a small store in the center (alternative 5). If it were known that the shopping center would become the primary shopping area, the choice is equally clear; the management would sell the downtown store and open one in the center (alternative 3). If the two shopping areas would become roughly equal in terms of women's clothing sales, management would again be well advised to keep the downtown store and open a small store in the center (alternative 5).

Sarah Gilligan had concluded that there was a good chance that at least one-half of the clothing purchases made in the area would be at Valley River Center stores within a year after the Center stores were opened. That is, her conclusion was that market conditions 2 and 3 were more likely than market condition 1.

None of the partners believed that they had enough information to make a decision in which they would have a high degree of confidence. It was not clear how they could develop more information themselves that would be of much help, and time was getting short. Ms. Gilligan suggested that they consider retaining a consultant, William George, a well-known and highly regarded professor from a school of retailing at a university in the East. From preliminary discussions it was estimated that George's fee and expenses would be about $8,500.

1. What decision should be made if no more information is obtained? Why?

2. What additional information might be helpful in making the decison?

3. Should the consultant be retained?

Case 2–2
Southern Equipment Manufacturing Company

The Product Development Committee of Southern Equipment Manufacturing Company (SEMC) recently began a review of a prospective new product. The product was basically a small version of the rotary engine. The engine would cost approximately 15 per cent more than a standard engine with the same performance characteristics. However, the new engine would provide better fuel utilization and require less maintenance, which would offset the increased initial costs of the engine within 18 months under normal operating conditions. In addition, the new engine would have an average "life span" approximately 10 per cent longer than the standard engine.

Engines in this size range are powered by gasoline, butane, or natural gas. The proposed engine would, like the standard engine, function with any of these fuel systems. The engines are used as stationary engines; that is, they do not power moving vehicles. Instead, they operate small irrigation wells, generators, and industrial and agricultural equipment.

The committee in conjunction with the director of marketing research worked out sales estimates for "optimistic," "most probable," and "pessimistic" market shares. These estimates relied heavily on a series of discussions held with the firm's sales force. Both the optimistic and pessimistic forecasts were based on the assumption that there was approximately a 25 per cent chance of their being realized.

The committee developed these sales forecasts for the six-year planning period used by the firm. SEMC uses a discount rate of 12 per cent on all such projects. The income projections for the six-year planning period are as follows.

Year	Pessimistic	Most Likely	Optimistic
1	<$ 50,000>*	<$ 50,000>	<$ 50,000>
2	< 200,000>	< 180,000>	< 170,000>
3	< 100,000>	< 60,000>	5,000
4	< 10,000>	75,000	100,000
5	100,000	300,000	400,000
6	125,000	350,000	440,000

* < > denotes loss.

1. Should the engine be developed under each of the following decision rules (assume a zero payoff for not introducing)? (a) Maximin, (b) Maximax, (c) Minimax Regret, (d) AMV, (e) EMV.

2. Which rule is most appropriate for this situation? Why?

Case 2–3
Harvest-Rich Fruit Growers

Harvest-Rich is a medium-sized cooperative of fruit growers in California that marketed its member's products. Oranges, lemons, avocados, grapefruit, fresh figs, and grapes were packed in fruit boxes and dried figs and raisins were packaged and marketed by the cooperative, all under the *Harvest-Rich* brand.

The management of the cooperative had become more and more concerned about the increase in packaging costs caused by inflation. The dried figs and raisins were packaged in boxes, the figs in 8 and 16 ounce box sizes and the raisins in 1, 8, and 16 ounce boxes. A research project that their advertising agency had conducted a few years before had indicated that those package sizes and the boxes used were both viewed favorably by consumers. The majority of users of the brand that were surveyed stated that they liked the box and that this form of packaging was an important reason for their purchase of the brand.

The packaging supervisor, John Eastman, had investigated other means of packaging raisins and dried figs and found that bags were much cheaper. Either cellophane or polyethlylene bags could be used with a substantial saving in cost. New packaging equipment would be required but, even with amortizing the equipment over a five-year period, he estimated that the cost savings would still be about $14,000 per year with sales at the same level as they were with the box.

The question that concerned the management was how consumers would react to the change in packaging. If the consumers were indifferent between bag and box, or preferred the bag, it seemed like a straightforward decision to make the change to bags. If, on the other hand, boxes were preferred, it might turn out to be false economy to switch to bags. The growers' supply of figs and grapes was fixed for the next several years by the trees and vines they now had in production. If there were any substantial reduction in demand for the *Harvest-Rich* dried figs and raisins, more would have to be packed and sold as fresh figs and grapes. This was a less profitable way of marketing and was to be avoided, if possible.

The cooperative did not have a marketing research department. The research that was conducted was usually done by (or, if done by a marketing research firm, it was coordinated by) their advertising agency.

Bill Martin, the agency account executive, met with the president, the vice president for marketing, and members of the marketing department staff to discuss the problem. After being told the reasons for considering the packaging change, he asked what their opinions were about consumer preferences concerning packaging. Did consumers prefer boxes, did they prefer bags, or were they indifferent between the two?

There was a surprising lack of unanimity in the answers. The marketing vice president felt strongly that boxes were preferred. Since both raisins and figs have a high sugar content they attract insects, he said, and housewives want a package that will keep them out. He pointed out that boxes were easier to close than bags, did not spill as easily, and could be more readily stored by stacking on cans or other boxes. He also cited the satisfaction with the *Harvest-Rich* box that users of the brand had expressed in the previous survey.

The sales manager was just as confident that bags would be preferred. He observed that most of the competitive brands of dried figs and several brands of raisins were packaged in cellophane bags. This allowed the housewife to see what she was buying. Since *Harvest-Rich* packaged only a uniformly high quality of both products, bags should increase sales. He observed that no comparison between boxes and bags had been asked for in the consumer survey done before, and the fact that consumers were satisfied with the *Harvest-Rich* box did not mean that they would not be as satisfied with a *Harvest-Rich* bag.

The advertising manager and the president both leaned toward favoring the box, but thought that consumers might be largely indifferent between the two.

Martin then asked for estimates of the effects on sales that consumer preferences in packaging might have. If consumers preferred boxes, and the switch was made to bags, what would the likely loss in sales be? If consumers preferred bags, and the change was made to bags, how much were sales likely to increase?

The sales estimates were averaged and profit estimates (after taxes) made for the next five years. The results were as follows:

	Consumers Prefer Boxes	Consumers Indifferent Between Boxes and Bags	Consumers Prefer Bags
Keep box	$265,000	$265,000	$265,000
Change to bag	210,000	333,000	414,000

Martin said that the data seemed to support the switch to bags. He suggested that if they wanted to test consumer acceptance of the bag before making the change, however, they could pack enough of both products in bags to supply a sample of wholesalers for a six-month test period and see what happened. He thought it was possible to lease bagging equipment but, if not, they could contract out the bagging for the test. Ten wholesalers were suggested as a reasonable number for the test.

John Eastman was asked to investigate ways of bagging the figs and raisins needed for the test. Later in the week he reported that, for the quantities involved, the cost of leasing equipment would be prohibitive but that the bagging could be contracted out for about $19,000. The savings in the cost of boxes was estimated at $6,400 but no savings in labor were expected.

What decision should have been made?

CHAPTER 3

Value and Cost
of Information

Information for decision making, whether for everyday matters or for executive concerns, is almost always insufficient. It may be in short supply because additional information is not available at any cost. A more prevalent reason for the lack of sufficient information, however, is that additional information could be obtained but the cost of obtaining it is considered to be too high.

A decision maker normally approaches a problem with some information. If the problem is, say, whether or not a new product should be introduced, he will usually have accumulated enough information through past experience with other decisions concerning the introduction of new products (both those of his own company and of competitors) and from various other sources to allow him to form some preliminary judgments about the desirability of introducing the product in question. He will rarely feel sufficiently confident in these judgments that he would not accept additional information relevant to the decision he has to make if it were available without additional cost or delay. He might feel confident enough, however, that he would not pay very much or wait very long for this additional information.

Willingness to buy additional information depends upon the quality of the information as well as the price. If perfect information, that is, information that would remove all uncertainty from the decision, were available, our decision maker would no doubt be willing to pay more than he would for information that would still leave some uncertainty about the proper decision.

The principle involved in deciding whether or not to do more research is *research should be conducted only when it is expected that the value of the information to be obtained will be greater than the cost of obtaining it.* Two kinds of errors can be made when deciding whether to *do more research or decide without more research.* One kind results when the expected value is *greater* than the cost of the research but the decision is *not to conduct* research. The other kind of error is made when the expected value is *less* than the cost of the research but the decision is *to conduct* the research.

This chapter is concerned with means of avoiding these errors. Both the *traditional* and the *decision theory* approaches to deciding whether to do research are examined. The two methods require that the same judgments be made in deciding whether research should or should not be conducted. Substantially different means of expressing and utilizing them are involved, however.

A Decision About Test Marketing a New Product

A few years ago a product manager and the marketing research manager of the Allied Mills Company disagreed about the need for having a potential new product test marketed. The research manager wanted to run a market test before deciding whether or not to introduce the new product, and the product manager thought that this would be a waste of time and money. Their disagreement was so strong and the discussion became so heated that the research manager accused the product manager of misleading management. The product manager in turn accused the research manager of not recognising a sound new product idea when he saw one.

After their tempers had cooled somewhat, they agreed to write down the estimates that were the basis for their respective conclusions. The estimates were as follows:

	Research Manager	*Product Manager*
Break-even sales volume for new product	500,000 units	500,000 units
Forecasts of sales and profits	"Good chance" (about 70 per cent) that sales for the 3 year planning period would be between 500,000 and 800,000 units with 650,000 units as the most likely level. With sales of 650,000 units profits are estimated to be $2,650,000. "Fair chance" (about 30 per cent) that sales for the 3 years will be between 300,000 and 500,000 units, with most likely level (if so) of 400,000 units. With sales of 400,000 units, losses are estimated to be $2,120,000.	"Very good chance" (about 85 per cent) that sales would be between 500,000 and 1,100,000 units during the 3 year planning period, with 800,000 units as the most likely level. With sales of 800,000 units profits are estimated to be $4,250,000. "Not very likely but some chance" (about 15 per cent) that sales will be between 400,000 and 500,000 units, with most likely level (if so) of 450,000 units. With sales of 450,000 units, losses are estimated at $1,100,000.
Cost of test marketing the product in four cities	$250,000	$250,000
Accuracy of market test	"Good." About 80 per cent chance of the test correctly indicating whether or not the break-even sales volume would be reached.	"Good." About 80 per cent chance of the test correctly indicating whether or not the break-even sales volume would be reached.
Conclusion	Run market test before deciding whether or not to introduce the product.	Introduce the product without running a market test.

As may be seen, the differences that had caused the dispute were concerned with both the *chance* and the *amount* of profits. The research manager was not as optimistic as the product manager, either with respect to the chance that the product would be profitable or, if it were, the amount of profit that would result. They had no disagreement about the break-even point in terms of sales, however, or the accuracy or estimated cost of the market test.

Suppose you were the chief marketing executive of the company that had developed the new product and that the disagreement concerning the next step to be taken had been brought to you for resolution. How would you have gone about making a decision on whether to conduct the market test? What would you have decided?

The Traditional Method of Making the Decision of Whether to Do Research

Two approaches can be taken to arrive at an assessment of whether the expected value of the information in a proposed research project is greater than its estimated cost: the *traditional* and the *decision* theory approaches to the problem.

The traditional approach was used by the research manager and the product manager in the Allied Mills case. This approach relies on the unaided judgment of the person making the assessment. Since it is a judgmental process, it is not susceptible to complete description. Presumably, however, the person making the judgment gathers information on (1) the *alternative actions* being considered in the problem the research will help solve, (2) the *payoffs* of each action, (3) the *degree of uncertainty* about which action to take, (4) the *additional information* needed to choose among the alternative actions, (5) the *predictive validity of the information* that would be provided by the research design of the proposed project, and (6) the *estimated cost of the project*. If there is more than one research design being considered, the manager will presumably obtain these kinds of information for each. He will then make a judgment about the expected value versus the estimated cost of the information for each design, and choose the one with the greatest positive difference.

The traditional method of making the *do research-decide without more research* decision was used almost universally until the early 1960s and remains by far the most commonly used procedure today. Its wide usage has stemmed from the ability of executives to make out-of-pocket cost estimates on explicit, more or less objective, bases and their inability to do so with respect to the value of information. The natural result has been for companies to use the cost estimates and to rely upon the private, informal judgmental process of the executives(s) concerned to determine whether value was likely to exceed cost.

Using the traditional approach made considerable sense as long as more systematic methods were not available. There is evidence to suggest, however, that this approach results in a persistent overevaluation of research information as compared to the decision theory approach.[1] (If you decided earlier that the market test *should* be conducted by Allied Mills, your evaluation of the information to be provided by the test was too high compared to the evaluation that an expected value decision maker should make.) Although such overevaluation may reflect only the fact that people are not using an expected monetary value rule when buying information, it nonetheless raises questions about the effectiveness of the traditional method of making the information purchasing decisions.

Other problems are associated with the traditional approach that make desirable a more explicit method of estimating the value of the information. One problem is that reasonable people reach different conclusions and have no basis for rationally determining which decision is correct. The research manager and the product manager described previously are an illustration. Another problem with the traditional approach is that it is very difficult to improve an implicit process. The executive himself cannot explain *how* he decided that value would probably exceed cost. So long as he does not understand the process it becomes almost impossible to improve it in any systematic way.

A method for determining the expected value of information for a particular problem situation that is much more explicit than the traditional method has been developed. It is a part of the general *decision analysis* approach and uses the same judgments as the traditional method. Before describing this approach and its application, however, it is necessary to review some of the basic concepts of probability.

Some Probability Concepts

A well-known economist has observed that "everyone knows what 'price' means except economists and lawyers." A probabilist would be equally justified in stating that "everyone knows what 'probability' means except probabilists and statisticians." In both instances a concept that lies at the heart of the discipline has disputed differences in interpretation.

The two major views of probability are the one held by the "relative frequentists" and the one held by the "personalists." We examine the underlying concepts of each.

---

[1] See P. E. Green, et al., *Experiments on the Value of Information in Simulated Marketing Environments* (Boston: Allyn & Bacon, Inc., 1967).

Relative Frequencies as Probabilities

A relative frequency view of probability is that the probability of a specified outcome of an event, say getting heads on the flip of a coin, is the limit of the relative frequency observed of that outcome as the number of trials approaches infinity. For example, if a fair coin were flipped an infinite number of times, the limit of the relative frequency of heads would be 50 per cent. Thus, the probability of obtaining a head on any given trial is .5. This has also been called a "physical probability," an "intrinsic probability," or "chance." It is this view of probabilty that has been held by the traditional statisticians and probabilists.

Stated as a set of axioms, we may say that probability is a measure of a set of events such that (1) the probability of any one event is greater than or equal to zero; (2) the sum of the probabilities of all events in the set that are mutually exclusive and collectively exhaustive is one; and (3) the probability of an event that consists of n mutually exclusive subevents is the sum of the probabilities of the n subevents.[2]

Personal Probability

A personalist interpretation of probability takes the form of a *degree of belief*. Although it is commonly used in an informal way, this interpretation has been institutionalized in such forms as parimutuel betting odds, announcement of rainfall probability by the weather bureau, and in the "beyond reasonable doubt" and "clear and abiding conviction" criteria in jury trials in criminal cases in the United States.[3]

Although several kinds of personal probabilities have been identified,[4] our interest centers on those that form a *consistent set*. A consistent set of probabilities, when applied to a betting situation, is one in which your opponent cannot obtain a "straddle"; he cannot change his bets in such a way that you will lose money regardless of what happens. A consistent

[2] An easily understood but rigorous discussion of elementary probability is given in S. Goldberg, *Probability: An Introduction* (Englewood Cliffs, N.J.: Prentice-Hall, Inc., 1960).

[3] An interesting discussion of the use of personal probability in the judicial system is given in J. Kaplan, "Decision Theory and Reasonable Doubt," in L. E. Allen and M. E. Caldwell, eds., *Communication Sciences and Law: Reflections from the Jurimetrics Conference* (New York: The Bobbs-Merrill Co., 1965), 251–259. 259.

[4] Another form of personal probability, suggested by Bertrand Russell, is the "logical probability." It is defined as a rational intensity of conviction such that any person who disagrees is wrong.

set of probabilities conforms to the same probability axioms given for the relative frequency concept of probability.[5]

Even though "probability" as defined by the relative frequentist and the personalist conform to the same set of axioms, there are important differences in the manner in which each applies it. The relative frequentist feels comfortable talking about probability only when counts of trials and successes can be made.[6] The proportion of good units of product produced on a given production line in a given period, for example, is a relative frequency and forms an objective basis for stating the "probability" of any particular proportion of 100 units of product coming off the line being of acceptable quality. He cannot, however, talk about unique events in probabilistic terms. The probability that a market test of a new product will predict actual sales volume within a given range of error is outside the relative frequency framework.

Yet, each of us, as well as executives in business firms or officials in governmental agencies or nonprofit organizations, must make decisions every day that rest on personal probability assessments. Social and economic and political problems seldom occur more than once under the same (or almost the same) conditions. Although everyone would like the assurance that relative frequency probabilities give, most situations simply do not permit it. A powerful argument for the use of personal probabilities in formal analytic methods therefore arises—if we are going to use them anyway, we may as well make the best possible use of them.

Means of Expressing Personal Subjective Probabilities

Phrases such as "there is a good chance that" and "it is highly probable that" are common in the conference room as well as in everyday conversation. No thought is usually given to whether the listener understands the degree of likelihood the speaker wants to convey. Yet, this means of expressing a probability is very imprecise. Is the probability connoted by "good chance" less than, equal to, or greater than that of "highly probable" or "very likely?" What *is* the probability that each describes?

The answer to this question is that there is no one generally understood level of probability associated with any of the three phrases. One study[7] shows that the median probability level assigned to the phrases "highly probable" and "very likely" was .90 and to "good chance" was .75. How-

[5] See L. J. Savage, *The Foundations of Statistics* (New York: John Wiley & Sons, Inc., 1954).

[6] Or, when he has reason to believe that the underlying process will generate a predictable relative frequency, he can calculate probabilities.

[7] S. Lichtenstein and J. R. Newman, "Empirical Scaling of Common Verbal Phrases Associated with Numerical Probabilities," *Psychonomic Science,* **9** (October 1967), 563–564.

ever, the probabilities assigned to the phrase "highly probable" ranged from .60 to .99, for "very likely" from .45 to .99, and for "good chance" from .25 to .96. Consider the communication problems that can result in a conversation between a person who is using "good chance" to mean a probability of .25 and another who is using it to mean a probability of .96.

In order to use personal probabilities in analytic methods involving computation, it is necessary to state them in quantitative form. It is this quantification of personal probabilities that has most concerned relative frequentists. They have raised two primary questions about the propriety of saying that an event has "a .15 probability" rather than that it has "little chance" or is "not very likely" to occur.

The first argument that is raised about numerical assignments to personal probabilities is that it implies a precision that is not likely to be there. Recall that the research manager stated that he thought there was about a "30 per cent chance" that the new product would not reach the break-even point during the three year planning period. Can the research manager really say that he believes that the probability is .30 rather than .29 or .31? Can he even distinguish between .30 and .25 or .35?

The argument really resolves to whether the person making the assessment should state this probability as an interval rather than as a single value. The answer is the same as that for relative frequency probabilities; it depends upon the use. If the marketing research manager thinks the probability of not reaching break-even may be as low as .25 or as high as .35 and wants to test the effect of this difference in the results of the analysis, he should state his assessment in interval form. A *sensitivity analysis* can be run using first one extreme value and then the other to determine if it makes any difference which one is used in the final decision. If it does not, the effect of the range of probabilities is nil. If it does make a difference, it will focus attention on one of the critical considerations affecting the decision. This is useful information in itself.

The second argument against quantifying personal probabilities is a variation of the first. It involves different assessments of probabilities when more than one person is involved in making the decision. The marketing research manager and the product manager assessed the probability of reaching break even differently; for example, their probability assignments were .70 and .85, respectively. The question must arise as to which figure is correct. Since no objective basis is available for resolving this uncertainty, it follows, so the argument goes, that the use of either numerical value is suspect.

Techniques for resolving differences in judgments such as this have been developed. An especially promising technique is known as the *Delphi* process.[8] Some differences are likely to remain however. The pro-

---

[8] This technique is discussed in Chapter 16.

cedure in such cases is the same as that just described for the interval estimate; conduct a sensitivity analysis to see if it makes any difference which is correct. The assessments of *both* the marketing research manager and the product manager may imply the same conclusion concerning conducting the market test; if so, the difference is of no practical consequence; if not, it highlights an important consideration in the overall introduction decision.

In the discussion that follows personal probabilities are used in calculations in the same way that relative frequency probabilities are used.

Evaluation of Information—Decision Analysis Approach

All information obtained through research has the possibility of being imperfect. For decisional research projects this means that there is always some chance that it will yield incorrect predictions. If we could determine the value of perfect information, we would know that imperfect information could only be worth something less. It would place an upper limit on any evaluation that could reasonably be made on the information we were seeking.

If we could evaluate the cost of the errors that might be made as a result of the imperfect nature of the information, and subtract such costs from the value the information would have if it were perfect, we would arrive at the value of the imperfect information. This is the logic that underlies the decision analysis approach to information evaluation.

Since we are dealing with chance events, and are assuming that we are using an expected monetary value maximization decision rule, we use expected values rather than direct ones. We first examine the expected value of perfect information and then consider the expected cost of errors.

Expected Monetary Value of Perfect Information—*EMVPI*

We can calculate the expected monetary value of a venture if perfect information were available. We can also calculate the expected value of the venture with no additional information. The difference between these two values is the expected monetary value of perfect information, or *EMVPI*. That is,

$$EMVPI = EMV \text{ of the venture with } - EMV \text{ of the venture with no} \\ \text{perfect information} \quad\quad \text{additional information}$$

In the Allied Mills problem, we have all the estimates we need from the research manager and the product manager to calculate EMVPI for

Table 3–1   Allied Mills—Conditional Payoff Table for Research Manager

Action	Market State 1 Sales > 500,000 units		Market State 2 Sales ≤ 500,000 units	
	Probability	Payoff	Probability	Payoff
A_1—Introduce	.70	$2,650,000	.30	<$2,120,000>*
A_2—Do not Introduce	.70	–0–	.30	–0–

* < > denotes loss.

each of them. The estimates of the research manager of the outcomes of introducing and not introducing the new product are shown in Table 3–1. Recall from Chapter 1 that this table is called a *conditional payoff table* since the payoffs shown are conditional upon the state of the market that actually exists.

Problems that have only two actions with one of the actions having zero payoffs are known as *venture analysis* problems. The Allied Mills problem has the two characteristics and so is an example of a venture analysis problem.

Suppose that the market test being considered would disclose with certainty which market state is the actual one. This would provide perfect information for making this decision since there could no longer be any doubt about which action to take. If the favorable market condition (market state 1) were shown to be the actual one, the decision would be to introduce the product. If the unfavorable state of the market were indicated, the product should not be introduced.

The best estimate of the probability that a perfect (completely accurate) test market will show market state 1 as the true state is .70 because that is the best estimate of the probability that market state 1 *is* the true state. By the same reasoning, there is a .30 probability of getting the indication that market state 2 is the actual state. Since the product would *not* be introduced if market state 2 were indicated, the payoff for that state in a situation in which perfect information is to be obtained may be shown as zero. The calculation of the *EMV* of the venture with perfect information using the research manager's estimates is then

$$EMV \text{ of the venture with perfect information} = .70(\$2,650,000) - .30(0)$$
$$= \$1,855,000$$

The *EMV* for the research manager if no additional information is obtained is a straightforward expected value calculation, for example,

$$EMV \text{ of the venture with no additional information} = .70(\$2,650,000)$$
$$- .30(<\$2,120,000>)$$
$$= \$1,219,000$$

EMVPI has already been defined as the difference between the two, or

$$EMPVI = \$1,855,000 - \$1,219,000$$
$$= \$636,000$$

Thus, the research manager, as an expected value decision maker, could reasonably agree to pay up to $636,000 for perfect information.

It should be noted that the amount of $636,000 is the expected loss conditional upon introducing the product with the unfavorable state of the market being the true one; that is, it is equal to .30 × |$2,120,000|, where the vertical bars indicate "absolute value." This makes intuitive good sense; one certainly would not spend more to get information to avoid loss than one would expect to lose in the first place.

Remember that the $636,000 represents the value of *perfect* information. It sets an upper limit on what can be spent to acquire information. Since the $250,000 cost of the test market is less than the value of perfect information, the marketing research manager would next have to determine the expected value of the *imperfect* information that will actually be provided by the market test. If this value is also greater than the cost, then he should recommend conducting the test.

The same methodology when applied to the estimates of the payoffs and their probabilities provided by the product manager yields an *EMVPI* of $165,000. (You should verify this amount by working through the problem in the same way used for the research manager.) Note that the expected monetary value of *perfect* information in the case of the product manager is less than the estimated cost of $250,000 of conducting the market test to obtain imperfect information. Therefore, he has no need to calculate the value of *imperfect* information. Instead, he should argue that the test *not* be conducted since even perfect information would not be worth the cost of the test (on an expected value basis using his estimates).

Expected Cost of Errors

Two kinds of errors are possible in the market test information. If T_1 is the designation for the market test indicating that market state S_1 is the true state and, similarly, T_2 is the indication for market state S_2, then we can get a T_1 indication from a market in which S_2 is the actual situation, or a T_2 indication given a market in which S_1 is the true state.

The error of T_1 given S_2 is known as a *Type I* error.[9] It is a conditional error since the indication T_1 is in error only under the condition that S_2

---

[9] The Type I error is the result of falsely rejecting the null hypothesis. In this case, the null hypothesis would be that the break-even point could not be reached, that is, that S_2 is the true market state.

is the true state of the market. The conditional probability of this error occurring is shown symbolically as

$$P(T_1|S_2),$$

where the vertical line means "conditional upon."

The probability of a Type I error is traditionally denoted as α. Therefore, in this context $\alpha = P(T_1|S_2)$.

A *Type II* error is the other kind of error possible, the one of the market test giving a T_2 indication when S_1 is the true state. It is denoted by β. We may, therefore, write $\beta = P(T_2|S_1)$.

The expected cost of an error is the conditional probability of the error times the prior probability of the state times the payoff of the state. The expected cost of the two types of errors are

$$\text{Expected cost of Type I error} = P(T_1|S_2) \cdot P(S_2) \cdot |V_2|$$
$$= \alpha P(S_2) \, |V_2|$$

where $|V_2|$ is the absolute value of the payoff for state 2, and

$$\text{Expected cost of Type II error} = P(T_2|S_1) \cdot P(S_1) \cdot V_1$$
$$= \beta \, P(S_1)V_1$$

where V_1 is the value of the payoff for state 1.

We can now determine the expected error costs for the marketing research manager's formulation of the Allied Mills problem. Recall that the research manager's assessment (and that of the product manager as well) of the predictive accuracy of the proposed market test was 80 per cent. That is, there was only a 20 per cent chance of the market test giving an incorrect indication of the sales volume in the three year planning period, or

$$P(T_1|S_2) = \alpha = .20$$
$$P(T_2|S_1) = \beta = .20$$

Using this information and that in Table 3–1, we may then calculate

$$\text{Expected cost of Type I error} = \alpha P(S_2)|V_2|$$
$$= 2.0 \times .30 \, |\$2,120,000|$$
$$= \$127,200$$

and

$$\text{Expected cost of Type II error} = \beta P(S_1) \cdot V_1$$
$$= .20 \times .70 \, |\$2,650,000|$$
$$= \$371,000$$

We have determined the expected monetary value of perfect information and the expected monetary costs of the errors. We now have all of the elements necessary to determine the expected monetary value of imperfect information.

Expected Monetary Value of Imperfect Information (EMVII)—Two Market States

For a problem formulation of the kind in the Allied Mills case *the expected monetary value of imperfect information (EMVII) is equal to the expected monetary value of perfect information less the expected costs of the two types of errors.* That is,

$$EMVII = P(S_2)|V_2| - \alpha P(S_2)|V_2| - \beta P(S_1)V_1 \qquad (3\text{-}1)$$

For this problem,

$$EMVII = \$636{,}000 - \$127{,}200 - \$371{,}000$$
$$= \$137{,}800$$

Recall that the estimated cost of the market test was $250,000. If the research manager is an expected monetary value decision maker, he must conclude that the test is *not* worth its estimated cost. It is important to note that the implications of the prior probabilities of the occurrence of the states, the estimates of the payoffs, and the assessment of the predictive validity of the market test by the marketing research manager differ from his judgment of the value versus the cost of the test using a traditional approach.

A direct assessment of expected value of a research project is very difficult to make. To illustrate this point, suppose that both error probabilities are lowered to .10, that is, $\alpha = \beta = .10$. With the other factors remaining as the research manager estimated them, would you argue that the market test should or should not be conducted?[10]

Expected Monetary Value of Imperfect Information (EMVII)—Three Market States

This method of finding *EMVII* also works for venture analysis problems that are formulated in three-state form. In a three-state venture analysis formulation, the states are usually defined such that S_1 denotes an "optimistic" market situation, S_2 a "most probable" one, and S_3 a

---

[10] Some research project should be conducted. The calculation is

$$EMVII = \$636{,}000 - .10 \times .30\,|-\$2{,}120{,}000| - .10 \times .70(\$2{,}650{,}000)$$
$$= \$636{,}000 - \$63{,}600 - \$185{,}550$$
$$= \$386{,}900$$

The *EMVII* is, therefore, greater than the estimated cost of $250,000. Some other design may be a better informational buy than the proposed market test and it should be conducted instead. If no such design can be found, then the proposed test should be run.

"pessimistic" state. The formula for *EMVII* in a three-state venture analysis problem is

$$EMVII = EMVPI - \alpha P(S_3)|V_3| - \beta_1 P(S_1)V_1 - \beta_2 P(S_2)V_2 \quad (3\text{--}2)$$

where

$$
\begin{aligned}
EMVPI &= P(S_3)|V_3| \\
\alpha &= 1 - P(T_3|S_3)\,^{11} \\
\beta_1 &= P(T_3|S_1) \\
\beta_2 &= P(T_3|S_2)
\end{aligned}
$$

$|V_3|$ = the absolute monetary value of the payoff for state 3, and

V_1, V_2 = the monetary values of the payoffs for states 1 and 2, respectively. Both V_1 and V_2 are positive.

The general logic of the *EMVII* being equal to *EMVPI* minus the expected cost of the errors also applies in multiple action problems where more than one action has nonzero payoffs. However, the *EMVII* in such problems must be worked out differently; the formulas for the two- and three-state venture analysis problems do not apply.

The use of *decision trees* provides a convenient way of visualizing and working with problems with any number of actions and states. The Allied Mills product introduction problem will also be used to illustrate the use of decision trees in *EMVII* problems.

Decision Trees and *EMVII*

The initial options of Allied Mills are diagrammed in Figure 3–1. This is the beginning of a decision tree (also sometimes called a *decision flow diagram*). Decision trees help to conceptualize problems of this type.

The three options shown are the minimum available in any problem situation. One always has at least one "go" alternative, one "no go" alternative, and the alternative to get more information before deciding. It is, of course, when the "get more information" option is exercised that research is conducted.

The analysis of the "introduce" branch using the research manager's estimates is added in Figure 3–2. The possible outcomes of introducing under market state 1 or state 2 and their associated payoffs and probabilities are added. They are added after a circle to indicate a *chance fork*. (A *decision fork* is indicated by a square.) The expected payoff of the "introduce now" branch is shown above the circle as $1,219,000. It is

---

[11] There are two possible α errors, $P(T_1|S_3)$ and $P(T_2|S_3)$. However, the sum of these errors is equal to $1 - P(T_3|S_3)$ since $P(T_1|S_3) + P(T_2|S_3) + P(T_3|S_3) = 1.0$.

the algebraic sum of the payoffs of each market state multiplied by the probability of the state occurring.

Evaluation of the "get more information" branch is somewhat more complicated but not unduly so. As shown in Figure 3–3, as we move out that branch the first fork encountered is the chance fork of indications from the market test if it were actually run. Under each of these branches a space has been left to show the probability of each possible indication,

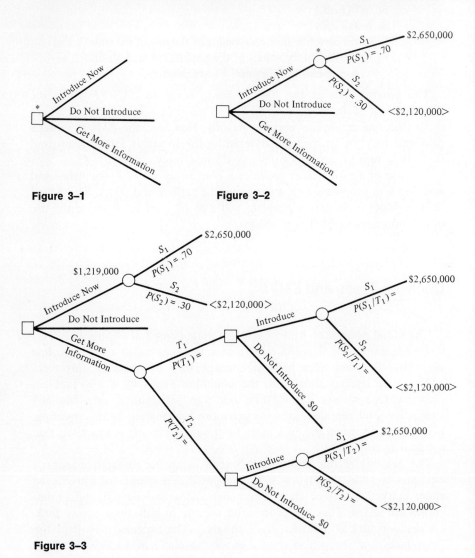

Figure 3–1

Figure 3–2

Figure 3–3

Decision tree for a new product—marketing research manager's estimates. (Note: □ indicates a decision fork and ○ a chance fork.)

$P(T_1)$ and $P(T_2)$. Implicit in the assessments of prior probabilities of states $P(S_1)$ and $P(S_2)$, and of errors of the $P(T_1|S_2)$ and $P(T_2|S_1)$, is the assessment of the probability of each of the possible test results, $P(T_1)$ and $P(T_2)$. We discuss shortly how the values for $P(T_1)$ and $P(T_2)$ may be calculated.

As we move out the T_1 branch in Figure 3–3 a decision fork is reached. Given that the market test is conducted and that the T_1 indication is obtained, a decision must be made as to whether the product is to be introduced. If it is not introduced, the payoff is zero. The expected payoff, if it is introduced, is yet to be determined.

At first thought it might seem that the expected payoff is no different than it would be if no market test had been run. That is, one might think it is still $1,219,000 as it is on the "introduce now" branch at the top of the tree in Figure 3–3. Further reflection indicates that this cannot be the expected payoff now, however, since the probabilities now being used are conditional on the indication to be received from the market test rather than the original probabilities of each of the market states occurring. The marketing research manager had assessed the probability of market state 1 occurring as $P(S_1) = .70$. Given that a market test were run and a T_1 indication were obtained, the probability will become higher than .70 that S_1 is the true market state. A revised probability is obtained that is shown as $P(S_1|T_1)$ and read as the "probability of S_1 given T_1."

Four such conditional probabilities exist in the Allied Mills problem. Two of them must be determined to evaluate the T_1 branch, that is, $P(S_1|T_1)$ and $P(S_2|T_1)$. The other two such probabilities apply to the T_2 branch, and are $P(S_1|T_2)$ and $P(S_2|T_2)$.

These conditional probabilities are calculated by using Bayes Theorem. It is necessary to have an understanding of this theorem to understand fully the determination of $EMVII$.

Bayes Theorem

Bayes Theorem is a means of revising an unconditional probability, such as $P(S_1)$, to a conditional probability, such as $P(S_1|T_1)$. This is an important and useful step in determining the expected value of information. We can see intuitively that if $P(S_1|T_1)$ is only slightly larger than $P(S_1)$, running a test and getting a T_1 indication would not be of much value. Conversely, if $P(S_1|T_1)$ is substantially higher than $P(S_1)$, conducting the test and getting a T_1 indication may be of considerable value.

Bayes Theorem as applied to a revision of one of the unconditional probabilities in the Allied Mills problem is

$$P(S_1|T_1) = \frac{P(T_1|S_1) \cdot P(S_1)}{P(T_1|S_1) \cdot P(S_1) + P(T_1|S_2) \cdot P(S_2)} \qquad (3\text{--}3)$$

or, in words,

	probability of the market test indicating a S_1 state when that is the actual state	· probability that S_1 is the actual state
probability of S_1 being the actual state after a = market test indicates it is		

$$\text{—————————————————}$$

probability of the market test indicating a S_1 state when that is the actual state · probability that S_1 is the actual state

+ probability that the market test will indicate S_1 when S_2 is the actual state · probability that S_2 is the actual state

Note that the marketing research manager (and the product manager) has made estimates of all of the values on the right-hand side of the equation. The marketing research manager's estimates were

$$P(S_1) = .70, \; P(S_2) = .30, \text{ and}$$
$$P(T_1|S_2) = P(T_2|S_1) = .20$$

These can be substituted in equation 3–3 in solving for the conditional probability, $P(S_1|T_1)$. (This calculation is made below.)

Three other conditional probabilities must be calculated in determining the *EMVII* for the marketing research manager. These are $P(S_2|T_1)$, $P(S_2|T_2)$ and $P(S_1|T_2)$ and can be calculated from the appropriate Bayes Theorem formulation. $P(S_2|T_2)$, for example, is calculated by

$$P(S_2|T_2) = \frac{P(T_2|S_2) \cdot P(S_2)}{P(T_2|S_2) \cdot P(S_2) + P(T_2|S_1) \cdot P(S_1)}$$

Calculation of EMVII

In calculating *EMVII* we must evaluate the conditional expected payoffs of each branch of the decision tree. Suppose we evaluate the T_1 branch first, which is represented in Figure 3–6. The missing probabilities for the evaluation are $P(S_1|T_1)$, $P(S_2|T_1)$ and $P(T_1)$. Using the research manager's probability assessments of

$$P(S_1) = .70, \; P(S_2) = .30, \text{ and}$$
$$P(T_1|S_2) = P(T_2|S_1) = .20$$

the first of these probabilities is calculated as follows:

$$P(S_1|T_1) = \frac{P(T_1|S_1) \cdot P(S_1)}{P(T_1|S_1) \cdot P(S_1) + P(T_1|S_2) \cdot P(S_2)}$$
$$= \frac{\cdot 80(.70)}{.80(.70) + .20(.30)} = \frac{.56}{.56 + .06} = \frac{.56}{.62}$$

The conditional probabilities are conveniently left as fractions to reduce the arithmetic computation. However, the conversion of .56/.62 to decimal form shows that $P(S_1|T_1)$ is slightly more than .90. This is considerably higher than the estimate of .70 for $P(S_1)$.

Since S_1 and S_2 are the only market states, $P(S_1|T_1) + P(S_2|T_1) = 1.0$. It therefore follows that

$$P(S_2|T_1) = 1.0 - P(S_1|T_1)$$
$$= 1.0 - .56/.62 = .06/52$$

The probability of T_1 is determined as

$$P(T_1) = P(T_1 \text{ and } S_1) + P(T_1 \text{ and } S_2).$$

Since $P(T_1 \text{ and } S_1)$ and $P(T_1 \text{ and } S_2)$ are joint probabilities, they comprise the only ways that a T_1 indication could be obtained (as S_1 and S_2 are the only market states being considered). When $P(T_1 \text{ and } S_1)$ and $P(T_1 \text{ and } S_2)$ are added, therefore, the result is the probability of a T_1 indication, or $P(T_1)$.

From the multiplication theorem in probability, we know that

$$P(T_1 \text{ and } S_1) = P(T_1|S_1) \cdot P(S_1) \text{ and}$$
$$P(T_1 \text{ and } S_2) = P(T_1|S_1) \cdot P(S_2).$$

We may, therefore, write

$$P(T_1) = P(T_1|S_1) \cdot P(S_1) + P(T_1|S_2) \cdot P(S_2)$$
$$= .80(.70) + .20(.30)$$
$$= .62$$

The T_1 branch of the tree with these probabilities added is shown in Figure 3–4. An evaluation of the expected payoff at the chance fork on the T_1 *indication—introduce branch* may be calculated as

Expected Payoff Conditional
Upon T_1 Indication and
Introduction of Product $= P(S_1|T_1)V_1 + P(S_2|T_1)V_2$
$= .56/.62 (\$2,650,000) + .06/.62 (<\$2,120,000>)$
$= 1,356,800/.62$

(The convenience of leaving the answer as a fraction will become apparent shortly.)

The expected payoff of the "Do not Introduce" portion of the T_1 branch is, of course, \$0 since the payoffs are \$0 regardless of market state. If we were to conduct the market test and get a T_1 indication, we would choose the "Introduce" rather than "Do not Introduce" alternative.

There is a .62 probability that a T_1 indication will be received. This probability must be multiplied times the conditional payoff calculated previously to remove the T_1 condition. The unconditional expected payoff at the beginning of the T_1 branch is then

Unconditional Expected $= .62 (\$1,356,800/.62)$
Payoff of T_1 Branch
$= \$1,356,800$

The T_2 branch may be evaluated by an identical procedure. The results of the completed evaluation are shown in Figure 3–5.

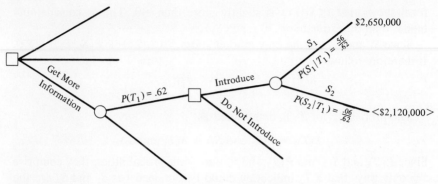

Figure 3–4 T_1 branch of decision tree—Allied Mills new product introduction problem—marketing research manager's payoff estimates and probability assessments.

As one would expect, the best decision given a T_2 indication is not to introduce. A payoff of zero results from not introducing while the expected payoff of introducing is negative. The "Introduce" branch is blocked off by a pair of wavy lines to show that it is the less desirable of the two actions if a T_2 indication results from the market test.

The overall expected monetary value of the venture with the market test being conducted is $1,356,800, and the expected monetary value with-

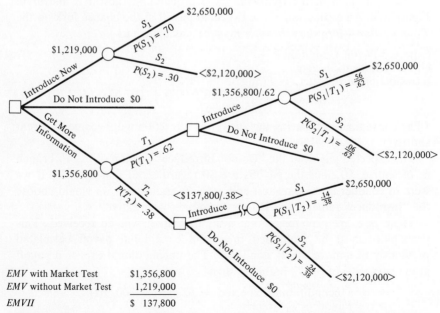

EMV with Market Test	$1,356,800
EMV without Market Test	1,219,000
EMVII	$ 137,800

Figure 3–5 Allied Mills new product introduction problem—research manager estimates.

out the market test is $1,219,000. The difference is $137,800, the same result obtained by the use of the method described earlier.

This method of solving for *EMVII* is the general method of solving for *EMVII*. It will work on multistate-multiaction problems regardless of complexity. The formula used earlier to solve the Allied Mills problem works only on two action problems where one of the actions has zero payoffs.

Correspondence of Traditional and Decision Analysis Approaches

The symbols and formulas used in the last few pages may have tended to obscure the fact that the underlying considerations used in the decision analysis approach are no different than those used in the traditional ap-

Table 3–2 Correspondence of Traditional and Decision Analysis Approaches to Deciding Whether Research Should Be Conducted

Step	*Traditional Approach*	*Decision Analysis Approach*
1.	Determine different actions that could be taken (a) possible results of each action (b) degree of uncertainty about each possible result	Prepare conditional payoff table (a) estimate payoffs (b) set prior probabilities for states—$P(S_j)$
2.	Decide what additional information is needed	Same
3.	Decide what research design to use	Same
4.	Estimate the predictive accuracy of the information to be provided by that design	Set conditional probabilities of research indication given state—$P(T_i|S_j)$
5.	Estimate the cost of the research project being considered	Same
6.	Decide whether the expected value of the research is greater than its estimated cost.	Compare the calculated expected value of the information with its estimated cost to determine which is greater.

proach. Both require the same judgments; they are only expressed and used differently.

The correspondence of the basic considerations in the two approaches is shown in Table 3–2.

Summary

A casual examination of the traditional and the decisional analysis approaches to deciding whether or not to do research may suggest that they differ substantially. However, closer examination of the two indicates that they require judgments of the same kind concerning the same elements. They differ only in the way these judgments are expressed and used in the decision-making process.

The traditional approach involves a direct judgment of whether the value will exceed the cost of a contemplated project. Judgments are made about possible outcomes of each of the actions being considered, the "chance" of each outcome occurring, how good the research information would be in predicting the true outcomes, and how much the project will cost. From these considerations an overall judgment is made of whether the information will be worth its cost. The decision analysis method formalizes these procedures.

The formula developed in the first approach illustrates the underlying logic of both decision analysis methods, namely, that the *expected value of imperfect information is equal to the expected value of perfect information minus the expected cost of the errors.*

The overall decision rule for deciding whether or not to conduct a research project can then be applied. It is to *conduct a research project when the expected value of the information to be obtained is greater than the estimated cost of obtaining it.*

Full decision analysis solutions are not required in all cases. A reasonable kind of procedure in making the research decision is to determine first the expected monetary value of perfect information and to make an estimate of the cost of the research. A comparison of these two values may well give a clear-cut answer to the question (as it did for the product manager in the Allied Mills case). If a reasonable degree of doubt remains, the full analysis should be run.

Questions and Problems

3.1. Decide what numerical probability you assign to each of the following phrases. Record these probabilities. Without indicating your answers, ask two other people to tell you what numerical probabilities they associate with each phrase.
   (a) It is unlikely that . . .
   (b) It is doubtful that . . .

(c) It may be that . . .
(d) It is improbable that . . .
(e) There is a good chance that . . .
(f) There is a possibility that . . .
(g) It is very likely that . . .
(h) It is probable that . . .
(i) It is very unlikely that . . .
(j) It is highly doubtful that . . .
(k) There is not a good chance that . . .
(l) It is very doubtful that . . .
(m) It is very improbable that . . .
(n) There is a good possibility that . . .
(o) It is uncertain that . . .
(p) It is likely that . . .
(q) It is highly probable that . . .

What conclusions do you draw about the precision with which your assessments of probabilities are communicated by these phrases?

3.2. Juries in criminal cases are instructed to find the defendant guilty only if they believe he is guilty "beyond a reasonable doubt."
(a) What probability do you assign to this phrase?
(b) There are two possible errors that a jury can make. It can find a guilty person innocent or an innocent person guilty. What effect does the previous instruction have on the relative size of these errors?
(c) Sometimes the phrase "clear and abiding conviction" is used instead of "beyond a reasonable doubt." Do the two phrases mean the same thing in numerical probabilities to you?

3.3. Shoppers continually make decisions about whether to get more information before they buy. How should the decision be made on whether to go to one more store before buying a
(a) record in the $5 price range?
(b) stereo set in the $500 price range?

3.4. The U.S. Postal Service is now operated as a publicly owned corporation rather than as a government agency. In 1972, a plan for selling stamps and stamped envelopes by mail was being considered. It was proposed that from $4 to $10 of these items could be ordered by filling out an order blank and mailing it to the local post office. A $.40 handling fee was to be charged. After the post office received the order, it would be filled and returned by mail.

Assume that the conditional payoff table for this program was as follows:

	S_1		S_2	
	probability	*payoff*	*probability*	*payoff*
A_1—Start mail program	.6	$500,000	.4	<$400,000>
A_2—Do not start mail program	.6	0	.4	0

A market test of this sale-by-mail program was proposed. Fourteen cities in the United States were to be included in the test. The estimated predictive accuracy of the proposed market test was as shown as follows. The estimated cost was $25,000. (These data are assumed, but the situation actually occurred.)

	$P(T_i|S_1)$	$P(T_i|S_2)$
T_1	.80	.15
T_2	.20	.85

(a) Using the traditional approach to evaluating the proposed market test, should it be conducted? Explain.
(b) What is the expected monetary value of perfect information?
(c) What is the expected monetary value of the information that would be provided by the market test?
(d) An important part of the consideration of whether or not to start the sale-by-mail program was the added convenience provided to customers. The "payoff" from this consideration is not included in the conditional payoff table. Could it be? Should it be? Explain.
(e) Using the decision analysis approach to evaluating the market test, should it be conducted? Explain.

3.5. Intercontinent Air, Inc., is considering adding an "excursion plan" on its New York–Paris–Rome flights. All passengers who travel on this plan must buy a round-trip fare and fly on a space available basis for which they will receive a 20 per cent fare reduction.

Management recognizes that the lower fare will attract some passengers from the regular flights. However, it believes that enough new passengers may be added to increase the average occupancy ratio by at least 5 percentage points. If so, it calculates that the added revenue will more than offset costs.

The conditional payoff table is estimated to be as follows:

	Market State 1 S_1 Occupancy Ratio Increases $\geq 5\%$ Points		Market State 2 S_2 Occupancy Ratio Increases $< 5\%$ Points	
Alternative	$P(S_1)$	Payoff	$P(S_2)$	Payoff
A_1—Establish Plan	.6	$2.0 M	.4	$< \$1.0$ M$>$
A_2—Do Not Establish Plan	.6	0	.4	0

Some members of management argue that a survey of present and potential passengers should be taken before a final decision is made. A design is proposed that will cost $50,000, inclusive of expected opportunity loss during the 3 months it will take to conduct it, and will give a 0.80 chance of correct prediction—$[P(T_1|S_1) = P(T_2|S_2) = 0.80;\ P(T_1|S_2) = P(T_2|S_1) = 0.20]$.

(a) Describe the steps involved in a traditional approach to deciding whether the survey should be done.
(b) Describe the steps involved in a decision analysis approach to deciding whether the survey should be done.
(c) Would you recommend the survey be conducted? Why?

3.6. Some years ago General Foods Corporation developed an instant ice cream soda. It consisted of ice cream packed in a container (shaped like an ice cream soda glass, as you might expect) along with two tablets that released carbon dioxide when water was added. It was designed to be kept in a freezer in the store and at home until used. It was then to be taken from the freezer, the lid removed, and warm water added. The water made the ice cream softer and released the carbon dioxide while it became chilled.

The research department had made some preliminary estimates of sales and profits if the product were introduced. It was not very confident about these estimates as it was difficult to decide in what markets the product would compete and what share it would obtain. Should the product be considered as vying only for part of the general home ice cream product market, the snack market, the market for sodas at soda fountains, or some combination of these markets plus others?

The estimates made by the research department are not available. However, suppose they were as shown in the following table. The dollar figures shown are in terms of discounted cash flows for the first three years after introduction. The probabilities shown are the best assessments the research department could make of the chance that each such amount would be realized.

Conditional Payoff Table for Instant Ice Cream Soda

	S_1 Market Condition 1		S_2 Market Condition 2		S_3 Market Condition 3	
Action	Proba-bility	Payoff	Proba-bility	Payoff	Proba-bility	Payoff
Intro-duce	.2	$2,600,000	.4	$1,500,000	.4	<$2,000,000>*
Do not intro-duce	.2	0	.4	0	.4	0

*< > denotes loss.

Since the research department was not very confident of its estimates, and the potential loss was fairly high, it proposed a market test. The test was to be conducted by an outside marketing research firm in Wichita, Kansas, and Cleveland, Ohio. It was to run for six months with the same level of promotional support that had been planned for the national introduction. The same price as planned for the national market was to be used.

The research department estimated that the predictive accuracy of the test would be as shown in the next table. (Again, these data are assumed.)

Estimated Predictive Accuracy of Proposed
Market Test

Test Indication	Actual Market Condition		
	S_1	S_2	S_3
T_1	.80	.15	.05
T_2	.15	.70	.15
T_3	.05	.15	.80

(T_1 in this table should be interpreted as indicating
market condition S_1, T_2 as indicating market condition S_2, and T_3 as indicating market condition S_3.
Thus, if market condition S_1 were actually the true
market situation, there was an 80 per cent probability, in the research department's estimation,
that the market test would correctly identify it
($P(T_1|S_1) = .80$). There was a 15 per cent chance it
would incorrectly identify it as market condition
S_2, however, ($P(T_2|S_1) = .15$) and a 5 per cent
chance as market condition S_3 ($P(T_3|S_1) = .05$).
The rest of the table is interpreted similarly.)

The market test was estimated to cost $400,000. Should General Foods
have authorized it (if these data are assumed to be correct)? Explain.

Selected Bibliography

BROSS, IRWIN D. J. *Design for Decision.* New York: The Free Press, 1953. A
well-written and interesting introductory treatment of statistical decision
making. Presents and develops several decision rules and discusses their
application. Also treats the subjects of models, measurement, and analysis
of data.

ENIS, BEN M., and CHARLES C. BROOME. *Marketing Decisions: A Bayesian
Approach.* Scranton, Pa.: Intext Educational Publishers, 1971. A concise
exposition of the principles of Bayesian analysis including a discussion of
the expected monetary value of information.

GOLDBERG, SAMUEL. *Probability: An Introduction.* Englewood Cliffs, N.J.:
Prentice-Hall, Inc., 1960. A lucid presentation of elementary probability
theory using set theory.

GREEN, PAUL E., and DONALD S. TULL. *Research for Marketing Decisions,*
3rd ed. Englewood Cliffs, N.J.: Prentice-Hall, Inc., 1975. A book dealing
with the application of Bayesian decision analysis to marketing research.

HADLEY, G. *Introduction to Probability and Statistical Decision Theory.* San
Francisco, Holden-Day, Inc., 1967. Probability theory and utility theory
and their applications to decision making are discussed in a clear and
incisive manner.

MOSTELLER, FREDERICK, and JOHN W. TUKEY. "Data Analysis, Including Statistics," in Gardner Lindzey and Elliot Aronson, eds. *The Handbook of
Social Psychology,* vol. II. Reading, Mass.: Addison-Wesley Publishing
Company, 1968, 80–200. A comprehensive but (understandably) condensed general treatment of analysis of data. Of immediate interest is the
section on "Bayesian Ideas," 160–183.

NEWMAN, JOSEPH W. *Management Applications of Decision Theory.* New York: Harper & Row, Publishers, Inc., 1971. A book that describes the application of the materials presented in this chapter to product introduction problems at the General Foods Corporation.

RAIFFA, HOWARD. *Decision Analysis.* Reading, Mass.: Addison-Wesley Publishing Company, 1968. An introductory but comprehensive treatment of decision making under uncertainty. Highly recommended for readers of this chapter who want a more extensive background. It is written in an informal style that is easily understood yet does not sacrifice rigor.

SCHLAIFER, ROBERT. *Analysis of Decisions Under Uncertainty.* New York: McGraw-Hill Book Company, Inc., 1971. Robert Schlaifer is a leading decision theorist. This book applies Bayesian statistics to real-world problems in a systematic way.

Case 3–1

Marblestone Company—Decision on Subscription to Syndicated Data Service

The Marblestone Company, the manufacturer of *Scour Power,* a kitchen cleanser, has been in the scouring cleanser field for over 100 years. *Scour Power* was one of the original powdered cleansers, and, although the product has been improved over the years, only a single brand and a single formulation of it is marketed. The market share of the cleanser began to decline after World War II. From a high of 8.1 per cent in 1948 it fell consistently and reached a low of 1.9 per cent in 1974. The market share has stabilized at about 2.0 per cent since that time.

Scour Power is distributed nationally through wholesalers and chains. Sales last year were $24,219,000 with profits (after taxes) of $514,000. A total of $372,000 was spent in advertising in women's magazines last year. There was no advertising in other media.

The Marblestone Company subscribes to the consumer panel reports compiled by a marketing research firm. Every month it receives a report of purchases of kitchen cleanser by a national panel of 7,500 families. The purchase data are reported by brands for households classified by such characteristics as total family income, occupation of head of household, age of housewife, education of head of household, number and age of children (if any), and region and city size of residence. Purchases are also reported by the types of stores at which they were made, whether food, drug, variety, general merchandise, or department stores, and whether they are part of a chain or are independently owned.

Purchase data are collected weekly from each household. Purchases of food, drug, and household items are recorded in a diary and mailed to the company headquarters. The number of units of each item purchased, the size of the units, the price paid, and whether or not cents-off-coupons or other "deals" were in effect are recorded. The weekly reports are cumulated into monthly reports for each product class. The reports on the product class(es) subscribed to are then sent air mail–special delivery to each client.

The vice-president for marketing of the Marblestone Company receives the report on "Kitchen Cleansers" each month. For this report the company pays $45,000 per year. An economy drive was started recently by the president of the company and justification is required for each expenditure by a department amounting to more than $250.

1. How should the vice-president for marketing go about determining the value of the monthly report?

2. What specific information will be needed for this evaluation?

Case 3–2
Sebring Tire Company: Market Test Division

Some years ago the Sebring Tire Company developed a substitute for snow tires and chains that was called "SNO-CHARGERS." It consisted of a series of one-inch wide polyurethane bands that could be attached over conventional tires or snow tires when needed. Tests indicated that when the bonds were attached at 12- to 14-inch intervals they provided about the same amount of traction as chains and enabled conventional tires to outpull snow tires by about 70 per cent.

Eight bands were used on most tires and were referred to as a "unit." Preliminary market research indicated that the total annual market for snow tires and chains in the United States was the equivalent of approximately 21 million SNO-CHARGER units. At that time Sebring had an estimated 19.2 per cent share of this market with its snow tires (new and retread) and chains sold through its company owned stores and dealer owned outlets.

Sebring owned and operated 1,350 tire stores and marketed its tires through 10,400 dealer owner outlets. The dealers were franchised and Sebring supplied tires, batteries, and automobile accessories (including chains) to them. The number of snow tires sold by each company-owned store (other than in the South and Southwest) ranged from 250 to 2,500 per year, with an average of about 800. (This included both new and retreaded snow tires). Each of the company-owned stores also sold an average of about 80 sets of chains per year. The dealer outlets were much smaller, on the average, than the company-owned stores. Their average volume of sales of snow tires and chains was only about 40 per cent of that of the company-owned stores.

A use test was run during that winter with 50 Sebring employees participating. Each was given four SNO-CHARGER units and asked to "use them in the same way you would if you had bought them." Each participating employee was asked to fill out a questionnaire every four weeks during the test to indicate usage of SNO-CHARGERS, snow tires, and chains, any problems they had encountered with the SNO-CHARGERS if they had used them, and to answer the question, *"If SNO-CHARGERS were available in a Sebring store or dealer outlet at $9.95 a set (for two tires) do you think you would buy them? Yes (__) No (__)."*

There had been a great deal of uncertainty in the marketing research department before the test was begun about how much information it would provide. In part, this was because the results were dependent on the amount and frequency of snowfall over the winter; if there were little or no snow during a reporting period, there obviously would be no need to use the SNO-CHARGERS and no information would be obtained. That winter turned out to be one with several heavy snowfalls, with a frequent need for cars in the area to use chains or snow tires. At least one snowfall came during each of the four reporting periods. The information on usages was tabulated for the four periods and cross tabulated with the responses at the end of the fourth period to the "would you buy?" question. The results are shown in the following table.

Usage of SNO-CHARGERS and Intention to Buy If Available

	Would Buy	Would Not Buy	Total
Kept Conventional Tires on			
Used SNO-CHARGERS but not chains	4	12	16
Used SNO-CHARGERS part of time, chains part of time	3	1	4
Used chains but not SNO-CHARGERS	0	0	0
Used neither chains nor SNO-CHARGERS	0	1	1
Subtotal	7	14	21
Put on Snow Tires			
Used SNO-CHARGERS but not chains when snow was heavy	14	4	18
Used SNO-CHARGERS part of time, chains part of time when snow was heavy	3	2	5
Used chains but not SNO-CHARGERS when snow was heavy	0	1	1
Used neither chains nor SNO-CHARGERS	0	5	5
Subtotal	17	12	29
Grand total	24	26	50
Recap:			
Used SNO-CHARGERS	24	19	43
Did not use SNO-CHARGERS	0	7	7
	24	26	50

The marketing research analyst believed that the small size of the sample and that the fact that the use test had been conducted in only one location permitted only tentative inferences to be drawn. He also believed that there was a favorable bias in the results since the sample was comprised of Sebring employees. In his report he stated these reservations and then added:

Taking the results of the use test at face value, however, it would appear that SNO-CHARGERS would compete primarily with chains rather than snow tires, and that they would compete successfully. Almost one-half of the sample of users (23 of 50) used them over snow tires. Three-fourths of those who used them this way said they would buy them (17 of 23). Of those who used them both SNO-CHARGERS and chains during the test, two-thirds (6 of 9) said they would buy SNO-CHARGERS.

Overall, these are *favorable* findings. The estimated gross margin on a set of SNO-CHARGERS is $2 *more* than for a set of chains, about the same as for a set of two retreaded snow-tires, but about $8 *less* than for two new snow tires.

After allowing for the favorable bias he believed was present in the use test results, the analyst concluded that "with good acceptance" sales of SNO-CHARGERS would replace about 40 per cent of the sales of chains through the Sebring stores and dealer outlets and about 10 per cent of the snow tire sales. With "poor acceptance" he estimated that SNO-CHARGERS might get no more than 15 per cent of the sales of chains and 5 per cent of the sales of snow tires. He estimated that if acceptance were "good" over a two-year introductory period, the profit (after taxes) would be about $750,000, after allowing for loss of profits on snow tires not sold because the customer bought SNO-CHARGERS instead. If it were "poor" the company could expect to lose about $300,000. He stated in the report that, "although the indications from the use test are encouraging, it is difficult to say which of these outcomes is more likely without more information about whether the average car owner would actually buy and use SNO-CHARGERS if they were on the market."

He recommended that a market test be conducted during the coming winter. A sample of Sebring owned stores would be selected, an inventory of SNO-CHARGERS provided, and the product advertised in local newspapers, radio, and television. He estimated that it would cost $30,000 plus about $800 per store (net of expected receipts from the sale of the SNO-CHARGERS) to conduct the test. He recommended that a sample of a total of 50 Sebring stores in the New England, North Atlantic, North Central, Rocky Mountain, and Pacific Coast regions be used for the market test. He stated in the report that a market test during the coming winter using 50 stores "should provide information which will allow us to make an accurate assessment of how good market acceptance for SNO-CHARGERS would be if we marketed them on a national basis."

Should the market test recommended by the analyst have been conducted?

Case 3–3

Scientific Educational Equipment
Market Survey Decision

In June, 1961, John Borton, president and one of the principal stock-holders of Scientific Educational Equipment (SEE), went to Japan to look for new supply sources for laboratory equipment. SEE was one of the two large mail-order houses that sold equipment and supplies for science laboratories to secondary schools and colleges in the United States. During the past three years, expenditures for science and science-related instruction had climbed substantially. This reflected the increasing interest and higher enrollments in science classes brought about by the launching of Sputnik by the Russians in 1957. Borton was looking for new products and for alternate sources of supply to serve this expanding market.

One of the products in which Borton was interested was a telescope. He was aware that there had been a sharp increase in the number of astronomy courses offered by schools in the United States since the Sputnik launching. SEE had never carried telescopes in the past but it now looked as if it might be a desirable line to add. During the spring of 1961 the purchasing department had written a number of potential suppliers inquiring about availability, prices and terms of sale, maintenance and service arrangements, and direct customer shipment. Sagaguchi, the president of Kobi Optical Company in Kobi, Japan, had replied personally to the first letter. In a subsequent exchange of letters with Borton, Sagaguchi had expressed interest in the possibility of an exclusive distributor arrangement between the two companies. Since Borton needed to talk to potential suppliers of other products in Japan, he agreed to meet and talk with Sagaguchi there.

Before leaving for Japan, Borton had asked the head of the accounting department, George Struthers, to gather what information he could on the educational market for telescopes in the United States. Struthers had been unable to find much information that related specifically to schools but had found some overall market data and had collected information on the telescopes then on the market.

He found that the market for telescopes and accessories in the United States in 1960 amounted to a total of about $6 million. Over 90 per cent of this market was supplied by importers of foreign telescopes. Although some telescopes were imported from Switzerland and Germany, most of them came from Japan. Data that he obtained from the U.S. Department of Commerce (given in the following table) showed Borton that the dollar value of imports of telescopes in 1958 had almost doubled as compared to 1957, and that there had been further increases in 1959 and 1960. Japanese imports had increased proportionately so that they had maintained a consistent share of 85 to 90 per cent of the telescopes imported into the United States during that period.

Imports of Telescopes and Parts and Accessories, 1956–1960 (millions of dollars)

Year	Imports from All Countries			Imports from Japan		
	Tele-scopes	Parts and Accessories	Total	Tele-scopes	Parts and Accessories	Total
1956	$1.81	$0.12	$1.93	$1.55	$0.11	$1.66
1957	1.99	0.16	2.15	1.78	0.14	1.92
1958	3.86	0.16	4.12	3.55	0.12	3.67
1959	4.00	0.34	4.34	3.59	0.28	3.87
1960	4.87	0.45	5.32	4.37	0.40	4.77

In one of his letters Sagaguchi stated that Kobi had an exclusive agency arrangement with N. R. Edmundson, an importer of cameras, binoculars, and telescopes, to distribute Kobi telescopes to retail stores. The exclusive agency agreement specifically precluded Edmundson from selling to schools or to industrial firms, however. Any inquiries Edmundson received from potential customers to these two markets were directed to Kobi. Edmundson maintained a service department for Kobi telescopes that industrial and institutional buyers could use, however.

From the promotional brochures that had been sent in response to the original enquiries, and from visiting local suppliers, Struthers had found that there were 11 other brands of telescopes on the market that were suitable for use by schools. Six of these were refractor telescopes, the more expensive type, and five were reflector telescopes. Kobi was rated by the suppliers as having the highest quality. It had no telescopes that sold at retail for less than $100, and most of their models were over $250. The price of a Kobi telescope was usually about 20 per cent more than for a comparable model of a competitor. Kobi offered most of the usual accessories (view finders, various powers of eyepieces, rack and pinion focusing, sun projecting screen, slow motion controls, and case). Kobi did not offer cameras and camera mounts for use with their telescopes, however.

In the discussion at the Kobi factory, Sagaguchi proposed to Borton that they sign an agreement whereby SEE would acquire exclusive rights to distribute Kobi telescopes to educational institutions in the United States. Kobi would agree to provide telescopes and accessories at cost plus 15 per cent (its agreement with N. R. Edmundson was at cost plus 30 per cent, he said). Kobi would arrange for Edmundson to handle all service and repair work at customer expense. SEE in return would agree not to sell any other line of telescopes to the educational market, to sell

Kobi telescopes to the educational market only, and to pay $50,000 for the exclusive rights to sell to this market for five years. After five years, SEE would have the option of renewing for another five years on the same terms. Any unused inventory could be returned if SEE did not exercise the option to renew.

Sagaguchi stated that, according to his sources, educational institutions in the United States were now buying about $300,000 worth of telescopes per year. He said that there were strong indications this would grow to at least $500,000 per year during the next five years, as the shortage of people trained to teach astronomy was reduced. This would mean a total market of at least $2 million over the five-year period. With the reputation and position of SEE in the science education equipment field, and the recognized high quality of Kobi telescopes, he believed that SEE should get at least one-half of this market. One million dollars of sales should provide a gross margin of half that, or $500,000, Sagaguchi said, for which $50,000 was a small price to pay.

He said he did not have to have an answer immediately but that conversations were being held with other interested parties and that he would need a reply by August 15. Borton promised to give an answer by that date. He returned to the United States uncertain about what reply to give, however. He was not convinced that Sagaguchi's estimates of the educational market for telescopes were correct. Borton suspected they might be high, but given the total market data that Struthers had supplied, it was possible they were realistic. Several other points concerned him as well.

The first was the desirability of the Kobi distributorship as compared with handling one or more other brands of telescopes on a nonexclusive basis. SEE could select one or two other brands initially, pay no fee, and see how sales were during the first year they were carried in the catalog. A decision would then be made about continuing or discontinuing the line, and if continued, on what brands to carry. If the agreement with Kobi were made, on the other hand, SEE would be committed to the line and to one brand for five years. It was the best quality telescope available, however, and the price concession SEE would get would allow it to price Kobi telescopes competitively with other telescopes with no loss of margin.

Borton was also not sure that marketing telescopes by mail order would be successful. Although SEE sold oscilloscopes, beam balances, and other expensive instruments by mail, they were all well-known brands of standard items with which the buyers had had previous experience. The buyers of an expensive telescope who had not bought one before might well want a demonstration, and even a trial period, before making a final decision.

He also was concerned about a camera mount and cameras as accessories. He did not know how classes in astronomy were conducted but suspected that taking pictures of the celestial bodies being studied might well be a requirement. If this proved to be the case, SEE would have to obtain cameras and mounts from another supplier. Although Sagaguchi had agreed to exempt this accessory from the exclusive agency agreement, Borton was not sure that a suitable mount and camera could be found easily.

He also was uncertain about what effect of "Buy America" preferences or legal requirements might have on sales of an item imported from Japan. He knew that at least part of the purchases of telescopes for schools would be financed from National Defense Education Act funds. He believed that there were restrictions on using NDEA funds to buy foreign products that were also produced in the United States. He also knew that there was still some anti-Japanese sentiment remaining from World War II, as well as questions about the general quality of their products.

Borton decided that he would try to get information on the size of the educational market for telescopes and on these other issues before making a decision concerning the Kobi distribution agreement. He called Paul McKittrick of McKittrick and Associates, a local marketing research firm, and arranged a meeting with him to discuss a possible research project.

McKittrick proposed that his firm conduct a study of the educational market for telescopes by doing a survey of a randomly selected sample of the secondary schools and of the colleges and universities on SEE's catalog mailing list. He stated that they would obtain information for the past three years and estimates for the next three years on the number of astronomy courses offered, the number of students, the number and kind of telescopes purchased, whether or not cameras are used, and on whether there were any restrictions on the purchases of Japanese built equipment.

McKittrick said that he believed that a telephone survey would be preferable to either personal interviews or a mail questionnaire for the study. Personal interviews would provide the most information but they would cost about five times as much as telephone calls. Mail questionnaires were unlikely to get a very high rate of response, he thought, because they would arrive during the summer vacation period. In addition, the probability of getting replies to a mail questionnaire back in time to prepare a report by early August did not look promising.

A formal proposal submitted two days later indicated that the telephone study would cost $6,000 and was to be finished by August 5. A sample of 100 secondary schools and 100 colleges and universities would be taken to obtain the required information.

1. How should Borton go about deciding whether or not to have the market study done?

2. What should his decision about the market study be? Why?

CHAPTER 4

Research Design

Research design is the *specification of procedures for collecting and analyzing the data necessary to define and/or solve the problem.* It is the blueprint for doing the research project.

The process of designing a decisional research project requires that a number of steps be taken. Although not always conducted in the exact sequence shown, these steps are to:

1. *Obtain agreement on the statement of the management problem.*
2. *Obtain background information on the problem situation.*
3. *Get information on the manager's problem situation model.*
4. *Formulate own problem situation model.*
5. *Restate management problem as a research problem.*
6. *Develop alternative ways of collecting and analyzing the data required.*
7. *Estimate the time and financial requirements of each design.*
8. *Choose among the contending designs.*
9. *Prepare a research proposal.*

These steps are each discussed in the first section, followed by a discussion of the sources and use of secondary information. A summary treatment is then presented of the types of errors that can reduce the accuracy of the research findings and strategies for dealing with them. The chapter is concluded with a discussion of the design requirements involved in various types of research, particularly causal research, as this is the most complex and ultimately the most important type of research.

This chapter is concerned with a general overview of the problem of research design. The technical research design considerations that center on sampling, measurement techniques, and data analysis are covered in Chapters 5 through 14.

The Steps in Research Design

1. Obtaining Agreement on the Statement of the Management Problem

In a meeting with a marketing research consultant, the president of a Chamber of Commerce discussed a research project that "will help us reduce the amount of shopping residents of our community do in two larger communities nearby." The management problem was apparently clear; how to reduce "outshopping" and so increase the amount of shopping done locally. Stated in this way, the task of the researcher was to help identify and evaluate various ways for increasing the local merchants' share of the shopping done by residents.

Although this seemed like a clear and straightforward statement of the problem, the consultant had learned that managers often cannot provide a complete statement of the problem when it is first discussed. In this case the chamber president's initial statement of his basic problem proved to be at least partially inaccurate. Further probing revealed that his underlying problem was to convince a majority of the local retailers that there was a sufficient outflow of local trade to warrant joint action to reverse the flow.

Only after the retailers were convinced of this would it be possible to utilize information on *why* local residents were shopping in surrounding communities. The more precise statement of the management problem implied a very different research problem than did the initial statement. Now, the researcher would become concerned with measuring the level of the retail trade outflow in addition to the reasons for the outflow.

The basic goal of *problem clarification* is to ensure that the decision maker's initial description of the management problem is accurate and reflects the appropriate area of concern for research. If the wrong management problem is translated into a research problem, the probability of providing management with useful information is low. One should *not* assume that the decision maker always has a clear understanding of the management problem he is attempting to solve. In fact, he is perhaps more likely to approach the researcher with problems that are not well defined. The researcher must satisfy himself that both he and the decision maker are in agreement as to what the management problem really is.

2. Obtain Background Information on the Problem Situation

The management problem can only be understood within the context of the problem situation. The *situational analysis* focuses on the variables that have produced the stated management problem. The factors that have led to the problem manifestations *and* the factors that have led to management's concern with the problem should be isolated. The situational analysis is seldom limited to an armchair exercise in logic, although this may be a valuable part of it. It also involves giving careful attention to company records, appropriate secondary sources such as census data, industry sales figures, economic indicators, and so on, and interviews with knowledgeable individuals both internal and external to the firm. The persons interviewed will include the manager(s) involved and may include salespersons, other researchers, trade association officials, professionals, and consumers.

In the retail trade study referred to previously, members of the Chamber of Commerce, local retailers, and consumers were interviewed. In addition, both applied and theoretical studies of shopping behavior were consulted.

A situational analysis may provide sufficient information to deal with the management problem or to indicate that what was initially perceived as a management problem is either not a problem at all or a different problem. Suppose that a researcher were asked to determine why ski wear and equipment sales were down in the Northwest in the fall of 1972. A thorough situational analysis would indicate that many of the ski areas did not open until late in the season and maintained only limited operating hours because of extremely mild weather. Information of this type, perhaps supported by additional data that industry sales were down at least as much as the firm's, should provide the decision maker with sufficient information to deal with this problem.

3. Get Information on the Manager's Problem Situation Model

Once the researcher has a sound understanding of the problem situation, he should get as clear an understanding as he can of the problem situation model of the manager. Specifically, he should try to get answers to the following questions:

1. *What objective(s) is desired?*
2. *What variables determine whether or not the objectives will be met?*
3. *How do they relate to the objective(s)?*
4. *What (general type of) decision rule is to be used?*

To say that the researcher should get answers to these questions is much easier than to obtain them. Often the manager will not have thought through the problem completely and will only have a "feel" for what is important in solving it. In these cases the manager may be *unable* to provide some of the information needed. In other instances he may be *unwilling* to do so. It is unlikely that the chamber president would have revealed his true objective for the research project if it were simply to impress fellow chamber members in order to ensure his re-election.

Although the best way of getting the desired information will depend upon the researcher and the manager(s) involved, as a general rule it is best to ask questions concerning the ultimate use of any resultant information. Specifically, the researcher should list the research findings that he thinks are possible and, in conjunction with the manager, trace the implications of each with respect to the decision. That is, the researcher must ask the question, "Given this finding, what would the firm do?" Note that the question is not stated in terms of capabilities. It does not help the researcher to know what the firm is capable of doing. He must determine *what it will do, or at least, is likely to do, given certain findings.* Often a firm may have a capacity for a certain action, such as increasing its advertising, but may be reluctant to do so because of other priorities.

A second type of information that the researcher should secure from the manager, directly or indirectly, is the nature of the decision rules that the manager will apply in this decision. As we saw in Chapter 2, different information is required for different kinds of decision rules. Some idea of how the manager will deal with the uncertainty involved in the decision is, therefore, required. If the researcher is a part of a company research department and has worked on other projects with the same executive(s), he will probably have already developed an understanding of risk preferences and methods of dealing with them that will apply to this decision. If not, he should attempt to learn them.

4. Formulate His Own Problem Situation Model

One of the early tasks of the researcher is to help the manager make his model explicit. Although this is often a difficult task, it is only the first step. The researcher should not be satisfied to operate with only the manager's model of the problem. Instead, he should attempt to develop the best possible model of the decision at hand. Although he will usually be bound by the objectives of the firm, he should examine carefully the list of variables developed thus far that are believed to be the determining ones. Are *all* of these variables relevant? Are these the *only* relevant variables? How does each affect the outcome of the decision?

At least three sources of information may be helpful in this phase of research design. First, *secondary data sources* beyond those concerned directly with the situational analysis should be reviewed. These sources range from trade journal articles and special reports focusing on the variable in a specific situation to more abstract theoretical treatments of the variable. For example, if a problem is concerned with sales force effectiveness, the researcher should not avoid theoretical academic works on salesmanship, interpersonal relations, and the like, simply because they tend to be abstract whereas he is concerned with a specific problem. They may well provide him with a viable alternative to consider.

A second approach for getting information to help the researcher in developing a problem situation model is the use of selected *case analyses*. The general approach to using case analyses for research purposes is described in Chapter 9. When used as an aspect of variable analysis, the goal is to isolate those variables that are relevant to the problem. Assume that a firm is concerned with the sales performance of its various branch offices. The case approach to variable analysis would suggest an in-depth comparison of a "successful" branch and an "unsuccessful" branch. Those variables that differed the most between the two branches would then be considered relevant for additional study.

Any new variables that are suggested by either of these two means should be discussed with *people who are knowledgeable about the problem*. This may require that one talk again with some of the people interviewed during the situation analysis.

5. Restate Management Problem as a Research Problem

Once the researcher and the decision maker are confident that they are both concerned with the same management problem and that it is properly defined, and the researcher has developed a problem situation model, the researcher must translate the management problem into a research problem. Management problems and marketing research problems are seldom identical. Management faces a problem when it must develop and choose among alternatives. These alternatives are typically courses of action to achieve a goal but may involve the selection of the goal itself. The *research problem is to develop information that will assist in the process of developing and choosing among alternatives*. The translation of the management problem into a research problem is one of the most critical tasks facing the researcher.

The shopping study provides an example. Here the management problem was to develop and select alternatives to increase the amount of shopping done locally. The research problem in this example is, at its broadest level, how to measure "why some consumers shop outside the local community." At a more specific level, it becomes one of how to measure the variables in the problem model, that is, who tends to shop outside, the attitudes that the consumers have about shopping locally versus in other communities, what kinds of appeals may be effective in changing their shopping habits, and so on.

6. Develop Alternative Ways of Collecting and Analyzing the Data Required

The two general ways of obtaining information are through *secondary* and *primary* sources. *Secondary data are data that were developed for some purpose other than helping to solve the problem at hand.* They may be *internal* (accounting records, sales invoices, salesmen call reports) or *external* (census data and other government reports, data collected by trade associations and trade publications, data collected by syndicated services) in nature. Secondary data sources are discussed in some detail in the section of this chapter that follows.

Primary data are data generated to help solve the problem being considered. They are developed through one or more of the following generic types of research designs: *observation, surveys, laboratory experiments, field experiments, and simulations.* An additional source of information that is part secondary and part primary in nature is the *statistical analysis of experience* data. These generic types of research design are discussed in detail in subsequent chapters.

There are many variations in size and complexity of each of these generic designs. A survey of consumers, for example, can be conducted by mail, by telephone, or by personal interview; it may be a one-time collection of information or a continuing panel with information obtained at periodic intervals. It can range in sample size from a few people informally selected to a sample of several thousand selected by an elaborate probabilistic sampling plan. A field experiment may range from an experiment conducted in a few supermarkets for a few days to a full-scale market test involving several cities for a year or more.

The researcher should develop alternative approaches for collecting the required data. The development of several approaches helps assure that a truly efficient and economic research design will be developed. All too often the first design a researcher creates will contain methodological weaknesses or overly expensive elements. Developing several alternative designs helps guard against this problem.

7. *Estimation of Time and Financial Requirements*

Once the competing research designs have been devised, the researcher must estimate the resource requirements. These requirements can be broken down into two broad categories: *time* and *financial*. Time refers to the time period needed to complete the project. The financial requirement is the monetary representation of manpower, computer time, and materials requirements. The time and financial requirements are not independent. As we shall see, on occasion, time and money are interchangeable.

Time Requirements and PERT

Program Evaluation Review Technique (PERT) coupled with the *Critical Path Method (CPM)* offers a useful aid for estimating the resources needed for a project as well as clarifying the planning and control process. CPM is, in reality, a part of PERT, so that in the following discussion PERT is referred to as including CPM.

PERT involves dividing the total research project into its smallest component activities, determining the sequence in which these activities must be performed, and attaching a time estimate for each activity. The activities and time estimates are presented in the form of a flow chart that allows a visual inspection of the overall process. The time estimates allow one to determine the *critical path* through the chart—that series of events whose delay will delay the completion of the project. Each of these aspects is discussed in more detail.[1] Before reading these descriptions, however, Figure 4–1 should be examined to get an idea of what a PERT chart looks like.

Activities, Events, and Time Requirement Estimates

Any research project can be broken down into a series of *activities* and *events*. An *activity* represents the allocation of time and resources to perform a particular task, such as training interviewers or pretesting a questionnaire. An *event* represents the completion of an activity. The first step in constructing a PERT analysis is to divide the total research project into its component activities. Every distinct activity that is relevant to the research project must be identified.

Once each activity has been identified and clearly defined, the researcher

---

[1] The following discussion of PERT is based on R. W. Miller, "How to Plan and Control with PERT," *Harvard Business Review,* **40** (March-April 1962), 93–104.

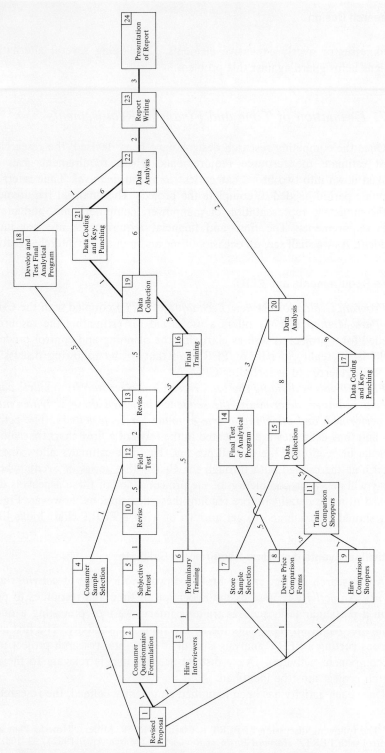

Figure 4–1 An example of a PERT chart. (— critical path)

must determine which activities are dependent upon the completion of other activities and which activities are independent of other activities. For example, sample selection can usually be performed independently of the training of the interviewers but both must be completed prior to data collection. The result of the activity sequence analysis is a PERT chart such as the one shown in Figure 4–1. This chart shows the researcher which activities must be completed first, which activities can be carried on simultaneously, and so forth.

Having isolated the various activities, the researcher must assign time estimates for the completion of each activity. These time estimates should be made by those most familiar with each particular activity. Of the four approaches to making the time estimates, the most frequently used estimate is the *most likely time*. This represents the normal or usual time such an activity would require. The *optimistic* estimate represents the *minimum time* an activity would take given exceptionally good luck. The *pessimistic* estimate represents the *maximum time* an activity would take given bad luck. *Combination* estimates are generally weighted averages of the three estimates.

The most commonly used combination estimate weights the most likely estimate by four and each of the other two estimates by one. The weights are multiplied by the appropriate time estimate, the products are summed, and the total is divided by 6. Assume that for the consumer interviewing activity in the project charted in Figure 4–1 the most likely time for completion is estimated to be 5.5 days, the optimistic estimate is 4 days, and the pessimistic estimate is 10 days. The combination estimate using the weights just stated would then be

$$\text{Combination estimate of time for interviewing} = \frac{4 \times 5.5 \text{ days} + 1 \times 4 \text{ days} + 1 \times 10 \text{ days}}{6}$$

$$= 6 \text{ days}.$$

Although the researcher will generally rely on either the most likely or combination estimate, he is well advised to develop contingency plans based on each of the other two estimates. That is, he should be prepared to take advantage of exceptionally good luck or to minimize the effects of exceptionally bad luck.

Once time estimates have been assigned to each activity, they should be placed on the PERT Chart. Although there are a number of possibilities for showing the time estimates, in Figure 4–1 the estimate is placed on the line connecting the activity with each subsequent dependent activity. Thus, in Figure 4–1, it can be seen that it will take an estimated six days to complete the consumer data collection so that final data analysis can begin.

Determination of Critical Path

After the time estimates have been attached to each activity, the researcher must trace each possible path through the network and estimate the total time for each path. The path with the greatest total time requirement is the *critical path.* Any delay in the completion of the activities composing this path will cause a delay in the completion of the project. In contrast, all other paths have *slack time,* which is the time difference between the critical path and any other path. This represents the amount of delay that can occur in the noncritical path without delaying the completion of the project. For relatively simple projects, the critical path can be determined by hand calculations. For more complex projects, computer programs are available.

In Figure 4–1, the heavy lines connecting events 1, 2, 5, 10, 12, 13, 16, 19, 21, 22, 23, and 24 represent the critical path. The time to complete this sequence of activities is 18.5 days. No other path through the network requires this much time. Therefore, any other path can experience delays up to the difference between its estimated total time and the time to complete the critical path without delaying the completion of the project. For example, the total time estimate for path 1, 9, 11, 15, 17, 20, 23, 24 is 16.5 days. The difference between the critical path and this path is 18.5 minus 16.5, or 2 days slack time. A delay in the noncritical path of up to a total of 2 days will not delay the project.

Graphic Evaluation and Review Technique (GERT)

An alternative to PERT has been developed that overcomes some of its shortcomings. The new approach, Graphic Evaluation and Review Technique (GERT), allows the introduction of probability estimates to the need to conduct specific activities. For example, a third wave in a mail survey might be needed only if the nonrespondents' replies could change the final decision. This cannot be known until after the second wave. GERT allows this branch to be established on a probability basis. The basic analysis of a GERT network is a computer simulation of the entire project. This can produce both time and cost estimates and ranges. For complex projects, GERT offers a rich potential.[2]

Financial Requirements

The PERT chart provides the time estimate. Estimates of financial requirements must include the direct and indirect manpower costs, materials,

---

[2] For details see A. C. Samli and C. Bellas, "The Use of GERT in the Planning and Control of Marketing Research," *Journal of Marketing Research,* **8** (August 1971), 335–339.

transportation, overhead, and other costs. Commercial research organizations, particularly those that specialize in specific types of research, are often able to derive accurate "rules of thumb."[3] A common approach to estimating the cost of a survey is to use a variable cost of Y dollars per completed interview plus a fixed cost of X dollars. Once the sample size is determined, the cost estimate can be quickly calculated.

For the unique research project, this is not a satisfactory solution. In cases of this type, the PERT technique becomes very useful as a starting point for analysis. As you will recall, PERT requires that every activity that goes into the research project be identified. The total man-days required for each activity is estimated and multiplied by the daily rate (including fringe benefits) of the workers that perform that activity. In addition, the materials and other direct expenses associated with each activity must be determined. The amount of time that the research director and other supervisory personnel will devote directly to the project must also be included. These various estimates are then totaled to provide an estimate of the *most likely direct cost* of the project.

Generally, it is wise to go through the procedure outlined previously also using the pessimistic time estimates. Then, a contingency or reserve can be budgeted based on the magnitude of the difference between the most likely costs and the highest anticipated costs.

The cost figures just described represent only direct costs. Indirect costs, such as rent, utilities, secretarial and staff assistance, and time of executives, must also be estimated. Indirect costs vary widely according to the type of operation involved. However, charges of 50 per cent or more of direct costs are typical.

When a firm is purchasing research from an outside research organization, it is common to solicit a limited number of competitive bids for the project. This allows the firm some control over the price and allows it to review different proposals. However, the practice has been criticized as leading to higher overall prices and lower quality research.[4] Competitive bids tend to produce a wide range of cost estimates even when relatively detailed specifications are provided to the bidders.[5] Ultimately, the firm must evaluate the quality of the proposal and the ability of the research firm to deliver the quality promised as well as the price.[6]

[3] J. R. Goodyear, "A Specialist Agency View," *Journal of the Market Research Society,* **14,** no. 4 (1972), 223–232.
[4] J. H. Myers, "Competitive Bidding for Marketing Research Services," *Journal of Marketing,* **33** (July 1969), 40–45.
[5] R. Gane and N. Spackman, "A Survey of Agency Costings," *Journal of the Market Research Society,* **14,** no. 4 (1972), 197–212.
[6] Goodyear, op. cit.; B. Hughes, "A Researcher Buyer's View," *Journal of the Market Research Society,* **14,** no. 4 (1972), 233–238; R. Roberts-Miller and F. Teer, "Costs and Pricing-Conclusions," *Journal of the Market Research Society,* **14,** no. 4 (1972), 239–241; and Myers, op. cit.

Other Benefits of PERT Analysis

PERT's most obvious advantage to the research planner is in making time estimates. However, its value extends far beyond this. PERT forces the researcher into a detailed plan and this is perhaps its greatest value. When three time estimates are made for *each* activity, the researcher is, in effect, forced to examine the assumptions that underlie the more common "most likely" time estimates. The activity sequence analysis often allows a given project to be completed in a shorter time period since independent activities can be identified and performed simultaneously. The isolation of each activity also allows for more accurate resource and manpower estimates. Critical path analysis allows a shift of manpower and/or resources from less critical to more critical areas as the need arises. In addition, the PERT chart can be a useful tool in controlling the research process.

An additional type of analysis that PERT helps expedite is the *time-cost analysis*. It is frequently possible to substitute financial resources for time. For example, it may be possible to gather information by personal interview or by mail. Although a number of variables may affect this decision, cost and time frequently play a major role. Personal interviews are generally faster and more expensive than mail questionnaires. However, if time is more critical in a given research project than the additional cost, personal interviews may be substituted. However, a PERT chart may indicate that this is worthwhile only if this part of the data collection procedure falls on the critical path. In other words, the completion of a projection can be advanced only by shortening the time requirements of the critical path. An excellent example and description of the methodology for this time-cost analysis is provided by Beckwith.[7]

8. *Choose Among the Alternatives*

Having developed several alternative research designs for collecting the required data, the researcher must select the "best" design. The principle that should guide this selection is: *that research design should be chosen from among the alternatives being considered that is expected to provide the greatest excess of value over cost.* More simply stated, one chooses what is believed to be the best informational buy.

The way that the value of each alternative is assessed will depend upon the type of decision rule being used and the preferences of the person(s) making the final decision. The evaluation may be made by the traditional method that will rest on the implicit judgment of the evaluator. If, on the other hand, an expected value decision rule is utilized, a full-scale Bayesian

[7] N. E. Beckwith, "The Costs of Crashing—A Comment," *Journal of Marketing,* **35** (October 1971), 63–66.

analysis may be run to determine the expected monetary value of imperfect information for each alternative. This, after the estimated cost of the alternative is subtracted, will give a direct basis for comparison of the contending designs.

We believe that a Bayesian analysis to the point of calculating the expected value of perfect information (*EMVPI*) is a useful guide in most decisions even if the expected value of imperfect information (*EMVII*) is not determined. *EMVPI* is easy to calculate and sets an upper limit on the value of the information. Some of the alternatives can automatically be eliminated (a $100,000 study for an *EMVPI* of $50,000, for example) if one is willing to apply the expected value rule for this purpose. It also provides some basis for judging the monetary value of added, or decreased, accuracy of designs.

The discussion thus far has focused on the value of information for the solution of *a specific management problem*. It is often possible to increase the value of a specific research project by generating information that is relevant to an *entire class of management decisions*. Consider a firm that has developed a new consumer product and is attempting to select an appropriate package design. The firm has developed three alternative package designs and the immediate problem is to select the package with the most "overall appeal" to the firm's target market. A rather simple preference study will most likely provide a good indication of which of the three packages is preferred. However, if the study focuses only on this one decision and not on the underlying dynamics influencing the consumers' preferences for packages in this product category, the same type study will have to be conducted each time a new package design is required. Furthermore, the firm will have gained only limited insights into what constitutes a "good" package. Therefore, the firm cannot expect to improve the absolute attractiveness of the next package it designs.

In such a situation, we may be able to generate information useful for the decision at hand that will be useful for future decisions of this type as well. That is, the design of the study should focus not only on selecting a package but also on obtaining data on what characterizes a "good" package. This approach may require a more complex and costly design and the expected value of the added information should be compared with this extra cost.

9. *Preparing the Research Proposal*

The research planning process provides the researcher with a blueprint or guide for conducting and controlling the research project. This blueprint is written in the form of a *research proposal*. A written research proposal should precede any research project. The word *precede* may be somewhat misleading. Obviously, a substantial amount of research effort is involved in the research planning process that must precede the research proposal. One writer estimates that the proposal may cost 5 to 10 per cent of the total cost of a project.[8]

The research proposal helps ensure that the decision maker and the researcher are still in agreement on the basic management problem, the problem model, and the research approach to the problem model. It also presents the researcher a chance to sell his product. In most firms, research funds are relatively scarce and the researcher must convince management that the money spent on a given research project will yield as high a return as any competing use of the funds. This is not to suggest that the researcher should overstate his case or request funds for research projects that he does not feel are warranted. However, it is meant to suggest that, if the researcher believes a project can make a contribution to the firm, he should present his views as clearly and forcefully as possible.

Elements of a Research Proposal

The basic elements of the research proposal are shown below and are discussed in the following paragraphs.

Elements of the Research Proposal
1. *Summary:* A brief statement of the major points from each of the other sections.
2. *Background:* A statement of the management problem and the factors that influence it.
3. *Objectives:* A description of the types of data the research project will generate and how these data are relevant to the management problem.
4. *Research Approach:* A description of the proposed methodology.
5. *Time and Cost Requirements:* An explanation of the time and costs required by the planned methodology.
6. *Technical Appendixes:* Any statistical or detailed information that only one or a few of the potential readers may be interested in.

Summary. The first section of the research proposal should be a brief summary. This summary should contain a short description of each of the sections of the overall proposal. Considerable effort should be spent in making the summary clear, concise, and convincing as it may be the only part of the proposal that is read by some portion of the relevant audience. It must contain enough information to allow those who read only the

[8] Myers, op. cit., 41.

summary to develop a feeling for the nature and value of the research project. Balanced against the need for information is the need for brevity. The purpose of the summary is to allow an executive to develop a basic understanding of the proposal *without* reading the entire proposal.

Background. The proposal should contain a detailed description of the management problem and the factors that influence it. This is necessary as those who must approve a proposal or who may have an interest in it are not necessarily the same person as the decision maker who initiated the process. This section serves to inform these individuals and to ensure that the researcher and the decision maker are still in agreement as to the nature of the basic management problem.

Objectives. The objectives section describes the translation of the management problem into a research problem. It makes explicit the model and the nature of information to be generated. This information is then related to the management problem. This section is a critical part of the proposal. The researcher must justify the information he will generate in terms of its ability to aid in the solution of the management problem. The expected value of information may be presented at this point. However, it should be explained in general terms and the computations presented in an appendix.

Research Approach. This section should contain a rather complete description of the tentative research methodology. Since this section may be fairly long, it should be preceded by a summary that provides more detail than the initial summary section of the proposal but much less than the detailed description that follows. The detailed description should provide a reasonably detailed statement of each aspect of the methodology. Technical discussions, questionnaire formats, and other complex and/or lengthy aspects of the design should be confined to appendixes, however.

Time and Cost Requirements. The PERT chart forms the basis for this section. The time requirements, including the range as well as the most likely time, are described in terms of this chart. In addition, the major activity clusters in the chart can serve as a useful way of describing the cost requirements. The costs should be justified in terms of the expected or potential value of the information.

Technical Appendixes. Any highly technical information or information that will appeal to only a few readers should be placed in appendixes at the back of the report. This is done to ensure that the proposal proper maintains its conciseness and readability without sacrificing potentially useful information.

Secondary Data

Advantages of Secondary Data

As defined earlier, *secondary data are data that were developed for some purpose other than helping to solve the problem at hand.* Secondary data can be gathered quickly and inexpensively compared to primary data. Even when reports or publications must be ordered, the time involved is generally substantially less than the time required to collect original data.

A thorough search of secondary data will often provide sufficient information to resolve the problem. If so, the researcher has produced a substantial time and cost savings. In those cases where the secondary data cannot solve the problem, they can often help structure the problem and eliminate some variables from consideration. Or, it may be possible to utilize the secondary data in conjunction with primary data. For example, a survey may be used to estimate the expenditure for a certain product by households with the head of the household in each of a series of age categories. Census data could be used to determine the number of households in each category. The two sets of figures could then be multiplied to determine total expenditures for the product.

Thus, secondary data can provide a complete or partial solution to many problems and may help us structure others. They tend to cost substantially less than primary data and can be collected in less time.

Problems Encountered with Secondary Data

Before secondary data are applied to a particular marketing problem, their *relevance* and *accuracy* must be assessed. *Relevance* refers to the extent to which the data fit the information needs of the research problem. Even when the data cover the same general topic as that required by the research problem, they may not fit the requirements of the problem.

Three general problems reduce the relevance of data that would otherwise be useful. First, there is often a difference in the *units of measurement*. For example, many retail decisions require detailed information on the characteristics of the population within their "trade area." However, available population statistics may focus on counties, cities, or census tracts that do not match the trade area of the retail outlet. The unit of measurement required by the problem, the trade area, does not coincide with the unit of measurement available in the secondary data.

A second general problem that can reduce the relevance of secondary data is the *definition of classes*. For example, a manufacturer may have a product that appeals to children 8 to 12 years old. If available secondary data are based on age categories 5 to 9 and 10 to 14, the firm will have a hard time utilizing it. Social class, age, income, firm size, and similar category-type breakdowns found in secondary data frequently do not coincide with the exact requirements of the research problem.

The final major factor affecting relevancy is *time*. Generally, research problems require current, if not future, data. Most secondary data, on the other hand, have been in existence for some time. For example, complete census reports are not available for several years. Data are frequently collected one to three years prior to publication. The publication itself may be several years old before it is utilized. It is not uncommon to find the exact data needed that are just too old to be relied upon.

Accuracy is the second major concern of the user of secondary data. The real problem is not so much obvious inaccuracy as it is the difficulty of determining how inaccurate the data are likely to be.

When using secondary data, the original source should be used if possible. This is important for two reasons. First, the original report is generally more complete than a second or third report. It often contains warnings, shortcomings, and methodological details not reported by the second or third source. Second, using the original source allows the data to be examined in context and may provide a better basis for assessing the competence and motivation of the collector.

Examine Table 4–1 before reading the rest of this paragraph. Did you notice the error? The total expenditure figure for each expenditure category should not be determined by multiplying the number of individuals in the category by the minimum expenditure in the next highest category. This procedure grossly overstates the total expenditures. The appropriate multiplier is the midpoint of each category. This error could not have been caught had one seen a secondhand report that provided only the total expenditure figure and did not show the computations.

Table 4–1 was taken from an actual research report that was circulated to business firms. Its purpose was to convince them to advertise in the sponsoring medium because of the high level of expenditures of their audience for selected product categories. Therefore, it would be to the sponsoring firm's advantage for these figures to be overstated.

Few sources "cheat" in the sense of supplying outright false data. However, writers with a strong point of view often report only those aspects of a study that support their position. In addition, some sources are more competent than others, both from a technical point of view and from the standpoint of having sufficient resources to adequately perform the task at hand. Thus, the reputation of the source is an important criterion for deciding whether or not to use a particular piece of secondary data.

Table 4–1   Annual Expenditures on Selected Products

Total Annual Expenditures	Per Cent Of Sample	Estimated Number	Projected Expenditures
$199 or less	6.4	1,000	$ 200,000
$200 to $399	15.3	2,300	920,000
$400 to $599	13.2	2,000	1,200,000
$600 to $799	9.1	1,350	1,080,000
$800 to $999	8.7	1,325	1,325,000
$1,000 to $1,199	11.1	1,675	2,010,000
$1,200 to $1,399	4.9	750	1,050,000
$1,400 to $1,599	6.6	1,100	1,980,000
$1,600 to $1,799	5.9	950	1,710,000
$1,800 or more	19.0	2,900	5,800,000
Total	100.0	15,350	$17,275,000

Sources of Secondary Data

There are two general sources of secondary data—*internal* sources and *external* sources. Internal data are available within the firm whereas external sources provide data that are developed outside the firm.

Internal Sources

Internal sources include sales records, sales force reports, operating statements, budgets, previous research reports, and the like. The most useful type of internal information is generally sales data. Unfortunately, many firms do not collect or maintain sales data in a manner that allows the researcher to tap their full potential. Depending on the type of business, sales records should be kept by customer or customer type, by payment type (cash versus credit), by specific product line and category, by sales territory or department, by sales person, and by as detailed time periods as possible.

Such records, if properly utilized, allow the researcher to isolate profitable and unprofitable customers, territories, and product lines, to identify developing trends, and perhaps to measure the effects of manipulations of marketing mix variables.

Internal data must be collected in a usable format and must be analyzed to be of value. For example, a student intern was asked to estimate the "best" price reduction for a store that frequently sold paint at a reduced price. An examination of the firm's advertising records allowed him to identify the timing of numerous sales at different discounts over the past several years. The firm's inventory records allowed a close estimate of the units sold during each sale. By combining these two data sources, the student was able to develop a useful estimate of the price elasticity of demand for the firm's paint. In addition, he was able to isolate one season of the year when the elasticity of demand was unusually high and one season when it was relatively low.

As this example should indicate, many firms have useful but unutilized data. By changing the format of collection forms (sales invoices, salesman call reports, and so on), other useful data can often be collected. They are available and inexpensive; internal data are usually the best information buy.

External Sources

Numerous sources external to the firm may produce data relevant to the firm's requirements. Four general categories of external secondary information are described in the sections that follow—(1) *trade associations,* (2) *government agencies,* (3) *other published sources,* and (4) *syndicated services.*

Trade Associations. Trade associations frequently publish or maintain detailed information on industry sales, operating characteristics, growth patterns, and the like. Furthermore, they may conduct special studies of factors relevant to their industry. Since trade associations generally have an excellent reputation for not revealing data on individual firms as well as good working relationships with the firms in the industry, they may be able to secure information that is unavailable to other researchers.

These materials may be published in the form of annual reports, as part of a regular trade journal, or as special reports. In some cases, they are available only on request from the association. Most libraries maintain reference works such as the *Encyclopedia of Associations,*[9] which list the various trade associations and provide a statement of the scope of their activities.

Government Agencies. Federal, state, and local government agencies produce a massive amount of data that is of relevance to marketers. In this section the nature of the data produced by the federal government is briefly described. However, state and local government data should not be overlooked by the researcher.

The federal government maintains five major agencies whose primary function is the collection and dissemination of statistical data: (1) *Bureau of the Census,* (2) *Bureau of Labor Statistics,* (3) *National Center for Educational Statistics,* (4) *National Center for Health Statistics,* and (5) *Statistical Reporting Service, Department of Agriculture.* There are also a

---

[9] *Encyclopedia of Associations* (Detroit: Gale Research Co., 1972).

number of specialized analytic and research agencies, numerous administrative and regulatory agencies, and special committees and reports of the judicial and legislative branches of the government.

These sources produce two broad types of data. First, statistics that focus on *people* are produced. These include demographics, vital and health statistics, labor, and social conditions. The second broad category focuses on *economic activity*—commerce, finance, government transactions, agriculture, and the like. Both types of data are widely used by business firms as an aid in decision making.

The data available may be standardized, such as census data, or it may be in the form of special reports. For example, a special report entitled *Who's Home When*[10] contains data on the time of day when individuals with given socioeconomic characteristics may be expected to be found at home. Such information is useful for planning telephone or personal interviews.

Census publications are one of the most widely used sources of secondary data. Some examples of the use of census tract data are as follows:

A department store used census tract data to help obtain the proper zoning and favorable financing for a new department store.

A savings and loan association used data by census tract to help determine the feasibility of applying for a new branch facility and in obtaining approval for it.

An automotive supply chain used census tract data to help in reorganizing a direct mailing system to obtain greater sales at less cost.[11]

Although there is no doubt that the government provides a tremendous amount of potentially useful data, it is sometimes rather difficult to find it. Steps are being taken to make this material more accessible. In 1973, the first volume of the *American Statistics Index* was published by the Congressional Information Service. The 1973 volume covered only statistics dealing with people. However, the 1974 volume deals with both people and economic activity. The goal of the *American Statistics Index* is to be a *comprehensive* index of statistical data available to the public by any agency of the federal government. The index will be issued annually and updated monthly. It should simplify the task of locating relevant data published by the government.

Another index of information useful to marketing researchers is the computerized search and reference service provided by the *National Technical Information Service* (NTIS) of the U.S. Department of Commerce. Over 300,000 documents dating back to 1964 are referenced. For the pay-

[10] Bureau of the Census, *Who's Home When* (Washington, D.C.: U.S. Government Printing Office, 1973).

[11] For details on these and other examples see W. McCann, *Some Uses of Census Tracts in Private Business* (Washington, D.C.: U.S. Government Printing Office, 1967).

ment of a fee (less than $100) a search will be made of documents relating to a specific topic. Pertinent documents are cited, an abstract provided, and a price quoted if NTIS has the document available.

Other Published Sources.   There is a virtually endless array of periodicals, books, dissertations, special reports, newspapers, and the like that contain information relevant to marketing decisions. Any attempt to list or describe even the more important of these sources would be beyond the scope of this book and the interests of the readers.

A starting point in a search for published sources on any particular topic is the subject heading in the local library's card catalog. This should be followed by consulting the relevant abstracts or literature guides such as *Dissertation Abstracts, Psychological Abstracts, Sociological Abstracts, Business Periodicals Index,* the *Social Science Citation Index,* and the *Reader's Guide to Periodical Literature.* After consulting these sources, the reader should ask the librarian to provide additional suggestions. The librarian can frequently produce references that even a thorough search by a person without specialized training would not reveal.

Syndicated Services.   A number of firms regularly collect data of relevance to marketers that they sell on a subscription basis. Two types of syndicated services are widely used by marketing researchers—channel information and omnibus surveys.

Channel information is available to the firm at four levels—manufacturers, intermediaries, retailers, and consumers. A manufacturer's sales and shipments are generally available only through the firm's own internal records. Therefore, although a firm can monitor its own activities at this level, it can only infer the output of other manufacturing firms.

At the intermediary or wholesale level, several syndicated firms provide information on the flow of products and brands to retail outlets. Selling Areas-Marketing, Inc. (SAMI) and Market Research Corporation of American (MRCA) are both involved in this area of research. Data of this nature allow the researcher to estimate market size and trend, brand share, and related information.

Store audits provide data on the movement of brands through retail outlets. For example, the A. C. Nielsen Company maintains a large sample of stores (food and drug stores) that are visited periodically. The stores' inventories for specific product categories are counted, and purchase invoices are examined. This allows the auditor to determine the inventory on hand and the amount sold since his last visit. Nielsen projects these sample data into estimates of total sales and inventories of specific brands for all outlets of a given type in the United States or various regions.

Audits and Surveys Company, Inc., also provides national auditing services. Other firms specialize in localized auditing services. Information of this type allows the manufacturer to estimate sales, sales trends, and market share. In addition, the researcher can quickly estimate the effect of variations in his own or the competitor's market mix. For example, one problem that a firm faces in conducting a standard test market is the fact its competitors may learn as much about the sales of the product as quickly as the sponsoring firm through its subscription to a store audit service.

At the consumer level, consumer panels provide data on both purchasing patterns and media habits. The Nielsen Company's television monitoring program provides information on consumer viewing habits. The Market Research Corporation of America, National Family Opinion, Inc., and Consumer Mail Panels, Inc., all provide a system whereby a large panel of consumers report their purchases of various products. The researcher can use these data in the same manner described for store audit data. Moreover, consumer panels also provide information on the sociodemographic characteristics and past purchasing patterns of the respondents. Therefore, the researcher can monitor not only shifts in sales or brand share but also the characteristics of purchasers-nonpurchasers, early purchasers, brand loyal purchasers, and so on.

Omnibus surveys collect data that are useful to a number of subscribers from a series of independent samples. Daniel Starch and Staff conduct interviews with consumers and businessmen to determine the impact of advertisements appearing in a wide range of publications. Both Gallup, Inc., and R. H. Bruskin Associates conduct periodic surveys that include topics of specific interest to business firms. For example, Bruskin Associates allows the insertion of a firm's slogan, trademark, package, and so on to determine the public's ability to identify it.

Syndicated services enjoy the same advantages of other types of secondary sources. Basically, they are substantially less expensive than similar primary research. The reason for this is that the cost is shared by a number of subscribers. In addition, the studies tend to be of high quality because the firm is able to develop considerable expertise in the type of service offered.

Research Design and Error Minimization

Secondary data are often adequate to satisfy the research requirements. When they are not adequate for this purpose, the researcher must generate primary or original data. Primary data, like secondary data, must be both relevant and accurate. Relevance is generally not a problem since the information is gathered to meet the specific requirements of the problem model.[12] Therefore, the researcher's basic concern with primary data is balancing the accuracy of the data with the cost of obtaining it.

Researchers *want* perfect information. Perfect information would provide a completely accurate prediction of what would happen if each alternative being considered were chosen. As we saw in Chapter 3, the expected monetary value of perfect information sets an upper limit on the amount a researcher should be willing to spend on a given research project.

Unfortunately, most research information contains errors. Why? First, some kinds of error are physically impossible to eliminate. For example, it is not possible to question everyone who purchased a new car last year if for no other reason than the fact that some have died since then. Yet this would be necessary in order to eliminate all nonresponse error in a study of that particular population. Second, with our current level of skill, we do not have the capacity to eliminate some kinds of error. We simply cannot measure motives, attitudes, or even preferences with perfect accuracy. Finally, it costs too much to eliminate certain kinds of error. A census will eliminate all sampling error but it may well be too expensive to justify the increase in accuracy.

The *goal of research design in applied research is to maximize the difference between the cost of obtaining various levels of accuracy with the expected value of information associated with each level of accuracy.* This statement recognizes two facts. First, the accuracy of research information is directly related to the cost of the information. For example, sampling error can be decreased by increasing the size of the sample. However, increasing the sample size increases the cost of the information. Second, the total error can often be reduced by intelligent manipulation of the research design *without* increasing total cost. Frequently, this involves trading a given amount of one type of error for a smaller amount of another type of error.

Types of Error

Before we can fully develop the concept of error trade-offs, we need to become aware of the various sources of error. A summary of eight types of error that may arise in a research project is presented, and then each type is briefly described. A more detailed treatment of each type of error is provided in the chapter concerned with the specific aspect of research design that is influenced by that error source.

---

[12] Misspecification of the problem model is considered to be one source of inaccuracy. See the discussion on surrogate information error on page 124.

Potential Sources of Error in Research Information

1. *Surrogate information error:* Noncorrespondence of sought to required information.
2. *Measurement error:* Noncorrespondence of achieved to sought information.
3. *Experimental error:* Measurement of the effects of the experimental situation rather than the effects of the independent variable.
4. *Population specification error:* Noncorrespondence of sought to required population.
5. *Frame error:* Noncorrespondence of sought to required sample.
6. *Sampling error:* Variable error resulting from the chance inclusion of population elements according to the sampling plan.
7. *Selection error:* Noncorrespondence of selected to sought sample.
8. *Nonresponse error:* Noncorrespondence of achieved to selected sample.

Surrogate Information Error   Asking the WRONG Question

Surrogate information error is the noncorrespondence of sought to required information. That is, it represents the results of seeking information that does not accurately represent the characteristic in which we are interested. The so-called "price-quality relationship" where a consumer uses the price of a brand to represent its quality level is a common example of a measure that is subject to surrogate information error since price level does not always reflect quality level.

In a marketing research framework, seeking information on past behavior as a predictor of future behavior and seeking verbal statements of brand preference as an indicator of "real" preferences are examples of data that are subject to surrogate information error. As these examples indicate, surrogate information error arises in the process of translating the management problem into a research problem. Since it is seldom possible to collect data that are perfectly suited to the management problem, most research projects contain some degree of surrogate information error.

Measurement Error (Design)

Measurement error reflects a lack of congruence between the achieved information and the desired information. In other words, not only is it possible to seek the wrong type of information (surrogate information error) but it is possible to gather information that is different than that which we are seeking. This is one of the most common and serious errors. For example, a respondent may exaggerate his income in order to impress an interviewer. The reported income will then reflect an unknown amount of measurement error. Measurement error is particularly difficult to control because it can arise from many different sources.

Experimental Error   *Testing Effects*

Experiments are designed to measure the impact of one or more independent variables on a dependent variable. Experimental error occurs when the impact of the experimental situation itself is measured rather than the impact of the independent variable. For example, an experiment that lasts several hours may produce fatigue in the respondents. The measurement of the experimental effects may reflect this fatigue rather than the effects of the independent variable.

Like measurement error, experimental error can arise from a number of sources. As discussed in Chapter 12, experimental designs allow for the control of specified sources of experimental error.

Population Specification Error   *Asking the WRONG people*

Population specification error involves selecting an inappropriate universe or population from which to collect data. This is a potentially serious problem in both industrial and consumer research. A firm wishing to learn the criteria that are considered most important in the purchase of certain machine tools might conduct a survey among purchasing agents. Yet in many firms the purchasing agents do not determine or necessarily even know the criteria behind brand selections. These decisions may be made by the machine operators, by committee, or by higher level executives. A study that focuses on the purchasing agent as the person who decides what brands to order may be subject to population specification error.

Population specification error is perhaps more common in consumer research. The relative ease of contacting females, particularly housewives, has led to a great deal of reliance on surveys of housewives. Yet for many purchasing decisions, husbands or children play the primary role. If the housewife is treated as the primary decision maker in these cases, as she often is, population specification error has occurred.

Frame Error   *(Design) Determined who going to ASK + need to Select people from list, but list is WRONG*

Frame error is the noncorrespondence of the sought to the required sample. The *sampling frame* is the list from which the sample units are selected. An ideal frame identifies each element once and only once. Obviously, perfect frames are difficult to obtain, particularly for human subjects. Any frame that is not representative of the desired population contains frame error. This may result in the final respondents not being an accurate reflection of the appropriate population. For example, using the telephone directory as a sampling frame for the population of a community contains a high potential for frame error. Those families who do not have listed numbers, both voluntary and nonvoluntary, are likely to differ from those with listed numbers in such respects as income, sex, and mobility.

Sampling Error   *LARGE SAMPle eRRoR is Design*

Sampling error is the focal point of concern in classical estimation and hypothesis testing. The nature of sampling error is treated in most introductory statistical texts and in the sampling chapters of this text. Sampling error for *probability samples* is the variable error resulting from the chance inclusion of population elements according to the sampling plan. Sampling error for probability samples can be readily measured and its implications for research design can be specified. Sampling error for *nonprobability samples* may be variable or systematic (or both) in nature and is not measurable. Variable sampling error can be reduced by increasing sample size and/or switching to a more efficient design. Increases in sample size generally increase costs. Larger sample sizes will not necessarily reduce any of the other types of error.

Selection Error   *Collection*

Selection error is the noncorrespondence of selected to sought sample. It arises when there is an improper selection of respondents in a nonprobability sample. It is a particularly acute source of error in convenience samples that often correspond more closely to the characteristics of the interviewers than to the population of interest to the researcher. Quota and judgment samples also suffer from this problem.

Nonresponse Error

Nonresponse error is composed of two elements: (1) respondents with whom contact was never made, and (2) refusals to respond to all or specific parts of the measurement instrument. It is apparent that people who are difficult to contact or who are reluctant to cooperate will differ, on at least some characteristics, from those who are relatively easy to contact or who readily cooperate. If these differences include the variable of interest, nonresponse error has occurred.

Strategies for Dealing with Errors

After such a cataloging of errors, one may begin to question the value of research information. The situation is not as gloomy as it may seem, however. Several remedies are available, including the strategies of (1) *minimizing individual errors* through careful research design, (2) *trade-offs to reduce total error, and* (3) *measurement,* (4) *estimation,* and (5) *ignoring* residual errors.

A description of the techniques available for minimizing the effects of each of the sources of errors occupies the central portion of this book (Chapters 5 through 14). The remaining error strategies are discussed as follows.

Error Trade-Offs

Assume that a researcher has initially selected a large sample for a mail survey. The sample is large enough to provide a low level of sampling error, but it has taken such a large proportion of the research budget that there are sufficient funds remaining for only one follow-up mailing. Past experience with surveys of this type indicates that with one follow-up mailing, the total response rate will reach 60 per cent whereas with four follow-ups it will climb to 85 per cent. Given the nature of the survey, the researcher thinks that the nonrespondents may differ significantly from the respondents.

One solution would be to ask for an increase in the budget. However, such funds may not be available or the resultant data may not justify additional expenditures. A second solution is to "trade" sampling error for nonresponse error. Sample size could be reduced, which would increase the probable amount of sampling error. However, the funds thus freed could provide additional mailed follow-up questionnaires and telephone calls to the final group of nonrespondents. These efforts may reduce nonresponse error more than enough to offset the increase in sampling error. Thus, the result is a reduction in total error and an increase in total accuracy.

Since eight major sources of error are possible, designing a research project so as to minimize the total error can be quite complex. The decisions as to exactly what level of error is associated with a particular aspect of the research project are quite subjective. However, this is *not* an argument for ignoring errors. A conscious attempt to minimize not only each individual type of error but also total error will almost always produce more accurate results than simply ignoring the potential errors or the possibilities of error trade-offs.

Strategies for Dealing with Residual Error

Several strategies are available for dealing with residual or nonreducible errors. These strategies may be applied to total error or they may be applied to individual error types. Basically, the three strategies are (1) *to measure the error,* (2) *to estimate it,* or (3) *to ignore it.*

Measurement and/or estimation of errors is to be preferred to ignoring them. Potential errors should never be completely ignored. It is possible and fairly common to estimate that the net effect of these errors is so small as to warrant no specific action. However, this is *not* the same as ignoring the potential errors. At a minimum, the researcher should *explicitly,* if subjectively, estimate the extent of each type of potential error. If individual errors or the combined effects of the errors are large, they should be reduced via the research design or their effects taken into account in the analysis of the data. While a complete discussion of estimating and measuring individual and total error is beyond the scope of this text,[13] both approaches are described in detail with respect to nonresponse error in Chapter 11.

Research Design and Research Goals

One can specify three general goals of which one or more are important in any research project. Each particular goal is associated with certain characteristic research designs.

Exploratory research is concerned with discovering the general form of the problem situation model. The situation analysis described earlier in this chapter is a common form of exploratory research, which is characterized by a high degree of flexibility. The researcher proceeds without a fixed plan, although he may have a tentative checklist or guide. His strategy is to follow each clue or idea as far as seems profitable. Although any approach to data collection and analysis can be utilized, exploratory research tends to rely on secondary data, convenience or judgment samples, small-scale surveys or simple experiments, case analyses, and subjective evaluation of the results.

Descriptive research is focused on the accurate description of the variables in the problem model. Studies such as consumer profiles, market potential studies, product usage studies, attitude surveys, sales analyses, media research, and price surveys are examples of descriptive research. All possible sources of information can be utilized in a descriptive study (secondary sources, surveys, natural experiments, controlled experiments, and simulation), although most studies of this nature rely heavily on secondary data sources and survey research.

In descriptive research projects it is generally assumed that an adequate functional or causal model of the system under consideration exists or at

---

[13] See D. S. Tull and G. S. Albaum, *Survey Research: A Decisional Approach* (New York: Intext Educational Publishers, 1973), 67–77.

least has been suggested. As our confidence in our knowledge of the functional relationships declines, the value of descriptive research declines. For example, it does little good to provide a merchant with a socio-demographic profile of an area for a potential store if he has no feel for *how* these variables relate to the success of the store.

In *causal research* studies, the attempt is made to specify the nature of the functional relationship between two or more variables in the problem situation model. For example, studies on the effectiveness of advertising generally attempt to discover the extent to which advertising causes sales or attitudes. The basic assumption underlying causal research is that some variables cause or affect the values of other variables. Experimentation and, to a lesser extent, survey research are used to produce evidence of causation.

We tend to think and act in terms of causation. Prices are reduced or advertising is increased to *cause* an increase in sales. Salespersons are paid on a commission plan to cause them to sell more. Our problem models all specify some form of causation. Yet the concept of causation is often not well understood. In the next section an attempt is made to clarify this important concept.

Nature of Causation

What is the nature of causation? What do we mean when we say that a price decrease causes an increase in sales? An event can be considered to be the cause of another event if its occurrence is both the necessary and sufficient condition for the occurrence of the second event. A *necessary* condition means that the caused event cannot occur in the absence of the causative event. A *sufficient* condition means that the causative event is all that is needed to bring about the caused event. In other words, in a simple causative relationship, the two events *never* occur in isolation.

The simple causative relationship described is obviously inadequate for marketing phenomena. A price decrease may sometimes be followed by an increase in unit sales. However, it may also be followed by no change or by a decrease in unit sales. In addition, sales may change when price is unaltered. Thus, the price-sales relationship, like other marketing relationships, is not amenable to a simple causative analysis. A broader concept of cause is required.

Contributory cause is defined as "the occurrence of one event increasing the likelihood or probability of the occurrence of a second event." Although a contributory cause will increase the probability of the occurrence of the second event, it does not make the second event certain since it is only one (or a subset) of the factors that jointly determine the outcome.

For example, offering a price discount to a given industrial purchaser may generally increase the probability of his purchasing a given brand. However, if he views the product as inferior and interprets the price discount as evidence of this, the probability of purchase may be decreased rather than increased. Obviously, price level does not *determine* the purchasing behavior, but it may *influence* it.

The presence of a number of contributory causes leads to a consideration of *alternative causes* that might also make the event more likely. In our example, it might be found that a well-documented justification for the current prices will also cause an increase in the probability of a purchase. Thus, we find that either a price discount or a justification of current prices increases the probability of a sale if the purchasing agent views the brand as being of high quality. These represent alternative contributory causes.

Determination of Cause

The preceding discussion has assumed that we had some measure of cause, some way of inferring that the price discount caused (at least on a contributory basis) the sales increase. How can we determine this? *Causation cannot be proven in the behavioral sciences.* All we can do is draw inferences about the probability of causal relations from our data. However, if certain conditions are met we can have a high degree of confidence that our inferences about causation are correct. We can use three types of evidence to make inferences about causation. These are (1) *concomitant variation,* (2) *sequence of occurrence,* and (3) *absence of other potential causal factors.*

Concomitant variation, or invariant association, is a common basis for ascribing cause. Suppose that we vary our advertising expenditures across a number of geographic areas and measure sales in each area. To the extent that high sales occur in areas with large advertising expenditures and low sales occur in areas with limited advertising expenditures, we may infer that advertising is a cause of sales. It must be stressed that we have only inferred this; we have not *proven* that advertising causes sales. At best, we have some evidence that suggests it might.

Sequence of occurrence can also provide evidence as to causation. For one event to cause another, it must always precede it. An event that occurs after another event cannot be said to cause the first event. The importance of sequence can be demonstrated in our last example of advertising causing sales. Suppose that further investigation showed that the advertising allocation to the geographic regions has been based on last period's sales such that the level of advertising was directly related to past sales. Suddenly, the nature of our causal relationship is reversed. Now, because of the sequence of events, we can infer that changes in sales levels cause changes in advertising levels.

A final type of evidence that we can use to infer causality is the *absence of other potential causal factors.* That is, if we could logically or through our research design eliminate all possible causative factors except the one we are interested in, we would have established that the variable we are concerned with was the causative factor. Unfortunately, it is never possible to control completely or to eliminate all possible causes for any particular event. Always we have the possibility that some factor that we are not aware of has influenced the results. However, if all reasonable alternatives are eliminated except one, we can have a high degree of confidence in the remaining variable.

The "Narrowing" Technique

One of the most common uses of causal marketing research is to determine why (the cause) some objective is not being met. A typical management question put to the researcher is "Why are our sales (market share, image, and so on) down?" This calls for causal research.

One highly successful consulting firm approaches problems of this nature by means of a *narrowing technique.* The preliminary investigation is utilized to suggest as many potential causes as possible. In terms of the problem situation model framework, an attempt is made to list all possible variables that might have affected the outcome.

This list is then narrowed by applying the criteria of concomitant variation and then sequence of occurrence to each potential cause. The first pass through the list utilizes only secondary data, known facts, and logic. This typically eliminates most of the potential causes. On the second pass through the list, any necessary primary data are gathered. Often survey type research can provide evidence on concomitant variation and on the sequence of occurrence. This procedure may leave several alternative causes. To eliminate any variables that have met both the criteria mentioned previously, some form of experimentation is generally required. Thus, although experimentation is not the only way to determine causation, it is uniquely suited to controlling for alternative causes.

Summary

This chapter has focused on *research design,* which involves the manipulation of data collection and analysis techniques so as to maximize the expected return on the research investment. Each of the nine steps involved in producing a research proposal, the final output of the research design process, was described in some detail. Particular attention was paid to the use of PERT as an aid in the estimation of the time and financial requirements of the study.

A major portion of the research design process centers on an analysis of secondary data. *Secondary data* are information gathered for some other purpose that might help solve the problem at hand. They are generally less expensive and can be obtained faster than primary data. However, they must be examined closely to ensure that they are *relevant* and *accurate*.

The two major types of secondary data are internal and external. Internal data are available from within the firm. Sales records are the most useful type of internal data. External secondary sources include trade associations, governments, other published sources, and syndicated services.

If primary data must be collected, the researcher must still be concerned with their accuracy. Eight types of error can reduce the accuracy of research data—*sampling, population specification, frame, selection, nonresponse, surrogate information, measurement,* and *experimental.* The next ten chapters focus on ways of controlling each individual type of error. However, total error can often be reduced through error trade-offs—trading a given amount of one type of error for a smaller amount of another type. Manipulating the research techniques so as to minimize both cost and total error is the essence of research design.

Research designs are often categorized by their goals. *Exploratory research* seeks to define the problem model. *Descriptive research* seeks to describe the variables in the problem model. *Causal research* attempts to determine the nature of the relationships between two or more variables in the problem model.

Simple concepts of cause are not adequate for marketing phenomena. Cause is inferred through *concomitant variation, sequence of events,* and an *absence of other causative factors.* The *narrowing technique* utilizes all three of these types of evidence in seeking the cause of marketing related phenomena.

Questions and Problems

4.1. A new product has been developed in this country by a corporation that specializes in food products. It is a very inexpensive staple food made from soya beans and ground plant stalks. It was developed to be sold to low income families all over the world. It has the consistency of mashed potatoes and can be flavored artificially to taste like rice, potatoes, ground corn, or wheat germ.

The product has now gone through development to the point that it could be produced and marketed. The company is willing to take a very low rate of return on this product because of its potential for alleviating hunger and improving diets. However, it will not intentionally subsidize the product. The company has decided that a safety profit margin of at

least $500,000 should be forecast to allow for contingencies before a "Go"
decision can be justified.
(a) What is the management problem?
(b) What is the research problem?
(c) What secondary sources would you consult to help develop a research
proposal to aid management?
(d) What other sources might be useful?
(e) What type of research—exploratory, descriptive, or causal—would
be most appropriate? Why?

4.2. As a one-man research staff for a manufacturer of men's shirts, you are
asked to do a study to recommend what market segments the marketing
program of the firm should concentrate on.
(a) How would you obtain a more precise problem statement?
(b) Give a plausible statement of the management's problem and translate it into a statement of the research problem to be conducted to
help solve it.

4.3. A research project was conducted for one of the major grocery chains to
determine what the best layout is for supermarkets. The method used was
to give a random sample of housewives a pad and a pencil and ask them
to "draw a supermarket" showing each of the departments. They then
analyzed the plans to find the relative location and size of each of the departments. The fresh vegetables and meat departments were usually a
larger proportion of the drawing than of actual store square footage; dry
groceries was usually smaller and often left out; dairy products were
usually at the back, and so on. What types of error are likely to be most
critical in such a study?

4.4. Give at least five *specific* potential sources of secondary information that
you would consult to estimate market potential for a new product.
(Choose a product of interest to you.) Give enough detail so that the
sources can be consulted directly from your description.

4.5. Which error strategies are appropriate for *basic* research projects? Which
error strategies are appropriate for *decisional* research projects? Is there
a difference? If so, why?

4.6. Refer to the PERT chart shown in Figure 4–1. Make the following
changes in the time estimates:

Activity Number	Time
2	3
12	4
18	3
15	9
17	9
8	1

Identify: (a) the critical path, (b) the path with the least slack, (c) the path with the most slack.

4.7. Select a specialty retail store type such as health foods, indoor plants, and so on that interests you. Assume that you are interested in opening such a store in the general area of the campus. Precisely what is your management problem? What is the research problem? Gather and summarize as much secondary data as are available that would help you decide on whether or not to open such a store. Identify the specific individuals you would want to consult with to help in this decision.

4.8. Suppose you are the marketing research manager for a firm that produces and markets frozen vegetables. Give examples of types of information that could be obtained from secondary sources (internal and external) that would be useful to management in making marketing decisions in the areas of (i) product, (ii) price, and (iii) promotion.

Selected Bibliography

BLALOCK, HUBERT M., JR. *Causal Inferences in Nonexperimental Research.* New York: W. W. Norton & Company, Inc., 1964. A detailed discussion of causation and the problems of inferring causation from nonexperimental data.

BROWN, REX V. *Research and the Credibility of Estimates.* Cambridge, Mass.: Harvard University Press, 1969. The pioneering text dealing with the analysis of research errors.

Journal of the Market Research Society, **14,** no. 4 (1972). This issue contains a valuable series of articles on the seldom discussed issue of the pricing of research.

MILLER, ROBERT W. "How to Plan and Control with PERT." *Harvard Business Review,* **40** (March/April 1962), 93–104. A brief but thorough exploration of the use of this valuable planning tool.

SIMON, JULIAN L. *Basic Research Methods in Social Science.* New York: Random House, Inc., 1969. A good treatment of research design as well as specific research techniques in the social sciences.

TULL, DONALD S., and GERALD S. ALBAUM. *Survey Research: A Decisional Approach.* New York: Intext Educational Publishers, 1973, Chap. 4. Contains a discussion of research errors and strategies for dealing with them. Although the material focuses on survey research, it can easily be applied to other areas.

WILSON, AUBREY. *The Assessment of Industrial Markets.* London: Hutchinson of London, 1968. An excellent presentation of research design as it is utilized to assess industrial markets.

Case 4–1

Liberty Savings Research Proposal*

Research Associates is a small consulting firm that has been in existence for two years. At a recent luncheon, Bill Brown, senior partner of Research Associates, was introduced to John Williams, assistant vice-president of Liberty Savings. Liberty Savings is the area's largest savings and loan association. During the course of their conversation, Brown learned that Williams' primary area of responsibility was marketing research and that the bank was considering a small-scale image study to pinpoint the strengths and weaknesses of the association in the minds of its customers. The information was to be used to help the annual review and one-year plan that was performed by management each January.

Brown asked to discuss the matter further with Williams and a two-hour meeting was subsequently held at Williams' office. During this meeting Brown learned that the study would have to be performed by an outside firm. He further found that the president felt that research of the type desired by the bank "is worth about $5,000 to us." With this information, Brown prepared the attached research proposal.

1. If you were Brown, what changes would you make in the proposal?

2. If you were Williams, would you recommend that Research Associates be hired?

Mr. John Williams
Assistant Vice-President
Marketing Department
Liberty Savings

Dear Mr. Williams:
The following pages present our proposal for the study we discussed with you on November 29. We feel that this study will give you a solid picture of your current and past customers' impressions of the strengths and weaknesses of Liberty Savings. This information can play a vital role in structuring the full spectrum of your marketing efforts ranging from advertising and premium offerings to "sales" orientation and training for your personnel.

The study we are proposing would be disguised as a survey of consumer impressions of savings and loan institutions in general. The study would be composed of three sections. The first section is designed to identify the competitive position of Liberty Savings in the minds of its customers. This will be done by examining customer awareness of Liberty Savings' prominent competitors and their feelings about the comparative images of these institutions. In addition to

* Prepared by K. A. Coney and J. E. Van Dyke. Used with permission of the authors.

comparing the images of Liberty Savings with its competitors, we will also obtain information regarding factors that describe the "ideal" savings and loan in the consumers' minds. Finally, the first section will identify the role of premium offers in attracting and holding savings and loan customers.

The second section of the study will identify savings deposit and withdrawal patterns among current and past Liberty Savings customers. The information obtained in this section will be related to demographic data in order to "profile" customers who are stable savers versus those who are less satisfied and more prone to close their accounts. In addition, this profile will examine reasons why customers save and why they make withdrawals and then relate this information to standard demographic variables.

The third section of the study would be different for each of the three customer groups to be examined. The focus of this section for customers who have recently opened accounts will be directed toward determining why they chose Liberty Savings as well as previous savings patterns. For interviews with customers who have had accounts with Liberty Savings for some time, the third section will be directed toward identifying the basis for their satisfaction with your institution. Finally, for customers who have recently closed their accounts, the third section will look at the reasons for leaving Liberty Savings, and the manner in which withdrawn funds were handled.

In order to provide a reliable picture of consumer impressions on the issues described above, we would propose to interview between 180 and 240 customers distributed among six to eight branches which have had either strong patterns of new account openings, stable continuing accounts, or relatively large number of closed accounts recently. The interview distribution is detailed by branches:

Option I:

Home Office	30 interviews
North Branch	30 interviews
Midtown Branch	30 interviews
Valley Branch	30 interviews
Primhill Branch	30 interviews
South Valley Branch	30 interviews
	180 interviews

Option II:

This would include the 180 interviews outlined in Option I and also add 30 interviews in each of the two upstate branches.

The 30 interviews from each of these branches would be balanced differently according to their relative strength or weakness. Branches with heavy withdrawal patterns would have 20 interviews with customers recently closing accounts, 5 with customers who have had accounts for some time, and 5 with customers who have recently opened new accounts. Branches which have had a large number of recently opened accounts would have 20 interviews with new customers, 5 with continuing customers, and 5 with customers who have recently closed accounts. Finally, the South Valley Branch, which has been fairly stable, would have 20 interviews with continuing customers, and 5 each with new customers, and customers who have closed accounts.

When the study is completed, we will provide you with 10 copies of our final report and conduct a formal presentation of our findings. This report would include our findings in each of the basic areas discussed and recommendations for action which may be operationalized directly by your firm and its advertising agency.

Our cost estimates for the proposed study may be broken down by the sample option your firm wishes to select. If the sample is restricted to Option I the total cost of the completed study would be $5,000. This figure represents $2,000 in interviewing costs, and our fee of $3,000 for questionnaire preparation, interviewer training, survey validation, analysis of results, and preparation and presentation of the final report. If the survey is extended to the upstate area the interview costs would be $2,750 and our professional fees would be $3,500 for a total cost of $6,250. The additional costs incurred by extending the study to the upstate area are necessitated by the problems of making interviewing arrangements and monitoring the interviews in that area. In addition, the analysis of data is more time consuming due to the 25 per cent increase in sample size.

We feel that the study we are proposing can help you make an important step toward an even better understanding of your customers and the directions you might take to increase your market share. Please feel free to contact us regarding any modifications to this proposal that you feel would improve the value of the study to your firm. Our only question is the same one that you ask of your customers—how may we best serve your needs?

Sincerely,

Bill Brown, Senior Partner
Research Associates

A Survey of Consumer Impressions of Savings and Loan Institutions

Section I—Savings and Loan Images
1. *Top of Mind Awareness of Savings and Loan Institutions*
   The relative standing of the four most prominent institutions (Liberty Savings, First Federal, Southern Savings, and Homestate Savings).
2. *Savings and Loan Competitive Profile*
   A comparison of Liberty Savings, First Federal, Southern Savings, and Homestate Savings against each other and also against the "consumer ideal" Savings and Loan institutions. The basic image dimensions to be investigated are as follows:
   General Image
   A. *Services*
         Number of services
         Number of branches
         Premium offers
         Convenience of location
         Interest rates
   B. *Appreciation for Customer*
         Treatment of Customers
           Personal
           Concern
           Helpful
           Friendly
           Understanding

    C. *Reputation*
        Trust
        Safe
        Size
        Age
        Progressive
        Competitive
  3. *Premium Offers*
    (a) The role of premiums in obtaining and retaining savings and loan customers.
    (b) Relative attractiveness of various premium offers.
Section II—Savings and Withdrawal Patterns
  1. Frequency of deposits and withdrawals
  2. Reasons for deposits and withdrawals
Section III—A Comparison of Liberty Savings Customers
  1. *Recently Opened Accounts*
    (a) Who are these customers?
    (b) What are their reasons for opening an account at this institution?
    (c) Have they had previous savings accounts? Where? How long ago?
  2. *Continuing Accounts*
    (a) How long have they had your account?
    (b) Why did they choose this institution?
    (c) What are their likes and dislikes about the institution?
    (d) Have they considered changing institutions and, if so, why?
  3. *Discontinued Accounts*
    (a) Why did they discontinue their last account?
    (b) What did they do with the money from the account?

Case 4–2

High Lake Resort

High Lake Resort is located on the shore of High Lake, 3 miles off a major highway. It is 65 miles from a medium-sized city in the Northwest. The lake is located near the summit of a 6,000-foot high pass through the Cascade mountains. The resort offers 25 individual cabins, a 40-room motel, a lounge and dining room, boat rentals, moorage, a small store, and other amenities. No other lodge operates on the lake.

    The primary business season is during the summer months when the resort operates at or near capacity. Spring and fall are also profitable. However, the winter season, although attracting almost as much business as the spring or fall season, has lost over $25,000 in each of the past 3 years. This has reduced the annual profits to slightly less than $100,000.

    The resort attracts substantial business during the winter. It is located within five miles of a small ski area that does not have dining or overnight facilities. In addition, many customers come to take advantage of the excellent cross-country skiing in the hills surrounding the lodge as well as along the shore of the lake. Others come to enjoy the winter scenery and the peace and quiet.

The reason for the loss of profits during the winter is not the lack of demand. Ample revenue is generated for a profitable operation except for one unusual expense item—maintaining the three miles of private road leading to the lodge. Throughout the winter season, the road must be snowplowed and sanded almost daily. Since state law prohibits the use of state equipment on private roads, the resort must maintain its own equipment. The expense of maintaining and operating this equipment is so great that the firm loses money heavily from December through March.

Unfortunately, the fixed expenses associated with maintaining the lodge are such that even greater losses would be incurred it it were to cease operations entirely during the winter months.

Ken Davis, owner and manager of High Lake Resort, has developed an idea that he hopes will solve his problem. There is a large parking area near the entrance to the road leading to the resort. The state highway department will maintain this parking area during the winter for no charge since it is state property (during the summer it is used by people hiking in a short distance to view a waterfall).

Davis proposes to not maintain his road. Instead, the cross-country skiers can park in the area at the highway and ski into the lodge. This he feels would give him a completely unique product—a resort devoted entirely to cross-country skiers. However, although cross-country skiing is very popular in the area, Davis is not certain that there will be adequate demand to maintain a sufficient sales volume. He is concerned that many of the skiers will not want to stay overnight because of the problems of packing in extra clothing or leaving small children with baby-sitters. Therefore, he is also considering running a sled pulled by a snowmobile to and from the lot either every hour or every two hours. Or, rather than maintaining a regular schedule, he could install a phone at the lot and pick customers up when they called.

The sled presents its own set of problems. He is afraid that the relatively easy accessibility provided by the sled will reduce the resort's appeal to some who would prefer maximum isolation. He is also not sure how much, if anything, he should charge for the sled ride into the lodge.

1. What is the management problem?

2. What is the research problem?

3. What type(s) of secondary data would help solve the research problem?

4. What type(s) of primary data are required?

5. What types of errors are likely to be most critical?

Case 4-3
Kermit Sand and Gravel

Ed Bailey, president of Kermit Sand and Gravel, was recently concerned over the fact that sales had shown only limited increases over the past two years. He called Market Research, a local marketing consulting firm and made an appointment with Mary Russell, a researcher for Market Research. During the discussion of the lack of sales growth, Bailey indicated four primary market segments that the firm attempts to serve: (1) general contractors, (2) residential contractors, (3) concrete contractors, and (4) homeowners.

Russell found out as much as possible during her conversation with Bailey but was not able to develop what she felt was an acceptable "feel" for the problem faced by Kermit Sand and Gravel. The most definitive statements she obtained from Bailey was that "sales just aren't growing the way they should." With this information, Russell agreed to prepare an informal research proposal to be discussed at their next meeting four days hence.

Prior to preparing the proposal, Russell examined various sources of secondary data such as building permits, road construction statistics, and home improvement loans for the area. These records revealed that the rate of growth of these areas that utilize large quantities of sand and gravel had been relatively constant over the past five years. Therefore, the leveling of Kermit Sand and Gravel's sales meant that the firm was losing market share. A telephone call to Ed Bailey confirmed comments made by the president of the Chamber of Commerce that no new sand and gravel firms had begun sales in the area in the past four years.

At their next meeting, Russell made the following proposal:

"We know that Kermit Sand and Gravel is losing market share. However, we do not have any firm ideas as to why this is happening. I propose that we engage in an exploratory research project to help us gain some insights into the following three areas:

1. Factors that influence the purchasers' decision-making process for concrete products.
2. Factors that specifically influence the sales of Kermit Sand and Gravel.
3. Potential courses of action to increase the sales of Kermit Sand and Gravel.

"Since each of the four market segments may have unique needs, we will examine each separately. The three categories of contractors will be stratified on the basis of size (large, medium, small) and the amount of their total business done with Kermit Sand and Gravel (all, part, none). This will produce a matrix like the following one. A random sample of two firms will be drawn from each cell and the person responsible for purchasing will be interviewed in a semistructured depth interview. That is, he will be encouraged to talk freely about how he uses sand and gravel, the problems he has with it, why he purchases it where he does, and so forth.

	General Contractors			Concrete Contractors			Residential Contractors		
	All	*Part*	*None*	*All*	*Part*	*None*	*All*	*Part*	*None*
Large									
Medium									
Small									

"The fourth market segment, howeowners, will be stratified on the basis of occupational category and age of home. This will produce a matrix such as the following one. A quota sample of households will be drawn until three households from each cell have been found that purchased one of the relevant products in the past year. The person who made the purchase will be interviewed in a semistructured depth interview.

	Older Homes	*Newer Homes*
Managerial–Professional		
Blue-Collar		

"This approach should allow us to gain insights into why consumers purchase these products. This will allow us to formulate a more extensive research proposal if necessary."

1. Did Russell make proper use of secondary data?

2. Is exploratory research called for in this situation?

3. Will this research design produce the data required?

4. How can Kermit Sand and Gravel determine the maximum value of the proposed research?

Case 4–4
Corona Corporation

One of the products being investigated by the market development group of the Corona Corporation for commercial possibilities was an electronic system for converting and recording signals from test instruments. Corona was one of the large manufacturers of rocket engines and its engineering department had developed the system to record measurements of thrust, temperatures, pressures, vibration, and other variables during test firings.

The market development group had investigated approximately 200 new commercial product possibilities during the past two years. It consisted of three marketing analysts and three application engineers. The manager of the group, Dave Dobbie, was one of the engineers. The group was attached to the marketing department for administrative purposes, but reported directly to the new products committee, comprised of the vice-presidents of marketing, finance, production, and engineering. During the two years the committee had been in existence, the company had licensed three products (a metal fastener, a riveting tool, and a new type of strain gauge) and one process (for bonding plastic to metal).

A preliminary investigation of the data converting and recording system showed promising results. A market analyst, Brooks Williams, and applications engineer, Bill Steelhammer, had been assigned to the project. They had found 13 different potential applications for the system, such as wind tunnel testing, structural analysis, process monitoring and control in nuclear reactors, oil refineries, chemical plants, and electrical power networks.

The new products committee was intrigued with the possibilities of the system and asked for a report on a complete market and engineering investigation as soon as it could be prepared. Dave Dobbie asked Williams and Steelhammer to provide an estimated date of completion of the project.

Williams and Steelhammer sat down to draw up the list of necessary activities and to assign responsibility for each of them. They estimated the time required for each activity on the basis of (1) the number of man-days that they would spend in working on each activity and (2) the number of elapsed workdays that the activity would require. (For example, the estimated time that Steelhammer would spend with cost analysts in the production department to prepare cost estimates for producing the commercial version(s) of the system was one day. They estimated that it would take five workdays for the cost estimates to be made, however.)

After they had completed the list of activities and the time estimates for each (see table), Williams and Steelhammer began to prepare an estimate

Activity and Department Concerned	Responsibility and Estimated Time Required			
	Williams		Steelhammer	
	Man-days	Elapsed work-days	Man-days	Elapsed work-days
Market Research and Applications Engineering				
1. Check out potential applications for system				
(a) wind tunnel testing	4	4		
(b) structural analysis	—	—	8	8
(c) process monitoring and control of nuclear plants	—	—	8	8
(d) process monitoring and control of oil refineries	6	6	—	—
(e) process monitoring and control of chemical plants	8	8	—	—
(f) process monitoring and control of power networks	5	5	—	—
(g) automotive			—	—
(h) flight testing	4	4	—	—
(i) turbojet engine testing	—	—	2	2
(j) turbine engine testing	—	—	2	2
(k) ramjet engine testing	—	—	2	2
(l) medical tests	5	5	—	—
(m) Cape Kennedy and Point Mogu launch sites.	5	5	—	—
2. Prepare estimates of potential number of systems that could be sold given specified numbers of signals to be converted and recorded, accuracy levels, and speeds of switching.	2	2	2	2
3. Check out competitive systems now under development or on the market to determine capabilities and price.			6	30
4. Estimate market share for different configurations of the commercial version of the system and make conditional forecasts of sales.	1	1	1	1
Engineering				
5. Coordinate commercial system design for different system specifications with engineering, production, and marketing departments	—	—	5	15

Activity and Department Concerned	Responsibility and Estimated Time Required			
	Williams		Steelhammer	
	Man-days	Elapsed work-days	Man-days	Elapsed work-days
6. Coordinate console and other packaging design with engineering, production, and marketing departments.	—	—	3	10
7. Obtain estimates of design and development costs.	—	—	1	5
Production				
8. Work with cost analysts in production to obtain estimate of production costs for system.	—	—	1	5
Legal				
9. Conduct patent check.	neg.*	60	—	—
10. Conduct trademark search for name.	neg.*	30	—	—
Marketing				
11. Coordinate selection of name for system.	2	6	—	
12. Prepare recommendation for distribution method.	2	2	—	—
13. Prepare recommendation on how customer systems are to be installed and repaired and estimate servicing costs.	—	—	3	3
14. Prepare recommendation on price of system for each configuration.	2	2	—	—
15. Prepare recommendation on advertising budget and media for system.	2	2	—	—
16. Estimate marketing costs.	4	4	—	—
Financial				
17. Coordinate preparation of *pro forma* income statements and balance sheets for commercial production and marketing of system, estimate payoff of venture.	3	9	—	—
New Products Committee				
18. Prepare report and give briefing to new product committee.	7	7	7	7
Total	62	162	51	100

* neg. = negligible

of the overall number of elapsed workdays that the project would require. When this estimate was made, they could give Dave Dobbie a date to schedule the presentation of the results of the project to the new products committee.

1. What are the number of workdays that are required for the project?

2. (a) What activities should be begun first by Williams and Steelhammer?
   (b) How much slack time will Steelhammer have during the project?
   (c) How much slack time will Williams have during the project?

3. Prepare a PERT chart for the project showing the critical path.

Case 4–5

Marblestone Company: Scour-Puff Market Test

In the mid 1970s the management of the Marblestone Company began to consider a diversification program. The company was then over 100 years old and had manufactured and sold only one product line (kitchen cleansers) and a single brand (*Scour-Power*) during that entire period.

Scour-Power had lost market share consistently after World War II. Competition in the cleanser field, always strong, became intense with the introduction of foaming cleansers and cleansers with new and more powerful bleaching agents. Advertising and sales promotion budgets for cleansers rose to levels that would not have been considered in earlier years. Marblestone did not have the financial capability to match its competitors' promotional program and, although it was doing some advertising, it had to rely heavily on price to move its product.

The market share of *Scour-Power* had fallen from a postwar high of 8.1 per cent to about 2.0 per cent. It appeared to have stabilized at that level but Marblestone management decided that protection against further decline was needed. That protection, they believed, lay in diversifying the Marblestone product line.

In assessing potential new products to add, the Marblestone management decided that other cleaning products and accessories were the most promising areas. The company had a well-known brand name and had always had good relations with the wholesalers and grocery chains through which *Scour-Power* was sold. By introducing related products, using a family brand name that would be identifiable with *Scour-Power,* and distributing through the same outlets, management believed it could take advantage of these assets and diversify successfully.

The company was approached by John Gilbert, the owner of a local firm that designed special-purpose machinery. His company had designed a machine for a client that would fasten nylon netting into a ball that was to be marketed for cleaning Teflon-coated pots and pans. The nylon net would not scratch the Teflon and the client had specified that the fastening for the netting had to be located so that it also would not cause scratches. Gilbert's firm had successfully designed a machine that met the client's specifications only to learn that he had gone into bankruptcy in the interim.

Gilbert had since applied for a patent on the machine and was interested in selling the machine and the patent rights, or licensing the machine and others like it that he would produce. He estimated that the nylon balls could be produced for 6.2 cents each in lots of 50,000. He believed that given the proper kind of marketing program, they could be a highly profitable item.

While discussions were being held with Gilbert, Fred Lewis, the marketing research manager of Marblestone, obtained a supply of 100 of the nylon net balls. He arranged to meet with two women's clubs to obtain reactions to the concept of the product, some idea of what it would be used for, whether it would be bought and at what prices, and what colors were preferred. He tentatively named the product *Scour-Puff* for these meetings. He was also interested in their reaction to this name.

The reactions were highly favorable. Most of the women said they would buy such a product and would use it as a dishcloth supplement on Teflon-coated cooking ware and fine glassware. They tended to favor pastel colors, with green and blue being the leading choices. A majority of the women said they did not think it should sell for more than $.29, but about half of them said they would pay $.29 for it. The name *Scour-Puff* seemed to be well received.

Based on the favorable results of these meetings, Lewis recommended to management that an exclusive licensing arrangement be made with Gilbert's firm for one year with an option to buy the patent to the machine at the end of that time. He believed that they could test market the product during the year and be in a better position to make the decision about whether to buy the machinery and the patent rights after the results of the test were known.

Gilbert was not interested in granting an exclusive license for a year for the quantities involved in a market test. He pointed out that this would cost his company the revenues they could receive from some other marketer of the product who was willing to introduce the product on a full-scale basis. A compromise of a six-month license period, with an option to buy the equipment and the patents at the end of that time, was suggested and an agreement was finally reached. Marketing research was to conduct a market test during this license period.

Fred Lewis knew that six months was a very short time in which to plan and to implement the market test. However, there seemed to be no possibility of extending the time so the best thing to do was to make as good use of it as possible. He started the planning of the test by compiling a list of activities (see table) and estimating the number of man-days of work involved by marketing research. He also obtained estimates of the elapsed number of workdays that would be required by the responsible department to complete each activity. He then began to prepare a PERT chart of these activities.

1. What is the activity that needs to be started first in order to get the market test underway in the shortest possible time?

2. On what day will the market test begin?

3. According to the schedule, will Fred Lewis need to assign more than one market analyst from his department to work on the activities for which marketing research is responsible?

4. Prepare the PERT chart for the test.

	Estimated Time Required	
Activity and Department Responsible	*Marketing Research Man-days*	*Elapsed Workdays Required by Responsible Department*

Marketing Research
1. Select test-market cities.

2 · · · 2

2. Forecast sales for each two-week period during the test, conditional on price, level of advertising, and promotion.

1½ · · · 3

3. Prepare questionnaire for consumer survey to be conducted one month before end of test, run pretest, and revise as required.

7 · · · 20

4. Arrange with research firms in test cities to conduct survey.

1½ · · · 10

5. Arrange to buy consumer panel data on purchases of product from syndicated data service.

¼ · · · 10

6. Conduct dealer survey one month after test begins to determine their acceptance, problems, and so on.

8 · · · 8

7. Analyze sales, consumer and dealer survey data, brief management on results.

6 · · · 6

Marketing
8. Select name for product.

2 · · · 8

9. Set advertising and promotions budget.

½ · · · 3

10. Prepare advertising program to be ready for start of test.

3 · · · 20

11. Prepare promotional campaign (coupons, samples, and so on) for test.

2 · · · 15

Activity and Department Responsible	Estimated Time Required	
	Marketing Research Man-days	Elapsed Workdays Required by Responsible Department
12. Set price and terms of sale.	3	8
13. Establish sales program for product, including sales budget.	1½	10
14. Prepare price lists and have these printed.	—	10
15. Have tags designed for product.	—	7
16. Decide on colors of product and relative amounts of each to be produced.	¼	¼
17. Make sales calls and initial shipments of product to wholesalers and chains (all shipments to be timed to arrive four days before test starts).	—	20
18. Estimate marketing costs.	½	1½
Production–Purchasing		
19. Decide on shipping containers.	—	5
20. Procure shipping containers.	—	15
21. Select supplier of tags.	—	1
22. Procure tags.	—	8
23. Select supplier of nylon netting.	—	½
24. Procure netting.	—	7
25. Estimate production costs.	—	1½
26. Produce initial quantity required.	—	12
Legal		
27. Conduct trademark search for name.	—	30
Total	39	241¾

CHAPTER 5

Sampling and Research: The Sampling Process

Sampling is a necessary and inescapable part of human affairs. Each of us samples and is sampled regularly. We sample the kind of performance and service we can expect from a new car by a test drive, a wine by a few sips, a restaurant by a first meal, and a new acquaintance by an initial meeting. We are parts of groups that are sampled to select juries, vote for political candidates, state opinions on issues, and record what television shows we watch and magazines we read.

If all possible information needed to solve a problem could be collected, there would be no need to sample. We can rarely do this, however, because of limitations on the amount we can afford to spend, the time we can take, or other reasons. We, therefore, must take samples.

This chapter is concerned with sampling and the sampling process as used for obtaining information that will help predict human behavior. It begins with a discussion of the reasons for sampling. The steps in the sampling process are then discussed, including a description of the various types of samples that may be taken, how they are selected, and the principal factors involved in the choice among the selected samples. A sample designed and taken by a consulting firm for a marketer of women's hair-grooming products is described to illustrate each of the steps involved in taking a sample. The issue of the size of the sample to take is covered in the next chapter.

Census versus Sample

It is sometimes possible and practicable to take a *census;* that is, to measure each element in the group or population of interest. Surveys of industrial consumers or of distributors of consumer products are frequently in the form of a census. More often than not, however, one or more of a number of reasons make it impractical or even impossible to take a census. These reasons involve considerations of *cost, time, accuracy,* and *destructive nature of the measurement.*

Cost and Census versus Sample

Cost is an obvious constraint on the determination of whether a census could reasonably be taken. If information is desired on grocery purchase and use behavior (frequencies and amounts of purchase of each product category, average amount kept at home, and so on) and the population of interest is all households in the United States, the cost will preclude a census being taken. The budget for the 1970 Decennial Census of Population was more than $240 million. As an approximation of the cost of a census of households to obtain the information on groceries, it is apparent that this cost would far exceed any conceivable value of such information for a marketer of this type of product. A sample is the only logical way of obtaining new data of this kind.

If one needed information on a proposed new product for use on commercial airlines, however, a census might be a highly practical solution. There are only about 25 major airlines in the United States and, if this were the population of interest, the cost of taking a census might well be less than the value of the information obtained.

Time and Census versus Sample

The kind of cost we have just considered is an *outlay* cost. The time involved in obtaining information from either a census or a sample involves the possibility of also incurring an *opportunity* cost. That is, delaying the decision until information is obtained may result in a smaller gain or a larger loss than would have been the case from making the same decision earlier. The opportunity to make more (or save more, as the case may be) is, therefore, foregone.

Even if a census of households to obtain information on grocery purchase and use behavior were practical from a cost standpoint, it might not be so when the time involved is considered. Data collection for the 1970 Decennial Census in the United States was begun in April, 1970, and yet the detailed characteristics of the population were not published until February, 1973. Most of the kinds of decisions made by business firms need to be made much faster than that.

Accuracy and Census versus Sample

A study using a census, by definition, contains no sampling error. It may contain any of the other types of error described in Chapter 4. A study using a sample may involve sampling error in addition to the other types of error. Therefore, *other things being equal,* a census will provide more accurate data than a sample.

However, it is often possible, given the same expenditure of time and money, to reduce substantially the nonsampling errors in a sample relative to those in a census. In fact, the nonsampling errors can often be reduced to the point where the sum of the sampling and nonsampling errors of the sample are *less* than the nonsampling error alone in the census. When this is the case, *it is possible to obtain a more accurate measurement from a sample than from a census.* This involves the concept of error trade-off discussed in Chapter 4.

The Decennial Census of the United States again provides a useful example. It has been argued that a more accurate estimate of the population of the United States could be made from a sample than from a census. Taking a census of population requires that about 165,000 temporary interviewers be recruited, trained, and supervised. They must be taught how to read maps, ask questions, and record information. The potential for error from missed assignments, poor interviewing, nonresponse, and faulty recording is large.

As examples, people interviewed by census takers have reported afterward they thought they had been visited by a representative of the Internal Revenue Service, a man from the County Assessor's Office, or a termite inspector. Open and unbiased responses seem unlikely in such a situation. Nonreporting of illegitimate babies is common, as is the presence of persons who have made an illegal entry into the country or have other reasons for wanting to conceal their location from the authorities.

With these kinds of problems, it is understandable how it could be argued that, given careful selection and training and supervision of interviewers, nonsampling errors in a sample of the population could be reduced to the point where the overall population estimate would be more accurate than one obtained from a census.

It is not always possible to reduce nonsampling error by an amount sufficient to compensate for sampling error. In the case of the company needing an evaluation of a potential new product for use by the major domestic airlines, this may not be the case. Given a total population of 25 airlines, missing just one of them raises the possibility of a sampling error in the estimation of the market potential for the product of (an average of) 4 per cent. It is unlikely that significant reductions could be made in the other types of errors by the expenditure of the funds freed by changing from a census to a sample in a case such as this.

Destructive Nature of the Measurement

Measurements are sometimes destructive in nature. When they are, it is apparent that taking a census would usually defeat the purpose of the measurement. If one were producing firecrackers, electrical fuses, or paint, performing a functional use test on all products for quality-control purposes would not be considered from an economic standpoint. A sample is then the only practical choice. On the other hand, if light bulbs, bicycles, or electrical appliances are to be tested, a 100 per cent sample (census) may be entirely reasonable.

The process of change that takes place in respondents to a survey or participants in an experiment is far more subtle and less dramatic than is the destructive test of a product. Yet changes do occur in the opinions and attitudes of homemakers who are given a new all-purpose detergent to use in lieu of an old detergent plus bleach, or an urban resident who is interviewed in depth about mass transportation. *The measurement process often induces change in respondents or experimental subjects.* When this occurs, the population after the census is different than it was before it was taken. This does not prevent taking a census for a single measurement but it does indicate a potential problem when a census is used for more than one measurement.

The Sampling Process

We have discussed briefly *why* samples are taken; it is now appropriate to consider *how* they are taken. The sampling process consists of seven sequential steps. These steps are listed and a brief summary description is

|model| = Reality + B + E

FRame

In picking sample first decide on frame   Marketing Research

Table 5–1 Steps in the Sampling Process

Step	Description
1. Define the population	The population is defined in terms of (a) element, (b) units, (c) extent, and (d) time.
2. Specify sampling frame	A specification of the means of representing the elements of the population, for example, telephone book, map, or city directory.
3. Specify sampling unit	A specification of the unit for sampling, for example, city block, company, or household. The sampling unit may contain one or several population elements.
4. Specify sampling method	Specification of the method by which the sampling units are to be selected.
5. Determine sample size	Decide how many elements of the population are to be sampled.
6. Specify sampling plan	Specification of the operational procedures for selection of the sampling units.
7. Select the sample	Carrying out the office and fieldwork necessary for the selection of the sample.

given in Table 5–1, and it will be useful to examine the table now. A more detailed treatment of each step of the sampling process is given in the sections that follow.

Step 1. *Define the Population*

The population for a survey of purchasing agents might be defined as "all purchasing agents in companies and government agencies that have bought any of our products in the last three years." The population for a price survey might be defined as "the price of each competitive brand in supermarkets in the Cleveland sales territory during the period July 15–30."

To be complete, a population must be defined in terms of *elements, sampling units, extent,* and *time.* In relation to these constituent parts, the population of purchasing agents defined is

(*element*)	purchasing agents in
(*sampling unit*)	companies and governmental agencies that have
(*extent*)	bought any of our products
(*time*)	in the last three years.

[handwritten: Does frame fit the model? — listing — criteria]

[handwritten: may be frame error because criteria is different from reality.]

Similarly, the population for the price survey is defined as

$\Big\{$ *(element)*   price of each competitive brand
    (sampling unit)   in supermarkets
    (extent)   in the Cleveland sales territory
    (time)   during the period July 15–30.

Note that eliminating any one of these specifications in either case leaves an incomplete definition of the population that is to be sampled.

The way the population is defined can play a very important role in determining how useful the information is. For example, suppose a senator from Oregon commissions a pre-election poll pitting him against his other major party opponent. Suppose further that this population is defined as

(element)	All registered voters
(sampling unit)	in households
(extent)	in Oregon
(time)	during the week of May 23–27.

It is apparent that potentially important segments of the electorate may have been missed. All voters who register between May 27 and the last date for registration for the November election are disregarded. This will exclude all people who become 18 and families who move into the state during this period. Both of these segments of the electorate are probably different in political views than the other segments. This is especially true if there is a concerted campaign by either candidate to register voters. In addition, restricting the units to households eliminates the polling of students who live in dormitories, which in many states (including Oregon) is a significant percentage of the electorate.

It is sometimes difficult to define the population properly. How would you define the population for a survey to determine the best features of a children's cereal to promote, an apartment complex for families, a station wagon, or a frozen dessert? To define any of these populations properly, one would have to know the role played by each family member in the purchase and consumption of the product as well as what types of families constitute the primary market. At times, a research project is required to define the population before the study for which it is to be used can begin.

Step 2. Specify the Sampling Frame

A sampling frame is a means of representing the elements of the population. It may be a telephone book, a city directory, an employee roster, or a listing of all students attending a university. If one wanted to take a sample of firms whose stock is listed on the New York Stock Exchange, a complete sampling frame is provided in almost all weekday and Sunday issues of any major metropolitan newspaper—the listing of stock prices on the financial page.

Maps also serve frequently as sampling frames. A sample of areas within a city may be taken and another sample of households may then be taken within each area. City blocks are sometimes sampled and all households on each sample block are included. A sampling of street intersections may be taken and interviewers given instructions as to how to take "random walks" from the intersection and select the households to be interviewed.

A perfect sampling frame is one in which *every element of the population is represented once but only once.* The listing of companies and their stock prices in the *Wall Street Journal* provides a perfect frame for sampling listed companies of the New York Stock Exchange. Examples of perfect frames are rare, however, when one is interested in sampling from any appreciable segment of a human population.

Probably the most widely used frame for sampling human populations is the telephone book. Although approximately 90 per cent of the households in the United States have telephones,[1] the distribution of telephone ownership is not even across all groups. Low income, rural, and city-center homes constitute the primary source of homes without telephones. In addition, many homes with telephones do not have their numbers listed in the telephone directory. The higher income households have a higher proportion of unlisted numbers than does the general population. Single women who live alone often have unlisted numbers for security reasons. These cases representing voluntarily unlisted numbers may constitute between 10 and 30 per cent of the telephone owners in a given area.[2]

Involuntarily unlisted numbers are caused by people moving into the area after the directory is issued. These numbers are not a problem immediately after the directory is issued but may become significant as the directory becomes older. Although techniques are available to deal with these problems,[3] a telephone directory is seldom a perfect frame.

These omissions and nonworking numbers may lead to *frame errors* in the study in which the telephone book is used as a sampling frame. This is true of city directories, maps, census tract information, or any other listing or representation of a population that is incomplete or out-of-date. Unfortunately, some frame error is probably unavoidable in most surveys of human populations.

---

[1] *Statistical Abstract of the United States: 1973,* 94th ed. (Washington, D.C.: U.S. Government Printing Office, 1973), 496.

[2] S. Cooper, "Random Sampling by Telephone—An Improved Method," *Journal of Marketing Research,* **1** (November 1964), 45–48; and G. J. Glasser and G. D. Metzger, "Random-Digit Dialing as a Method of Telephone Sampling," *Journal of Marketing Research,* **9** (February 1972), 59–64.

[3] See Glasser and Metzger, op. cit., and Chapter 11.

Step 3. Specify Sampling Unit

The sampling unit is the basic unit containing the elements of the population to be sampled. It may, of course, be the element itself or a unit in which the element is contained. For example, if one wanted a sample of males over 13 years of age, it might be possible to sample them directly. In this case, the sampling unit would be identical with the element. However, it might be easier to select households as the sampling unit and interview all males over 13 years of age in each household. Here the sampling unit and the population element are not the same.

The sampling unit selected is often dependent upon the sampling frame. If a relatively complete and accurate listing of elements is available—a register of purchasing agents, for example—one may well want to sample them directly. If no such register is available, one may need to sample companies as the basic sampling unit.

The selection of the sampling unit is also partially dependent upon the overall design of the project. If a telephone survey is to be conducted, the sampling unit will necessarily be telephone numbers. A mail questionnaire requires a sampling unit of addresses (names if available). Personal interview studies, on the other hand, permit considerably more flexibility in choosing the sampling unit.

Step 4. Selection of Sampling Method

The sampling method is the way the sampling units are to be selected. Sampling units may be selected in many ways; a useful way of classifying them is shown in Figure 5–1.

The diagram is developed from five basic choices that must be made in deciding upon a sampling method. These are, the order in which they are considered in the diagram,

   i. *probability versus nonprobability,*
   ii. *single unit versus cluster of units,*
   iii. *unstratified versus stratified,*
   iv. *equal unit probability versus unequal probability,* and
   v. *single stage versus multistage.*

These five choices, when combined, give 32 possible combinations. Only 16 of these are shown in Figure 5–1 because of space limitations. The other 16 combinations are the same as the 16 shown with the exception that they are nonprobability in nature.

These classification criteria are not meant to be exhaustive. Other classification criteria could be used (sequential versus nonsequential sampling,

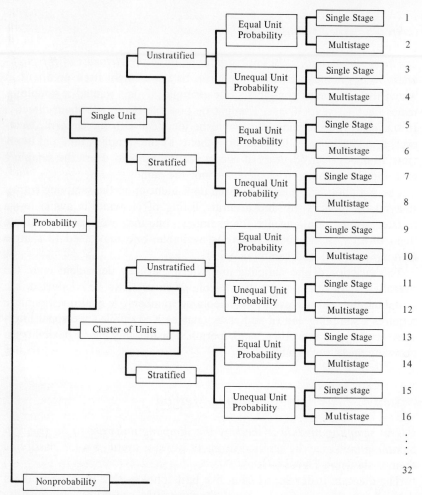

Figure 5–1 Diagram of sampling methods.

for example), which would result in more than 32 different sampling methods. However, the five criteria listed are the most important ones in the sampling of human populations, and we limit our consideration to them.

nonprobability gives no way to measure random sample error

✳ Probability versus Nonprobability Sampling

We have listed the most crucial decision first: the choice of a probability versus a nonprobability selection procedure. *A probability sample is one in which the sampling units are selected by chance and for which there is a known chance of each unit being selected. A nonprobability sample is one in which chance selection procedures are not used.*

Probability Samples. Probability samples are selected by use of a stable, independent data generating process. The table of random numbers in Appendix E is the result of the use of such a process. Tables of random numbers such as this are commonly used for selecting the sampling units to be included in a probability sample.

Suppose a major oil company wants to sample its credit card holders to test a "travel club" program by sending promotional flyers with the next billing to the customer. Further suppose that the first seven numbers on the card identify each customer.

A probability sample could be taken by starting at a preselected place in a table of random numbers and selecting seven digit numbers by a designated procedure. The preselected place in the table might be, for example, the top righthand corner of page 719 if one were using the table in this book. An example of an appropriate procedure for selecting seven digit random numbers would be to take each seven digits in sequence as one moves down the righthand column, go to the top of the adjoining column, move down it, and so forth.

This would result in a particular kind of random sample being taken. It is known as a *simple random sample* (often abbreviated as *srs*) and, in addition to being a *probability* sample, it would have the characteristics of consisting of *single units* each of which was drawn from an *unstratified* population with an *equal probability of each unit's being selected* by a *single-stage* procedure. This is sampling method 1 in Figure 5–1.

A sampling method that is very similar to the simple random sample is called *systematic* sampling. This involves picking a random starting point and then taking every kth unit in the frame. In the case of the oil company, the researcher may have decided to take a sample that amounted to 1 per cent of the credit card holders. The systematic sample would be taken by starting at a randomly selected number between 001 and 100 and then taking every 100th name on the list. k in this example is 100. In the more general case, k is equal to the number of sample units divided by the sample size in units, or $k = \dfrac{N}{n}$.

This is the equivalent of a *srs* so long as one can be assured that changes in the population do not occur at intervals equal to k. For example, a k of 7 when applied to a study of daily retail sales for department stores would result in always measuring sales for the same day of the week. Yet retail sales are consistently higher on some days of the week than others. A biased measurement would result.

Nonprobability Samples. Several kinds of nonprobability samples are possible. A *convenience* sample (sometimes called a *chunk*) is one in which the only criterion for selecting the sampling units is the convenience of the sampler. An example of convenience sampling is the testing by food product manufacturers of potential new products by adding them to the menu of the company cafeteria. A potential new cake mix, for example, can be tested by adding it to the dessert section and noting how well it sells relative to the other kinds of cake offered.

Convenience samples are often used in exploratory situations when there is a need to get only an approximation of the actual value quickly and inexpensively. Commonly used convenience samples are associates and "the man on the street." Such samples are often used in the pretest phase of a study, such as pretesting a questionnaire.

Convenience samples contain unknown amounts of both variable and systematic selection errors. These errors can be very large when compared to the variable error in a *srs* of the same size. This possibility should be considered both before and after using convenience samples.

Another kind of nonprobability sample is the *purposive* sample. Here the sample units are selected with some specific objective(s) in mind. An example is the sample of automobile drivers selected to test drive one of the limited number of turbine automobiles produced by the Chrysler Corporation a few years ago. The sample was selected by a national accounting firm from among applicant automobile owners. The drivers were to be given a car to drive for three months in return for providing evaluative information on its performance. The drivers selected were those who individually gave evidence of maturity and responsibility and collectively represented geographic locations that provided the range of road and traffic conditions desired for the test.

A *quota* sample of a human population is one selected in such a way that the demographic characteristics of interest are represented in the sample in the same proportion as they are in the population. If one were selecting a quota sample of persons for a use test of pizza-flavored catsup, for example, one might want to *control* by ethnic background, age, income, and geographic location. That is, the sample taken would have the same proportion of people in each income bracket, ethnic group, age group, and geographic area as the population. Quota samples are widely used in consumer panels.

The controls used in quota samples of human populations (1) *must be available and should be recent,* (2) *should be easy for the interviewer to classify by,* (3) *should be closely related to the variables being measured in the study,* and (4) *should be kept to a reasonable number so as not to produce too many cells.* Each possible set of controls produces a separate *cell* in a quota sample. If the selection of respondents is controlled by five income brackets, three ethnic backgrounds, four age brackets, and six areas, for example, there would be $5 \times 3 \times 4 \times 6 = 360$ different cells in the sample. The interviewers would have trouble filling the quota assigned to many of these cells, and the costs of taking the sample would rise as a result.

The fact that a quota sample resembles a proportional stratified probability sample (this type of sample is discussed later in the chapter) should not be used for concluding that the variances of the two are the same. In a study of the results of election polls, Stephan and McCarthy[4] found that the sampling variance of the quota samples used averaged about one-and-one half times that of an equivalent sized *srs*. Sizable selection errors can arise from the way interviewers select the persons to fill the quota for each cell, incorrect information of the proportions of the population in each of the control variables, biases in the relationship of the control variables to the variables being measured, and from other sources.[5]

Quota samples are usually "validated" after they are taken. The process of validation involves a comparison of the sample and the population with respect to characteristics not used as control variables. In a quota sample taken to form a consumer panel for which income, education, and age were used as control variables, for example, a comparison of the panel and the population might be made with respect to such characteristics as average number of children, the occupation of the chief wage earner, and home ownership. If the panel differed significantly from the population with respect to any of these characteristics, it would be an indication of potential bias in the selection procedures. It should be noted that similarity with respect to the validating characteristics does not necessarily mean the absence of bias, however.

A *judgment* sample is one in which there is an attempt to draw a representative sample of the population using judgmental selection procedures. An example is a sample of addresses taken by a municipal agency to which questionnaires on bicycle-riding habits were sent. A judgment sample was taken after looking at traffic maps of the city, considering the tax assessment on houses and apartment buildings (per unit), and keeping the location of schools and parks in mind.

The amount of variable and systematic selection error present in a judgment sample depends upon the degree of expertise of the person making the selection. These errors *can* be substantially less than the variable error present in a *srs* of the same size, particularly if the sample is small. In test-market situations where the new product is to be introduced in a small number of cities (usually two to four) to see how well it sells, the selection of cities is almost always made on a judgmental basis. Anyone who has a general knowledge of the product and of cities in the United States is likely to choose a more representative sample than would be selected by a random process. As sample size increases, however, judgment becomes less trustworthy compared to random selection procedures.

[4] F. Stephan and P. J. McCarthy, *Sampling Opinions—An Analysis of Survey Procedures* (New York: John Wiley & Sons, Inc., 1958), Chap. 10.

[5] See L. J. Kish, *Survey Sampling* (New York: John Wiley & Sons, Inc., 1965), 562–566 for a discussion of errors that can be present in quota sample measurements.

A sample of 100 counties in the United States is likely to be more representative if selected by random procedures (particularly if there is stratification) than if drawn by judgment, for example.

All of the nonprobability sampling techniques are subject to selection error. One of the authors was recently interviewed at his home. The interviewer had considerable flexibility in selecting households to interview. She stated that she had initially selected the house next door until she saw that the family owned a dog. Since she was afraid of dogs, she avoided all houses where such animals were visible. If the ownership of a dog was correlated with any of the variables in this survey (a very likely occurrence given the subject matter), the results would contain errors because of the interviewer's selection criteria.

The Choice Between Probability and Nonprobability Samples. The selection between probability and nonprobability samples is based on the *cost versus value* principle. We will want to take whichever kind of sample yields the greatest margin of value over cost.

No one would question this principle; the problems come in applying it. The real question at issue is, "How can I estimate with a reasonable degree of confidence whether a probability sample will give more or give less value for its cost than a nonprobability sample?"

This question is not answered fully in this chapter. We suggest here some factors to consider in estimating relative value. In the next chapter we describe an analytic framework for helping make the decision.

Several considerations affect the potential value of the information. These include the following:

1. *"What kind of information is needed—averages and/or proportions or projectable totals?"*
   Do we need to know only the proportion of users and/or the average amount used or do we need to estimate the overall market share and/or the total market for the product?
2. *"What kind of error tolerance does the problem allow?"*
   Does the problem require highly accurate estimates of population values?
3. *"How large are the nonsampling errors likely to be?"*
   How sizable are the population specification, frame, selection, nonresponse, surrogate information, measurement, and experimental errors likely to be?
4. *"How homogeneous is the population with respect to the variables we want to measure?"*
   Is the variation likely to be low among the sampling units, or will it be high?
5. *"What is the expected cost of errors in the sample information?"*

What is the cost to me if the average(s)/proportion(s) I obtain from the data are above the error tolerance on the high side? The low side?

Generally speaking, the need for *projectable totals, low errors, high population heterogeneity, and high expected costs of errors* favor the use of probability sampling. A tight error tolerance means that the elimination of selection bias and the ability to calculate sampling error become more important considerations in the selection of the sampling plan and favor a probability sample. Small nonsampling errors likewise favor probability samples; the sampling error becomes relatively more important the smaller the other errors are. The more diversified and heterogeneous the population is the greater is the need to assure representativeness through a probability sampling procedure.

The first four of the questions are concerned with *error probabilities;* they help in making assessments of the α and β error probabilities discussed in Chapter 3. Question 5 is concerned with the *expected cost* of such errors. The higher the cost of errors the greater is the premium on accuracy. The higher the error costs the more inclined one should be toward choosing a probability sample, other factors being equal.

Single Unit versus Cluster Sampling

In *single unit sampling* each sampling unit is selected separately; in *cluster sampling* the units are selected in groups. If the unit is a household, for example, single unit sampling would require that each household be selected separately. One form of cluster sampling would be to change the sampling unit to city blocks and to take every household on each block selected.

The choice between single unit and cluster sampling is again an economic tug-of-war between cost and value. Cluster sampling usually costs less (and often substantially less) per sampling unit than does single unit sampling. For samples of the same size, the sampling error for a cluster sample will usually be greater than that of a single unit sample because of less within-cluster variability than for the population as a whole.

The lower cost per unit and higher sampling error potential of a cluster sample is illustrated by considering a sample of 100 households to be selected for personal interviews. If the 100 households are selected on a single unit basis they will most likely be scattered around the city. This will increase the chance of getting a representative cross section of the various ethnic groups, social classes, and so on. In contrast, a cluster sample in which ten blocks are selected and ten households interviewed on each block will be likely to miss more of the social groups. The reason for this is that members of social groups tend to live in neighborhoods where others of the same group live. The within-cluster variability is likely to be low since the family backgrounds are similar. The costs of personal interviews per unit in a cluster sample will be low, however, because of the close proximity of the units in each cluster.

The decision between single unit and cluster samples is made on many of the same grounds as those for choosing between probability and nonprobability samples. Low error tolerance, high population heterogeneity, and high expected costs of errors all favor single unit sampling.

Unstratified versus Stratified Sampling

A *stratum* in a population is a segment of that population having one or more common characteristics. It might be an age stratum (age 35–49), an income stratum (all families with incomes over $25,000 per year), or a part of the population identified with some other characteristic of interest.

Stratified sampling involves treating each stratum as a separate subpopulation for sampling purposes. If the head-of-household age strata "18–34," "35–49," "50 and over" are of interest in a study on household furnishings, each of these age groups could be treated separately for sampling purposes. That is, the total population could be divided into age groups and a separate sample drawn from each group.

The reasons for stratifying a population for sampling purposes are two: (1) it may help to ensure representativeness (and thus reduce sampling error) and (2) the required sample size for the same level of sampling error will usually be smaller than for a nonstratified sample. A *srs* is not necessarily a representative sample whereas with stratification, representativeness to some degree is forced.

The saving in the size of the sample, while still obtaining the same level of sampling error as a nonstratified sample, may not be as intuitively obvious but it is easily explained. In the household furnishings study referred to previously, the age group 18–34 is that of family formation and initial acquisition of most furnishings; age 35–44 is the time of replacement of original purchases and acquisition of more marginal items, and age 50 and over is generally a time of limited purchasing of any kind of furnishings. To the extent that these generalizations hold, the households falling within each of these strata should be more like each other than they are to those in any other stratum.

The greater the degree to which this within-stratum similarity holds the smaller is the sample size required in each stratum to provide information about that stratum. Consider the extreme case where all units in each stratum were *identical*. If this were true, a sample of *one* would be all that was required from each stratum to give complete information on the subpopulation of interest. Thus, the more homogeneous each stratum is with respect to the variable of interest the smaller is the sample required.

Equal Unit Probability versus Unequal Unit Probability Sampling

"Most of the gross errors of bad sampling are violations of simple common sense. The methods of good sampling are not obvious to common sense."[6] One of the methods of good sampling that is intuitively not obvious is that it is often better to have *unequal* probabilities of selection. The example of the household furnishing study just described affords an example.

Suppose we are interested in the average amount spent on household furnishings by families in each of the age strata. It seems reasonable to assume that the variation in expenditures of the 18–34 and the 35–49 age group households are likely to be higher than those for the 50-and-over group. If this is the case, it is more efficient statistically to take a disproportionately smaller sample of the 50-and-overs and allocate part of its proportionate share to the two groups with the higher variation in purchase amounts.

Stated differently, it is only when we have no reason to believe that the variation (variance) is different among the strata that we would take a proportional sample and thus give an equal chance of representation to each sampling unit.

Single Stage versus Multistage Sampling

The number of stages involved in the sampling method is partially a function of the kind of sampling frame available. If a perfect frame were always available complete with all the associated information one might want for purposes of clustering and/or stratifying, there would be far fewer multistage samples taken than there are now. In practice, it is not uncommon to have a first stage area sample of, say, census tracts, followed by a second stage sample of blocks, and completed with a systematic sample of households within each block. With the help of census maps, city maps, or aerial photographs, one can always generate a sampling frame composed of geographic areas. These stages would often not be necessary if a complete listing of households were available.

There are other reasons for taking multistage samples, however. One reason is to obtain a better estimate of the variance of the population to determine final sample size and/or whether or not to stratify. A sample that is known to be too small is taken to obtain this information. The decisions concerning final size and/or stratification are then made and the remaining units sampled.

[6] Quoted from a privately circulated manuscript written by H. V. Roberts.

Another reason for multistage sampling involves economic considerations. The results may be such that a first sample will provide sufficiently definitive information that a second sample will not be required. If this does not prove to be the case, however, the second stage is conducted.

Suppose a taste test on a new soft drink is to be given. It has been decided that it must be concluded that at least 50 per cent of the population like the taste (at a confidence level of 70 per cent) before proceeding with the development will be worthwhile. An initial sample of 100 respondents is taken in a probability sample. If less than 40 or more than 60 report they like the taste, the test can be terminated; if the number is between these two extremes, another sample of 100 will be taken.

Step 5. Determination of the Sample Size

The determination of the proper sample size has traditionally been taught by one method in statistics classes and often practiced by an entirely different approach in the field. The reason for this is that traditional sampling theory has included only in a very circuitous and indirect way (if indeed it is considered at all) the concept of the cost versus the value of the information to be provided by various sized samples. Practitioners have been forced to deal with the realities of sampling economics regardless of whether theory recognizes them or not.

The problem of determination of sample size is dealt with in the next chapter. Both the traditional and the decision analysis approaches to determining sample size are presented.

Step 6. Specify Sampling Plan

The *sampling plan* involves the specification of how each of the decisions made thus far are to be implemented. It may have been decided that the household will be the element and the block the sampling unit. How is a household defined operationally? How is the interviewer to be instructed to distinguish between families and households in instances where two families and some distant relatives of one of them are sharing the same apartment? How is the interviewer to be instructed to take a systematic sample of households on the block? What should the interviewer do when a housing unit selected is vacant? What is the callback procedure for households at which no one is at home? What age and/or sex of respondents speaking for the household are acceptable?

These are only a few of the questions that must be answered in a survey of respondents involving personal interviews. A lot of tedious, unglamorous work is involved in providing the necessary answers. If the project is to be a competently conducted one, however, answers *must* be provided. Furthermore, answers to as many questions as can be anticipated must be provided *before* the project is completed.

An example of a part of the preliminary planning that is necessary to prespecify adequately the sampling plan for a systematic sample is provided in Table 5–2. The special situations that are shown in the table represent problems that an interviewer might encounter while "starting with the first occupied dwelling unit to the left of the preliminary address, attempt to interview every third occupied dwelling unit in the block until four completed interviews are obtained in homes with listed phone numbers."

Table 5–2 Special Situations Encountered in Systematic Sampling by Circling a Block*

In the instructions that follow, reference is made to following your route around a "block." In cities this will be a city block. In rural areas, a "block" is a segment of land surrounded by roads.

1. If you come to a dead end along your route, proceed down the opposite side of the street, road, or alley, traveling in the other direction. Continue making right turns, where possible, calling at every third occupied dwelling.

2. If you go all the way around a block and return to the starting address without completing four interviews in listed telephone homes, attempt an interview at the starting address. (This should seldom be necessary.)

3. If you work an entire block and do not complete the required interviews, proceed to the dwelling on the opposite side of the street (or rural route) that is *nearest* the starting address. Treat it as the next address on your Area Location Sheet and interview that house only if the address appears next to an "X" on your sheet. If it does not, continue your interviewing to the left of that address. Always follow the right turn rule.

4. If there are no dwellings on the street or road opposite the starting address for an area, circle the block opposite the starting address, following the right turn rule. (This means that you will circle the block following a clockwise direction.) Attempt interviews at every third dwelling along this route. (Illustrated in block 2 of diagrams that follow.)

5. If, after circling the adjacent block opposite the starting address, you do not complete the necessary interviews, take the next block found, *following a clockwise direction*. (Illustrated as block 3 in diagrams that follow.)

6. If the third block does not yield the dwellings necessary to complete your assignment, proceed to as many blocks as necessary to find the required dwellings; these blocks follow a clockwise path around the primary block. (Blocks 4, 5, 6 and so on in diagram.)

---

* Reprinted from an actual interviewer guide by permission of Belden Associates, Dallas, Texas. The complete guide was over 30 pages long and contained maps and other aids for the interviewer.

Table 5–3 Selection of a National Probability Sample

A national sample of women was taken to obtain information on the media viewing and reading habits of women. It was sponsored by a well-known company marketing women's hair grooming products. The sampling plan and the actual selection were both done by a consulting firm specializing in marketing research.

Definition of population	The population was defined as white females 15 years and older (*element*) in households (*unit*), in the continental United States (*extent*) during the month the sample was taken (*time*).
Sampling frame used	Three frames were used: (1) a list of the counties and (2) the Standard Metropolitan Statistical Area (SMSA) in the continental United States with (3) maps of the counties/ metropolitan areas selected.
Sampling unit used	Households
Sampling method used	*Probability* A sampling of 228 counties was taken. When a sample county was part of a Standard Metropolitan Statistical Area it (the SMSA) was used in lieu of the county. Individual blocks and country open segments were then selected by probability sampling methods. *Single unit* selection was used. A systematic sample of households was taken from each block. A systematic procedure for selecting households from road intersection starting points was devised for the country open segment. The population was *unstratified*. However, age group and geographic area comparisons were made with census data to determine the representatives of the sample. *Unequal probability of element selection* was used. For example, in the metropolitan areas of the Northeast where the company had high per capita sales, one woman was interviewed for (approximately) every 15,-600 women. In the metropolitan areas of the South Atlantic states where per capita sales were lower, one woman was interviewed for each 3,900 women. The sample was obviously of a *multistage* design: County/SMSA to block or open country segment and then systematic selection of households.
Desired sample size	A sample of 6,000 women was specified.
Sampling plan	An entire notebook of materials was prepared and used for training interviewers and field supervisors.
Selection of the sample	Only 5,493 of the interviews were actually completed. A quota sample of 500 cases was added to make up the deficit. The quotas stipulated were such as to compensate in age groups that were underrepresented and to provide added cases if subgroups were special analysts were desired (for example, girls attending colleges and universities.) Only 442 cases were obtained of the 500 specified. Returns from the quota sample were included with returns from the probability sample in calculations.

The Selection of a Sample—An Actual Situation

We have discussed the steps involved in the sampling process as a general procedure. An actual situation in which these procedural steps were followed is shown in Table 5–3.

The company conducting the study was a well-known marketer of products for the grooming of women's hair. At the time the sample was taken the products they were selling were used predominantly by white women and so the sample did not include women of other races.

As indicated in Table 5–3, a sample size of 6,000 women was desired. The original probability sampling provided only 5,493 cases. A quota sample of 500 was then added to compensate for the loss in size and to bolster representation in some of the age groups that were unrepresented. Some 442 cases were obtained in the quota sample, which were included with the probability sample for analysis.

Summary

This chapter has been concerned with the reasons for sampling and the process by which samples are taken. We first discussed *cost, time, accuracy,* and the *destructive nature of (such) measurements* as reasons for sampling.

The sampling process involves elements of both artistry and scientific knowledge. It consists of making and implementing decisions with respect to *defining the population, selecting the sampling frame(s), specifying the sampling unit, selecting the sampling method, determining the sample size, drawing up the sampling plan, and, finally, actually selecting the sample.* These steps were each discussed at some length. An example of a company that had a national probability sample selected to study media exposure and purchases of hair grooming products by women was described to illustrate the application of each of the steps.

In the next chapter we examine the problem of determining sample size.

Questions and Problems

5.1. For each situation (a) critique the method used and (b) suggest alternatives you consider better where appropriate.
   (i) To study attitudes toward a chain of supermarkets, interviewers were stationed in the parking lots of stores in the chain and questioned all those willing to answer.
   (ii) In studying the results of a screening method for credit card applica-

tions for a department store, folders of applicants were selected at a
fixed interval beginning at the front of each file drawer.

(iii) To study the effect of opinion leaders on product purchases, each of
a (simple random) sample of housewives were asked to name the
three women whose opinion influenced them the most in purchases
and the three women they felt they influenced the most. These
women were then asked the same question and the results were
cross matched.

(iv) To form an estimate of how many households had been exposed to a
particular television program the night before, a random sample of
telephone subscribers was called. A sample of 1,000 subscribers was
telephoned of which 800 responded. Of the 800, 200 reported having
seen the program and 600 said they had not seen it. The researcher
estimated that 50 of the 200 families not at home when called had
also seen the program.

5.2. Define the appropriate population for a sample to determine the effectiveness of an antialcoholism campaign on television sponsored by Alcoholics
Anonymous.

5.3. Suppose you were asked to design a probability sample to obtain names
and address of 100 households in your city for a product use test. (Unmarked containers of your product and competitive products are to be
given to the housewives to use in return for a later evaluation of each.)
How would you select the sample?

5.4. A national quota sample of 4,000 persons is to be taken to determine the
level of knowledge and opinions of AMTRAK passenger service.
(AMTRAK is the government corporation that subsidizes and supervises
passenger train service.) What quota variables and level of variables
should be used and how many persons should be included in each cell?

5.5. In the national sampling of women described on p. 168 the data from a
quota sample of 442 cases were added to the data from a probability
sample of 5,493 for purposes of analysis. What assumptions are implicit
in this way of treating the data?

5.6. A telephone survey of 300 randomly picked listed subscribers is to be
conducted in your city. The data are to be supplemented by 100 personal
interviews of respondents selected in a purposive sample. How would you
select the purposive sample?

5.7. A telephone company conducts an annual survey to determine customer
reaction to the telephone service received during the year. Would their
telephone book be a perfect frame for such a study? Explain.

Selected Bibliography

KISH, LESLIE. *Survey Sampling*. New York: John Wiley & Sons, Inc., 1965. A
book that blends the experience of the author as program director of the
Survey Research Center at the University of Michigan and the theory of
sampling. Well written and recommended.

LANSING, JOHN B., and JAMES N. MORGAN. *Economic Survey Methods*. (Ann Arbor: Ann Arbor Institute for Social Research, 1971, Chap. III. A book on surveys to obtain economic data, and as the pun in the name suggests, a book which is concerned with how to conduct surveys in economically efficient ways. It is a book worth reading including the chapter on sampling.

PETERSON, PETER G., and WILLIAM F. O'DELL. "Selecting Sampling Methods in Commercial Research." *Journal of Marketing,* **15** (October, 1950). An aging article that is as timely now as when it was written. The authors were consultants in a marketing research firm when the article was written. The practitioner's view is reflected.

STEPHAN, FREDERICK F., and PHILLIP J. McCARTHY. *Sampling Opinions*. New York: John Wiley & Sons, Inc., 1958. A book that presents much of the available information (after almost 20 years) on empirical measurements of sampling and nonsampling errors. Every research practitioner should read it.

Case 5–1
Greenville, South Carolina, 4th Brand Inventory

The Greenville News periodically conducts a "brand inventory" of certain household items in its market area as a service to its customers, clients, and other interested parties. The survey focuses on the *brands* of food and household items in the home at the time of the study. In addition, data on shopping preferences, housing, family composition, and saving habits are collected.

A recent Brand Inventory questionnaire was sent to all subscribers of *The Greenville News* on June 3 and had to be returned no later than June 8. The questionnaire was part of an eight-page (tabloid) contest inserted in the newspaper. The first part of the contest required the respondent to provide "5 Reasons Why I Read *The Greenville News.*" Each reason had to be expressed in one sentence not exceeding 12 words. The second part of the contest required the respondent to complete the brand inventory questionnaire.

Entries were to be judged on neatness and completeness. Only one entry per family was allowed. There were 29 total prizes with a total value of approximately $5,000. The prizes ranged from a new car to a transistor radio.

Approximately 5,100 usable questionnaires were returned. As the questionnaires were received, they were grouped into county of residence (there were nine counties in the paper's circulation area). From these groups of questionnaires, a total sample of 1,737 questionnaires (2 per cent of the paper's circulation in the area) was randomly selected for analysis. The questionnaires were selected from each county in proportion to circulation in that county compared to total circulation.

All projections of the sample data were made to the circulation of the paper in various areas.

1. What types of errors, if any, are likely to be present in the projections because of the sampling process?

2. What type of sample was taken from the completed questionnaires?

Case 5–2
Sampling Plan for a Brand Preference Survey

The sampling part of the methodology section of a recently completed brand preference study is presented as follows.

A sample was drawn from telephone directories for the telephone exchanges serving the 25 county market area. The proper geographical distribution of the sample was ensured through the weighting of each directory on the basis of its percentage of total telephone subscribers in the market area under study. After the number of names to be drawn from any directory was determined, the third name of the "*n*th" column was selected. The value of *n* was determined by dividing the total number of columns in the telephone directory by the number of names to be selected from that directory. Whenever the third name in the column was "commercial," the next "individual" name following was selected.

Based upon estimated returns and the required number of completed returns required to provide adequate statistical validity for the study, a total of 2,010 names were drawn for the sample. The area being studied contains 222,000 homes.

1. What type of sample was drawn?

2. What types of errors, if any, were likely to be present because of the sampling process being used?

3. What concept of nonresponse error is implied in the last paragraph?

Case 5–3
Ward's Book Services

Ward's Book Services is a large book wholesaler that deals primarily with academic libraries. The firm has grown from a small regional operation in 1955 to a multinational firm with sales of over $60 million. This growth has been achieved through a heavy emphasis on providing service to the academic libraries. The firm not only responds to orders received from the libraries but can also evaluate the adequacy of a library's collection in any specific area or automatically maintain a library collection at a specified level of coverage for any given subject area. Ward's can ship books with no preparation or it can provide any level of preparation, through supplying indexing on the jacket, the inside folder, and a complete set of catalog cards.

The last two years have resulted in stable sales at a time when industry sales have been growing. Ward's has some evidence to indicate that it is losing sales to a new firm that emphasizes price discounts rather than service. Gerald Ward, founder and president of Ward's, is concerned that the budget pressure facing most academic libraries has caused them to opt for the identifiable savings of a lower priced book rather than the less visible savings associated with the free or inexpensive services provided by his firm. If this is the case, he is willing to lower both the level of his service and the price of his books.

Ward requested Sharon Reed, a newly hired MBA from a nearby college, to prepare a study of the feasibility of reducing prices and services. Reed was convinced that the academic library market was not a single market as Ward's management had always assumed. It was her opinion that the market could be segmented on the basis of size of the library. She found an academic research report that contained responses from 2,400 libraries (approximately 85 per cent of the total). From this report, she estimated that those libraries responding spent $110 million for books in the past year. Furthermore, she estimated that the 465 libraries that spent $50,000 or more accounted for $79 million or 72 per cent of the total.

It was Reed's contention that these larger libraries generally had graduate programs in the library fields and large fixed staffs. They would therefore have much less need for the special services provided by Ward's than the smaller libraries. If this were the case, Ward's would be wise to adopt one price-service strategy for the larger libraries and another for the smaller libraries.

In order to test these ideas, Reed decided to conduct a survey. For a sampling frame she had the list of respondents to the earlier study (85 per cent of all academic libraries), which contained information on last year's expenditures, number of staff personnel, and total number of books. As an alternate frame, she had a directory that contained the names and addresses of all the academic libraries in the United States. Finally, she had the list of Ward's accounts (1,600) and their purchases during the past year. Two hundred of these accounts produced about 70 per cent of the firm's sales.

1. Which sample frame should she use?

2. How should she select the sample?

Case 5–4

Tower Hills Shopping Center

Tower Hills Shopping Center (THC) is located in a small city (population 150,000). The city is located 125 miles south of the only other large city (population 450,000) in the area. It is over 300 miles in any direction to another city with more than 25,000 population.

THC has three large department stores and over 50 smaller stores clustered about its all-weather shopping mall. Each store maintains its separate promotional budget and engages in its own advertising and sales promotion activities. Each store also pays a fixed fee for every square foot of floor space it leases. A total of $75,000 of these fees go to the advertising budget of the THC Management Group.

The management group is responsible for promoting the welfare and growth of THC itself. A major activity has been the creation and promotion of special "theme" activities, generally sales. Thus, in addition to standard holiday sales, back-to-school sales, and so forth, THC has sales celebrating such events as the anniversary of Paul Revere's ride or the opening of the Panama Canal. Approximately $60,000 of the advertising budget goes to promote either traditional holiday or "special day" sales. The remaining $15,000 is spent to promote the overall image of THC through such community-oriented activities as placing advertisements carrying the THC name and promoting the United Fund or the Big Brother program.

The management group spends all of its "image" funds on local newspaper, radio, and television advertising. However, almost $15,000 of the funds spent to promote "sales" are allocated to some 23 newspapers, 12 radio stations, and 2 television stations located in small towns within 150 miles of the center. Many of these communities also receive the city's newspaper and radio and television broadcasts.

This information was available to Paul Bowers of Bowers Advertising, Inc., when his agency was asked by the THC management group to handle the THC account. The request came on October 15 and his agency was asked to handle all THC advertising beginning February 1. Paul somewhat reluctantly agreed to assume the account. His was the fourth agency in six years to handle the THC account. In discussing the high rate of agency turnover with a member of the management group, Paul found that the allocation of specific sums to media in each small community produced considerable tension among the five directors of the management group. Since the members of the management group could not agree on the appropriate allocation, the agency was quickly placed in the difficult position of alienating some of the directors no matter what it recommended.

Further inquiry revealed that the management group had no empirical data on where customers came from or why they shopped at THC. Paul decided that he had to convince the center to collect these data. Since his agency frequently conducted surveys for clients, he believed that this represented an important opportunity to impress the THC management group with the diversity and quality of services available from his firm. A good research proposal to this group might result in additional work from individual stores within the center as well.

Shortly after he began work on the research proposal, Paul faced a problem. He was not sure which of two sampling approaches to utilize. One option would be to hand people the questionnaire as they left the center through one of its eight exits. Or, he could draw a sample from the names in the local telephone directory and the 27 smaller community directories that appeared relevant.

1. How would Bowers implement each of the two sampling strategies?

2. Which is most appropriate for the case at hand? Why?

Case 5–5

The Gallup Organization: Design of a National Probability Sample*

The Gallup Organization, Inc., maintains a national probability sample of interviewing areas that is used for all TRENDS surveys. TRENDS is the Gallup "omnibus" service. For each survey, a minimum of 1,500 individuals is personally interviewed. An independent sample of individuals is selected for each survey.

The sampling procedure is designed to produce an approximation of the adult civilian population, 18 years and older, living in the United States, except for those persons in institutions such as prisons or hospitals.

The design of the sample is that of a replicated, probability sample down to the block level in the case of urban areas, and to segments of townships in the case of rural areas. Approximately 300 sampling locations are used in each survey. Interpenetrating samples can be provided for any given study when appropriate.

---

* The material for this case was supplied by and is used with the permission of The Gallup Organization.

The sample design included stratification by these four size-of-community strata, using 1970 census data: cities of population of (a) 1 million and over; (b) 250,000 to 999,999; (c) 50,000 to 249,999; (d) less than 50,000. Each of these strata is further stratified into seven geographic regions: New England, Middle Atlantic, East Central, West Central, South, Mountain, and Pacific. Within each city size–regional stratum, the population is arrayed in geographic order and zoned into equal sized groups of sampling units. Pairs of localities are selected in each zone, with the probability of selection of each locality being proportional to its population size in the 1970 census, producing two replicated samples of localities.

Within localities so selected for which the requisite population data are reported, subdivisions are drawn with the probability of selection proportional to size of population. In all other localities, small definable geographic areas are selected with equal probability.

Separately for each survey, within each subdivision so selected for which block statistics are available, a sample of blocks or block clusters is drawn with probability of selection proportional to the number of dwelling units. In all other subdivisions or areas, blocks or segments are drawn at random or with equal probability.

In each cluster of blocks and each segment so selected, a randomly selected starting point is designated on the interviewer's map of the area. Starting at this point, interviewers are required to follow a given direction in the selection of households until their assignment is completed.

Interviewing is conducted at times when adults, in general, are most likely to be at home, which means on weekends, or if on weekdays, after 4:00 P.M. for women and after 6:00 P.M. for men.

Allowance for persons not at home is made by a "times-at-home" weighting[15] procedure rather than by "callbacks." This procedure is a standard method for reducing the sample bias that would otherwise result from underrepresentation in the sample of persons who are difficult to find at home.

The prestratification by regions is routinely supplemented by fitting each obtained sample to the latest available Census Bureau estimates of the regional distribution of the population. Also minor adjustments of the sample are made by educational attainment by men and women separately, based on the annual estimates of the Census Bureau (derived from their Current Population Survey) and by age.

Describe each of the procedural sampling steps (as listed in Table 5–1) used by Gallup in the design of the sample.

[15] A. Politz, and W. Simmons, "An Attempt to Get the 'Not at Homes' into the Sample Without Callbacks," *Journal of the American Statistical Association,* **44** (March 1949), 9–31.

CHAPTER 6

Sampling and Research: Determining Sample Size

An inescapable part of taking a sample is determining what size it should be. Any sample that is large enough for the research director is almost certain to be too large for the comptroller. It is the trade-off between added information and added costs that makes sample size determination difficult.

In this chapter we grapple with this problem using three differing approaches. The *traditional method* of determining sample size is introduced following a discussion (and simulation) of the sampling distribution. Sample size determination for both estimation and hypothesis testing problems are discussed. The logic of the *Bayesian method* for determining sample size is then examined. (The computation techniques are presented in Appendix A.) Sample size is determined by the Bayesian approach for the same case problem used to illustrate the traditional approaches and the results obtained are compared.

Finally, we discuss the problems and techniques involved in determining the sample size of a *nonprobability sample*. This is an important area since many, if not most, applied studies use some form of a nonprobability sample.

The Sampling Distribution

Sampling theory, including that concerned with how large a sample to take, rests on the concept of a *sampling distribution*. Having a basic understanding of what a sampling distribution is and how it is used removes much of the mystery from sampling theory. If the sampling distribution is itself somewhat mysterious, the rest of sampling theory is almost certain to be so.

A simulation is used as a means of reviewing the concept of a sampling distribution. A *sampling distribution of the mean* is simulated for samples drawn from the population of 1,250 invoice values. We utilize a simple random sample of size 50 ($n = 50$) for the simulation.

The definition of a *sampling distribution of the mean* is "the relative frequency distribution of the sample means of all possible samples of size n taken from a population of size N."[1] The definition specifies that *all* possible samples of size *n* from population size *N* should be taken. With a sample of size 50 from a population of size 1,250, this would require approximately 2×10^{91} samples. Since such an undertaking is possible in theory but not in practice, we have to settle for a more modest number of samples in the simulation.

Simulated Sampling Distribution of the Mean

Five hundred simple random samples of size 50 were taken from the invoice values in Table 6–1 and the means were calculated for each. The means were sorted into intervals based on the value of the sample mean. (The symbol we use for the sample mean is $\bar{x}$.) The resulting frequency distribution is shown in Table 6–2.

The relative frequencies in Column 2 of Table 6–2 were calculated by dividing the absolute number in each interval (the figure in Column 1) by the total number of samples taken, 500. Thus, a relative frequency for a class (interval) in this example is nothing more than the number of times means with values falling within the class limits occurred *relative* to the total number of means.

A relative frequency, then, is a measure of a *probability*. If one were

[1] This definition assumes that the sampling is from a population of finite rather than infinite size. This is usually the situation in marketing and, if the sampling is from an infinite population, presents no conceptual problem.

asked to predict the probability of a random sample of size 50 taken from this population having a mean between $50.00 to $51.99, the best estimate would be .22 based on the table. That is, we would expect that about 2 out of each 10 means chosen will fall within this range.

The relative frequencies in Table 6–2 are shown in a histogram in Figure 6–1. A normal curve is shown in the same figure. It may be seen that the relative frequency distribution is very close to being normally distributed. Had all possible samples been drawn rather than only 500, it *would* have been normally distributed. The normal curve in Figure 6–1 is the sampling distribution of the mean for the sampling problem with which we are work-ing. A sampling distribution of the mean for *simple random* samples that are large (30 or more) has

1. *a normal distribution*
2. *a mean equal to the population mean (M)*
3. *a standard deviation, called the standard error of the mean (σ_x), that is equal to the population standard deviation (σ) divided by the square root of the sample size ($\sqrt{n}$). That is*

$$\sigma_{\bar{x}} = \frac{\sigma}{\sqrt{n}} \qquad (6\text{–}1)$$

The only reason that a standard error of the mean is called that instead of a standard deviation is to indicate that it applies to a sampling distribu-tion of the mean and not to a sample or a population. The standard error formula shown applies only to a *simple random* sample. Other kinds of probability samples have more complicated standard error formulas. Their meaning and use are the same, however.

A basic characteristic of any normal curve is that the area under it be-tween two points can be calculated if the mean and standard deviation are known. This is also true of a sampling distribution of the mean since it is normally distributed. In Figure 6–2, for example, we can calculate what proportion the shaded area under the curve is to the total so long as we know what the mean and standard error are.

The mean and standard deviation of the population of the 1,250 values are $M = \$50.97$ and $\sigma = \$28.06$ as determined by actual calculations. The standard error of the mean is then

$$\sigma_{\bar{x}} = \frac{\sigma}{\sqrt{n}} = \frac{\$28.06}{\sqrt{50}} = \$3.97$$

The shaded area in Figure 6–2 is that area under the curve between the points $50.97 and $54.94. When the distance between these two points is expressed in units of standard errors, it is referred to as Z and is calculated as

$$Z = \frac{\bar{x} - M}{\sigma_{\bar{x}}} = \frac{54.94 - 50.97}{3.97} = 1.0 \text{ standard errors.}$$

Table 6-1 Values of 1,250 Sales Invoices (to nearest dollar)

44	17	81	63	93	91	52	43	50	74	61	99	02	19	94	26	77	28	14	95	39	22	25	30	53
88	67	13	65	42	16	55	42	78	81	12	66	58	07	30	20	59	47	14	96	78	59	58	69	07
53	18	13	47	12	81	71	93	43	14	45	90	39	29	77	47	92	81	23	69	70	56	79	90	60
88	57	56	97	96	24	63	95	32	41	90	43	48	61	52	05	74	80	89	89	12	76	37	73	88
49	37	69	38	27	16	62	64	95	32	63	31	18	12	21	68	08	84	16	48	33	93	67	46	23
66	00	15	15	06	86	14	07	70	69	84	86	88	40	08	58	63	87	36	88	19	90	93	66	98
17	07	89	49	45	65	08	01	23	92	30	67	99	66	81	88	60	41	47	47	28	53	64	08	23
73	99	60	72	28	09	19	34	62	10	49	62	95	68	60	91	13	06	88	83	46	64	87	59	12
11	33	21	44	43	15	91	22	07	59	28	42	12	76	76	20	27	24	24	70	78	93	67	51	24
43	08	41	21	85	32	51	09	47	54	45	23	51	66	66	50	41	27	63	67	16	08	28	32	61
57	56	85	67	62	97	61	49	23	51	35	95	77	49	03	10	42	91	43	94	50	57	03	49	25
62	38	42	48	72	35	81	64	85	19	29	39	03	71	60	19	86	80	21	92	34	33	81	80	38
21	73	14	67	12	30	23	68	19	78	55	90	37	25	71	03	99	59	12	51	47	82	45	25	35
75	65	33	81	82	13	23	96	76	82	86	23	82	51	50	61	17	55	28	41	95	03	63	62	58
61	13	17	91	71	77	05	72	82	73	67	68	45	97	77	51	16	78	93	01	91	17	66	61	95
72	56	13	65	11	38	13	00	50	56	82	09	31	33	12	41	61	84	23	92	13	13	55	38	26
97	53	14	68	19	44	44	70	74	30	71	77	35	63	80	55	10	31	95	97	17	11	39	44	14
35	79	16	21	57	81	75	53	33	60	94	09	79	29	49	07	35	47	83	12	22	55	88	46	32
22	64	20	80	44	28	22	09	90	58	41	77	16	23	35	36	38	02	23	49	46	95	65	00	13
87	88	39	37	23	99	34	19	32	45	33	06	30	66	95	80	65	92	68	67	31	91	29	79	07
50	76	04	65	30	15	56	76	70	61	88	70	27	70	46	09	46	73	04	94	55	24	55	10	83
02	76	80	86	96	52	36	31	74	80	76	33	60	20	92	29	77	41	81	86	05	73	24	28	12
34	36	90	26	29	39	20	76	95	42	67	34	58	69	47	56	81	35	65	16	23	82	53	24	13
69	47	26	60	28	33	65	51	63	91	41	07	85	54	48	47	89	89	28	03	53	63	25	95	47
36	14	60	08	90	71	30	34	43	18	96	70	86	34	51	06	11	11	14	29	33	67	85	71	88
62	16	07	76	94	09	32	30	74	76	86	78	75	52	70	37	57	13	08	95	32	23	91	70	90
75	46	96	99	49	03	54	32	74	20	58	77	01	14	85	16	66	99	99	97	46	57	76	48	56
32	53	72	54	45	60	27	14	38	61	94	74	32	19	78	12	00	75	28	27	32	75	62	45	08
66	09	42	47	16	57	33	95	50	67	41	75	79	43	09	79	78	39	85	77	21	30	48	49	62
12	56	30	19	62	47	50	43	44	05	13	13	95	58	36	73	10	71	01	99	56	92	66	44	20
93	63	44	62	76	44	76	82	45	38	09	46	79	96	66	80	57	46	17	23	32	05	27	34	43
99	96	66	76	57	19	62	73	25	37	61	76	95	17	07	61	40	57	23	99	54	85	84	40	08
92	95	55	56	71	43	33	26	00	73	43	15	01	66	82	74	35	10	28	92	17	90	92	95	63

90	03	83	63	43	49	75	22	59	90	27	58	39	97	80	67	60	87	60	16	13	08	70	77	88
79	73	88	37	87	25	71	86	49	70	53	95	98	16	73	88	95	18	48	08	65	44	59	43	71
54	49	32	48	74	48	52	10	61	90	65	95	07	77	83	17	39	95	95	00	32	68	50	71	81
56	34	19	78	13	19	96	10	75	77	42	91	79	93	21	65	07	07	99	57	65	54	17	35	85
47	16	59	19	85	88	30	73	37	84	68	18	21	42	25	35	61	12	81	58	00	17	88	98	97
67	14	22	28	49	34	30	65	49	27	38	88	17	80	15	71	82	91	21	51	66	89	04	50	40
92	25	25	25	55	14	68	11	33	61	20	54	67	46	19	89	46	85	87	14	82	48	51	73	22
48	37	69	24	63	26	95	07	40	16	30	44	43	46	18	84	00	42	45	64	69	31	99	29	21
94	97	85	61	41	87	31	99	51	35	62	39	64	34	31	92	05	35	33	82	79	67	80	09	18
42	68	05	64	93	43	56	64	53	34	53	05	97	92	38	62	54	28	75	44	46	60	96	72	26
82	87	34	93	44	57	86	11	11	37	92	56	36	27	17	63	50	46	11	43	71	86	80	28	66
70	07	18	86	49	85	52	12	12	22	78	08	87	00	63	75	31	10	25	78	85	99	58	99	62
43	61	36	28	96	11	08	19	28	00	02	19	99	12	59	67	50	83	41	19	48	69	57	60	55
11	54	98	12	65	96	31	96	63	84	16	85	51	06	59	81	03	12	09	58	48	95	89	62	76
02	97	58	70	58	16	47	78	12	63	79	81	54	16	15	32	40	39	59	40	23	20	26	66	94
37	09	49	51	81	94	72	12	55	99	65	07	87	30	81	37	14	93	66	54	98	48	51	73	50
90	94	93	15	66	11	29	14	41	75	23	53	53	85	01	57	08	83	49	92	22	04	04	11	94

Table 6–2 Frequencies and Relative Frequencies
of 200 Sample Means

	Column 1	Column 2
	Frequency of Sample Means	*Relative Frequency of Sample Means*
$38.00–39.99	1	$1/500 = $ .002
40.00–41.99	2	$2/500 = $ .004
42.00–43.99	17	$17/500 = $ .034
44.00–45.99	39	$39/500 = $ .078
46.00–47.99	52	$52/500 = $ .104
48.00–49.99	85	$85/500 = $ .170
50.00–51.99	110	$110/500 = $ .220
52.00–53.99	77	$77/500 = $ .154
54.00–55.99	64	$64/500 = $ .128
56.00–57.99	37	$37/500 = $ .074
58.00–59.99	10	$10/500 = $ .020
60.00–61.99	4	$4/500 = $ .008
62.00–63.99	2	$2/500 = $ .004
Total	500	1.000

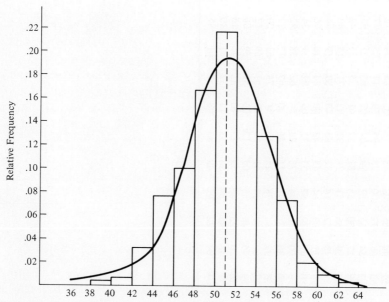

Figure 6–1 Simulated and actual sampling distribution of the mean for
sales invoice problem ($n = 50$).

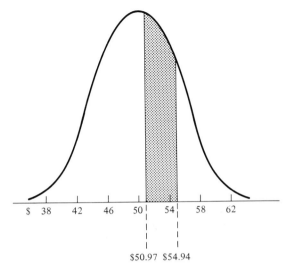

Figure 6–2 Determination of probability of getting sample mean with a value of $50.97 to $54.94.

We may use a table to look up the area. Such a table is given in Appendix B. We see that the area is .3413.

For sampling distributions this area is a *probability*. In our example if we took all possible samples of size 50 from the population, the relative frequency of the occurrence of those with means falling from $50.97 to $54.94 would be .3413. That is, slightly more than one-third of them would fall between $50.97 and $54.94.

The fact that the *relative frequency* of occurrence of *all possible* samples of size 50 with a mean of plus (or minus) one standard error from the population mean is .3413 means that the *probability* of *one* sample with a mean falling within this range is .3413 (or 34.13 per cent). That is, if we know the population mean and the standard error we know that the probability of any given sample mean being within 1 standard error ($Z = 1.0$) of the population mean is .3413. We know the comparable probability for any Z value (number of standard errors) from the table of areas under the normal curve.

Statistical Estimation and the Sampling Distribution of the Mean

In statistical estimation problems involving the mean, we want to estimate a *population mean* that *we do not know* from a sample mean that *we do know*. Two kinds of estimates of a population mean may be made, *point* and *interval*.

A *point estimate* of the mean is an estimate involving only a single value. If a random sample is taken, the sample mean is the best estimate that can be made from the sample data. If we have taken a random sample of 50 invoices from the population of 1,250 in Table 6–1 and want to estimate the population mean, we simply use the sample mean as the best guess, or estimate, of the value of the population mean.

A visual examination of the sampling distributions of the mean of Table 6–2 shows that the mean of a *srs* of size 50 is likely to be quite close to the actual population mean. However, on some occasions it will be a substantial distance from the true value. Thus, *a srs is not always a representative or accurate sample.* The distance between the sample value and the true value of the mean is the *sampling error.*

Increasing sample size will reduce the potential sampling error. This is because as sample size increases, the sampling distribution becomes clustered more closely around the true population value. Or, stated another way, the standard error of the mean becomes smaller as the sample size increases.

The fact that point estimates based on sample means are seldom *exactly* correct makes the *interval estimate* quite useful. As the name implies, it is an estimate concerning an interval, or range of values. A statement of the probability that the interval will enclose the true value of the mean is also given. This probability is called a *confidence coefficient* and the interval is often called a *confidence interval.*

The interval estimate of the mean is arrived at by the following procedure. A sample is taken and the sample mean is calculated. We know that this sample mean falls somewhere within the sampling distribution, but not at what location. We do know, however, that there is a probability of .3413 (34.13 per cent) that it lies within one standard error above and a probability of .3413 (34.13 per cent) that it lies within one standard error below the actual population mean. We may, therefore, make an interval estimate that: *We may be 68.26 per cent confident that the population mean (M) lies within the interval formed by the sample mean ($\bar{x}$) plus one standard error ($\sigma_{\bar{x}}$) and the sample mean minus one standard error.*

In symbols this interval may be shown as

$$\bar{x} - 1.0\sigma_{\bar{x}} \leq M \leq \bar{x} + 1.0\sigma_{\bar{x}}$$

The 68.26 per cent is the confidence coefficient of the estimate.

We may extend the interval to be more confident that the true value of the population mean is enclosed by the estimating process. We might enlarge the interval to plus or minus two standard errors. Reference to Appendix B indicates that the appropriate confidence coefficient is 95.44 per cent. Although we are more confident of our interval estimate now, it is a larger interval and, therefore, may not be as useful. The same observation applies to the estimate formed by the sample mean and three standard errors on either side (99.74 per cent confidence coefficient.)

The question may be asked, "This seems all right if you know the value of the standard deviation of the population. But what do you do when you don't know that either?" One answer is that you may estimate it from the sample. If we let $\hat{\sigma}$ stand for an *estimate* of the standard deviation of the population and s represent the sample standard deviation, an estimate is given by

$$\hat{\sigma} = \sqrt{\frac{n}{n-1}}\, s, \quad \text{where} \quad s = \sqrt{\frac{\sum_{i=1}^{n}(x_i - \bar{x})^2}{n}} \qquad (6\text{-}2)$$

When the sample gets large (say 30 or more), the term $\sqrt{\dfrac{n}{n-1}}$ is so close to 1.0 that it can be disregarded and the sample standard deviation used as a direct estimate of the population standard deviation.

The Sampling Distribution of the Proportion

Researchers are often interested in proportions as well as in means. For example, marketers are concerned about the percentage of magazine readers who remember a specific advertisement, the percentage of a group that prefers Brand A over Brand B, and so on. Therefore, marketing researchers are often dealing with proportions and, of necessity, with the sampling distribution of the proportions.

The definition of a *sampling distribution* of the proportion is "the relative frequency distribution of the sample proportions (p) of all possible samples of size n taken from a population of size N."[2]

The same basic reasoning we have gone through with respect to the sampling distribution of the mean applies to the sampling distribution of the proportion. A sampling distribution of a proportion for a simple random sample has a

1. *normal distribution,*
2. *a mean equal to the population proportion (P), and*
3. *a standard error (σ_p) equal to*

$$\sigma_p = \sqrt{\frac{P(1-P)}{n}} \qquad (6\text{-}3)$$

We could simulate a frequency distribution of the proportions (say of invoices with a value over $20) exactly as we did for the mean. Like the

[2] This definition also assumes that the sampling is from a population of finite size.

histogram for the mean, the histogram of relative frequencies of the proportion would approximate a normal curve with the classes nearest the population proportion being the largest. Estimation procedures similar to those described for the mean are applicable.

The estimated standard error of the proportion (given a large sample size) is

$$\hat{\sigma}_p = \sqrt{\frac{p(1-p)}{n}} \qquad (6\text{-}4)$$

where p represents the sample proportion.

Having briefly reviewed the critical concept of the sampling distributions, we now turn our attention to how this concept can be used in the determination of sample size.

Traditional Methods of Determining Sample Size

In the introduction to this chapter, reference was made to *traditional* and to *Bayesian* approaches to determining sample size. There are many similarities between the two. Both rely heavily upon the concept of the sampling distribution. Both are concerned with being able to measure sampling errors so that the chance of a wrong conclusion because of sampling variation will be known. Both are also concerned with how much error can be tolerated in each problem situation.

There are significant differences between the two, however. The Bayesian approach involves an explicit consideration of the cost of errors whereas the traditional approach does not. The prior judgments of the investigator are used in the Bayesian approach but are not allowed by the traditionalists.

In this section we consider the traditional approach for determining sample size in problems of estimation and problems involving hypothesis tests. We examine the Bayesian approach in a later section.

Determination of Sample Size in Problems Involving Estimation

Specifications Required for Estimation Problem Involving Means

Suppose an estimate of the mean dollar amount per invoice is required for a decision concerning the frequency with which sales calls should be scheduled. A simple random sample is to be taken from the 1,250 invoices in Table 6–1 to make the estimate. Further, suppose that the marketing research department is conducting the study and you are the analyst assigned. What information would you need before you could determine the size of sample to take?

In the traditional approach, three kinds of specifications have to be made before the sample size necessary to estimate the population mean can be determined. These are

1. *Specification of error* $(\bar{x} - M)$ *that can be allowed*—how close must the estimate be?
2. *Specification of confidence coefficient*—what level of confidence is required that the actual sampling error does not exceed that specified?
3. *Estimate of the standard deviation* (σ)—what is the standard deviation of the population?

Note that there is no specification required of either costs of errors or of prior judgment about the mean.

The first two of these specifications are matters of judgment involving the *use* of the data. As the analyst in the invoice sampling project you would be well advised to talk with the person or persons who will be using the information you develop. The questions of "How much error in the estimate is acceptable?" and "How confident do you want to be that the error really isn't any greater than that?" need to be raised.

Suppose that after discussing these questions, it is decided that the allowable error is ± $10.00 and that a confidence level of 90 per cent is desired.

The third specification, the estimate of the standard deviation of the population, is the responsibility of the analyst. Estimates of the standard deviation sometimes are available from previous studies. Most government agencies that collect data report means and deviations as well. If not, the population standard deviation can be calculated easily from the summary tables in which the data are reported.[3] Standard deviations are either available directly or can be calculated for such demographic and other variables as personal income, corporate income, age, education, labor rates, housing values, and most other information collected and reported by the Bureau of the Census, Bureau of Labor Statistics, and other government agencies.

If other sources are not available for estimating standard deviation, one can sometimes design the sampling plan so that a small sample is taken for

---

[3] A formula for calculating the standard deviation from a frequency table is

$$\sigma = \sqrt{\frac{\sum_{i=1}^{h} f_i(x_i - M)^2}{N}}$$

where h is the number of classes, x_i is the midpoint of class i, f_i is the frequency of class i, and N is the size of the population.

that purpose. The sample standard deviation is calculated and used to estimate population standard deviation and the final sample size is determined. The initial sample is included as a part of the total sample so that the only loss is the extra time involved.

Assume that, based on past studies, we estimate the standard deviation of the population of invoice values to be $28.60. With the allowable error already set at $10.00 and the confidence coefficient at 90 per cent, all the specifications needed to calculate sample size are complete.

Calculation of Sample Size in Estimation Problems Involving Means

The three specifications made are related in the following way:

$$\frac{\text{number of standard errors implied by confidence coefficient}}{} = \frac{\text{allowable error}}{\text{standard error}}$$

or, in symbols,

$$Z = \frac{\bar{x} - M}{\frac{\sigma}{\sqrt{n}}} \tag{6–5}$$

The only unknown variable is the sample size.

This equation is the direct result of the logic of the sampling distribution. We know that the sample mean $(\bar{x})$ lies somewhere on the sampling distribution, which has as its mean the population mean (M). In order to

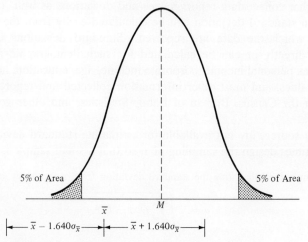

5% of Area   5% of Area

M

$\bar{x}$

$\left|\longleftarrow \bar{x} - 1.640\sigma_{\bar{x}} \longrightarrow\right|\longleftarrow \bar{x} + 1.640\sigma_{\bar{x}} \longrightarrow\right|$

Figure 6–3 Sampling distribution and 90 per cent confidence interval—estimate of mean.

be 90 per cent confident that the population mean will be included, we
must construct an interval that will include the population mean in all
cases except those in which the sample mean happens to fall in the last 5
per cent of the area at the two ends of the distribution. This interval is
shown in Figure 6–3.

What is the number of standard errors (Z) required to give a 90 per
cent level of confidence? Reference to Appendix B indicates that 1.64
standard errors cover 45 per cent of one side of the sampling distribution;
$\pm 1.64\sigma_{\bar{x}}$, therefore, covers 90 per cent of the entire distribution.

The calculation remains. Substituting in the equation 6–5, we obtain a
required simple random sample size of 23 as follows

$$Z = \frac{\bar{x} - M}{\dfrac{\sigma}{\sqrt{n}}}$$

$$1.64 = \frac{\$10.00}{\dfrac{\$28.90}{\sqrt{n}}}$$

$$\sqrt{n} = \frac{\$28.90 \times 1.64}{\$10.00} = 4.74$$

$$n = 23$$

A formula for the size of simple random samples can be derived from
equation 6–5. It is

$$n = \frac{Z^2\sigma^2}{(\bar{x} - M)^2} \tag{6–6}$$

This formula can be used for calculating sample size without the requirement of doing the algebraic manipulations required if equation 6–5 is
used.[4]

For some problems we may want to set the allowable error in relation
to the mean rather than in absolute terms. That is, we may want to avoid
an error any larger than, say, 1/10th or 1/5th or some other fraction of
the mean. It, therefore, makes sense to set the tolerable error in these
terms. This is known as the *relative allowable error* and is denoted by the
letter R. Mathematically, R is equal to the allowable error divided by the
mean, or

$$R = \frac{(\bar{x} - M)}{M} = \text{relative allowable error.}$$

[4] These formulas assume an infinite rather than a finite population. If the population is finite and sample size calculated by equation 6–6 is 5 per cent or more of the
population, it is larger than necessary. In such cases, the formula that should be used
for calculating sample size is

$$n = \frac{\hat{\sigma}^2}{\dfrac{(\bar{x} - M)^2}{Z^2} + \dfrac{\hat{\sigma}^2}{N}}$$

The standard deviation may also be estimated relative to the mean. The relative standard error is called the *coefficient of variation* and is denoted by the letter *C*. Mathematically, *C* is equal to the standard deviation divided by the mean, or

$$C = \frac{\sigma}{M} = \text{coefficient of variation.}$$

Expressing the allowable error and the standard deviation in relative rather than in absolute terms permits equation 6–6 to be shown as

$$n = \frac{Z^2 C^2}{R^2} \tag{6-7}$$

A *nomograph* has been developed from equation 6–7 to allow one to read off the sample size rather than having to calculate it for estimation problems. It is shown in Figure 6–4.

As an example of the use of the nomograph, assume that a sample size is to be determined for a simple random sample for a situation in which it has been specified that (1) *the allowable error is to be no more than 20 per cent of the population mean* — *R* = .20; (2) *the confidence level is to be 95 per cent;* and (3) *the standard deviation of the population is estimated to be 60 per cent of the mean* — *C* = .60. By placing a ruler on the values *R* = .20 and *C* = .60, the sample size can be read off where it crosses the column of sample sizes for a 95 per cent confidence level. It is found that *n* = 35.

Specifications Required for Estimation Problems Involving Proportions

Suppose an estimate of the proportion of invoices that have dollar amounts of $20.00 or more is to be made. A simple random sample is to be taken from the population of 1,250 invoices represented by Table 6–1 on pages 180–181. What additional information is needed before you determine the sample size to take?

The specifications that must be made to determine the sample size for an estimation problem involving proportion are very similar to those for the mean. They are:

1. *Specification of error* $(p - P)$ *that can be allowed*—how close must the estimate be?
2. *Specification of confidence coefficient*—what level of confidence is required that the actual sampling error does not exceed that specified?
3. *Estimate of population proportion* (P)—what is the approximate or estimated population proportion?

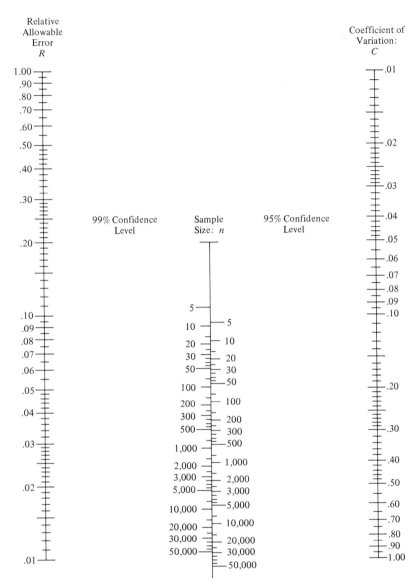

Figure 6–4 Nomograph for determining size of a simple random sample in estimation problems of the mean—infinite population. (Used with the permission and through the courtesy of Audits and Surveys, Inc.)

The reasoning for these specifications and the methods of obtaining them are the same as those for the mean. They, along with the sample size, collectively determine the sampling distribution for the problem. Since the sample size is the only remaining unknown, it can be calculated.

As was the case with the sample mean, the three specifications made are related as follows:

$$\begin{array}{l} \text{number of} \\ \text{standard errors} \\ \text{implied by} \\ \text{confidence} \\ \text{coefficient} \end{array} = \frac{\text{allowable error}}{\text{standard error}}$$

The formula for the estimated standard error of the proportion is

$$\hat{\sigma}_p = \sqrt{\frac{p(1.0 - p)}{n}}$$

The relation among specifications may be shown symbolically as

$$Z = \frac{(p - P)}{\sqrt{\dfrac{p(1.0 - p)}{n}}} \qquad (6\text{--}8)$$

Since the logic for this relationship is the same as it is for problems involving estimation of means, we do not repeat it here. The calculation of sample size can also be made in the same way.

The formula[5] for determining n directly is

$$n = \frac{Z^2[p(1.0 - p)]}{(p - P)^2} \qquad (6\text{--}9)$$

The sample size required for estimating the proportion of invoices with dollar amounts of $20.00 or more where the specification of *error that can be allowed* $(p - P)$ is .08 (8 percentage points), *the confidence level* is 95.4 per cent (thus, $Z = 2.0$) and the estimate of the *population proportion* is $P = .20$ (20.0 per cent) is

$$\begin{aligned} n &= \frac{2^2[.20(1.0 - .20)]}{(.08)^2} \\ &= \frac{4[.16]}{.0064} \\ &= 100 \end{aligned}$$

Figure 6–5 may also be used for reading the (simple random) sample size directly after the necessary specifications have been made for a prob-

---

[5] These formulas assume an infinite rather than a finite population. If the population is finite and sample size calculated by equation 6–8 is 5 per cent or more of the population, it is larger than necessary. In such cases, the formula that should be used for calculating sample size is

$$n = \frac{p(1 - p)}{\dfrac{(p - P)^2}{Z^2} + \dfrac{p(1 - p)}{N}}$$

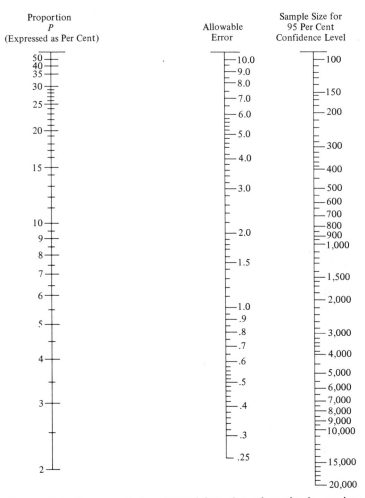

Figure 6–5 Nomograph for determining size of a simple random sample in estimation problems of the proportion—infinite population. (Used with the permission and through the courtesy of Audits and Surveys, Inc.)

lem involving estimation of a proportion. Determine the sample size for the problem stated using the nomograph and see if the answer is the same.

Sample Size Determination for Non-srs Random Samples in Problems Involving Estimation

Thus far we have considered only simple random samples (*srs*) in the determination of the size sample to take. The reasons for limiting the discussion to *srs* are two: (1) it is the simplest of all the methods, and (2) the principles that apply to it are applicable to all methods of probability sampling.

As described in the last chapter, however, simple random sampling is but one of a large number of probability sampling methods. Samples are often taken of human populations that involve several stages, many areas, different strata, clusters of sampling units, or some combination of these characteristics.

The complexities of determining the proper size of a several-stage sample of a human population involving areas, strata, and clusters is well beyond the scope of this book. In Appendix A a discussion is given of the determination of the sample size for stratified random samples for purposes of estimating the mean or a proportion for a population. Reference to more advanced books dealing with sampling will be necessary for a discussion of the determination of sample size for other types of non-*srs* random sampling methods.

Thus far we have dealt only with determining sample sizes for problems in which means or proportions were to be estimated. Although estimation is an important aspect of marketing research, hypothesis testing is also important. We now turn our attention to the traditional approach to determining sample size for problems involving hypothesis testing.

Determination of Sample Size in Problems Involving Hypothesis Testing

A few years ago a major oil company was considering initiating a program of selling low priced durable items (clock radios, typewriters, binoculars, and the like) by direct mail to its credit card holders. The mailing piece was to be sent out with the monthly statements. Those who decided to buy the item each month could do so by returning a card on which their name, address, and credit card number had already been entered.

The marketing research analyst assigned to investigate this potential new venture reported that an order rate of about 4 per cent of the credit card holders was necessary in order to break even. He stated that if the program were begun, merchandise purchase schedules dictated that it be run for three mailings.

He recommended that the company run a market test consisting of an item judged to be representative of those the company was considering for the program. He recommended further that the test be run using order rates of 3.5 and 5.0 per cent; if 3.5 per cent were the estimated average order rate, the idea should be dropped. If 5.0 per cent turned out to be the indicated rate, the company should proceed.

How large a simple random sample of credit card holders should be taken?

Specification Required and Calculation of Sample Size for Hypothesis Testing Problems Involving Proportions

In order to determine the sample size in a hypothesis testing problem involving proportions, the following specifications must be made:

1. *the hypotheses to be tested,*
2. *the level of sampling error permitted in the test of each hypothesis,* and
3. *the test statistic to be used.*

1. *The Hypotheses to be Tested.*   A *null* and an *alternate* hypothesis are involved in each hypothesis test. A *null hypothesis,* designated by H_0, *is one that, if accepted, will result in no opinion being formed and/or action being taken that is different from those currently held or being used.* The null hypothesis in the problem just described is

$$H_0: \text{order rate} = 3.5\%$$

If it is accepted, the program being considered will not be initiated.

The *alternate hypothesis,* designated by H_1, *is one that will lead to opinions being formed and/or actions being taken that are different from those currently held or being used.* The alternate hypothesis here is

$$H_1: \text{order rate} = 5.0\%$$

Although the null hypothesis is always explicitly stated, this is sometimes not true of the alternate hypothesis. In those instances when it is not stated it is understood that it consists of all values of the proportion not reserved by the null hypothesis. In this situation if the alternate hypothesis were not explicitly stated, it would be understood that it would be

$$H_1: \text{order rate} \neq 3.5\%$$

2. *The Level of Sampling Error Permitted in the Test of Each Hypothesis.*   Two types of error can be made in hypothesis testing problems. An error is made when the null hypothesis is true but the conclusion is reached that the alternate hypothesis should be accepted. This is known as a Type I error. The Type II error is made when the alternate hypothesis is true but the null hypothesis is accepted. The two possible states along with the two possible conclusions about them are shown in Table 6–3.

The probability of making a Type I error is designated as α (alpha) and of making a Type II error as β (beta). These errors are commonly specified at the .10, .05, or .01 levels, although there is nothing other than

Table 6-3 Conclusions and Errors

Conclusion	H_0 is true	H_1 is true
Accept H_0	Correct conclusion	Type II error
Accept H_1	Type I error	Correct conclusion

convention to recommend these values over others that could be chosen. In this problem we assume that $\alpha = .05$ and $\beta = .05$.

The specification of the hypotheses to be tested and the allowable error probabilities results in the testing situation shown in Figure 6-6. The α and β levels specified result in a rejection region for H_0 and H_1, respectively. The boundary of each is common and defines a *critical value* in the test. Any sample value higher than the critical value in our example means that H_1 will be accepted; any lower sample value will result in H_0 being accepted.

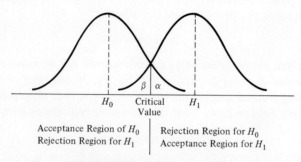

Figure 6-6 Test of H_0 and H_1.

3. *The Test Statistic to Be Used.* The test statistic to be used in this case is

$$Z = \frac{(p - P)}{\sqrt{P(1.00 - P)/n}}$$

The determination of the Z values associated with α and β, designated as Z_α and Z_β, respectively, is similar to that of the Z values associated with a confidence coefficient in an estimation problem. The distance to the critical value from the center of the sampling distribution is $Z_\alpha \sigma_{p_0}$ for the null hypothesis distribution and $Z_\beta \sigma_{p_1}$ for the alternate hypothesis distribution.

We can see from Figure 6-7 that this distance covers one half of the total area of the distribution minus α. If $\alpha = .05$, then .45 (45 per cent) of the

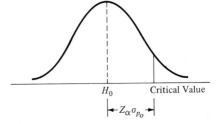

Figure 6–7 Distance of critical value
—null hypothesis distribution.

curve is covered by $Z_\alpha \sigma_{p_0}$. Looking in Appendix B we find that the corresponding Z value is $Z_\alpha = 1.64$.

We have now specified all that is required to determine the sample size for the problem being considered.

From the specifications that have been made we can determine the appropriate sample size using the formula

$$n = \frac{[Z_\alpha\sqrt{P_0(1.0 - P_0)} + Z_\beta\sqrt{P_1(1.0 - P_1)}]^2}{(P_1 - P_0)^2} \qquad (6\text{–}10)$$

Substituting the specifications made earlier, we obtain

$$n = \frac{[1.64\sqrt{.035(1.0 - .035)} + 1.64\sqrt{.05(1.0 - .05)}]^2}{(.05 - .035)^2}$$

$$n = \frac{[1.64\sqrt{.0338} + 1.64\sqrt{.0475}]^2}{(.015)^2}$$

$$n = 1932$$

Specifications Required and Calculation of Sample Size for Hypothesis Testing Problems Involving Means

For hypothesis testing problems involving means, the following specifications are required:

1. *the hypothesis to be tested,*
2. *the level of sampling error permitted in the test of each hypothesis,*
3. *the standard deviation of the population,* and
4. *the test statistic to be used.*

These specifications are the counterparts of those required for problems involving proportions.

The logic of the calculation of sample size in mean problems is the same as that for proportions. The equation determining the sample size in mean problems is

$$n = \frac{(Z_\alpha + Z_\beta)^2\sigma^2}{(M_1 - M_0)^2} \qquad (6\text{–}11)$$

Bayesian Method of Determining Sample Size

It can be argued that the traditional method of determining sample size is better adapted to basic research than to decisional research. A basic researcher involved in a study to estimate a population value, or to test a hypothesis, needs to take a sample of a size that will allow him to state that the sampling error is within some specified limit with a given level of confidence. As we have just seen, the traditional method of determining sample size meets that requirement.

In decisional research the size of the sample becomes an *economic problem* rather than one concerned primarily with the probable limits of sampling error. Here the emphasis shifts to taking the size of sample that will provide the best informational buy. The *value of the information* and the *cost of the sample* both come into consideration in determining the appropriate size of sample to take.

In Chapter 3 a general method for determining the expected monetary of imperfect information (EMVII) for a research project was presented. Intuitively, it can be seen that if there were two research designs for a project, one with a large sample and one with a small one but otherwise the designs were the same, the *EMVII* would be more for the design with the large sample than for the small one. The sampling error would be less for the larger sample and the information would be of more value for making the decision involved. It would also cost more to take the larger sample, however, and the added value of the information might or might not be worth the extra cost.

The difference between the expected value of the information (*EMVII*) and the estimated cost of taking the sample (*CS*) is called *the expected net gain from sampling (ENGS)*. That is

$$\begin{array}{ccc} \text{expected net gain} & = & \text{expected monetary} & - & \text{cost of} \\ \text{from sampling} & & \text{value of imperfect} & & \text{sampling} \\ & & \text{information} & & \end{array}$$

or

$$ENGS \quad = \quad EMVII \quad - \quad CS$$

The principle involved in the Bayesian method of determining sample size is to *take that size sample that gives the greatest expected net gain from sampling*. This involves determining the *EMVII* and estimating the cost of sampling for each of a large number of sample sizes and choosing the one with the largest *ENGS*.[6]

This has been done for the oil company direct-mail merchandising pro-

---

[6] For some problem formulations this can be done using the methods of the calculus to find a maximum value for *ENGS* rather than having to calculate *ENGS* for various sized samples.

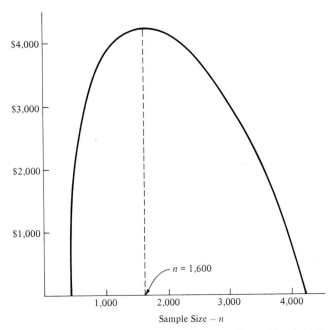

Figure 6–8 Expected net gain from sampling—Direct Mail Merchandising Program.

gram. The method of making the calculations involved is given in Appendix A. The results are shown in Figure 6–8. As shown in the figure, *ENGS* is highest with a sample size of about $n = 1,600$. This compares with the sample size of 1,932 arrived at by the traditional method in the preceding section (when α and β were specified to be .05).

The specifications necessary for this approach are *a conditional payoff table for the problem, the values of P_0 and P_1 (or M_0 and M_1), and the estimated costs of sampling.*

The calculations involved are not overly complex but they can become tedious. Fortunately, a computer program is available for calculating the optimal sample size using the Bayesian approach.[7]

Determining the Size of Nonprobability Samples

Thus far we have considered only probability samples. However, it is likely that more nonprobability than probability samples are taken each

---

[7] R. Schlaifer, *Computer Programs for Elementary Decision Analysis* (Cambridge, Mass.: Harvard University Press, 1971).

year. Despite their widespread usage, little is known about their characteristics and there is no available theoretical basis for determining sampling
error. Stephan and McCarty's empirical investigation of quota samples is
the only systematic effort of which we are aware that has been made to
determine the extent of nonprobability sample sampling errors encountered
in practice.[8]

Yet the fact that nonprobability sampling is widely used is itself evidence that the lack of an analytical or experimental basis for determining
sampling error has not been an insurmountable deterrent to its use. Both
descriptive and prescriptive questions need to be raised about sample size
determination in practice, namely, "How *are* the sizes of nonprobability
samples determined?" and "How *should* the sizes of nonprobability samples
be determined?"

The Determination of Nonprobability Sample Size: Some Observations on Practice

Observation suggests that most sample size decisions for nonprobability
samples are made on a resources available-sampling costs basis. That is,
if $10,000 is available for a project, the estimated fixed costs of sampling
and the costs other than sampling total $5,000, and sampling costs are
$50.00 per element, the sample size is very likely to be ($10,000 −
$5,000)/$50.00, $n = 100$.

This approach to setting sample size is open to criticism on at least two
counts. It does not take into account the difference in *value* of the information of the sample of 100 as opposed to that for other sample
sizes. In addition, there is (usually) no explicit consideration of the trade-
off between reducing nonsampling and sampling errors in the data.

The Determination of Nonprobability Sample Size: Some Prescriptions

The following prescriptions are based primarily upon a Bayesian approach to sample size determination. After having read Chapter 3 and the
section on Bayesian sampling, it will not be surprising to learn that the
suggestions center around the concept of taking a sample size that will
provide the greatest difference between the value of the sample information
and its cost.

[8] F. Stephan and P. J. McCarthy, *Sampling Opinions—An Analysis of Survey
Procedures* (New York: John Wiley & Sons, Inc., 1950), Chap. 10.

Five steps need to be taken in determining the sample size of a non-probability sample. They are

1. *Estimate the standard error for various sizes of samples.*
2. *Estimate the selection bias.*
3. *Estimate the expected monetary value of information for various sizes of samples.*
4. *Estimate the cost of taking various sizes of samples.*
5. *Determine the difference in expected value and estimated cost for each size sample.*

1. Estimate the Standard Error for Various Sizes of Samples

The sources of variation that are relevant to the estimate of standard error are the *population standard deviation* and variations caused by *sampling, measurement,* and *selection* errors.

By making allowance in the sampling plan for calculation of a standard deviation of the first portion of the sample, a direct estimate can be obtained of the composite effects of all of these sources of variation. This is the simplest and best method of estimating the variable errors in a sample and should be used whenever possible. This sample standard deviation can be used as an estimate of the population standard deviation which in turn is used to determine the final sample size.

Mayer[9] and Brown[10] propose a way of arriving at an estimate of variation that can be used when it is not possible to obtain a standard deviation from the first portion of the sample. They recommend making separate estimates of each constituent source of variation and combining them.

2. Estimate The Selection Bias

A *selection bias* exists whenever interviewers or research supervisors or anyone else selects sample elements by nonprobability means. There is a tendency for interviewers to select people with their own socioeconomic background who are: (a) well groomed, (b) cheerful in appearance, and (c) easily and quickly reached.

Estimation of bias is a difficult and uncertain task. Yet it must be done if nonprobability samples are used. To ignore selection bias is, in effect, to estimate it as being insignificant. A discussion of selection bias estimation is given in Chapter 11.

[9] C. S. Mayer, "Assessing the Accuracy of Marketing Research," *Journal of Marketing Research,* **7** (August 1970), 285–291.
[10] R. V. Brown, *Research and the Credibility of Estimates* (Cambridge, Mass.: Harvard University Press, 1969).

3. Estimate the Expected Value of Information for Various Sizes of Samples

As we saw in Chapter 3, the value of information is a function of both the expected cost of errors and the likelihood of making them. The higher the sampling and nonsampling errors are the less the information is worth.

The procedure for estimating the expected value of information from sampling is described in Appendix A.

4. Estimate the Cost of Taking Various Sizes of Samples

As in most cost incurring activities, there are fixed and variable costs associating with sampling. The devising of the sampling plan, the preparation of the measurement instrument, and the programming of the computer to run analyses are examples of fixed cost. The addition of each element in the sample to be taken adds variable costs, both for obtaining the measurement and for analyzing the data.

5. Determine the Difference in Expected Value and Estimated Cost for Various Sizes of Samples

This difference is the expected net gain from sampling (*ENGS*). That sample size should be chosen that has the largest *ENGS*. A discussion of *ENGS* determination (with a probability rather than a nonprobability sample) was given in the Bayesian section of the chapter and elaborated upon in Appendix A.

Although these prescriptions are general guidelines, they do represent a start toward a rational approach to the determination of sample size in nonprobability samples. This is a critical area since nonprobability samples are widely used in marketing research.

Summary

The *traditional,* the *Bayesian,* and the *nonprobability* methods of determining sample size were discussed in this chapter.

The *traditional* method involves the concept of a sampling distribution and results in a randomly selected sample. A *sampling distribution* is a relative frequency distribution of a sample statistic of all possible samples of size *n* taken from a population of size *N*.

Sample sizes for various kinds of random samples can be determined based on the sampling distribution and the specifications necessary for that kind of sample. For a simple random sample for a problem involving the estimation of a population mean, the specifications required are the *error that can be allowed* $(\bar{x} - M)$, the *confidence coefficient,* and an *estimate of the population standard deviation* (σ).

The *Bayesian method* of sample size determination involves finding that sample size that will give the greatest *expected net gain of sampling* (*ENGS*). This *ENGS* for a given sample size is determined by calculating the expected value of imperfect information (*EMVII*) and subtracting the cost of sampling (*CS*) for a sample of that size. This process is repeated for enough samples of varying sizes to find the sample size that gives the highest *ENGS.*

A sizable proportion of the samples taken in decisional research are *nonprobability* samples. A reasonable approach to the determination of the sample would seem to be (1) estimate the standard error for various sizes of samples, (2) estimate the biases, (3) estimate the expected value of information for various sizes of samples, (4) estimate the cost of taking various sizes of samples, and (5) determine the difference in expected value and estimated cost for various sized samples (*ENGS*). That sample size should be chosen that has the largest *ENGS.*

Questions and Problems

6.1. A simple random sample is to be taken from a population of 50,000 sales invoices to estimate the mean amount per invoice. Suppose that the population mean is actually $8,150 and the standard deviation of the population is $4,000. The allowable error is set at $200 and the confidence coefficient at 95 per cent.
   (a) What size sample is required? (You may ignore the finite population correction factor.)
   (b) Suppose the sample mean turns out to be $8,396. What is the interval estimate?

6.2. A survey is being designed to obtain information about television viewing habits. In addition to writing and pretesting the questionnaire, it is necessary to plan the type and size of sample. The decision is made to use a simple random sample. It is also decided that the two most important aspects of the survey are the percentage of households owning television sets and the average viewing time per week. (The basic time interval of one week is chosen because it eliminates day-to-day variation.) It is desired to estimate with a confidence level of 95 per cent the percentage of television ownership within plus or minus 3 per cent and the mean viewing time per week within plus or minus 1 hour. A previous survey, done on a small scale, indicates that the percentage of households owning television sets is about 90 per cent and the mean number of hours of viewing time per week is about 20, with a standard deviation of 3 hours.
   (a) How large a sample should be taken when considering the percentage of households owning television sets and ignoring mean viewing time?
   (b) How large a sample should be taken when considering mean viewing time and ignoring percentage of households owning television sets?
   (c) Which sample size should be chosen? Explain.

(d) Assume that a sample of the size indicated in (c) is taken and the following sample values obtained:

percentage of households owning television sets = 92.6 per cent
mean viewing time per household per week = 19.1 hours
standard deviation of viewing time = 3.4 hours

i. What is the interval estimate of percentage of households owning television sets?

ii. What is the interval estimate of mean viewing time?

6.3. The Catalonian Cutlery Company decides to do a study of sales of stainless steel razor blades by type of outlet. It is decided that a stratified proportional random sample of 1,000 retail stores will be taken. Preliminary study indicates that three different types of retail stores should be sampled: drugstores, grocery stores, and "all other." The population of each of these types of stores is as follows:

Drugstores	100,000
Grocery stores	500,000
All other	1,400,000
Total	2,000,000

(a) How many of each type of store should be included in the sample?

(b) Suppose the following estimates had been made by Catalonian Cutlery before the sample in problem 6.3 was taken. (All values shown are in gross per week.) If a non-proportional stratified random sample were taken, how many of each type of store should be included? (See Appendix A for description of solution method and formula.)

	Mean Sales	Standard Deviation
Drugstores	5.0	2.0
Grocery stores	4.0	1.0
All other	1.0	.2

6.4. Compumap, Inc., has developed a computerized method of converting street addresses to geographic coordinates and displaying them on maps. The bulk of the potential market for such a device is believed to lie in four applications: electrical utilities, telephone companies, city and county planning departments, and police departments.

The company is planning on taking a sample of these potential customers to determine the number of planned acquisitions of this type of equipment within the next year. It has compiled lists of the companies/departments and has made estimates of the variance of the proportion of planned acquisitions for each type of application. These data are as follows:

	Number of Potential Customers	Estimated Proportion of Planned Acquisitions Within Next Year
Electrical Utilities	705	.10
Telephone Companies	35	.15
City and County Planning	2,125	.05
Police Departments	3,135	.05

It plans to take a stratified, nonproportional sample that will yield an interval estimate of the proportion of customers planning to acquire units within the next year with a confidence coefficient of 95.4 per cent.

(a) What is the overall size of sample that should be taken?

(b) What size sample should be taken in each of the strata?

6.5. The office of development of a university is considering a special telephone solicitation follow-up of its annual mail campaign for contributions from alumni. Each alumnus who did not respond to the mail campaigns and who could be reached by telephone would be called and asked to contribute to this year's Alumni Fund. An additional packet would be mailed if the first one had been misplaced or discarded.

The average gift per contributor from the mail solicitations in the past had been almost exactly $9.00. Since the calls were to be placed by volunteers, no costs were involved other than the costs of the telephone call and any additional packets sent out. It was estimated that these costs would average $.45 per alumnus. Assuming that the contributions resulting from the telephone calls were of the same average amount as those from the mail solicitation, the break-even contribution response rate from the telephone calls was then $.45/$9.00 = .05.

The director of development did not want to start the campaign if the prospects were not reasonably good that contributions would exceed costs. He estimated that if the campaign did not break even, the expected response rate would be .03 and the loss would be $3,000. He assessed the probability of this happening at .4. He believed that, if the telephone campaign were a success, the expected response rate would be .08 with a "profit" of $13,500. He thought there was a probability of .6 that this would be the result.

Before making a final decision about calling all of the alumni, he decided to take a sample. He estimated there would be about 50,000 alumni who had not responded to the mail solicitation.

(a) Assuming a fixed size simple random sample was to be taken, what size should it have been?

(b) Would some other kind of sample have been preferable to that in (a)? Explain.

Selected Bibliography

COCHRAN, WILLIAM G. *Sampling Techniques,* 2nd ed. New York: John Wiley & Sons, Inc., 1963. A book that is written at a somewhat more advanced theoretical level than Kish (*infra.*) but has less material dealing with application.

KISH, LESLIE. *Survey Sampling.* New York: John Wiley & Sons, Inc., 1965. A carefully written book that presupposes a sound understanding of elementary sampling theory. Much of the extensive field experience of the author is reflected in the book.

Sampling Lectures: Supplemental Courses for Case Studies in Surveys and Lectures, Bureau of the Census, U.S. Department of Commerce, 1968. A simply written, authoritative manual of elementary sampling theory as applied to the problems of sampling human populations. Describes simple random, stratified random, and cluster sampling and the practical problems encountered in taking such samples. There is no discussion of the Bayesian approach to estimating sample size.

SCHLAIFER, ROBERT. *Analysis of Decisions Under Uncertainty.* New York: McGraw-Hill, Inc., 1969, chap. 14. Robert Schlaifer has done more than anyone else to develop and apply Bayesian statistics to business problems. Chapter 14 in this book deals wih the determination of optimal sample size using the Bayesian approach.

TULL, DONALD S. and GERALD S. ALBAUM. *Survey Research: A Decisional Approach.* New York: Intext Educational Publishers, 1973, chap. 4. Chapter 4 is concerned with nonsampling errors and strategies for dealing with them.

Case 6–1

Brand Usage Survey

The following paragraphs were contained in the methodology section of a recently completed brand usage survey.

The current study examines consumer purchases and/or usage. Consumers were asked to indicate the *brands* that they purchased or used during the two weeks prior to receiving the mailed questionnaire.

Statistical calculation resulted in the decision that a return of 500 responses would give a validity of minimum acceptability. Consequently, the decision was made to send out 1,500 questionnaires in the hope of receiving an acceptable return. Actually, the original mailing and follow-up resulted in a total return of 791 questionnaires of which 739 were usable. The unused questionnaires were not tabulated since they were either incomplete, incorrectly filled out, or received after the tabulation deadline.

By using accepted statistical techniques, the researcher estimates that the maximum possible error on reported results is just over three per cent (3%). To be more precise, there is a ninety-five per cent (95%) probability that each observation is within a maximum of 3.6 percentage points of the true value.

The 1,500 name sample was drawn in the following manner. An allocation was given to individual counties within the area according to *Sales Management Magazine* statistics on households per county. After this stratification, names were drawn from city directories and telephone books. Selection of specific names was made by choosing the first name on the first column of each *"nth"* page. The value of *"n"* was determined by dividing the number of names to be drawn into the number of pages in the directory or directories that covered a county. Only individuals were chosen. When the first name that appeared on a page was "commercial," the first "individual" appearing thereafter was chosen.

A mailing was sent to 1,500 persons on March 1. After one week, those persons who had not responded were sent a follow-up questionnaire stamped "Second Request, PLEASE." Identification for both the first and second mailer was indicated by numbering the "No Postage Necessary" Business Reply Envelope. The tabulation included all questionnaires received through March 25.

1. What type of sampling process was used?

2. What types of errors are likely to be present because of the sampling plan?

3. Is this the proper approach to sample size determination?

4. How did they arrive at the 95 per cent confidence interval being equal to the sample percentage plus or minus 3.6 percentage points?

Case 6–2
Marketing of Dormitory Housing

From the mid-1960s into the early 1970s, the occupancy rate of university dormitory housing at the University of Oregon had been declining. As rules requiring students to live in university housing were relaxed, the university dorms found themselves unable to compete with private housing alternatives. To market university dorms effectively the university believed that it needed a better understanding of the factors that influenced the students' selection of a place to live. To this end, a private consulting firm was hired to investigate the following issues.

—Initial motivations for selection of dormitory housing.
—The relative role that parents play in determining housing selection.
—Reasons for defection from the dormitories.
—Satisfaction with present housing, both on and off campus.
—Evaluation of dormitory housing on key acceptance factors, such as food, furnishings, facilities, freedom, privacy, and social life.
—Analysis of potential effect of improvements on student acceptance of dormitory housing.

The consulting firm identified six separate population groups that they believed should be subjected to separate sampling and analysis. The groups and the final sample size are presented as follows.

Population Group	Number of Interviews
Dormitory Occupants	251
Parents of Dorm Occupants	100
Dormitory "Dropouts" of Last Year	153
Parents of Dorm "Drop-Outs"	100
"Never" Dorm Occupants	245
Parents of "Never" Occupants	100
Total	949

All the samples were randomly selected from computer files except for the "last year dropouts." A census was taken of all available dropout students who moved from dormitory housing in the past year.

The following statements concerning sampling error were made in the final report:

All sample surveys are subject to ranges of variability, or the chance that results might vary, within known limits, from those that a complete enumeration would produce.

The finite universe formula was used to compute variability ranges for dormitory occupants, whereas the normal standard error formula was used for other sample groups.

The sampling variability ranges for all of the sample groups except "dropouts" are presented as follows. The ranges are not presented for dormitory "dropouts," since this group represents a census rather than a sample.

	Sampling Variability		
Percentage in Report:	Dorm Occupants	"Never" Occupants	Parents
10% or 90%	3.6%	3.8%	6.0%
20% or 80%	4.8	5.0	8.0
30% or 70%	5.4	5.8	9.2
40% or 60%	5.8	6.2	9.8
50%	5.9	6.4	10.0

Example: Seventy per cent of dorm occupants rated the cleanliness of their housing as either "excellent" or "good." Chances are 19 out of 20 that this figure (70%) is within 5.4 per cent, plus or minus, of the result that would accrue from interviewing every dormitory occupant at the University of Oregon.

Variability ranges for subgroup breakdowns by sex, class, and residential hall are somewhat wider, because of reduced sample sizes.

1. What was the management problem facing the university?

2. Was this management problem properly restated as a research problem?

3. Were the "populations" identified by the consultants the proper ones?

4. Were any of the sample sizes too large? too small?

5. Comment on the consultant's treatment of sampling variability.

field work & data tabulation

Case 6–3

Sebring Tire Company Market Test Design

The Sebring Tire Company had been one of the leaders in developing and marketing tires with high quality and new improved features since the company was started in 1915. Sebring had also been one of the first major tire manufacturers to open its own retail stores and to franchise independent dealers to sell Sebring brand tires, batteries, and a line of automobile accessories.

With this tradition of progressive management, executives of the company had mixed reactions to the development of SNO-CHARGERS (see Case 3–2 for the necessary background). They believed that the new product might be successful in getting a substantial share of the tire chains-snow tire market if it were introduced, but were afraid it might be *too* successful. Every set of SNO-CHARGERS sold was a potential substitute for a set of Sebring Snow Tires. Since the average gross margin of new snow tires at current prices was four times as much as that estimated for SNO-CHARGERS (approximately $8 per new snow tire versus an estimated $2 per SNO-CHARGER unit), their concern was easy to understand. In order for the company to break even, *three* SNO-CHARGER units would have to be sold that were not bought as substitutes for Sebring snow tires for every *one* SNO-CHARGER unit that was bought as a substitute. Some of the older executives still remembered what had happened to new tire sales when retreaded tires came on the market and did not want to duplicate that situation, even on a small scale.

Given this concern, and the limited information the company had on both the potential sales of SNO-CHARGERS and the likely substitution rate for Sebring Snow Tires, the management tentatively decided to go ahead with a market test of SNO-CHARGERS during the coming winter. The marketing research manager was asked to prepare an overall plan for the market test and to present it at a meeting of the executive vice-president and vice presidents of marketing, production, and finance. The meeting was to be held in two weeks.

1. What data should be obtained from the market test?

2. Prepare a sampling plan for the market test including the recommended number of Sebring owned stores and/or franchised dealer outlets that should participate in the test.

Measurement and Research: Concepts of Measurement

Measurement is a familiar and common activity for all of us. College entrance examinations represent an attempt to measure an individual's potential to successfully complete college. Aptitude tests are used in an attempt to measure an individual's interest and skill areas. Automobile speedometers measure the velocity of the automobile. Cooking recipes call for measures of the quantity of the various ingredients. Gasoline pumps are used to measure the quantity of the gasoline delivered to the car. Watches and calendars are used to measure the passage of time. Even the numbers on football players' jerseys represent a form of measurement (they indicate whether the player is a lineman, an end, or a member of the backfield).

Measurement is the process of assigning numbers to represent some characteristic of objects, persons, states, or events. In this chapter a discussion of the principles and problems involved in measurement as they apply to decision-oriented marketing research is presented. In the first section we attempt to clarify exactly what measurement is. This is followed by a discussion on the distinction between the characteristic being measured and the actual measurement operations.

As the list of common measurements at the beginning of this section indicated, there are several types of measurement. One approach to classifying the various type scales used in measurement—*nominal, ordinal, interval,* and *ratio* scales—is described in the second section of this chapter.

As we all know from experience, measurements are often not correct: the gasoline guage shows a quarter of a tank when we run out of gas or the 10 o'clock news comes on at 9:45 according to our clock. The third major section deals with an analysis of the various components of a measurement that may affect its final value. Included in this section are discussions of validity and reliability. The chapter concludes with a discussion of the need for predictive capability and the costs of obtaining it.

Concept of Measurement

Measurement Defined

Measurement may be defined as *the assignment of numbers to characteristics of objects, persons, states, or events according to rules.* What is measured is not the object, person, state, or event itself but some characteristic of it. When objects are counted, for example, we do not measure the object itself but only its characteristic of being present. We never measure a person, only his age, height, weight, or some other characteristic. A study to determine whether a higher percentage of males or females purchase a given product, for example, measures the characteristics *male-female* and *purchaser-nonpurchaser* attributes of the persons sampled. It is important to remember that we are always measuring some characteristic of the object or event and *not* the object or event itself.

The term *number* in the definition of measurement does not correspond to the usual meaning given this term by the nonresearcher. It does not necessarily mean numbers that can be meaningfully added, subtracted, divided, or multiplied. Instead, it means that numbers are used as symbols to represent certain characteristics of the object. The nature of the meaning of the numbers—symbols—depends upon the nature of the characteristics they are to represent and how they are to represent them. This issue is developed in some depth in the section on scales of measurement.

The most critical aspect of measurement is the creation of the rules that specify how the numbers are to be assigned to the characteristics to be measured. Once a measurement rule has been created and agreed upon, the characteristics of events, persons, states, or objects are described in terms of this rule. Thus the statement: "Company A increased its market share from 12 per cent to 15 per cent during the past year" has a meaning that is common among those who know the measurement rule that is being applied. However, those not aware of the rule will not always be able to understand what has been measured.

This problem arises because the rules that specify *how* to assign the numbers to the characteristics to be measured are arbitrary. Numbers are assigned based on created or invented rules, not as a result of some divine revelation or undeniable natural law. Consider the accounting problem involved in measuring sales. When is an item considered sold? Is it when an order is received, when the item is shipped, when the customer is billed, when the customer pays, or is it after the period for return expires? Are sales to be measured in units or in dollars? Are dollar sales to be in terms of amount of current dollars or is the dollar value to be deflated to some base year? Each of these questions implies a *different measurement rule,* and unless one knows which rule is being applied, a monthly sales figure is not completely understandable.

Measurement and Reality

If measurement is a procedure performed to a set of arbitrary rules, how do we evaluate measurements? Can the quality of a measurement be measured? The answer to the latter question is a qualified "yes." Two aspects of the quality of a measurement can be evaluated.

First, *we can evaluate the extent to which the measurement rule has been followed.* Errors may be made from either *misunderstanding* or *misapplication* of the rule. For example, a researcher may decide on a measurement rule and instruct his assistants to count the total number of people who walk past a point-of-purchase display and the number of people who "examine" the item. An assistant who counts only those who physically handle the item as "examiners" has applied one interpretation of the rule. A second assistant who counts those who either look at or pick up the item as "examiners," applies another interpretation of the rule. A third assistant who fails to count a number of examiners because of distractions has made errors in applying the rule. The count of "examiners" of either the first or second assistant is in error because of misunderstanding the rule. The count of the third assistant is in error because of misapplication of the rule.

Second, we can evaluate how closely the rule corresponds to some aspect of "reality." The extent of the correspondence required depends on the purpose of the research. Consider the example shown in Table 7–1.

There is a perfect correspondence between the characteristic relative size or rank as measured and as it actually exists. If the researcher is interested only in rank order, perhaps to decide in which market to concentrate marketing efforts, there is satisfactory correspondence. This is true despite the errors in measuring the exact size of market potential that served as the basis for deriving the ranks.

Table 7-1   Measurement and Reality

	Actual		Measured	
Area	Rank	Size	Rank	Size
A	1	24,800,000	1	29,600,000
B	2	16,500,000	2	25,300,000
C	3	15,200,000	3	14,900,000
D	4	12,100,000	4	6,300,000
E	5	1,700,000	5	4,900,000

If the researcher is concerned with preparing a sales forecast based on the size of market potential, however, the correspondence to reality is probably insufficient for all except Area C. Thus, it is possible to have a "good" measurement when one level of measurement is considered and a "bad" measurement when another level is considered. The rule of measurement in this case was adequate to determine rank but inadequate to determine absolute level. It is important that "good" measurements occur on those characteristics that will influence the decision. This issue is explored more fully in the final section of this chapter.

Measurement and Concepts

A *concept* is simply an invented name for a property of an object, person, state, or event. The term *construct* and *concept* are sometimes used interchangeably. We use concepts such as *sales, market share, attitude,* and *brand loyalty* to signify abstractions based on observations of numerous particular happenings. Concepts aid in thinking by subsuming a number of events under one heading.[1] Thus, the concept *car* refers to the generalization of the characteristics that all cars have in common. The concept *car* is closely related to a physical reality.

Many concepts utilized in marketing research do not have such easily

[1] C. Selltiz, et al., *Research Methods in Social Relations,* rev. ed. (New York: Holt Rinehart and Winston, Inc., 1959), 41.

observed physical referents. It is impossible to point to a physical example of an *attitude, product image,* or *social class.* Therefore, particular attention must be devoted to precisely defining exactly what is meant by a given concept. Two definitional approaches are necessary to adequately define a concept: (1) *conceptual definition* and (2) *operational definition.*

Conceptual Definitions

A *conceptual definition* defines a concept in terms of other concepts. It states the central idea or essence of the concept. Very often it is the equivalent of a definition found in a dictionary. A good conceptual definition clearly delineates the major characteristics of the concept and allows one to distinguish the concept from similar but different concepts. Consider *brand loyalty* as a concept. How do you define it? Under your definition, is the person loyal to a brand who consistently buys it because it is the only brand of the product that is available at the stores at which he shops? Is he brand loyal in the same sense as the person who consistently selects the same brand from among the many carried at his store? An adequate conceptual definition of brand loyalty should distinguish that concept from some other concept such as "repeat purchasing behavior." A lack of such a conceptual definition has hindered research into brand loyalty.[2]

Operational Definitions

Once a conceptual definition has been established, an *operational definition* must be designed that will reflect accurately the major characteristics of the conceptual definition. An operational definition describes the activities the researcher must complete in order to assign a value to the concept under consideration in a given instance. Concepts are abstractions; as such they are not observable. Operational definitions translate the concept into one or more observable events. Thus, a conceptual definition should precede and guide the development of the operational definition.

Consider the conceptual definition of brand loyalty offered by Engel, et al.: "The preferential attitudinal and behavioral response toward one or more brands in a product category expressed over a period of time by a consumer (or buyer)."[3] Brand loyalty defined in this way can be measured in a number of different ways. However, it is sufficiently precise to rule out many commonly used operational definitions of brand loyalty. For example, an operational definition involving purchase sequence in which brand

---

[2] For an excellent discussion of this particular problem see J. Jacoby and D. Kyner, "Brand Loyalty vs. Repeat Purchasing Behavior," *Journal of Marketing Research,* **X** (February 1973), 1–9.

[3] J. Engel, et al., *Consumer Behavior* 2nd ed. (New York: Holt, Rinehart and Winston, Inc., 1973), 552.

loyalty is defined as X consecutive purchases (usually 3 or 4) of one brand is often used. This definition is not adequate because it ignores the attitudinal component specified in the conceptual definition.

Table 7–2 shows a conceptual definition of *social class* and a number of operational definitions of this concept found in the marketing literature. Which of these operational definitions is best? Traditional theory would suggest that we should utilize the approach that most closely matches the conceptual definition. This idea is discussed further in the later subsection on validity. For decisional research, we must consider not only the accuracy of the operational definition but also the cost of each method in relation to objectives of the research project. This approach is treated with more detail in the final section of this chapter.

Table 7–2   Conceptual and Operational Definitions of Social Class

---

Conceptual definition: Social classes are relatively permanent and homogeneous divisions in a society into which individuals or families sharing similar values, lifestyles, interests, and behavior can be categorized.

Operational definitions:
1. Reputational: Individuals are assigned to social classes based on how people who know them rank them.
2. Sociometric: Individuals are placed into social classes based on whom they associate with.
3. Subjective: Individuals are placed into social classes based on their self-ranking.
4. Objective: Individuals are placed in a social class based on their possession of some objective characteristic or combination of characteristics such as occupation, education, and income.

As Table 7–2 indicates, it is possible, and in fact common, to have several operational definitions for the same concept. This fact requires us to specify clearly the operational definitions we are utilizing. Such terms as *sales, profit, social class,* and *market share* should always be accompanied by precise operational definitions when used in a research context.

Even an obvious concept such as the sex of an individual can vary according to the operational definition. Three general categories of operational definitions of sex can be identified: psychological, anatomical, and genetic. Using psychological traits as a definition of sex type will result in classifying some individuals differently from the more traditional anatomical approach. An example of an operational definition of sex determined by characteristics of genes rather than by anatomy is provided by Runkel and McGrath:

We find even more interesting the 1967 decision by officials of the Olympic games that sex of apparently female athletes shall be corroborated no longer by inspection of genitalia but by analysis of chromosomes. At least one ostensible woman was found to have the chromosomes of a male, and the Olympic officials preferred the latter operational definition of sex for the purposes of enforcing the Olympic rules.[4]

Scales of Measurement

In the preceding section, we found that numbers were assigned to characteristics of objects or events in such a way as to reflect some aspect of reality. The goal then is to assign numbers so that the properties of the numbers are paralleled by the properties of the objects or events that we are measuring. This implies that we have different kinds of numbers. A moment's reflection will indicate that this is indeed the case. In a large university or class you may be identified by your university ID card number or your seat number. A number used in this manner is very different from the number that represents your score on the final exam. And the score on the final examination is different in nature from your final rank in the class.

It is common to distinguish four different types of numbers or scales of measurement *nominal, ordinal, interval,* and *ratio.* The characteristics of these four types of scales are summarized in Table 7–3 and discussed in the following paragraphs. The rules for assigning numbers constitute the essential criteria for defining each scale. As we move from nominal to ratio scales, we must meet increasingly restrictive rules. As the rules become more restrictive the kinds of arithmetic operations for which the numbers can be used are increased. The following discussion is nontechnical and somewhat simplified. More complex treatments may be found in Guilford[5] and Siegel.[6]

Nominal Measurements

Nominal scales are comprised of numbers used primarily to categorize objects or events. Perhaps the most common example is when we assign a male the number 1 and a female the number 0. Numbers used in this man-

[4] P. Runkel and J. McGrath, *Research on Human Behavior* (New York: Holt, Rinehart and Winston, Inc., 1972), 151.

[5] J. P. Guilford, *Psychometric Methods,* 2nd ed. (New York: McGraw-Hill Book Company, Inc., 1954).

[6] S. Siegel, *Nonparametric Statistics* (New York: McGraw-Hill Book Company, Inc., 1956).

Table 7–3   Types of Measurement Scales

Scale	Basic Empirical Operations	Typical Usage	Typical Statistics*	
			Descriptive	Inferential
Nominal	Determination of equality	Classification: Male–Female, Purchaser–Nonpurchaser, Social Class	Percentages Mode	Chi-square Binomial test
Ordinal	Determination of greater or less	Rankings: Preference data, market position, attitude measures, many psychological measures	Median	Mann-Whitney U, Friedman two-way ANOVA, Rank-Order correlation
Interval	Determination of equality of intervals	Index numbers, attitude measures, level of knowledge about brands	Mean, Range, Standard Deviation	Product-moment Correlation, T-tests, Factor analysis, ANOVA
Ratio	Determination of equality of ratios	Sales, units produced, number of customers, costs, age		Coefficient of variation

* All statistics applicable to a given scale are also applicable to any scale below it in the table. For example, all the statistics applicable to an ordinal scale are also applicable to interval and ratio scales.
Source: Adapted from S. S. Stevens, "On the Theory of Scales of Measurement," *Science*, **103** (June 7, 1946), 677–680.

ner differ significantly from those used in more conventional ways. We could have just as easily assigned the 0 to the males and the 1 to the females or we could have used the symbols *A* and *B* or the terms male and female. In fact, in the final research report, terms are generally substituted for nominal numbers.

A nominally scaled number serves only as a label for a class or category. The objects in each class are viewed as equivalent with respect to the characteristic represented by the nominal number. In the example given, all those placed in category 1 would be regarded as equivalent in terms of "maleness;" those in category 0 would be equivalent in "femaleness." The number 1 *does not* imply a superior position to the number 0. The only rules involved are that (1) all members of a class (every object that has a certain characteristic) have the same number and (2) no two classes have the same number.

Although nominal scales are used for the "lowest" form of measurement in that they require the fewest restrictive rules, they are widely used in marketing research. Such nominal classifications as sex, geographic location, social class (sometimes treated as ordinal measurement), purchaser–nonpurchaser, saw the commercial–did not see the commercial, and so on are used in many applied research reports. In addition, more advanced forms of measurement, such as age, income, and educational categories, are often treated as nominal data.

An example of the use of nominal measurement is the case of a manager of a restaurant located in a shopping center who wants to determine whether his noon customers select his establishment primarily because of its location or primarily because of its unique menu. He randomly selects and questions 100 customers and finds that 70 state that they eat there because of the location and 30 because of the menu. This represents a simple analysis using nominal data. The manager has formed a two-category scale, counted the number of cases in each category, and identified the modal category.

If our restaurant manager had also noted the sex of each respondent, he could array his data as shown in Table 7–4. Without doing a formal statistical analysis, it can be seen that females prefer the restaurant because of the menu and males because of the location.

Table 7–4 Restaurant Selection Criteria by Sex

| *Primary* | *Sex Classification* | | |
Reason	*Male*	*Female*	*Total*
Location	55	15	70
Menu	5	25	30
Total	60	40	100

Any arithmetic operations performed on nominally scaled data can only be carried out on the *count* in each category. Numbers assigned to represent the categories (1 for male, 0 for female, for example) cannot meaningfully be added, subtracted, multiplied, or divided.

A *mean* or a *median* cannot be calculated for nominal data. A *mode* is the only average that can be used. In the example given, *location* was the modal reason for choosing the restaurant among males and the menu was the modal reason among females. The *percentages* of items falling within each category can also be determined.

A number of inferential statistical techniques can be used on nominally scaled data. These are discussed in Chapter 14.

Ordinal Measurements

Ordinal scales represent numbers used primarily to rank items. This is essentially an advanced form of categorization. Items can be classified not only as to whether they share some characteristic with another item but also whether they have more or less of this characteristic than some other object. However, ordinally scaled numbers do not provide information on *how much* more or less of the characteristic various items possess. For an example, refer to the "actual" column of Table 7–1. Here five markets have been ranked in terms of market potential. The difference in rank between markets A and B is 1 as it is between markets B and C. However, the difference in scales between A and B is approximately $8 million, whereas the difference between B and C is approximately $1 million. This information is not conveyed with an ordinal scale.

A significant amount of marketing research, particularly consumer-oriented research, relies on ordinal measures. The most common usage of ordinal scales is in obtaining preference measurements. For example, a consumer or a sample of experts may be asked to rank its preferences for several brands, flavors, or package designs. Attitude measures are also often ordinal in nature. The following attitudinal questions will produce ordinal data, for example:

How would you rate the selection of goods offered for sale in Mission Hills as compared to the selections offered for sale in Denver or Boulder?

( ) Good   ( ) Average   ( ) Poor

Read the list of brands of cake mix on the card I just gave you. Tell me which brand you think has the highest quality. . . . Now tell me the one you think is next highest in quality. . . .
Continue until all brands are named or until the respondent says she does not know the remaining brands. Record DK if she does not know the brand.
(1) ——————————— (3) ——————————— (5) ———————————
(2) ——————————— (4) ———————————

Suppose that *Betty Crocker* is one of the brands of cake mix. Further suppose that the quality ratings it receives as compared with four other brands from a sample of 500 housewives are as follows:

Quality Rating	Number of Respondents Giving Rating
1	100
2	200
3	100
4	50
5	50

What kind of descriptive statistics may be used on these data?

As indicated in Table 7–4, a *mode* or a *median* may be used, but not a *mean*. The modal quality rating is "2," and the median rating is "2." It is possible to calculate a mean (its value is 2.1) but, unless one assumes that the data are interval rather than ordinal in nature, it is meaningless (no pun intended). This is because the differences between ordinal scaled values are not necessarily the same. The *percentages* of the total appearing in each rank may be calculated and are meaningful.

The inferential statistical techniques that can be applied to ordinally scaled data are discussed in Chapter 14. The branch of statistics that deals with ordinal measurements is called nonparametric statistics. Siegel[7] provides an excellent treatment of nonparametric statistics.

Interval Measurements

Interval scales represent numbers used to rank items such that numerically equal distances on the scale represent equal distances in the property being measured. However, the location of the zero point is not fixed. Both the zero point and the unit of measurement are arbitrary. The most common examples of interval scales are the temperature scales, both centigrade and Fahrenheit. The same natural phenomenon, the freezing point of water, is assigned a different value on each scale, 0 on centigrade and 32 on Fahrenheit. Thus, the 0 position is obviously arbitrary. The difference in the volume of mercury is the same between 20 and 30 degrees centigrade and 40 and 50 degrees centigrade. Thus, the measure of the underlying phenomenon is made in units as nearly equal as the measuring instrument permits. A value on either scale can be converted to the other by using the formula: $F = 32 + 9/5C$.

The most common form of interval measurement in marketing is index numbers. Index numbers require an arbitrary zero point and equal intervals between scale values. Other common types of data treated as interval measurements are attitudinal and personality measures. However, data of this type are usually ordinal if a strict interpretation of measurement rules is applied. A Likert scale (described in Chapter 10), for example, requires the respondent to state his degree of agreement or disagreement with a statement by selecting a response from a list such as the one presented:

1. Agree very strongly
2. Agree fairly strongly
3. Agree
4. Undecided

[7] Ibid.

5. Disagree
6. Disagree fairly strongly
7. Disagree very strongly

It is doubtful if the interval between each of these items is exactly equal. However, most researchers treat the data from such scales as if they were interval. The results of most standard statistical techniques are not affected greatly by small deviations from the interval requirement, and if the deviations are in fact small, no serious damage is done. However, this does not excuse the researcher from examining closely the nature of the measurement instrument and the responses he obtains to assure himself that he does indeed have measurements that closely approach being interval.

Virtually the entire range of statistical analysis can be applied to interval scales. Such descriptive measures as the *mean, median, mode, range,* and *standard deviation* are applicable. Bivariate correlation analyses, t-test, analysis of variance tests, and most multivariate techniques applied for purposes of drawing inferences can be used on intervally scaled data. The applicable techniques are discussed in Chapter 14.

Ratio Measurements

Ratio scales consist of numbers that rank items such that numerically equal distances on the scale represent equal distances in the property being measured *and* have a meaningful zero. In general, simple counting of any set of objects produces a ratio scale of the characteristic "existence." In this case, the number 0 has an absolute empirical meaning—none of the property being measured exists. Thus, such common measurements as *sales, costs, market potential, market share, number of people,* and *age* are all made using ratio scales.

All descriptive measures and inferential techniques are applicable to ratio scaled data. However, this produces only a minimal gain in analytic technique beyond those available for interval data.

Components of Measurements

Assume that an individual has completed an attitude questionnaire that "measured" his attitude toward Ford automobiles. His score or number on this measurement instrument was 47. We can assume any scaling system— nominal through ratio. The question that the researcher must ask is: What factors or characteristics are reflected in this score?

In an ideal situation, there would be only one component in the score and this component would be a direct reflection of the characteristic of interest—the individual's attitude toward Ford automobiles. Unfortunately, such a state of affairs is seldom achieved. The researcher must, therefore, be concerned about the extent to which any single measurement reflects the characteristic under consideration versus other characteristics.

The following list summarizes the components that may be reflected in any given measurement.

COMPONENTS OF MEASUREMENTS

1. *True characteristic:* Direct reflection of the characteristic of interest.
2. *Additional stable characteristics of the respondent:* Reflection of other permanent characteristics such as social class, intelligence, or response set.
3. *Short term characteristics of the respondent:* Reflection of temporary characteristics such as hunger, fatigue, or anger.
4. *Situational characteristics:* Reflection of the surroundings in which the measurement is taken.
5. *Characteristics of the measurement process:* Reflection of the interviewer, interviewing method, and the like.
6. *Characteristics of the measuring instrument:* Reflection of ambiguous or misleading questions.
7. *Characteristics of the response process:* Reflection of mistaken replies caused by checking the wrong response, and the like.
8. *Characteristics of the analysis:* Reflection of mistakes in coding, tabulating, and the like.

As the list indicates, the characteristic of interest is only one of eight possible components of a single measurement. The paragraphs that follow describe each of these components in more detail.

Reflection of Additional Stable Characteristics

Perhaps the most troublesome measurement error occurs when the *measurement reflects a stable characteristic of the object or event in addition to the one of interest to the researcher.* Thus, the score of "47" in our earlier example may reflect the respondents' tendency to be agreeable by marking positive responses as well as his "true" attitude toward Ford. Such "extraneous" variables as social class, intelligence, and need for social acceptance may operate to influence various measurements that are designed to measure other characteristics. This problem is most acute in research dealing with consumer behavior such as attitudes, preferences, and opinions. However, it also occurs in such instances as comparing changes in dollar sales over time that reflect inflation as well as changes in sales levels.

Temporary Characteristics of the Object

An equally common source of error is the *influence of short-term characteristics of the object*. Such factors as fatigue, health, hunger, and emotional state may influence the measure of other characteristics. In the attitude measure example, some of the "47" could reflect the fact that the respondent was almost struck by a car on his way to the measurement session. Or, a measure of sales may reflect the short-term "stocking up" on the part of purchasers in anticipation of a price increase. Researchers frequently assume that such temporary fluctuations are randomly distributed in their effect on the measurement and will cancel each other out. However, if such an assumption is made, it should be explicitly stated and clearly justified.

Situational Characteristics

Many *measurements that involve human subjects reflect both the true characteristic under consideration and characteristics under which the measurement is taken*. For example, husbands and wives tend to report one level of influence in a purchase decision if their spouse is present and another level if the spouse is absent. Our 47 score may reflect a pleasant test situation in which coffee has been served, comfortable chairs provided, and the interview conducted by an unusually personable interviewer. In such a case, the individual may be indicating his attitude toward the interview situation as well as toward Ford.

Characteristics of the Measurement Process

The *measurement can also include influences from the method of gathering the data*. Sex, age, ethnic background, and style of dress of the interviewer have all been shown to influence individual's response patterns on certain questions. In addition, various methods of interviewing—telephone, mail, personal interview, and the like sometimes alter response patterns. Thus, the score of 47 could reflect the respondent's like, or dislike, of the interviewer.

Characteristics of the Measuring Instrument

Aspects of the measuring instrument itself can cause constant or random errors. Unclear instructions, ambiguous sentences, and confusing terms can all introduce errors. For example, the term *dinner* causes some people to think of the noon meal and others to think of the evening meal. If our respondent thought primarily of *Pinto* automobiles when completing the questionnaire, his responses would most likely be different than if he were referring to *Torinos.*

Characteristics of the Response Process

Response errors are another reason why responses may not reflect the "true" characteristic accurately. For example, our respondent may have inadvertently checked a positive response when he intended to check a negative one. Part of his "47" would be caused by this mistake rather than his true attitude.

Characteristics of the Analysis

Finally, *mistakes can occur in interpreting, coding, tabulating, and analyzing an individual's or group's response.* In our attitude example, a keypuncher might punch an eight rather than a three for one of the questions. Again, the "47" would be composed of an error component in addition to the characteristic of interest.

The measurement errors described are subject to varying degrees of control by the researcher. The material in Chapters 8, 9, and 10 provide explicit discussions of various approaches for controlling measurement error. The next section of this chapter describes the impact of the error components in terms of the validity and reliability of the measurement.

The Concepts of Validity and Reliability

The everyday conceptual definition for validity is the extent to which a measure reflects only the characteristic of interest. A valid measure is one that provides an accurate representation of what one is trying to measure. In this conceptual definition, validity includes both *systematic* and *variable* error components. However, researchers have found it useful to limit the meaning of the term *validity* to refer to the degree of consistent or systematic error in a measurement. Therefore, we define *validity* as the "extent to which a measurement is free from systematic error."

The term *reliability* is used to refer to the degree of variable error in a measurement. We define *reliability* as "the extent to which a measurement is free of variable errors." This is reflected when repeated measures of the same stable characteristic in the same objects show variations.

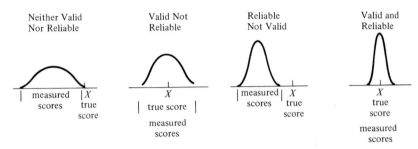

Figure 7–1   Reliability and validity.

Any measurement or series of measurements may be: (1) *neither valid nor reliable,* (2) *valid but not reliable,* (3) *reliable but not valid,* or (4) *valid and reliable.* In the first instance, we have extensive systematic and variable errors. The second case signifies extensive variable and limited systematic errors. The third case involves extensive systematic and limited variable errors. The final example reflects limited errors of both types. Figure 7–1 depicts these situations graphically. It should be noted, however, that reliability and validity are not "either-or" categories. Rather, they can vary over a wide range.

Reliability

Marketing researchers have historically shown only a limited interest in measures of reliability. Part of this stems from false reasoning on the nature of reliability. This reasoning is basically as follows: "Reliability is concerned with consistency or stability over time. Most applied research studies are one time affairs. Therefore, we need not be concerned about reliability." Although reliability is concerned with consistency and stability over time, this concern should be used *as evidence of variable errors in the measurement.* The presence of random errors in any measurement, even if it is a single measurement, can cause the decision maker to reach incorrect conclusions. Therefore, the reliability of a measurement is of importance to the marketing researcher.

The major operational approaches to the estimation of reliability are summarized in the following list and discussed in the next sections.

Major Operational Approaches to Reliability

1. *Test-retest reliability* involves applying the same measure to the same objects a second time.
2. *Alternative-forms reliability* involves measuring the same objects by two instruments that are designed to be as nearly alike as possible.
3. *Split-half reliability* involves comparing the responses from half the items on a multiitem or multitrial measuring instrument with the responses from the remaining half.

Test-retest Reliability. Test-retest reliability estimates are obtained by repeating the measurement using the same instrument under as nearly equivalent conditions as possible. The results of the two administrations are then compared on an item by item basis and the degree of correspondence is determined. The greater the differences the lower the reliability. The general philosophy behind this approach is that the presence of random fluctuations will cause the items being measured to score differently on each administration.

A number of practical difficulties are involved in measuring test-retest reliability. First, *some items can only be measured once.* It would not be possible, for example, to remeasure an individual's initial reaction to a new advertising slogan. Second, in many situations, *the initial measurement may alter the characteristic being measured.* Thus, an attitude survey may focus the individual's attention on the topic and cause him to form new or different attitudes about it. Third, *there may be some form of a carry-over effect from the first measure.* The retaking of a measure may produce boredom, anger, or attempts to remember the answers given on the initial measurement. Finally, *factors extraneous to the measuring process may cause shifts in the characteristic being measured.* These four factors may operate to increase or decrease the measured reliability coefficient. Despite these problems, the technique remains a useful approach to estimating reliability, particularly when it can be used in conjunction with other methods or with various test groups in different situations.

Alternative Forms Reliability. Alternative forms reliability estimates are obtained by applying two "equivalent" forms of the measuring instrument to the same subjects. As in test-retest reliability, the results of the two instruments are compared on an item by item basis and the degree of similarity determined. The basic logic is the same as in the test-retest approach. Two primary problems are associated with this approach. The first is the extra time, expense, and trouble involved in obtaining two equivalent measures. The second, and more important, is the problem of constructing two truly equivalent forms. Thus, a low degree of observed similarity may reflect either an unreliable instrument *or* nonequivalent forms.

Split-half Reliability. Split-half reliability estimates are obtained by comparing the results of half the items on a multiitem measure with the results from the remaining items. It is in reality a version of the alternate forms technique. In this case the entire test is assumed to consist of two or more equivalent subsets that can then be compared. This technique can only be used with multiitem or multitrial measures that measure a unidimensional characteristic. That is, each item is assumed to represent an independent measure of the same characteristic. The usual approach to split-half reliability involves dividing the total number of items into two groups on a random basis and computing a measure of similarity (a correlation coefficient—see Chapter 14). A low coefficient means that all of the items are not measuring the same characteristic. Another approach to computing a coefficient based on internal consistency in effect compares every item to every other item. The resulting coefficient is the average split-half correlation for all possible ways of dividing the test into two parts.[8] A computer program is available to perform these computations.[9]

Importance of Reliability

As discussed earlier, reliability is important even when the measurement will not be repeated over time because it is an estimate of the level of those measurement errors that are variable in nature. How reliable should a particular measure be? For basic research projects one would be tempted to claim that reliability should be maximized. However, this is clearly not appropriate from a decisional point of view. Since increasing measurement reliability generally increases costs and may increase other forms of error, the desired level of reliability has to be judged by the requirements of the problem at hand.

Although no precise rules can be specified for what level of reliability should be sought in a decisional research project, a number of general considerations need to be kept in mind.[10] First, the more homogeneous the group with respect to the characteristic being measured, the more difficult it is to obtain high reliability. If most members of the group being studied possess similar attitudes toward a product, slight random errors may result in substantial misclassifications. Second, the finer the distinctions we want to make among objects the more we need high reliability. Relatively unreliable measures will distinguish holders of strongly favorable and strongly

[8] Selltiz, op. cit., 175.
[9] G. Vigderhous, "Coefficient of Reliability Alpha," *Journal of Marketing Research,* **XI** (May 1974), 194.
[10] Selltiz, op. cit., 178–182.

unfavorable attitudes toward a product. However, a highly reliable measure is required to effectively discriminate between holders of neutral and slightly favorable attitudes. Third, estimates of reliability are based on the average reliability of scores of individuals in a group. The reliability of an average score is always higher than the reliability of the individual scores. Therefore, when we are interested in group results, we can, to some extent, compensate for low measurement reliability by increasing sample size.[11]

Finally, variable error is one component of the total variance. As seen in Chapter 3 and again in Chapter 6, the greater the variance the less the information is worth. The cost versus the value of increasing the reliability of data, therefore, is highly dependent on the conditional payoff table of the problem.

Validity

Validity, like reliability, is concerned with error. However, it is concerned with consistent or systematic error rather than variable error. A valid measurement reflects only the characteristic of interest and random error. One must be sure that the characteristic of interest in the research project and the one in the problem are the same, however. For example, occupation is often used as a surrogate measure of social class. No matter how accurately occupation is measured, to the extent that it does not reflect the conceptual definition of social class, it is not a valid measure.

The four most common approaches to the determination of validity are presented in the following list and discussed in the next sections.

1. *Construct validity* involves understanding what factors lie behind the obtained measurement.
2. *Content validity* involves assessing the appropriateness of the measurement technique primarily on logical grounds.
3. *Concurrent validity* involves the assessment of how closely this measure of the characteristic is correlated with other measures of the same characteristic.
4. *Predictive validity* involves the assessment of the ability of the measure to predict the existence of some additional characteristic associated with the same item.

Construct Validity

Construct validity—understanding the factors that underlie the obtained measurement—is the most complex form of validity and is the ultimate

---

[11] Other methods of increasing reliability are described by Selltiz, ibid., 182–186.

concern of the basic researcher. It involves more than just knowing *how well* a given measure works; it also involves knowing *why* it works. In addition to a strictly logical approach to construct validity, researchers interested in this approach often attempt to tie their concept into a network of related concepts. Construct validity of a measure is then determined by the extent to which the measurement of the concept of interest correlates in the predicted manner with measures of related concepts. Thus, in construct validation both the measure and the theory relating the construct to other constructs are being evaluated.

The emphasis on theoretical relationships, coupled with a lack of well-developed marketing theory, has reduced the usefulness of this approach in applied marketing research. However, it remains a useful goal.

Content Validity

Content validity estimates are essentially subjective judgments of the appropriateness of the measurement instrument. The term *face validity* is often used when the measurement instrument contains only one measurement of the characteristic in question. For example, a pantry audit in which the presence of an item is assumed to mean that the item is used in that household is often justified as having face validity. Face validity can be challenged on logical grounds. In the example, an alternative explanation could be advanced that the item was acquired as a mistake, gift, or experiment and is still on hand because it was not liked and is not used in the household.

The more common form of content validity applies to multiitem measures. In this case, the reseacher or some other individual or group of individuals assesses the representativeness or sampling adequacy of the included items in light of the purpose of the measuring instrument. Thus an attitude scale designed to measure the overall attitude toward a shopping center would not be considered to have content validity if it omitted any major attributes such as location, layout, and so on. Content validation is the most common form of validation in marketing research. Unfortunately, there is a tendency for the researcher to also serve as the judge rather than acquiring outside opinions.

Concurrent Validity

Estimates of *concurrent validity* are probably the most common type in the behavioral sciences. This technique involves comparing the results of two different measures of the same characteristic in the same objects, usually through some statistical measure of correlation. This is particularly useful when a new measuring technique has been developed. For example, when a new measure of anxiety was developed, measures of correlation between the new measure and three more established measures of the same construct were reported.[12]

Concurrent validation is seldom used in marketing. A primary reason is the lack of well-established alternative measuring techniques. Marketing researchers have had a tendency to either borrow measuring instruments from the behavioral sciences and assume that they were valid or develop a unique measurement tool for each specific problem and rely on face validity.

Predictive Validity

Predictive validity is frequently characterized as the most important form of validation for decisional purposes because decisions, by their very nature, require predictions of uncertain events. As the term is used by many marketing researchers, predictive validity simply refers to the ability of a measure of one characteristic to predict another characteristic or the same characteristic at a future point in time. This actually refers to *predictive accuracy* rather than predictive validity. Predictive validity seeks to validate the measure of one concept or characteristic by observing the relationship between the measure of the concept of interest and the measure of some concept that has a known or assumed relationship to the original concept. The remainder of this section seeks to clarify the nature of predictive validity. The next section discusses predictive accuracy.

Figure 7–2, focusing on the predictive validity of social class as indicator of brand usage, may help clarify the nature of predictive validity, which is an attempt to confirm link 3 by assessing link 4, or to confirm link 1 by assessing link 4. However, even a brief examination of the figure indicates that link 2 and either link 3 or link 1 must be assumed to be valid and links 5 and 6 must be assumed to have minimal impact. Thus, in a strict sense, one is seldom certain exactly what has been validated or has failed validation when predictive validity is used.

Strict predictive validation procedures are seldom used in marketing research. However, estimates of predictive accuracy are common. This is the topic of the next section.

Predictive Accuracy

Marketing researchers measure in order to predict. The more accurate a measure is, the better it predicts the characteristic it is measuring. If the characteristic being measured is associated with another characteristic that

---

[12] C. D. Spielberger, et al., *STAI Manual* (Palo Alto, Calif.: Consulting Psychologists Press, 1970), 10.

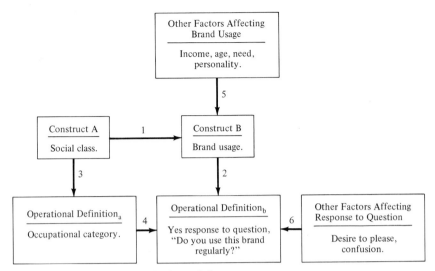

Figure 7–2 Nature of predictive validity.

cannot be measured, an accurate measure of the first allows an accurate estimation of the second. For example, if buying intentions are closely associated with future purchases (which cannot be measured in the present), an accurate measure of buying intentions will allow an accurate prediction of future purchases. Referring back to Figure 7–2, we can see that predictive accuracy is strictly a function of link 4. The researcher is concerned only with how well his measure predicts the characteristic in which he is interested. The applied researcher often means predictive accuracy when he talks about predictive validity. However, a concern for prediction involves verifying link 4 with no concern for link 3 or link 1.

The target level of predictive accuracy is a function of the decision to be made. The more precise the decision, that is, setting a production schedule as opposed to a go-no go type decision, the more accurate is the information requirement. Consider the decision to enter or not enter a given market. Assume that 1 million units must be sold in order to make entering the market worthwhile. A 10 or 20 per cent error becomes critical only at values close to the 1 million unit level. The required level of accuracy can be balanced against cost estimates for obtaining such an accuracy through the use of Bayesian analysis.

The forecast made of the number of units that would be sold if the decision is to enter the market is, in effect, treated as if it were nominally scaled data with two categories—(1) more than 1 million units will be sold and (2) less than 1 million will be sold. In contrast, decisions such as setting the production level require interval or ratio scaled predictions. *How much* to be produced at *what times* must be decided. These kinds of decisions require more accurate information. Again, however, the cost of the errors should be balanced against the cost of obtaining better information so they can be reduced.

Summary

This chapter has been concerned with concepts of measurement. *Measurement is the process of assigning numbers to the characteristics of objects, persons, states, or events according to rules.* It is the *characteristics* of items that are measured, not the items themselves. The numbers used in measurement serve as symbols rather than as numbers in the everyday sense of the term. Since the numbers are applied to the characteristics of interest according to arbitrary rules, the quality of measurement can be evaluated only by (1) the extent to which the measurement rule has been applied correctly and (2) the extent of correspondence between the rule and some aspect of reality. The statement of measurement rules for a given concept constitutes the *operational definition* of that concept. These rules should be derived from the *conceptual definition* or central idea of the concept.

Four different types or scales of measurement were described—*nominal, ordinal, interval,* and *ratio.* Each has its unique uses in marketing research. As we move from nominal to ratio measurements, we encounter increasingly restrictive measurement rules. However, as the rules become more restrictive, the range of permissible arithmetic operations becomes larger.

Any single measurement can be composed of the characteristic of interest and the impact of various error components. Seven such error components were described in this chapter: (1) additional stable characteristics of the respondent, (2) short-term characteristics of the respondent, (3) situational characteristics, (4) characteristics of the measurement process, (5) characteristics of the measurement instrument, (6) characteristics of the response process, and (7) characteristics of the analysis.

Reliability and *validity* are concerned with variable errors and systematic errors, respectively. Test-retest, alternative forms, and split-half measures of reliability were described. Construct, content, concurrent, and predictive validity approaches were analyzed.

Questions and Problems

7.1. For each of the measurements described, indicate whether a *nominal, ordinal, interval,* or *ratio* scale was used. Briefly explain why you believe your answer is correct.
   (a) A measurement of brand preference between *Prestone* and *Zerex* antifreeze.

(b) A compilation of total industry antifreeze sales (in gallons) for the year 1973.

(c) A determination of the temperature at which a mixture of one gallon of *Prestone* and three gallons of water will freeze.

7.2. What kind(s) of scale(s) is/are involved in the following statements? Is the anaylsis consistent with the scale(s) used?

(a) "Children under 10 receive aspirin as the most widely prescribed drug reducing the temperature of a fever. Most doctors prescribe aspirin when the temperature reaches 100°F or more. It reduces temperature at an average rate of 0.77°F per hour."

(b) "A sample of 300 adults was asked to rank aspirin, *Bufferin, Emperin, Excedrin,* and *Anacin* in order of preference for treatment of headaches. The most preferred was given a ranking of '1' and the least preferred a ranking of '5.' The average for aspirin was 1.72."

(c) "Adults over 60 use 2.43 times as many grains of aspirin per year as adults between the ages of 20 and 30."

7.3. Give one conceptual and two or more operational definitions for each of the following concepts: (a) profit, (b) brand image, (c) attitude, (d) market, (e) market share, (f) preference.

7.4. What measurement components do you think were or would be most important in the following situations?

(a) Your performance on your college entrance exam.

(b) Your performance on your last hourly exam.

(c) Your response the last time someone asked you how he/she looked or what you thought of a new purchase he/she had made.

(d) The response of a rushed Christmas shopper to a "man in the street" interview on the topic, "Have we taken the *Christ* out of *Christmas?*"

(e) A brand preference interview given by telephone.

7.5. Is reliability or validity more important or are they of equal importance to the decisional researcher? Why?

Selected Bibliography

KERLINGER, F. N. *Foundations of Behavior Research.* New York: Holt, Rinehart and Winston, Inc., 1973, Chaps. 3, 25, 26, 27. Excellent treatments of conceptual and operational definitions, measurement theory, and reliability and validity.

RUNKEL, P. J., and J. E. MCGRATH. *Research on Human Behavior.* New York: Holt, Rinehart and Winston, Inc., 1972, Chap. 6. A good discussion of operational definitions and reliability and validity.

STEVENS, S. S. "On the Theory of Scales of Measurement." *Science,* **103** (June 7, 1946), 677–680. A classic paper on the nature of measurement scales.

TORGERSEN, W. S. *Theory and Methods of Scaling.* New York: John Wiley & Sons, Inc., 1958. A comprehensive but fairly technical and theoretical treatment of measurement.

Case 7–1

Willamette Bakeries
Data Collection Procedure

Far West Research Associates, a marketing research and consulting firm, was approached by Williamette Bakeries concerning a survey of purchase and consumption patterns for bread in its market area. Williamette is a small, independent bakery that, like most independents, had been losing market share for several years to the private brand breads of the food chains. The purpose of the survey was to obtain information about its market to help the bakery take action to reverse this declining trend in market share.

After some discussion it was agreed that Far West Research would conduct a survey as a part of an overall consulting project. The objectives of the survey were "to determine if there are viable market segments for bread based upon (1) characteristics of purchasing families and amounts of purchase, (2) communication media and appeals, and (3) distribution outlets."

Jack Brown, an analyst for Far West, began to prepare the questionnaire that would be used for the survey. Personal interviews were to be conducted and, to meet the objectives of the survey, information on amount of bread and where it was purchased, occupation, stage of life cycle, level of education, and income of the chief wage earner of the family, print and electronic media exposure, and attitudes toward bread and its use would have to be obtained.

Brown believed that the information that would be the most difficult to obtain with the accuracy needed was on amounts of bread purchased. The information required was the average amount of bread purchased as measured by some standard unit, such as a pound, by type of bread, for some standard time period, such as a week. Two major problems were involved in obtaining this information, as Brown saw it.

First, most people who buy bread buy it by loaf rather than by weight. They would know the size of the loaf they usually buy by sight but might not know how much it weighed. Second, many people buy bread on an "as needed" rather than on a regular basis. They may also buy different numbers of loaves as well as making irregular purchases. To obtain an accurate report on the average amount of bread purchased each week under such circumstances would be difficult.

Brown considered two alternative ways of obtaining information on bread purchases. The way that would give the most accurate information, he believed, was to have the housewife keep a diary of her bread purchases for ten weeks. She could be asked to look at the bread wrapper to obtain the weight of the loaf before recording it. The diary could be either picked up or mailed in at the end of the period.

Even though the information obtained in this way would be more accurate, Brown knew that it would still have inaccuracies. People who keep consumer diaries of this kind sometimes forget to record their purchases. Others agree to keep a diary of purchases and then change their minds. Still others wait until the end of the recording period to record purchases and make mistakes in the amounts shown.

A panel of this sort would also be considerably more expensive than just asking the housewife questions about bread purchases. Some premium would have to be given to obtain cooperation from a large enough proportion of the sample to make it worthwhile. Callbacks would have to be made to check questionable entries if the diaries were mailed in, or a second call would be required if the diaries were collected by an interviewer. In either case, added costs would be incurred.

The second alternative considered by Brown was that of obtaining the information solely by interview. To explore this possibility he drew up a tentative list of questions that could be used for obtaining the information and tried them on his wife. The questions appeared to serve the desired function with her. The questions for white bread that he had drawn up were as follows:

1. *Do you usually do the shopping for food?*
   Yes _____ No _____
2. *(Do you) (Does your family) eat white bread?*
   Yes _____ No _____
3. *About how often would you say you buy white bread?*
   Three times a week _____
   Twice a week _____
   Once a week _____
   Once a month _____
   Twice every three months _____
   Once every three months _____
4. *About how many loaves of white bread do you buy each time?*
   One loaf _____
   Two loaves _____
   Three loaves _____
   Four loaves _____
   More than four loaves (list number) _____
5. *What size of loaves of white bread do you buy each time?*
   Extra large (approx. 32 oz.) _____
   Large (approx. 22 oz.) _____
   Medium (approx. 15 oz.) _____
   Small (less than 15 oz.) _____

Brown was undecided as to which method to use.

1. Are there likely to be systematic errors in the diary method of measuring bread purchases? If so, is the measurement likely to be high or low?

2. Are these likely to be systematic errors in the questionnaire method of measuring bread purchases? If so, is the measurement likely to be high or low?

3. Evaluate the tentative list of questions that Brown prepared. Could they be improved? If so, how?

4. Which method do you think Brown should use? Why?

Case 7-2
Marlin Advertising Agency: Testing Advertising Effectiveness

Marlin Advertising Agency specializes in retail advertising. The firm is located in a city of approximately 750,000 and has enjoyed moderate success over its 15-year history. Current billings are slightly over $1,300,000. Over time, Ann Mobley, founder and president of the agency, evolved a policy of working with the management of the retail firm to help create a distinct store image. She has stressed to management that advertising is only one part of the marketing mix. In her opinion, a successful firm must convey a strong, distinct image that can only be developed through consistency in all aspects of the marketing mix.

Mobley has found little difficulty in persuading potential clients of the wisdom of her philosophy. However, she has had difficulty in persuading them of the ability of her agency to help them create this strong image. A number of the larger retail accounts have recently opted for one of the two major advertising agencies in town.

In order to strengthen the agency's competitive position, Mobley hired Charles Cole to establish a marketing research department within the agency. The department would be used to assist in preparing presentations to potential new accounts and to provide free or low cost services to existing accounts.

Cole had received a degree in marketing from the city college two years earlier and had worked in the marketing research department of a large bank until accepting the offer to work for the agency. After spending a month becoming familiar with the operations of the agency and its information requirements, he made the following recommendations in a note to Mobley.

What we need is a way to measure each aspect of a retail store's image. Then, prior to a presentation to a potential client or in cooperation with an existing client, we can take a random sample of 100 customers from the client's target market and measure their images of the store. We can use this information to identify weaknesses in the store's image and, in conjunction with management, we can isolate those weaknesses that advertising can help correct. After each advertising campaign we can take a new random sample and apply the same measuring instrument. In this way, we can demonstrate the effectiveness of our advertising. In addition, we can use this second measurement to identify areas of concern for the next advertising campaign.

I have developed a measuring instrument for this purpose. A copy is attached. The instrument can be sent by mail or we can use personal interviews. The agree-disagree responses will be assigned values of 1 through 5 such that the high score is always associated with a positive response regardless of whether it is an agree or disagree response. That is, disagreeing with a negative statement and agreeing with a positive statement will both produce a high score. The scores for each of the 100 individuals will be summed for each of 12 items and an average computed for each item. A "perfect" store would have an average of 5 for every item. The lower the score, the more concerned the store's management should be.

Customer Attitudes Toward Store A

Please indicate how accurately you believe each of the following statements describes Store A by indicating your level of agreement or disagreement with the statement. There are no right or wrong answers. We are interested in your *opinion* of the store. Therefore, your frankness will be appreciated. Please respond to each item.

1. The products carried by Store A are high-quality products.
   __Strongly Agree __Agree __Neutral __Disagree __Strongly Disagree
2. Considering the nature of the products, Store A's prices are extremely high.
   __Strongly Agree __Agree __Neutral __Disagree __Strongly Disagree
3. The service in Store A is extremely bad.
   __Strongly Agree __Agree __Neutral __Disagree __Strongly Disagree
4. Store A is an exceptionally dependable store.
   __Strongly Agree __Agree __Neutral __Disagree __Strongly Disagree
5. Store A is basically a dishonest store.
   __Strongly Agree __Agree __Neutral __Disagree __Strongly Disagree
6. Store A is an exceptionally clean store.
   __Strongly Agree __Agree __Neutral __Disagree __Strongly Disagree
7. The employees in Store A are very helpful.
   __Strongly Agree __Agree __Neutral __Disagree __Strongly Disagree
8. It is very difficult to find items in Store A.
   __Strongly Agree __Agree __Neutral __Disagree __Strongly Disagree
9. Store A is a very old-fashioned store.
   __Strongly Agree __Agree __Neutral __Disagree __Strongly Disagree
10. Store A is an extremely pleasant store.
    __Strongly Agree __Agree __Neutral __Disagree __Strongly Disagree
11. Store A has a wide selection of items.
    __Strongly Agree __Agree __Neutral __Disagree __Strongly Disagree
12. Store A is a very unfriendly store.
    __Strongly Agree __Agree __Neutral __Disagree __Strongly Disagree

Upon receipt of Cole's note, Mobley called him into her office and made the following statement: "This is very impressive and seems to have real possibilities. However, what if people are not consistent in how they respond to it? That is, how can we be sure that it is reliable?"

1. How should Cole respond to this question?

2. Is this a valid measure of store image? Why?

3. Is Cole's requirement that the responses be averaged a sound one?

4. What types of measurement components are likely to be a problem for Cole's instrument?

CHAPTER 8

Measurement and Research: Questionnaire Design

In the preceding chapter a number of issues involved in measurement were discussed. In this chapter and the next two, the more commonly used measurement techniques are described. These techniques must, of course, be evaluated in light of the requirements imposed by the measurement task described in Chapter 7.

This chapter is concerned with *questionnaire design*. Although the design of questionnaires is more of an art form than a scientific undertaking, the accumulated experience of survey researchers has resulted in the development of a number of principles. These principles are set forth and described in this chapter.

Nature of Questionnaire Design

Suppose we are curious about some aspect of another individual. Our curiosity could involve his behavior, his knowledge, his personal characteristics, or his attitudes. How would be satisfy this curiosity? For any one of a fairly wide range of topics, we would simply ask the individual to tell us. Most of us, at one time or another, have asked complete strangers for "the time." Most people consider this an entirely proper question and respond freely and as accurately as possible.

However, there are other questions that we would hesitate before asking a stranger, or even a friend. We might, for some reason, be interested in how much money an individual is carrying with him. However, few of us would ask a stranger, "How much money do you have with you?"

Even if we obtained an answer such as: "I left all my money at home," we would most likely suspect some distortion.

The point is that questioning is a common, everyday approach to obtaining information. There are, however, some types of information for which questioning is appropriate and other types for which it is less appropriate.

Questionnaires are simply a formalized approach to asking someone for information. As such, their function is measurement[1] and they represent the most common form of measurement in marketing research. Although questionnaires are generally associated with survey research, they are also frequently the measurement instrument in experimental designs as well. When questionnaires are administered by means of the telephone or by a personal interviewer, they are often termed *interview schedules,* or simply *schedules*. However, the term *questionnaire* will be used throughout this text to refer to a list of questions regardless of the means of administration.

Questionnaires can be used to measure (1) *behavior*—past, present, or intended, (2) *demographic characteristics*—age, income, occupation, (3) *level of knowledge,* and (4) *attitudes and opinions*. All four areas are frequently measured by questionnaire and often on the same questionnaire. Exhibit 8–1, for example, contains a questionnaire that was used to measure all four areas. The measurement of attitudes has become so important, both to marketing and the behavioral sciences in general, that a number of specialized questioning techniques has been developed to measure them. These specialized techniques are treated in detail in Chapter 10. However, they are often administered as a part of a general questionnaire and the rules for questionnaire design must be kept in mind

---

[1] A. N. Oppenheim, *Questionnaire Design and Attitude Measurement* (London: Heinemann Educational Books, Ltd., 1966), 24.

when developing and applying attitude scales. The same is true for projective techniques described in the next chapter.

Three types of error are influenced by the questionnaire itself (as opposed to the sampling strategy or method or administration). *Surrogate information* error can be a problem if the researcher has not clearly defined the types of information needed to solve the management problem. However, this is generally a problem in specifying the research problem rather than in designing the questionnaire.

The questionnaire design can affect the *response rate* both to the overall instrument and to specific items on the questionnaire. Overall response rate issues are dealt with in the chapter on survey research (Chapter 11). Techniques to improve the response rate to specific questions are described in the following pages.

The most critical problem in questionnaire construction is *measurement error*. For example, consider two alternative ways of asking what appears to be the same question to a group of nonworking housewives: *"Would you like to have a job, if this were possible?"* and *"Would you prefer to have a job, or do you prefer to do just your housework?"* The second version merely makes explicit the implied alternative in the first. Will such a minor change make any difference? "Probably not" is the common response from those unfamiliar with questionnaire design. When these two questions were read to two random samples of nonworking housewives, the first version (implicit alternative) produced 19 per cent who stated that they would not like to have a job. However, the second version (explicit alternative) produced 68 per cent who would prefer not to have a job![2]

Obviously, questionnaire construction is of critical importance. Only in rare instances will sampling error produce distortions as extreme as that just described. Yet numerous volumes have been written on sampling techniques and relatively little on questionnaire design.[3] Thus, although we may approach sampling from a reasonably scientific standpoint, questionnaire design remains very much an art form. In the following pages an attempt is made to provide a rough guideline for questionnaire design.[4] However, ultimately a sound questionnaire depends upon *common sense, concern for the respondent, a clear concept of the needed information,* and *thorough pretesting.*

The discussion on questionnaire construction techniques focuses on

[2] E. Noelle-Neumann, "Wanted: Rules for Wording Structured Questionnaires," *Public Opinion Quarterly,* **34** (Summer 1970), 200.

[3] For an outstanding, humorous exception see S. L. Payne, *The Art of Asking Questions* (Princeton: Princeton University Press, 1951).

[4] The following sections are based in large part on A. Kornhauser and P. B. Sheatsley, "Questionnaire Construction and Interview Procedure" in C. Selltiz, et al., *Research Methods in Social Relations* (New York: Holt, Rinehart and Winston, Inc., 1959), 546–587.

Table 8–1 A Summary of the Major Decisions on Questionnaire Design

---

I. *Preliminary Decisions*
   A. Exactly what information is required?
   B. Exactly who are the target respondents?
   C. What method of communication will be used to reach these respondents?

II. *Decision About Question Content*
   A. Is this question really needed?
   B. Is this question sufficient to generate the needed information?
   C. Can the respondent answer the question correctly?
   D. Will the respondents answer the question correctly?
   E. Are there any external events that might bias the response to the question?

III. *Decisions Concerning Question Phrasing*
   A. Do the words used have but one meaning to all the respondents?
   B. Are any of the words or phrases loaded or leading in any way?
   C. Are there any implied alternatives in the question?
   D. Are there any unstated assumptions related to the question?
   E. Will the respondents approach the question from the frame of reference desired by the researcher?

IV. *Decisions About the Response Format*
   A. Can this question best be asked as an open-ended, multiple-choice, or dichotomous question?

V. *Decisions Concerning the Question Sequence*
   A. Are the questions organized in a logical manner that avoids introducing errors?

VI. *Decisions on the Layout of the Questionnaire*
   A. Is the questionnaire designed in a manner to avoid confusion and minimize recording errors?

VII. *Decisions About the Pretest*
   A. Has the final questionnaire been subjected to a thorough pretest using respondents similar to those that will be included in the final survey?

---

seven areas: (1) *preliminary considerations,* (2) *question content,* (3) *question wording,* (4) *response format,* (5) *question sequence,* (6) *physical characteristics of the questionnaire,* and (7) *the pretest.* These topics and the major issues under each are shown in Table 8–1.

Although these topics are discussed in the general order that the researcher should consider them, the decisions are, in fact, interrelated. Not only do decisions made during the early stages influence the types of decisions that can be made later but decisions made during the final stages may compel the reconsideration of earlier choices. For example, decisions on question sequence will often influence the wording of the questions involved. Therefore, although the following discussion of the steps in the design of questionnaires implies that they are sequential, it must be recognized that in fact they are interactive.

In order to provide an initial awareness of the nature of questionnaires and to help illustrate points to be made in the chapter, a complete questionnaire is reproduced in Exhibit 8–1. The questionnaire was used by *need to capture respondents attention at the beginning.*

Exhibit 8–1 U.S.D.A. Study Questionnaire*

Hello, I'm (Name) from Haug Associates, a consumer survey and public opinion firm. We are making a survey to find out how people feel about different public and private organizations. (GO DIRECTLY TO Q. 1a)

1a. (HAND CARD I) Here are some symbols, or pictures, which different organizations and companies have used. (FOR EACH SYMBOL ASK) Have you seen this one before? (RECORD BELOW) *OK (p231)*

1.b (FOR EACH ONE SEEN) What do you think this symbol stands for?

	Q.1a Seen Before Yes	No	Stands For	
TB Seal	6–1	7–1		8–
				9–
Jolly Green Giant	–2	–2		10–
				11–
Smokey the Bear	–3	–3		12–
				13–
Bell Telephone	–4	–4		14–
				15–
Edison Electric Institute/ Gold Medallion Homes	–5	–5		16–
				17–
Quaker Oats Man	–6	–6		18–
				19–

2. (HAND CARD II) (FOR EACH SYMBOL AWARE OF, ASK) Which of these phrases best describes how you feel about this symbol or picture. (POINT TO EACH SYMBOL) *Confusing*

Are we looking for symbol or what it represents?

	TB Seal	Green Giant	Smokey	Bell Tele-phone	Edison/ Gold Med.	Quaker Oats Man
It's my favorite	20–1	21–1	22–1	23–1	24–1	25–1
I like it	–2	–2	–2	–2	–2	–2
It's no better or worse than the rest	–3	–3	–3	–3	–3	–3
I don't like it as well as the others	–4	–4	–4	–4	–4	–4
I don't like it at all	–5	–5	–5	–5	–5	–5
No answer/ don't know	–6	–6	–6	–6	–6	–6

(IF RESPONDENT HAD *NOT* IN Q. 1a SEEN *SMOKEY* BEFORE, SKIP TO Q.*3b*)

Used by permission of Haug Associates, Inc.

Exhibit 8–1 *(Continued)*

3a. (POINT TO PICTURE OF SMOKEY ON CARD I) Who is this a picture of?
Do you know his name?

His name: —————————————————— 26–

3b. (IF "SMOKEY," "SMOKEY BEAR," OR "SMOKEY THE BEAR" NOT
MENTIONED, ASK) This is a picture of "Smokey the Bear"; have you heard
his name before?

Yes   27–1   No –2   (SKIP TO Q. 10)

4. (SHOW TAT #1 SHEET) Here is a picture of two people talking. The first one
asks, "Why do they have Smokey the Bear—what is he supposed to do?" What
do you think the other person would answer? (PROBE)

——————————————————————————————

——————————————————————————————
                                                              28–
—————————————————————————————— 29–
                                                              30–
——————————————————————————————

——————————————————————————————

5. How do you feel about Smokey the Bear? (PROBE HOW FEEL AND WHY)

——————————————————————————————

——————————————————————————————
                                                              31–
—————————————————————————————— 32–
                                                              33–
—————————————————————————————— 34–

6. Here are some phrases about Smokey the Bear that have not been completed.
As I show you each phrase, please tell me how you would complete it. Just give
me the first thought that comes to your mind.

6a. (CARD III) The kinds of people who would like Smokey the best are   35–
                                                              36–
                                                              37–
——————————————————————————————

6b. (CARD IV) Smokey is a————————————————kind of 38–
a character.   39–
                                                              40–
——————————————————————————————

6c. (CARD V) The thing people like best about Smokey is———————— 41–
                                                              42–
                                                              43–
——————————————————————————————

Exhibit 8–1 *(Continued)*

6d. (CARD VI) Adults feel that Smokey is_____ ___ 44–
                                                                45–
                                                                46–

6e. (CARD VII) The thing that people do *not* like about Smokey is   47–
                                                                      48–
                                                                      49–

6f. (CARD VIII) Teen-agers feel that Smokey is_____ ___ 50–
                                                               51–
                                                               52–

6g. (CARD IX) Smokey's *voice* sounds_____ ___ 53–
                                                                54–
                                                                55–

6h. (CARD X) The way Smokey looks is_____ ___ 56–
                                                             57–
                                                             58–

6i. (CARD XI) People would like Smokey better if_____ ___ 59–
                                                               60–
                                                               61–

6j. (CARD XII) Children feel that Smokey is_____ ___ 62–
                                                            63–
                                                            64–

7. (CARD XIII) Here is a list of words. Please take your time to look it over. Which of these words do you think describe Smokey? Pick as many as you feel could be used to describe him.

a.	Friendly	65–1	j.	Slow	66–1
b.	Weak	–2	k.	Clever	–2
c.	Old-fashioned	–3	l.	Modern	–3
d.	Effective	–4	m.	Silly or "corny"	–4
e.	Lazy	–5	n.	Cautious	–5
f.	Daring	–6	o.	Full of pep	–6
g.	Ugly	–7	p.	Unfriendly	–7
h.	Fast	–8	q.	Not effective	–8
i.	Strong	–9	r.	Pleasant looking	–9

7a. Where have you seen or heard about Smokey the Bear? (PROBE "Any others?")

Friends	67–1	Newspapers	67–5
Signs in parks or		Parades	–6
along highways	–2	Other:	
Television	–3		
Magazines	–4		

7b. Have you seen or heard any advertising for Smokey the Bear?

Yes   68–1   No   –2   (SKIP TO Q.8a)

Exhibit 8–1 (*Continued*)

7c. What do you remember about any advertising you have seen with Smokey in it? (PROBE)

_____

_____   69–

_____   70–
                                                            71–
_____
                                                            72–

_____

_____

7d. How do you feel about the advertising which shows Smokey—do you like it *better*, *worse*, or *about the same* as most advertising you see?

                     Better   73–1
                     Worse   –2
                     About the same   –3

7e. Why do you feel that way? (PROBE)

_____

_____

_____   74–
                                                            75–
_____   76–
                                                            77–
_____

Adults

8a. Smokey the Bear has a slogan or saying which he uses. This slogan is a reminder about forest fire prevention. Do you happen to know what it is?

The slogan:_____   78–

8b. (IF "ONLY YOU CAN PREVENT FOREST FIRES" NOT MENTIONED, ASK) This slogan is "Only you can prevent forest fires." Are you familiar with this slogan?

                    Yes 79–1   No –2

8c. How do you feel about this slogan, "Only you can prevent forest fires?" (PROBE HOW FEEL AND WHY)

_____

_____

_____   11–
                                                            12–
_____   13–
                                                            14–
_____

Exhibit 8–1   *(Continued)*

9a. (HAND CARD XIV) Overall, how good a job do you think Smokey the Bear is doing in *trying* to prevent forest fires?

An excellent job	15–1
A good job	–2
A fair job	–3
A poor job	–4
A very poor job	–5

9b. Why do you feel that way? (PROBE)

_____

_____ 16–
_____ 17–
_____ 18–
_____ 19–

10. (HAND CARD XV) Here is a list of items which causes damage in our country every year. Which one do you think causes the *most* damage? (RECORD BELOW) Which causes the next most damage? (RECORD BELOW) And the next most? (RECORD BELOW) And the next most? (RECORD BELOW)

	Most Damage	2nd Most Damage	3rd Most Damage	4th Most Damage
Floods	20–1	21–1	22–1	23–1
Earthquakes	–2	–2	–2	–2
Forest Fires	–3	–3	–3	–3
Plane Crashes	–4	–4	–4	–4
Hurricanes	–5	–5	–5	–5

11a. What one thing do you think causes most forest fires? (IF "CARELESSNESS" MENTIONED, PROBE "What kind?")

_____ 24–

_____ 25–

11b. What other things do you think cause forest fires?

_____ 26–
_____ 27–

_____ 28–

Exhibit 8–1   *(Continued)*

12. In what ways are forest fires a serious problem? (PROBE HOW SERIOUS AND WHY FEEL THAT WAY)

29–

30–
31–

13. What do you feel is the main damage done by forest fires? (PROBE MAIN DAMAGE AND WHY FEEL THAT WAY)

32–

33–
34–

14. What kinds of benefits do you think would result from more efficient fire prevention and control programs? (PROBE)

35–

36–
37–

15. In your opinion, what can be done to cut down the number of forest fires? (PROBE)

38–

39–
40–

Exhibit 8–1 *(Continued)*

16a. (HAND CARD XVI) Suppose someone accidentally starts a forest fire through carelessness. What do you think should be done to him?

Nothing		41–1
Given a warning		–2
Put in jail for:	1 month	–3
	6 months	–4
	1 year	–5
	2 years	–6
	5 years	–7

16b. Why do you say that? (PROBE)

_____

                                                        42–
_____
                                                        43–
                                                        44–
_____

16c. (HAND CARD XVI) What about the person who deliberately starts a forest fire—what do you think should be done to him?

Nothing		45–1
Given a warning		–2
Put in jail for:	1 month	–3
	6 months	–4
	1 year	–5
	2 years	–6
	5 years	–7

16d. Why do you say that? (PROBE)

_____

                                                        46–
_____
                                                        47–
                                                        48–
_____

16e. (HAND TAT #2 SHEET) Here is a picture of two people talking. The first one says, "Someone I know has been asked to testify in court against a person he saw starting a forest fire. What should he do?" How do you think the other person would answer? (PROBE)

_____

                                                        49–
_____
                                                        50–
                                                        51–
_____

Exhibit 8–1   *(Continued)*

17a. During the last year, have you visited or driven through any forests?

Yes   52–1   No   –2   (SKIP TO Q.18)

17b. About how many times have you driven through a forest area in the last year?

_____times   53–

17c. About how many times have you camped out in a forest area during the last year?

_____times   54–

17d. Altogether, how many days or parts of days would you say that you spent in forests or forest areas during the last year?

_____days   55–

17e. Have you ever seen a forest fire burning?

Yes   56–1   No   –2

17f. Have you ever seen a forest *after* a fire?

Yes   57–1   No   –2

18.   Respondent's age: Under 25   58–1
                                 25–34   –2
                                 35–44   –3
                                 45–54   –4
                                 55 and over   –5

19.   Family size: 1 person   59–1
                                 2 persons   –2
                                 3 persons   –3
                                 4 persons   –4
                                 5 or more persons –5

20.   Sex: Male   60–1
                                 Female   –2

21.   Occupation of male head of house_____ 61–
      If no male head of house check here ☐

22.   Income: Under $3,000   63–1
                                 $3,000–$4,999   –2
                                 $5,000–$7,999   –3
                                 $8,000–$9,999   –4
                                 $10,000–$11,999   –5
                                 $12,000 and over   –6

Respondent's Name:_____

Address:_____

Phone:_____

Interviewer:_____

symbols

Card I

TAT #1 Sheet

Haug Associates, Inc., a marketing research firm, in a study for the co-operative Forest Fire Prevention Program of the U.S. Department of Agriculture (U.S.D.A.) It should be read carefully prior to reading the remainder of the chapter.

The purpose of the study was to measure the public's knowledge of *Smokey the Bear* and the *Smokey* campaign as well as attitudes toward

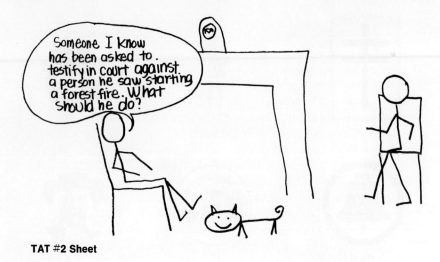

TAT #2 Sheet

forest fires and fire prevention programs.[5] To avoid repetition, specific
questions on the questionnaire are referred to in the text by their number
with no direct reference to the title of the questionnaire.

Preliminary Decisions

Prior to constructing the actual questionnaire, the researcher must know
exactly *what information* he will attempt to collect from *which respondents*
by *what techniques.* We have already discussed (Chapter 1) the critical
importance of clearly specifying exactly what information is needed.
Obviously, the data gained from a questionnaire are of limited value if
they are on the wrong topic (surrogate information error) or if they are
incomplete. The gathering of data that are not specifically required increases the cost of the project. The researcher must begin with a precise
statement of what information is required to deal with the management
problem at hand.

The specific objectives for the U.S.D.A. questionnaire were to determine:

[5] The complete report, which contains two other versions of the questionnaire and
the sampling plan and data analysis, is Haug Associates, Inc., *Public Image of and
Attitudes Toward Smokey the Bear and Forest Fires* (Washington, D.C.; U.S. Department of Agriculture, June, 1968).

a. *Awareness of Smokey the Bear Campaign and Smokey*
   - Aided and unaided recall of Smokey
   - Association of Smokey with fire prevention
   - Sources of awareness of Smokey
   - Awareness of the slogan, "Only You Can Prevent Forest Fires"
   - Advertising recall

b. *Attitudes Toward the Campaign and Smokey*
   - Attitudes and feelings toward Smokey
   - Smokey's image
   - Elements particularly liked and disliked about Smokey
   - Attitudes toward the slogan
   - Attitudes toward the campaign
   - Perception of the effectiveness of the Smokey campaign

c. *Knowledge of and Attitudes Toward Forest Fires*
   - The extent to which forest fires are viewed as a serious national problem and reasons why
   - Factors believed responsible for forest fires
   - Knowledge of the damage caused by forest fires
   - Steps that can be taken to reduce forest fires
   - How the accidental and deliberate starters of forest fires are viewed in terms of the punishment that should be imposed upon them

d. *Exposure to Forests*
   - Number of visits per year
   - Number of times camped

It is also essential to have a clear idea of exactly who our respondents are to be. Questions that are appropriate for a group of college graduates might not be appropriate for a group of high school graduates, and almost certainly would not be appropriate for grade schoolchildren. In general, the more diversified the potential respondents, the more difficult it is to construct a sound questionnaire that is appropriate for the entire group. For example, the U.S.D.A. questionnaire reproduced in Exhibit 8–1 was designed for adult respondents. A second version was prepared for grade school children and a third version for high school students.[6]

Finally, we need to decide on the method or technique of administering the questionnaire prior to designing it. However, it may be necessary to

---

[6] For discussions of special problems in questioning specific subgroups see P. M. Vaillancourt, "Stability of Children's Survey Responses," *Public Opinion Quarterly,* **37** (Fall 1973), 373–387; S. Welch, J. Comer, and M. Steinman, "Interviewing in a Mexican-American Community: An Investigation of Some Potential Sources of Response Bias," *Public Opinion Quarterly,* **37** (Spring 1973), 115–126; and R. A. Peterson, "Selected Marketing Research Techniques—Potentials and Pitfalls," paper presented at the 1974 Southwestern Marketing Association Meetings.

alter the method of administration if attempts at designing an effective questionnaire for the initial method of administration are unsuccessful. The nature of the decision involving which method of administration to use is described in the chapter on survey research. The U.S.D.A. questionnaire was administered in person at the respondent's home.

In addition, the researcher must be aware of the general approach that is to be taken with the respondents. This involves such issues as identification of the sponsor, what the respondents are told the purpose of the research is, and whether the respondents are to be treated anonymously. The conditions under which the questionnaire is administered are, in effect, part of the measuring instrument and may affect the results.

Decisions About Question Content

Decisions concerning question content center on the general nature of the question and the information it is designed to produce rather than the form or specific wording of the question. Five major issues, or problem areas, are involved with question content. For each question, the researcher must ascertain (1) *the need for the data,* (2) *the ability of the question to produce the data,* (3) *the ability of the respondent to answer accurately,* (4) *the willingness of the respondent to answer accurately,* and (5) *the potential for external exents to bias the answer.*

The Need for the Data Asked for by the Question

In general, every question on a questionnaire should make a contribution to the information on which the recommendation(s) to management is based. Therefore, the first question a researcher should ask about each question is: "Exactly how am I going to use the data generated by this question?" If he cannot provide a precise answer, the question should *not* be retained on the questionnaire. Vague answers such as "It might come in handy later" are not sufficient. Each question should play a definite, precise role.

The greatest mistake make by inexperienced questionnaire designers is to ask a large number of questions about the topic of interest without carefully considering how each will be used. Then, when it comes time to analyze the results, they find that most of the data generated are not needed for the analysis and that some essential information has not been generated. The researcher must ensure that each question contributes information to the analysis and that there is a question to generate each separate type of data needed for the analysis. The best way to approach this problem is to make up responses (dummy data) to each question, analyze the results, and ensure that the results of the analysis provide sufficient information for the resolution of the management problem.

In certain situations we may ask questions that are not part of our planned analysis. There are two acceptable reasons for doing this. The first is that it may occasionally be useful to ask a series of relatively neutral questions at the beginning of a questionnaire or interview in order to obtain respondent involvement and rapport prior to asking more sensitive or controversial questions. However, these questions should be used only when necessary and for an explicit purpose.

The second acceptable reason for using questions that will not play an explicit role in our analysis is to help disguise the purpose or sponsorship of a study. People tend to exaggerate their positive feelings toward a store, brand, or company if they are aware that it is sponsoring the survey. Therefore, it is sometimes necessary to ask questions about competing brands or products even though the information thus gained will not aid in the management decision. Such questions are also frequently used in the first part of a questionnaire but are omitted from later stages when it is no longer possible or necessary to disguise the purpose and/or sponsorship of the study. This approach was used in the U.S.D.A. study although the other symbols utilized in questions *1* and *2* did provide reference points for interpreting the responses to *Smokey*.

Ability of the Question to Produce the Data

Once we have assured ourselves that the question is necessary, we must make sure that it is sufficient. That is, will this one question generate the information we need or should we utilize two or more separate questions? For example, many questions ask individuals to express choices or preferences. If the researcher is also interested in how *strongly* or *intensely* the respondent holds these views, a separate question should be asked to ascertain this: *How strongly do you feel about this—very strongly, somewhat strongly, or not at all strongly?*

Or consider the "double-barreled" question, *"Do you prefer a small, economy car or a larger, sporty car?*" Would a response of "larger, sporty car" mean that the individual preferred larger cars, sporty cars, or larger, sporty cars? Here several questions or a different questioning technique are needed to avoid confusion. Each question should, to the extent possible, provide data that are subject to only one interpretation. Therefore, if two or more types of information are needed about a topic, such as a respondent's preference and how strongly he holds that preference, a specific question should be designed for each type of information.

Ability of the Respondent to Answer Accurately

Once we are sure that our question content is necessary and sufficient, we must consider the respondent's ability to provide an accurate answer. Inability to answer a question arises from three major sources: (1) *having never been exposed to the answer,* (2) *having been exposed to the answer but forgetting,* and (3) *being unable to verbalize the answer.* The first two categories are concerned primarily with "factual" information whereas the third is concerned more with attitudes and motives.

Uniformed Respondents

Respondents are frequently asked questions on topics about which they are uninformed. "Uninformed" in this sense means that they have never known the answer to the question. Wives may be asked about their husband's gross income or the annual cost of insurance premiums, or husbands may be asked about their wive's gross income or credit purchases. In both of these cases, the spouse may have never known the answer. Another common example is to ask an individual's opinion about a product, store, or brand that he has literally "never heard of."

Uninformed respondents become a source of measurement error because of a reluctance of people to admit a lack of knowledge on a topic. This becomes particularly acute when the content or wording of the question implies that the individual *should* know the answer. In one study, 70 per cent of the respondents expressed an opinion about "the Metallic Metals Act" even though no such act had ever existed or been proposed![7]

Any time there is a possibility that the respondent may have no knowledge of the information requested, an attempt should be made to verify this fact. Consider the two following sets of questions: *"Do you know the current assessed value of your home?"* and *"What is the current assessed value of your home?"* and questions *1a* and *1b* from Exhibit 8–1. The second question in each set, if it were the only one asked, would imply that the respondent should know the answer. This, in turn, will encourage guessing on the part of the respondent.

On the other hand, the first question implies that at least some people do not know the assessed value of their home or may not have seen one or more of the symbols. This makes it somewhat easier for the respondent to admit his own lack of knowledge. If a third question were also asked— *"How confident are you that the figure you gave is within $100 of the actual figure?"* extremely confident, quite confident, not too confident—the researcher would be much better equipped to evaluate the responses.

[7] S. Gill, "How Do You Stand on Sin?" *Tide,* **XXI** (March 14, 1947), 72.

Forgetful Respondents

A more common type of problem arises when the respondent is forced to rely upon memory for facts that he had been exposed to in the past. A simple test will indicate the delicate nature of memory. Answer the following questions from memory and then check the answers. Who was the defeated vice-presidential candidate in the 1972 election? Who are the senators from your state? How many credit cards (of all types) do you own? How much money is in your wallet? How many pairs of shoes do you own? What color shirt did you wear three days ago? Most of us do not know the answer to one or more of these rather simple questions. Yet we confidently ask housewives to report on not only the last brand of peas purchased but also on why they purchased them, and how many advertisements they had noticed about them.

Memory decays rapidly with *time*. That is, we forget most things very soon after they occur.[8] After a few days, the rate of forgetting drops rapidly. The further in the past an event occurred, the higher is the probability that it has been forgotten. Counteracting the rate of forgetting induced by time are "pressures" to remember caused by *repetition* and *impression*. Studies involving repetition suggest that the more often we perform a task, see an advertisement, and the like, the more likely we are to remember. This does *not* mean that we are likely to remember any one exposure to the advertisement or the performance of the task. It only means that we are likely to remember the advertisement or the task itself.

The impression that a particular situation makes on us influences the probability of our remembering it. The greater the impression, the greater is the likelihood of remembering. Impression value is determined by the psychological importance of the event, the importance of the events with which it is associated, and the nature of other events occurring in the same time frame. Many of us can remember even unimportant details about buying a first car, a wedding ring, or perhaps a house, even though these events occurred a number of years ago.

Unfortunately, many of the events of interest to marketing managers, and thus to marketing researchers, are of only minor importance to the average consumer. A brand manager may invest a year or more of his life in shepherding a new snack food through development and into an introduction campaign. However, the consumer who is exposed to the television advertisement or who tries the product sees it only as a $.69 item that might satisfy a relatively minor need or desire. The odds of a consumer remembering a great deal about the purchase, or even if he made one, two weeks later, are not substantial.

---

[8] J. F. Engel, D. T. Kollat, R. D. Blackwell, *Consumer Behavior*, 2nd ed. (New York: Holt, Rinehart, and Winston, Inc., 1973), 340–341.

Numerous studies have indicated that questions that rely on *unaided recall* (questions that do not provide any clues to potential answers) result in an understatement of specific events such as shows watched or small items purchased.[9] In addition, more popular and well-known brands tend to be overstated in response to questions asking for this kind of information. For example, a respondent may vaguely remember seeing an advertisement for soup and so he reports seeing an advertisement for Campbell's Soup as this is the only brand name that comes to his mind. Questions *3a, 7a,* and *7c* rely on unaided recall.

Attempts to overcome problems with simple memory questions—unaided recall—focus on providing cues or aids to help the individual recall more accurately. *Aided recall* provides the respondents with all or some aspects of the original events. The difference between an aided recall and an unaided recall question is similar to the difference between a multiple choice and an essay examination question. Questions *3b* and *8b* are examples of aided recall questions.

One measure of billboard advertising effectiveness would be to ask respondents to *"name or describe any billboards that you have noticed while commuting to and from work."* This would be unaided recall. A second way of measuring the effectiveness of billboard advertisements would be to present a list of product categories and ask the respondents to indicate whether they had noted billboards for each category and, if so, for which brands. A third approach would be to present a list of brand names for each product category and ask the respondents which, if any, of these brands were advertised on billboards along their route to work. Finally, a picture of a billboard for each brand could be shown and the respondents asked to identify those that appeared along their route to work.

The level of "aid" increases at each stage in this example and, in general, so will the number of billboards identified. Unfortunately, the number identified may exceed the number along the route the individual takes to work and even worse, the correspondence between those identified and those actually on the individual's route may not be particularly high. It has been suggested that researchers warn the respondents in advance that some of the items they will be shown are bogus, that is, billboards that are not in the area. The results of this approach have been mixed.[10]

To the extent possible, researchers should avoid requiring respondents to attempt to recall events that occurred beyond the past few days or that

[9] J. H. Myers and W. H. Reynolds, *Consumer Behavior and Marketing Management* (Boston: Houghton Mifflin Company, 1967), 65–67.

[10] D. Starch, *Measuring Advertising Readership and Results* (New York: McGraw-Hill Book Co., 1966), 20; and E. M. Smith and J. B. Mason, "The Influence of Instructions on Response Error," *Journal of Marketing Research,* **7** (May 1970), 254–255.

were not of importance to the respondent. The researcher should also be alert to the fact that his involvement with a firm or product will have a tendency to make it seem much more important to him than it will to the average respondent.

When recall must be used, several levels should be used. Unaided recall questions should be followed by questions with additional cues. This practice was followed in the U.S.D.A. questionnaire in question sequences *3a, 3b; 7a, 7b;* and *8a, 8b.* The researcher might want to use some middle ground between the unaided and aided recall questions if his purpose is merely to compute an aggregate measure. If the recall data are used to classify individual respondents, for example, to compare the attitudes of those who report seeing a given advertisement with those who do not, the problem is more complex. The best remedy (other than to avoid the situation) is to take both unaided and aided recall measures, analyze each separately and see if the conclusions differ. If not, there is no problem. If they do, other evidence or more extensive interviewing must be done to determine which measure is more accurate.

Inarticulate Respondents

Many times respondents fail to give meaningful answers to researchers' questions because they are not able to verbalize the answers. Questions such as, *"Why did you buy that style of car?"* or *"Why did you decide to shop here?"* cannot always be answered by the respondent. If we think closely, each of us can remember instances when we made purchases for which we did not really understand our motives. We can also think of instances in which we probably purchased an object for some reason other than the one we admitted to ourselves.

We buy things from habit, for vanity, and other reasons that we are not consciously aware of. However, when asked *why* we buy a given product or brand we may respond with conventional reasons rather than the actual reasons. A researcher who accepts these conventional reasons is operating with substantial measurement error. A method for overcoming a respondent's inability to verbalize answers to particular questions involves projective techniques. These techniques are discussed in the next chapter. Question 4 in the U.S.D.A. questionnaire is an example of a projective technique.

Willingness of the Respondent to Answer Accurately

Assuming that the respondent *can* answer the question, we must still assess the likelihood that he *will* answer it. A refusal to answer a question may take one of three forms. First, the respondent may refuse to answer the specific question or questions that offend him and still complete the remainder of the questionnaire. This is called *item nonresponse.* The seriousness of item nonresponse depends upon how critical the particular question is to the overall analysis. However, since the researcher would be ill-advised to include any potentially sensitive questions that were not absolutely essential for his analysis, *item nonresponse* can result in the information from the entire questionnaire being of limited value.

Another effect of an improper question (from the respondent's viewpoint) is a refusal to complete the remainder of the questionnaire. In mail surveys, this generally results in a failure to return the questionnaire. In telephone interviews, it may result in a broken connection.

The third way of "refusing" to answer a question is to provide an incorrect answer deliberately. Thus, rather than "hanging up on" or "throwing out" the interviewer, the respondent may avoid a particular question by providing acceptable but inaccurate information. This type of refusal is perhaps the most difficult of the three with which to deal because, unlike the other two forms, it is hard to detect.

Why would a respondent refuse to answer one or more questions accurately? There are a host of particular reasons. However, most of these specific reasons fall into one of three categories. The information request may be perceived by the respondent as (1) *"none of the interviewer's business,"* (2) *embarrassing,* or (3) *reflecting on his prestige.*

Requests for Personal Information

Most people will provide answers to questions that they think are legitimate. By legitimate we mean that the questions are reasonable in light of the situation and the role of the person asking the question. Thus, people will answer very personal questions posed by their doctor but would consider the same questions quite improper if asked by a casual acquaintance. Researchers of sexual behavior patterns have been able to obtain cooperation in gaining extremely personal data in part because the types of questions they asked were perceived as appropriate given their role as researchers into sexual behavior.

Unfortunately, too many marketing researchers seem to believe that a brief introduction and the fact that they are with a reputable marketing research firm (which very few respondents will have heard of) makes any question they wish to ask legitimate in the eyes of the respondent. Experience indicates that many respondents who have willingly answered a lengthy series of questions on purchasing and shopping patterns may balk when suddenly asked for their income, age, occupation, or other data without an explanation. The common phrase, "Now I would like to ask you a few questions about yourself," is seldom an adequate explanation for why someone should reveal his age or income to a stranger. A limited explanation of why a particular piece of information is required will often suffice: *"To help us understand how people in different age and income groups view the shopping process, we need to know . . ."*

Requests for Embarrassing Information

Answers to questions asking for embarrassing information are subject to distortion, especially when either personal or telephone interviews are used. Questions on the consumption of alcoholic beverages, use of personal hygiene products, readership of certain magazines, and sexual or aggressive feelings aroused by particular advertisements are examples of topics on which questions are subject to refusals or distortions by the respondents.

Two techniques are possible for dealing with this problem aside from asking the questions in the normal manner and hoping for the best. They are the use of *counterbiasing statements* and *randomized response* techniques.

Counterbiasing Statements. These involve beginning the question with a statement that will make the potentially embarrassing response seem common or hard to deny. For example, *"Recent studies have shown that a high percentage of males utilize their wife's hair spray to control their hair. Have you used your wife's hair spray in the past week?"* Another approach is to ask, *"When was the last time you used your wife's hair spray?"* Both of these types of questions make it easy for the respondent to admit the potentially embarrassing behavior. However, not all respondents will be so inclined. Furthermore, leading questions such as these may cause some to admit to behavior they did not engage in because it may suddenly seem embarrassing to *not* have engaged in the behavior.

Randomized Response Techniques. A second approach for overcoming nonresponse and measurement error caused by embarrassing questions is the randomized response technique.[11] It presents the respondent with two questions, one sensitive or potentially embarrassing, the other harmless or even meaningless. The respondent then flips a coin, looks at the last number on his Social Security card to see if it is odd or even, or in some other random manner selects which question to answer. The chosen question is then answered with a "yes" or "no" *without telling the researcher which question is being answered.*

Consider the problem of the researcher who needs information on the number of students who engage in shoplifting. It is unlikely that many

[11] C. Campbell and B. L. Joiner, "How to Get the Answer Without Being Sure You've Asked the Question," *The American Statistician,* **27** (December 1973), 229–231.

students would answer this question even if asked in an anonymous mail survey (because of a fear that the survey might not be truly anonymous). Therefore, the randomized response technique is appropriate. The two following questions could be used:

A. *"Have you shoplifted anything in the past four weeks?"*
B. *"Were you born during the month of June?"*

The students are instructed to check their Social Security cards. If the last two digits are 60 or above, they are to answer question A with the single word, "yes" or "no," on a separate, blank card. If the last two digits are 59 or less, they are to answer the question B with a "yes" or "no" on the card. From these responses the researcher, without knowing who answered which question or even which answer is associated with which question, can estimate the percentage of students who reported shoplifting in the previous four weeks. The appropriate formula is:

P("yes") $= P$(Question A is chosen) $\cdot P$(Yes answer to question A)
$\qquad\qquad + P$(Question B is chosen) $\cdot P$(Yes answer to question B)

If we assume that we receive 16 per cent "yes" replies, we can easily compute the best estimate of the percentage of students who reported they engaged in shoplifting. Assume that from the registrar's office we determine that 10 per cent of the students were born in June (it is essential that the percentage of respondents who could be expected to answer "yes" to the nonsensitive question be known). The formula then contains only one unknown—the percentage of respondents who answered "yes" to the sensitive question:

$$.16 = (.4)(X) + (.6)(.1)$$
$$.10 = .4X$$
$$X = .25$$

Thus, we can estimate that 25 per cent of those who answered the sensitive question answered positively. This is also the estimate of the percentage of the total student body that would report engaging in shoplifting.

The reported uses of this technique involve unreported automobile accidents[12] and abortions.[13] It appears to offer a useful approach to obtaining sensitive information from respondents while completely protecting the respondent's anonymity.

Requests for "Prestige" or "Normative" Information

Questions that reflect on the respondent's prestige or that have a socially desirable choice among the answers are subject to measurement error.

---

[12] Ibid.
[13] Ibid.

Prestige-oriented questions, such as those dealing with education obtained, income earned, or amount of time spent in reading newspapers, typically produce answers with an upward bias. For example, readership of high prestige magazines is frequently overstated and readership of low prestige magazines is frequently understated when self-report techniques are utilized.[14]

Similarly, questions with a normative or socially accepted answer tend to have a consistent bias toward social norms. For example, surveys generally indicate strong support for educational television; yet, relatively few people consistently watch educational channels according to research using observational techniques. Many shoppers report price to be an important variable yet behave in a manner that casts doubt upon these reports.

When possible, it is best to avoid questions with prestige or normative answers. When unavoidable, the "leading" questions technique or the randomized response technique can sometimes be used to reduce measurement error. Careful wording and frequent pleas for candor, coupled with explanations of why candor is needed, can also reduce measurement error on these questions.

Sometimes indirect questions can be employed. For example, *"Have you read the latest nonfiction best seller?"* will probably result in an overstatement of the number of readers. An indirect approach such as *"Do you intend to read _____?"* allows those who have not a graceful way to say so by indicating that they intend to read it. Those who say they do not intend to read the book can then be asked why. Those who have already read the book can then so indicate. This approach will often produce a more accurate measurement than the more direct approach.

The Impact of External Events

A final issue involving question content is potential bias or error that a question may reflect because of factors outside of the questionnaire itself. The time at which a question is asked is such a variable. A traffic planning commission was considering the need for bicycle paths. A questionnaire was designed and mailed to a sample of the population. One question asked for information on bicycle riding during the past week, which, in and of itself, was a reasonable question. However, the questionnaire was sent out in the winter after a week of particularly bad weather. Therefore, the bicycle usage figures were most likely much less than would have been obtained had the weather been more nearly normal the preceding week.

[14] J. I. Engel, H. G. Wales, and M. R. Warshaw, *Promotional Strategy* (Homewood, Ill.: Richard D. Irwin, Inc., 1971), 288.

Decisions Concerning Question Phrasing

Question phrasing is the translation of the desired question content into words and phrases that can be understood easily and clearly by the respondents. The central concern is to ensure that the respondents and the researcher assign exactly the same meaning to the question. The following are five general issues with which we must be concerned when we evaluate question phrasing: (1) *Are the words, singularly and in total, understandable to the respondents?* (2) *Are the words biased or "loaded" in any respect?* (3) *Are all the alternatives involved in the questions clearly stated?* (4) *Are any assumptions implied by the question clearly stated?* and (5) *What frame of reference is the respondent being asked to assume?*

The Meaning of Words

Most of us would agree that questions designed for 12 year olds should utilize a simpler vocabulary than similar questions designed for adult respondents. What we tend to overlook is the fact that the reading and vocabulary skills of most 12 year olds surpass those of many adults. The researcher must take the vocabulary skills of his intended respondent group into account when designing a question. It is obvious that such terms as *innovations, psychographics,* and *advertising medium* should be used only when dealing with specialized respondent groups.

Unfortunately, common words sometimes create equally serious problems. *"How many members are there in your family?"* Does "family" mean "nuclear family?" If so, will it have the same meaning to all respondents? Is a grandmother, aunt, or the spouse of one of the children that lives with the nuclear family to be counted? The word *kind* can cause similar problems. *"What kind of razor do you use?"* will result in some respondents identifying the type (safety or electric) whereas others name brands.

Usually is also subject to several interpretations. How should one respond to the question *"Do you usually use aftershave lotion?"* if he always uses it prior to going on a date (say three times a week) and never uses it otherwise? *Regularly* causes the same problem of interpretation. What type of transportation does an individual use "regularly" if he rides a bicycle to work five days a week, goes shopping in the car every Saturday, and takes the city bus each week to a downtown lecture series?

What is meant by the term, *forest area,* in question *17b?* Does its meaning differ from the term *forests,* in question *17a?* What about the term *burning* in question *17e?* Do you need to see the flames or just the smoke from a distance? How much time is implied by the term *after* in question *17f?*

Terms such as these may elicit different responses from people with identical behavior patterns and identical responses from people with different behavior patterns. Furthermore, the researcher may attach an interpretation that does not coincide with that of the majority of the respondents.

Even more critical problems can be introduced when the same term takes on different meanings to different groups of people. In some regions of the United States middle- and upper-class individuals apply the term *dinner* to the evening meal and refer to the noon meal as *lunch.* However, working-class families tend to call the evening meal supper and the noon meal dinner. Therefore, a question eliciting information about eating habits at "dinner" would receive evening meal information from one group and noon meal information from the other. If social class were then used as a classification variable, the two groups would most likely report vastly different eating habits at "dinner."

The impact that unclear words or phrases can have is demonstrated in a study that compared two versions of a question on wig ownership among women. The first version of the question was used to ask half the sample whether or not the respondent owned a wig made of genuine hair. Eight per cent of the respondents indicated that they did. The second version was used to ask the second half of the sample if the respondent owned a wig *or* hairpiece made of genuine hair, and allowed a separate response for wig and hairpiece. This version of the questions showed that only 1 per cent of the respondents owned wigs whereas 15 per cent owned hairpieces.[15] Thus, the first question identified eight times more "wig" owners than the second because many women did not distinguish between a wig and a hairpiece until this distinction was indicated in the question itself.

How do we ensure that the words we select are likely to be clear to our respondents? A number of graded vocabulary lists are available that contain "well-known" words but these are generally too old to place a great deal of confidence in today.[16] In the absence of a current word list of this type, a good first step is to follow Payne's advice and consult a reputable, up-to-date dictionary and a thesaurus and ask the following six questions of each word (including the common ones whose meaning may seem obvious to us):

1. Does it mean what we intend?
2. Does it have any other meanings?
3. If so, does the context make the intended meaning clear?

---

[15] Noelle-Neumann, op. cit., 198.
[16] E. L. Thorndike and I. Large, *The Teacher's Word Book of 30,000 Words* (New York: Columbia University Press, 1944). See also Payne, op. cit., 151–176.

4. Does the word have more than one pronunciation?
5. Is there any word of similar pronunciation that might be confused?
6. Is a simpler word or phrase suggested?[17]

After this process, two or more alternative wordings for a given question may exist. Pretesting and the *split ballot* technique (sending out two or more versions of the same questionnaire) can help decide on which wording to utilize.

Biased Words and Leading Questions

Biased or loaded words and phrases are emotionally colored and suggest an automatic feeling of approval or disapproval.[18] Leading questions suggest what the answer should be or indicate the researcher's own point of view. Both result in a consistent measurement error that would not exist if a more neutral phrasing were used.

Consider the following two questions: "How many times in the past month have you purchased gasoline on the black market?" versus "How many times in the past month have you been able to secure gasoline beyond your allocation?" It is easier for most respondents to accurately answer the second version than it is the first. A phrase such as *the black market* is objectionable to most people and leads to considerable bias in the response.

Loaded phrases are difficult to deal with because phrases that are neutral to one group may be emotionally charged to another. Phrases such as *luxury items* and *leisure time* are neutral to many people yet carry negative overtones to others. This fact illustrates the need to pretest with respondents as similar as possible to those to be included in the final survey.

"Do you think that General Motors is doing everything possible to reduce air pollution from the cars it manufactures?" is a loaded question. General Motors is not doing "everything possible" in this area. This does not mean that it is not doing everything *reasonable*. However, few firms or individuals ever do "all that is possible." The use of phrases such as *everything possible* (or its opposite, *anything*) tend to produce biased responses.

Identification of the sponsor can introduce measurement error into the results. The sponsor may be identified in the request for cooperation, in a specific question, or the respondent may infer sponsorship from the relative frequency that one brand is covered in the questions. The tendency is to exaggerate one's positive feelings toward the sponsor. Even in mail surveys, respondents are reluctant to "hurt someone's feelings" by saying negative things about the sponsor. In addition, some respondents feel flat-

[17] Payne, op. cit., 141.
[18] Oppenheim, op. cit., 59.

tered by the attention and thus feel grateful to the sponsoring company. For these reasons, in most research projects the research organization conducting the study is identified but not the firm sponsoring the study. This was the case in the U.S.D.A. study.

Introductory materials that accompany the questionnaire can also bias the response. One of the authors recently received a questionnaire, which, in the introduction, contained statements that implied that the FTC, consumer groups, and progressive advertisers all supported comparative product advertising. The questionnaire then asked for opinions concerning comparative advertising. It would have made one feel almost un-American to state anything negative about comparative advertising following that introduction.

Organizations and groups as well as words can take on emotional meanings. Groups such as the Boy Scouts, the Heart Association, the Communist party, the Teamster's Union, and the American Medical Association have acquired strong emotional connotations for many people. Consider the probable response to the following versions of a question: "Do you agree with the Boy Scouts' (Communist party, AMA, and so on) statement that . . ." In the previous question, the response involves an evaluation of the statement and an evaluation of the organization that supposedly made the statement.

The use of examples to clarify a question can sometimes introduce a bias. "Do you believe that people should eat at least one leafy vegetable, such as spinach, each day?" will produce different answers than "Do you believe that people should eat at least one leafy vegetable, such as lettuce, each day?" Examples such as those mentioned previously are sometimes necessary to make the meaning of the question clear. However, they also tend to draw attention away from the question itself and to focus it on the example. Thus, the answers to the first questions posed will reflect, in part, the respondent's perceptions of spinach whereas answers to the second question will reflect their perceptions of lettuce.

Implied Alternatives

At the beginning of this section, an example was presented that showed that making an implied alternative explicit increased the selection of that alternative from 19 per cent to 68 per cent. Other studies have produced equally impressive results.[19] For example, the question "Do you think workers should have the right to elect a representative on the board of directors of the company they work for?" produced 61 per cent "yes" answers. However, when the phrase "or should all the directors be elected

[19] See Noelle-Neumann, op. cit., 200–201, and Payne, op. cit., 55–74.

by the owners of the company?" was added, the percentage that indicated that the workers should have the right to elect a representative dropped to 53 per cent.[20]

Parten cites evidence that indicates that the order in which alternatives are mentioned will affect the results. If the respondents do not have strong opinions on the issue or if the alternatives are long or complex, the alternative presented last will be chosen more often than it would if presented earlier.[21]

A thorough examination of the literature dealing with this issue leads to two major conclusions. First, all relevant alternatives should be clearly stated unless there is an explicit reason for not doing so. Second, when practical, a split-ballot technique should be used to ensure that each alternative appears in the last position on an equal number of questionnaires.

Implied Assumptions

Questions are frequently asked in such a way that the answer depends upon assumptions about factors outside the question itself. "Are you in favor of curtailing the amount of advertising allowed on television?" will elicit differing responses depending on the respondents' assumptions concerning the effects this might have on the quantity and quality of television programming. A more effective way of wording the question would be: "Are you in favor of curtailing the amount of advertising allowed on television if this would have (such and such an impact) on television programming?"

Failure to state essential assumptions often produces (not always accidentally) inflated estimates of the public's demand for various products, social programs, or services. One more example should make the importance of this issue clear. "Are you in favor of requiring all new refrigerators to be built with the most effective insulation available as an energy conservation measure?" will elicit substantially more positive responses in that form than it will when "even though it will mean a 25 per cent increase in the retail price of the refrigerator" is added.

Frame of Reference

The wording of the question will determine which frame of reference or viewpoint the respondent will assume. Consider the following versions

[20] M. Parten, *Surveys, Polls, and Samples* (New York: Harper & Row Publishers, Inc., 1950), 210.
[21] Ibid., 211.

of a question to be answered by recent claimants of an automobile insurance company.

> "Does Allstate provide satisfactory or unsatisfactory settlement of claims"
> "Do you believe that Allstate provides satisfactory or unsatisfactory settlement of claims?"
> "Were you satisfied or unsatisfied with Allstate's settlement of your recent claim?"

Each of these versions provides the respondent with a somewhat different frame of reference. The first version calls for an objective answer that may include the respondent's perceptions of other people's standards for claim settlement and how adequately Allstate meets these expectations. The third question involves only the individual's own standards and his perceptions of the firm's reaction to his last claim. The second question probably elicits responses somewhere between the first and the third. Which question is best depends entirely on the purposes of the research. However, if the researcher is interested in personal responses to specific situations he must be sure that this is what the question asks for. The focus throughout most of the U.S.D.A. questionnaire is on the individual respondent.

Decisions About the Response Format

"Who do you think will win the Super Bowl this year?" "Who do you think will win the Super Bowl this year, the Cowboys, the Redskins, or the Dolphins?" "Do you think the Cowboys will win the Super Bowl this year?" These three questions represent the three basic response formats that questions can assume. The first question is an example of an *open-ended* question. The respondent is free to choose any response he deems appropriate within the limits implied by the question. The second question is an example of a *multiple-choice* response format. Here the respondent must select from among three or more prespecified responses. The final question represents a *dichotomous* question.

The decision as to which form of question to use must be based on the objective for the particular question. Each has its particular uses, advantages, and disadvantages.

Open-Ended Questions

Open-ended questions leave the respondent free to offer any replies that seem appropriate to him in light of the question. The relative freedom in choosing which response to make leads some researchers to refer to questions of this nature as *free-response* or *free-answer* questions. Questions *5* and *7e* are examples of open-ended questions.

The degree of openness will vary from question to question. The question, "What do you think about cigarettes?" allows almost total freedom to the respondent who may discuss cigarettes in general, particular brands, advertising slogans, health issues, ethics, and/or a host of other related issues. The question, "What brand of cigarettes do you generally smoke?" offers much less freedom. In this case the respondent is constrained (we hope) to merely naming the brand that he generally smokes. Questions *5* and *11a* are characterized by equally dramatic differences in openness.

Advantages of Open-ended Questions.   Open-ended questions have a number of desirable features. The respondent is not influenced by a pre-stated set of response categories. Thus, he is able to express his opinion even though it might be quite divergent from what the researcher expected or what others had expressed. Related to this is the fact that open-ended questions elicit a wide variety of responses. This variety comes from both the diversity of responses across the total group and from individuals giving several responses to the same question. Both of these properties make open-ended questions particularly suitable for exploratory and problem identification research.

Open-ended questions also serve as an excellent introduction to a topic area. They allow the respondent to express any pertinent feelings he may have on the topic and also get him accustomed to the topic and the process of answering questions. Open-ended questions help reduce potential frustration, particularly when mail surveys are used. Anyone who has examined the returns from mail surveys that did not contain some open-ended questions can testify to people's desires to express themselves as evidenced through margin notes and additional handwritten questions and answers.

Finally, open-ended questions can provide the researcher with a basis for judging the actual values and views of the respondents that is often difficult to capture with more structured techniques. This "feel" for the quality of the information can often be conveyed in the final report by the inclusion of quotes from representative samples. This was done in the U.S.D.A. study report.

Disadvantages of Open-ended Questions.   Unfortunately, the open-ended question is subject to a number of problems. It is generally inappropriate for self-administered questionnaires since most respondents will not write elaborate answers. Furthermore, it is subject to two important sources of error. First, it may measure respondent articulateness rather than the real issue. Some respondents will answer clearly and in depth on almost any topic, whereas others, who may have equal knowledge, may be more reluctant to express themselves.[22]

A second critical source of error is interviewer effects. Interviewers will vary in their ability to record the respondents' answers, in their intensity of probing, and in their objectivity. Ability to record answers is a function of writing speed and ability to summarize (if allowed).[23] Probing is a more complex issue. Some interview situations allow or require the interviewer to "probe" the respondent by asking such questions as "Why do you say that?" or "Can you tell me any more about that?" (See questions *12* through *16* for examples of probing instructions.) However, even when probing is expressly prohibited, the length of time the interviewer waits after a respondent stops speaking before asking the next question can introduce biases that are hard to detect.

Assume an interviewer believes that everyone should consider safety features as an important attribute in selecting an automobile. When a respondent answers an open-ended question concerning the attributes he considers important and mentions safety features, the interviewer quickly moves to the next question. However, when the respondent does not initially mention safety features, the interviewer hesitates a brief moment before asking the next question. Some of the respondents will take this as a cue to continue talking and some will finally mention safety features. Thus, safety features will end up being overstated even though the interviewer was perhaps not even aware of the bias being introduced.

An additional problem with open-ended questions is that, except for very small surveys, the responses must eventually be coded or categorized.[24] Obviously, most researchers cannot read 1,000 responses to an open-ended question and have a secure grip on all of the ramifications of the data. If the interviewers record the answers verbatim or nearly so, the time and cost of coding becomes a sizable proportion of the total cost of the research.

As an alternative to central coding, each interviewer can code or categorize the respondent's answer without showing the respondent the list of response alternatives. This technique is generally called *precoding*. The interviewer has, in effect, a multiple-choice question that he presents to the respondent as an open-ended question. The interviewer must then select the appropriate response category based on the respondent's verbal reply. Thus, the question "Which brand of cigarettes did you last pur-

---

[22] See B. S. Dohrenwend, "Some Effects of Open and Closed Questions," *Human Organization,* **24** (Summer 1965), 175–184.

[23] For example, see W. A. Collins, "Verbal Idiosyncracies as a Source of Bias," *Public Opinion Quarterly,* **34** (Fall 1970), 416–422.

[24] For a sophisticated approach to this problem see P. E. Green, Y. Wind, and A. K. Jain, "Analyzing Free-Response Data in Marketing Research," *Journal of Marketing Research,* **X** (February 1973), 45–52.

chase?" can be treated as open-ended by the respondent but the interviewer may, instead of recording the response, have a list of the most popular brands and simply check which brand the respondent names or an "other" category. Question *7a* utilizes this approach.

This technique works reasonably well with relatively simple questions such as the number of members in a family or monthly expenditures for given product categories. However, questions that require more complex answers present a high probability of interviewer bias. For example, a respondent might talk for several minutes in response to a question about why he purchased the brand he did. During this time he may mention several reasons or make statements that could fit into several response categories. The interviewer must then check one or a limited number of answers. It is virtually impossible to prevent the interviewer's personal preferences and expectations from affecting the results.

It seems best generally to restrict the use of open-ended questions to preliminary research and to research designed to develop categorical questions.[25] This assumes that the alternative to the open-ended question is a well-developed multiple-choice question. As we see in the next section, good multiple-choice questions are not easy to prepare. Nonetheless, for any large-scale survey, the cost and effort involved in developing such questions is worth the effort.

Multiple-Choice Questions

Approximately how much money do you spend on gasoline each month?
__$0–$1.00   __$1.01–$7.50   __$7.51–$12.50   __$12.51–$17.50
__$17.51–$22.50   __$22.51–$27.50   __over $27.50

Do European, Japanese, or American cars represent the highest level of workmanship?

Do you plan to buy a new refrigerator in the next 6 months?
__Definitely Yes   __Probably Yes   __Probably No   __Definitely No

What was the brand name of the last package of cigarettes you purchased?
__Winston   __Marlboro   __Salem   __Camel   __Vantage   __Kent
__Lucky Strikes   __Tareyton   __Chesterfield   __Old Gold   __Other

These questions represent versions of the multiple-choice question as do questions *9a, 10,* and *16a.* The essential feature of a multiple-choice question is that it presents, either in the question proper or immediately following the question, the list of possible answers from which the respondent must choose.

[25] This recommendation is consistent with S. L. Payne, "Are Open-ended Questions Worth the Effort?" *Journal of Marketing Research,* **2** (November 1965), 417–418.

Advantages of Multiple-Choice Questions.   Multiple-choice questions offer a number of advantages over open-ended questions. They are generally easier for both the field interviewer and the respondent. Indeed, they are almost essential for securing adequate cooperation in self-administered surveys. They also tend to reduce interviewer bias and bias caused by varying levels of respondent articulateness. In addition, tabulation and analysis are much simpler. Multiple-choice questions have an advantage over dichotomous questions whenever the answer naturally involves more than two choices or when some measure of gradation or degree is desired.

Disadvantages of Multiple-Choice Questions.   Balanced against these advantages are a number of problems. The development of a sound set of multiple-choice questions (or dichotomous questions) requires considerable effort, generally including the preliminary use of open-ended questions. In addition, showing the respondents the list of potential answers can cause several types of distortion in the resulting data.

If all possible alternatives are not listed, no information can be gained on the omitted alternatives. Even if an *"Other* (Specify)" category is included, there is a strong tendency for respondents to choose from among those alternatives listed. This may occur simply because one of the alternatives sounds familiar or logical and not because it is the proper answer to the question. All alternatives listed tend to be given equal consideration. Alternatives that the respondent had not thought about before may be selected over alternatives that he would have thought of on his own. This particular feature may be good or bad depending on the precise purpose of the question.

Number of Alternatives.   A crucial issue in multiple-choice questions is how many alternatives to list. The standard answer to this question is that the list of alternatives should be "mutually exclusive and collectively exhaustive." In other words, each alternative should appear only once and all possible alternatives should be included. However, it is frequently impractical to include all possible alternatives. A list of all possible brands of cigarettes, for example, would have to include not only American brands but also all foreign brands that are available in local tobacco shops. A researcher is seldom interested in those brands or alternatives that only a few people will select. Therefore, the general approach is to list the more prevalent choices and an "Other" category, which is often accompanied by a "Please Specify" and a short space to write in the answer. If the original list somehow excluded a major alternative, the "Other" category may uncover it.

Alternatives may also be omitted when one alternative would overwhelm the others and hide valuable information. Thus, one might ask, "Aside from honesty, which of the following characteristics is most important for a politician?" This is also a good way to avoid receiving socially acceptable answers rather than those that are perhaps more germane: "Not considering patriotism and support for the U.S. economy, which of the following reasons best justifies purchasing products made in the United States?"

Balanced or Unbalanced Alternatives. Another important issue concerns the number of alternatives on each side of an issue. For example, consider the following two lists of alternatives for the same question:

Is Sears' advertising truthful or misleading?
____Extremely misleading
____Very misleading
____Somewhat misleading
____Neither misleading nor truthful
____Truthful

versus

Is Sears' advertising truthful or misleading?
____Extremely truthful
____Very truthful
____Somewhat truthful
____Neither truthful nor misleading
____Misleading

The results obtained from the two sets of response categories will differ significantly. Although the preceding example is an extreme one, it is not difficult to find cases where a high degree of imbalance exists. A balanced treatment may tend to produce some central position bias, but the resulting error will generally be much smaller than that introduced by a heavily unbalanced design. The U.S.D.A. study utilized balanced lists, for example, in question *9a*. However, questions *16a* and *16c* appear somewhat unbalanced.

Position Bias. Position bias is also an important issue with multiple-choice questions. A list of numbers, such as amount of money spent, or estimates of facts, such as the number of outlets in a given chain store, is almost always subject to a strong middle position bias. That is, respondents tend to select those values that are near the middle of the range presented. Furthermore, an examination of most questionnaires indicates that this is a reasonably good strategy on the respondent's part. Many researchers, when one figure is known to be correct, include that figure in the list of alternatives and then select two or three figures for inclusion above and below the correct figure. This seems logical in that it gives the respondent an equal chance to overstate and understate the correct figure. What this logic ignores is the tendency of respondents to guess when they do not know an answer and to use the center positions as a safe guessing strategy.

This type of error can become especially critical when there is no "correct" answer and the researcher is merely attempting to ascertain some fact that should be unique to each respondent. For example, suppose the researcher, interested in the number of trips to the grocery store that a group of respondents makes in an "average" week, constructs a multiple-choice question to measure this. His judgment is that the average is two trips per week and very few people make more than four trips. Therefore, his alternatives are "Less than 1," "One," "Two," "Three," and "Four or more." The natural tendency of people to select the middle position will tend to confirm his hypothesis even though it may be incorrect. Split-ballot techniques should be used that place the "correct" or "expected" answer at various places along the list of numbers.

Table 8–2   Position Bias for Alternatives—Visual Presentation*

	Per Cent Selecting a Given Alternative			
Position of Alternative	*A*	*B*	*C*	*D*
Top	27	11	24	23
Middle	17	7	20	16
Bottom	23	7	21	18

* Adapted from S. L. Payne, *The Art of Asking Questions* (Princeton: Princeton University Press, 1951), 84.

It has been found that if three or four relatively long or complex alternatives are read to the respondents, there will be a bias in favor of the last alternative. However, if the alternatives are presented visually and all at the same time, the bias shifts to the alternative appearing at the top of the list. This effect can easily be seen in Table 8–2, which shows the percentage of samples of matched respondents that chose each of four alternatives when the position of the alternatives was rotated. As can be seen, there are strong position effects. Again, a split ballot technique is called for.

The construction and application of multiple-choice questions is not a simple task. Yet it is undoubtedly the best technique for collecting certain types of data (natural multiple answers or degrees) in large-scale survey research.

Dichotomous Questions

Dichotomous questions, which represent an extreme form of the multiple-choice question, allow only two responses; such as yes-no, agree-disagree, male-female, and did-did not. Questions *1a* and *7b* are dichotomous questions. Often the two categories are supplemented by a third neutral category such as "don't know," "no opinion," "both," or "neither."

Advantages of Dichotomous Questions. The advantages of the dichotomous question are similar to those of the multiple-choice question. It is quick and easy for the field interviewers to ask and for the respondents to answer. It is also easy to code and there is less opportunity for interviewer bias than with open-ended questions. The dichotomous question is well suited to determining certain points of fact, such as *"Did you purchase a new model car in the past year?"* and to clear-cut issues on which the respondents are likely to hold well-crystallized views.

Disadvantages of Dichotomous Questions. The critical point in the decision on whether or not to use a dichotomous question is the extent to which the respondent group approaches the issue in dichotomous terms. Although decisions themselves can often be broken down into a series of "yes-no" type responses, the thought process that leads up to them may be characterized by "maybes," "ifs," and "probablys." A simple dichotomous question, such as "Do you plan to purchase a new car within the next three months?", may elicit a "yes" from one individual and a "no" from another. Yet both individuals may "plan" to buy a car *if* they get a promotion. Furthermore, each may be equally likely to receive the promotion. However, the optimistic individual responds with "yes" and the pessimistic one responds with a "no."

Dichotomous questions are particularly susceptible to error caused by implied rather than stated alternatives (refer to the discussion of this issue in the section of question wording). Stating the question in a positive or negative manner can also have a strong effect. In one study, a change from "should allow" to "should forbid" resulted in a change from 21 per cent to 39 per cent in favor of allowing the proposed activity.[26]

Should the Response Be Forced? A final issue that the researcher must consider is whether or not to force a response. That is, should a third neutral category be allowed and, if it is allowed, should it be shown to the respondent? If the neutral category is allowed and, especially if it is shown to the respondent, the number of nonresponses will decline and the number of neutral responses will increase. The neutral category may increase the accuracy of the results if a number of people are truly neutral. Unfortunately, many who are not completely neutral will select the neutral

[26] D. Rugg, "Experiments in Wording Questions: II," *Public Opinion Quarterly,* **5** (March 1941); see also A. M. Falthzik and M. A. Jolson, "Statement Polarity in Attitude Studies," *Journal of Marketing Research,* **XI** (February 1974), 102–105.

category rather than expend the mental effort required to choose one alternative or the other. The decision in this instance should be based on the researcher's estimate of the percentage of respondents who are truly neutral. If this percentage is very high, a neutral position should be used. An alternative approach is to use a split ballot with half of the respondents receiving a neutral category and half being forced to choose.

Decisions Concerning the Question Sequence

Question sequence, the specific order in which the respondents receive the questions, is a frequent source of error. Like the other areas of questionnaire design, no unalterable rules are available. However, a number of general guidelines will reduce the probability of generating measurement error caused by the sequence of the questions.

The first questions should be simple, objective, and interesting. If the respondent cannot answer the first questions easily or if he finds them uninteresting, he may refuse to complete the remainder of the questionnaire. Similarly, if the questions arouse his suspicions in any way, such as causing him to think that the interview is perhaps really a sales call, he may be very guarded or may even distort the answers to later questions. Therefore, it is essential that the first few questions relax and reassure the respondent. This may make it necessary to use introductory questions that will not be part of the final analysis.

In general, *the overall questionnaire should move from topic to topic in a logical manner with all questions on one topic being completed before moving to the next.* Questions that are difficult to answer or that ask for controversial or sensitive information should be placed near the end of the questionnaire. By this time the interviewer, if one is being used, will have had ample opportunity to establish rapport with the respondent. Furthermore, the respondent, having put forth the effort to answer the preceding questions, will be more likely to feel committed to completing the questionnaire. In addition, any suspicion or resentment caused by these questions will not influence the answer to preceding questions. Classification data, such as age, income, and educational level, should be requested at the end of the interview for the same reasons. This practice was followed in the U.S.D.A. questionnaire.

Within groups of questions on a given topic, general questions should be asked first and more specific ones later. Consider the two following questions: "How many miles per gallon does your present car get?", "What things would you like to see improved in your car?" If these questions are asked in the order presented, gas economy will be mentioned many more times in the second question than it would if the order were reversed. Questions *7a* and *7b* illustrate the same point.

Asking general questions first reduces the likelihood that answers to later questions will be biased. An impressive example of the impact of previous questions is provided by Gross.[27] He described a new product, a combination pen and pencil, that would sell for $.29. All of the respondents were asked to indicate their level of buying interest. One group was asked to indicate this immediately after hearing a description of the product; a second group was first asked to describe the advantages of such a product and then indicate their buying interest; a third group first described the disadvantages; a fourth group described both advantages and then disadvantages, and a fifth group described both disadvantages and then advantages. The percentage of respondents expressing "very much interest" in purchasing the product was 0 per cent when asked after naming disadvantages, 2.8 per cent when asked immediately, 5.7 per cent when asked after describing advantages and then disadvantages, 8.3 per cent after describing disadvantages and then advantages, and 16.7 per cent after describing advantages.

Preceding questions not only indicate the answer to following questions, they also set the frame of reference or point of view that the respondent uses in answering following questions. For example, Parten reports a study on advertising in which part of the respondents were initially asked a question on dresses. When these respondents were then asked a question on advertising, they responded in terms of dress advertising and gave more favorable responses than those who did not receive the dress question.[28] Thus, it is important to avoid establishing a biased frame of reference prior to asking critical questions.

Physical Characteristics of the Questionnaire

The physical characteristics of the questionnaire should be designed to make it easy to use. In self-administered questionnaires, particularly mail surveys, appearance is an important variable in securing cooperation from the respondent. When interviewers are utilized, a properly designed questionnaire is important in reducing recording error.

The form of the questionnaire itself can influence the responses. For example, the more space that is left after an open-ended question, the

[27] E. J. Gross, "The Effect of Question Sequence on Measures of Buying Interest," *Journal of Advertising Research,* **4** (September 1964), 41.
[28] Parten, op. cit., 213.

longer the replies will be regardless of whether the respondent or an interviewer is recording the answer.

Decisions About the Pretest

Only on rare occasions and for specific, explicit reasons should a questionnaire be administered without a *thorough* pretest. A thorough pretest
involves much more than merely administering the questionnaire to some
fellow researchers, friends, and spouses, however helpful they may have
been in developing the questionnaire. A thorough pretest must use respondents who are as similar as possible to the target respondents. This
typically involves drawing a subsample from the larger sample. Obviously,
the more heterogeneous the target respondent group, the larger is the
sample needed for a reasonable pretest.

The questionnaire should be administered in the same manner as the
final survey. In addition, some of the pretest respondents should be interviewed after they have completed the questionnaire. During the interview,
the respondents should be asked to explain, precisely and in detail, *why*
they answered each question as they did. This should uncover most of the
weaknesses that may have slipped past the researcher.

The pretest should also make extensive use of the split ballot technique.
Many types of error, such as prestige suggestion, often will not be apparent even when respondents are asked to justify each answer. The
researcher must be alert to the potential of such errors and use the
split-ballot technique whenever he suspects a potential source of error. In
addition, the split-ballot technique should be used in the final administration of almost all questionnaires to combat position bias, to build up knowledge on alternative approaches, and to allow the use of mean or median
responses when two techniques produce different results. Even though this
will require that two or more different questionnaires be printed, this cost
is usually small compared to the added accuracy obtained.

Summary

Table 8–1 contains a brief listing of the more critical issues discussed
under the general topic of questionnaire design. It is worth rereading as an
overview of the problems of questionnaire design.

Although this discussion has been reasonably complete, the reader who
anticipates extensive involvement in questionnaire design should consult
the more detailed treatments referred to in the bibliography. For those
whose main contact with questionnaire design will be the approval of

proposals containing questionnaires or the utilization of data generated from questionnaires, the discussion in this chapter should be sufficient.

Questions and Problems

8.1. The manufacturer of a certain brand of nationally advertised and distributed frozen fruit juices has retained you as a consultant to advise on a questionnaire that is being prepared. The purpose of the survey is to determine consumer opinions and attitudes about frozen versus fresh fruit juices. Personal interviews are to be conducted on a randomly selected sample of families.

The questions listed are being considered for the questionnaire. Comment on each, indicating whether you would leave the question as it is or would change it. If you think it should be changed, rewrite it as you believe it should be asked.

(1) Do you or any of your family drink fruit juices? Yes___ No___
(2) Is the juice drunk at a meal or between meals or both?
      At a meal___   Between meals___   Both___
(3) What advantages, if any, do you believe using fresh juice has to using frozen juice?
(4) What brand or brands of juice do you regularly buy?
      _____   Don't know___
      _____
      _____

(5) On this card is a list of fruit juices. Tell me which is your family's first, second, and third choice.
      grape   ___
      tomato   ___
      lime   ___
      lemonade   ___
      orange   ___
      V-8   ___
      other   ___

8.2. What are the advantages and disadvantages of using aided recall in a questionnaire?

8.3. Develop a questionnaire that will allow you to estimate:
      (a) the total amount of beer consumed by full-time students on your campus;
      (b) the amount of money spent on beer;
      (c) the top five brands in terms of amount of money spent on each brand,
      (d) each of the preceding three for freshmen, sophomores, juniors, seniors, and graduate students;
      (e) for women; and
      (f) for those with above-average income compared to those with below-average income.

8.4. Evaluate the following questions.
      (a) We would like to know if anything you read or saw in *Travel and Travelers* during the past year or two interested you sufficiently to

induce you to talk about it or to take any of the following actions. You may check one or more boxes.

1. Discussed articles with others ☐
2. Visited a country or area ☐
3. Decided on or modified a travel plan ☐
4. Stayed at a hotel, motel, etc. ☐
5. Asked for more information on a product or service ☐
6. Bought or ordered a product ☐
7. What else? _____

(b) Please indicate how much of an average issue of *High Walker* you usually read.
1. Less than 1/3 ___
2. 1/3 to 1/2 ___
3. Over 1/2 ___

(c) Do you think federal control should be increased or decreased in the field of environment protection and antipollution?
Should be increased ☐   Should be decreased ☐

(d) Please check the following activities in which you participate *as a private citizen* interested in environment protection.
Read books and articles on the subject ☐
Membership in business or professional groups on environment ☐
Membership in conservationist, antipollution, ecology groups ☐
Attend lectures, meetings on subject ☐
Wrote letters to legislators, newspapers, or government officials ☐
Made speeches, published articles on subject ☐
Other (Please specify)_____

(e) Have you bought powdered milk this week? ☐ Yes ☐ No
(f) Where do you buy *most* of your meat?
(g) Where do you do *most* of your grocery shopping?
(h) How many times during the week do you usually eat breakfast?
(i) When you eat dinner out, do you usually eat at the same place?
(j) Are you currently planning any additions or expansions to your existing food services at this location? ☐ Yes ☐ No
(k) What percentage of your employees utilize this service?
☐ Under 25%   ☐ 50%–74%
☐ 25%–49%   ☐ 75%–100%
(l) What brand(s) of antifreeze have you bought in the past 12 months?

8.5. Develop questions to elicit information on the following topics from (1) first graders, (2) high school sophomores, (3) college seniors.
(a) Food preferences and dislikes and the underlying reasons for these likes and dislikes.
(b) Opinions about the seriousness of air and water pollution.
(c) Opinions about television advertising and how many hours a week the respondent spends watching television.

Selected Bibliography

ERDOS, P. L. *Professional Mail Surveys.* New York: McGraw-Hill Book Company, 1970, Chaps. 6 and 7. Good guidelines for self-administered questionnaires from a leading practitioner.

KORNHAUSER, A., and P. B. SHEATSLEY. "Questionnaire Construction and Interview Procedure," in C. Selltiz, et al. *Research Methods in Social Relations.* New York; Holt, Rinehart and Winston, Inc., 1959. An outstanding practical guide to questionnaire design.

OPPENHEIM, A. W. *Questionnaire Design and Attitude Measurement.* London: Heinemann Educational Books, Ltd., 1966. A thorough discussion of issues and problems in questionnaire design from a European perspective.

PAYNE, S. L. *The Art of Asking Questions.* Princeton; Princeton University Press, 1951. A detailed, humorous guide to question phrasing. It should be required reading for those who design questionnaires.

Case 8–1

Smokeless Tobacco

The United States Tobacco Company is a leading marketer of smokeless tobacco, or snuff. Although total consumption of snuff in the United States underwent a long period of decline, aggressive marketing activities by United States Tobacco in the late 1960s appears to have reversed this trend. These activities have included the development of new flavors, intensive "sampling" (giving away free samples), and a greatly expanded advertising program.

The firm's advertising program relied heavily on print media and focused on three brands—Skoal, Happy Days, and Copenhagen. All three brands were mentioned in each advertisement. The bottom of each advertisement contained a relatively inconspicuous offer to supply additional information on these products and an address. Anyone requesting additional information received a letter expressing thanks for the request, a flyer showing how to use the product, and a can of each of the three advertised products. Approximately 8,000 requests were received each year.

To help evaluate the effects of sending the free samples, a program of survey research was initiated. A mail questionnaire, which follows, was sent to a random sample of 400 of those who had requested information. The questionnaire was sent approximately eight weeks after the respondent was mailed the free sample. The firm plans a follow-up survey with a smaller sample every six months to monitor any shifts in the respondents' characteristics.

1. Evaluate the questionnaire.

2. Is the sample size adequate?

3. How useful do you feel the resultant information will be to management?

Exhibit 1

Moist Brands Advertising Offer Survey*

1. In what magazine or newspaper did you see our advertisement offering information about moist tobacco?
2. If you DID NOT write us because of the advertisement, how did you learn of our offer?
3. Did you use tobacco of any kind before you wrote us for the moist tobacco information?
4. If you do use tobacco would you please record the percent of your use—favorite brand and how long used for each type in the following list:

Type of Tobacco	Percent of Your Use	Favorite Brand	How Long Used
Pipe	_____	_____	_____
Cigarette	_____	_____	_____
Cigar	_____	_____	_____
Cigarette Size Cigars	_____	_____	_____
Snuff Moist (type we sent)	_____	_____	_____
Snuff Scotch (dry powdered)	_____	_____	_____
Chewing Tobacco	_____	_____	_____

5. What were your reasons for wanting information about moist tobacco?
6. (a) Has this introduction to our moist tobaccos caused you to buy and use any of the three brands we sent you?
   (b) If your answer is YES, which brand?
      Why did you select this brand over the other two?
   (c) Have you been favorably impressed with this sampling opportunity, even though you may not wish to use moist tobaccos regularly?
      What is your reason for this answer?

Moist Brands Product Preference

1. (a) Did you use *ALL* of *EACH* sample of moist tobacco we sent you?
   (b) What did you do with the samples you did not use?
2. Of the three sample brands, which did you prefer?

1st choice	*Copenhagen*	*Skoal*	*Happy Days*
2nd choice	*Copenhagen*	*Skoal*	*Happy Days*
3rd choice	*Copenhagen*	*Skoal*	*Happy Days*

  * NONE OF THEM (if NONE record dislikes in spaces provided in questions 4, 6, 8)
3. What do you *like* about *Copenhagen?*
*4. Is there anything you *dislike* about *Copenhagen?*
5. What do you *like* about *Skoal?*
*6. What do you *dislike* about *Skoal?*
7. What did you *like* about *Happy Days?*
*8. What do you *dislike* about *Happy Days?*
9. Will you continue to buy and use the sample you preferred?

  * (Condensed from two legal-size pages.)

Case 8–2

Daily Emerald Newspaper Readership Survey*

Late in the spring 1973 term, the *Daily Emerald,* the student newspaper on the University of Oregon campus, decided to conduct a survey of the student body. The survey had two basic goals. First, it would be used to develop estimates of the monthly expenditures of the student body for selected product categories. These estimates would then be used to help persuade local and national advertisers to purchase advertising space in the paper. Second, the survey would measure students' attitudes and opinions toward various aspects of the newspaper itself. The management of the paper had a substantial list of both products and aspects of the newspaper about which it was eager to receive information.

The questionnaire (Exhibit B) involved three segments (although these segments were not separately identified on the questionnaire). The first six questions sought basic demographic data. The second group of questions (numbers VII through XVII) gathered data on students' shopping patterns, income, and expenditure patterns. The final group of questions (numbers XVIII through XXX) gathered information on the students' media preferences and attitudes toward the *Emerald.*

Prior to mailing the questionnaire, it was pretested in a class of senior marketing students. These students first completed the questionnaire as respondents. They then noted any problems they had with specific questions or the overall questionnaire. As a result of this procedure, several ambiguous questions were clarified. A cover letter (Exhibit A) was drafted with the characteristics of the university student and the time of the year (immediately prior to final exams) in mind.

The specific student population of interest to the newspaper was those students who were full-time resident students during all three terms of the 1972–73 academic year. A sampling frame was available that contained the names and mailing addresses of all students who had registered as full-time students during the appropriate time period.

The sampling frame was on a computer tape and, therefore, could be stratified according to one or more of the following criteria at no additional cost: age, sex, year in school, or marital status. It was decided to draw a simple random sample of 750.

The survey took the form of an anonymous mail survey. The researcher provided a number of reasons for this decision. First, the budget would support an estimated 75 completed personal interviews, 125 completed

* Originally prepared by D. I. Hawkins and G. Albaum. Used with permission of the authors.

telephone interviews, or a one-shot mailing of 750 questionnaires. Not-at-homes and refusals would be a severe problem with all three methods. However, a response rate of 33 per cent was anticipated with the mail questionnaire. Furthermore, given the personal and complicated nature of some of the questions, it was believed that measurement error would be less with a mail questionnaire.

Each returned questionnaire was thoroughly analyzed for internal consistency prior to being coded for analysis. For example, students who reported living in a university dorm and reported a monthly expenditure for rent that was outside the range charged by university dorms were dropped from the analysis. The screening resulted in the rejection of 30 of the returned questionnaires. However, a number of these were dropped because of unique characteristics of the student. For example, several returned questionnaires were from students who were enrolled full time but who spent one or more terms off campus doing special research. Others were dropped because of a large number of incomplete questions or for obviously failing to treat the questionnaire seriously.

Some respondents left one or several questions unanswered even though the overall questionnaire was filled out correctly. These answers were treated in the analysis as missing data. In addition, some otherwise valid questionnaires had one or more responses that indicated that the respondent either misinterpreted the question or made a mistake in coding his answer. These specific responses were also coded as missing data and excluded from the analysis of that particular question.

The following data show the response rate for the sample:

Total number of questionnaires mailed	750
Number undeliverable	25
Number delivered	725
Number returned by respondents	366
Unusable questionnaires	30
Total number of usable questionnaires	336

1. Was the sampling plan the best one to use considering the circumstances?

2. Is the informal nature of the cover letter a proper approach to an audience of this nature?

3. What changes would you recommend in the questionnaire itself?

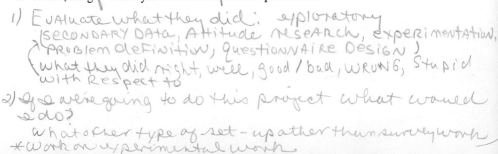

Exhibit A Questionnaire Cover Letter

Dear Student:

Gads, not another form to fill out! Yes, we would like to ask you to help us one last time this year. We realize that you are busy with final exams, term papers, and preparing to leave for the summer. However, we hope you can find about 15 minutes to complete and return the attached questionnaire.

The purpose of the questionnaire is to help us understand some of the impact students have had on the economic community in which they reside. In addition, we want to look at the role that various media play in students' lives.

Your name was selected randomly from a list of all University of Oregon students. Since we have a very limited budget, a small sample was drawn. Therefore, it is very important to us that everyone return the completed questionnaire. You are not asked to identify yourself on the questionnaire, and no one will contact you concerning it. So please take a few minutes to accurately complete and return the questionnaire in the envelope provided.

If you have any questions concerning the questionnaire, please feel free to call Iam A. Researcher at 999-9999.

Thank you for your time and cooperation.

Sincerely,

Iam A. Researcher

Exhibit B Student Expenditure Survey

I. How long have you been a student at the University of Oregon?
— (1) One year
— (2) Two years
— (3) Three years
— (4) Four years
— (5) More than four years

II. Sex: __ (1) Male __ (2) Female

III. Age: __

IV. Marital status:
— (1) Single
— (2) Married
— (3) Divorced or separated

V. Number of children living with you:
— (1) None
— (2) One
— (3) Two
— (4) Three or more

VI. (a) Where do you live?
— (1) Eugene
— (2) Springfield
— (3) Other (specify)____

(b) In what type of housing do you live?
— (1) University dormitory
— (2) Fraternity or sorority house
— (3) University married student housing
— (4) Apartment
— (5) Other (specify)____

VII. At which store did you *last purchase* groceries?
— (1) Albertsons
— (2) Big C
— (3) Drive and Save
— (4) Growers Market
— (5) Mayfair
— (6) McKays

___ (7) Safeway
___ (8) Shoppers Market
___ (9) 7–11 Stores
___ (10) Stop and Save
___ (11) 24-Hour Market
___ (12) Warehouse Foods
___ (13) Other
___ (14) Do not remember

VIII. At which type of store did you *last purchase* sundries (personal grooming products, etc.)?
___ (1) Grocery store
___ (2) Drug store
___ (3) Discount store
___ (4) Variety store
___ (5) University Co-op
___ (6) Other
___ (7) Do not remember

IX. What percentage of your clothes do you buy in Eugene and Springfield?
___ (1) 100%
___ (2) 75–99%
___ (3) 50–74%
___ (4) 25–49%
___ (5) Less than 25%
___ (6) Do not buy clothes in Eugene and Springfield

X. Do you use regularly (check answer/s):
___ (1) Automobile
___ (2) Motorcycle
___ (3) Bicycle
___ (4) City bus

XI. For each of the shopping areas listed, indicate the number of times within a typical month that you visited the area for purposes of purchasing some item:

	None	1–3	4–6	7–9	10 or more
Campus village	___	___	___	___	___
Eugene downtown	___	___	___	___	___
Franklin Blvd.	___	___	___	___	___
Valley River Center	___	___	___	___	___
Willamette Plaza	___	___	___	___	___
Springfield downtown	___	___	___	___	___
Mohawk Shopping Center	___	___	___	___	___
Oakway Mall	___	___	___	___	___
River Road area	___	___	___	___	___
Big Y Shopping Center	___	___	___	___	___

XII. (a) Do you have a *checking* account in your name?
___(1) No
___(2) Yes, in Eugene or Springfield
___(3) Yes, in other area

(b) Do you have a *savings* account in your name?
___(1) No
___(2) Yes, in Eugene or Springfield
___(3) Yes, in other area

XIII. What is your monthly income? _____ (Please do your best to break income down to a monthly figure. Include all sources of income: part-time jobs, scholarships, loans, work grants, gifts, allowances from home, and any other including drawing from personal savings.)

XIV. Where do you usually eat each meal? (If you regularly use more than one place, rank the first three with 1 representing the most frequently used.)

	Breakfast	Lunch	Dinner
(1) Dorm cafeteria			
(2) Student Union			
(3) Fraternity or sorority house			
(4) Apartment or place of dwelling			
(5) Off-campus restaurant			
(6) Seldom eat this meal			
(7) Other _____			

XV. What have been your average monthly expenditures for the following products during the past academic year? (Please do your best to break down any semester costs into *monthly* amounts.)

___ (1) Groceries
___ (2) School supplies (exclude textbooks)
___ (3) Jewelry, watches, etc.
___ (4) Film
___ (5) Other photographic equipment and supplies
___ (6) Housing (rent/payments)
___ (7) Hamburgers/sandwiches at restaurants
___ (8) Other meals at restaurants
___ (9) Laundry, cleaning, pressing
___ (10) Furniture/appliances
___ (11) Gasoline
___ (12) Other automotive expenses
___ (13) Sundries (shampoo, deodorant, etc.)

___ (14) Rented items (furniture, tools, etc.)
___ (15) Personal (beauty shop, barber)
___ (16) Flowers
___ (17) Bars and taverns
___ (18) Movies
___ (19) Theater
___ (20) Records, tapes
___ (21) Music supplies/instruments
___ (22) Sports equipment
___ (23) Hobbies
___ (24) Non-textbooks/magazines
___ (25) Gifts
___ (26) Coke or coffee breaks
___ (27) Medicinal drugs (aspirin, cough medicine, etc.)

XVI. Which of the following items do you own? Which have you purchased since you have been at the University of Oregon? Which have you purchased in the past nine months? (Check all that apply.)

	Currently own	Purchased since at UO	Purchased in past 9 months
(1) Automobile			
(2) Motorcycle			
(3) Bicycle			
(4) Camera			
(5) Black and white TV			
(6) Color TV			
(7) Stereo phonograph			
(8) Stereo tape deck			
(9) Washer			
(10) Dryer			

	Currently own	Purchased since at UO	Purchased in past 9 months
(11) Refrigerator			
(12) Range			
(13) Electric razor			
(14) Other small appliance			
(15) Bookcase			
(16) Typewriter			
(17) Lamp			
(18) Desk			
(19) Radio			
(20) Insurance			

XVII. (a) What classification and amount of insurance coverage have you purchased since first enrolling at the UO?

Life Insurance
__ (1) None
__ (2) $4,999 or less
__ (3) $5,000–$9,999
__ (4) $10,000–$14,999
__ (5) $15,000–$19,999
__ (6) $20,000 or more
__ (7) Don't know

Automobile Insurance
__ (1) Liability
__ (2) Collision
__ (3) Comprehensive
__ (4) None

Personal Property
__ (1) None
__ (2) Less than $1,000
__ (3) $1,000–$2,999
__ (4) $3,000 or more

(b) What type of insurance was purchased through an agent or salesman located in Eugene or Springfield?
__ (1) Life
__ (2) Automobile
__ (3) Personal property
__ (4) None

XVIII. What radio stations do you listen to? (Rank your top three preferences with 1 representing most preferred.)
__ (1) KORE (1050)
__ (2) KASH (1600)
__ (3) KATR (1320)
__ (4) KBMC (94.5)
__ (5) KUGN (590)
__ (6) KFMY (97.9)
__ (7) KERG (1280)
__ (8) KEED (1450)
__ (9) KZEL (96.1)
__ (10) Other _____

XIX. What newspapers do you read regularly?
__ (1) *Daily Emerald*
__ (2) *Eugene Register Guard*
__ (3) *Oregonian*
__ (4) *Springfield News*
__ (5) *Valley News*
__ (6) Other _____

XX. How often do you read the *Emerald?*
__ (1) Never
__ (2) Once weekly
__ (3) Twice weekly
__ (4) Three times weekly
__ (5) Four times weekly
__ (6) Five times weekly

XXI. Where do you most often pick up your copy of the *Emerald?*
__ (1) Student Union
__ (2) Dorm cafeteria or lobby
__ (3) Fraternity or sorority

— (4) Co-op
— (5) Classroom building
— (6) Other _____

XXII. For *each* of the following general topics, please indicate *both* your interest *and* your satisfaction with the *Emerald's* coverage (check answers):

My Level of Interest			Topics	Emerald's Coverage			
Highly Inter-ested	Moder-ately Inter-ested	Un-inter-ested		Exces-sive	Good	Fair	Poor
———	———	———	General news	———	———	———	———
———	———	———	National news	———	———	———	———
———	———	———	State news	———	———	———	———
———	———	———	Community news	———	———	———	———
———	———	———	University news	———	———	———	———
———	———	———	Sports news	———	———	———	———
———	———	———	Feature articles	———	———	———	———
———	———	———	Editorials	———	———	———	———
———	———	———	Commentary	———	———	———	———
———	———	———	General adver-tising	———	———	———	———
———	———	———	Classified adver-tising	———	———	———	———

XXIII. In terms of sports, please indicate your evaluation of the *Emerald's* cover-age of the following areas:

	Much More Em-phasis Needed	Slightly More Em-phasis Needed	About Right	Slightly Less Em-phasis Needed	Much Less Em-phasis Needed
UO men's intercol-legiate	———	———	———	———	———
UO women's inter-collegiate	———	———	———	———	———
Pac 8	———	———	———	———	———
Men's intramurals	———	———	———	———	———
Women's intramurals	———	———	———	———	———
Local sports news	———	———	———	———	———
National sports	———	———	———	———	———
Feature articles on athletes	———	———	———	———	———

XXIV. How useful do you find the *Emerald's* weekly entertainment section in terms of planning activities and purchases?
— (1) Extremely useful   — (3) Slightly useful
— (2) Somewhat useful   — (4) Not useful

XXV. What kinds of reviews would you like to see in the entertainment section?

	Extensive Coverage	Moderate Coverage	Limited Coverage	No Coverage
(1) Concerts	_____	_____	_____	_____
(2) Plays	_____	_____	_____	_____
(3) Films	_____	_____	_____	_____
(4) Books	_____	_____	_____	_____
(5) Albums and tapes	_____	_____	_____	_____
(6) Restaurants	_____	_____	_____	_____
(7) Bars and taverns	_____	_____	_____	_____
(8) Other _____	_____	_____	_____	_____

XXVI. How many letters to the editor have you submitted in the past academic year?
— (1) 1
— (2) 2
— (3) 3
— (4) 4
— (5) 5 or more
— (6) None

XXVII. Approximately how many *Emerald* classified ads have you responded to in the past academic year?
— (1) 1
— (2) 2–4
— (3) 5–9
— (4) 10–14
— (5) 15 or more
— (6) None

XXVIII. How much would you be willing to pay *per issue* to continue receiving the *Emerald?*
— (1) 1¢ per issue
— (2) 2¢ per issue
— (3) 3¢ per issue
— (4) 4¢ per issue
— (5) 5¢ per issue
— (6) 6¢ per issue
— (7) 7¢ per issue
— (8) 8¢ per issue
— (9) 9¢ per issue
— (10) 10¢ per issue
— (11) Nothing

XXIX. Approximately how many *Emerald* general ads have you responded to in the past academic year?
— (1) 1
— (2) 2–4
— (3) 5–9
— (4) 10–14
— (5) 15 or more
— (6) None

XXX. In general, how would you rate the *Emerald* on the following factors:

	Ex- tremely	Mod- erately	Slightly	Not at all
Accurate	_____	_____	_____	_____
Fair	_____	_____	_____	_____
Widely read by students	_____	_____	_____	_____
Influential with students	_____	_____	_____	_____
Liberal	_____	_____	_____	_____
Student oriented	_____	_____	_____	_____
Commercial	_____	_____	_____	_____
Useful	_____	_____	_____	_____
Entertaining	_____	_____	_____	_____

Case 8–3

West Side Beauty Salon

George and Cheri Richards have operated the West Side Beauty Salon for nearly three years. During that time, business has shown a slow but steady rate of growth. Cheri recently read an article in a trade journal about the marketing concept. As she and George discussed this article, it occurred to them that they actually knew very little about their customers or what their customers thought of them. Therefore, they constructed the questionnaire shown below. For two weeks, each customer was handed a copy of the questionnaire as she left the store.

1. What changes, if any, would you make in the sampling plan?

2. Evaluate the questionnaire.

Questionnaire

Dear Customer:
   Would you help us to improve our salon? We are constantly trying to better our services, and we would be most grateful for your candid appraisal on the form below. Any additional criticism or suggestions you may be able to offer will also be appreciated:

WHAT INFLUENCED YOU TO COME TO OUR SALON?

For what reason or reasons did you leave the salon where you had been going?

How would you rate our telephone manners?
Friendly and courteous? _____
Do we need improvement? _____
Are our business hours convenient to you? _____
Would you like us to be open at any time during which we are now closed?

Do you like the arrangement and the decor of our salon?

Are there any changes or improvements you could suggest?

What is your opinion on our prices?

Do you believe we charge fairly?

Are there any prices you feel should be adjusted?

Are there any services you would like us to perform that are not available now?

In your opinion, which employees in this salon are performing well?
Names:

How could our employees improve their service to you? _____
Sally Smith—How could this employee improve to serve you and the patrons
better?

Judy Jones—How could this employee improve to serve you and the other
patrons better?

Linda Greer—How could this employee improve to serve you and the other
patrons better?

Rita Washington—How could this employee improve to serve you and the
other patrons better?

Sam West—How could this employee improve to serve you and the other patrons better?

Owners:
Cheri Richards—How could I improve to serve you and the other patrons
better?

George Richards—How could I improve to serve you and the other patrons
better?

Is there anything else you would like to suggest; is there something else we
could do for you?

Thank you for taking the time and effort to complete this questionnaire. It
will be evaluated with the greatest care and we will do everything possible to
make you more beautiful and your salon visit more enjoyable. Please do not
bring the questionnaire to our salon; just drop it into the mail in the attached,
stamped envelope. There is no need to give us your name as we are solely interested in your true opinion. Of course, if you prefer to give us your name,
feel free to sign the questionnaire. Thank you.

Cheri and George Richards

Case 8–4

Woodburn Market Analysis*

In 1972, the Woodburn, Oregon, Chamber of Commerce commissioned a
survey of the local community. The survey had three primary objectives as
specified by a consensus of the Chamber members: (1) to evaluate the

* This case was prepared by C. M. Lillis and D. I. Hawkins. Used with permission of the authors.

competitiveness of retail businesses in Woodburn relative to those in Portland and Salem, (2) to estimate the value of the retail expenditure outflow for selected product categories from Woodburn, (3) to assess the buying habits and motivations of the Woodburn residents with regard to the three trade areas. The study was conducted as a service for the local business community.

Woodburn has three major shopping areas. The old downtown area contains over 50 per cent of the total retail outlets but is showing obvious signs of deterioration. Senior Estates, a large retirement development, has a small shopping center catering primarily to residents of Senior Estates although anyone may shop there. Finally, there is a relatively new shopping center located at the edge of town.

Although Woodburn is not a large town, it does draw business from a number of smaller communities nearby and from the rather large rural farm population. Therefore, its trading area contains over 20,000 people. However, although Woodburn is able to draw from smaller communities, Woodburn retailers must compete with two nearby cities. Located approximately 20 miles away by freeway is Salem, the state's capital, which has a population of approximately 70,000. Portland is located approximately 25 miles away by freeway in the opposite direction from Salem. It has a population of almost 400,000 and a well-developed retail sector that serves as a regional trading center.

Time and budget constraints dictated the use of a telephone survey. The Woodburn city telephone directory served as the sampling frame. The questionnaire used in the survey is attached. It was developed following discussions with the Chamber as to the most important products to cover. In addition, a number of depth interviews were conducted with local citizens and retailers to provide guidance in the construction of the questionnaire.

The interviewers began each interview by reading a request for cooperation. This request included the interviewer's name, the fact that the survey was being conducted for the Woodburn Chamber of Commerce, and the fact that the study dealt with the respondent's shopping patterns.

1. Evaluate the questionnaire.

2. Will this questionnaire provide the required data?

3. Is frame error likely to be great in this situation?

Interviewer's
Name _____

Questionnaire

Included throughout this questionnaire are instructions to the interviewer. These instructions are set in italics. It is necessary that these instructions be followed to gain uniformity in the questioning process.

1. On your last trip out of Woodburn, where did you go?
   a. Portland
   b. Salem
   c. Other (_____)
2. On that last trip to (_____) what was your reason for going?
   a. Shopping
   b. Entertainment
   c. Visiting
   d. For professional services
   e. Vacation
   f. Other (_____)
3. Who went with you?
   a. Went alone
   b. Spouse
   c. Children
   d. Friends
   e. Neighbors
   f. Relatives
   g. Other (_____)
4. What types of goods, if any, were purchased?
   a. Shoes
   b. Clothing
   c. Household furnishings
   d. Appliances
   e. Groceries
   f. Other (_____)
5. Do you usually purchase groceries in Woodburn?
   a. Yes (GO TO 7)
   b. No (GO TO 6)
6. Do you purchase groceries in:
   a. Salem
   b. Portland
   c. Other (_____)
7. Of your total monthly food purchases, about how much of that total do you spend in Woodburn? For examples, would you say it is:

Read list of possible answers to interviewee.

   a. Less than 1/10
   b. About 1/4
   c. About 1/2
   d. About 3/4
   e. More than 3/4

8. In what city do you *usually* buy clothing (other than shoes) for adults in your family?
   a. Woodburn
   b. Salem
   c. Portland
   d. Woodburn and Salem
   e. Woodburn and Portland
   f. Other (_____)

9. What proportion of your total annual adult clothing purchases are made in Woodburn? For example, would you say it is:

   Read list of possible answers.

   a. Less than 1/10
   b. About 1/4
   c. About 1/2
   d. About 3/4
   e. More than 3/4
   Do you have any children?
   ___ Yes—continue   ___ No—skip to 12

10. In what city do you usually buy clothing (other than shoes) for children in your family?
    a. Woodburn
    b. Salem
    c. Portland
    d. Woodburn and Salem
    e. Woodburn and Portland
    f. Other (_____)

11. What proportion of your total annual children's clothing purchases are made in Woodburn? For example, would you say it is:

    Read list of possible answers.

    a. Less than 1/10
    b. About 1/4
    c. About 1/2
    d. About 3/4
    e. More than 3/4

12. Do you do most of your Woodburn clothing shopping in:
    a. The downtown area
    b. The Highway 99 shopping district
    c. The Senior Estates Shopping Center

13. In what city do you usually buy shoes for the adults in your family?
    a. Woodburn
    b. Salem
    c. Portland
    d. Woodburn and Salem
    e. Woodburn and Portland
    f. Other (_____)

14. What proportion of your total annual adult shoe purchases are made in Woodburn? For example, would you say it is:

    Read list of possible answers.

    a. Less than 1/10
    b. About 1/4

    c. About 1/2
    d. About 3/4
    e. More than 3/4

If they previously indicated having no *children—skip to 17.*

15. In what city do you usually buy shoes for the children in your family?
    a. Woodburn
    b. Salem
    c. Portland
    d. Woodburn and Salem
    e. Woodburn and Portland
    f. Other (_____)
16. What proportion of your total annual children's shoe purchases are made in Woodburn? For example, would you say it is:

Read list of possible answers.

    a. Less than 1/10
    b. About 1/4
    c. About 1/2
    d. About 3/4
    e. More than 3/4
17. Do you do most of your Woodburn shoe shopping in:
    a. The downtown area
    b. The Highway 99 shopping district
    c. The Senior Estates Shopping Center
18. In what city do you buy appliances such as stoves, refrigerators, washing machines, and the like?
    a. Woodburn
    b. Salem
    c. Portland
    d. Woodburn and Salem
    e. Woodburn and Portland
    f. Other (_____)
19. What is the proportion of your total annual appliance purchases made in Woodburn? For example, would you say it is:

Read list of possible answers.

    a. Less than 1/10
    b. About 1/4
    c. About 1/2
    d. About 3/4
    e. More than 3/4
20. Do you do most of your Woodburn appliance shopping in:
    a. The downtown area
    b. The Highway 99 shopping district
    c. The Senior Estates Shopping Center
21. In what city do you buy home-furnishings such as carpets, draperies, chairs, and the like?
    a. Woodburn
    b. Salem
    c. Portland
    d. Woodburn and Salem

    e. Woodburn and Portland
    f. Other (_____)

22. What is the proportion of your total annual home-furnishings purchases made in Woodburn? For example, would you say it is:

Read list of possible answers.

    a. Less than 1/10
    b. About 1/4
    c. About 1/2
    d. About 3/4
    e. More than 3/4

23. Do you do most of your Woodburn home-furnishings shopping in:
    a. The downtown area
    b. The Highway 99 shopping district
    c. The Senior Estates Shopping Center

24. In what city is your family doctor located?
    a. Woodburn
    b. Salem
    c. Portland
    e. No family doctor

25. In which city is your family dentist located?
    a. Woodburn
    b. Salem
    c. Portland
    d. No family dentist

26. In which city does your lawyer have his practice?
    a. Woodburn
    b. Salem
    c. Portland
    d. No family lawyer

27. What is the approximate age of the head of your household?
    a. Below 20
    b. 21–25
    c. 26–30
    d. 31–35
    c. 36–40
    f. 41–45
    g. 46–50
    h. 51–55
    i. Over 55

28. In what city is he/she employed?
    a. Woodburn
    b. Salem
    c. Portland
    d. Not employed
    e. Retired

If retired. Is head of household a

    f. Retired resident of the City of Woodburn
    g. Retired resident of Senior Estates
    h. Other (_____)

If answer to 28 is d *or* e, *skip to 30.*

29. What type of work does the head of the household do?
    a. Farm laborers (farmhand, general farm worker)
    b. Service worker (waiters, cooks, service station people)
    c. Craftsmen (plumbers, carpenters)
    d. Office workers (clerical and other nonprofessionals)
    e. Sales (salesmen of all types)
    f. Clerks (cashiers, retail clerks)
    g. Managerial (business, own stores)
    h. Farmers and Farm Managers
    i. Professional/Technical (doctors, lawyers, and so on)
    j. Local and County (teachers, policemen)
    k. State and Federal (social worker, forest service)
30. Is spouse also employed?

    If yes, indicate full-time or part-time.

    a. Yes
    b. No
    c. Full-time
    d. Part-time
    e. Not married/deceased *omit question 31.*
31. What type of work does spouse do?
    a. Office
    b. Sales
    c. Professional/Technical
    d. Manufacturing/Production
    e. Farm laborer
    f. Self-employed
32. How many individuals (including adults and children) are living in the household?
    a. 1–2
    b. 3–4
    c. 5–6
    d. 7–8
    e. 9–10
    f. Over 10
33. How many years have you been living in Woodburn?
    a. 0–2
    b. 3–5
    c. 6–10
    d. 11–15
    e. 16–20
    f. Over 20

On the next question you will be asked to compare Woodburn stores to similar types of stores in Portland or Salem. I will read a statement to you and you should respond with a rating of either "good," average," or "poor" (again, remembering that you are comparing *Woodburn* stores to those of Portland or Salem). For example, I might say, "How would you rate the selection of goods offered for sale in Woodburn as compared to selections offered in Salem or Portland?" You should then respond with a rating of "good," "average," or "poor."

OK, let's begin—

34. How would you rate the *selection* of goods offered for sale in Woodburn as compared to *selections* offered in Salem or Portland?
    a. good
    b. average
    c. poor
35. How would you rate the *quality* of goods offered for sale in Woodburn as compared to the *quality* of goods offered in Salem or Portland?
    a. good
    b. average
    c. poor
36. How would you rate the *availability* of professional people (doctors, lawyers, dentists) in Woodburn as compared to Salem or Portland?
    a. good
    b. average
    c. poor
37. How would you rate the *pleasantness* of Woodburn sales personnel as compared to those of stores in Salem or Portland?
    a. good
    b. average
    c. poor
38. How would you rate the *convenience* in location of shopping areas (or centers) in Woodburn as compared to those in Salem or Portland?
    a. good
    b. average
    c. poor
39. How would you rate the *availability of ample parking* facilities near stores in Woodburn as compared to *availability of parking* near stores in Portland or Salem?
    a. good
    b. average
    c. poor
40. Do you think, in general, prices charged for goods sold in Woodburn are:

    Read all possible answers.

    a. Higher than those in Salem or Portland
    b. Lower than those in Salem or Portland
    c. The same as those in Salem or Portland

Thank you for your time and patience in responding to these questions.

CHAPTER 9

Measurement and Research: Observation, Depth Interviews, Projective Techniques, and Case Analyses

The most common method of obtaining information about the behavior, attitudes, and other characteristics of people is to ask them. In the last chapter we were concerned with the preparation of structured, direct questionnaires for that purpose.

It is not always possible, or desirable, to use direct questioning to obtain information. People may be either *unwilling* or *unable* to give answers to questions they consider to be an invasion of their privacy, that adversely affect their self-perception or prestige, that are embarrassing, that concern motivations that they do not fully understand or cannot verbalize, that concern facts they have forgotten, or for other reasons. Therefore, additional approaches to obtaining such information may be desirable or necessary.

Observation is one method that can be used in lieu of direct questioning. Like questioning, observation is a common, everyday activity. Like questionnaire design, the design of observation studies is oriented primarily toward the reduction of measurement error. Observation techniques are described in terms of the basic decisions the researcher must make when utilizing these techniques.

Depth interviews and projective techniques can, on occasion, be used to obtain information from respondents that is difficult or impossible to infer from either questionnaires or observation. The nature and uses of depth interviews are discussed. The major types of projective techniques and their uses in marketing research are also described in this chapter.

The in-depth analysis of a specific situation or activity is the basis for *case studies,* which are particularly useful in exploratory research. The role of this activity is described in the last section of the chapter.

Observation

In speaking of the effects of Oregon's "bottle bill" (an antilitter measure), William Wessinger, board chairman of Blitz Weinhard Co., reported: "While driving to work (from out of town) on Monday morning, I used to be able to make a 'market survey' distinguishing market share and volume."[1] Wessinger's use of informal observation to gain relevant marketing information is not unusual. At the informal level, observation is probably used more than questioning to gain information. The manufacturer notices changes in competitors' advertising, the salesman observes changes in competitors' prices, the retail manager notices long lines forming around a register. The list of common, day-to-day observations that provide useful information to marketing managers is virtually endless.

However, casual observation, like casual questioning, is likely to produce excessive measurement error. The purpose of this section is to describe "scientific" observation as opposed to casual observation.

Scientific observation differs from casual observation to the extent that it (1) serves a specifically formulated research purpose, (2) is planned systematically, (3) is recorded systematically and related to more general propositions, and (4) is subjected to checks and controls on its total accuracy.[2]

---

[1] "Ecology Law Ends Oregon Brewer's 'Market Survey,'" *Marketing News,* **7** (December 15, 1973), 5.

[2] C. Selltiz, M. Jahoda, M. Deutsch, and S. W. Cook, *Research Methods in Social Relations* (New York: Holt, Rinehart and Winston, Inc., 1959), 200.

General Characteristics of the Observational Approach

Conditions for Use

Before observation can be used in applied marketing research, three minimum conditions must be met. First, the *data must be accessible* to observation. Motivations, attitudes, and other "internal" conditions cannot be readily observed, if at all. However, it may be possible to make *inferences* about attitudes and motivations from behavior that can be observed. For example, facial expressions have been used as an indicator of babies' attitudes or preferences for various flavorings of food. Furthermore, when we use direct questioning or attitude scales, we are still involved in a process of *inferring* the underlying attitude from the verbal report. Nonetheless, attitudes are not well suited for measurement by observation. Nor are a host of private or intimate activities such as sexual activities, eating, worshipping, or playing with one's children.

A second condition is that the *behavior must be repetitive, frequent, or otherwise predictable.* Although it is, of course, possible to observe infrequent, unpredictable occurrences, such as train wrecks, the amount of time that would have to be spent waiting would be excessive for most purposes. Even Jane van Lawick-Goodall was forced to alter the probability of certain behavior occurring to observe more effectively chimpanzees in the wild.[3]

Finally, an *event must cover a reasonably short time span.* To observe the entire decision-making process that a couple might go through as they consider purchasing a new home could easily take months, if not years. The time and monetary costs associated with this are beyond the value of most applied studies. Thus, we are usually restricted to observing activities that can be completed in a relatively short time span or to observing phases, such as store visits, of activities with a longer time span.

Reasons for Preferring Observational Data

The fact that a given type of data *can* be gathered by observational techniques does not imply that it *should* be gathered by such techniques. There are two conditions under which observational techniques are preferred over alternative methods. In some cases, *observation is the only technique that can be used to collect the information.* The most obvious example is food or toy preferences among children who cannot talk yet. At other times, people either are not aware of, cannot remember, or will not admit to certain behaviors. For example, many retailers monitor the

[3] J. van Lawick-Goodall, *In the Shadow of Man* (New York: Dell Publishing Co., Inc., 1971).

prices and advertising effort of their competitors. In this way, they can remain informed despite the fact that the competitors would not voluntarily supply them this information.

The other reason for preferring observational data is that in some situations the *relationship between the accuracy of the data and the cost of the data is more favorable for observation than for other techniques*. For example, traffic counts, both of in-store and external traffic, can often be made by means of observational techniques more accurately and for less expense than using some other technique such as a survey.

The above discussion should not be interpreted as meaning that observation techniques are always in competition with other approaches. On the contrary, observation techniques can supplement and complement other techniques. For example, observation is frequently useful in exploratory research. When used in combination with other techniques, each approach can serve as a check on the results obtained by the other.

Sampling Problems

Sampling for observational techniques poses some unique problems. Consider the sampling process involved in observing consumer reactions to a point-of-purchase display. It is not practical to take a probability sample of consumers and follow them until they pass the display. Instead, the researcher must sample the stores that contain the displays. He must also sample (or take a "census") of the times of the day, week, and month during which he will make his observations. Then, during the selected time period he observes all, or some proportion, of those who pass the display.[4]

Types of Observational Approaches

There are five basic dimensions along which observational approaches can vary: (1) natural or contrived situation, (2) open or disguised observation, (3) structured or unstructured observation, (4) direct or indirect observation, and (5) human or mechanical observers. These five dimensions are not dichotomies as presented above. Instead, they represent continuums. That is, a situation is more or less natural, not natural *or* contrived.

Natural versus Contrived Situation

The researcher who sits near the entrance to a restaurant and notes how many couples, groups of couples, or families of various sizes enter during

[4] A more complete discussion of sampling for observational studies is contained in F. Kerlinger, *Foundations of Behavioral Research*, 2nd ed., New York: Holt, Rinehart and Winston, 1973, 544–546.

specified time periods is operating in a natural situation. He has done nothing to encourage or restrain people from entering. It is likely that those entering the restaurant view the situation as being natural in every way.

Unfortunately, many behaviors that a researcher might like to observe occur so seldom or under such specialized conditions that it is impractical for the researcher to attempt to observe them in the natural state. Exhibit 9–1 provides an example of a contrived situation, in which the "applicant" was a trained observer with no intention of opening an account at the bank. In this instance the respondent is unlikely to notice the contrived nature of the study. At the other extreme are situations such as where the respondent is asked to view an advertisement shown on a tachistoscope[5] while being monitored by an eye camera, a pupilometer, and a psychogalvanometer.

In general, the more natural the situation, the more likely is the behavior being observed to be an accurate reflection of the individual's nor-

---

Exhibit 9–1   An Example of Contrived Observation*

Bank:	Competitor B	Date:	6/8/72
Location:	Cranston	Time:	10:20 A.M.
Clerk:	Mrs. L.	Account:	Savings

I entered the bank and approached a teller, Miss I., and asked who I would see to find out about a savings account. She said I should see Mrs. L., indicating her. Mrs. L. had a customer at her desk, so the teller suggested I have a seat and wait. She said, "There's a pamphlet on savings accounts on the rack over there you might like to look over while you're waiting." I thanked her, took a pamphlet, and sat down. After about two minutes Mrs. L. was free and I told her I was interested in a savings account. She took out a pamphlet and said, "I see you have one of these; maybe it would be best if we go through it together." She then went over each type of savings plan offered, adding comments on each that were not in the brochure. She told me I could save by mail or come in to the office and gave me their hours. She also mentioned that if I had a checking account I could have money saved automatically. I said I did not have a checking account, so she went over them fully, giving me literature. At the end she said, "We're a full service bank—we have loans, safe deposit boxes, even a credit card!" I had already told her I wouldn't be opening anything "until payday." She said, "right over where you got that first brochure, we have literature on all our services; why don't you take one of each and look them over, and come back and see me on payday?"

Mrs. L. was extremely knowledgeable, well organized, and very pleasant.

---

* Source: *Specialized Marketing Services for the Banking Industry.* A special report by Bank Marketing Group, a division of Sheldon Spencer Associates, Inc., Warwick, Rhode Island. Used with permission.

[5] See J. Guttman, "Tachistoscopic Testing of Outdoor Ads," *Journal of Advertising Research,* **12** (August 1972), 21–28.

mal or standard behavior. Against this must be measured the sometimes greater cost of waiting for the desired behavior to occur or the impossibility of using certain measurement instruments such as a pupilometer in a natural setting.

Open versus Disguised Observation

One of the potential strengths of the observation method is that it can measure behavior without any direct effects being caused by the measuring instrument. The example presented in Exhibit 9–1 was basically a disguised approach. Had the teller known she was under observation, she would probably have altered her behavior in some manner. Two-way mirrors, observers dressed as stock clerks or repairmen, and hidden cameras are a few of many ways that are used to prevent respondents from becoming aware that they are being observed.

It is not always possible to prevent the respondent from being aware of the observer. For example, in observing salesmen's behavior on sales calls, it would be difficult to remain effectively disguised. Similarly, in laboratory studies disguise is seldom practical. The audiometer (a device attached to a radio or a television set that records when and to what station a set is tuned) is a form of another observational method that cannot be used in a disguised form.

Researchers disagree as to the extent to which the known presence of an observer affects the behavior being observed. Kerlinger believes that the effects are minimal and short term: ". . . it is more of a problem to the uninitiated who seem to believe that people will act differently, even artificially, when observed."[6] Other researchers assign much more importance to the observer effect.[7]

The known presence of an observer offers the same potential for error as the presence of an interviewer in survey research. The observer may vary in how "obviously present" he is. An audiometer attached to a television set is unobtrusive, whereas an observer who travels with a salesman is obvious to the salesman. The magnitude of observer effects is probably closely related to how obvious the observer is to the subject. Therefore, it seems wise to always minimize the presence of the observer to the extent possible.

Structured versus Unstructured Observation

In structured observation, the observer knows in advance precisely which aspects of the situation he is to observe or record. All other behav-

[6] Kerlinger, op. cit., 538.
[7] See A. C. Samli, "Observation as a Method of Fact Gathering in Marketing Decisions," *Business Perspectives,* **4** (Fall 1967), 19–23, and E. J. Webb, D. T. Campbell, K. D. Schwartz, and L. Sechrest, *Unobtrusive Measures: Nonreactive Research in the Social Sciences* (Chicago: Rand McNally & Co., 1966), 113–114.

iors are to be "ignored." Exhibit 9–2 provides an example of part of a form for use in a structured observation. Note that the form specifies the behaviors that are to be observed.

Highly structured observations typically require a considerable amount of inference on the part of the observer. For example, in Exhibit 9–2 the observer is required to note whether or not the teller is well-groomed. This is sometimes a difficult judgment task and one that is strongly influenced by personal tastes. However, well-trained observers can achieve a high degree of agreement as to which category a given individual should be placed in.

Exhibit 9–2   An Example of Structured Observation*

Bank_____   Date_____
Location_____   Time_____
Teller_____   Transaction_____

Appearance
  Well-groomed   Yes_____   No_____

Behavior
  Chewing gum or eating_____
  Smoking_____
  Personal conversations:
    with customer_____
    with other employees_____
    on telephone_____
  Other poor behavior_____

Window
  Nameplate visible   Yes_____   No_____
  Loose cash or checks   Yes_____   No_____
  Cluttered work area   Yes_____   No_____
  Personal belongings visible   Yes_____   No_____

Transaction (General)
  Waited on immediately   Yes_____   No_____
    if no, waited (_____) minutes
      presence acknowledged   Yes_____   No_____
      teller was:
        helping customer_____
        talking with employee:
          business_____
          personal_____
        working:
          at station_____
          at back counter_____
          at drive-in window_____
        other_____

* *Source: Specialized Marketing Services for the Banking Industry.* A special report by Bank Marketing Group, a division of Sheldon Spencer Associates, Inc., Warwick, Rhode Island. Used with permission.

Completely unstructured observation places no restriction on what the observer should note. Thus, an observer for a department store might be told to mingle with the shoppers and notice whatever seems relevant. Completely unstructured observation is often useful in exploratory research. However, it is seldom utilized in more advanced studies.

Direct versus Indirect Observation

We can generally observe current behavior directly. That is, if we are interested in purchasing behavior, we can observe people actually making purchases. Most of the examples described so far have focused on direct observation. However, to observe other types of behavior, such as past behavior, we must turn to some record of the behavior or indirect observation. That is, we must observe the effects or results of the behavior rather than the behavior itself.

One type of indirect observation is the examination of *archives* or secondary sources. This type of observation is so critical to applied research that a large part of Chapter 4 was devoted to it. Another type of indirect observation involves *physical traces*. The roadside litter "survey" mentioned at the beginning of this section is an excellent example of the informal use of this technique.

Physical traces have been used to study the consumption of alcoholic beverages in a town without package stores. Since the researcher believed that questionnaire techniques alone would not provide an adequate estimate, he focused on the number of empty liquor bottles in the trash from area homes.[8] An automobile dealer who based his selection of radio stations for advertising on those radio stations shown on the position of the dial in cars brought in for service was making an applied use of physical traces.[9]

Another frequent use of physical traces is known as the pantry audit. In a pantry audit, respondents' homes are examined (with their permission, of course) for the presence and quantity of certain prespecified items. The basic assumption of this approach is that possession is related to purchase and/or usage. Unfortunately, this is often a tenuous assumption. For example, one of the authors has had a bottle of hot sauce in his pantry for several years, and it is likely to remain there for several more years. To infer that this product is liked or consumed because of its presence would be incorrect. This problem, coupled with the rapidly developing use of panel techniques, has reduced the use of pantry audits.

[8] H. G. Sawyer, "The Meaning of Numbers," speech before the American Association of Advertising Agencies, 1961. Reported by Webb, et al., op. cit., 41–42.
[9] "Z-Frank Stresses Radio to Build Big Chevy Dealership," *Advertising Age,* **35** (November 2, 1964), 35.

Human versus Mechanical Observations

Most of the examples and discussions thus far have emphasized human observers. However, it is sometimes possible and desirable to replace the human observer with some form of mechanical observer. This may be done because of accuracy, cost, or functional reasons.

Traffic counts of automobiles can generally be performed more accurately and for less expense by machine than by human observers. Even these machines are subject to some error. One of the authors remembers, rather shamefully, being in a group as a teen-ager that took great delight in finding traffic counters and driving back and forth across them.

Cameras may be used to supplement human observers in studies of shelf facings, package designs, and the like. In this case, human observers must still evaluate the actions recorded on the film. However, the permanent record allows for repeated viewing by different observers and should lead to a more accurate assessment of the behavior.

Mechanical devices may also be used when it would be functionally impossible to use human observers. It would not, for example, generally be possible to have human observers monitor a family's television viewing habits. However, the audiometer used by a syndicated research service does this effectively. In addition, measures of physiological reactions to advertisements, package designs, and the like rely on mechanical observers that can "observe" or measure changes that are beyond the capabilities of human observers.

The *psychogalvanometer* measures emotional reactions to various stimuli by measuring changes in the rate of perspiration. Since this reaction is beyond the control of the subject, there is no chance for the respondent to deliberately distort his response. Through the use of this device, researchers can determine if subjects have an emotional reaction to various slogans, brand names, or advertisements. Unfortunately, the machine provides only limited information about the nature of the response.

The *eye-camera* records movements of the eye. It is used to determine which parts of a newspaper or magazine page are read first, the order and amount of time an individual spends looking at the various parts of an advertisement or package, or which of two competing stimuli receives the most attention.

The *pupilometer* measures changes in the size of the pupils of the subject's eyes. A change in the size of the pupil is apparently an involuntary reaction and reflects the subject's interest in whatever he is looking at (assuming that brightness and distance are held constant).[10] This device is used to measure interest or preference for various advertisements, slogans, product designs, and packages.

[10] A. S. King, "Pupil Size, Eye Direction, and Message Appeal: Some Preliminary Findings," *Journal of Marketing,* **36** (July 1972), 55–58.

Conclusions

Observational techniques are both underdeveloped and underutilized. Little research has been focused on assessing the accuracy of the observation method, and few attempts have thus far been made to utilize, in a formal sense, the vast array of relatively inexpensive sources of observational data. Exhibit 9–3 provides an example of an exception to this tendency.

Exhibit 9–3   An Example of the Formal Use of Readily Available Observational Data*

Description of Neighborhood—What is the typical occupation of the people in the block? Are there mixed types and qualities of home and apartment buildings? Is this neighborhood holding its own or going downhill?

Description of Home—Apartment, house? Brick, frame, stucco, duplex, row house, above store, etc.? About how old is it? What style? If house, try to estimate the current market value, or give approximate rental figure for apartment.

Interior—How large is it—how many rooms? How many people seem to be living here, sharing R's home or apartment? Are furnishings expensive, moderaate, sparse? Is the home immaculate, neatly kept, a mess?

Describe the Respondent—Tell us something of R's personality (the way R struck you), manner, appearance, etc. Add anything you feel might help in giving us your picture of the respondent.

   * *Source:* Social Research, Inc., *A Study of Working-Class Women in a Changing World* (Chicago: Social Research, Inc., 1973), 20. Used with permission.

The questions contained in Exhibit 9–3 were answered by interviewers after a substantial semistructured interview with the respondent. These data are used to supplement and substantiate similar data collected directly from the respondent. Such information can prove useful in the analysis of standard survey data. Yet it is unusual for a firm to take explicit advantage of the observations of its interviewers.

Firms also often fail to systematize and utilize the observations of other potential sources of information. In a study to determine how accurately information flows from salesmen to decision makers, Albaum "planted" six pieces of market information with a firm's sales force. Of these six highly useful bits of information, only one arrived in a useful form; and that took ten days.[11] This is not an unusual condition. One of the areas most susceptible to improvement is the formalization of casual observation systems.[12]

   [11] G. S. Albaum, "Horizontal Information Flow: An Exploratory Study," *Acad-*
   [12] D. H. Robertson, "Sales Force Feedback on Competitors' Activities," *Journal of Marketing,* **38** (April 1974), 69–71.

Depth Interviews and Projective Techniques

One of the primary reasons for using observation techniques is to gather information that respondents are either unable or unwilling to provide in response to direct questioning. However, observational techniques are not generally suitable for generating data on attitudes, motives, or opinions. Projective techniques and depth interviews are designed to uncover information that direct questioning and observation approaches cannot generate. Their focus is on the *reasons why* individuals buy or use various products and what the act of buying, owning, or using the product *means* to them.

Depth interviews and projective techniques are frequently categorized as *motivation research* techniques.[13] Actually, motivation research is somewhat of a misnomer since the most common applications are oriented toward attitudes rather than motives.

Motivation research became popular among researchers in the 1950s. During this time, some of its supporters made such enthusiastic claims for the powers of the techniques that other researchers listed "overexpectations" as one of the major problems with motivation research.[14] As a result of overenthusiastic claims and misuse of the techniques, the use of motivation research declined during the 1960s. However, both projective techniques and depth interviews have become a standard part of most marketing researchers' repertoires.

Depth Interviews

Depth interviews are designed to "uncover basic predispositions—unconscious feelings, needs, conflicts, fears, and the like."[15] Depth interviews achieve this result by creating a "completely permissive atmosphere, in which the subject is free to express himself without fear of disapproval, admonition, or dispute, and without advice from the interviewer."[16] Depth interviews can involve one respondent and one interviewer or they may involve a small group, 5 to 25 respondents, and an interviewer. The latter are called *group depth interviews,* and the former are termed *individual*

[13] For a review of the history of motivation research, see L. Collins and C. Montgomery, "The Origins of Motivational Research," *British Journal of Marketing,* **3** (Summer 1969), 127–135.

[14] S. H. Butt, "Some Hazards of Motivation Techniques," in R. Ferber and H. G. Wales, *Motivation and Market Behavior* (Homewood, Ill.: Richard D. Irwin, Inc., 1958), 89–93.

[15] J. W. Newman, *Motivation Research and Marketing Management* (Cambridge, Mass.: Harvard University Press, 1957), 405.

[16] Selltiz, et al., op. cit., 269.

depth interviews or just depth interviews. Both types are also referred to as *qualitative* and *in-depth* interviews.[17]

Individual Depth Interviews

Individual depth interviews involve a one-to-one relationship between the interviewer and the respondent. The interviewer does not have a specific set of prespecified questions that he must ask according to the order imposed by a questionnaire. Instead, he is free to create questions, probe those responses that appear relevant to him, and generally to try to develop the best set of data in any way practical. However, the interviewer must follow one rule. He must not consciously try to affect the content of the answers given by the respondent. The respondent must feel free to reply to the various questions, probes, and other, more subtle ways of encouraging responses in the manner he deems most appropriate.

Nondirective Interviews.   The amount of guidance the interviewer provides the respondent can serve to classify the interview. In a completely *nondirective interview,* the interviewer's function is to encourage the respondent to talk about a given topic with a minimum of direct questioning.[18] For example, a researcher may ask for a person's feelings about clothing, Ford *Pinto,* instant coffee, or whatever is his main topic of interest. He will then refrain from directing the course of the conversation along any prespecified lines. Instead, he will probe statements that interest him with such questions as *"Why do you say that?", "Can you tell me more?", "That's interesting,"* and so forth. The basic idea, however, is to let the respondent lead the interview and determine what topics will be discussed.

The nondirective interview is particularly useful in the early stages of exploratory research. During this period, the researcher is attempting to discover whatever variables and relationships may exist that could help him solve his particular problem. The almost complete lack of structure in the nondirective interview increases the probability that unanticipated or unique findings will result.

Focused Interviews.   As the researcher develops more of a feel for the problem and the variables associated with it, he will generally move to a more *focused interview*. The focused interview concentrates on a given experience and its effects. The researcher typically has a list of topics or

[17] For a number of applied examples of both individual and group depth interviews, see J. R. Goodyear, "Qualitative Research Studies" in J. Aucamp, ed., *The Effective Use of Market Research* (London: Staple Press, 1971), 47–65.
[18] Selltiz, et al., op. cit., 268.

subareas that he wishes to cover during the interview. However, the choice of questions and the timing of these questions is left to his discretion.

For example, in a focused depth interview to learn more about decisions to purchase carpeting, the interviewer might be instructed to cover such areas as financing, husband-wife interaction, the role played by children, life-style, views on entertaining, style consciousness, and so on. Within each of the areas, the interviewer would be instructed to probe until he is certain that he has uncovered the underlying attitudes associated with that area.

The problems associated with the individual depth interview are similar to those faced by the group interview. These problems are described after the next section.

Group Depth Interviews

Curlee Clothing recently undertook a major marketing research effort to help management evaluate current advertising and product strategy. As part of this effort, they brought together various groups of six or seven young men with similar demographic characteristics such as college students, blue collar workers, or salesmen. These groups were placed in comfortable surroundings, provided refreshments, and asked to discuss clothing in terms of why and how they purchased it, their likes and dislikes, and so forth. Each session was taped and analyzed.

Management anticipated that the discussions would focus on styles, prices, quality, and perhaps advertising. However, what emerged from each session was a critical discussion of the retail sales personnel. Most of the individuals, once relaxed, expressed a feeling of insecurity in purchasing men's fashion-oriented clothing. This insecurity was coupled with a distrust of both the intentions and competence of the retail salesperson. As a result of these findings, Curlee embarked on a major effort at training the retail sales personnel through specially prepared films and training sessions.[19]

Curlee Clothing made excellent use of the *group depth* interview. Group depth interviews can be applied to: (1) basic need studies for product idea creation, (2) new product idea or concept exploration, (3) product positioning studies, (4) advertising and communications research, (5) background studies on consumers' frames of reference, (6) establishment of consumer vocabulary as a preliminary step in questionnaire development, and (7) determination of attitudes and behaviors.[20]

---

[19] D. I. Hawkins, "Curlee Clothing Company," Harvard Intercollegiate Case Clearing House, #9–572–618, Cambridge, Mass., 1972.

[20] Market Facts, Inc., *Qualitative Group Research* (Chicago: Market Facts, Inc., undated).

Advantages of Group Interviews.   Group depth interviews possess a number of advantages over individual depth interviews or more structured interviews.[21] Basically, the group depth interview, which can involve anywhere from 5 to 25 members, operates in the same fashion as the individual depth interview. However, in this case, the interviewer, often called the moderator, plays a limited, but critical, role. He introduces the topic and sees that the conversation remains on the general topic. However, beyond that he relies primarily on the group interaction to produce useful insights into the underlying attitudes and motivations of the participants.

The interaction process induced by the group situation produces a number of potential advantages.[22] Each individual is able to expand and refine his opinions in the interactions with the other members. This process provides more detailed and accurate information than could be derived from each individual separately.

Snowballing occurs when a comment, perhaps random, by one member triggers an idea or similar feeling in others. The idea may spread through the group, changing and developing as it goes. An excellent example of this process is provided by Goldman:

A study of the factors that determine which of several supermarkets were used by shoppers in a particular neighborhood illustrates the definitive and lasting reaction to subliminal stimuli. Some of the women in each of four group sessions were adamant in their intention not to shop in one of the markets, although they did not appear able to express their reasons in a clear or consistent manner. Some mentioned a vague feeling that the market in question was somehow messy or even dirty. Yet, upon further exploration, these same women agreed that the shelves were neatly stacked, the personnel clean, the floors swept, the counters well dusted. They could not point out anything to support their charges of uncleanliness. Further, they readily agreed that the store they did shop in was more messy than the one in which they refused to shop. A casual reference by one of the women to a peculiar odor evoked immediate recognition from the others. This occurred spontaneously in several of the groups and led to the consensus that it was a "bloody" or "meaty" odor. This process of "concensual validation" suggested that this vague impression of untidiness stemmed not from anything that could be seen, but rather from this faint yet pervasive and offensive odor. Later this information served to bring to the attention of the management an ineffective exhaust-and-drainage system in the supermarket's meat room.[23]

[21] For a more complete discussion of this technique, see A. E. Goldman, "The Group Depth Interview," *Journal of Marketing,* **26** (July 1962), 61–68; and G. H. Smith, *Motivation Research in Advertising and Marketing* (New York: McGraw-Hill Book Co., 1954).

[22] Based on J. M. Hess, "Group Interviewing," in R. L. Kind, ed., *Marketing and the New Science of Planning* (Chicago: American Marketing Association, 1968), 193.

[23] Goldman, op. cit., 61.

A group interview situation is generally more exciting and offers more *stimulation* to the participants than a standard depth interview. This heightened interest and excitement makes more meaningful comments likely. In addition, the *security* of being in a crowd encourages some members to speak out when they otherwise would not. Since any questions raised by the moderator are to the group as a whole rather than to individuals, the answers contain a degree of *spontaneity* not produced by other techniques. Furthermore, individuals are not under any pressure to "make up" answers to questions.

Disadvantages of Group Interviews.   Given all of these benefits, why isn't group interviewing more widely used? Unfortunately, it also has a number of serious flaws. Although group interviews can uncover the existence of various attitudes, opinions, motivations, and emotions, it is often not safe to project the findings from group depth interviews into the larger population. Those who attend group interviews and actively participate in them are likely to be different in many respects from those who do not. That is, nonresponse can be a serious source of error. In addition, the interpretation of group interview data is of necessity a subjective process. Different analysts may reach different conclusions from the same data.

The problems in conducting such interviews are also severe. Arranging for groups of people to meet at specified times is a surprisingly complex task. It is generally necessary to pay the participants, use a highly trained interviewer, and have a specialist interpret the interview results. These factors all add to the cost of the project. The interviewer must keep the conversation moving, and he must prevent a few individuals from dominating it. The "depth" at which a group interview will operate is often substantially less than that obtainable in individual interviews.

Nonetheless, the group interview is a useful technique,[24] particularly in exploratory research. As the examples of Curlee Clothing and the supermarket indicate, the group interview can also provide information for final decisions. Its use, like the individual depth interview, depends on the nature of the problem at hand.

Projective Techniques

Projective techniques are based on the theory that the description of either real or imagined events requires interpretation, and this interpreta-

---

[24] See P. H. Berent, "The Depth Interview," *Journal of Advertising Research,* **6** (June 1966), 32–39.

tion can only be based on the individual's own background, attitudes, and values. The more vague or ambiguous the object to be described, the more the respondent must reveal of himself in order to complete the description.

The following general categories of projective techniques are described: *association, completion, construction,* and *expression.*[25] All of these techniques have been adopted from psychology, particularly clinical psychology. Marketing researchers have tended to utilize these techniques out of context and to expect more from them than they were designed to deliver. However, when properly used, projective techniques can provide useful data.[26]

Association Techniques

Association techniques require the subject to respond to the presentation of a stimulus with the first thing or things that come to mind. The *Rorschach* inkblot test is perhaps the most widely known version of this approach. However, its use is largely restricted to clinical work, and it has little to offer the marketing researcher.

A more useful tool for the applied researcher is the *word association* technique. This technique requires the respondent to give the first word or thought that comes to his mind after the researcher presents him with a word or phrase. In *free word association* only the first word or thought is required. In *successive word association* the respondent is asked to give a series of "first" words or thoughts that occur after hearing a given word. The respondent is generally read a number of relatively neutral terms to establish the technique. Then the words of interest to the researcher are presented, each separated by several neutral terms. The order of presentation of the key words is randomized to prevent any position or order bias from affecting the results.

The most common approach to analyzing the resulting data is to analyze the frequency with which a particular word or category of word (favorable, unfavorable, neutral) is given in response to the word of interest to the researcher.

Word association techniques are widely used in testing potential brand names and occasionally for measuring attitudes about particular products or product attributes or existing "brand" images. For example, a study by McCann-Erikson, Inc., on the use of zippers in home sewing presented the words *zippers, buttons, hook and eyes,* and others in a form of successive word association.[27] The responses were analyzed according to their

[25] Based on Kerlinger, op. cit., 515; and G. Lindzey, "On the Classification of Projective Techniques," *Psychological Bulletin,* **56** (1959), 158–168.
[26] For a critical view of the value of projective techniques, see W. A. Yoell, "The Fallacy of Projective Techniques," *Journal of Advertising,* **3,** No. 1 (1974), 33–36.
[27] Newman, op. cit., 264–319.

favorable or unfavorable nature. The technique also can be applied to phrases describing activities. Examples are "buying a car," "eating out," and "stopping at the new shopping center."

In addition to providing useful information for decision making, word associations can provide useful insights into the types of adjectives that should be included in a more structured technique such as the semantic differential.

Completion Techniques

Completion techniques require the respondent to complete an incomplete stimulus. Two types of completion techniques are of interest to marketing researchers—*sentence completion* and *story completion.*

Sentence completion, as the name implies, involves requiring the respondent to complete a sentence (see question 6 in Exhibit 8–1 for examples). To some extent, it merely rephrases an open-ended question. For example, the questions "What kind of people prefer filter cigarettes?" and "People who prefer filter cigarettes are _____" represent two approaches to the same information. However, in direct questioning, the respondent is giving *his* answer. In most sentence completion tests, the respondent is asked to complete the sentence with *a* phrase. Generally he is told to use "the first thought that comes to your mind" or "anything that makes sense." Since the individual is not required to directly associate himself with the answer, his conscious and "subconscious" defenses are more likely to be relaxed and to allow a more revealing answer.

Newman provides additional examples of incomplete sentences used in actual research studies. Among them are:

Insurance of all kinds is . . .
The Pan-American Coffee Bureau is . . .
People who drive convertibles . . .
A woman who never sews . . .
Jewel brand products . . .[28]

Like word association responses, sentence completion responses are typically analyzed to determine the frequency of various response categories. For example, the analysis of responses to question *6f* in Exhibit 8–1 (Teen-agers feel that Smokey is . . .) produced the following results:

Good/fine/cool/groovy	17%
Square/corny/outdated/silly	11
Symbol of fire prevention	7
Cute/likeable/appealing	7
Valuable helper/teacher	6

[28] Ibid., 426.

Sentence completion can be used to study the same general areas for which word association is used. This technique typically provides a more complete expression of the respondent's thought but may not be quite as spontaneous.

Story completion is an expanded version of sentence completion. As the name suggests, part of a story is told and the respondent is asked to complete it. In a study on the role of husbands and wives in the purchase of furniture, for example, the respondents could be presented a story that included a visit to a furniture store and a disagreement as to which brand to purchase. The respondents would be asked to complete the story. Since the respondent does not know how the people in the story will react, he must create the end of the story based on his own experiences and attitudes.

Story completion is a potentially useful projective technique. It offers the researcher a chance to introduce slightly more structure, or at least a clearer focus, than most of the other techniques. This makes it well suited for identifying underlying attitudes and motivations.

For example, consider a manufacturer who introduces a major appliance innovation that generates a great deal of consumer interest but few sales. A story could be created about a couple who were interested in the product but did not purchase it. The respondents would then be asked to complete the story beginning as the couple were driving home after looking at the product and one was saying to the other: "That whidgit was nice,' but . . ." This would serve to direct the remainder of the study along the lines of interest to the researcher.

Construction Techniques

Construction techniques focus on the product of the respondent.[29] The respondent is required to produce or construct something, generally a story, dialogue, or description. An analysis is then made of this output. We examine *cartoon, third person,* and *picture-response* versions of construction techniques.

Cartoon techniques present cartoon type drawings of one or more people in a particular situation. Often one or more of the individuals is shown with a sentence in bubble form above his head and one of the others is shown with a blank bubble that the respondent is to fill in. Question *4* in Exhibit 8–1 is an example of this approach. Other opening phrases could include such statements as: "My boyfriend bought a new Ford Pinto," "The Joneses are building a new swimming pool," "We are thinking about carpeting the living room," and the like. The reply of the other person would be supplied by the respondent.

[29] Kerlinger, op. cit., 516.

One study utilized a version of this technique in a study of the motives in industrial buying. In this case, the cartoon showed a conference with several comments on the possibility of changing the firm's suppliers. The respondents, purchasing agents, were to react to these comments.[30]

Instead of having the bubble showing replies or comments, it can be drawn to indicate the unspoken thoughts of one or more of the characters. This device allows the respondent to avoid any restraints that she might feel against having even a cartoon character *speak,* as opposed to *think,* certain thoughts.

The basic idea in this technique is the same as in other projective techniques. The individual is allowed to "project" any "subconscious" or socially unacceptable general feelings onto the cartoon character. The analysis is the same as it is for word association and sentence completion.

Third person techniques allow the respondents to project their attitudes onto some vague third person. This third person is generally "an average woman," "your neighbors," "the guys where you work," "most businessmen," or the like. Thus, instead of asking the respondent why he did something or what he thinks about something, the researcher asks him what his friends, neighbors, or the average person thinks about the issue. His answer will hopefully reveal more about himself than would the response to a more direct question.

A useful version of this technique is to provide a description of a set of positions, purchases, or activities of an individual and ask the respondents to describe the individual's personality, interests, or other characteristics of interest. The respondents' feelings toward the items on the list will be reflected in his description of the owner. Mason Haire provides a now classic example of the use of this technique.[31]

When instant coffee was first introduced, many housewives refused to use the product. When questioned why, the standard response was "It doesn't taste good." Haire, who was not willing to accept such a surface reason, prepared two brief shopping lists. The lists were identical except that one contained "Nescafé instant coffee" and the other "Maxwell House coffee (drip grind)." One group of 100 women was given one list and a second group received the second list. Each woman was asked to "write a brief description of the personality and character" of the woman who would purchase the set of items on the list.

The differences in the descriptions provided by the two lists (which differed only in the type of coffee) were both striking and revealing. The

---

[30] G. M. Robertson, "Motives in Industrial Buying," in R. S. Hancock, *Dynamic Marketing for a Changing World* (Chicago: American Marketing Association, 1960), 266–276.

[31] Mason Haire, "Projective Techniques in Marketing Research," *Journal of Marketing,* **14** (April 1950), 649–656; see also C. R. Hill, "Haire's Classic Instant Coffee Study—18 Years Later," *Journalism Quarterly,* **45** (August 1968), 466–472.

hypothetical woman whose shopping list contained drip grind coffee was described as being more or less average. In contrast, the woman with instant coffee on her shopping list was characterized as being lazier, more of a spendthrift, and not as good a wife. These responses undoubtedly were more revealing about the women's attitudes toward instant coffee than the "I don't like the taste" response generated by direct questions.

This technique can be easily adapted to a wide range of objects. Woodside utilized a shopping list of items for a party and varied the brands of beer on the list;[32] other approaches could involve descriptions of billfold owners whose wallets contain a BankAmericard compared to those without such a card. This could provide useful insights for determining the image associated with owning a BankAmericard. A little imagination can provide lists for virtually any product or product category.

Picture response, another useful construction technique, involves using pictures to elicit stories. These pictures are usually relatively vague so that the respondent must use his imagination to describe what is occurring. Exhibit 9–4 shows a version of this technique that was used by a research firm in a study of the attitudes of working-class women. The interviewer handed the respondent the picture shown in the exhibit and gave the following instructions and questions:

Now make up a story about who these people are and what's going on. Make up any kind of story you want. (Probe with:) How does each one feel about what they are doing? What (else) are they saying to each other? Why?

What happens afterwards—how does it turn out for them in the long run?[33]

A typical response to this picture was:

The woman buys a wig because the salesgirl suggests a change is what she needs. Getting home, the woman shows her family the wig and they laugh at her. She gets mad and tells them she is going to change, she is not going to let them bully her around any more. She has confidence in her new self. (Her motto becomes) never worry about today, just live it.[34]

A number of stories similar to this one led to the conclusion that "the wig has become an important symbol (as well, in effect, as a working tool) of a woman's right to change her identity if and when she sees fit. The wig is symbolic of her declaration of feminine independence."[35]

The potential value of information of this type, not only to wig manu-

---

[32] A. G. Woodside, "A Shopping List Experiment of Beer Brand Images," *Journal of Applied Psychology,* **56** (December 1972), 512–513.

[33] Social Research, Inc., *A Study of Working-Class Women in a Changing World* (Chicago: Social Research, Inc., 1973), Appendix II, 16.

[34] Social Research, Inc., op. cit., 142.

[35] Ibid., 141.

Exhibit 9-4   An example of a picture response technique. Social Research, Inc., *A Study of Working-Class Women in a Changing World* (Chicago: Social Research, Inc., 1973), Appendix II, p. 22. Used with permission.

facturers but to anyone interested in communicating with the working-class woman, is obvious. Yet it would be exceedingly difficult to obtain such information from standard questioning techniques since the woman herself is probably unaware of the symbolic meaning that her wig has for her.

Expressive Techniques

In expressive techniques, the respondent is again required to produce or construct something. Now, however, the emphasis shifts from *what* is constructed to the *manner in which* it is constructed. Such activities as play, drawing, and role playing are commonly used expressive techniques. However, role playing is the only expressive technique utilized to any extent by marketing researchers.

In *role playing,* the consumer is asked to assume the role or behavior of another person, such as a salesperson for a particular department store. The role-playing customer can then be asked to try to sell a given product to a number of different "consumers" who raise varying objections. The means by which the role player attempts to overcome these objections can reveal a great deal about her attitudes. Another version of the technique involves studying the role player's approach to shoppers from various social class backgrounds. This could reveal the role player's attitudes on what type of people "should" shop at the store in question.

Role playing can be adapted to a wide variety of situations. The primary problem is to secure representative respondents who are also willing to engage in role playing. They may well consider such an activity to be demeaning, embarrassing, or simply child's play. Those who are willing to participate may differ on a number of key variables from those who refuse to participate.

Problems and Promise of Projective Techniques

Both sampling and selection error often play a critical role in studies using projective techniques. Since projective techniques generally require personal interviews with highly trained interviewers and interpreters to evaluate the responses, they tend to be very expensive. This, in turn, has led to small sample sizes that increase the probability of substantial sampling error.

Furthermore, the reliance on small samples has often been accompanied by nonprobability selection procedures. Thus, selection error is also likely to be present. These potential errors are not an integral aspect of the technique. They have become associated with projective techniques because of the costs and the predispositions of some of the practitioners, not because of the techniques themselves. These problems can be minimized with proper sampling.

Nonresponse is more serious. Some of the projective techniques require the respondents to engage in behavior that may well seem strange to them. This is particularly true for techniques such as role playing. Therefore, it is reasonable to assume that those who agree to participate differ in a number of ways from those who refuse to participate. This is a strong argument for testing the findings generated by projective techniques with other techniques that may generate a more representative sample. However, it should be noted that, with the possible exception of role playing, these techniques can generate response rates as high as those obtained in many surveys. The appropriate approaches for dealing with nonresponse are basically the same as they are for standard survey techniques and are discussed in the chapter on survey techniques.

Measurement error is also a serious issue with respect to projective techniques. The possibility of interpreter bias is obvious. The responses to all except the word association techniques are open-ended. The opportunity for error in attempting to decide what a fairly vague and contradictory story or phrase means is great.

The typical approach to analyzing the responses of all the techniques is to look for common, underlying themes. Each stimulus type (Ford, Plymouth) or respondent group (blue-collar, white-collar) is scored based on the percentage of the respondents who mention the key theme. This can be developed into a relatively efficient and reliable scoring system.[36]

Projective techniques are a valuable and useful marketing research tool.[37] As the examples presented indicate, they can help to uncover information not available through direct questioning or observation. They are particularly useful in the exploratory stages of research. They can generate hypotheses for further testing and provide attribute lists and terms for more structured techniques such as the semantic differential. The results of projective techniques can also be used directly for decision making. However, the techniques are complex and should not be used naïvely.[38]

Case Analyses

A *case* or *case study* refers to the intensive analysis of a single situation. Case studies used for research purposes, as opposed to teaching purposes, are most applicable in exploratory research. Because of the intensive level of analysis, variables and relationships may be suggested that would otherwise be overlooked. The case approach is particularly useful for generating hypotheses concerning the factors influencing the success of various marketing activities or units.

An insurance company may be concerned with discovering the facts that are associated with effective salesmanship. As part of the exploratory research, two successful and two unsuccessful salesmen, according to the company's criteria, are selected for in-depth analysis. The salesmen are observed making their calls for a period of two weeks. They are given a series of personality tests in which both structured and unstructured questionnaires are administered. Any differences found between the two successful salesmen and the two unsuccessful salesmen can then be tested in the overall group of company salesmen using less intensive techniques. The results can then be used to guide the hiring, training, and managing of the sales force. This same general approach can be used to generate research

[36] D. C. McClelland, *The Achieving Society* (New York: The Free Press, 1961); see also M. M. Nacuas, "Objective Scoring of the T.A.T.: Further Validation," *Journal of Projective Techniques and Personal Assessment,* **29** (December 1965), 456–460.

[37] See H. L. Steck, "On the Validity of Projective Questions," *Journal of Marketing Research,* **1** (August 1964), 48–49.

[38] P. Sampson, "Qualitative Research and Motivation Research," in R. M. Worcester, *Consumer Market Research Handbook* (London: McGraw Hill Book Co. (UK), Ltd., 1972), 7–28.

ideas any time the firm can isolate successful and unsuccessful units to which it has access.

Using cases for more than the generation of ideas for further testing is risky. The problems of small sample size, nonrandom selection, the lack of similarity in some aspects of the problem situation, and the subjective nature of the measurement process combine to limit the accuracy of a few cases. However, when used for generating hypotheses, they can often produce valuable insights.

Summary

In this chapter a variety of methods for obtaining information not readily available through direct questioning have been examined. *Observation, depth interviews, projective techniques,* and *case analysis* were described.

Observation is widely used informally but is probably underutilized in formal marketing research. The use of observation requires that the behaviors: (1) be accessible to observation; (2) be repetitive, frequent, or otherwise predictable; and (3) cover a reasonably short time span. Observation is used rather than, or in conjunction with, questionnaires in order to increase the accuracy or decrease the cost of the resultant data. Observational studies can vary along five basic dimensions: (1) natural or contrived situation, (2) open or disguised observation, (3) structured or unstructured observation, (4) direct or indirect observation, and (5) human or mechanical observers.

Depth interviews are designed to uncover basic predispositions, unconscious feelings, emotions, and so forth. They can be either individual or group interviews. The individual depth interview has the potential advantage of a close rapport between the interviewer and the respondent. This allows a detailed examination of the respondent's reasons for behaving in certain ways. Group interviews do not have the same degree of closeness between the interviewer and the respondent. However, they gain the advantages of group interaction. Individual and group interviews vary in the amount of focus or structure provided by the interviewer. Most marketing studies utilize relatively structured interviews. Depth interviews are subject to a high nonresponse rate and substantial measurement error through both interviewer effects and the subjective interpretation of the results.

Projective techniques are based on the premise that an individual's description of real or imagined events requires interpretation, and this interpretation can only be based on the individual's own attitudes and values. Four broad categories of projective techniques were described. *Association techniques* include Rorschach, free word association, and successive word association. *Completion techniques* of interest to applied marketing researchers are sentence completion and story completion. *Construction techniques,* which focus on the product of the respondent, include cartoon techniques, third person techniques, and picture-response techniques. *Expressive techniques* are not widely used in marketing research. Projective techniques should be used with caution. However, when properly applied, they can provide valuable insights into the underlying reasons for specific behavior patterns.

A *case* or *case study* refers to the intensive analysis of a single business situation and is most commonly used in marketing research in the exploratory stages. It is not uncommon to conduct case studies of successful and unsuccessful units in order to isolate differences between them.

Questions and Problems

9.1. Observe shoppers in the fresh vegetable section of a local supermarket. What hypotheses or insights have you gained from this observation concerning the purchasing of fresh vegetables?

9.2. A regional grocery chain has 25 stores. All the stores are located in middle income areas and are open from 9 A.M. until 9 P.M., seven days per week. Management would like to test a new point-of-purchase display for its own brand of soft drinks. The display is large, brightly colored, and has several moving parts. Design an observational study of the display, including:
   (a) The sampling plan.
   (b) Details on each of the five dimensions involved in an observational study.
   (c) What other research technique(s), if any, would be more suitable for this problem?

9.3. Describe two managerial problems and the associated research problem for which each of the following techniques would be appropriate. Tell why you believe the technique is appropriate:
   (a) Observation, (b) depth interviews, (c) projective techniques, (d) case analysis.

9.4. Conduct a depth interview with one person (not a student) to determine his feelings on the purchase of fresh fruits.
   (a) Report your findings to the class.
   (b) What types of error do you believe might be present in your findings?

9.5. Select a product and brand of interest to you. Administer each of the following techniques to five fellow students (different students for each technique) to develop an idea of their feelings toward the product category and/or brand.
   (a) Successive word association, (b) sentence or story completion, (c) cartoon, (d) third person.

Selected Bibliography

Observation:

BRANT, R. M. *Studying Behavior in Natural Settings.* New York: Holt, Rinehart and Winston, Inc., 1972. A recent, detailed treatment of the area.

WEBB, E. J., D. T. CAMPBELL, K. D. SCHWARTZ, and L. SECHREST. *Unobtrusive Measures: Nonreactive Research in the Social Sciences,* Chicago: Rand McNally & Co., 1966. The classic work in this area. The book is essential for anyone seriously involved in observational studies.

WEICK, K. E. "Systematic Observational Methods," in G. Lindzey and E. Aronson. *The Handbook of Social Psychology,* 2nd ed., VII. Menlo Park, N.J.: Addison-Wesley Publishing Co., 1968, 357–451. A very good discussion of techniques and methods of observational studies.

Depth Interviews:

GOLDMAN, A. E. "The Group Depth Interview." *Journal of Marketing, 26* (July 1962), 61–68. A brief, informative description of the group depth interview.

GOODYEAR, J. R. "Qualitative Research Studies," in J. Aucamp. *The Effective Use of Market Research.* London: Staple Press, 1971, 47–65. Provides a number of applied examples of both individual and group depth interviews.

Projective Techniques:

BERENT, P. H. "The Depth Interview." *Journal of Advertising Research, 6* (June 1966), 32–39. A brief description of the depth interview along with advice on "how to do it."

MURSTEIN, B. I. *Handbook of Projective Techniques.* New York: Basic Books, Inc., 1965. A detailed description of a number of potentially useful projective techniques.

NEWMAN, J. W. *Motivation Research and Marketing Management.* Cambridge, Mass.: Harvard University Press, 1957. Perhaps the best book written on motivation research in marketing. It contains a number of detailed descriptions of successful marketing applications of these techniques.

Case 9–1

Lohmann Brewery

Lohmann Brewery, established in 1934, produces and markets Lohmann beer. Although the firm has been in existence for over 40 years, the distribution of Lohmann beer is limited to the Midwestern state in which it is produced. Even within this limited area, the firm has never achieved more than a minor share of the market. Lohmann's market share had stabilized at approximately 10 per cent after World War II and remained at that level until the mid 1950s. Major advertising campaigns by national and regional competitors began to sharply reduce Lohmann's market share until it had fallen to 6 per cent by 1960.

In 1960, Lohmann's management elected to utilize a low-price policy in an attempt to compete with the larger firms. This tactic appeared to work for several years. Sales of Lohmann beer stabilized at 5 per cent of the market. Since 1970, however, a slow but steady erosion of market share has occurred. The firm has shown small losses each of the last three years since 1972.

Mack Lohmann, sole owner of the brewery, recently hired Doug Andrews to take over the management of the brewery. Andrews had acquired an MBA seven years earlier and had spent the years since his graduation working for a major marketing consulting firm in Chicago.

Andrews spent his first five weeks on the job analyzing the firm's cost structure, distribution system, and sales patterns. He also examined the overall patterns and trends in the brewery industry and the activities of the major breweries operating in the state. Finally, he held telephone discussions with the owners or executives of five small breweries that had failed in the past three years. At the end of his analyses, he made the following report and recommendations to Lohmann and the chief executive officers of the firm.

Beer is purchased as much for the brand's image as it is for its taste. Research shows that most consumers cannot distinguish one brand from another in blind taste tests. Price also plays a very limited role. Every one of the five recent brewery failures that I contacted had relied on price as its primary competitive weapon. Unfortunately, we know from firsthand experience that a reduced price policy will not work for us. The *only* answer is to compete on an image basis.

As you realize, we do not have the resources to compete with the major breweries in the general marketplace. However, we *can* compete successfully if we can concentrate *all* of our efforts on one submarket. Furthermore, there is a perfect submarket which we can easily reach with specialized media. This is the college student market. The recent lowering of the legal drinking age from 21 to 18 makes this a substantial market. In fact, the college student market is estimated to consume approximately three times our current sales.

To reach this market effectively, we must understand what they think of beer in general and of our brand in particular. In addition, we want to measure their feelings toward Coors beer, which appears to enjoy substantial acceptance on campuses. To gain the information we need, we will measure students' attitudes at the state university, at one of the larger community colleges, and at one of the private colleges. One hundred students from each campus will be randomly selected and divided into four groups. The students in each group will be asked to describe the type of person who would purchase certain items for a small party (three couples). The four lists will contain several types of chips, dips, and other snack items. The lists will be identical except for the beverage. One list will contain "a case of soft drinks," one "a case of beer," the third "a case of Lohmann beer," and the fourth "a case of Coors beer." We can analyze the differences in the resulting descriptions to determine the students' attitudes toward beer, toward Lohmann's, and toward a popular brand. We can use these data to design an image campaign directed at the college student market.

1. Will this study provide the needed information?

2. What changes, if any, would you recommend?

3. Could these data be gathered through depth interviews?

4. What sampling technique would you utilize to select the individual students for inclusion in the study?

Case 9–2
Why Do People Litter?

The Highway Department of a large state has become increasingly concerned about the annual costs of cleaning litter from the state's roadways. Littering is prohibited by law and carries a maximum fine of $500. However, it is difficult for law enforcement officers to apprehend litterers, and the state and local police tend to believe that littering is a minor offense compared to the many other violations they must attempt to control.

The Highway Department has sponsored a number of publicity and advertising campaigns aimed at reducing littering. Two basic themes have been utilized—pride in the state, and the cost to taxpayers for removing litter. Neither theme appears to have had a substantial impact on the amount of litter being deposited on the state's highways. The state legislature is considering a number of potential programs to deal with the problem. These programs range from instituting special police "litter patrols," whose primary duty is to apprehend litterers, to starting a major educational campaign on littering in the state's schools.

Stu Billington, director of the state's Highway Department, recently testified before a subcommittee investigating litter. In his testimony he stated that: "The reason our programs don't work is that we have absolutely no idea why people litter. If we don't know why they do it, how can we persuade them to stop?" The Senate subcommittee decided that Billington was correct in his assessment, and four months later he received authorization to spend $15,000 to isolate the underlying reasons why people litter.

Billington asked Motivation Research, Inc.,* to submit a proposal on this problem. Parts of the proposal are presented in the paragraphs that follow.

Littering, though all too widely practiced, is not socially acceptable to the general society. Most individuals will not openly admit to littering even on anonymous questionnaires. Littering on the surface appears to be a simple act.

* This is a fictitious name.

One removes something from one's car in a simple, convenient, and direct manner. However, we do not believe that littering is, in reality, such a simple process. Otherwise, it would not persist in the face of so much stated opposition.

We do not pretend to know the underlying dynamics of littering at this time. However, we can venture several guesses. Littering may be viewed subconsciously as an act of rebellion. Children rebel against parental commands, including the command to clean up. Governmental agencies issue orders ("do not litter") much like parents. Therefore, littering may be an act of rebellion against authority. Other factors may be involved. The private automobile is cherished for the amount of freedom it provides the individual. Littering while in an automobile may represent an extension of this freedom. In this case it is freedom from the rules of neatness that generally apply in the home.

Other potential motives could be suggested. However, it is the purpose of this study to discover the underlying motives. Therefore, we will begin with an open mind rather than a prespecified set of hypotheses.

The research will involve two approaches. First, group depth interviews (ten respondents per group) will be conducted, with one group selected from each of the relevant populations described earlier. These interviews will last approximately 2.5 hours. Since littering is not a socially acceptable activity, one member of each group will actually be a member of our organization. This member will admit to littering early in the discussion, which will make it easier for others to confess. In addition, the "plant" will admit to or agree with antisocial motives for littering. Again, this will make it easier for others to admit to the same feelings.

The second approach to the problem will involve separate samples of 50 from each of the relevant population groups. These groups will complete several projective techniques. First, each group will complete a successive word association test involving ten words. *Litter, highway,* and *cleanliness* will be the key words. The remaining seven terms will be relatively neutral.

The second projective technique is a version of the picture technique. Half of each sample will see a vague drawing of a car traveling down a highway. The car will have a male driver and a female passenger in the front seat and two children in the back seat. The other half of each sample will see the same picture except that several pieces of litter will be shown coming from the car. The respondents will be asked to tell a story about the people in the car, including where they are going, where they have been, what they are like, what they are thinking, and so forth. The stories will be analyzed to reveal differences between those who saw the car with litter and those who saw the car without litter.

The final projective technique will utilize the cartoon approach. Two characters (line drawings) will be shown in conversation. One will be saying: "I threw some junk out of the window of my car on the Interstate the other day and got a $20 ticket." The respondents will be asked to provide *both* the verbal reply and the unspoken thoughts of the second character.

The depth interviews and the three techniques described will provide us a clearer understanding of the underlying dynamics of the behavior that results in littering.

1. Should Billington authorize the study?

2. Will the "plants" in the group depth interviews introduce any potential error?

3. Is it ethical to use "plants" in an interview situation of this type?

4. Are both depth interviews *and* projective techniques required? What information will each give that the other will not?

5. What other specific projective techniques could be used?

6. Are all three projective techniques required? Explain.

Case 9–3

Braverman Toys, Inc.

Jerome Braverman, founder and principal stockholder of Braverman Toys, Inc., was considering a proposal that had been made by Thomas Ash, his market research manager. Ash had recommended that a nursery school be set up by the company in a residential area to serve as a means of "field testing" potential new toys. Children would be admitted for six-week sessions. There would be only a nominal charge for each session and so a substantial waiting list of applicants could be expected. Children from families comprising a cross section of socioeconomic backgrounds and age groups could be selected for each session. One-way mirrors would be installed to allow observation of the children at play. Observers could study which toys were selected initially, how often the child returned to them, how they were used in play, what problems were encountered in playing with them, and what learning experiences each toy appeared to provide without in any way intruding in or affecting the children's play.

Ash's report stated that the company would have to get a license from the state to operate such a school and it would have to hire professionally trained teachers to staff it. An estimate of $42,000 in initial capital outlay and $65,000 in operating expenses per year for the school was given in the report.

Braverman was aware that the recommended school was patterned after a similar operation by a leading company in the industry, Fisher-Price. Fisher-Price, which established such a school a number of years before, had since become the largest and most profitable company in the business. Although there was no necessary reason for concluding that the operation of the school had contributed substantially to its success, Fisher-Price seemed to have fewer failures among the toys it introduced than did any of the other companies in the business.

Braverman Toys specialized in toys for preschool children as did Fisher-Price. Braverman was also a strong believer in toys with educational value and in advertising them to the mother rather than to the child. With sales of slightly more than $3 million last year, the Braverman advertising budget had been more than $450,000 and its net profit for the year was $187,000.

Braverman was concerned about the cost of the proposed school. The capital outlay of $42,000 to start the school did not bother him especially but he was reluctant to commit the company to a recurring operating expenditure of $65,000 per year, particularly at a time when the industry was facing a shrinking market because of the drop in the birth rate. Still, toys that failed were also expensive. The difference in profit between a successful and an unsuccessful toy averaged about $40,000 per year.

1. Should Braverman accept Ash's recommendation?

2. Are there any ethical issues involved in an observational study of this type?

Measurement and Research: Attitude Scales

What do you think about this year's football team? How do you like your new car? Do you prefer red or blue? All of us ask and respond to questions such as these every day. Basically, these questions are attempts to measure attitudes. As we have seen in earlier chapters, marketing researchers also make use of such questions. However, such questions are, for the reasons discussed in Chapter 9, often inadequate for measuring attitudes. This chapter is focused on developing more exact self-report measures of attitudes.

In the first section, the nature of attitudes is briefly sketched and the general approaches to attitude measurement are described. The second section provides a reasonably detailed description of the various rating scales used by marketing researchers to measure attitudes. This section is followed by sections on attitude scales and multidimensional scaling. In the fifth section the appropriate approach to choosing an attitude scaling technique is discussed. The final section describes the role of attitude measures in marketing decisions.

The Nature of Attitudes

What is an attitude? Perhaps the most widely known conceptual definition is "an enduring organization of motivational, emotional, perceptual, and cognitive processes with respect to some aspect of the individual's world."[1] Another common conceptual definition is "a person's basic orientations for or against some psychological object."[2] Attitudes are generally conceived of as having three components: (1) a *cognitive* component—a person's beliefs or information about the object; (2) an *affective* component—a person's feelings of like or dislike concerning the object; and (3) a *behavioral* component—action tendencies or predispositions toward the object.

Each component—cognitive, affective, and behavioral—tends to remain in balance with the other two components. That is, if a person holds favorable beliefs toward an object and likes the object, he will generally behave in a supportive manner toward the object. This might be reflected in protecting the object from harm, praising the object, or moving to acquire it. This presumed consistent relationship between the components of attitudes makes the concept interesting to marketers. For example, if we can measure the cognitive or affective components of an individual's attitude, we might be able to predict behavior that has not yet occurred. Furthermore, by changing one of these components we may be able to change behavior.

General Approaches to Attitude Measurement

Attitudes do not exist in the physical sense of that term. There is, to our knowledge at least, no physical component to an attitude. Therefore, measuring an attitude is substantially more difficult than measuring a physical characteristic such as weight. The problem is made even more complex by the many conceptual definitions of attitude. Furthermore, the operational definitions often have at best a limited relationship to any specific conceptual definition.

[1] D. Krech and R. S. Crutchfield, *Theory and Problems in Social Psychology* (New York: McGraw-Hill, Inc., 1948), 152.
[2] J. G. Engel, D. T. Kollat, and R. D. Blackwell, *Consumer Behavior* (New York: Holt, Rinehart and Winston, Inc., 1968), 165.

Operational Approaches to Attitude Measurement

There are five general operational approaches to the measurement of attitudes.[3] These are: (1) *inferences based on self-reports of beliefs, feelings, and behaviors;* (2) *inferences drawn from observation of overt behavior;* (3) *inferences drawn from responses to partially structured stimuli;* (4) *inferences drawn from performance of objective tasks;* and (5) *inferences drawn from the physiological reactions to the attitudinal object.* This chapter is concerned with the first of these approaches. The other four approaches were discussed in Chapter 9.

In this chapter, we examine the more common attitude scaling techniques. Our treatment is divided somewhat arbitrarily into three major subsections—*rating scales, attitude scales,* and *multidimensional scaling.*

Rating Scales

The use of a *rating scale requires the rater to place the object* (perhaps himself) *being rated at some point along a numerically valued continuum, or in one of a numerically ordered series of categories.* Rating scales are widely used in marketing research. Their application extends beyond the measurement of attitudes into such areas as the rating of past, present, or future behaviors. When used to measure attitudes, rating scales can be focused on the overall attitude toward an object or on the attitude toward some specific attribute of the object.

Each of the two types of rating scales—*noncomparative* and *comparative* is described along with specific examples of the more popular forms of each scale.

Noncomparative Rating Scales

With a noncomparative rating scale, the respondent is not provided with a standard to use in assigning the rating. If he is asked to rate a product, for example, he does so based on whatever standards he may desire to use. The researcher does *not* provide a comparison point such as an "average

[3] S. W. Cook and C. Selltiz, "A Multiple-Indicator Approach to Attitude Measurement," *Psychological Bulletin,* 62 (1964), 36–55.

brand" or "your favorite brand." The respondent must, of course, use some standard, but the researcher has not provided it for him.

Graphic Rating Scales

A *graphic rating scale* is a type of noncomparative scale that requires the respondent to indicate his rating by placing a mark at the appropriate point on a line that runs from one extreme of the attitude in question to the other. Although the researcher may provide scale points, that is, numbers, and brief descriptions along the continuum, their purpose is to assist the respondent in localizing his rating rather than to provide distinct categories. After the respondent has indicated his attitude by placing a mark on the line, the researcher divides the line into as many categories as he desires and assigns the individual a score based on which category his mark fell into.

Graphic rating scales are relatively easy to construct and use. Two precautions should be observed, however. First, the end statements should not be overly extreme. One generally should not use terms or phrases as "the worst possible," "never," and so forth. Second, descriptive aids, if used, should correspond as closely as possible with the points on the scale.[4] A detailed treatment of the construction and use of rating scales is provided by Guilford.[5] The following are two examples of a graphic rating scale, the first without and the second with descriptive aids.

Overall, how would you rate the taste of Mr. Pips?

Excellent————————————————————————————————————*Very Poor*

Overall, how would you rate the taste of Mr. Pips?

Probably the very best.	*Very Good. I like it.*	*All right. Neither good nor bad.*	*Not at all good. I do not like it.*	*Probably the very worst.*

1	2	3	4	5	6	7	8	9	10	11	12	13	14	15

Itemized Rating Scales

Itemized rating scales, or specific category scales, are probably the most popular scales in marketing research. Itemized rating scales are noncomparative scales that force the rater to select one of a limited number of categories that are ordered in terms of their scale positions. Questions *2* and *9a* in Exhibit 8–1 are examples of itemized rating scales.

[4] C. Selltiz, M. Jahoda, M. Deutsch, and S. W. Cook, *Research Methods in Social Relations* (New York: Holt, Rinehart and Winston, Inc., 1959), 346.

[5] J. P. Guilford, *Psychometric Methods* (New York: McGraw-Hill Book Co., 1954), 263–301.

Itemized rating scales are the basic building blocks for the more complex attitude scales. Therefore, we examine the issues surrounding the use of itemized rating scales in some detail. The major issues are: (1) *degree of verbal description,* (2) *number of categories,* (3) *balanced versus unbalanced scale,* (4) *odd or even number of categories,* and (5) *forced versus nonforced choice scales.*

Researchers have a tendency to provide at least a brief *verbal description of each category.* This is not a requirement, and often only the end categories are labeled. However, some researchers believe that the more clearly defined each category is, the more reliable the ratings will be.[6] The precise wording used to describe each category also has a major impact on the responses.[7] Instead of verbal descriptions, pictures have been used for special respondent groups. For example, scales for use by children have utilized "a set of cartoon facial expressions which range from ecstasy at one end to a Bronx cheer at the other."[8]

Any *number of categories* may be created, depending upon the nature of the attitude being investigated. In some cases, a dichotomous (favorable—unfavorable) type scale may provide sufficient detail. An example of this approach is provided in the section on adjective checklists. For other problems, ten or more categories may be required. If the researcher is interested in averages across people or in averaging or aggregating several individual scales to produce a new scale for each individual, two or three scale categories may be adequate. However, if the focus is on individual behavior, five- to seven-category scales may be needed.[9] In addition, the more homogeneous the population of interest is, the greater is the need for four or more categories.[10] Since it is generally as easy to design and administer five- to seven-point scales as it is to administer two- or three-point scales, it is best to utilize at least five categories unless there is a specific reason not to do so.

---

[6] Selltiz, et al., op. cit., 349.

[7] R. Mittelstaedt, "The Distribution of Opinion as a Function of the Semantic Properties of Response Categories," in B. W. Becker and H. Becker, *Marketing Education and the Real World and Marketing in a Changing World* (Chicago: American Marketing Association, 1973), 479–483; and P. Bartram and D. Yelding, "The Development of an Empirical Method of Selecting Phrases Used in Verbal Rating Scales: A Report on a Recent Experiment," *Journal of the Market Research Society,* **15** (July 1973), 151–156.

[8] W. D. Wells, "Communicating with Children," *Journal of Advertising Research,* **5** (June 1965), 2–14; see also J. W. Cagley, "Advertising Reference Testing in Middle Childhood," a paper presented at the 1973 Southwestern Social Science Association meeting.

[9] D. R. Lehmann and J. Hulbert, "Are Three-Point Scales Always Good Enough?" *Journal of Marketing Research,* **9** (November 1972), 444–446; see also M. S. Matell and J. Jacoby, "Is There an Optimal Number of Alternatives for Likert-Scale Items," *Journal of Applied Psychology,* **56** (December 1972), 506–509.

[10] J. R. Masters, *Reliability as a Function of the Number of Categories of a Summated Rating Scale,* unpublished dissertation, University of Pittsburgh, 1972.

The researcher also must decide whether or not to use a *balanced* or *unbalanced* set of categories. A *balanced* scale provides an equal number of favorable and unfavorable categories. The decision to use a balanced scale should hinge on the type of information desired and the assumed distribution of attitudes in the population being studied. For example, in a study of current consumers of a firm's brand, it may be reasonable to assume that most have a favorable overall attitude toward the brand (this would *not* be a safe assumption if we were measuring attitudes toward specific attributes). In this case, an unbalanced scale with more favorable categories than unfavorable categories might provide more useful information. General Foods, Ltd., makes frequent use of this approach by means of a product evaluation scale with these categories: (1) *excellent,* (2) *extremely good,* (3) *very good,* (4) *good,* (5) *fair,* and (6) *poor.* However, this scale has caused difficulties in the company's attempts to predict new product success.[11]

Any time a summary of rating scale data is presented, the scale that was used to generate it should be examined. As an extreme example, a rating scale could be so unbalanced as to contain only positive categories. The respondent with a negative attitude is forced to either leave the question blank or to mark the least favorable (but still positive) category. This can then lead to such promotional claims as "100 per cent of those responding indicated a favorable attitude toward our product." Unbalanced attitude rating scales offer the possibility of biasing responses and should be used with this potential measurement error in mind.

The issue of an *odd* or *even number of scale categories* is an unresolved problem. If an odd number of scale items is utilized, the middle item is generally designated as a neutral point. Proponents of even-numbered categories prefer to avoid neutral points, arguing that attitudes cannot be neutral and individuals should be forced to indicate some degree of favorableness or unfavorableness. A recent research effort attempted to determine the relationship between even (six-point) and odd (seven-point) scales. The researchers concluded that there was no significant difference in the results of using these two approaches.[12]

Another issue of importance with rating scales is the use of *forced versus nonforced scales.* A forced scale requires the respondent to indicate an attitude on the item. In this situation respondents often mark the midpoint of a scale when in fact they have no attitude on the object or characteristic being rated. (In some cases the instructions even request the

[11] G. Brown, T. Copeland, and M. Millward, "Monadic Testing of New Products— An Old Problem and Some Partial Solutions," *Journal of the Market Research Society,* **15** (April 1973), 112–131.

[12] G. S. Albaum and G. Munsinger, "Methodological Questions Concerning the Use of the Semantic Differential," paper presented at the spring 1973 meeting of the Southwestern Marketing Association.

respondent to mark the midpoint when he has no opinion.) If a sufficient portion of the sample has no attitude on a topic, utilization of the midpoint in this manner will distort measures of central tendency and variance.[13] On those occasions when the researcher expects a substantial portion of the respondents to have no opinion, as opposed to merely being reluctant to reveal it, he may obtain more accurate data by providing a "no opinion" or "no knowledge" type category.

Table 10–1 presents a number of examples of itemized rating scales that illustrate some of the points that we have been discussing.

Despite the simplicity of itemized rating scales, they may provide very useful and economical data. In one study, the accuracy of predictions of future aggregate purchases based on responses to an itemized rating scale (similar to number two in Table 10–1) were compared to a more complex

Table 10–1   Examples of Itemized Rating Scales*

1. Balanced, forced-choice, odd-interval scale focusing on an attitude toward a specific attribute.
   How do you like the taste of Wonder Bread?

Like it very much	Like it	Neither like nor dislike it	Dislike it	Strongly dislike it
_____	_____	_____	_____	_____

2. Balanced, forced-choice, even-interval scale focusing on an overall attitude.
   Overall, how would you rate Ultra Bright toothpaste?

Extremely good	Very good	Somewhat good	Somewhat bad	Very bad	Extremely bad
_____	_____	_____	_____	_____	_____

3. Unbalanced, forced-choice, odd-interval scale focusing on an overall attitude.
   What is your reaction to this advertisement?

Enthusiastic	Very favorable	Favorable	Neutral	Unfavorable
_____	_____	_____	_____	_____

4. Balanced, nonforced, odd-interval scale focusing on a specific attribute.
   How would you rate the friendliness of the sales personnel at Sears' downtown store?

Very friendly	Moderately friendly	Slightly friendly	Neither friendly nor unfriendly	Slightly unfriendly	Moderately unfriendly	Very unfriendly	Don't know
_____	_____	_____	_____	_____	_____	_____	_____

* When used in a written format, the scales may appear either horizontally, as shown in this table, or vertically. In general, the particular layout can be based on how the scale will best fit on the questionnaire.

[13] G. D. Hughes, "Some Confounding Effects of Forced-Choice Scales," *Journal of Marketing Research,* **6** (May 1969), 223–226.

weighted multiattribute model forecast. In two of three product categories, the itemized rating scale outperformed the more complex approach.[14]

Rating scales have been used in such diverse tasks as the development of a new typewriter,[15] the evaluation of television commercials,[16] the measurement of flavor preferences,[17] and the establishment of sales goals.[18]

Comparative Rating Scales

In the graphic and itemized rating scales described previously, the rater evaluates the object without direct reference to a specified standard. This means that different respondents may be applying different standards or reference points. When asked to rate the overall quality of a particular brand, one respondent may compare it to his ideal brand, another to his current brand, and a third to his perception of the average brand. This approach may provide an accurate reflection of each individual's attitude since he will presumably use those reference points that are most salient to him. However, it can become difficult for a researcher to interpret a group's scores on a rating scale if each individual is employing a distinct standard. Therefore, when the researcher wants to ensure that all respondents are approaching the rating task from the same known reference point, some version of a comparative rating scale should be used.

Graphic and Itemized Comparative Rating Scales

Noncomparative graphic and itemized rating scales can be converted to comparative scales by simply introducing a comparison point. Often it is not even necessary to change the category descriptions. The issues and applications discussed under noncomparative scales also apply to comparative scales.[19] The following examples should make the nature of comparative graphic and itemized rating scales clear.

[14] F. B. Kraft, D. H. Granbois, and J. O. Summers, "Brand Evaluation and Brand Choice: A Longitudinal Study," *Journal of Marketing Research,* **10** (August 1973), 235–241.

[15] B. G. Wolfsie, "Marketing Research in the Development of a New Typewriter," *Journal of Marketing Research,* **1** (February 1964), 35–37.

[16] L. E. Crane, "How Product Appeal and Program Affect Attitude Toward Commercials," *Journal of Advertising Research,* **4** (March 1964), 15–18.

[17] J. L. Eastlack, "Consumer Flavor Preference Factors in Food Product Design," *Journal of Marketing Research,* **1** (February 1964), 38–42.

[18] G. D. Hughes, "A New Tool for Sales Managers," *Journal of Marketing Research,* **1** (May 1964), 32–38.

[19] See for example, D. Harris, "Predicting Consumer Reaction to Product Designs," *Journal of Advertising Research,* **4** (June 1964), 34–37.

Compared to the beer I generally drink (Budweiser, most brands, my ideal brand), Coors is:

Vastly superior	Neither superior nor inferior	Vastly inferior

How do you like the taste of Gleem compared to Ultra Bright (your regular brand)

Like it much more	Like it more	Like it about the same	Like it less	Like it much less	Don't know

Paired Comparisons

Paired comparisons are a special type of comparative rating scale. The use of the *paired comparison technique involves presenting the respondent with two objects at a time and requiring him to select one of the two according to some criterion* such as overall preference, taste, or style. Thus, the respondent must make a series of judgments of the nature: A tastes better than B, overall B is better than A, or A is more stylish than B.

Each respondent must compare all possible pairs of objects. If the researcher is interested in 5 brands ($n = 5$), there will be 10 comparisons $[n(n - 1)/2]$. If he is interested in 10 brands, the number of required comparisons increases to 45. Furthermore, there must be a comparison for each attribute of interest. Thus, if we are interested in 10 brands and 5 attributes, our respondents will each be required to make 220 comparisons. This rapid increase in the number of comparisons required for more than 5 or 6 objects limits the usefulness of the technique.

Table 10–2 presents the output generated by comparing 5 brands on 1 attribute. This output can be analyzed in a number of ways. A simple visual inspection reveals that Brand B is preferred over each other brand. Visual analysis will also provide the basis for judging the rank order of the 5 brands. The data in Table 10–2 can also be converted into an interval scale through the application of Thurstone's Law of Comparative Judg-

Table 10–2 Proportions Preferring Brand I (Top of Table) to Brand J (Side of Table)

	A	B	C	D	E
A	—	.81	.68	.26	.37
B	.19	—	.28	.08	.14
C	.23	.72	—	.15	.26
D	.74	.92	.85	—	.57
E	.63	.86	.74	.43	—

ment. A treatment of Thurstone's law is beyond the scope of this text, but a number of excellent treatments are readily available.[20]

Advantages of the Paired Comparison Technique.   The paired comparison technique offers a number of advantages. For fairly small numbers of brands, it does not induce respondent fatigue. It involves a direct comparison, requires overt choice, and places the compared experiences as close together in time as possible. Its potential for conversion into an interval scale is also an advantage. For these reasons, it is widely used in tests of competing advertisements, product and package versions, and so forth.

Disadvantages of the Paired Comparison Technique.   However, the paired comparison technique is not without disadvantages. Its use is generally restricted to fewer than ten objects and the order in which the items are presented may bias the results.[21] The comparison of two objects at a time bears little resemblance to the more common multialternative situation found in the marketplace. An item may do well in a paired comparison situation and yet not do well when placed in an actual market situation. The finding that one object is preferred over certain others does not mean that any are "liked" in an absolute sense. One may just be disliked less than the others.[22] Finally, simpler noncomparative rating scales will often provide similar results.[23]

On balance, the paired comparison technique appears to offer a viable approach to gathering preference type attitude data. The weaknesses described indicate that it is not a universally useful technique. Nonetheless, it is a valuable tool in the attitude researcher's set of techniques.

Rank Order Rating Scale

The *rank order method requires the respondent to rank a set of objects according to some criterion.* Thus, a respondent may be asked to rank

[20] See H. A. David, *The Method of Paired Comparisons* (London: Charles Griffin and Co., Ltd., 1963), A. L. Edward, *Techniques of Attitude Scale Construction* (New York: Appleton-Century-Crofts, 1957), 20–29; P. E. Green and D. S. Tull, *Research for Marketing Decisions* (Englewood Cliffs, N.J.: Prentice Hall, Inc., 1974), 184–191; L. L. Thurstone, *The Measurement of Values* (Chicago: University of Chicago Press, 1959), 39–49. For an alternative approach, see R. L. Day, "Systematic Paired Comparisons in Preference Analysis," *Journal of Marketing Research,* **2** (November 1965), 406–412.

[21] P. Daniels and J. Lawford, "The Effect of Order in the Presentation of Samples in Paired Comparison Tests," *Journal of the Market Research Society,* **16** (April 1974), 127–133.

[22] A. B. Blankenship, "Let's Bury Paired Comparisons," *Journal of Advertising Research,* **6** (March 1966), 13–17.

[23] R. Seaton, "Why Ratings Are Better Than Comparisons," *Journal of Advertising Research,* **14** (February 1974), 45–48.

five brands of a snack food based on his overall preferences, taste, saltiness, or package design. This approach, like the paired comparison approach, is purely comparative in nature. An individual may rank ten brands in descending order of preference and still "dislike" the brand he rates as 1 because the ranking is based solely on the individual's reactions to the *set of objects presented for evaluation*. Thus, a brand might be ranked number 5 when compared with brands A, B, C, and D, and yet be ranked first when compared to brands E, F, G, and H. Therefore, it is essential that the researcher include at least the most relevant competing brands, product versions, or advertisements.

The rank-order method is widely used. For example, General Foods, Ltd., found it useful to add a version of the rank-order approach to its consumer evaluations of new products.[24] It forces respondents to discriminate among the relevant objects and does so in a manner closer to the actual shopping environment than does the paired comparison technique. It is also substantially less time consuming than paired comparisons. Ranking 10 items is considerably faster and easier for most people than making the 45 judgments required to generate paired comparison data for 10 brands. The instructions for ranking are also easily understood by most individuals, a fact that makes it useful for self-administered questionnaires where more complex instructions may reduce the response rate or increase measurement error.

The major shortcoming of the technique is the fact that it produces only ordinal data. (However, rank-order measurements can also be converted to interval data using Thurstone's Law of Comparative Judgment.)

The Constant Sum Scale

The *constant sum scale* is gaining popularity in marketing research.[25] This technique *requires the respondent to divide a constant sum, generally 100, among two or more objects or attributes so as to reflect the respondent's relative preference for each object*. The constant sum approach can be applied to either the paired comparison or rank-order format. Although the technique was originally developed to provide data that could be converted into a ratio type scale,[26] marketing applications generally utilize the technique to provide an approximate interval scale.

[24] Brown, et al., op. cit.; see also J. B. Mason and M. L. Mayer, "Insights into the Image Determinants of Fashion Specialty Outlets," *Journal of Business Research,* **1** (Summer 1973), 72–80.

[25] An example of its use can be found in J. W. Udell, "The Perceived Importance of the Elements of Strategy," *Journal of Marketing,* **32** (January 1968), 34–40; see also G. David Hughes, *Attitude Measurement for Marketing Strategies* (Glenview, Ill.: Scott, Foresman and Company, 1971), 105.

[26] J. P. Guilford, *Psychometric Methods* (New York: McGraw-Hill, Inc., 1954), 214–220.

Hughes[27] provides a simple formula for converting constant sum data using a paired comparison format into interval data:

$$S_i = \sum_1^c S_{ic}/[n(n-1)/2]$$

where S_i is the interval scale value of brand i, S_{ic} is the score or points given brand i during comparison c, and n is the number of brands being compared.

Perhaps the most useful role for this technique in marketing research is with the rank-order format. In this situation, the respondent is asked to divide the 100 points among *all* the brands of attributes under consideration. The resulting values can be averaged across individuals to produce an approximate interval scale value for the brands or attributes being considered. The following example indicates the potential value such data may have.

Divide 100 points among the characteristics listed so that the division will reflect how important each characteristic is to you in your selection of a new automobile:
Economy
Style
Comfort
Safety
Social status
Price
Dependability
   Total   100

Even though the constant sum technique can generate valuable information beyond that provided by the standard paired comparison and rank-order methods, it has several weaknesses. The accuracy of the interval assumptions of the constant sum technique have not yet been thoroughly tested. When used with the rank-order format, only a limited number of objects may be compared because of the difficulty that many respondents may have in assuring that their divisions sum to 100. In conjunction with this problem is the fact that the instructions must be very carefully phrased to avoid confusion. One approach to overcoming confusion has been to work with 10, or in some cases 100, pennies, which the respondent can physically allocate to the objects.

Attitude Scales

At stated earlier, the distinction between rating scales and attitude scales is blurred. *Attitude scales* represent carefully standardized questionnaires.

[27] Hughes, op. cit., 106–107.

Instead of describing himself directly in terms of his position on the attitude in question, the respondent expresses his agreement or disagreement with a number of statements relevant to it. On the basis of these responses, he is assigned a score.[28]

In general, interest is focused on the total score or particular subscores that an individual or group obtain rather than the responses to the individual items. However, on occasion the responses to the individual items become central, as in profile analysis with the semantic differential scale or the overall array of items in the Q-sort.

In selecting items to include on an attitude scale, two criteria must be considered.[29] First, *the items must elicit responses that reflect the attitude being measured*. Second, *the total set of items must differentiate among people who hold different levels of the attitude*. In applied research, the level of discrimination required is a function of the problem at hand. It is often possible to utilize a rather gross level of discrimination for many marketing problems.

In the remainder of this section, we examine six attitude scales— *Q-sort, Thurstone, Guttman, Likert, semantic differential,* and *Stapel*. A close examination of each technique, except perhaps the Q-sort, indicates that the itemized rating scale is the basic building block. Therefore, we should keep in mind the various issues and problems discussed in relation to the itemized rating scales as they are applicable to most of the more advanced scales.

The Q-Sort Technique

The *Q-sort technique*[30] is, in essence, an efficient rank ordering process. It requires the respondent to sort, that is, to divide into piles or groups, a large number of statements or other objects according to a specified criterion. The technique, as originally developed, was used to measure an individual's response to psychological therapy. However, its marketing applications center on segmenting individuals with similar attitudes about a given object or determining which objects have similar attitude profiles by some group of respondents.[31] Q-sort procedures can be best understood by going through the steps involved in designing and administering one.

[28] Selltiz, et al., op. cit., 357.

[29] Ibid.

[30] For a more detailed discussion see F. N. Kerlinger, *Foundations of Behavioral Research* (New York: Holt, Rinehart and Winston, Inc., 1973), 582–600; O. H. Mowrer, "Q-Technique Descriptions, History, and Critique," *Psychotherapy: Theory and Research,* ed. by O. H. Mowrer (New York: The Ronald Press Company, 1953); and M. J. Schlinger, "Cues on Q-Technique," *Journal of Advertising Research,* **9** (September 1963), 53–60.

[31] See W. Stephenson, "Public Images of Public Utilities," *Journal of Advertising Research,* **3** (December 1963), 34–39.

1. *The researcher must select the criterion along which the items are to be sorted.* Widely used criteria include "most like/least like my present brand" (or ideal brand; brand X) and "most pleasing/least pleasing to me." The criterion used must, of course, meet the needs of the specific problem. It is sometimes useful to have the same individual make two or more sorts of the same items according to different criteria. The most common application of this is when the respondent is required to sort based on his ideal brand, his current brand, and perhaps the brand of interest to the researcher.

2. Next, *the specific items for sorting must be selected.* Examples for product research include "stylish, economical, functional . . ."; for advertising copy research "amusing, interesting, informative . . ."; for store image research "friendly, convenient, expensive . . ."; and so forth. Selecting enough appropriate items for sorting can be difficult since this type of scale generally requires between 60 and 120 items. Once the items are selected, they are printed (or otherwise attached) on cards.

3. *The respondent is instructed to sort the items into 11 groups or piles, placing a specified number in each pile.* The groups range from one extreme of the sorting criteria to the other. The respondent is "forced" to place the items in the piles in such a way as to yield an approximate normal distribution. This allows for the use of parametric statistics. The following example may help clarify the sorting process.

Divide the 100 terms on the cards into the 11 groups so that they will describe your view of an ideal cake mix. Those terms that most closely describe your ideal cake mix should be placed in the groups to the left, and those that are least like it should be placed in the groups to the right. Be sure to place exactly the number required in each group.

Group 1	Group 2	—	—	—	—	—	—	—	—	Group 11
Most like my ideal cake mix	—	—	—	—	—	—	—	—	—	—	Least like my ideal cake mix
# of cards per group	2	4	8	12	14	20	14	12	8	4	2

4. *The items are assigned the score of the group they are placed in* and are analyzed by special correlational techniques.[32]

The Q-sort technique takes less respondent time than rank order and paired comparisons of a similar number of items. It has a well-developed set of analytical techniques that permit the respondent to gain potentially useful insights into the meaning of Q-sort data. These techniques make it possible to classify respondents on the basis of overall attitude similarity rather than a summed attitude score.

[32] Kerlinger, op. cit., 582–597.

Despite these advantages, the technique has not been widely used by marketing researchers, in part, because of its relative newness and the specialized nature of the analysis of Q-sort data. Furthermore, few computers have sufficient capacity to analyze more than 200 respondents.[33] There has also been some criticism of the statistical nature of Q-sort results.[34]

Cost is a major drawback for the applied researcher. The technique requires cards, sorting boards or other aids, and personal or group interviews. All of these factors increase both the time and cost requirements of the technique to a point where few applied researchers utilize it. Despite this drawback, the Q-sort is useful as an exploratory technique and for certain specialized research problems. It will probably receive increasing attention as more marketing researchers gain familiarity with it.

The Guttman Scale

The *Guttman scale* is the name applied to the technique of scalogram analysis developed by Louis Guttman.[35] The respondents are presented a series of items, generally statements about a product or product attribute, and are asked to indicate their degree of agreement or disagreement with each item. The primary goal of the technique is to determine after the fact if a cumulative, unidimensional scale has been achieved.

For example, if we asked respondents to agree or disagree with the following five statements, we would achieve the indicated response pattern:

		A	B	C	D	E
A.	I am over 20	X	X	X	X	X
B.	I am over 30		X	X	X	X
C.	I am over 40			X	X	X
D.	I am over 50				X	X
E.	I am over 60					X

Anyone over 60 must, of necessity, be over 50, 40, 30, and 20. Likewise, anyone over 40 must also be over 30 and 20. Age is an "unidimensional" phenomenon—it involves one and only one factor. To determine whether or not a series of attitude statements measures only one dimension of an attitude, the responses of a sample are arrayed as shown. If most of the responses fit the pattern, a unidimensional scale exists.

[33] Schlinger, op. cit., 54.
[34] Kerlinger, op. cit., 595.
[35] For a more detailed treatment of scalogram analysis, see A. Edwards, *Techniques of Attitude Scale Construction* (New York: Appleton-Century-Crofts, 1957), 172–200; Selltiz, et al., op. cit., 370–371; and G. F. Summers, *Attitude Measurement* (Chicago: Rand McNally, & Co., Inc., 1970), 174–213.

Despite a strong statement of its potential[36] and an example of its use by the W. A. Sheaffer Pen Company,[37] the Guttman technique is seldom used in marketing research.[38] The technique provides only limited assistance in scale construction since it must be applied after the data have been gathered. However, it can be used on pretest data to help develop unidimensional scales. Perhaps the primary reason for its relative lack of use is the fact that marketing researchers do not feel a need for this type of data. As several researchers have noted, a perfect Guttman scale may not be the most effective means for measuring attitudes or for predicting behavior.[39] Furthermore, a given scale may be unidimensional for one group and not for another. For these reasons, the Guttman scale is unlikely to be used in marketing unless the researcher has a specific reason for desiring a cumulative, unidimensional scale.

Thurstone Equal-Appearing Interval Scale

The *Thurstone equal-appearing interval scale* was an early attempt to devise an indirect measure of attitudes that would result in interval data.[40] The construction and use of such a scale require the following steps:

1. *The researcher generates a "large number" (more than 100) of statements that he thinks are related to the attitude being investigated.* The statements should range from one extreme of the attitude in question to the other.

2. *A "large number" of judges independently classify the statements into 11 groups ranging from "most favorable" through "most unfavorable."* Group six is defined as a neutral group that is neither favorable nor unfavorable. The number of judges is generally 50 or more, but recently fewer judges, 20 to 50, are being used with reasonable results.

3. *The scale value of each statement is the median position (some researchers use the mean) to which it is assigned by all of the judges.* Those statements with a wide variance—that is, those that are placed in a large number of groups by the various judges—are discarded as ambiguous.

4. *A final scale is composed of 10 to 20 statements that represent a fairly uniform distribution of scale values from 1 to 11.* The items are

[36] M. N. Manfield, "The Guttman Scale," in G. Albaum and M. Venkatesan, eds., *Scientific Marketing Research* (New York: The Free Press, 1971), 167–178.

[37] E. A. Richards, "A Commercial Application of Guttman Attitude Scaling Techniques," *Journal of Marketing,* **22** (October 1957), 166–173.

[38] For a critical view of the value of the technique, see J. P. Robinson, "Toward a More Appropriate Use of Guttman Scaling," *Public Opinion Quarterly,* **37** (Summer 1973), 260–267.

[39] Selltiz, et al., op. cit., 376.

[40] For a detailed treatment, see L. L. Thurstone, *The Measurement of Values* (Chicago: University of Chicago Press, 1959).

typically randomized and the underlying scale value is not shown to the respondent.

5. *The respondent is asked to check or mark those items that most closely approximate his own position.* He is then assigned as a score the median (some researchers use the mean) of the scale values of the items he has checked.

Thurstone equal-appearing interval scales are not widely used in marketing research. Two potential weaknesses in the technique reduce its usefulness. First, since the individual's score is the median (or mean) of the scale values of the items he checks, essentially different attitudinal patterns may be expressed by the same score. That is, an individual who agreed with items having values of 4, 5, and 6 would score 5 as would the individual who checked items 2, 5, and 8. However, if the scale is well constructed, such an occurrence is unlikely. A more serious weakness is the possibility that the scale values themselves are dependent on the attitudes of the original judges.[41]

A more critical problem for the applied researcher is the fact that Thurstone scales are both expensive and time consuming to construct. This makes it inappropriate for those problems where alternative methods are available. However, a few "generalized" Thurstone scales may prove useful to applied research. A generalized scale has a series of statements that are applicable to a certain *type* of object. For example, the Kelley-Remmers "Scale for Measuring Attitudes Toward Any Institution" can be applied to advertising (as an institution) as well as to the church, business, or government. There does not appear to be any reason why a firm or trade association could not develop a "generalized" Thurstone-type scale for its particular product category. The costs of developing the instrument could then be written off over many applications. However, such an undertaking would make sense only if no equally useful and less expensive techniques were available.

Likert Scales

Likert scales, sometimes referred to as Likert-type scales or summated scales, are widely used in marketing research. A Likert scale requires a respondent to indicate a degree of agreement or disagreement with each of a series of items, generally statements, related to the attitude object. These levels of agreement-disagreement are then scored in such a way as to consistently reflect positive and negative attitudes, and the scores are summed for each individual. The following two examples should help clarify the nature of Likert scales.

[41] Selltiz, op. cit., 364–365.

1. *Macy's is one of the most attractive stores in town.*

__Strongly agree	__Agree	__Neither agree nor disagree	__Disagree	__Strongly disagree
(5)	(4)	(3)	(2)	(1)

2. *The service at Macy's is not satisfactory.*

__Strongly agree	__Agree	__Neither agree nor disagree	__Disagree	__Strongly disagree
(1)	(2)	(3)	(4)	(5)

The score or value for each response is shown in parentheses below the response. These values are *not* shown on the regular questionnaire but are presented here to illustrate the scoring system. Notice that the scale values are switched so that a high score on an item will reflect a favorable attitude rather than agreement with the item itself.

There are five steps in the construction of a Likert scale.[42]

1. The researcher generates a substantial number of items, generally statements that are relevant to the attitude of interest. These statements should be either clearly favorable or clearly unfavorable. They should also be of approximately equal attitude value. That is, each statement should reflect equally important aspects of the attitude under examination (although there is no inherent reason why individual items could not be weighted to reflect unequal attitude value).

2. A number of response categories (agree-disagree type categories) ranging from 3 to 10 are attached to each item. The problems involved in selecting the number of response categories are the same as those discussed in the earlier section on rating scales.

3. The initial set of items is presented to a group of respondents who are representative of those whose attitudes the researcher is interested in.

4. These respondents are scored in the same manner shown in the example, and each individual is assigned a total score that is the sum of his scores on the individual items.

5. The individual items are then analyzed to ascertain which ones discriminate most clearly between the high scorers and the low scorers on the total score. Those items that do not show a substantial correlation with the total score or that do not elicit different responses from those who score high and those who score low on the overall test are eliminated. This procedure increases the internal consistency or reliability of the instrument. The remaining items, or a sample of them, serve as the final Likert scale.

The Likert scale offers a number of advantages over the Guttman and Thurstone scales. First, it is relatively easy to construct and administer. The instructions that must accompany the scale are easily understood,

---

[42] Based on Selltiz, op. cit., 367–368.

which makes the technique useful for mail surveys of the general population. The Likert scale can also contain items that do not bear an obvious relationship to the attitude in question. The only requirement is that each item be consistent with the total score (see number 5). This technique also tends to be quite reliable and, because of the wide range of responses, it provides fairly precise information on the individual's attitude.

The scale is frequently criticized because a number of unique response patterns can result in the same total score. (This is one of the problems that Guttman attempted to solve in devising his scale.) However, this may not represent as much of a problem as many of the critics claim, particularly if the scale is well developed initially. Furthermore, there is no reason why Likert scale data cannot be subjected to profile analysis. (See the following section on the semantic differential for a discussion of profile analysis.)

In general, the advantages of Likert-type scales outweigh the disadvantages as long as only ordinal data are required.[43] In fact, many researchers believe that this type of data is close enough to interval data to justify the use of normal statistical routines. Its ease of construction and simplicity of administration are additional advantages for applied marketing studies.

The Semantic Differential Scale

The *semantic differential scale* is the most frequently used attitude scaling device in marketing research.[44] In its most common form, it requires the respondent to rate the attitude object on a number of itemized, seven-point rating scales bounded at each end by one of two bipolar adjectives. For example:

BUICK RIVIERA

Fast	_X_:	__:	__:	__:	__:	__:	__:	Slow
Bad	__:	__:	__:	__:	__:	_X_:	__:	Good
Large	__:	__:	__:	_X_:	__:	__:	__:	Small
Inexpensive	__:	__:	__:	__:	_X_:	__:	__:	Expensive

The instructions indicate that the respondent is to mark the blank that best indicates how accurately one or the other term describes or fits the attitude object. The end positions indicate "extremely," the next pair

[43] For a description of an improved version of the Likert scale, see G. Kundu, "A Comparison of the Likert and a New Technique of Attitude Measurement," *Indian Journal of Psychology,* **47** (September 1972), 245–258.

[44] For example, see T. R. Wotruba and J. S. Breeden, "The Ideal Company Image and Self-Image Congruence," *Journal of Business Research,* **1** (Fall 1973), 165–172.

indicate "very," the middle-most pair indicate "somewhat," and the middle position indicates "neither-nor" or "not applicable." Thus, the respondent in the example described the Buick Riviera as extremely fast, very good, somewhat expensive, and neither large nor small.

The original work by Osgood[45] shows that three factors can explain most of the results obtained with the semantic differential. These three factors are: (1) *evaluative*—good versus bad, (2) *activity*—active versus passive, and (3) *potency*—strong versus weak. However, marketing researchers tend to concentrate on the evaluative factor as this seems most appropriate for understanding attitudes toward products, brands, and stores.

Semantic differential data can be analyzed in a number of ways. The versatility is increased if the assumption is made that the resultant data are interval in nature. This assumption is widely accepted among researchers.[46] Two general approaches to analysis are of interest to us— aggregate analysis and profile analysis. The first step in either approach is to assign each blank a value of one through seven. For aggregate analysis, it is essential (and helpful for profile analysis) if the larger numbers are consistently assigned to the blanks nearer the more favorable terms.

Aggregate analysis requires that all the scores across all adjective pairs be summed for each individual (this should be done only for adjectives reflecting the same factor or attitude dimension as determined by factor analysis). Each individual is thus assigned a summated score. The individual or group of individuals can then be compared to other individuals on the basis of their total scores, or two or more objects (products, brands, or stores) can be compared for the same group of individuals. Aggregate analysis is most useful for predicting preference or brand share. However, disaggregate or profile analysis appears to provide more useful data for marketing decision making.

Profile analysis involves computing the mean value assigned to each adjective pair for an object by a specified group. This profile can then be compared, usually visually, with the profile of another object or of another group. Figure 10–1 provides an example of a profile comparison of two retail department stores. Both stores would receive similar aggregate scores. However, these profiles are quite different even though both are favorable. Store A is at a disadvantage in terms of "price," "service," "helpful employees," "pleasantness," and "friendliness." All of these factors except price appear to be related to the store personnel and the

[45] C. Osgood, G. Suci, and P. Tannenbaum, *The Measurement of Meaning* (Urbana: University of Illinois Press, 1957).

[46] For a more detailed discussion of analytical approaches as well as the nature of semantic differential data, see Kerlinger, op. cit., 566–581; and C. Holmes, "A Statistical Evaluation of Rating Scales," *Journal of the Market Research Society,* **16** (April 1974), 87–107.

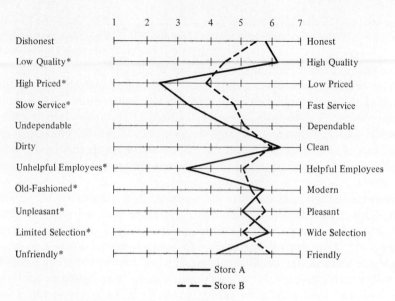

*Indicates a statistically significant difference ($p < .05$)

Figure 10–1   Profile analysis using semantic differential data.

general manner of their dealing with customers. Store B is at a disadvantage with regard to "quality," "selection," and "modernness." These factors seem to be related primarily to product line decisions.

Stapel Scale

The *Stapel scale* is a simplified version of the semantic differential. The original Stapel scale was described as a unipolar ten-point nonverbal rating scale with values ranging from $+5$ to -5, which measures direction and intensity simultaneously.[47] Unlike the semantic differential, the scale values are used to indicate how accurately *one* adjective describes the concept in question.

Table 10–1 shows the format of a Stapel scale that has been altered from 10 to 6 points.

The advantages of this technique lie in the ease of administration and the absence of any need to pretest the adjectives or phrases to ensure true bipolarity.[48] The ability of the Stapel scale to produce results

[47] I. Crespi, "Use of a Scaling Technique in Surveys," *Journal of Marketing,* **25** (July 1961), 69–72.

[48] The need for bipolarity in the semantic differential is described in E. J. Lusk, "A Bipolar Adjective Screening Methodology," *Journal of Marketing Research,* **10** (May 1973), 202–203.

Table 10–1 Format of the Stapel Scale

	Sears		
	+ 3	+ 3	+ 3
	+ 2	+ 2	+ 2
	+ 1	+ 1	+ 1
Large	Friendly	Low Priced	
	− 1	− 1	− 1
	− 2	− 2	− 2
	− 3	− 3	− 3

equivalent to those produced by the semantic differential has been verified empirically.[49] The scale has been utilized in studies focusing on department store images, new food products, and advertising copy.[50]

The results of the Stapel scale can be analyzed in the same ways as semantic differential data. Figure 10–2 presents a visual profile analysis

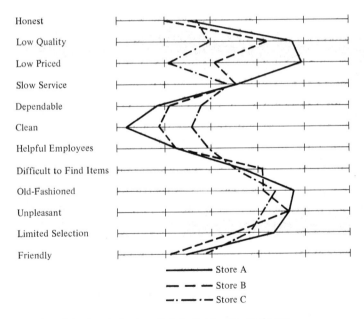

Honest
Low Quality
Low Priced
Slow Service
Dependable
Clean
Helpful Employees
Difficult to Find Items
Old-Fashioned
Unpleasant
Limited Selection
Friendly

——————— Store A
— — — Store B
—·——·— Store C

*The closer the line is to the descriptor, the better that descriptor fits the store.

Figure 10–2 Comparative profiles—Stapel scale.

[49] D. I. Hawkins, G. Albaum, and R. Best, "Stapel Scale or Semantic Differential in Marketing Research?" *Journal of Marketing Research,* **11** (August 1974), 318–322: and J. J. Vidali, "Single-Anchor Stapel Scales versus Double-Anchor Semantic Differential Scales," *Psychological Reports,* **33** (October 1973), 373–374.

[50] J. Stapel, "Predictive Attitudes," in L. Adler and I. Crespi, *Attitude Research on the Rocks* (Chicago: American Marketing Association, 1968), 96–115.

of three stores using six-point Stapel scale data. It seems likely that the Stapel scale will gain an accepted place in marketing research, particularly since it appears to produce good results when administered over the telephone.[51]

Adjective Checklist

The adjective checklist is somewhat like a two-category Stapel scale. This approach presents the respondent with a list of adjectives or phrases from which he is to check the ones that describe the object. The following instructions (see Question 7, Exhibit 8–1) are typical:

Here is a list of words. Please take your time to look it over. Which of these words do you think describe Smokey? Pick as many as you feel could be used to describe him.[52]

The typical analytical approach is to compute the percentage of respondents that check each adjective and compare these figures across various groups or objects. Although this is not a rigorous technique, it can frequently provide useful insights, particularly in exploratory research.

Philip Morris International made effective use of a version of the checklist that required the respondents to select one word or the other from each of 14 pairs of words that could be used to describe cigarettes.[53] The test involved three groups of 800 people in the Canadian market. One group, the control group, smoked unmarked Parliament cigarettes from completely blank white packages and expressed their attitudes toward the cigarettes by means of the checklist. The same procedure was followed for the other two groups except for the packages. One of the remaining groups received packages labeled "American Type Cigarettes" whereas the third group received packages labeled "Cigarettes Blended with the Darker Colored Burley Tobacco for Better Filter Smoking and Lower Tar Delivery."

The "blended-burley-low tar" claim did not produce significantly different responses from those elicited by the cigarettes in the plain package. This was true among both the English and French-speaking Canadians. However, the "American-type cigarette" claim lowered the percentage of

[51] Hawkins, et al., op. cit.

[52] U.S. Department of Agriculture, Forest Service, "Public Image of and Attitudes Toward Smokey the Bear and Forest Fires," a study conducted by Haug Associates, Inc., June 1968, p. 184.

[53] W. J. Keegan, *Philip Morris International*, 9–571–641 (Boston: Intercollegiate Case Clearing House, 1968).

positive responses among English-speaking Canadians but increased the percentage of positive responses among French-speaking Canadians.

Multidimensional Scaling

The various attitude scales described in the previous section are all based on one of two simplifying assumptions. Several scales, such as the Guttman scale, assume that only one attitude dimension such as like/dislike or high quality/low quality is relevant. Others, such as the semantic differential scale, assume that several dimensions may be relevant *and* that the researcher knows in advance what these attitude dimensions are (since he must provide the relevant adjectives).

Multidimensional scaling (MDS) is a term that is applied to a variety of computer-based techniques that have as their goal the representation of an object in multidimensional space based on one or more respondent's perceptions of or attitudes toward the object. It assumes that neither the respondent nor the researcher can accurately identify the number or the nature of the dimensions a respondent utilizes to evaluate a product or store. Therefore, MDS utilizes relatively simple data—typically judgments of similarity or preference for brands or stores—and attempts to disclose the dimensions or attributes that underlie these judgments. Each brand or store is then plotted on these dimensions so that the researcher can compare objects along any particular dimension.

Examine the multidimensional map shown in Figure 10–3. This map was generated from one individual's ranking of his preferences for the eight brands and from his judgments about which pair of brands were most similar, which pair was next most similar, and so forth until he ranked all possible pairs of brands according to their similarity.

The map indicates that the individual utilizes two primary dimensions in evaluating these soft drinks—"colaness" and "dietness." MDS techniques *do not provide the names of the dimensions.* This must be done by the researcher based on his experience, the nature of the output, and any other data he may have available. The ideal point for this individual, shown on the map as *I,* was derived from his preference rankings of the brands. As can be seen, 7-Up is closest to his ideal brand, followed by Sprite, and Tab is most distant from it. When both ideal points and perceptual points are plotted on the same map as in Figure 10–3 (a process that requires special techniques), we have what is called a *joint space configuration.*

As stated earlier, MDS is not a single technique. Rather, it represents an entire array of techniques. All of the techniques are dependent on the

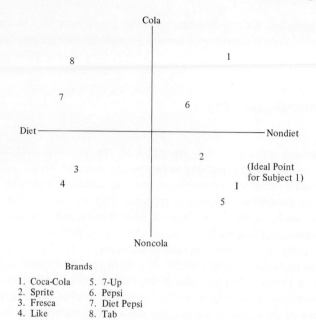

Brands

1. Coca-Cola	5. 7-Up
2. Sprite	6. Pepsi
3. Fresca	7. Diet Pepsi
4. Like	8. Tab

Figure 10–3 Multidimensional space for soft drinks.

computer to perform the necessary computations. Over a dozen different computer programs are available to perform multidimensional scaling. One study that compared a number of these techniques concluded that there is generally a high degree of consistency of results regardless of the technique used.[54] However, another study reached the opposite conclusion.[55] Thus, conclusions on the compatibility of the various techniques must await further testing.

MDS techniques can be broken into the following three broad categories.[56]

1. *Fully Metric MDS.* These techniques require ratio-scaled measures of the distances between the objects. The basic task is: Given a set of interpoint distances, find the dimensionality (number of dimensions) and configuration of points whose distances most closely match the numerical input values. The output is in ratio scale form.

2. *Fully Nonmetric MDS.* These techniques require only a rank order of the distances between the objects. The objective is to find a space of

---

[54] P. E. Green and V. R. Rao, *Applied Multidimensional Scaling* (New York: Holt, Rinehart and Winston, Inc., 1972).

[55] C. M. Lillis, *An Investigation of the Use of Nonmetric Multidimensional Scaling in Identification and Analysis of Market Segments,* unpublished doctoral dissertation, Eugene, Oregon, 1972.

[56] P. E. Green and F. J. Carmone, *Multidimensional Scaling* (Boston: Allyn & Bacon, Inc., 1970), 10–11.

minimum dimensionality and the rank order of each point on each dimension in turn. The results are *not* the configuration of points (that is, their positions in space) but only the rank order of the objects on each dimension. Thus the output, like the input, is in ordinal form.

3. *Nonmetric MDS.* These approaches require only ordinal input data but generate ratio output. Given a rank order of "psychological distance" data, the objective of these approaches is to develop a configuration whose rank order of ratio scaled distances best reproduces the original input ranks.

Nonmetric multidimensional scaling (NMDS) is currently the most popular MDS technique for marketing applications. Its ability to convert ordinal input into ratio output is the primary reason for this interest. The potential usefulness of NMDS is illustrated by the following applied example.

A wholesale firm wished to determine how it was perceived by its market (35 regional distributors). Exploratory research indicated that the relevant purchasing agents could compare the wholesaler to its five major competitors but were vague in explaining exactly what criteria they were using in making these comparisons. As a result, the firm decided to use NMDS. The purchasing agents were asked to rank the various pairs of wholesalers in terms of perceived similarity. They also ranked the five wholesalers in terms of their preference for them.

These data were fed into a computerized NMDS program that produced, in this case, the two-dimensional output shown in Figure 10–4. The six wholesalers, *A* through *F,* are arrayed around the two axes. The meaning assigned to the axes was based on the researcher's and management's intuition and knowledge of this market.

Figure 10–4 also shows the ideal points for three purchasers (1, 2, and 3). These points represent that particular combination of price competitiveness and sales assistance that each of these purchasers would like to receive from a supplier. Thus, no firm appears to be meeting purchaser 1's need for sales assistance or purchaser 2's desire for low prices.

It has been suggested that MDS will eventually provide valuable assistance to the marketing researcher in such areas as product life-cycle analysis, market segmentation, vendor evaluation, advertising evaluation, test marketing, salesman and store image research, and brand switching, as well as various other forms of attitude scaling. For example, Dupont utilized the technique to investigate market segments for 45 different products between 1963 and 1968.[57] Nonetheless, the techniques still have computational, empirical, and conceptual problems. Although the tech-

[57] D. H. Doehlert, "Similarity and Preference Mapping: A Color Example," in R. L. King, *Marketing and the New Science of Planning* (Chicago: American Marketing Association, 1968), 250–258.

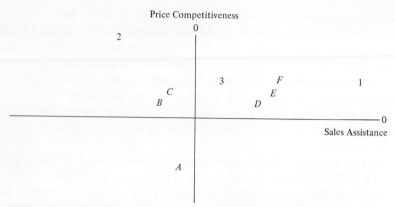

Figure 10–4 NMDS solution to dissimilarities data between pairs of wholesalers.

niques are undergoing rapid development and expansion, their use is limited primarily to larger firms. The newness of and the techniques the lack of researchers trained in this methodology are possible causes. In addition, the entire set of techniques is computer based so that access to a computer and the appropriate programs are an essential prerequisite to applying the technique.

Which Scale to Use?

The preceding pages have contained descriptions of a number of techniques, all of which purport to measure some aspect of attitudes. In addition to these techniques, numerous less well-known techniques and various versions and alterations of the popular scales are available. Each technique has its own unique strengths and weaknesses; there is no best technique for all situations. The researcher must select the technique that will best meet his information requirements and cost constraints.

When various scaling techniques have been compared, the results generally have been equivalent across the techniques. Kassarjian and Nakanishi compared seven attitude measurements and found that all seven produced high intermethod correlations.[58] Hughes compared the ability of a 9-item Thurstone scale, a 20-interval semantic differential scale, and a version of the itemized rating scale in order to determine their ability to detect attitude change under field conditions. The semantic

[58] H. H. Kassarjian and M. Nakanishi, "A Study of Selected Opinion Measurement Techniques," *Journal of Marketing Research,* **4** (May 1967), 148–154.

differential and the rating scales performed similarly and better than the Thurstone scale.[59] Another study compared the semantic differential and the Stapel scales and found no differences in the results.[60] Dawes compared the ability of five attitude type scales to reflect the height of a person when the respondents personally knew the individual. The correlations between the average ratings and actual physical height ranged from .88 to .94,[61] indicating a very satisfactory performance for all scales in this situation.

As the studies cited indicate,[62] when one or more techniques are applicable to a given measurement task, they tend to produce similar results. Therefore, the selection of the scaling technique to use should depend on the nature of the information required, the cost of the technique, how well the technique adapts to the preferred method of administration, and ease of use for the respondent.

Attitudes and Marketing Decisions

In the preceding pages a number of self-report attitude measurement techniques have been described. Marketing has an intense interest in attitude measurement because of the assumed relationship between attitudes and behavior. Attitude measures are used in two general ways by marketing practitioners. One is to predict market reaction to new products, commercials, package designs, and the like. This approach is frequently extended to a comparison of two or more versions of the marketing variable to predict which version will most likely prove successful in the market. It generally requires a measure of overall preference for the object or for some particular attribute of the object. Most of the techniques described in the preceding section can be readily adapted to this task. However, in general, the simpler and less expensive rating techniques will suffice.

The other general use of attitude measures is to measure specific components of a group's attitude toward an object or group of objects in order to devise a strategy to alter the attitude *or* to alter the product to match the attitude. For example, Dupont has used semantic differential type scales to measure the impact of an advertising campaign on the

[59] G. D. Hughes, "Selecting Scales to Measure Attitude Change," *Journal of Marketing Research* (February 1967), 85–87.

[60] Hawkins, et al., op. cit.

[61] R. M. Dawes, *Fundamentals of Attitude Measurement* (New York: John Wiley & Sons, Inc., 1972), 109.

[62] See also J. L. Phillips and R. B. Coates, "Two Scales for Measuring Attitudes Toward Police," *Wisconsin Sociologist,* **8** (Spring 1971) 3–19.

firm's corporate image.[63] Again, most of the techniques we have described can be adapted to this purpose. Currently, the semantic differential is the most widely used technique for this purpose.

Both of the uses of attitude measurements described are based on the assumption that attitudes influence behavior. Indeed, the most widely accepted conceptual view of the attitudes ascribes a behavior component to them. Yet frequent findings reveal that attitude measures do not accurately predict future behavior or even stated past behavior, particularly on an individual as opposed to an aggregate basis.[64] Other studies have found reasonably high correlations between attitudes and behavior.[65] Therefore, the researcher must be concerned with the issue of whether a lack of correspondence between attitude measures and individual behavior reflects a measurement problem or a theoretical problem. That is, do we frequently fail in our behavioral predictions because we do not adequately measure attitudes or because the link between attitudes and behavior is not as direct as we had thought?

Attitudes cannot be measured exactly. Not only are our instruments crude but it is virtually impossible to control for all the "noise" or external factors that may affect our measurements. For example, responding to an attitude scale is a form of behavior that is influenced by our attitude toward the object being rated *and* our attitude toward the situation in which we are rating it. When we then have an opportunity to purchase this item, our attitude toward the object might still be the same, but our attitude toward the situation may be vastly different since the situation itself is different.[66]

However, the major problem lies in expecting too much from a knowledge of attitudes. Attitudes are only one factor that influence purchasing behavior. Economic constraints certainly play a role. Many of us probably have highly favorable attitudes toward certain sports cars and expensive vacations. However, without the economic ability we cannot acquire them. Need likewise exerts a strong influence; even the most wealthy can only consume a certain amount of steak and caviar.

Other attitudes may influence behavior in a manner different from that which would be predicted from knowledge of one attitude alone. For example, one of the authors has a negative attitude toward almost all aspects of a store near his home. However, the store is several miles closer than any competitor, and he also has negative attitudes toward excess

[63] R. C. Grass, D. W. Bartges, and J. L. Piech, "Measuring Corporate Image Ad Effects," *Journal of Advertising Research,* **12** (December 1972), 15–22.

[64] For a detailed discussion of this issue, see G. S. Day, *Buyer Attitudes and Brand Choice Behavior* (New York: The Free Press, 1970).

[65] Kraft, et al., op. cit.

[66] See M. Rokeach, *Beliefs, Attitudes, and Values* (San Francisco: Jossey-Bass, Inc., 1968).

driving. Therefore, he makes most of his small purchases of hardware items at this store. This appears to be relatively logical behavior. However, if a researcher measured the author's overall attitudes, the store would score lower than any competitor's. If the researcher also measured shopping behavior in terms of trips per month, this store would be the most shopped at by the author. Thus, the researcher would note that the least liked store was also the store most shopped at.

Clearly, the relationship between attitudes and behavior is complex and should be treated cautiously by the researcher. The previous example is a good reason why aggregate predictions of behavior based on attitudes are generally accurate, whereas individual predictions frequently are not. Fortunately, marketing is most often concerned with aggregate rather than individual behavior. Therefore, attitude measures can provide a useful aid for predicting behavior and designing strategies. However, attitudes should not be naïvely considered as the only or even primary influence on behavior in any given situation.

Summary

Attitudes reflect a person's basic orientation for or against some object. Since attitudes presumably both influence and predict behavior, they are of great interest to marketing researchers. Inferences about attitudes can be based on: (1) *self-reports*, (2) *observations of overt behavior*, (3) *reactions to partially structured stimuli*, (4) *performance on objective tasks*, and (5) *physiological reactions*. This chapter has focused on the special forms of self-reports that require the respondent to utilize scales.

Self-report scales are divided into three broad categories, *rating scales*, *attitude scales*, and *multidimensional scaling*. *Rating scales*, both comparative and noncomparative, require the respondent to place the object being rated at some point along a continuum or in one of an ordered series of categories and a numerical value is attached to the point or category. *Noncomparative rating* scales do not provide the respondent with an explicit reference or comparison point, whereas comparative rating scales do. Graphic and itemized rating scales are the primary noncomparative rating scales. Itemized scales form the basic building block for most of the more complex attitude scales. Researchers utilizing itemized scales must deal with the issues of: (1) type of category description, (2) number of categories, (3) balanced versus unbalanced categories, (4) odd versus even number of catgeories, and (5) forced versus nonforced choice.

Comparative scales include versions of the graphic and itemized rating scales, paired comparison techniques, rank-order rating scales, and the constant sum scale. Of these techniques, the rank order or preference scale is the most widely used in marketing. The constant sum technique, which may be able to provide approximate interval scale data, is useful in a number of situations.

Attitude scales, the second broad category of scaling techniques, assign an individual a score based on his response to a series of items or statements relevant to the attitude object. Most of these techniques have been borrowed from psychology and have a wide range of supporting research. This area includes Q-sorts, Guttman, Thurstone, Likert, semantic differential, Stapel, and adjective checklist scales. The Q-sort technique, although seldom used, appears to offer a great deal of potential, particularly for exploratory research. Neither the Guttman nor the Thurstone techniques offer unique advantages to the marketing researcher. The Likert and semantic differential scales are widely used, with profile analysis of the semantic differential being particularly useful. The Stapel scale produces results similar to semantic differential and offers some advantages in ease of administration. The adjective checklist can often provide useful information on product images and is extremely easy to administer.

The final broad category of scaling techniques is termed *multidimensional scaling*. This is a computer-based set of techniques designed to isolate the underlying dimensions or attributes that individuals use in evaluating brands, stores, or products. The most popular of these approaches, nonmetric multidimensional scaling, has the ability to generate ratio-scaled output describing a multidimensional configuration of brands, firms, or other objects of interest, from simple ordinal input data.

The selection of the appropriate scaling technique should be based on the information requirements of the problem, the abilities of the respondents, and the time and cost constraints of the study. In those cases where the results from various scaling techniques have been compared, they generally produced similar findings.

The researcher should not assume that behavior is a direct function of attitudes or that attitudes accurately predict behavior. However, in most cases aggregate attitude measures *do* predict aggregate behavior measures. Furthermore, knowledge of attitude components *can* provide a useful guide to alter behavior or products as long as this knowledge is not assumed to be the only cause of behavior.

Questions and Problems

10.1. How would you select a set of items (adjectives, phrases, and the like) for use in a semantic differential or Stapel scale to study the image college students have of banks and savings and loan institutions?

10.2. Use the following techniques to measure a sample of 20 students' attitudes toward beer and wine. (Use a separate sample for each technique.)

(a) Semantic differential, (b) Stapel scale, (c) Likert scale, (d) adjective checklist.

10.3. Use the following techniques to measure a sample of 20 students' attitudes toward: (1) Coca-Cola, (2) Tab, (3) 7-Up, (4) Sprite, (5) Dr. Pepper. (Use a separate sample for each technique.) Compare the results.
(a) Paired comparison, (b) rank order, (c) constant sum.

10.4. Assuming the three stores in Figure 10–2 are attempting to sell to the same market using the same basic approach (products, advertising, and price), what are the managerial implications of this figure for Store A? Store B? Store C?

10.5. Develop a scale for administration to second grade children to measure their attitudes toward breakfast.

10.6. What type of scale would you use to identify needs that current brands in a product category are not meeting?

10.7. What type of scale would you use to predict the initial market share of a new product designed to appeal to middle-income individuals? Would your answer differ if the product were aimed at fourth graders?

Selected Bibliography

DAY, G. S. *Buyer Attitudes and Brand Choice Behavior*. New York: The Free Press, 1970. An excellent study of the relationship between attitudes and behavior in the marketplace.

EDWARDS, A. L. *Techniques of Attitude Scale Construction*. New York: Appleton-Century-Crofts, 1957. A thorough but fairly technical discussion of attitude scales.

GREEN, P. E., and F. J. CARMONE. *Multidimensional Scaling*. Boston: Allyn & Bacon, Inc., 1970. A good treatment of the issues and promises of multidimensional scaling.

GUILFORD, J. P. *Psychometric Methods*. New York: McGraw-Hill, Inc., 1954. Another detailed technical discussion of a number of scaling approaches.

HUGHES, G. D. *Attitude Measurement for Marketing Strategies*. Glenview, Ill.: Scott, Foresman and Company, 1971. A brief but very good treatment focusing on the utilization of attitude measurements for marketing decisions.

KERLINGER, F. N. *Foundations of Behavioral Research*. New York: Holt, Rinehart and Winston, Inc., 1973, Chap. 34. A complete, up-to-date treatment of the use and analysis of the Q-sort technique.

KIESLER, C. A., B. E. COLLINS, and N. MILLER. *Attitude Change*. New York: John Wiley & Sons, Inc., 1969. A thorough treatment of attitudes, attitude models, and attitude change. Deals with both theoretical and research issues.

OSGOOD, C., G. SUCI, and P. TANNENBAUM. *The Measurement of Meaning*. Urbana: University of Illinois Press, 1957. The original, classic work on the semantic differential. Still required reading for the serious attitude researcher.

THURSTONE, L. L. *The Measurement of Values*. Chicago: University of Chicago Press, 1959. A complete treatment of the development of the Thurstone equal-appearing interval scale is contained in this volume.

Case 10–1

Williams & Sloan Department Store: Comparative Image

Williams & Sloan (W&S) is an independent department store located in an Eastern city of approximately 150,000 population. It faces competition from three national chain outlets—Penneys, Sears, and Wards. However, management considers the local branch of Ramseys, a regional chain, to be its primary competitor. Both W&S and Ramseys stress quality and service and appeal to the upper-income segments of the market.

Cheri Sloan, granddaughter of one of the founders of the firm, recently assumed the title of director of marketing research. Cheri had graduated from one of the better private colleges on the east coast with a degree in marketing one year earlier. She spent her first year with the firm going through the same training program as all other newly hired management trainees. After a year, however, she felt, and was able to convince her father who was executive vice-president of the firm, that she could make a major contribution to the firm by starting a small marketing research department. Prior to this time, W&S had not utilized any type of formal research.

Cheri's first project as director was an image study of her firm and its chief competitor, Ramseys. She knew from experience that approximately 80 per cent of both firms' customers were women and that virtually 100 per cent came from families with a greater than average income. Therefore, she decided to sample women residing in census tracts with a median income higher than the median income for the entire city. With these census tracts as a guide, she used a systematic random sample to select 1,000 names from the appropriate areas as listed in the most current city directory.

In reviewing the discussion of image studies in her college marketing research text, she found a reference to a journal article that used the semantic differential to compare the images of two retail outlets. The article concluded that the semantic differential was an extremely useful tool for this purpose. Therefore, she decided to use the semantic differential as her measuring instrument. She also decided to use the same bipolar items used in the journal article and to use six intervals as was done in the article.

A cover letter requesting cooperation, the two semantic differential scales (one for each store), a brief questionnaire asking about the frequency of shopping at the various stores and for demographic data (age of each family member living at home, income, occupation of chief wage earner) and a hand-stamped return envelope were sent to the 1,000 person sample. Fifty-seven were returned as undeliverable for various reasons. After two weeks, 383 replies were received. Ms. Sloan believed that this was a sufficiently large sample, so no additional attempts to increase the response rate were made. The images obtained for each store are presented as follows.

| | Store* | |
Scale Items	W&S	Ramseys
Honest—Dishonest†	1.97	1.93
High Quality—Low Quality	2.26	2.63‡
Low Priced—High Priced	5.07	3.42‡
Fast Service—Slow Service†	4.56	4.03‡
Dependable—Undependable†	1.96	2.05
Clean—Dirty	1.33	1.47
Helpful Employees—Unhelpful Employees	3.61	3.02‡
Easy to Find Items—Hard to Find Items†	2.83	2.87
Modern—Old-Fashioned	1.86	2.32‡
Pleasant—Unpleasant†	2.15	1.91
Wide Selection—Limited Selection	2.41	2.96‡
Friendly—Unfriendly	3.17	2.61‡

* The scores are computed such that a low score indicates agreement with the item on the left in the table.
† These items were in reverse order on the actual questionnaire.
‡ A difference between the two means this large or larger would occur less than one time in ten by chance.

1. Evaluate the sampling procedure used.

2. Evaluate the semantic differential scale items used.

3. What conclusions and recommendations would you suggest based on the images presented?

4. What additional types of data and/or analyses would be useful?

Case 10–2

Williams & Sloan Department Store: Shopping Frequency Study

Cheri Sloan, marketing research director of Williams & Sloan Department Store (W&S), was considering further analysis of the comparative image data she had collected on W&S and Ramseys (Case 10–1). She decided that a comparison of the images of W&S held by those who shop there regularly with those who do not shop at W&S regularly might provide some useful insights. An examination of the shopping frequency questions revealed that approximately one third of the 383 respondents shopped regularly (two or more times per month) at W&S.

The image of W&S held by the two groups is presented as follows.

| | Shopper Type* | |
| | Regular | Infrequent |
Scale Items		
Honest—Dishonest†	1.93	1.99
High Quality—Low Quality	2.15	2.32
Low Priced—High Priced	3.97	5.61‡
Fast Service—Slow Service†	4.40	4.67
Dependable—Undependable†	1.88	2.03
Clean—Dirty	1.31	1.34
Helpful Employees—Unhelpful Employees	3.46	3.89‡
Easy to Find Items—Hard to Find Items†	2.71	2.87
Modern—Old-fashioned	1.87	1.86
Pleasant—Unpleasant	2.04	2.23
Wide Selection—Limited Selection	2.33	2.49
Friendly—Unfriendly	2.87	3.38‡

* The scores are computed such that a low score indicates agreement with the item on the left in the table.
† These items were in reverse order on the actual questionnaire.
‡ A difference between the two means this large or larger would occur less than one time in ten by chance.

1. What conclusions and recommendations would you suggest based on the images presented?

Case 10–3

Attitudes Toward Fresh Strawberries*

The California Strawberry Advisory Board (CSAB) has as its primary objective the promotion of California strawberries. It engages in a number of activities based on this overall objective such as the preparation of merchandising aids, consumer and trade advertising, and research. A recent research study was conducted for CSAB by Elrick and Lavidge, a marketing consulting firm. The goal of the study was to provide information about consumers' use and opinions of fresh and frozen strawberries that would be of value "in planning future advertising and promotion directed to the consumer market."

The study was conducted by telephone in 16 cities located throughout the United States. A systematic sample of female homemakers was interviewed from each city. The results of *one* part of the study are presented.

The information in the exhibit was secured by asking each respondent

---

* Used with permission of the California Strawberry Advisory Board.

to indicate whether she generally agrees or generally disagrees with each of the characteristics of fresh strawberries shown in the exhibit. For purposes of simplification, only the percentage of respondents agreeing is shown in the exhibit.

1. Evaluate the technique used.

2. Develop a questionnaire suitable for administration by mail that will fulfill the objective of the study.

3. What conclusions and recommendations would you make based on the material provided in the exhibit?

Extent of General Agreement* About Certain Characteristics of Fresh Strawberries

	Total	*Fresh Strawberry Use*		
		Heavy Users	*Moderate Users*	*Light Users*
Qualities:				
Low calorie fruit	62%	65%	61%	59%
Extra special/gourmet fruit	56	53	57	60
Rich in Vitamin C	49	50	52	45
Most delicious flavor of any fruit	48	53	49	42
Spoil more quickly than other fruits	74	69	76	77
Expensive compared with most fresh fruit	43	40	43	48
Season:				
Best ones come in the spring	73	72	75	72
Except in springtime, almost never in the stores	57	52	55	63
Uses-versatility:				
More ways to use than most other fruit	67	71	68	61
Very few recipes for using them	13	11	13	16
California Quality:				
Best strawberries come from California	20	23	16	21
Flavor-appearance Relationship:				
Very difficult to judge their taste by how they look	65	66	64	65
(Number of respondents)	(1,172)	(426)	(367)	(379)

* Difference between percentages shown and the 100 per cent is accounted for by "disagree" or "don't know" answers.

Case 10–4

Trio Toyota New Car Purchaser Survey

The management of Trio Toyota was concerned by the fact that it was not aware of who its current customers were and why they bought at Trio. Trio is one of two Toyota dealers currently operating in a community of 250,000 population. A local marketing consultant was asked to make recommendations. He proposed a mail survey of recent new car buyers with the objective of "determining the present and potential market for Trio Toyota and defining those factors that have attracted or might attract customers to Trio."

The questionnaire he proposed using is shown below.

1. Will the questionnaire generate the required data?

2. What weaknesses, if any, are present in the questionnaire?

3. What types of attitude measurement scale are used?

Questionaire

This is a questionnaire on automobile purchases. Please answer the questions and follow directions carefully.

Types and Number of Cars
  1. How many cars do you presently own?
     a. 1
     b. 2
     c. 3
     d. 4 or more
  2. What make and model are they?
     Make _____ Model _____ Year _____
     Make _____ Model _____ Year _____
  3. Which of the cars did you purchase most recently? _____
  4. Did you purchase the most recent car, New _____ or Used _____?
  5. Who did you purchase this car from? Private party _____ dealer _____
  6. Do you classify this car primarily as,
     a. economy
     b. luxury
     c. sport
     d. utility
     e. other (explain) _____

Uses and User
  1. Who is the principal user of the car?
     a. yourself
     b. wife
     c. children
     d. husband
     e. other (explain) _____

2. For what reason did you purchase the automobile?
   a. business
   b. pleasure
   c. transportation
   d. other (explain) _____

Purchase Procedure
   1. When purchasing the car, approximately how many different brands of cars did you consider?
      a. 1
      b. 2–3
      c. 4–6
      d. 7–9
      e. 9 or more
   2. Approximately how many different dealers did you visit while shopping for the car?
      a. 1
      b. 2–3
      c. 4–6
      d. 7–9
      e. 9 or more
   3. When visiting the dealer(s) in question, which of the following factors did you consider important? (For example, if the item on the list was most important, circle 1. If it was unimportant, circle 5. The other numbers correspond to different degrees of importance).

		Most Impor.		No Opinion		Least Impor.
a.	availability of financing	1	2	3	4	5
b.	delivery date of new car	1	2	3	4	5
c.	personality of salesman	1	2	3	4	5
d.	service reputation	1	2	3	4	5
e.	recommendation of dealer by friend or relative	1	2	3	4	5
f.	advertising	1	2	3	4	5
g.	personal friend in dealership	1	2	3	4	5
h.	previous experience with dealer	1	2	3	4	5
i.	added incentives (free gifts, options, etc.)	1	2	3	4	5
j.	size of dealer inventory selection	1	2	3	4	5
k.	trade-in allowance	1	2	3	4	5
l.	test drive	1	2	3	4	5
m.	price	1	2	3	4	5

   4. Could you list from the statements above, the three most important factors to you in order of importance.
      1. _____
      2. _____
      3. _____

Please circle the responses to the following statements in terms of your agreement or disagreement with them. (For example, if you agree strongly with the statement in question, circle number 1. If you strongly disagree, circle number 5. The other numbers correspond to different degrees of agreement.)

5. New car dealers use sales gimmicks to influence you to buy a car.

Strongly agree	Agree	No basis for opinion	Disagree	Strongly Disagree
1	2	3	4	5

6. New car suggested "sticker" prices are reasonable.

   1   2   3   4   5

7. New car dealers are hard to bargain with.

   1   2   3   4   5

8. New car salesmen are "pushy."

   1   2   3   4   5

9. New car financing is honest.

   1   2   3   4   5

10. New car dealers are honest.

   1   2   3   4   5

11. Financing a car is better than paying cash for it.

   1   2   3   4   5

12. Dealer service is important when you buy a car.

   1   2   3   4   5

13. Which dealer did you finally purchase your car from?

The following statements refer to the dealer you bought your car from. Please respond to them the same way you did in the statements above.

14. I liked the trade-in offer.

   1   2   3   4   5

15. I was pressured into buying a car I didn't want.

   1   2   3   4   5

16. The price I paid was less than I expected.

   1   2   3   4   5

17. The model I wanted was readily available.

   1   2   3   4   5

18. The salesman was hard to bargain with.

   1   2   3   4   5

19. The salesman was not interested in my needs, only in selling me a car.

   1   2   3   4   5

20. I felt at home in the showroom.

   1   2   3   4   5

21. The dealer advertising reflects a true picture of the dealer.

   1   2   3   4   5

22. I would buy another car from this dealer.

   1   2   3   4   5

23. Are there any other dealers in this area that sell the same make of car you bought?

   Yes _____   No _____   Don't know _____

24. Please respond to the following factors in terms of whether they were better or worse in comparing the dealership you bought your car from, to the other dealers you visited. (For example, if the dealer you bought from is better, circle 1, if they were worse, circle 3.)

	Better	*The Same*	*Worse*
a. opinion of friends	1	2	3
b. advertising	1	2	3
c. price quote for car	1	2	3
d. trade-in offer	1	2	3
e. physical appearance of dealership	1	2	3
f. size of dealer inventory	1	2	3
g. delivery date of car	1	2	3

Personal Information

For purposes of our own information, could you please answer the following questions about yourself? Your answers will remain anonymous and strictly confidential.

1. What is the age of the principal user of the car?
   a. 16–25
   b. 25–39
   c. 40–55
   d. 55 and over
2. What is your marital status?
   a. single
   b. married
   c. divorced
   d. widowed
3. How long have you lived in this county? _____
4. What is your annual total income?
   a. under $5,000
   b. $ 5,000–$10,000
   c. $10,000–$15,000
   d. $15,000–$20,000
   e. $20,000 and over.
5. How many people in your household? _____
6. What is your occupation?

_____

If you would be interested in helping us further with our study, please write your name and address in the space provided below.

Name: _____

Address: _____

Phone #: _____

Additional Comments:

CHAPTER 11

Survey Research Panels, and Ex Post Facto Research

The preceding four chapters have focused on the concept and techniques of measurement. In this chapter and the next, the emphasis is shifted. Instead of examining the measuring instruments, these chapters are concerned with the conditions or environment in which measurement takes place.

Survey research is concerned with the administration of questionnaires (interviewing). In this chapter a number of issues associated with administering a questionnaire are examined. First, the issues of degree of structure and degree of directness of the interview are addressed. Attention then moves to the types of survey: personal, mail, and telephone. The criteria relevant for judging which type of survey to use in a particular situation are described in some detail. Finally, an in-depth treatment of the problem of nonresponse error is provided.

Panel studies represent a special type of survey. In continuous panels, individuals report specific aspects of their behavior on a regular basis. Interval panels are composed of people who have agreed to respond to questionnaires as the need arises. Both types of panel are described in the second major section of this chapter.

The final section treats *ex post facto* (a Latin term meaning "after the fact") research. In *ex post facto* research, data are used after being collected as if they were experimental data without having been collected under the conditions of an experimental design. Despite this flaw, it is widely used in marketing research since it is the only practical approach to many problems.

Survey Research

Survey research is the systematic gathering of information from respondents for the purpose of understanding and/or predicting some aspect of the behavior of the population of interest.[1] As the term is typically used, it implies that the information has been gathered with some form of a questionnaire.

The survey researcher must be concerned with sampling, questionnaire design, questionnaire administration, and data analysis. This portion of this chapter is focused on questionnaire administration. Sampling, questionnaire design, and data analysis are covered in separate chapters.

The administration of a questionnaire to an individual or group of individuals is called an *interview*. Surveys are commonly categorized by the method of interviewing used. For example, a telephone survey is so labeled because the interviews are conducted by telephone.

Types of Interviews

Interviews are classified according to their degree of structure and directness. *Structure* refers to the amount of freedom the interviewer has in altering the questionnaire to meet the unique situation posed by each interview. *Directness* involves the extent to which the respondent is aware of (or is likely to be aware of) the nature and purpose of the survey.

Characteristics of Structured and Unstructured Interviews

As stated earlier, the degree of *structure* refers to the extent to which an interviewer is restricted to following the question wording and instructions in a questionnaire. An interviewer can alter interviews by omitting or

[1] D. S. Tull and G. S. Albaum, *Survey Research: A Decisional Approach* (New York: Intext Educational Publishers, 1973), 3.

adding questions, probing (asking for an elaboration of a response), changing the question sequence, or changing the wording of the questions. Most marketing surveys fall toward the structured end of the continuum. That is, most marketing surveys allow the interviewer little or no latitude in how the questions are to be asked. The questionnaires are generally fixed in terms of questions, sequence, and wording. The interviewer is restricted to reading the questions to the respondent and recording the answers.

Structured interviews offer a number of advantages to the marketing researcher. Interviewer bias, although potentially present, tends to be at a minimum in structured interviews. If an interview is viewed as a stimulus-response situation, all the respondents in a structured survey receive roughly the same stimulus (series of questions). Therefore, we may have more confidence that differences in responses represent underlying differences in the variable of interest rather than shifts in the stimulus. In addition, it is possible to utilize less skilled (and less expensive) interviewers with a structured format since their duties are basically confined to reading questions and recording answers. Of course, mail surveys are necessarily completely structured.

These advantages of structured interviews may be purchased at the expense of richer or more complete information that skillful interviewers could elicit if allowed the freedom. Relatively unstructured interviews become more important in marketing surveys as *less* is known about the variables being investigated. Stated differently, a fairly high level of prior knowledge or intuition is required for a structured survey. Thus, unstructured techniques are widely used in exploratory surveys.

There appears to be a trend toward allowing the interviewer to ask unstructured questions at given points of the interview. The order and wording of most of the questionnaire remains fixed. However, at specified points the interviewer is allowed to probe and ask additional questions until he is satisfied with the response. The questionnaire in Exhibit 8–1 utilized this approach.

Characteristics of Direct and Indirect Interviews

Direct interviewing involves asking questions such that the respondent is aware of the underlying purpose of the survey. Most marketing surveys are relatively direct. That is, although the name of the sponsoring firm is frequently kept anonymous, the general area of interest is often obvious to the respondent. For example, the general purpose of a series of questions on cars owned, driving habits, and likes and dislikes about automobiles would be fairly obvious to the respondent even though the sponsor's name and the exact purpose of the research were not revealed.

Direct questions are generally easy for the respondent to answer, tend to have the same meaning across respondents, and the responses are relatively easy to interpret. However, occasions may arise when respondents are either unable or unwilling to answer direct questions. For example, respondents may not be able to verbalize their subconscious reasons for purchases or they may not want to admit that certain purchases were made for socially unacceptable reasons. In these cases, some form of indirect interviewing is required.

Indirect interviewing involves asking questions such that the respondent does not know what the objective of the study is. A person who is asked to characterize an individual who rides a motorcycle to work may not be aware that the characterization is a measure of his attitudes toward motorcycles and this use of them.

Completely indirect interviews are generally used only when more direct techniques are not available. These interviews are largely restricted to the method of personal administration, and the interpretation of the responses requires trained specialists. Therefore, they tend to be expensive to administer. Both structure and directness represent continuums rather than discrete categories. However, it is sometimes useful to categorize surveys based on which end of each continuum they are nearest. This leads to four types of interviews: *structured-direct, structured-indirect, unstructured-direct,* and *unstructured-indirect.*

Four Categories of Interview

The *structured-direct* interview is the most commonly used technique in marketing surveys. It is simply a prespecified set of relatively direct or obvious questions. Virtually all mail surveys are of this type as are many telephone and personal surveys. The construction of questionnaires of this type was the focus of Chapter 8. Structured-direct techniques are used more often in the final stages of research projects than in the earlier, more exploratory stages. This type of interview requires extensive initial preparation but allows the use of less highly trained interviewers and interpreters.

Unstructured-direct interviews enjoy some use in marketing research, particularly in preliminary or exploratory campaigns. The most common form of this approach is the individual or group depth interview. These interviews were described in detail in Chapter 9.

Structured-indirect interviews are exemplified by the various projective techniques, such as word association and picture response. This technique was also described in Chapter 9. Like unstructured-direct interviews structured-indirect interviews are somewhat more popular in preliminary research than in the final stages.

Unstructured-indirect interviews are seldom used in marketing research. The prototype example of this approach is a "psychiatrist's couch" interview. In this situation, the respondent is encouraged to talk about whatever interests him with only occasional probing by the interviewer. Obviously, such an approach is seldom appropriate for the marketing researcher.

Figure 11–1 is a flow diagram that illustrates the decisions leading to the selection of a type of interview.

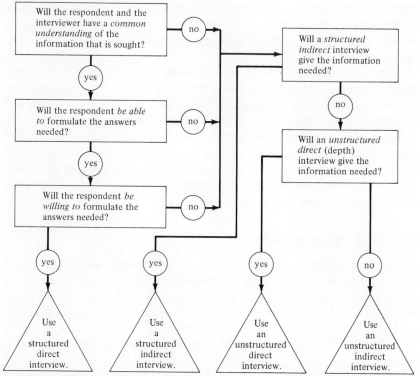

Figure 11–1 Flow diagram for decision on type of interview to use.

Types of Survey

Surveys are generally classified according to the method of communication used in the interviews: personal, telephone, or mail. *Personal interviews* represent the oldest type and they are still widely used in marketing research. In a personal interview, the interviewer asks the questions of the respondent in a face-to-face situation. This interactive situation may induce a number of social motives (such as, a desire to please or impress the interviewer) in the respondent.[2] The implications of the presence or absence of these social motives are discussed in more detail in the section on the criteria for selecting a survey method.

Telephone interviews involve the presentation of the questionnaire by telephone. Telephone interviewing has become much more practical and widespread during the past 20 years. The two primary reasons are the widespread incidence of telephone ownership and the increased costs for personal interviews. As the problems associated with unlisted numbers are reduced by recently developed techniques for dealing with them, telephone interviewing may become even more widespread.

In telephone interviewing, social motives on the part of the respondent are greatly reduced. By its very nature, a telephone call involves less social interaction than a personal visit. Nonetheless, social motives are still an important consideration since respondents may react to the *interviewer* in addition to the questions.

Mail interviews may be delivered in any of several ways. Generally, they are mailed to the respondent and the completed questionnaire is returned by mail to the researcher. However, the forms can be left and/or picked up by company personnel.[3] They can be also distributed by means of magazine and newspaper inserts or they can be attached to products. The warranty card attached to many consumer products serves as a useful source of survey data for many manufacturers.

Social motives are almost entirely lacking in mail surveys since there is no interaction between the respondent and the interviewer.

Criteria for the Selection of a Survey Method

A number of criteria are relevant for judging which type of survey to use in a particular situation. These criteria are: (1) *complexity,* (2) *required amount of data,* (3) *desired accuracy,* (4) *sample control,* (5) *speed,* (6) *acceptable level of nonresponse,* and (7) *cost.* The following discussion is organized around these criteria.

Complexity of the Questionnaire

Although researchers generally attempt to minimize the complexity of a questionnaire, some subject areas still require relatively complex questionnaires. For example, the sequence or number of questions asked often

---

[2] J. B. Lansing and J. N. Morgan, *Economic Survey Methods* (Ann Arbor: The University of Michigan Press, 1971), 160.

[3] R. V. Stover and W. J. Stone, "Hand Delivery of Self-Administered Questionnaires," *Public Opinion Quarterly,* **38** (Summer 1974), 284–287.

depends on the answer to previous questions. Consider the following questions:*

2 a. Have you ever read a copy of the evening _____?	YES	1
	NO (GO TO Q. 3a)	2
b. Did you happen to read or look into a weekday copy— that is, a Monday to Friday copy of _____ during the past seven days?	YES, HAVE READ	3
	NO, HAVE NOT READ (GO TO Q. 3a)	4
	DON'T KNOW (GO TO Q. 3a)	5
c. *Not counting today*, when was the last time you read or looked into a weekday copy of _____?	YESTERDAY	6
	EARLIER THAN YESTERDAY	7
	DON'T KNOW	8
(IF TODAY, ASK:) And when was the last time before today?		

* Taken from a survey conducted for a metropolitan newspaper by Belden Associates, Dallas, Texas. Used with permission.

It would make very little sense to ask someone question 2b if he responded "No" to question 2a. A trained interviewer who has practiced administering a given questionnaire can easily handle many such "skip" questions. However, a respondent, seeing a questionnaire of this type for the first time can easily become confused or discouraged. Thus, personal and telephone interviews are better suited to collect this type of information than mail interviews.

In addition to structured questionnaires with specified but variable question sequences, unstructured questionnaires cannot be administered through the mail. In general, such unstructured techniques as depth interviews require personal interviews because of the need for close rapport between the interviewer and the respondent. Such rapport can generally be developed only in face-to-face interaction.

Other aspects of complexity also tend to favor the use of personal interviews. Visual cues are necessary for many projective techniques such as the picture response. Multiple-choice questions often require a visual presentation of the alternatives since the respondent cannot remember more than a few when they are presented verbally. Similarly, most attitude measurement scales require visual cues for completion,[4] which renders them inappropriate for telephone interviews.

[4] For two exceptions to this see D. I. Hawkins, G. Albaum, and R. Best, "Stapel Scale or Semantic Differential in Marketing Research," *Journal of Marketing Research*, **11** (August 1974), 318–322, and J. J. Wheatley, "Self-Administered Written Questionnaires or Telephone Interviews?" *Journal of Marketing Research*, **10** (February 1973), 94–96.

Techniques that require relatively complex instructions, such as the Q-sort technique, are best administered by means of personal interviews. Similarly, if the response required by the technique is extensive, as with picture response projective techniques, personal interviews are better.

From this discussion, it can be seen that personal interviews are the most flexible of the three techniques. They can be used to administer any type of questionnaire. The interviewer can provide the respondent with visual cues on those questions that require them and can withhold them on other questions. One reason for the continuing widespread utilization of this technique is the fact that many complex questionnaires simply cannot be handled in any other manner.

Telephone interviews are less flexible than personal interviews. Their primary drawback is the impossibility of presenting visual cues to the respondent. In addition, the interviewer cannot observe the respondent to ensure further that he understands the instructions. These factors tend to limit telephone interviewers to relatively simple questionnaires.

Mail interviews are the least flexible. Questions must be presented in fixed order. All respondents receive the same instructions. This procedure may increase standardization but also may increase confusion on the part of some respondents. However, with well-developed instructions relatively complex questions and attitude scales can be administered by means of mail surveys.

Amount of Data

Closely related to the issue of complexity is the amount of data to be generated by a given questionnaire. The amount of data actually involves two separate issues: (1) *How much time it will take to complete the entire questionnaire?* and (2) *How much effort is required by the respondent to complete the questionnaire?* For example, one open-ended question may take a respondent 5 minutes to answer and a 25-item multiple-choice questionnaire may take the same length of time. Moreover, much more effort may go into writing down a 5-minute essay than in checking off choices on 25 multiple-choice questions.

Personal interviews can, in general, be longer than either telephone or mail interviews. Again, we see the impact of social motives on the part of the respondent. It would be "impolite" to terminate an interview with someone in a face-to-face situation; this is much easier to do in a telephone or mail survey.

In addition, the amount of effort required of the respondents is generally less in a personal survey than in a mail survey and often less than in a telephone survey. Answers to open-minded questions, responses to projective techniques, and other lengthy responses are recorded by the interviewer. This relieves the respondent of the tedious task of writing out long answers. Both telephone and personal interviews share this advantage. However, personal interviews have the additional advantage of allowing the presentation of visual cues that can reduce the effort required by the respondent.

> I am going to name eight different stores in this area. After I name each store, please indicate whether you think its prices are extremely high, somewhat high, neither high nor low, somewhat low, or extremely low.

This question could be successfully asked over the telephone. However, the respondent would have to remember the five response categories. In a personal interview, the respondent could be handed or shown a card listing the five alternatives, which he could look at as each store is named. This greatly reduces the mental effort required of the respondents.

Telephone interviews are traditionally shorter than either personal or mail interviews. The ease of terminating a telephone conversation, coupled with the more suspicious nature of a telephone call, tends to limit the length of time a person will spend on a telephone. Thus, most researchers tend to limit telephone interviews to less than 15 minutes.

Mail surveys are probably affected more by the type of questions than by the absolute length of the questions. Long, open-ended questions require considerable effort on the part of the respondents, whereas an equally long multiple-choice response will take much less effort. However, one study compared the response rate of 10-, 25-, and 35-page mail questionnaires and found that length did not have a significant impact.[5]

In general, we can conclude that the largest amount of data can be gathered by personal interviews, followed by mail questionnaires, with telephone interviews weakest on this criterion. In those cases where the respondents are likely to be highly interested in the topic, substantial amounts of data can be collected by all three methods. However, as the respondents' interest in the topic declines, the advantage of personal interviews increases.

Accuracy of the Resultant Data

Well-constructed and administered questionnaires will generally yield similar results regardless of the method of administration. This is particularly true when the subject matter is relatively neutral. For example, one

---

[5] R. F. Sletto, "Pretesting of Questionnaires," *American Sociological Review,* **5** (April 1940), 193–200. See also W. S. Mason, R. J. Dressel, and R. K. Bain, "An Experimental Study of Factors Affecting Response to a Mail Survey of Beginning Teachers," *Public Opinion Quarterly,* **25** (Summer 1961), 296–299; C. Scott, "Research on Mail Surveys, *The Journal of the Royal Statistical Society,* Series A, 124 (Part 2, 1961), 143–205; and D. R. Berdie, "Questionnaire Length and Response Rate," *Journal of Applied Psychology,* **58** (April 1973), 278–280.

study obtained similar results measuring store images with the semantic differential using mail and personal interviews.[6] The same study also obtained equivalent results with the Stapel scale being applied by means of mail, telephone, and personal interview. Another study reported similar results in the accuracy of reporting treatment for socially embarrassing diseases, with a personal interview and a *signed* self-administered questionnaire.[7]

However, other researchers have found substantial differences between the techniques, particularly when sensitive or potentially embarrassing questions are involved. In one study, 17 per cent of the respondents reported borrowing money at a regular bank in response to a personal interview. This percentage jumped to 42 per cent when a mail survey was used.[8] A study of sexual behavior found that, compared with anonymous questionnaires, interviews may lessen the expression of deviance.[9]

Thus, there is evidence that, for sensitive questions, mail surveys may develop more accurate answers than personal interviews.[10] Telephone surveys would most likely fall somewhere between mail and personal interviews.

Other types of inaccuracies can have a differential impact on the different methods of administration. The respondent cannot seek clarification of confusing questions or terms when mail surveys are used. In a personal or telephone interview, the interviewer can clarify various questions. In addition, in a personal interview he can, by observing the respondent closely, assure himself that the respondent understands the question. Thus, mail surveys offer the greatest chance for respondent confusion followed by telephone and personal interview.

Another potential problem with mail questionnaires is the fact that the respondent can read the entire questionnaire prior to answering the questions or he can change his answer to earlier questions after seeing later questions. This may result in less spontaneous and less revealing answers.

[6] Hawkins, et al., op. cit.

[7] C. Connell and F. Fowler, "Comparison of a Self-Enumerative Procedure and a Personal Interview: A Validity Study," *Public Opinion Quarterly,* 27 (Summer 1963), 250–264. See also E. C. McDonagh and L. A. Rosenblum, "A Comparison of Mailed Questionnaires and Subsequent Structured Interviews," *Public Opinion Quarterly,* 29 (Spring 1965), 131–136, and R. P. Butler, "Effects of Signed and Unsigned Questionnaires for Both Sensitive and Nonsensitive Items," *Journal of Applied Psychology,* 57 (June 1973), 348–349.

[8] W. F. O'Dell, "Personal Interviews or Mail Panels," *Journal of Marketing,* 26 (October 1962), 34–39.

[9] D. D. Knudsen, H. Pope, and D. P. Irish, "Response Differences to Questions on Sexual Standards: An Interview-Questionnaire Comparison," *Public Opinion Quarterly,* 31 (Summer 1967), 290–297.

[10] See also B. Dunning and D. Cahalan, "By Mail versus Field Self-Administered Questionnaires: An Armed Forces Survey," *Public Opinion Quarterly,* 34 (Winter, 1973–74), 618–624; and F. Wiseman, "Methodological Bias in Public Opinion Surveys," *Public Opinion Quarterly,* 36 (Spring 1972), 105–108.

Interviewer Effects. The ability of the interviewer to alter the questions, his appearance, his manner of speaking, the intentional and unintentional cues he gives, and the way he probes in personal and telephone interviews can be a disadvantage. It means that, in effect, each respondent may receive a slightly different interview. Thus, both interviewer effects and respondent-interviewer interaction can reduce the accuracy of personal and telephone interviews. Since the interviewer is much more of a force in personal interviews, the danger is greatest here. One study indicated that as many as one out of every four completed interviews may contain relatively serious interviewer errors.[11]

Self-enumeration was introduced on a large scale in the 1960 census to reduce interviewer effects.[12] Depending on the topic of the survey, the interviewer's social class, age, sex, race, authority, and degree of deference can affect the results.[13] With open-ended questions, the interviewer's vocabulary and verbosity can bias the data.[14] A number of studies have confirmed the fact that most interviewers deviate markedly and frequently from their instructions.[15] The primary implication of findings such as those described[16] is that the researcher must pay considerable attention to interviewer selection, training, and control.[17] In addition, a number of approaches for detecting interviewer effects have been developed.[18]

[11] P. B. Case, "How to Catch Interviewer Errors," *Journal of Advertising Research,* **11** (April 1971), 39–43.

[12] U.S. Department of Commerce, Bureau of the Census, Evaluation and Research Program of the U.S. Censuses of Population and Housing, 1960 Series ER 60 No. 7 *Effects of Interviewers and Crew Leaders* (Washington, D.C.; 1968), 1.

[13] For example, see E. R. Athey, J. E. Coleman, A. P. Reitmans, and J. Long, "Two Experiments Showing the Effect of the Interviewer's Racial Background in Responses to Questionnaires Concerning Racial Issues," *Journal of Applied Psychology,* **44** (December 1960), 381–385; M. Benney, D. Riesman, and S. A. Star, "Age and Sex in the Interview," *The American Journal of Sociology,* **62** (September 1956), 143–152; G. E. Lenski and J. C. Leggett, "Caste, Class, and Deference in the Research Interview," *The American Journal of Sociology,* **65** (March 1960), 463–467; and C. H. Weiss, "Interviewing Low-Income Respondents," *Welfare in Review,* **4** (October 1966), 3.

[14] W. A. Collins, "Verbal Idiosyncracies as a Source of Bias," *Public Opinion Quarterly,* **34** (Fall 1970), 416–422.

[15] W. A. Belson, "Increasing the Power of Research to Guide Advertising Decisions," *Journal of Marketing,* **29** (April 1965), 35–42; and B. W. Schyberger, "A Study of Interviewer Behavior," *Journal of Marketing Research,* **4** (February 1967), 32–35.

[16] For a more detailed summary, see H. W. Boyd, Jr., and R. Westfall, "Interviewer Bias Once More Revisited," *Journal of Marketing Research,* **7** (May 1970), 249–253.

[17] For details see *Interviewer's Manual: Survey Research Center,* Ann Arbor, Michigan, The University of Michigan, 1969; M. Hauck and S. Steinkamp, *Survey Reliability and Interviewer Competence* (Urbana, Ill.: University of Illinois Press, 1964); S. Sudman, "Quantifying Interviewer Quality," *Public Opinion Quarterly,* **30** (Winter 1966), 664–667; and S. Sudman, *Reducing the Cost of Surveys* (Chicago: Aldine Publishing Company, 1967).

[18] P. H. Benson, "A Paired Comparison Approach to Evaluating Interviewer Performance," *Journal of Marketing Research,* **6** (February 1969), 66–70; Case, op. cit.;

One final problem that arises with the use of telephone and particularly personal interviews is interviewer cheating. That is, for various reasons, interviewers may falsify all or parts of an interview. This is a severe enough problem that most commercial survey researchers engage in a process called *validation*. Validation involves reinterviewing a sample of the population that completed the initial interview. In this reinterview, verification is sought that the interview took place and was conducted properly. In addition, several of the original questions are asked again to ensure that the interviewer went through the entire questionnaire.

There has been a tendency to use postcards or letters for reinterview purposes because of the cost savings possible. However, this method has been found inadequate for detecting even rather gross interviewer malpractice.[19] Instead, it is recommended that the telephone or personal verification be used. The American Association for Public Opinion Research has developed the following "initial" guidelines for conducting validation studies:

1. Assume the interview was conducted.
2. Start the validation with recognition of the respondent's contribution to the research.
3. Use the validation interview as an extension of the initial interview, using the need for additional information as justification for the validation interview.
4. Provide respondents with an indication of how long the interview may take.
5. Avoid the cross-examination effect of investigation questions. If such questions are essential, they should be used after rapport has been firmly established.
6. Make no calls at unreasonable hours.
7. Avoid multiple validations—more than one validation call to a respondent.
8. Avoid overly long validations. To determine whether and how interviews have been conducted, use "fact" questions likely to have high interview-reinterview reliability.
9. Avoid delay between the initial interview and the validation interview.[20]

C. S. Mayer, "A Computer System for Controlling Interviewer Costs," *Journal of Marketing Research,* **5** (August, 1968), 312–318; and M. J. Shapiro, "Discovering Interviewer Bias in Open-Ended Survey Responses," *Public Opinion Research,* **34** (Fall 1970), 412–415.

[19] M. Hauck, "Is Survey Postcard Verification Effective?" *Public Opinion Quarterly,* **33** (Spring 1969), 117–120.

[20] M. N. Manfield, "AAPOR Standards Committee Study of Validation Practices: Pilot Study on Designs, Introductions, Questions, and Practices," *Public Opinion Quarterly,* **35** (Winter 1971–72), 635.

Despite an increased potential for error with personal interviews, well-developed questionnaires administered by highly trained personnel will generally give similar results by means of mail, telephone, or personal interview. This, of course, assumes that each method of administration will reach equivalent groups of respondents. As is demonstrated in the next section, this is not always a valid assumption.

Sample Control

Each of the three techniques allows substantially different levels of control over who is selected in the final sample. Telephone surveys are obviously limited to households with direct access to telephones. However, this is no longer a major restriction. Estimates of the percentage of households with telephones of 87 per cent in 1970[21] and 93 per cent in 1971[22] have been made. Except for low-income, city-center and rural homes, telephone ownership is almost 100 per cent.

However, the fact that telephones are almost universally owned does not mean that lists of telephone numbers such as telephone directories are equally complete. Estimates of the percentage of phones not listed in a current telephone directory run as high as 30 per cent for some areas.[23] The percentage of unlisted telephones is at its lowest point immediately after the telephone directory is issued. Most of the unlisted numbers at this point are "voluntarily" unlisted. That is, the owners explicitly requested that their telephone numbers not be placed in the directory. Recent research has shown significant differences between those with voluntarily unlisted numbers and those with listed numbers on such variables as ownership of luxury items and automobiles, housing characteristics, family composition, and other demographic variables.[24]

As the current telephone directory becomes older, the percentage of households with unlisted numbers increases because of new families moving into the area and others moving within the area. People who move frequently are thus most likely to have unlisted numbers. These families differ from less mobile families on a number of dimensions.

[21] *Housing Characteristics for States, Cities and Counties, Part I, United States Summary,* vol. I (Washington, D.C.: U.S. Bureau of the Census, 1970), 1–53.

[22] *Statistical Abstract of the United States:* 1973, 94th ed. (Washington, D.C.: U.S. Bureau of the Census, 1973), 496.

[23] G. J. Glasser and G. D. Metzger, "Random-Digit Dialing as a Method of Telephone Sampling," *Journal of Marketing Research,* **9** (February 1972), 59–64.

[24] J. A. Brunner and G. A. Brunner, "Are Voluntary Unlisted Telephone Subscribers Really Different?" *Journal of Marketing Research,* **8** (February 1971), 121–124; S. Roslow and L. Roslow, "Unlisted Phone Subscribers Are Different," *Journal of Advertising Research,* **12** (August 1972), 35–38; and D. A. Leuthold and R. Scheck, "Patterns of Bias in Samples Based on Telephone Directories," *Public Opinion Quarterly,* **35** (Summer 1971), 249–257.

Thus, we find that telephone surveys permit only limited control over the sample. Low income families are underrepresented among telephone owners. Unlisted numbers cannot be reached if the standard approach of using a telephone directory as a sampling frame is followed.

Random-digit dialing allows the researcher to overcome some of the problems associated with unlisted numbers in telephone surveys. This technique requires that at least some of the digits of each sample telephone number be generated randomly.[25] However, even with advanced techniques involving random digit dialing, simple random sampling or systematic sampling are generally the only approaches that can be used. As we saw in the sampling chapter, other approaches often offer substantial advantages.

Like the telephone, mail questionnaires require an explicit sampling frame composed of addresses, if not names and addresses. Such lists are particularly difficult to acquire for the general population. In fact, the telephone directory, or street directories where available, are generally used for this purpose. The problems associated with this type of sampling frame have already been described.

Mail panels represent one approach to obtaining representative samples for mail surveys. Mail panels are maintained by commercial research firms and consist of lists of families who have agreed to answer mail questionnaires. These panels are described in more detail in a later section. However, there is some suspicion that those who agree to serve on such panels are indeed different from the rest of the population even if they do match on certain demographic variables.

Lists of specialized groups are more readily available. At one extreme, a bank can easily compile a mailing list of its current checking account customers. Often specific mailing lists can be purchased from firms that specialize in this area. For example, one catalog contains approximately 25,000 lists, many of which can be subdivided on a state-by-state basis.[26] A good specialized mailing list can overcome many of the problems associated with sampling for a mail survey.

However, even with a good mailing list, one potentially serious problem remains. The researcher maintains only limited control over *who* within

---

[25] See S. Sudman, "The Uses of Telephone Directories for Survey Sampling," *Journal of Marketing Research,* **10** (May 1973), 204–207; Glaser and Metzger, op. cit.; J. O. Eastlack, Jr., and H. Assael, "Better Telephone Surveys Through Centralized Interviewing," *Journal of Advertising Research,* **6** (March 1966), 2–7; S. Cooper, "Random Sampling by Telephones: A New and Improved Method," *Journal of Marketing Research,* **1** (November 1964), 45–58; and M. Hauck and M. Cox, "Locating a Sample by Random Digit Dialing," *Public Opinion Quarterly,* **38** (Summer 1974), 253–260.

[26] *1973–1974 Catalog of Mailing Lists* (New York: Fritz S. Hofheimer, Inc., 1972).

the mailing address completes the questionnaire. Husbands and wives frequently provide divergent answers to the same question.[27] Although the researcher can address the questionnaire to a specific household member, he cannot be sure who completes the questionnaire. An additional complicating factor is that some respondents will seek assistance from their spouses whereas others will not. This will also result in different answers.[28]

Mailings to organizations face similar problems. It is difficult to determine an individual's sphere of responsibility from his job title. Thus, in some firms the purchasing agent may set the criteria by which brands are chosen, whereas in other firms this is either a committee decision or is made by the person who actually uses the product in question. Thus, a mailing addressed to a specific individual or job title may not reach the individual most relevant for the survey. In addition, busy executives may often pass on questionnaires to others who are not as qualified to complete the questionnaire.

Personal interview surveys, on the other hand, do not require an explicit list of individuals or households. Although such lists are desirable, various forms of area sampling can overcome most of the problems caused by the absence of a complete sampling frame (see Chapters 5 and 6). In addition, the researcher can control who is interviewed within the sampling unit, how much assistance from other members of the unit is permitted, and, to a limited extent, the environment in which the interview occurs.

Time Requirements

Telephone surveys generally require the least total time to complete. The number of telephone calls possible per hour greatly exceeds the number possible in personal interviewing. Although this is true regardless of the length of the individual questionnaire, the telephone's advantage is greatest with short questionnaires. In addition, it is generally easier to hire, train, control, and coordinate telephone interviewers.[29] Therefore, the number of interviewers can often by expanded until any time constraint is satisfied.

The number of personal interviewers can also be increased to reduce the total time required. However, training, coordinating, and control problems tend to make this uneconomical after a certain point. Since personal interviewers must travel between interviews, and often set up appointments, they take more time than telephone interviews.

[27] C. Safilios-Rothschild, "The Study of Family Power Structure: A Review 1960–69," *Journal of Marriage and the Family,* **33** (August 1971), 445–458.
[28] R. C. Nuckols and C. S. Mayer, "Can Independent Responses Be Obtained from Various Members in a Mail Panel Household?" *Journal of Marketing Research,* **7** (February 1970), 90–94.
[29] Eastlack, Jr., and Assael, op. cit.

Mail surveys tend to take the longest time. Furthermore, there is relatively little the researcher can do to shorten this interval except reduce the number of follow-up attempts. It generally requires two weeks to receive most of the responses to a single mailing. Although there is some evidence to suggest that follow-up efforts should be made at one week intervals,[30] a mail survey with only one follow-up mailing will require an absolute minimum of two weeks.

Response Rate

The *response rate* refers to the percentage of the original sample that is interviewed. The potential impact of a low response rate is so critical for survey research that it is treated in some depth in a later section of this chapter. The purpose of this section is to indicate that the probable response rate should enter into the decision of which survey technique to use.

Nonresponse is composed of two basic elements, *refusals* and *not-at-homes*. Since there are relatively few not-at-homes for mail surveys, the response rate for a single mailing is often higher than for a *single* telephone or personal interview. However, in general, personal and telephone interviews generate a higher response rate than mail surveys because of callbacks.

Cost

The cost of the survey varies with the type of interview, nature of the questionnaire, the response rate required, the geographic area covered, and the time at which the survey is made. However, personal interviews are generally much more expensive than the other two approaches. Telephone interviews are usually more expensive than those conducted by mail. However, for short interviews this relationship may not hold. Cost considerations for selecting a survey approach must include not only the costs of initial contacts but also the costs of any callbacks, remailings, or added telephone calls designed to increase the response rate.

Which Method to Use?

Obviously, no one method of survey data collection is best for all situations. The specific information requirements, the information that can be provided by each method, and time and monetary constraints determine

---

[30] W. E. Cox, Jr., "Response Patterns to Mail Surveys," *Journal of Marketing Research,* **3** (November 1966), 392–397.

which approach to use. The primary consideration is which technique is capable of generating appropriate information from the appropriate sample at the lowest cost. Table 11–1 provides a summary of the *general* strengths of the three techniques. It must be emphasized that the ratings shown in the table are of a general nature and will not hold true in all situations.

Thus far we have been considering the three techniques as though they were mutually exclusive. However, two or all three of the techniques often may be combined in a single survey. This approach, if properly performed, may allow the weaknesses of each technique to be offset by the strengths of the others. Unfortunately, selection of a data collection approach is still treated as an either-or situation in most survey studies.

Table 11–1   Strengths of the Three Survey Methods

Criterion	*Mail*	*Telephone*	*Personal*
1. Ability to handle complex questionnaires	Poor	Good	Excellent
2. Ability to collect large amounts of data	Good	Fair	Excellent
3. Accuracy of the resultant data	Good	Fair	Fair
4. Control of interviewer effects	Excellent	Fair	Poor
5. Degree of sample control	Fair	Fair	Excellent
6. Time required	Poor	Excellent	Fair
7. Probable response rate	Fair	Fair	Fair
8. Cost	Good	Good	Poor

Nonresponse Error in Survey Research

Table 11–2 indicates the median income of the respondents reached on each of a series of calls. As can be seen, a no callback policy would have produced an estimated income 25 per cent lower than that finally obtained. A difference of this magnitude could easily lead the researcher to erroneous conclusions.

Error caused by a difference between those who respond to a survey and those who do not is termed *nonresponse error*. It is one of the most significant problems faced by the survey researcher.[31]

---

[31] For example, see P. Ognibene, "Traits Affecting Questionnaire Response," *Journal of Advertising Research,* **10** (June 1970), 18–20; M. J. Gannon, J. C. Nothern, and S. J. Carroll, Jr., "Characteristics of Nonrespondents Among Workers," *Journal of Applied Psychology,* **55** (December 1971), 586–588, and R. L. Day and J. B. Wilcox, "A Simulation Analysis of Nonresponse Error in Survey Sampling" in F. C. Allvine, *Relevance in Marketing: Marketing in Motion* (Chicago: American Marketing Association, 1971), 478–483.

Table 11–2 Variations in Median Income on
Various Calls in a Survey*

Number of Call at Which Interviewed	Median Income	Number of Interviews
1	$4188	427
2	5880	391
3	6010	232
4	6200	123
5	6010	77
6+	7443	59
All	$5598	1309

* *Source:* J. B. Lansing and J. N. Morgan, *Economic Survey Methods* (Ann Arbor; The University of Michigan Press, 1971), 161. Used with permission of The University of Michigan Press.

In general, the lower the response rate to a survey the higher is the probability of nonresponse error. However, a low response rate does not automatically mean that there has been significant nonresponse error. One study concluded that "when surveys are made of homogeneous populations (persons having some strong group identity) concerning the group, significant response-rate bias is probably unlikely."[32]

Unfortunately, most marketing surveys are focused on groups that do not have strong group identity about questions concerning the group. Instead, consumer surveys tend to reach heterogeneous groups with questions that are concerned with individual-relevant behavior (as opposed to group-relevant behavior). This is not to deny the tremendous role that groups play in the individual consumer's behavior. Rather, it suggests that the survey researcher cannot assume that respondents are representative of nonrespondents because of a strong group identification in both segments.

Causes of Nonresponse

Not-at-homes and refusals are the major factors that reduce response rates.[33] Not-at-homes affect personal and telephone interviews but have only a limited impact on mail surveys. Not-at-homes are generally less of a factor for telephone interviews than for personal interviews as most people will answer a telephone even though they may be reluctant to open a door to a stranger.

[32] L. L. Leslie, "Are High Response Rates Essential to Valid Surveys?" *Social Science Research,* **1** (1972), 323.
[33] S. S. Kegeles, C. F. Fink, and J. P. Kirscht, "Interviewing a National Sample by Long Distance Telephone," *Public Opinion Quarterly,* **33** (Fall 1969), 412–419.

Assuming that the initial request for cooperation was well designed, little can be done to reduce refusals in personal and telephone interviews. If refused, the interviewer should offer to call again at a more convenient time. Beyond this, there is little that can be done once the interview is refused.

Except for holidays and the summer vacation period, not-at-homes are not a major problem for mail surveys. Moreover, a failure to return a questionnaire within a reasonable time after it is delivered is not as final as an explicit refusal to cooperate in a personal or telephone survey. Many respondents intend to return mail questionnaires but "just never get around to it."

Methods of Reducing Nonresponse

The major focus in reducing nonresponse in telephone and personal interview situations centers on *contacting* the potential respondent. The social motives present in a face-to-face or verbal interactive situation operate to minimize refusals. The reduction to nonresponse in mail surveys focuses on *motivating* the respondent to complete the questionnaire and return it. The emphasis on motivation is necessary since social motivations are largely absent and since there is no pressure on the respondent to complete the task immediately.

Reducing Nonresponse in Telephone and Personal Surveys. The percentage of not-at-homes in personal and telephone surveys can be reduced drastically with a series of callbacks. In general, the second round of calls will produce only slightly fewer contacts than the first call.[34] One review found that, for personal interviews, the first call yielded 25 to 30 per cent of the original sample, and the second call yielded about the same, with a rapid decline beginning with the third call.[35]

The minimum number of calls in most consumer surveys is three. Callbacks should generally be made at varying times of the day and on different days of the week. There is, as one might suspect, a definite relationship between both the day of the week and the time of day and the completion rate of telephone and personal interviews. One study of housewives and female heads of households found that Mondays, followed by Wednesdays and Thursdays, produced a higher completion rate than other days.[36] As Table 11–3 indicates, the time of day was found to influence both the percentage of not-at-homes and the refusal rate.

[34] L. Kish, *Survey Sampling* (New York: John Wiley & Sons, Inc., 1965), 532–548.

[35] W. C. Dunkelberg and G. S. Day, "Nonresponse Bias and Callbacks in Sample Surveys," *Journal of Marketing Research,* **10** (May 1973), 160.

[36] A. M. Falthzik, "When to Make Telephone Interviews," *Journal of Marketing Research,* **9** (November 1972), 451–452.

Table 11–3 Telephone Interviews of Housewives and Female Heads of Households by Time of Day*

Response	9:00 A.M.–12:00 noon	2:30 P.M.–5:30 P.M.	7:00 P.M.–10:00 P.M.	Total
Completed				
Frequency	136	75	105	316
Percentage	35.1	18.0	26.2	26.2
Refused				
Frequency	68	126	146	340
Percentage	17.6	30.2	36.5	28.2
Not at home				
Frequency	183	216	149	548
Percentage	47.3	51.8	37.3	45.6
Total				
Frequency	387	417	400	1204
Percentage	100	100	100	100

* $\chi^2 = 58.241$, $p < .01$, $d.f. = 4$.
Source: A. M. Falthzik, "When to Make Telephone Interviews," *Journal of Marketing Research*, **9** (November 1972), 452. Used with permission of the author and publisher.

A more detailed analysis of the best time to contact individuals at home has been conducted by the Bureau of the Census.[37] This analysis provides estimates of the percentage of people at home between 8:00 A.M. and 9:00 P.M. on an hourly basis. The findings are broken down by sex, poverty versus nonpoverty level, population, rural versus urban, race, and age. This study, based on a large sample, is an excellent guide for scheduling telephone and personal interviews.

Reducing Nonresponse in Mail Surveys. As stated earlier, attempts to increase the response rate to mail surveys focuses on increasing the potential respondents' motivation to reply. Two factors play an important role in this area. The first is to increase the motivation as much as possible in the initial contacts with the respondent.[38] The second approach is to remind the respondents through repeated mailings or other contacts.

The initial response rate to a mail survey is strongly influenced by the respondent's interest in the subject matter of the survey. For example, one study found a range of response rates from 13 per cent to 75 per cent de-

[37] Bureau of the Census, *Who's Home When* (Washington, D.C.: U.S. Government Printing Office, 1973).

[38] H. H. Blumberg, C. Fuller, and A. P. Hare, "Response Rates in Postal Surveys," *Public Opinion Quarterly*, **38** (Spring 1974), 113–123; and R. A. Eisinger, W. P. Janicki, R. L. Stevenson, and W. L. Thompson, "Increasing Returns in International Mail Surveys," *Public Opinion Quarterly*, **38** (Spring 1974), 124–130.

pending on how relevant the subject of the survey was to the sample population.[39]

Interest level can induce a serious source of nonresponse bias into the survey results. Consider a firm that is evaluating the potential for introducing a new athlete's foot remedy. A survey is conducted to determine the incidence and severity of the problem among the general population. Those individuals most interested in athlete's foot, and thus most likely to respond to the survey, are probably currently or recently suffering from the problem. Therefore, initial returns are likely to overstate the incidence of the disease. This could easily lead the firm to the wrong conclusion concerning the size of the market.

Researchers have tested a wide variety of ways to increase the response rate to mail surveys. Some of their more important findings are summarized in the paragraphs that follow.

An *advance letter or telephone call* that informs the respondent that he will receive a questionnaire shortly and requests his cooperation has been found to increase the response rate.[40] It apparently does not affect the timing of the replies, the number of unanswered questions, or the answers of the respondents.[41]

The *type of postage used,* both on the outgoing envelope and the return envelope, can affect the return rate. Both first-class outgoing mail and hand-stamped return envelopes have been found to produce higher return rates than third-class outgoing mail or metered return envelopes.[42] Special delivery postage also has been found to produce higher response rates than regular postage.[43]

Surprisingly, the *length of the questionnaire* does not appear to have an

[39] R. F. Mautz and F. L. Neumann, "The Effective Corporate Audit Committee," *Harvard Business Review,* **48** (November–December 1970), 58.

[40] See N. M. Ford, "The Advance Letter in Mail Surveys," *Journal of Marketing Research,* **4** (May 1967), 202–204; J. H. Myers and A. F. Haug, "How a Preliminary Letter Affects Mail Survey Returns and Costs," *Journal of Advertising Research,* **9** (September 1969), 33–39; J. E. Stafford, "Influence of Preliminary Contact on Mail Returns," *Journal of Marketing Research,* **3** (November 1966), 410–411.

[41] J. E. Stafford, ibid. For contradictory evidence see D. A. Dillman and J. H. Frey, "Contribution of Personalization to Mail Questionnaire Response as an Element of a Previously Tested Method," *Journal of Applied Psychology,* **59** (June 1974), 297–300.

[42] J. E. Gullahorn and J. T. Gullahorn, "An Investigation of the Effects of Three Factors on Response to Mail Questionnaires," *Public Opinion Quarterly,* **27** (Summer 1963), 294–296. See also W. E. Hensley, "Increasing Response Rate by Choice of Postage Stamps," *Public Opinion Quarterly,* **38** (Summer 1974), 280–284; W. C. Hewett, "How Different Combinations of Postage on Outgoing and Return Envelopes Affect Questionnaire Response Rates," *Journal of the Market Research Society,* **16** (January 1974), 49–50. For contradictory evidence see F. I. Landy and F. Bates, "The Noneffect of Three Variables on Mail Survey Response Rates," *Journal of Applied Psychology,* **58** (February 1973), 147–148.

[43] D. J. Champion and A. M. Sear, "Questionnaire Response Rate: A Methodological Analysis," *Social Forces,* **47** (March 1969), 335–339.

impact on the response rate. Studies comparing 10, 25, and 35 pages,[44] 6 and 8 pages,[45] 2 and 53 items,[46] and 1, 2, and 4 pages[47] all found no differences in the return rates. One study found that six-page and nine-page questionnaires were returned more often than three-page questionnaires.[48]

Overall, the evidence seems to indicate that a *monetary incentive* included with the questionnaire, particularly if it is as much as $.25, will increase the response rate.[49] However, there is some contradictory evidence.[50] Other variables such as the *color of the questionnaire*[51] or the *degree of personalization of the request for cooperation*[52] do not seem to have a significant impact on the return rate.

In addition to attempting to maximize the *initial* return of mail questionnaires, most mail surveys also utilize follow-up contacts to increase the overall response rate. Follow-up contacts generally consist of a postcard or letter requesting the respondent to complete and return the questionnaire.[53] If the survey is anonymous, any follow-up must necessarily be sent to the entire original sample. One technique for avoiding this problem is to provide a separate postcard with the questionnaire. The respondent is asked to return this postcard, which has his name printed on it, at the

---

[44] Sletto, op. cit., 193–200.

[45] Mason, et al., op. cit., 296–299.

[46] H. Durant and I. Maas, "Who Doesn't Answer," *British Psychological Society Bulletin,* **29** (1965), 33–34.

[47] Berdie, op. cit., 278–280.

[48] Champion and Sear, op. cit., 335–339.

[49] See W. M. Kephart and M. Bressler, "Increasing the Responses to Mail Questionnaires: A Research Study," *Public Opinion Quarterly,* **22** (Summer 1958), 123–132; T. R. Wotruba, "Monetary Inducements and Mail Questionnaire Response," *Journal of Marketing Research,* **3** (November 1966), 398–400; and S. W. Huck and E. M. Gleason, "Using Monetary Inducements to Increase Response Rates from Mailed Surveys: A Replication and Extension of Previous Research," *Journal of Applied Psychology,* **59** (April 1974), 222–225.

[50] R. D. Brennan, "Trading Stamps as an Incentive in Mail Surveys," *Journal of Marketing,* **22** (January 1958), 306–307.

[51] Gullahorn and Gullahorn, op. cit., 296; M. T. Matteson, "Type of Transmittal Letter and Questionnaire Color as Two Variables Influencing Response Rates in a Mail Survey," *Journal of Applied Psychology,* **59** (August 1974), 535–536.

[52] See A. R. Andreasen, "Personalizing Mail Questionnaire Correspondence," *Public Opinion Quarterly,* **34** (Summer 1970), 273–277; M. B. Kawash and L. M. Aleamont, "Effect of Personal Signature on the Initial Rate of Return of a Mailed Questionnaire," *Journal of Applied Psychology,* **55** (December 1971), 589–592; R. Simon, "Responses to Personal and Form Letters in Mail Surveys," *Journal of Advertising Research,* **7** (March 1967), 28–30; W. M. Weilbacher and H. R. Walsh, "Mail Questionnaires and the Personalized Letter of Transmittal," *Journal of Marketing,* **16** (July 1952), 331–336; and Landy and Bates, op. cit. For contradictory results, see G. Frazier and K. Bird, "Increasing the Response of a Mail Questionnaire," *Journal of Marketing,* **23** (April 1958), 186–187, Matteson, op. cit.; Dillman and Frey, op. cit.; and R. A. Kerin, "Personalization Strategies, Response Rate, and Response Quality in a Mail Survey," *Social Science Quarterly,* **55** (June 1974), 175–181.

[53] M. J. Etzel and B. J. Walker, "Effects of Alternative Follow-up Procedures on Mail Survey Response Rates," *Journal of Applied Psychology,* **59** (April 1974), 219–221.

same time that he returns the questionnaire. This protects the respondent's anonymity and provides the researcher with a list of the nonrespondents.

Follow-up efforts are not limited to postcards or letters. The questionnaire may be sent again or telephone, telegraph, or personal contacts can be used to increase the response rate. However, letters and postcards are the most common approach. In general, three or four mailings, including the original, are needed. When these are skillfully done, the final response rate may reach 80 per cent or higher.[54]

A five contact system for increasing the response rate to mail surveys has been proposed by Robin. This system includes (1) *a prequestionnaire letter,* (2) *a questionnaire with cover letter,* (3) *a follow-up letter,* (4) *a second questionnaire,* and (5) *a third follow-up letter.*[55] Robin recommends a seven-day interval between each mailing.[56] An application of this technique with a sample of 1,695 dentists as potential respondents produced a 77.8 per cent response rate.[57]

In any system of callbacks for personal, telephone, or mail surveys, the researcher must attempt to balance the increased cost of each successive wave against the benefits of a more representative sample.[58] The critical issue is how alike or different the respondents are from the nonrespondents. Methods of estimating the probable impact of nonrespondents are described in the next section.

Strategies for Dealing with Nonresponse

Sensitivity Analysis. After *each* successive wave of contacts with a particular group of potential respondents, the researcher should run a sensitivity analysis. That is, he should ascertain how different the nonrespondents would have to be from the respondents in order to alter the decision he would make based on the data supplied by the current respondents.

As an example, consider the decision rule, *If 20 per cent or more of the population appears favorable, we will introduce the new product.* A mail survey is launched and provides a 50 per cent return rate by the end of the second week. Of those responding, 80 per cent favor the new product. If the remaining 50 per cent of the potential respondents were unfavorable,

[54] Kish, op. cit., 539.

[55] S. S. Robin, "A Procedure for Securing Returns to Mail Questionnaires," *Sociology and Social Research,* **50** (October 1965), 24–35.

[56] Others have recommended a three-day interval. See R. C. Nichols and M. A. Meyer, "Timing Postcard Follow-ups in Mail Questionnaire Surveys," *Public Opinion Quarterly,* **30** (Summer 1966), 306–307.

[57] A. F. Williams and H. Wechsler, "The Mail Survey: Methods to Minimize Bias Owing to Incomplete Response," *Sociology and Social Research,* **54** (July 1970), 533–535.

[58] See Myers and Haug, op. cit., for a discussion of, and empirical evidence on, this point. Also Dunkelberg and Day, op. cit.

the projected percentage of favorable attitudes would still be 40 per cent. Since this is more than twice the amount needed for a *go* decision, any attempt to generate additional responses would be a waste of resources.

Subjective Estimates. When it is no longer practical to increase the response rate, the researcher can estimate the nature and effect of the nonrespondents.[59] The most common approach to this procedure, other than simply ignoring it, is purely subjective. That is, the researcher, based on his experience and the nature of the survey, makes a subjective evaluation of the probable effects of the nonresponse error.

For example, the general finding that those most interested in a product are most likely to return a mail questionnaire, gives the researcher some confidence that nonrespondents are less interested in the topic than respondents. Likewise, the fact that young married couples with no children are at home less than couples with small children provides the researcher a basis for evaluating some aspects of not-at-homes in personal or telephone interviews.

Measurement Using Subsamples. Subsampling of nonrespondents, particularly when a mail survey was the original methodology, has been found effective in reducing nonresponse error.[60] Concentrated attention on a subsample of nonrespondents, generally using telephone or personal interviews, can often yield a high response rate within that subsample. Using standard statistical procedures, the values obtained in the subsample can be projected to the entire group of nonrespondents and the overall survey results adjusted to take into account the nonrespondents. The primary drawback to this technique is the cost involved. Although it can often be used with local surveys, the cost of taking personal or telephone subsamples with regional or larger surveys tends to be prohibitive.

Trend Projections. The data in Table 11–4 represent a fairly common finding when the results of several waves of a survey are compared to known characteristics of the total sample. As can be seen, each successive wave more closely resembles the final group of nonrespondents.

Findings such as these have led a number of researchers to recommend that the trend, if present, in a series of calls be used to estimate the characteristics of the nonrespondents.[61] Unfortunately, we can never be sure

[59] See C. S. Mayer, "Integrating Nonsampling Error Assessments in Research Design," in R. L. King, *Marketing and the New Science of Planning,* (Chicago: American Marketing Association, 1968), 184–190.

[60] P. Ognibene, "Correcting Nonresponse Bias in Mail Questionnaires," *Journal of Marketing Research,* **8** (May 1971), 233–235.

[61] For relevant research see E. C. Lehman, Jr., "Tests of Significance and Partial Returns to Mail Questionnaires," *Rural Sociology,* **28** (September 1963), 284–289; J. E. Kivlin, "Contributions to the Study of Mail-Back Bias," *Rural Sociology,* **30**

Table 11–4 Using Trend in Responses to
Estimate Nonresponses*

	Percentage Response	Average Number of Fruit Trees
First Mailing	10	456
Second Mailing	17	382
Third Mailing	14	340
Nonresponse	(59)	290
Total	100	329

* Adapted from Leslie Kish, *Survey Sampling* (New York, John Wiley & Sons, Inc., 1965), 545. Used with permission of the publisher.

that such trends will hold. For example, one study obtained the following proportions of "yes" answers to the question, *"Have you attended more than four meetings of* (a particular club) *in the past year?"* on each of four waves of mailings: 54.8, 44.7, 27.0, and 30.4.[62] Obviously, a trend prediction made after the third wave would have underestimated the percentage of positive responses obtained on the fourth wave. A number of other studies have found similar problems in using trend analysis to estimate nonrespondent characteristics.[63]

How, then, should nonresponse be dealt with? First, the researcher should determine if the nonrespondents *could* alter his decision. If they could, further mailings or call-backs should be made until they are no longer economically feasible. If the nonresponse error *potential* is still large enough to affect the final decision, the researcher must attempt to estimate it. He can utilize a subjective estimate, a subsample estimate, or a trend estimate. Which technique is best depends on the costs and risks involved and the researcher's knowledge of the situation.

Conclusions on Survey Research

Survey research is a major approach to gathering information for marketing decisions. Despite the problems of error induced by interviewer effects and nonresponse error, survey research will be used even more in

(September 1965), 322–326; C. H. Fuller, "Weighting to Adjust for Survey Nonresponse," *Public Opinion Quarterly,* **38** (Summer 1974), 239–246; and L. Mandell, "When to Weight: Determining Nonresponse Bias in Survey Data," *Public Opinion Quarterly,* **38** (Summer 1974), 247–252.

[62] M. N. Donald, "Implications of Nonresponse for the Interpretation of Mail Questionnaire Data," *Public Opinion Quarterly,* **14** (Spring 1960), 99–114.

[63] For example, see R. A. Ellis, C. M. Endo, and J. M. Armer, "The Use of Potential Nonrespondents for Studying Nonresponse Bias," *Pacific Sociological Review,* **13** (Spring 1970), 103–109; and Ognibene, op. cit., 234.

the future than it is currently. However, this increased popularity will generate new problems with a public that is increasingly concerned about privacy and the right of formal organizations to obtain data of the type desired by marketing researchers.[64]

The next section of this chapter presents one potential answer to the problem described previously. Panels may enable researchers to collect data without many of the problems associated with standard surveys.

Panels

A *panel,* as the term is used in marketing research, *refers to a group of individuals who have agreed to provide information to a researcher over a period of time.* Two basic types of panels are in use today, *continuous* panels and *interval panels.* In a *continuous* panel, the members report specified behaviors, on a regular basis. Media exposure or purchase behavior are the usual kinds of behavior reported by consumer panels. Inventory level and planned capital expenditures are the most common types of information requested of industrial panels.

Radio and television viewing patterns may be monitored automatically through the use of *audimeters.* The A. C. Nielsen Radio-Television Index is based on this approach. Alternatively, media habits can be recorded in a self-administered diary such as the one used by the American Research Bureau.[65] Purchase patterns and industrial data are generally self-recorded in a diary and returned to the researcher at intervals ranging from one to four weeks. A *diary* is a self-administered questionnaire in which the consumer is asked to record prespecified information on a periodic basis. Evidence indicates that diaries yield more complete and accurate data than do other approaches such as daily telephone calls.[66]

A recently developed panel technique that is becoming increasingly popular consists of a sample of respondents who have agreed to complete a number of mail questionnaires during their tenure as panel members. Since these individuals respond only when particular information is needed, we refer to this type of panel as an *interval panel.*

---

[64] T. Sheets, A. Ralinski, J. Kohne, and G. A. Brunner, "Deceived Respondents: Once Bitten, Twice Shy," *Public Opinion Quarterly,* 38 (Summer 1974), 261–263.

[65] H. W. Boyd, Jr., and R. L. Westfall, *An Evaluation of Continuous Consumer Panels as a Source of Marketing Information* (Chicago: American Marketing Association, 1960), 7.

[66] S. Sudman and R. Ferber, "A Comparison of Alternative Procedures for Collecting Consumer Expenditure Data for Frequently Purchased Products," *Journal of Marketing Research,* 11 (May 1974), 128–135.

Panel Characteristics and Uses

Most panels are maintained by commercial research organizations such as *NPD Research, Inc., Market Research Corporation of America, National Family Opinion, Inc., Consumer Mail Panels, Inc.,* and *Home Testing Institute, Inc.* The cost of establishing and maintaining a viable panel is so great that subscriptions by a number of firms are generally required to make it economically feasible.

Continuous panels offer the advantage of allowing the firm to monitor shifts in an individual's or market segment's purchasing patterns over time. This allows the firm to evaluate the effects of both its own and its competitor's marketing activities on specific market segments. For example, if a competitor introduces a larger size package, the firm can tell what type and how many people are switching to the new size.

Continuous panel data are also beginning to serve as an important basis for forecasting the sales level or market share of a new product. A new product will often attract a number of purchasers simply because it is new. However, its ultimate success depends on how many of these initial purchasers become repeat purchasers. A number of forecasting models for products with relatively short repurchase cycles have been developed that require the type of purchase information generated by continuous panels.[67]

A recent survey of large advertisers found that monitoring trends and establishing demographic profiles of particular subgroups were the most common uses of continuous panels. These uses were followed by brand-switching analyses, new tryer-repeat buyer patterns, combination purchase analysis, early prediction of test markets, and promotion evaluation.[68]

The advantages associated with *interval panels* are different in nature from those of panels whose members report on a continuous basis. It is possible to survey the same interval panel members several times to monitor changes in their attitudes and purchase behavior. However, interval panels, are used more often for cross section (one time) surveys. A major advantage is the high response rate obtained by most mail panels. Return rates in the range of 85 to 90 per cent are often obtained.[69] In addition, the

---

[67] See G. J. Eskin, "Dynamic Forecasts of New Product Demand Using a Depth of Repeat Model," *Journal of Marketing Research,* **10** (May 1973), 115–129; D. H. Ahl, "New Product Forecasting Using Consumer Panels," *Journal of Marketing Research,* **7** (May 1970), 160–167; W. F. Massy, "Forecasting the Demand for New Convenience Products," *Journal of Marketing Research,* **6** (November 1969), 405–412; and J. H. Parfitt and B. J. K. Collins, "Use of Consumer Panels for Brand-Share Prediction," *Journal of Marketing Research,* **5** (May 1968), 131–145.

[68] D. K. Hardin and R. M. Johnson, "Patterns of Use of Consumer Purchase Panels," *Journal of Marketing Research,* **8** (August 1971), 365.

[69] "The Validity of Mail Panel Research," *NFO Digest,* published by National Family Opinion, Inc., **12** (September 1969).

firm does not have to generate a sampling frame, an activity that is both time consuming and costly.

As with a continuous panel, the research firm generally gathers a detailed demographic record of each respondent. This record may also contain a number of attitudinal and product ownership items. It allows researchers to obtain more relevant information from each respondent since they need not recollect the basic demographic data.

These basic demographic data also allow the researcher to select very specific samples. For example, a researcher can select only those families within a panel that have one or more daughters between age 12 and 16. This allows a tremendous savings over a random survey procedure if a study is to be made for a magazine for teen-age girls. Most firms that operate interval panels also make it economically feasible to survey unique groups such as heavy users of Tabasco sauce, owners of tropical fish, and tennis players.

Panels have a number of potential weaknesses and practical problems.[70] One serious problem is their degree of representativeness; that is, the extent that members of a panel can be considered representative of the broader population. *Market Research Corporation of America* had less than one-third of an original national probability sample serving as members of a continuous panel six months after it was initiated (40 per cent of those contacted refused to cooperate at all).[71] The panel of *National Family Opinion* consists of only 10 per cent of the families invited to join.[72] It is difficult to maintain representativeness given such low cooperation rates.

The basic approach to achieving representativeness is to ensure that the demographic characteristics (age, income, geography, family size, population density) of the panel match those of the national market. Therefore, the major distinction between the panel members and the general population is a willingness to serve on a panel. This aspect of cooperativeness may or may not be related to other variables that are of concern to the marketing researcher.

There is not a great deal of evidence concerning the relationship between panel members and the general population on factors other than demographics. One panel was found to be composed of substantially more

[70] See D. M. Crider, F. K. Willits, and R. C. Bealer, "Panel Studies: Some Practical Problems," *Sociological Methods and Research*, 2 (August 1973), 3–19.

[71] United States Department of Agriculture, *Establishing a National Consumer Panel from a Probability Sample*, Marketing Research Report 40 (Washington, D.C.: U.S. Government Printing Office, 1953).

[72] "The Validity of Mail Panel Research," op. cit., 1. For an example of a higher completion for a 12-week continuous panel see B. J. LaLonde and J. Herniter, "The Effect of a Trading Stamp Discontinuance on Supermarket Performance: A Panel Approach," *Journal of Marketing Research*, 7 (May 1970), 205–209. Techniques for increasing cooperation are presented in S. Sudman and R. Ferber, "Experiments in Obtaining Consumer Expenditures by Diary Methods," *Journal of the American Statistical Association*, 66 (December 1971), 725–735.

Table 11–5 Percentage of Large Advertisers Describing Potential Problems in Continuous Panels as "Fairly Severe" or "Critical Defects"*

	Among All Respondents (N = 84)	Among Regular Users (N = 25)
Inaccurate volume projections	39	36
Infrequent purchase	36	28
Biased samples	36	28
Cost of data collection	36	16
Instability of data	33	16
Incomplete reporting	32	16
Not cover out-of-home purchase/use	27	16
Cost of analysis	24	12
Field work too long	19	12
Continuity	19	20
Analysis too long	18	12
Lack analytic resources	16	16
Inflexible analysis programs	16	12

* *Source:* D. K. Hardin and R. M. Johnson, "Patterns of Use of Consumer Purchase Panels," *Journal of Marketing Research*, **8** (August 1971), 366. Reprinted by permission of the authors and the American Marketing Association.

owner occupied homes (75 versus 62 per cent) and more automobile owners (90 versus 74 per cent) than the estimate for the United States as a whole.[73] The percentage of home owners in panels has been found to increase over time unless specifically controlled for.[74] These findings probably reflect the difficulty of recruiting and maintaining representation from highly mobile families.

Those who initially join a panel and then withdraw from it have been found to be different from those who remain. When the panel is focused on no more than a few products, interest in the product(s) seems to be the primary distinction between the two groups. For example, one study found that 40 per cent of the users of cosmetics withdrew from a panel concerned with cosmetic usage after the first interview whereas 59 per cent of the nonusers withdrew.[75] On other factors including demographics, attitudes, and media habits, those remaining in a panel have been found to resemble closely either those leaving the panel or the general population.[76]

[73] O'Dell, op. cit., 268.

[74] M. G. Sobol, "Panel Mortability and Panel Bias," *Journal of the American Statistical Association,* **54** (March 1959), 52–68.

[75] M. Rosenberg, W. Thielens, and P. F. Lazarsfeld, "The Panel Study" in M. Jahoda, M. Deutsch, and S. Cook, eds., *Research Methods in Social Relations,* Part II (New York: Dryden Press, 1951), 599.

[76] Sobol, op. cit.; and W. N. Cordell and H. A. Rahmel, "Are Nielsen Ratings Affected by Non-Cooperation, Conditioning or Response Error?" *Journal of Advertising*

Table 11–5 indicates the major criticisms of continuous panels that appeared in a survey of the nation's 125 largest advertisers (84 usable questionnaires were returned). As can be seen, five of the top seven complaints are focused primarily on the *accuracy* of the data. One concerns costs and one indicates that panels are not appropriate for infrequently purchased items. However, it should be noted that only one-third of the respondents considered any of these potential problems to be either "fairly severe" or "critical defects."

Conclusions Concerning Panels

There is no empirical evidence concerning the utilization of interval panels. However, the number of commercial research firms offering interval panels and the sophisticated approach of these firms suggests widespread acceptance among researchers. Many people refuse to cooperate and thus these panels are not completely representative. Yet most random surveys have a large nonresponse error that also reduces their representativeness. As interval panel methodology develops, the rate of utilization will also increase.

Ironically, continuous panels may be producing more data that marketing decision makers can utilize. The survey of the 125 largest advertisers on their utilization of continuous panels led to the conclusion that:

Yet the dynamics of brand switching, new trial and repeat buying, combination purchases, and creation of new business by promotional activities rank relatively far down the list of purposes to which national panel data are put. The full utilization of these data may depend on the development of better marketing decision models.[77]

Ex Post Facto Research

A group of department stores in seven Midwestern states share details of their operations in order to improve their efficiency. A researcher selected one highly successful store and a relatively unsuccessful store. The "hypothesis" was that "differences between the two stores' buyers help explain the differences in sales performance of the two firms." The study

---

Research, **2** (September 1962), 45–49. For contradictory evidence see G. W. Paul and B. M. Enis, "Psychological and Socio-Economic A-typicality of Consumer Panel Members," in P. R. McDonald, *Marketing Involvement in Society and the Economy* (Chicago: American Marketing Association, 1969), 387–391.

[77] Hardin and R. M. Johnson, op. cit., 367.

found "demographic differences, and differences in self-confidence, aggressiveness, and fashion leadership" between the two stores' buyers. The researcher concluded that "balance in the buyer team and the discretion given to buyers may be two of the keys to success."[78]

The study described is an example of *ex post facto* research. In this type of research we start with "the present situation as an effect of some previously acting causal factors and attempt to trace back over an interval of time to some assumed causal complex of factors. . . ."[79] Thus, this study began with the conditions "successful store" and "unsuccessful store" and examined one potential causative factor—characteristics of store buyers.

The *ex post facto* nature of this study is fairly clear. If a survey had been conducted among 100 department stores and the characteristics of the buyers of the "successful" stores were compared with those of the "unsuccessful" stores, the research would also be of an *ex post facto* nature. Thus, any time survey results are analyzed after the fact in a manner designed to "show" causal relationships, it can be characterized as *ex post facto* research.

A recent study concerned with the acceptance of the midi dress utilized a telephone survey to gather data for an *ex post facto* analysis. Coeds were classified on the basis of their responses to three questions focusing on ownership and purchase intentions concerning the midi. Cross-classification analysis (discussed in Chapter 13) was utilized to compare those who indicated a high degree of acceptance with those who indicated lesser acceptance. The study found that those with the highest degree of acceptance of the midi were the younger, unmarried, sorority members whose parents had high annual incomes. They also attended fewer movies and more fashion shows.[80]

The critical weakness of this type of research is the fact that the various groups are *self-selected*. That is, the subject rather than the researcher determines who will be assigned to the various groups. Therefore, it is not possible to demonstrate a causative relationship using this methodology.

In this fashion study, there is no control in the research design over whether or not the coeds actually owned midis (as opposed to reporting the ownership) or whether they actually attended more fashion shows or simply *recalled* more fashion shows. This lack of control over the variables involved in the situation means that any causative conclusions must be viewed with caution.

Even in cases in which it is possible to ascertain positively the occur-

[78] C. R. Martin, Jr., "The Contribution of the Professional Buyer to a Store's Success or Failure," *Journal of Retailing,* **49** (Summer 1973), 69–80.

[79] F. S. Chapin, *Experimental Designs in Sociological Research,* rev. ed. (New York, Harper & Row Publishers, Inc., 1955), 95.

[80] J. B. Mason and D. Bellenger, "Analyzing High Fashion Acceptance," *Journal of Retailing,* **49** (Winter 1973–1974), 79–96.

rence of one or all of the major variables, one still cannot generalize the results to other groups. For example, a study of recent purchasers of national versus private brands of major appliances found "substantive" differences in purchase behavior and purchaser characteristics. Since store records were used, there is no doubt that the purchasers were correctly identified as national or private brand purchasers.[81] However, since recent purchasers are not a random sample of the larger population, the results cannot be projected statistically to that larger population. This does not mean that the researcher or decision maker cannot or should not subjectively project such results to the larger population. If the researcher is confident that the recent purchasers do, in fact, constitute a representative sample of the larger population, he should explicitly state the reasons for his belief and proceed to project the results.

Ex post facto projects such as those described are common and useful in marketing research. They will continue to enjoy widespread utilization because they can provide *evidence* of causation in situations where other techniques such as experimentation would be impractical or impossible. For example, *ex post facto* research has provided the primary evidence that smoking cigarettes "causes" lung cancer. However, since the "smoker" and "nonsmoker" groups are self-selected, it has been possible to suggest that some other factor, as yet unknown, "causes" or encourages *both* smoking and lung cancer.

The marketing researcher often is unable to conduct experiments for ethical, monetary, and practical reasons. Such variables as product ownership, media habits, income, social class, and personality do not lend themselves to experimental manipulation. Therefore, *ex post facto* research designs will continue to be important in marketing research.

Summary

Survey research is the systematic collection of data from respondents for the purpose of understanding and/or predicting some aspect of behavior of the population of interest by the administration of questionnaires. The administration of a questionnaire is called interviewing. Interviews may vary in structure—the degree of freedom the interviewer has to alter the questionnaire, and directness—the extent to which the respondent is aware of the purpose of the interview. These two variables lead to *four types of interviews:* (1) *structured-direct,* (2) *structured-indirect,* (3) *unstructured-direct,* and (4) *unstructured-indirect.*

Surveys are generally labeled according to the method of communica-

---

[81] J. T. Rothe and L. M. Lamont, "Purchase Behavior and Brand Choice Determinants," *Journal of Retailing,* **49** (Fall 1973), 19–33.

tion used in the interview: *personal, telephone,* or *mail.* Seven criteria are relevant for selecting the type of survey to use in a particular situation: (1) *complexity of the questionnaire,* (2) *required amount of data,* (3) *desired accuracy,* (4) *sample control,* (5) *speed of administration,* (6) *level of nonresponse,* and (7) *cost.* No single method of survey data collection excels on all seven criteria. The appropriate technique to use is the one that will generate the appropriate information from the desired sample at the least cost.

Nonresponse error, a difference on the characteristic of interest between those who respond to a survey and those who do not, is one of the most critical problems faced by the survey researcher. In general, the lower the response rate to a survey the higher is the probability of nonresponse error. *Nonresponse is caused by refusals and not-at-homes.* Not-at-homes are the primary problem in personal and telephone surveys. Refusals, intentional and unintentional, are more critical in mail surveys. Thus, the approach for reducing nonresponse in telephone and personal surveys centers on contacting the respondent. In mail surveys, the focus is on motivating the respondent.

Proper timing and a series of callbacks are the main ways of increasing the initial contacts in personal and telephone surveys. Repeated mailings, advance letters, special postage, monetary inducements, and personalized requests for cooperation are used to motivate respondents to return mail surveys.

After a set of responses is received, the researcher should run a *sensitivity analysis* to determine if the nonrespondents could alter the results enough to change the decisional implications. If they could, all economically feasible attempts to increase the number of respondents should be utilized. Then, the researcher must attempt to estimate the impact of any remaining nonresponse error. He can utilize *subjective estimates,* a *subsample estimate,* or a *trend estimate.*

A *panel* is a group of individuals that have agreed to provide information to a researcher over a period of time. Members of *continuous panels* report specified behaviors on a regular basis whereas members of *interval panels* provide data on request. Panels are typically maintained by commercial research firms and are widely used. The primary concern with panels is whether or not those individuals agreeing to serve on a panel are representative of the larger population.

Ex post facto research starts with a current situation and works backward in time in an attempt to find the cause. Analyzing survey results after the fact in a manner designed to "show" causal relationships is a common example of *ex post facto* research. Although causal links established by *ex post facto* research are always suspect, the technique is and will continue to be widely used in marketing research since it is the only practical approach to many problems.

Questions and Problems

11.1. All forest industry firms with sales over $50 million were surveyed in a recent study. The definition of a forest industry firm and the minimum sales level produced a total population of 50 firms. The major purpose of the survey was to determine the percentage of these firms that used on-line computer simulation to aid in strategic planning decisions. Twenty-nine of the 50 firms returned the questionnaire and 10 of these reported they used the technique. A random sample of six of those firms that did not respond were contacted by telephone. None of these six firms reported using the technique. What percentage of the total population (50 firms) would you estimate use the technique? Justify your answer.

11.2. Write a cover letter to accompany a four-page questionnaire to be sent to a national sample of working mothers with preschoolchildren. The questionnaire will focus on their attitudes toward work, the home, the level of assistance the husband (if married) provides with managing the home, and their use of certain convenience foods and household products.

11.3. What advantages, if any, would an interval panel offer in the situation described in Problem 11.2?

11.4. Design an *ex post facto* study to determine why some students are marketing majors and others are accounting majors. Will this design allow you to determine what causes an individual to select one field over the other? Why?

11.5. What biases, if any, might be introduced by offering to give respondents $5 upon receipt of the questionnaire? The purpose of the payment is to ensure a high response rate. Will it work?

11.6. People tend to respond to surveys that deal with topics that interest them. How can this fact be used to increase the response rate from a mail survey of the general public on attitudes toward and usage of a toilet bowl cleaner?

11.7. The manager of a shopping center recently conducted a survey to provide information on the types of stores that should be sought for the center's new wing that was under construction. The surveys were distributed by placing them on tables near the entrances to the center. A large sign above each table said: "Help Us Plan the New Wing." Deposit boxes for completed questionnaires were provided at each table. The tables were left up for a two-week period.

What type of errors are likely to be present in this study?

Selected Bibliography

ERDOS, P. L. *Professional Mail Surveys*. New York: McGraw-Hill, Inc., 1970. An outstanding practical guide to conducting mail surveys based on the author's extensive professional experience in the area.

HAUCK, M., and S. STEINKAMP. *Survey Reliability and Interviewer Competence.* Urbana: University of Illinois Press, 1964. A good treatment of the role of the interviewers in affecting the quality of data obtainable in personal interview surveys.

Interviewer's Manual. Ann Arbor: The University of Michigan, 1969. A detailed description of the responsibilities, methods, and techniques that interviewers for the Institute for Social Research must know.

KERLINGER, F. N. *Foundations of Behavioral Research.* New York: Holt, Rinehart and Winston, 1973, Chap. 22. A brief but complete description of the nature of *ex post facto* research.

LANSING, J. B., and J. N. MORGAN. *Economic Survey Methods.* Ann Arbor: University of Michigan, 1971. A thorough treatment of all aspects of survey research.

O'BARR, W. M., D. H. SPAIN, and M. A. TESSLER, eds. *Survey Research in Africa.* Evanston: Northwestern University Press, 1973. An excellent collection of readings devoted to the practical problems involved in doing survey research on the African continent.

RICHARDSON, S. A., B. S. DOHRENWEND, and D. KLEIN. *Interviewing.* New York: Basic Books, Inc., 1965. A thorough and detailed description of the interviewing process.

TULL, D. S., and G. S. ALBAUM. *Survey Research.* New York: Intext Educational Publishers, 1973. A fairly technical treatment of all aspects of surveys in decisional research.

Case 11–1

Travel & Leisure Readership Profile*

In March, *Travel & Leisure* magazine retained Erdos and Morgan, Inc., to conduct a second survey among American Express Money Cardmembers who were surveyed the previous year. The basic purpose of the survey was to bring the readership and demographic data up to date.

The first survey was conducted among a systematic sample of 2,000 Cardmembers who received the publication. A complete verification of these 2,000 persons, made in March, had shown that 1,843 of them were Cardmembers at that date. This group of current Cardmembers constituted the sample for the current survey.

On April 17, an advance postcard (Exhibit A) was mailed to the group, advising them of the forthcoming survey. Three days later the questionnaire (Exhibit B), accompanied by a cover letter (Exhibit C) and a $1.00 incentive, was mailed. Thirty-two pieces were returned as undeliverable, making a net mailing of 1,811. A follow-up letter was sent on May 18 (Exhibit D). By the closing date, June 4, 1,352 completed questionnaires, or 75 per cent of the net mailing, were returned.

* Research for this survey was conducted by Erdos and Morgan, Inc. of New York.

Telephone interviews were attempted with all nonrespondents between June 5 and June 20. During this period 167 nonrespondents were reached and interviewed, and 20 late mail returns were received. This second wave of responses (telephone plus late mail) represented 10 per cent of the total mailing, bringing the total response to 85 per cent.

Erdos and Morgan, Inc., although pleased with the high response rate, were concerned that the nonrespondents might alter the conclusions of the study. They, therefore, used the following logic to control for potential nonresponse error.

If we consider the mail responses that arrived before starting the telephone interviews as the "first wave," and the combined telephone interviews and the late mail returns as the "second wave," we have two comparable sets of tabulations.

Examination of the two waves indicated that there were some differences in the response patterns. It is reasonable to assume that the remaining 15 per cent nonrespondents are closer to the respondents of the second wave than to those of the first wave. Accordingly, the second wave was weighted by the number of nonrespondents and then added to the tabulations of the first wave to arrive at the figures shown in this report.

As an example, consider those whose answers to the education question indicated that they went to college. This would include those who checked "Attended," "Graduated," or Postgraduate studies."

	First Wave		Second Wave		Weighted Second Wave		Weighted Total (Sample)	
	#	%	#	%	#	%	#	%
Went to college	1129	83.5	134	71.7	329	71.7	1458	80.5
Base (100.0%)	1352		187		459		1811	

Since we consider the 187 second wave answers reasonably representative of all 459 nonrespondents to the first wave, the 134 respondents who went to college, comprising 71.7 per cent of the second wave, were expanded to 329, which is 71.7 per cent of 459. Adding these 329 to the 1,129 college repliers to the first wave gives the weighted total of 1,458, or 80.5 per cent of the total sample.

The following tables show some of the other questions to indicate the differences between the total sample (as adjusted) and the results of the first wave, based on a 75 per cent mail response.

Q. *Did you read or look through any part of the current issue of* Travel & Leisure *shown on this page?*

	Total Sample	First Wave
Yes	66.7%	73.2%
No	21.9	15.0
Haven't received it yet	10.9	11.1
No answer	0.5	0.7
Base (100.0%)	(1,811)	(1,352)

Q. *In addition to yourself and your spouse, how many other adult (over 18) members of your household read or looked at your copy of the above issue of* Travel & Leisure? *How many adults outside your household?*

	Average number of readers per copy	
	Total Sample	First Wave
In Household		
Males	0.9%	0.8%
Females	0.6	0.6
Total	1.5	1.4
Outside Household		
Males	0.4	0.4
Females	0.3	0.3
Total	0.7	0.7
All Readers		
Total Males	1.3	1.2
Total Females	0.9	0.9
Total	2.2	2.1

Q. *How many of the last three issues of* Travel & Leisure *have you read or looked through?*

	Total Sample	First Wave
One	5.6%	5.3%
Two	18.7	17.8
Three	68.2	71.6
None	6.6	4.4
No answer	0.9	0.9
Base (100.0%)	(1,811)	(1,352)
Average number of issues read	2.5	2.6

Q. *What was your total household income before taxes in 1972? (Please include income from all household members and from all sources, such as wages, profits, dividends, rentals.)*

	Total Sample	First Wave
Under $7,500	0.9%	1.1%
$7,500–9,999	1.2	1.3
$10,000–14,999	10.1	11.0
$15,000–19,999	17.2	18.1
$20,000–24,999	17.6	19.7
$25,000–29,999	14.6	14.8
$30,000–39,999	13.8	13.7
$40,000–49,999	5.5	5.8
$50,000 or over	10.2	10.6
No answer	8.9	3.9
Base (100.0%)	(1,811)	(1,325)
Median Income	$24,591	$24,201

1. Evaluate the procedures used to ensure a high response rate.
2. Evaluate the procedures used to adjust for nonresponse.
3. Evaluate the questionnaire.

Exhibit A Advance Postcard.

Dear Mr. Horn,

You are one of a small but representative group of *Travel & Leisure* readers whom we are asking to participate in a special survey that is being conducted throughout the United States.

In a few days you will receive a questionnaire. It will only take a short time to complete, and your answers will be completely confidential.

I will be most grateful for your cooperation.

Sincerely yours,

John S. Connors
Publisher

Exhibit B

CONFIDENTIAL SURVEY OF READERS OF
TRAVEL & LEISURE

1. Did you read or look through any part of the current issue of TRAVEL &
   LEISURE shown on this page?

   Yes ☐   No ☐   Haven't received it yet ☐

   If "Yes," please continue.
   If "No," skip to question 3; if "Haven't received it yet," skip to question 5.

2. Have you read or do you plan to read any of the following articles and features which appear in the
   current issue of TRAVEL & LEISURE? (Please check 1 box for each line.)

	Have read	Plan to read	Do not plan to read
WHAT TO DO AFTER A SERIOUS ACCIDENT by Ann Cutler (P. 20)	☐	☐	☐
TRAVEL & LEISURE by Caskie Stinnett (P. 31)	☐	☐	☐
THE ENDLESS DRAMA OF AMERICA by Alistair Cooke (P. 32)	☐	☐	☐
ARISTOTLE CONTEMPLATING THE BUST OF HOMER by Thomas Hoving (P. 40)	☐	☐	☐
EL BOOM ON COSTA DEL SOL by William A. Krauss (P. 42)	☐	☐	☐
THE GENTLE THAW OF THE FOUR SEASONS by Silas Spitzer (P. 46)	☐	☐	☐
THE STRANGE RHAPSODY OF FLIGHT by Richard Bach (P. 48)	☐	☐	☐
DIAL-A-KING by Neil Morgan (P. 51)	☐	☐	☐
VICTORIA, B. C. by James Morris (P. 56)	☐	☐	☐
THE SMALL HOTELS—OF ROME by Al Hine (P. 59)	☐	☐	☐

3a. Has your spouse read this issue? .... Yes ☐   No ☐

 b. In addition to yourself and your spouse, how many other adult (over 18) members of your house-
    hold read or looked at your copy of the above issue of TRAVEL & LEISURE? How many adults
    outside your household?

	Number of men readers	Number of women readers
In your household (others than you or your spouse)	_____	_____
Outside your household	_____	_____

4. After you have finished reading this issue of TRAVEL & LEISURE, what will you do with it?

   Keep it .... ☐   It goes into a waiting room ☐
   Give it to a friend or relative ☐   Discard it .... ☐
   Give it to a hospital or school ☐   Other .... ☐

5. How many of the last three issues of TRAVEL & LEISURE have you read or looked through?

   One ☐   Two ☐   Three ☐   None ☐

6. Please indicate how much of an average issue you usually read.

   Less than 1/3 ☐   1/3 to 1/2 ☐   Over 1/2 ☐

7. How do you obtain your copies of TRAVEL & LEISURE?

   Paid subscription ☐   Buy at newsstand ☐

   Other (please specify)_____

(Please turn)

Exhibit B   Page 2

8. We would like to know if anything you read or saw in TRAVEL & LEISURE during the past year or two interested you sufficiently to induce you to talk about it or to take any of the actions below. You may check one or more boxes.

        a. Discussed articles with others .... ☐
        b. Visited a country or area .... ☐
        c. Decided on or modified a travel plan .... ☐

        d. Stayed at a hotel, motel, etc................................... ☐
        e. Asked for more information on a product or service .... ☐
        f. Bought or ordered a product .... ☐

        g. What else?_____

If you gave any answer from "b" through "g," please jot down a short "case history" of the last time this happened.

_____

_____

ABOUT YOU AND YOUR FAMILY (Confidential information, for the statistical analysis of previous data.)

1. Are you male or female? .... Male ☐   Female ☐

2. What is your age? .... Under 30 .. ☐   45 - 49 ... ☐
                             30 - 34 ... ☐   50 - 54 ... ☐
                             35 - 39 ... ☐   55 - 64 ... ☐
                             40 - 44 ... ☐   65 or over ☐

3. Please indicate the highest level of schooling you reached. (Check one.)

        Grade school .... ☐
        Attended high school .... ☐
        Graduated from high school ☐

        Attended college .... ☐
        Graduated from college .... ☐
        Postgraduate study .... ☐

4. What is your title or position?

    Manager-official ☐   Proprietor ☐   Professional ☐   Sales/clerical ☐

    Other (please specify)_____

5. What was your total household income before taxes in 1972? (Please include income from all household members and from all sources, such as wages, profits, dividends, rentals, etc.)

    Under $7,500..... ☐ $15,000 - $19,999 ☐ $30,000 - $39,999 ☐
    $ 7,500 - $ 9,999 ☐ $20,000 - $24,999 ☐ $40,000 - $49,999 ☐
    $10,000 - $14,999 ☐ $25,000 - $29,999 ☐ $50,000 or over ... ☐

Thank you for your help.

Exhibit C

132 WEST 31 STREET
NEW YORK, N.Y. 10001
(212) 868-2600

CABLE ADDRESS AMEXPUB

JOHN S. CONNORS
Publisher

April 27, 1973

Will you do us a favor?

From time to time we conduct a survey among
readers of TRAVEL & LEISURE. It is a great help to
our publication to know something about you and about
some of your reading interests.

It will take only a short time to fill out the
enclosed questionnaire and return it in the stamped
reply envelope provided.

Since your name was included in our scientifically
selected sample, your answers are essential to the
accuracy of our survey, <u>whether or not you have had
time to read our latest issue</u>.

Of course all replies are confidential and will
be used only in combination with others from every state
of the Union.

We will be most grateful for your help.

Sincerely yours,

John S. Connors
Publisher

P. S. The enclosed dollar bill is just a token of our
appreciation. You may want to add it to your next
charitable contribution.

Exhibit D

TRAVEL & LEISURE

132 WEST 31 STREET
NEW YORK, N.Y. 10001
(212) 868-2600

CABLE ADDRESS AMEXPUB

JOHN S. CONNORS
Publisher

May 18, 1973

Recently we asked you to participate in a nationwide survey among our readers. If you were among the many who have already answered, please consider this our way of saying "Thank you".

If, on the other hand, you did not have a chance to fill out the form when you first received it, perhaps you will be so kind as to do so now. As we have already started to process the returns for analysis, we enclose a special delivery envelope along with another copy of the questionnaire to speed your replies to us.

Since the validity of every survey depends on the greatest possible number of replies, you can understand why we want to make certain that your answers are included, whether you have had an opportunity to read our latest issue or not.

Of course all answers are confidential and will be used only for statistical analysis.

TRAVEL & LEISURE, and I personally, will be most grateful for your help.

Thank you in advance.

Sincerely yours,

John S. Connors
Publisher

P.S.   The enclosed dollar bill is just a token of our appreciation. You may want to add it to your next charitable contribution.

Case 11–2

The *Denver Post* Consumer Analysis

Each year the *Denver Post* conducts a "consumer analysis" as a service to its advertisers. The primary data generated by the analysis is brand preference as inferred from brand owned, last brand bought, or brand(s) bought in a specified time period.

In 1970, the area covered by the survey was the Denver City Zone as defined by the Audit Bureau of Circulations. The overall area was subdivided into 16 control areas, homogeneous as to income, family characteristics, and density of population in Denver County and surrounding incorporated cities.

The questionnaire was mailed to families whose names were listed in the current Denver and suburban cities directories. Since these directories were reasonably current, most family units in the overall population were included in the sampling frame. A systematic random sample was drawn that gave each family in the sampling frame an equal chance of being selected.

Both the husband and wife were required to fill in the various sections of the questionnaire, which was six pages long. The questions focused on the brand or brands of specified products that were on hand or had been purchased in a specified time period. Since the questionnaire required the efforts of both the husband and wife, was long, and required that brands on hand be checked, a mail survey was used.

Respondents were given five days to complete the questionnaire and return it, *in person,* to the *Post's* survey headquarters (See Exhibit A). At the headquarters, trained interviewers went over each questionnaire with the respondent to ensure that it was complete and accurate. The respondent was then presented with a large shopping bag filled with 47 grocery and drug items as promised in the instructions to the questionnaire.

As the questionnaires were returned, the percentage return from each of the 16 control areas was tabulated. Additional mailings to new respondents were made at the conclusion of each five-day return period until approximately 1 per cent of the total households in each area had returned a questionnaire.

1. What type of sampling process was used?

2. What type of errors are likely to be present as a result of the sampling process?

3. What type of errors may be generated by the requirement that the questionnaire be returned in person?

4. What problems, if any, may be caused by the reward of a "large shopping bag of groceries?"

Exhibit A Instructions for the *Denver Post Consumer Analysis Questionnaire**

CONFIDENTIAL QUESTIONNAIRE

**For a survey of the buying
habits of Greater Denver families to be compiled by**

THE DENVER POST

AREA NO.
Do not write in this space.

~~~~~~~~~~ **INSTRUCTIONS** ~~~~~~~~~~

1. This questionnaire applies ONLY to family groups maintaining a household. It will be accepted from **single persons or widows IF** they maintain a household and prepare their own meals regularly
2. **Each** major question should be answered YES or NO with an "X" or other checkmark. Give brand names only for products which you have bought within specified time periods. If your answer to the main question is NO, do not answer any of the subquestions.
3. **PLEASE do not guess** in answering questions. Look up the BRAND NAME if you don't remember it. In each case list the brand you, yourself, BOUGHT LAST.
4. **IF YOU DO NOT KNOW THE BRAND NAME, AND CAN'T FIND OUT, WRITE "DON'T KNOW" ON THE BRAND LINE.**
5. Do not mail in questionnaire or send it by children.
6. Please write plainly. Use ink if possible.

Street Address _____ Zip Code_____

City _____ Telephone No._____
(Your name is not needed, but we must have your address so that we can be sure we have the correct number of questionnaires from each section of metropolitan Denver.)

The Consumer Analysis Dept. is at

444 14th St.
(Corner, 14th and Glenarm)

SURVEY OFFICE HOURS
9:00 a.m. to 8:00 p.m., Monday through Friday.
9:00 a.m. to 5:00 p.m. Saturday. Closed Sundays.

You will receive—FREE—a large shopping bag of grocery products if you fill in this questionnaire and bring it to the Consumer Analysis Dept. **NO LATER THAN** _____ **1969**

* Reproduced by permission of the *Denver Post*.

Case 11–3
Oregon Bicycle Usage Study*

In January the Oregon State Highway Division undertook a survey to gain information on bicycle usage in the Eugene-Springfield area. Since the University of Oregon is located in Eugene and bicycle usage is high among students, a separate questionnaire was designed for students living in university dorms. Both the student and the general population questionnaires had three parts. The first page was a request for cooperation and several questions on the number and characteristics of bicycles owned. The second section was a "one day trip report," and the third an opinion questionnaire. A copy of the general public version of each of these is included at the end of the case. In addition, a postage free return envelope was provided. The methodology and rationale for the study, as contained in a report by the highway department, are provided as follows.

* Used by permission of the Oregon State Department of Transportation.

It became increasingly evident that more information was needed to properly administer the bicycle path program. No estimates were available as to the number of bicycles, the types of bicycles, or their usage for any city in Oregon.

The first attempt at sampling for information on bicycles or bicyclists' attitudes was a limited survey addressed to organized bicycle clubs and groups. It was subsequently decided that a bicycle survey of the general public was needed. The Eugene-Springfield area was the first area chosen because of the keen interest in bicycling in that area, and because a base for conducting the study already existed. This base was the Eugene-Springfield Area Transportation Study, which already had adequate zoning and other technical data so that it was possible to proceed promptly with such a study.

Three separate objectives were selected for the study; information was desired on: (1) numbers and types of bicycles, (2) the weekday trips made by bicyclists, and (3) opinions of bicycle riders on bicycle usage and bicycle paths.

The preliminary work on the questionnaire was completed at the end of the year. There was a question as to whether to proceed with the survey during winter months or wait until more favorable bicycling weather before sending out the questionnaires. As the first and third objectives could be met regardless of the weather or time of the year, it was decided to go ahead with a January survey. A follow-up survey was considered for May to ascertain differences in bicycle usage because of season.

During the course of the January survey, there was some unfavorable publicity, undoubtedly because of a misunderstanding of the intent of the survey and proper statistical sampling methods. The controversy mainly centered around one question that asked that only "Yesterday's" bicycle trips be reported. The adverse publicity was unfortunate and probably had a detrimental effect on the study. (Author's note: The publicity was rather intense and negative. The weather was inclement throughout most of the survey period. Furthermore, a number of bicycle riders had believed for some time that the Highway Department did not support bicycle paths.)

In order to represent all of the bicycle trips in the study area, it is necessary to expand the trip information obtained by the sampling process. This must be done for a common time period, a time span that is common to all replies received. "Yesterday" was selected because it was learned previously in Origin-Destination Interviews for Motorists that the previous day's trips are better remembered, and more accurately reported, than trips made at any earlier time.

The questionnaires for the January survey were mailed in such a controlled-delivery manner that about 10 per cent of them were delivered to "Occupant" each day, Tuesday through Saturday, over a two-week period. This prevented a rainy day, or two, from seriously biasing the survey.

The January survey questions were a composite of questions from: (1) the California Bicycle Report, (2) questions resulting from the earlier limited survey of bicycle clubs, and (3) questions similar to those asked of the motoring public concerning the origin and destinations of trips. One question concerning whether or not the trip crossed the Willamette River was used to provide a "screenline" check of the replies received. This was done in the following manner. During the controlled mailing, and on the days on which trips could be reported, the bicycles crossing the Willamette River were counted by observers during the daylight hours at all bridge crossings. These observed crossings will be compared for accuracy with crossings reported in the questionnaires.

Sampling

The study area selected for the January Eugene-Springfield Area Bicycle Survey was that of the Eugene-Springfield Area Transportation Study (E-SATS). This was done for convenience, as zoning and other data were already available from E-SATS and duplicate efforts could be avoided.

Sample addresses were selected on a random and systematic basis to which the interview forms were mailed. Students living in the University of Oregon dormitories were sampled by having dormitory monitors place a questionnaire in every fifth mailbox.

The remainder of persons in the study area were sampled in the following manner. From 1970 census data, a printout was obtained of all block faces and their individual address ranges. Each block face in the area that contained dwelling units furnished one sample address. The current Johnson and Polks City Directories were used for the actual sample address within the block face address range. By the following procedure, care was taken to select samples in an orderly manner so that corner and midblock sections were equivalent. Beginning with the lowest address on the first block, each succeeding selection on each succeeding block was of higher address. This system was used on even numbered calendar days. On odd numbered calendar days, the reverse system was used beginning at the high numbered end of the block. This procedure resulted in a combination of random and systematic sample selection. In addition, all apartment houses with 20 or more units were sampled separately on a one-to-five ratio.

The sampling process described resulted in a selection of approximately 20 per cent of all dwelling units in the study areas as sample addresses. For the January survey, a total of 9,749 samples were mailed out. Of these, 493 were returned as being not deliverable for one of several reasons.

Some sampling error probably occurred near the fringes of the study area or those areas where new housing tracts were recently occupied. Although dwelling unit growth since 1970 was taken into account, it is believed that the city directories were not as current, despite recent dates on the covers. Also, the sampling method probably allowed greater influence to be shown proportionally by dormitory students than by the general public.

The return of questionnaires from dormitory students and the general public was close to being equal. Of the 9,749 questionnaires sent out, 494 went to dormitories and the remaining 9,255 mailed to "Occupant" for both houses and apartments. From dormitories 181 replies were received (36.6 per cent). From the general public there were 2,916 replies (33.3 per cent).

Completeness of Replies

The survey produced many incomplete forms. However, it would be unrealistic to expect from a mailout survey the quality and completeness that would be produced by trained interviewers.

For the January survey, a random sample of returns was examined to document the completeness of filling out the forms. Returns from 200 households showed that most (90 per cent) filled out the first and second pages (the bicycle inventory and the trip report). Only 50 per cent filled out the third page (the opinion questionnaire) reasonably well; 35 per cent did it poorly and 15 per cent left it blank.

1. Evaluate the sampling procedure.

2. Evaluate the questionnaires.

3. Evaluate the request for cooperation and the means used to increase the response rate.

4. If there had been no unfavorable publicity, would the data have been likely to contain any bias?

5. With the unfavorable publicity, how accurate are the data?

1

Sample Number

☐☐☐☐

2   6

OREGON STATE HIGHWAY DIVISION
Salem, Oregon, 97310

Sample Address _____

7 – 35   house number and street   36–41 city & zip code

BICYCLE SURVEY

Please help us plan bicycle paths and increased bicycle safety by answering all questions below. All replies are kept confidential and no names are used or recorded.

Please answer the first four questions whether or not there are bicycles or bicycle riders at this address. (Write numbers in boxes to the right of each question).

1. How many persons live at this address?

2. How many automobiles or pickups are available for use at this address? (Include "Company" cars)

3. How many persons living at this address have a motor vehicle drivers license?

4. How many persons living at this address ride a bicycle?
   (Do not count persons that can ride, but almost never do)
   For identification purposes, each bike rider will be called Bike Rider No. 1, Bike Rider No. 2, and so forth.

5. What type of bicycle is owned or ridden by each Bike Rider? (The Sting-Ray type has small wheels, highrise handlebars, banana seat. Touring is a multi-speed light weight, usually with down-turned handlebars. Standard is a one to three speed bike, ridden in a more upright position).
   How is each bike equipped? Please fill in boxes or check as required to describe each bike located at this address.

42
45

CHECK BOXES TO SHOW BICYCLE TYPE
& EQUIPMENT INSTALLED

BICYCLE RIDDEN BY:	Sting-Ray	Touring	Standard	Fenders	Headlight	Tail-light or Reflector	Write number of gear speeds in box
Bike Rider No. 1	☐ 46	☐	☐	☐	☐	☐	☐ 52
Bike Rider No. 2	☐ 53	☐	☐	☐	☐	☐	☐ 59
Bike Rider No. 3	☐ 60	☐	☐	☐	☐	☐	☐ 66
Bike Rider No. 4	☐ 67	☐	☐	☐	☐	☐	☐ 73
Bike Rider No. 5	☐ 74	☐	☐	☐	☐	☐	☐ 80

Each person at this address who rides a bike should use a separate Bike Riders Trip Report and list all bike trips he or she made yesterday.

In reporting where bike trips began and ended, please give a full address; house number and street name. If exact address number is not known, please estimate the number as close as you can. This will enable us to process your questionnaire with a computer, saving time and money.

If a bike rider made no bike trips yesterday, there is a place to say so. Also, each bike rider should answer the questions on the other side of the BIKE RIDERS ONE DAY TRIP REPORT.

Thank you for your help.

Oregon State Highway Division

BIKE RIDERS OPINION QUESTIONNAIRE

1. On the list below, please write a 1 beside the main reason you ride a bike. If you have other reasons write a 2 by the next most important reason, a 3 by the next, and so on. You don't have to fill all the blanks, so stop when you have listed all the reasons that are important to you.

For transportation to or from work	☐ 32	For recreation or exercise	☐ 33
For transportation to or from shopping	☐ 34	No other way to get around besides walking	☐ 35
For transportation to or from school	☐ 36		

2. Please estimate the number of round trips per week you will make during each season, for the next year, for any of the following kinds of trips. Also, estimate the mileage for one of each such trips (one way mileage). Please write answers in boxes.

	Number of round trips per week				Approx. one way Distance in miles
	Spring	Summer	Fall	Winter	
To and from work	☐ 37	☐	☐	☐	☐ 41
To and from school	☐ 42	☐	☐	☐	☐ 46
Shopping trips	☐ 47	☐	☐	☐	☐ 51
Recreational trips	☐ 52	☐	☐	☐	☐ 56

3. Do you feel that you encounter serious problems while riding a bike? (circle one) 57 YES₁ NO₂

If you do feel that you encounter serious problems while riding place a 1 in the box beside the most serious in the list below. If you encounter more than one serious problems put a 2 in the box beside the next most serious problem, and so on. You do not have to fill all boxes, so stop when you have listed all the problems that are serious to you.

Inconsiderate auto drivers	☐ 58	Rocks or litter in streets	☐ 59
Dogs	☐ 60	Lack of places to park bikes	☐ 61
Wet or icy pavement	☐ 62	Night riding hazards	☐ 63

4. Are you in favor of an Oregon State Bicycle Registration and license? (circle one) 64 YES₁ NO₂

If your answer was YES, how many dollars would you consider a reasonable fee? Please write answer in box. ☐ 65

If your answer was YES, write a 1 in the box showing the main purpose for which you think the registration funds should be spent. Put a 2 in the box for the second most important purpose, and so on. You do not have to fill all boxes, so stop when you have shown the purposes important to you.

| Bicycle route construction | ☐ 66 | Bicycle rider education | ☐ 67 |
| Bicycle Safety inspection | ☐ 68 | Install bike parking racks | ☐ 69 |

5. If new bike routes were built, which routes would benefit you the most? Write a 1 by your first choice, a 2 by your second, and so on. You do not have to fill all boxes, so stop when you have shown the choices important to you.

Routes in downtown metropolitan areas	☐ 70	Routes through parks	☐ 71
Routes along major arterial streets	☐ 72	Routes along highways for touring	☐ 73
Routes along residential or secondary streets	☐ 74		

6. If a new bikeway were built parallel to a route that you now take for non-recreational purposes, how many blocks would you be willing to go out of your way to ride the new bikeway?

Not at all ☐ 75   Number of Blocks ☐ 76

7. If one, and only one, new bikeway was to be built in your community from where to where would you want it to go? For what purpose would you use it? Tell us in your own words.

_____

_____

2 1

BIKE RIDERS ONE DAY TRIP REPORT

BIKE RIDER NUMBER 7 _____ AGE 8 _____ SEX 10 M₁ or F₂ (circle one)

Each person at this address who is a BIKE RIDER should fill out a separate "BIKE RIDERS ONE DAY TRIP REPORT" for all bike trips made yesterday. Please do not list any trips unless they were made YESTERDAY. Use extra sheets if more than 7 trips were made.

IF YOU MADE NO BIKE TRIPS YESTERDAY PLEASE PUT AN "X" HERE. 11

Sample Number 2 ____ 6

BIKE RIDERS ANNUAL TRIP REPORT

To the best of your memory write the number of times per week that you made any of the same trips you made yesterday. Do this for each trip for each season of the past year.

TRIP No.	Was this trip made primarily for exercise or recreation? (circle one)	Address where trip began	The purpose of this trip was to go FROM (circle one)	The purpose of this trip was to go TO (circle one)	This trip was made during: (circle one)	This trip crossed the Willamette River (circle one)	Spring	Summer	Fall	Winter
1	YES NO₂ 13	Address where trip ended — No. & Street or Route & Box No. — City 14 / 17	home school work college shopping other place	1 home 4 school 2 work college 5 3 shopping other place 6	daylight 1 dark 2 22	YES NO 23 1 2	24	26	28	30
2	YES NO	No. & Street or Route & Box No. — City	home school work college shopping other place	home school work college shopping other place	daylight dark	YES NO				
3	YES NO	No. & Street or Route & Box No. — City	home school work college shopping other place	home school work college shopping other place	daylight dark	YES NO				
4	YES NO	No. & Street or Route & Box No. — City	home school work college shopping other place	home school work college shopping other place	daylight dark	YES NO				
5	YES NO	No. & Street or Route & Box No. — City	home school work college shopping other place	home school work college shopping other place	daylight dark	YES NO				
6	YES NO	No. & Street or Route & Box No. — City	home school work college shopping other place	home school work college shopping other place	daylight dark	YES NO				
7	YES NO	No. & Street or Route & Box No. — City	home school work college shopping other place	home school work college shopping other place	daylight dark	YES NO				

PLEASE ANSWER THE ADDITIONAL QUESTIONS ON THE OTHER SIDE OF THIS SHEET.

Case 11–4

Survey of Student Eating Patterns

A new, private dormitory complex was being constructed near the campus of the University of Texas at Austin. The developers were considering placing a complex of six to eight specialty restaurants with a common kitchen area on the first floor. Before doing so, they needed information on the students' eating patterns and preferences. They requested a local marketing consulting firm to generate the required data. The consultant constructed the following questionnaire for administration by telephone. Personal interviews were too expensive for the available budget, and time constraints made the use of mail impractical.

Female interviewers were used to administer the survey. Each interviewer was assigned a sequence of pages from the student directory. She was also provided a random starting point and was told to contact every nth name. All of the information above the introduction section of the questionnaire was recorded directly from the student directory except for the "code," which was simply a predetermined questionnaire identification number. The name and telephone number of each respondent were recorded on the questionnaire so that 10 per cent of each interviewer's respondents could be verified. The verification involved checking to ensure that the systematic sampling plan was being followed and a call to ensure that the respondent had actually been interviewed. A verification was deemed essential since the interviewers were paid on a completed interview basis. They were to make a minimum of four callbacks and no substitutes were allowed.

All of the questions in the questionnaire were open-ended except for Questions IIIb, IVc, IVg, Vc, and VI.

1. Evaluate the sampling plan.

2. Evaluate the interviewing procedure.

3. Evaluate the questionnaire.

Questionnaire of Student Eating Patterns

Code _____   Interviewer _____
Name _____   Phone _____
Classification _____   (Freshman = 1, . . . , Grad = 5)
Marital Status _____   (1 if yes; 2 if no)
Fraternity/Sorority _____   (1 if yes; 2 if no)
Sex _____   (1 if male; 2 if female)

Hello, is _____ there?
I am conducting a survey in order to determine certain factors concerning the eating patterns of University of Texas students. I would like to ask you a few questions if I may.

Ia. Do you have an automobile in Austin?
    __ 1. Yes   __ 2. No

Ib. In what type of housing do you currently live?
    __ 1. Private home   __ 4. Fraternity/Sorority house
    __ 2. University dorm   __ 5. Apartment or duplex
    __ 3. Private dorm   __ 6. Co-op
             __ 7. _____

IIa. Are you currently under any type of contract for any of your meals?

    __ 1. Yes [Go to IIb]   __ 2. No [Go to III]

IIb. What type of place provides these contracted meals?
    __ 1. University dorm   __ 4. Fraternity/Sorority
    __ 2. Private dorm   __ 5. Univ. cafeteria meal ticket
    __ 3. Boarding house   __ 6. _____

IIc. During the week (Mon.–Fri.), what meals are covered by this contract?
    __ 1. Breakfast, lunch, dinner
    __ 2. Lunch, dinner
    __ 3. Lunch only
    __ 4. Dinner only
    __ 5. _____

IId. What meals are covered on Saturdays?
    __ 1. Breakfast, lunch, dinner
    __ 2. Lunch, dinner
    __ 3. Breakfast, lunch
    __ 4. Lunch only
    __ 5. Dinner only
    __ 6. _____

IIe. What meals are covered on Sundays?
    __ 1. Breakfast, lunch, dinner
    __ 2. Lunch, dinner
    __ 3. Breakfast, lunch
    __ 4. Lunch only
    __ 5. Dinner only
    __ 6. _____

IIf. What single feature do you like best about your current contractual arrangement?
    __ 1. Price   __ 6. Location
    __ 2. Advanced planning   __ 7. Atmosphere
    __ 3. Quality of food   __ 8. Variety of food
    __ 4. Quantity of food   __ 9. Convenience
    __ 5. Service   __ 10. _____

IIg. What single feature do you like least about your current contractual arrangement?

— 1. Price
— 2. Quality of food
— 3. Quantity of food
— 4. Service
— 5. Location
— 6. Atmosphere

— 7. Variety of food
— 8. Too many meals
— 9. Too few meals
— 10. No choice in contract
— 11. _____

IIh. Approximately how much does this arrangement cost per month?

— 1. Under $30
— 2. $30–$39
— 3. $40–$49
— 4. $50–$59

— 5. $60–$69
— 6. $70–$79
— 7. $80 or more
— 8. No Response

[If the respondent's contract includes all three meals during the week, skip to question No. VI. If it does not include all three meals, complete the questions dealing with the meals *not* covered by the contract.]

Breakfast

IIIa. How many times during the week (Mon–Fri) do you usually eat breakfast?

— 0
— 1
— 2

— 3
— 4
— 5

[If the response is 0 go to question No. IV, if 1–5, go to IIIb.]

IIIb. At which of the following types of places do you usually eat breakfast?

— 1. At your place of residence
— 2. At a university operated place
— 3. At a privately operated place you usually walk to
— 4. At a privately operated place you usually drive to
— 5. Other _____

[If the response is No. 1 above, proceed to question No. IV. If 2–5 proceed to IIIc.]

IIIc. What single feature do you like best about the type of place in which you usually eat breakfast?

— 1. Price
— 2. Quality of food
— 3. Quantity of food
— 4. Service
— 5. Location

— 6. Atmosphere
— 7. Variety of food
— 8. Type of food
— 9. Convenience
— 10. _____

IIId. What single feature do you like least about the type of place in which you usually eat breakfast?

— 1. Price
— 2. Quality of food
— 3. Quantity of food
— 4. Service

— 5. Location
— 6. Atmosphere
— 7. Variety of food
— 8. _____

IIIe. About how much do you usually pay for breakfast?

— 1. Less than $.50
— 2. $.50– $.74
— 3. $.75–$.99
— 4. $1.00–$1.24

— 5. $1.25–$1.49
— 6. $1.50 or more
— 7. No Response

Lunch

IVa. Out of the five weekdays, how many days do you usually eat lunch away from where you live?

  — 0   — 3
  — 1   — 4
  — 2   — 5

[If the response is 0 go to Question No. V, if 1–5, go to IVb.]

IVb. Do you usually eat lunch out at the same place most of the time?
  — 1. Yes [Go to IVc]   — 2. No [Go to IVg]

IVc. Which of the following types of places is it?
  — 1. A university operated place
  — 2. A privately operated place you usually walk to
  — 3. A privately operated place you usually drive to
  — 4. Other _____

IVd. What single feature do you like best about it?
  — 1. Price   — 6. Atmosphere
  — 2. Quality of food   — 7. Variety of food
  — 3. Quantity of food   — 8. Type of food
  — 4. Service   — 9. Convenience
  — 5. Location   — 10. _____

IVe. What single feature do you like least about it?
  — 1. Price   — 5. Location
  — 2. Quality of food   — 6. Atmosphere
  — 3. Quantity of food   — 7. Variety of food
  — 4. Service   — 8. _____

IVf. Approximately how much do you usually pay for lunch?
  — 1. Less than $.50   — 5. $1.25–$1.49
  — 2. $.50–$.74   — 6. $1.50–$1.75
  — 3. $.75–$.99   — 7. $1.75 or more
  — 4. $1.00–$1.24   — 8. No response
[Go to V]

IVg. At which of the following types of places do you usually eat?
  — 1. At university operated place
  — 2. A privately operated place you usually walk to
  — 3. A privately operated place you usually drive to
  — 4. Other _____

IVh. What single feature do you consider most important in choosing a place to eat lunch?
  — 1. Price   — 6. Atmosphere
  — 2. Quality of food   — 7. Variety of food
  — 3. Quantity of food   — 8. Type of food
  — 4. Service   — 9. Convenience
  — 5. Location   — 10. _____

IVi. Approximately how much do you usually pay for lunch?
  — 1. Less than $.50   — 5. $1.25–$1.49
  — 2. $.50–$.74   — 6. $1.50–$1.75
  — 3. $.75–$.99   — 7. $1.75 or more
  — 4. $1.00–$1.24   — 8. No response

Dinner

Va. Out of the five weekdays, how many days do you usually eat dinner away from your residence?

— 0   — 3
— 1   — 4
— 2   — 5

[If the response is 0, go to question No. VI, if 1–5, go to Vb.]

Vb. Do you usually eat dinner out at the same place?
    — 1. Yes [Go to Vc]   — 2. No [Go to Vg]

Vc. Which of the following tyes of places is it?
    — 1. A university operated place
    — 2. A privately operated place you usually walk to
    — 3. A privately operated place you usually drive to
    — 4. Other _____

Vd. What single feature do you like best about it?
    — 1. Price   — 6. Atmosphere
    — 2. Quality of food   — 7. Variety of food
    — 3. Quantity of food   — 8. Type of food
    — 4. Service   — 9. Convenience
    — 5. Location   — 10. _____

Ve. What single feature do you like least about it?
    — 1. Price   — 5. Location
    — 2. Quality of food   — 6. Atmosphere
    — 3. Quantity of food   — 7. Variety of food
    — 4. Service   — 8. _____

Vf. About how much do you usually pay for dinner?
    — 1. Less than $.50   — 6. $1.50–$1.74
    — 2. $.50–$.74   — 7. $1.75–$1.99
    — 3. $.75–$.99   — 8. $2.00–$2.24
    — 4. $1.00–$1.24   — 9. $2.25 or more
    — 5. $1.25–$1.49   — 10. No Response
    [Go to VI]

Vg. Which of the following types of places do you usually eat dinner out at?
    — 1. A university operated facility
    — 2. A privately operated place you usually walk to
    — 3. A privately operated place you usually drive to
    — 4. Other _____

Vh. What single feature do you consider most important in choosing a place to eat dinner?
    — 1. Price   — 6. Atmosphere
    — 2. Quality of food   — 7. Variety of food
    — 3. Quantity of food   — 8. Type of food
    — 4. Service   — 9. Convenience
    — 5. Location   — 10. _____

Vi. Approximately how much do you usually pay for dinner?

__ 1. Less than $.50
__ 2. $.50–$.74
__ 3. $.75–$.99
__ 4. $1.00–$1.24
__ 5. $1.25–$1.49
__ 6. $1.50–$1.74
__ 7. $1.75–$1.99
__ 8. $2.00–$2.24
__ 9. $2.25 or more
__ 10. No Response

VI. If a meal ticket were available which could be exchanged at any of six to eight specialty restaurants in one area three blocks west of campus for breakfast, lunch, or dinner, how interested would you be in purchasing one?

__ 1. Definitely interested
__ 2. Probably interested
__ 3. Probably not interested
__ 4. Definitely not interested

Experimentation means:
1) *manipulating independent var.*
2) *acct. for effect of extraneous variables*

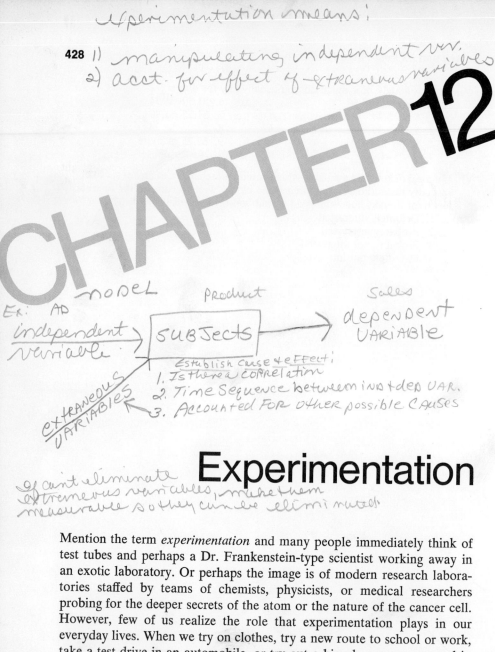

Ex: AD → MODEL
independent variable → SUBJECTS → Product → Sales *dependent VARIABLE*

EXTRANEOUS VARIABLES

Establish Cause + Effect:
1. Is there a CORRElation
2. Time Sequence between ind + deD VAR.
3. Accounted FOR other possible CAuses

Experimentation

If can't eliminate extraneous variables, make them measurable so they can be eliminated.

Mention the term *experimentation* and many people immediately think of test tubes and perhaps a Dr. Frankenstein-type scientist working away in an exotic laboratory. Or perhaps the image is of modern research laboratories staffed by teams of chemists, physicists, or medical researchers probing for the deeper secrets of the atom or the nature of the cancer cell. However, few of us realize the role that experimentation plays in our everyday lives. When we try on clothes, try a new route to school or work, take a test drive in an automobile, or try out a bicycle, we are engaged in experimentation.

Experimentation is also a common feature in the marketing activities of most firms. A grocer decides to utilize new point-of-purchase material to see how it works. A manufacturer offers an additional bonus for sales of certain products. An advertising agency compares the cost of a computer-generated media schedule with the cost of a schedule generated manually. All of these represent forms of experimentation.

Experimentation — Causal
We are researching what caused this result

In this chapter we consider the nature and principles of formal experimentation as opposed to the casual experimentation that most of us engage in. The characteristics of a controlled experiment are first described. Then the various types of errors that might affect an experiment are analyzed. The central section of the chapter is devoted to a description of the more common types of experimental designs that have been developed to control or reduce experimental errors. Then the environments—laboratory, field, and computer simulation—in which experiments are conducted are examined. Finally, the role that experimentation should play in decision making is discussed.

The Nature of Experimentation

Experimentation involves *the deliberate manipulation of one or more variables by the experimenter in such a way that its effect upon one or more other variables can be measured.* The variable being manipulated is called the *independent variable.* (It is sometimes also called the *treatment.*) The variable that will reflect the impact of the independent variable is called the *dependent variable.* Its level is dependent upon the level or magnitude of the independent variable.

Consider a retailer who has always charged $1.00 a unit for a particular product and has consistently sold 100 units per week. Curious about the effect of price level on sales, he increases the price to $1.20 a unit for a week and monitors sales. Sales drop to 50 units during the week. Price in this example is the independent variable and sales level is the dependent variable. Since sales changed, the retailer might be willing to conclude that price level does indeed affect sales level.

Before our retailer could reach such a conclusion, however, he would have to be sure that no other variable could have caused the change in sales. For example, if the area had had unusually bad weather, if the mass transit system had been closed because of a strike, if there had been street repairs in front of the store, or if a competitor had had a major sale, our retailer could not with any confidence attribute the cause of the sales decrease to the price increase.

Experimentation then is oriented toward the establishment and measurement of causal relationships among the variables under consideration. Well-designed experiments are uniquely equipped to demonstrate causal relations because they allow for or control other potential causal factors (extraneous variables). However, an experiment must be carefully designed to avoid a number of types of potential error.

Types of Errors Affecting Experimental Results

As briefly described in Chapter 4, a number of errors are unique to the experimental approach. In this section, nine types of errors that can confound experimental results are described: (1) *premeasurement,* (2) *maturation,* (3) *history,* (4) *instrumentation,* (5) *selection,* (6) *mortality,* (7) *interaction,* (8) *reactive error,* and (9) *measurement timing.*[1]

Premeasurement Error (Design)

Assume that an interviewer knocks on your door and requests your cooperation for a marketing study. You agree and proceed to complete an attitude questionnaire containing a number of open-ended questions, some multiple-choice items, and a 20-item semantic differential scale. The questions are concerned with a brand of soft drinks that you have heard of but have not tried. Shortly afterwards, you describe the interview to a friend and the next day try one of the firm's soft drinks.

Two weeks later the interviewer returns and asks you to complete another questionnaire. This questionnaire is an alternative form of the one you completed earlier. You have continued to consume the firm's soft drinks and the second questionnaire reflects both increased consumption and a more favorable attitude toward the brand.

What caused the shift in your behavior? Although the firm might have increased advertising, decreased price, altered the package design, or manipulated any of a number of other variables, the "cause" of your interest in and sampling of the product was the initial measurement. *Premeasurement effects occur anytime the taking of a prior measurement has a direct effect on the performance in a subsequent measurement.* This can occur because the respondents become more skilled at completing the measuring instrument, are annoyed at being measured twice on the same topic, or for any of a number of other reasons.

Premeasurement is a major concern if the respondents realize they are being measured. However, if inanimate factors such as sales are being measured or if disguised measurement of human subjects is used, premeasurement no longer represents a potential error source and can be ignored. In addition, a number of the experimental designs described later in the chapter reduce or eliminate premeasurement effects.

---

[1] Several additional but relatively minor error types are described in D. T. Campbell and J. C. Stanley, *Experimental and Quasi-Experimental Designs for Research* (Chicago: Rand McNally College Publishing Company, 1963).

Maturation (*Collection*)

Maturation represents *biological* or *psychological processes that systematically vary with the passage of time, independent of specific external events.*[2] Respondents may grow older, more tired, or thirstier between the pre- and postmeasurements.

For example, an experiment that begins at 2:00 P.M. and ends at 5:00 P.M. will begin with most of the respondents just having eaten and perhaps somewhat sleepy from lunch. By the time the experiment ends, the respondents will, on the average, be hungrier, thirstier (unless fluids were provided), less sleepy, and more fatigued. Maturation can also be a severe problem in those experiments that persist over months or years, such as market tests and experiments dealing with the physiological response to such products as toothpaste, cosmetics, and medications. Fortunately, most experimental designs control for any effects that maturation might have.

History (*Collection*)

History is a somewhat confusing term. It does *not* refer to the occurrence of events prior to the experiment. Rather, *history refers to any variables or events, other than the one(s) manipulated by the experimenter, that occur between the pre- and postmeasures and affect the value of the dependent variable.* For example, a gasoline manufacturer may measure its level of sales in a region, launch a promotional campaign for four weeks, and monitor sales levels during and immediately after the campaign. However, such factors as a price cut by competitors, a number of independent stations going out of business, or unseasonably warm or cold weather could each cause (or nullify) a change in sales. These extraneous variables are referred to as history and represent one of the major concerns in experimental design.

Instrumentation (*Analysis*)

Instrumentation refers to changes in the measuring instrument over time. These changes are most likely to occur when the measurement involves humans, either as observers or interviewers. Thus, during a premeasurement, interviewers may be highly interested in the research and may take great care in explaining instructions and recording observations. By the time the postmeasurements are taken, the interviewers may have lost most or all of their interest and involvement, and their explanations may be less thorough and their recording less precise. Alternatively, inter-

[2] Campbell and Stanley, op. cit., 7–8.

viewers or observers may become more skilled with practice and perform better during the postmeasure.

In either case, any recorded change between the pre- and post-measures is a function of the change in the measuring instrument rather than the independent variable.

Selection (Design)

In most experimental designs, at least two groups are formed. *Selection error occurs when the groups formed for purposes of the experiment are initially unequal with respect to the dependent variable or in the propensity to respond to the independent variable.*

Random assignment to groups, the *matching* of subjects assigned to each, or *blocking* (this technique is described later) can minimize this problem. However, random assignment to groups still leaves the potential for selection error. In this case it would be equivalent to the sampling error.

Selection is a critical problem in *ex post facto* research as described in Chapter 11. It is also common in many basic research studies done at universities where students serve as experimental subjects. An unfortunately common occurrence is to assign students in one class to one group and students in another class to a second group. Even if the classes are different sections of the same course, the fact that they are taught at different times or by different professors indicates that the students in the classes may also vary, particularly on attitudinal dimensions.

Selection error occurs in applied studies as well. Any time subjects volunteer for particular groups, regardless of the basis for making the decision, that is, time of day, location, pay, or other reasons, the possibility of selection error may occur. For example, an experiment that requires three hours to complete and requires three groups could run one group from 9 to 12 in the morning, one group from 2 to 5 in the afternoon, and the third group from 7 to 10 in the evening. The experimenter could then request volunteers for each of these time periods. However, it is likely that people able and willing to volunteer for a morning session differ in a number of respects from those who come at a different time. Therefore, the researcher would need to control for possible selection error in this situation. An initial measurement of each group on the variable of interest can be used to ensure that the groups are equivalent on this variable.

Mortality (maturation) special case of mortality

Mortality does not imply that some experiments reduce the population. Rather, *mortality refers to the differential loss (refusal to continue in the experiment*) *of respondents from the various groups.*[3] By a differential loss we mean that some groups lose respondents that are different from those lost by other groups.

Assume that a company has developed a new toothbrush that although somewhat inconvenient to use, should greatly reduce the incidence of cavities. A number of children, aged 8 to 15, are selected and randomly assigned to two groups, one of which will receive the new toothbrushes. The respondents in each group are given dental checkups and told to brush their teeth in their normal manner for the following year. During the year's time, both groups will lose some members because of moving, accidents, loss of interest, and so forth. This may not involve any mortality error since, if the sample is large enough, it will affect both groups more or less equally.

However, the treatment group with the new "inconvenient" toothbrush will lose some members because of this inconvenience. Furthermore, those remaining in the treatment group are likely to be more concerned about their teeth than those who quit. Therefore, by the end of the year, the treatment group will have a higher percentage of respondents who are concerned about their teeth. These respondents are likely to brush more often, eat fewer sweets, and generally take better care of their teeth than the control group. This may be sufficient to cause a difference between the groups even if the new toothbrush itself has no effect.

Interaction   Collection

Interaction occurs when a premeasure changes the respondents' sensitivity or responsiveness to the independent variables(s). This sensitizing effect is particularly important in studies involving attitudes, brand awareness, and opinions.

A group of individuals may be given a questionnaire containing several attitude scales concerned with a particular brand or product category. These individuals are then likely to be particularly interested in, or sensitive to, advertisements and other activities involving these products. Thus, an increase, decrease, or change in, say, advertising is more likely to be noticed and reacted to by these individuals than by a group who did not receive the initial questionnaire. This heightened sensitivity will often increase the effect of whatever change was made in the marketing variable and will be reflected in the postmeasurement.

It is important to note how interaction differs from direct premeasurement effects. In the example on direct premeasurement effects, the individual involved was never exposed to the independent variable. *All* of the change was caused by the initial measurement itself. In contrast, inter-

---

[3] Campbell and Stanley, op. cit., 5.

action does *not* require any direct effects from the initial measurement. It simply means that the independent variable is more likely to be noticed and reacted to than it would be without the initial measurement. This distinction is important as experimental designs that will control direct premeasurement effects will not necessarily control interaction effects.

Reactive Errors   *Problem definition*

Reactive errors occur when the artificiality of some experimental situations or the behavior of the experimenter cause effects that emphasize, dampen, or alter any effects caused by the treatment variable.[4] The reason for this is that human subjects do not respond passively to experimental situations. Rather, for some subjects at least, the experiment takes on aspects of a problem-solving experience in which the subject must first discover the experimental hypothesis and then produce the anticipated behavior.[5]

Reactive errors cannot be controlled for by the experimental design. Rather, they must be controlled for by the structure of the experimental situation. Since reactive arrangements are most critical in laboratory experiments, a detailed discussion of the problem they pose is delayed until the section on laboratory experiments.

Measurement Timing   *Problem definition*

We often have an unfortunate tendency to assume that the impact of any independent variable is both immediate and permanent. Thus, experimenters occasionally manipulate an independent variable (price or advertising, for example), take an immediate measure of the dependent variable (sales), and then move on to the next problem. The danger in such an approach is that the immediate impact of the independent variable is different from its long range impact. For example, the short-run effect of point-of-purchase displays is generally greater than the long-run effect.[6]

Errors of measurement timing occur when postmeasurement is made at an inappropriate time to indicate the effect of the experimental treatment. Consider the following example. Weekly sales of a product are measured in two equivalent groups of stores. Average sales in each group equal 100 units per week per store. The product is placed in a point-of-purchase

---

[4] An excellent discussion of this area is provided by M. T. Orne, "On the Social Psychology of the Psychological Experiment: With Particular Reference to Demand Characteristics and Their Implications," *American Psychologist,* **17** (1962), 776–783; also see C. A. Kiesler, B. E. Collins, N. Millar, *Attitude Change* (New York: John Wiley & Sons, Inc., 1969), 44–81.

[5] Orne, op. cit., 779.

[6] J. F. Engel, D. T. Kollat, and R. D. Blackwell, *Consumer Behavior,* 2nd ed. (New York: Holt, Rinehart and Winston, Inc., 1973), 473–478.

display in one group (treatment group) and is left in its usual shelf location in the second group (control group) of stores. Sales are measured for each group during the first week of the point-of-purchase display. Average sales for the treatment group are 120 units compared to 105 for the control group. The point-of-purchase display appears to have caused an average sales increase of 15 units per store.

If the researcher stops here, however, he is likely to reach an incorrect conclusion concerning the magnitude of the effect of the display. Measurements made after the first week or so of a point-of-purchase display typically show a decline in sales, often below the initial level. Thus, a part of the impact is simply a result of consumers stocking up on the product. Table 12–1 illustrates the general nature of these findings.

The researcher must be certain that his measurements, both before and after, are made over a sufficient time period to indicate the effect of the independent variable.

Table 12–1   Impact of Measurement Timing on Point-of-Purchase Experiments

	Measure-ment (1)	Intro-duction of P-O-P	(2)	Measurement (3)	(4)	(5)
Point-of-Purchase Group	100	X	120	110	105	112
Control Group	100		105	105	108	109

Summary of Types of Experimental Errors

The nine types of experimental errors, summarized in the following list, represent potential sources of error and do not necessarily affect all experiments. In general, experiments that utilize human respondents who are aware of some or all aspects of the experiment are most subject to these types of error. Those experiments that are concerned with nonhuman units, such as stores or geographic territories, are least subject to the various types of experimental error.

Potential Sources of Experimental Error

I. Premeasurement: changes in the dependent variable that are solely the result of the impact of the initial measurement.

II. Maturation: biological or psychological processes that systematically vary with the passage of time, independent of specific external events, and affect the measurement of the dependent variable.

III. History: the impact of extraneous variables on the dependent variable.

IV. Instrumentation: changes in the measuring instrument over time.
 V. Selection: assignment of experimental units to groups such that the groups are initially unequal on the dependent variable or in the propensity to respond to the independent variable.
 VI. Mortality: the loss of a unique type of respondent from one of the experimental groups.
 VII. Interaction: an increase (or decrease) in the effect of the independent variable because of a sensitizing effect of the premeasure.
VIII. Reactive error: effect(s) on the dependent variable caused by the artificiality of the experimental situation and/or the behavior of the experimenter.
 IX. Measurement timing: measuring the dependent variable at a point in time that will not reflect the actual impact of the independent variable(s).

All of the various types of error, except reactive errors and measurement timing, can be controlled for by the experimental design. In general, the more controls that are built into the design the more costly the experiment becomes. In addition, a design that is very efficient in controlling for some types of errors may be relatively inefficient with respect to others. Therefore, experiments should be designed to control for those errors that are *most probable* and are believed to be *most serious* in a given situation, not for all potential sources of error.

Experimental Designs

A number of experimental designs have been developed to overcome or reduce the various types of experimental errors. Experimental designs can be categorized into two broad groups: *basic* designs and *statistical* designs. Basic designs consider the impact of only one independent variable at a time whereas statistical designs allow the evaluation of the effect of more than one independent variable. Before any specific designs can be described, it is necessary to introduce the symbols that are used in their descriptions:

MB = *before measurement:* a measurement made on the dependent variable prior to the introduction or manipulation of the independent variable.
MA = *after measurement:* a measurement made on the dependent variable after the introduction or manipulation of the independent variable.
 X = *treatment:* the actual introduction or manipulation of the independent variable.
 R = designation that the group is selected randomly.

Any symbol that is to the *right* of another symbol indicates that the activity represented occurred *after* the one to its left.

A group in which the independent variable is manipulated is called a *treatment group*. A *control group* is one in which the independent variable remains unaltered. The following discussion of experimental designs does not include comments on measurement timing or reactive errors since the experimental design itself cannot control these forms of experimental error.

Basic Experimental Designs

After-Only Design

The *after-only* design involves manipulating the independent variable and following this with an after measurement, or

$$X \quad MA$$

This is often called a "tryout" rather than an experiment. However, it is a useful starting point and it does approximate a common "experiment" conducted by businessmen. Consider a retailer who decides to take out a full-page advertisement in the student newspaper at a nearby university. The advertisement features a one-day sale on slacks. The retailer records the number of pairs of slacks sold on the sale day. He believes that this is substantially above the amount he would have sold had he not advertised in the student newspaper and decides to continue using this medium to advertise slacks.[7]

After-only designs are subject to a number of potential errors, particularly *history*. This is a critical problem because it is difficult to separate the effects, if any, of the independent variable from those of extraneous variables. This shortcoming makes the after-only design one of the least useful experimental designs.

Before-After Design

The before-after design is like the after-only except that it also involves a before measurement:

$$MB \quad X \quad MA$$

The result of interest is the *difference* between the before and after measurements $(MA - MB)$. This comparison gives this design a considerable advantage over the after-only design. If no errors exist, the difference between the two measures is caused by the independent variable.

[7] A report of a similar utilization of this approach is presented by A. S. Donnahoe, "The Great Roe Herring Experiment," *Richmond Times Dispatch* (undated).

Unfortunately, the before-after design is subject to a number of experimental errors. *History, maturation, pretest, instrumentation, mortality,* and *interaction* all *may* effect the results of this design. However, if our experimental units are stores and we are measuring sales, the only source of error that is likely to be important is history.

One study used this approach to estimate the effect of a price increase on market share. The price of two leading brands of piecrust mix was increased by $.02 per box within a supermarket chain. The prices of the other three brands remained the same. Market share was measured both before and after the price change and it was found to drop almost 4 per cent for the leading brand and 13 per cent for the second leading brand.[8]

Since history was not controlled for, attributing the market share decline to price involves judgment. The decline *may* have been caused by competitors' actions, quality control problems, or other factors. The researcher may be willing to estimate subjectively the impact of any of these variables rather than going to the expense of adding a control group. There are many occasions when this is a very reasonable procedure. However, the researcher must be alert to the possibility that extraneous variables caused the results rather than the independent variable.

The before-after design is a common approach in decision making. Prices are increased, packaging is altered, advertising is expanded, and commission systems are installed without the use of control groups. Before measures are compared to after measures, and after allowing judgmentally for the effects of other variables, the differences are attributed to the independent variable. However, unless the researcher is confident that extraneous variables are not operating, or that he can make estimates of their effects within acceptable limits of error, before-after designs should be avoided.

Simulated Before-After Design

In the *simulated before-after design,* an attempt is made to control some of the errors that influence the standard before-after design when individuals serve as respondents. The design controls for premeasurement and interaction errors by using separate groups for the before and after measurements:

$$R \quad MB \quad X$$
$$R \quad\quad\quad X \quad MA$$

As in the standard before-after design, the measure of interest is the difference between *MA* and *MB*. Since different individuals receive the before and after measurements, there can be no *premeasurement* or *interaction*

[8] E. W. Hawkins, "Methods of Estimating Demand," *Journal of Marketing* (April 1957), 428–438.

effects. However, the remaining problems associated with the standard before-after design, particularly *history,* remain.

This design is common in advertising research. A typical application of it involves giving a large sample of respondents a questionnaire to measure their attitude toward the product (premeasurement). An advertising campaign is then conducted (change in the independent variable). Finally, a *second* sample of respondents are given the same attitude questionnaire as the first group (postmeasurement). If the sampling is done properly and the two samples are large enough, they should be similar in terms of their initial attitude. Thus, any difference in the two scores can be attributed to the effects of the advertising campaign *and* any effects produced by history.

Before-After with Control Design

The *before-after with control* design involves the addition of a control group to the standard before-after design discussed previously:

$$R \quad MB_1 \quad X \quad MA_1$$
$$R \quad MB_2 \quad\quad MA_2$$

The addition of the control group allows for the control of all the potential sources of experimental error, except *mortality* and *interaction.* For example, assume that a firm wishes to test the impact of a point-of-purchase display.[9] Ten retail stores in the firm's trade area are selected at random for inclusion in the treatment group and 10 are selected for the control group. Sales are measured in each group of stores before and after the introduction of the new point-of-purchase display. The *change* in sales between the two groups is compared. That is, the measure of interest is

$$(MB_1 - MA_1) - (MB_2 - MA_2).$$

This comparison controls for any initial inequalities between the sales of the two groups. Similarly, direct premeasurement effects are controlled. Both groups receive the premeasurement, and any changes caused by this should influence both after measures equally. In this example, premeasurement effects are unlikely to influence sales (unless the sales personnel suspect that *their* performance is being monitored). *History, maturation,* and *instrumentation* should also affect both treatment and control groups equally.

The before-after with control group design is subject to *interaction* effects. Suppose a researcher is interested in the effect on attitudes of a single direct mail advertisement. He selects a group of respondents and

[9] For examples of the use of this design to test point-of-purchase promotions see *Motion Moves More Merchandise* (New York: Point-of-Purchase Advertising Institute, undated), and M. L. Mckenna, "The Influence of In-Store Advertising," in J. Newman, *On Knowing the Consumer* (New York: John Wiley & Sons, Inc., 1966), 114–115.

administers a premeasurement to all of them. Half of the respondents then receive the direct mail advertisement (treatment group) and half receive nothing (control group). One week after the advertisement is delivered, both groups of respondents are remeasured.

Any direct effect, that is, learning or attitude change, caused by the premeasurement should affect both groups equally. However, if the premeasure serves to increase the respondent's interest or curiosity in the brand, the treatment and the control group may be affected differently. Those respondents in the treatment group will receive a direct mail advertisement from the firm that they may read simply because of the interest generated by the premeasurement.

The effect of the premeasurement (increased interest) *interacts* with the independent variable (advertising) to influence the aftermeasurement (change of attitude). The control group may also experience increased interest because of the premeasure. However, since the control group will not be exposed to the advertising, the increased interest will dissipate without influencing the aftermeasurement of attitudes. The overall result of this is that any conclusions about the effects of the advertising campaign may only be generalized to individuals who have taken the premeasurement.

In cases where interaction is unlikely and control for possible selection error is important, the before-after with control group design is probably the best design in terms of cost and error control. One example of this design involved a comparison of various channels of distribution for reaching low volume accounts.[10] Two treatment groups (mail-order and wholesale distributors) and one control group (the current distribution method —direct sales) were used:

$$
\begin{array}{cccc}
R & MB_1 & X_1 & MA_1 \\
R & MB_2 & X_2 & MA_2 \\
R & MB_3 & & MA_3
\end{array}
$$

The measures were of net profit contribution so interaction was not a problem. The before measures were needed to ensure initial equality between the groups since small samples were used. The findings resulted in a shift to wholesale distributors for low volume accounts.

After-Only with Control

The before measure in the before-after with control group design introduces the possibility of uncontrolled *interaction* effects. In addition, before measures generally cost money and may increase the artificiality of the overall situation. They are necessary whenever there is a reasonable

[10] C. H. Sevin, *Marketing Productivity Analysis* (New York, McGraw-Hill Book Company, 1965), 96–98.

probability that the treatment and control groups are not initially equivalent on the dependent variables. If it is likely that the groups are in fact initially equal on the variable of interest, then there is no reason to go to the expense of a before measure and an *after-only with control* design can be used:

$$R \quad X_1 \quad MA_1$$
$$R \qquad\quad MA_2$$

This design explicitly controls for everything that the before-after with control does except selection error. That is, even using random assignment, it is possible for the two groups to be initially unequal on the variable of interest. However, it does eliminate the possibility of interaction. It is appropriate any time selection error is not likely to be a problem. It is uniquely appropriate when selection error is not a problem *and* interaction is.

One application of this technique in measuring advertising effectiveness involved approximately 1,200 consumers randomly divided into two treatment groups and one control group.[11] The large number of respondents in each group (approximately 400) and the use of random assignment should minimize selection error. Each group was given a redeemable coupon for the product of interest. The two treatment groups each saw a different commercial for the product whereas the control group did not see the commercial. The aftermeasure was the percentage of coupons redeemed by each group. Comparisons were made between the control group after measurement and each treatment group after measurement.

Solomon Four-Group Design

The *Solomon four-group design,* often called the *four-group six-study design,* has been described as the "ideal model for controlled experiments."[12] It consists of four groups, two treatment and two control, and six measurements, two before measurements and four aftermeasurements. Hence, the *four-group six-study* designation. An examination of the following diagram shows the overall design to consist of a before-after with control experiment and an after-only with control experiment run simultaneously.

$$R \quad MB_1 \quad X \quad MA_1$$
$$R \quad MB_2 \qquad\quad MA_2$$
$$R \qquad\qquad X \quad MA_3$$
$$R \qquad\qquad\qquad MA_4$$

[11] W. J. Jennsen, "Sales Effect of TV, Radio, and Print Advertising," *Journal of Advertising Research,* **6** (June 1966), 2–7.

[12] S. L. Payne, "The Ideal Model for Controlled Experiments," *Public Opinion Quarterly,* **XV** (Fall 1951), 557–562.

This design explicitly controls for all sources of experimental error except *measurement timing* and *reactive error,* which are not subject to control by designs. No single method of analysis makes use of all six measurements simultaneously.[13] However, direct estimates of the effect of interaction and selection, as well as other experimental errors, can be made by various between group analyses.

Despite the virtues of this design, no instances of its use in applied marketing research have been reported. The only time such an approach would be needed is when both selection error and interaction are likely to cause serious distortions of the data. Even in this case, the cost of securing two additional groups and making four additional measurements may well exceed the cost of controlling for selection error through a larger sample size and using an after-only with control group design to control for interaction.

Conclusions Concerning Basic Designs

Table 12–2 summarizes the *potential* errors that may affect each design. A + indicates that the design controls for this type error, a − indicates

Table 12–2   Experimental Designs and Potential Errors*

	History	*Maturation*	*Premeasurement*	*Instrumentation*	*Selection*	*Mortality*	*Interaction*	*Reactive Error*	*Measurement Timing*
1. After-Only	−	−	+	+	−	0	+	0	0
2. Before-After	−	−	−	−	+	0	−	0	0
3. Simulated Before-After	−	−	+	−	−	0	+	0	0
4. Before-After with Control	+	+	+	+	+	+	−	0	0
5. After-Only with Control	+	+	+	+	−	−	+	0	0
6. Solomon Four-Group	+	+	+	+	+	+	+	0	0

* A + indicates that a method of controlling for the error is provided by the design; a − indicates no method of controlling is incorporated in the design; and an 0 indicates that the error is irrelevant to the design.

[13] Campbell and Stanley, op. cit., 25.

that it is vulnerable to it, an 0 indicates that the type of design is irrelevant for this type of error. *Potential errors* are not the same as *actual errors*.

Statistical Designs

Statistical designs permit the measurement of the impact of more than one independent variable. They also allow the researcher to control for specific extraneous variables that he believes may confound his results. Finally, statistical designs permit an economical design when more than one measurement will be conducted on each respondent.

Completely Randomized Design

The *completely randomized design (CRD)* is the basic before-after with control group described in the preceding section expanded to contain more than one level or form of the independent variable.[14] The critical feature is that the experimental units are assigned to the groups on a random basis. Thus, a fairly large sample size and/or a relatively homogeneous population are needed for the CRD design to function effectively.

The control group need not consist of an absence of the independent variable. For example, three versions of a new product, advertisement, or package could be tested. The researcher is interested in *which* version is most acceptable to the market.

The standard form of analysis for a CRD is a one-way analysis of variance. This technique indicates the probability of obtaining observed differences between treatment means given random assignment to groups. (Analysis of variance is discussed in Chapter 14.)

Completely randomized designs are not widely used in field experiments in marketing. The general use of small samples, the presence of strong confounding variables, and a wide divergence among experimental units on common dependent variables such as sales limits its applicability. However, it is a useful model for many laboratory experiments where individuals serve as the experimental units.

Randomized Blocks Design

Completely randomized designs are based on the assumptions that the experimental groups are relatively similar on the dependent variable and

---

[14] A detailed examination of the CRD is provided by C. M. Dayton, *The Design of Educational Experiments* (New York: McGraw-Hill Book Company, 1970), Chap. 2.

that the members of these groups will react to the independent variable in a similar manner. These assumptions are frequently invalid.

Consider the following two experimental situations:

1. A field experiment to determine which of three price levels to utilize has a total of 27 stores available as experimental units. The sales volume of the stores ranges from $300,000 to $800,000 per month. Sales of the product in question tend to vary closely with total store sales. In this situation, a CRD would not be appropriate since the probability of randomly selecting equivalent samples would be small.
2. A field experiment is to be conducted to decide upon an advertising theme for a new liquour. The primary issue is whether to use a masculine theme, a feminine theme, or a more sexually neutral theme. Six advertisements are prepared that represent different positions along a masculine-feminine appeal dimension. Management suspects that the reaction of the advertisement will be strongly influenced by the gender of the respondent. Again, a CRD would not be appropriate since the effects of the respondent's sex could not be easily determined.

Randomized blocks designs (*RBD*) are appropriate for situations in which the researcher suspects that there is one major external variable, such as total sales or sex of the respondents, which might influence his results. Of course, he must be able to identify or measure this variable before he can utilize a RBD. In RBD, the experimental units are *blocked,* that is, grouped or stratified, on the basis of the extraneous, or *blocking, variable.*

The basic idea behind RBD is the same as that underlying stratified random sampling. By ensuring that the various experimental and control groups are matched as closely as possible on the extraneous variable, we are assured that it affects all groups more or less equally. Furthermore, by isolating statistically the impact of the independent variable on the blocks, we can determine if the independent variable interacts with the blocking variable.

The principles and advantages of RBD can be seen by re-examining the two research situations presented at the beginning of this section. In the first situation, the researcher was faced with the problem of selecting 3 groups from 27 stores with a wide range of sales. Total sales were believed to be an extraneous variable that could confound the experimental results. A RBD is appropriate since the stores can be grouped by sales level.

First, the stores are rank ordered in terms of sales. The total number of experimental units, 27, is divided by the number of experimental groups, 3, to determine how many blocks are needed, 9. The experimental units are then systematically assigned to the 9 blocks such that the top 3 ranked stores are assigned to the first block, the second 3 to the second block, and so forth. Finally, 1 unit from each block is *randomly* assigned to each of the treatment groups. Table 12–3 illustrates this process.

In the situation involving the masculine versus feminine advertisements, the concern is somewhat different. In this situation, it is possible to secure a large enough group of men and women to assure adequate comparability of test and control groups. Rather than lack of comparability, the concern here is with isolating the impact of type of theme on the male and female subgroups as well as the total group. Again, a RBD represents an efficient approach.

Assume that a total sample of 800 males and 400 females is available. Individuals are assigned to blocks based on their gender, producing one block of 400 females and one block of 800 males. The individuals within each block are *randomly* assigned to treatment groups. The use of analysis of variance then allows the researcher to determine the impact of the

Table 12–3   RBD to Increase Experimental Precision

Block Number	Store Rank	Treatment Groups		
		X_1	X_2	X_3
1	1, 2, 3	3	2	1
2	4, 5, 6	4	5	6
3	7, 8, 9	9	7	8
4	10, 11, 12	10	11	12
5	13, 14, 15	14	13	15
6	16, 17, 18	17	18	16
7	19, 20, 21	20	19	21
8	22, 23, 24	22	23	24
9	25, 26, 27	25	26	27

commercial on the overall group, the impact of gender on the measurement, and the impact of any interaction between gender and the commercial (that is, a differential impact on males and females).

An RBD was used in a test of the effects of a countertop carousel display for a Dacron felt tip marker.[15] The marker was distributed through drugstores, stationery stores, and a number of similar outlets. The researchers, who wanted to estimate both the total impact of the new display and its effect in each store type, blocked on store type.

A judgment sample of four drugstores and four stationery stores was selected. Two stores from each block were randomly selected to receive the new display whereas the remaining two stores in each block main-

[15] P. J. McClure and E. J. West, "Sales Effects of a New Counter Display," *Journal of Advertising Research,* **9** (March 1969), 29–34. For additional examples see S. Banks, *Experimentation in Marketing* (New York: McGraw-Hill Book Co., 1965), Chap. 4.

tained the old displays. Average weekly sales for the three weeks prior to the new display served as a premeasure and average sales for the three weeks following the new display functioned as the postmeasure.

The results were a 16.1 per cent increase in sales in drugstores with the new display; a 15.8 per cent increase in stationery stores with the new display, and a 4.1 per cent decline in both drug- and stationery stores with the old display. The conclusion was, subject to sample size and other limitations, that the new display increased sales and did so equally well in both types of stores.

In general, RBDs are more useful than completely random designs since most marketing studies are affected by such extraneous variables as store type or size, region of the country, and sex, income, or social class of the respondent. The major shortcoming of RBDs is that they can only control for *one* extraneous variable. When there is a need to control for or block on more than one variable, the researcher must utilize Latin square or factorial designs.

Latin Square Designs

Latin square designs allow the researcher to control statistically for two noninteracting extraneous variables in addition to the independent variable.[16] This control is achieved by a blocking technique similar to that described in the previous section on randomized blocks designs.

This design requires that each extraneous or blocking variable be divided into an equal number of blocks or levels, such as, drug stores, supermarkets, discount stores. The independent variable must be divided into the same number of levels, such as, high price, medium price, low price. A Latin square design is shown in the form of a table with the rows representing the blocks on one extraneous variable and the columns representing the blocks on the other. The levels of the independent variable are then assigned to the cells in the table such that each level appears once (and only once) in each row and each column.

The rule that requires an equal number of blocks in each extraneous variable forces the table described to be perfectly square. Thus, the name for the design. Latin square designs are described on the basis of the number of blocks on the extraneous variables. A design with three blocks is called a *3 × 3 Latin square,* four blocks is a *4 × 4 Latin square,* and so forth.

The first step in constructing a Latin square design is to construct a table with the blocks on the extraneous variables associated with the rows and columns such as the following example:

[16] K. K. Cox and B. M. Enis, *Experimentation for Marketing Decisions* (Scranton, Pa.: International Textbook Co., 1969), 48.

Time Period	Store Type		
	Drug	*Supermarket*	*Discount*
1			
2			
3			

Next, we randomly assign the levels of the independent variable (say, price) to the nine cells of the table such that each of the three price levels is assigned once and only once to each row and each column.

This is, in fact, a simple procedure. The first step is to assign the three price levels randomly to each cell in row 1:

1	price 2	price 3	price 1

Next, price level 1 or 3 should be randomly assigned to row 2, column 1. Since price 2 is already in column 1, it is not eligible to appear again.

1	price 2	price 3	price 1
2	price 1		

These four random assignments completely determine a 3×3 Latin square since the "once to each row and column" rule will automatically specify which treatment goes into each of the remaining cells:

Time Period	Store Type		
	Drug	*Supermarket*	*Discount*
1	Price 2	Price 3	Price 1
2	Price 1	Price 2	Price 3
3	Price 3	Price 1	Price 2

Latin square designs are widely used in marketing research. They are particularly useful in retail oriented studies where the need to control for store type or size and time period is particularly acute.[17] The Latin square

[17] For example, see J. R. Kennedy, "The Effect of Display Location on the Sales and Pilferage of Cigarettes," *Journal of Marketing Research,* **7** (May 1970), 210–215; J. A. Kotzan and R. W. Evanson, "Responsiveness of Drugstore Sales to Shelf Space Allocations," *Journal of Marketing Research,* **6** (November 1969), 465–469; and H. F. Kruedeberg, "The Significance of Consumer Response to Display Space Reallocation," in P. R. McDonald, *Marketing Involvement in Society and the Economy* (Chicago: American Marketing Association, 1969), 336–339.

design also allows the minimization of sample size by allowing the same experimental units to react to all the different levels of the independent variable.

A 4 × 4 Latin square design was used to measure the impact of three common promotional claims on consumers' product evaluations.[18] The researchers were interested in the influence of the claims: (X_1) NEW!, (X_2) IMPROVED!, and (X_3) NEW! IMPROVED! A comparison group (X_4) with no such claims added to the basic package served as the fourth level of the independent variable.

Since the researchers wanted to see if product type had any impact, four blocks of the extraneous variable "products" were used. Four groups of subjects were exposed to each advertising claim. The final design was:

	Subject Groups			
Products	A	B	C	D
Facial Tissue	X_1	X_2	X_3	X_4
Hosiery	X_2	X_3	X_4	X_1
Scouring Cleanser	X_3	X_4	X_1	X_2
Underarm Deoderant	X_4	X_1	X_2	X_3

Respondents evaluated the "brands" on a semantic differential instrument. The resulting data were analyzed by the analysis of variance technique. Based on this study, the researchers concluded that " 'new' and 'improved' promotional package claims (compared to no claims) have no significant effect on evaluations of certain household and personal care products."[19]

Latin square designs suffer from several limitations. First, the requirement of an equal number of rows, columns, and treatment levels can sometimes pose problems for specific research tasks. For example, if we want to test four versions of a product and to control for time and store type, we must be able to isolate four store types. Furthermore, we must run the study for four time periods. If there are only three types of stores that carry this product, or if time is of critical importance, the Latin square must be altered.

Another drawback to the Latin square design is that only two extrane-

---

[18] M. L. Dean, J. F. Engel, W. W. Talarzyk, "The Influence of Package Copy Claims on Consumer Product Evaluations," *Journal of Marketing Research,* **36** (April 1972), 34–39.
[19] Dean, et al., op. cit., 38.

ous variables can be controlled for at once. However, there is a relatively simple expansion of the technique, called a *Graeco-Latin square,* which permits the control of an additional variable.[20]

When several versions of a treatment variable, such as price, are applied to one control variable, such as a store, Latin square designs assume that there are no "carry-over" effects from one condition to another. Thus, the design assumes that a low price in time period 1 will not affect the sales in time period 2 when a higher price is in effect. Clearly such assumptions are not always valid, and there have been several versions of the Latin square design created to deal with this type of problem. One such version, called the *double change-over* design, consists of standard Latin squares in which the sequence of treatments in the two squares is reversed.[21]

A final weakness of the Latin square design is the restriction that the control variables cannot interact with each other or with the independent variable. As the next section demonstrates, interaction between variables is fairly common in marketing.[22]

Factorial Design

Factorial designs are used to measure the effect of two or more independent variables at various levels. They are particularly useful when there is some reason to believe that the various levels of the independent variables might interact to produce results that neither could produce alone.[23] For example, assume that we are testing a new carbonated fruit drink designed for the preteen-age market. We need to decide how much carbonation and how much sweetener to put into the drink. Five levels of carbonation and five levels of sweetener cover the range of each of these variables.

How do we determine which combination of carbonation and sweetener to use? We could select one level of sweetener and add the five levels of carbonation to this level of sweetener, have a group of preteen-agers taste test the resulting five combinations and select their favorite version. Then we could repeat this operation in reverse to determine the level of sweetener. Unfortunately this approach does not take into account any interaction between the level of sweetener and the level of carbonation.

It is possible that low-carbonation drinks should be very sweet and high-carbonation drinks should not be very sweet. The most preferred

---

[20] Banks, op. cit., 168–179.

[21] See Banks, op. cit., Chap. 6, and S. K. Plasman, "Single Sample Commercial Testing," *Journal of Advertising Research,* **13** (December 1973), 39–42.

[22] C. W. Holland and D. W. Cravens, "Fractional Factorial Experimental Designs in Marketing Research," *Journal of Marketing Research,* **X** (August 1973), 272.

[23] Cox and Enis, op. cit., 62.

combination might lie somewhere between these extremes. A factorial design can uncover this type of information.

In depicting a factorial design in a table, each level of one variable can represent a row and each level of another variable can represent a column. Factorial designs require a cell for every possible combination of treatment variables. Therefore, this example would require a table such as Table 12–4 with 5 × 5 or 25 cells. The hypothetical values in the cells shown in Table 12–4 represent measurements of the taste reactions of 100 preteenagers who sampled all 25 versions of the product. The rating scale ranged from 0 (strongly dislike) to 20 (strongly like).

Table 12–4 5^2 Factorial Design

	Sweetness				
Carbonation Level	1	2	3	4	5
1	2	4	7	10	12
2	2	3	4	7	8
3	4	6	8	5	5
4	10	15	11	6	4
5	13	9	6	3	2

Statistically, an analysis of variance can determine the effect on stated preference of carbonation level, sweetness, and the interaction beween the two. Obviously this is of great value in many research studies.[24] However, the increase in measurement capabilities gained by using factorial designs is purchased at the expense of greater complexity, more measurements, and higher costs.

For example, if a third variable were included in the example, such as color or flavoring, with 5 levels the number of cells would increase to 125. The same 3 variables could be analyzed experimentally by means of a Latin square design with only 25 cells. However, the Latin square design will not detect interaction. Therefore, in cases where interaction is suspected, some form of a factorial design is required.

A 2 × 3 factorial design was used in a study of the effectiveness of "corrective" advertising.[25] The "2 × 3" description means that two vari-

[24] For example see W. D. Barclay, "Factorial Design in a Pricing Experiment," *Journal of Marketing Research,* **VI** (November 1969), 427–429; B. R. Miller and C. E. Strain, "Determining Promotional Effects by Experimental Design," *Journal of Marketing Research,* **VII** (November 1970), 513–516; and F. Wiseman, "Factor Interaction Effects in Mail Survey Response Rates," *Journal of Marketing Research,* **X** (August 1973), 330–333.

[25] R. F. Dyer and P. G. Kuehl, "The 'Corrective Advertising' Remedy of the FTC: An Experimental Evaluation," *Journal of Marketing,* **38** (January 1974), 48–54.

ables were involved, one with two levels and one with three. (A 2 × 3 × 5 factorial would involve three variables with 2, 3, and 5 levels, respectively.) One variable was the source of the message; (1) FTC-source message and (2) company-source message. The second variable was the strength of the message; (1) high-strength, (2) low-strength, (3) zero-strength. The dependent variables were "similar to widely used measures of advertising's communication effectiveness."[26] Although it is not possible to summarize all the findings of this research, it is of particular interest that interaction between source and message strength was critical for understanding the effect of corrective advertising. This finding could not have occurred without the use of a factorial design.

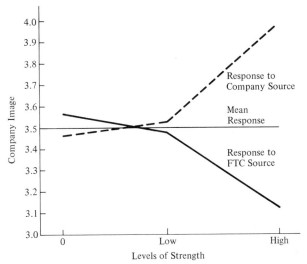

Figure 12–1 Source/strength interaction for trust-worthy-unscrupulous image. [R. F. Dyer and P. G. Kuehl, "The 'Corrective Advertising' Remedy of the FTC: An Experimental Evaluation," *Journal of Marketing, 38* (January 1974), 53. Reprinted by permission of the publisher.]

Figure 12–1 illustrates the interaction impact on one dimension—the firm's "trustworthy-unscrupulous" image. Notice that neither message strength nor company source has a differential impact on this dimension until the high strength condition is reached.

The primary disadvantage of factorial designs is the large number of treatments required when there are more than a few variables or levels of each variable. These large numbers are required if all interactions and main effects are to be measured separately. However, in many situations,

[26] Ibid., 50.

the researcher is interested in only a few of the possible interactions and main effects. In these cases a *fractional factorial design* may be used. As the title suggested, these designs consist of only a portion of a full factorial design.[27]

Conclusions Concerning Experimental Designs

The preceding sections have described a number of experimental designs. These designs have ranged from simple after-only design to factorial designs. No one design is *best*. The choice of the experimental design must balance cost constraints with accuracy requirements. Accuracy is related, of course, to the amount of error. However, we must avoid the habit of assuming that the possibility of an experimental error means that the error *will* occur. It *is* possible that history will *not* bias the results in a before-after design even though the design itself does not control for it. The researcher and the decision maker should apply judgment in deciding which errors represent sufficient potential danger to warrant additional outlays for control.

Experimental Environment

In the discussion of errors affecting experiments, the impact of the experimental environment (reactive error) was discussed briefly. There is ample evidence that the results of many marketing experiments are determined as much by the experimental environment as by the independent variable(s). This is a particularly severe problem for experiments using humans as the response group. To control for this type of error, we attempt to reduce the demand characteristics of the situation and to introduce as much realism into the study as possible.

Experimental environments can be classified according to the level of artificiality or realism that they contain. Artificiality involves eliciting behavior from the respondents in a situation that is different from the normal situation in which that behavior would occur. Thus, a taste test in which respondents are brought to a firm's product development laboratory, given three different versions of a soft drink in glasses labeled *L, M,* and *P,* asked to complete an eight-item semantic differential scale about each

---

[27] Holland and Cravens, op. cit., 270–276. For an applied example see R. C. Curhan, "The Effects of Merchandising and Temporary Promotional Activities on the Sales of Fresh Fruits and Vegetables in Supermarkets," *Journal of Marketing Research,* **11** (August 1974), 286–294.

"brand," and asked of which version, if any, they would like to receive a free carton, contains a high degree of artificiality.

At the other extreme, the three versions could be introduced into a number of stores or geographic areas accompanied by regular point-of-purchase displays, advertising, and pricing. Such an experiment is characterized by a high degree of realism.

The first study described represents a *laboratory experiment* whereas the second represents a *field experiment*. Laboratory experiments are characterized by a high degree of artificiality. Field experiments have a high level of realism. A given experiment may fall anywhere along this artificiality-realism continuum. Those nearer the artificiality end are termed laboratory experiments and those nearer the realism end are termed field experiments. Each general type of experiment has its particular strengths and weaknesses that are described in the following sections. In addition, a third type of experimental environment, *simulation,* is briefly described.

Laboratory Experiments

Laboratory experiments are widely used in marketing research in the initial testing of new products, package designs, advertising themes and copy, as well as in basic research studies. Laboratory experiments minimize the effects of history by "isolating the research in a physical situation apart from the routine of ordinary living and by manipulating one or more independent variables under rigorously specified, operationalized, and controlled conditions."[28] This degree of control is seldom possible in field experiments.

This isolation allows the researcher to be sure that the same experimental procedures will produce the same results if repeated with similar subjects. An advertisement, which elicits a positive response from a subject group when viewed under strictly controlled conditions through a pupilometer, will elicit the same, or nearly the same, positive response when replicated with other groups of similar subjects.

However, the executive in charge of advertising is not concerned with the ability of the advertisement to elicit positive responses from other groups of respondents looking into a pupilometer. His ultimate concern is the response of the individual when he is faced with the complexity of real world diversions such as children wanting to play, noise from the television, and projects needing completion. It is in situations such as this that the advertisement (or product or package) must finally perform.

The ability of the results in an experimental situation to predict the

---

[28] F. N. Kerlinger, *Foundations of Behavioral Research,* 2nd ed. (New York: Holt, Rinehart and Winston, Inc., 1973), 398.

results in the actual situation of interest to the researcher is called *predictive validity*. Unfortunately, laboratory experiments are generally somewhat weak in predictive validity. This weakness is a direct consequence of their primary strength. That is, the physical removal of most extraneous variables provide laboratory experiments with a high degree of *replicability* at the same time that it limits their predictive validity.

Laboratory experiments tend to cost substantially less in terms of resources and time than field experiments.[29] This has led many researchers to utilize laboratory experiments in the early stages of their research projects when they are concerned with developing one or a limited number of advertisements or products that excel under controlled conditions. Then, if the costs and risks warrant it, these versions are subjected to further tests in field experiments.

Reactive Arrangements in Laboratory Experiments

The very nature of a laboratory experiment may cause the respondent to react to the situation itself rather than to the independent variable (reactive error). There are two aspects to reactive errors: the *experimental situation* and the *experimenter*.

Subjects do not remain passive in an experimental situation. They attempt to understand what is going on about them. In addition, they typically attempt to behave as "expected." If there are cues in the environment suggesting that a certain type of behavior is appropriate, many subjects will conform in order to be "good" subjects.

For example, a group of volunteers are brought to a room and given an attitude questionnaire that focuses on several products. They then view a 30-minute tape of a television series with several commercials. One of these commercials relates to one of the products on the premeasure. The respondent may guess that an objective of the research is to try to change his attitude toward this product. And, if he does, he is likely to comply with the researcher's wishes.

This cannot be controlled by the experimental design. An after-only with control group would be the most appropriate design for this situation. Yet even with that design, some respondents would deduce that seeing a commercial about a product and then being asked about the product means that they should like the product. Thus, they may base their evaluations on what they think is expected of them rather than on their true reactions.

The only control for errors of this type is to use creative environments

---

[29] Cox and Enis, op. cit., 107.

and/or to design separate control conditions for suspected reactive arrangements. In the example, a relatively neutral advertisement for the same product could be shown to one group. If their attitudes are significantly more positive than those of a control group that saw no advertisement, we can assume that the reactive arrangements are causing at least some of the shift.

The impact of the *experimenter* is very similar to the influence of the personal interviewer in survey research. For example, a number of studies have shown that experimenter's expectations or hypotheses tend to be confirmed.[30]

In one study,[31] respondents were asked to estimate the level of success or failure of individuals shown in photographs. All of the experimenters were told that the purpose of the study was to replicate "well-established experimental findings." They were also paid a bonus to do a "good" job. Half the experimenters were led to expect a high rating (an average of + 5) from their respondents. The remaining experimenters were led to expect a low rating (an average of − 5) from their respondents. The respondents were, in fact, randomly assigned to each experimenter.

The mean rating obtained by those experimenters expecting a high rating was 4.05. The mean obtained by those expecting a low rating was − .95. Thus, when the experimenter's expectation is coupled with some form of vested interest in seeing it confirmed, the results should be viewed with suspicion. Yet, in many marketing experiments, the experimenter is involved in the formulation of the experimental hypothesis and certainly has a stake in seeing it confirmed.

Experimenter effects can be limited by some of the same techniques used to reduce interviewer bias. For example, the experimenter should, to the extent possible, remain unaware of the hypotheses of the research. Of course, experimenters, like respondents, do not remain passive in an experimental situation. Therefore, it is likely that they will form hypotheses of their own early in the experiment. The best answer appears to be to use highly trained experimenters, keep them uninformed about the research hypotheses, and minimize their contact with the respondents. Tape recordings, written instructions, and other impersonal means of communication should be used whenever feasible.

[30] See M. Venkatesan, "Laboratory Experiments in Marketing: The Experimenter Effect," *Journal of Marketing Research,* **4** (May 1967), 142–146; J. P. Sutcliffe, "On the Role of Instructions to the Subject in Psychological Experiments," *American Psychologist,* **25** (August 1972), 755–758; and R. W. Johnson and J. G. Adair, "The Effects of Systematic Recording Error versus Experimenter Bias on Latency of Word Association," *Journal of Experimental Research in Personality,* **4** (October 1970), 270–275.

[31] R. Rosenthal and K. L. Fode, "Psychology of the Scientist: Three Experiments in Experimenter Bias," *Psychological Reports,* **12** (April 1963), 491–511.

Field Experiments

Field experiments are characterized by a high degree of realism. The typical manner of obtaining this realism in marketing studies is to vary the independent variable in the marketplace. Unfortunately, field experiments are also characterized by a relative lack of control.[32] This lack of control often extends to the independent variable as well as extraneous variables.

For example, many field experiments require cooperation from wholesalers and/or retailers. However, this cooperation is often difficult to secure. Retailers who have a policy of price cutting may refuse to carry a product at the specified price, or they may be reluctant to assign prime shelf-facings to an untried product.

Control of extraneous variables is even more difficult. Such factors as bad weather, adverse legal decisions, strikes in pertinent industries, and campaigns by competitors are beyond the control of the researcher. In fact, such occurrences may occur without the researcher becoming aware of them.

Field experiments are probably less common in marketing than are laboratory experiments. However, greater reliance tends to be placed on their results and they are often used as a final "check" on new products prior to nationwide introduction. This procedure is known as *test marketing*.

Test Marketing

Test marketing represents a particular type of field experiment that is often conducted in conjunction with the development of a new consumer product. Test marketing involves the duplication of the planned national marketing program for a product in one or more limited geographical areas, usually cities. Often, differing levels of marketing mix variables are used in the test markets to help management isolate the best combination for the national introduction.

The two primary goals of most test market programs are the determination of market interest in the product and the testing of alternative marketing mixes.[33] A major additional value comes from alerting management to unsuspected problems and opportunities associated with the new prod-

---

[32] See K. P. Uhl, "Field Experimentation: Some Problems, Pitfalls, and Perspective," in *Science, Technology and Marketing* (Chicago: American Marketing Association, Fall 1966), 561–572.

[33] P. Kotler, *Marketing Management,* 2nd ed. (Englewood Cliffs, N.J.: Prentice-Hall, Inc., 1972), 498.

uct.[34] This value is reflected in the comment of a leading test marketer: "We want to see if the market plan meshes and get a gut feel about the risks of national rollout."[35]

This statement is probably an accurate appraisal of the type of information that most test markets generate although it may understate the ability of test marketing to improve specific aspects of the marketing plan. In one survey, it was found that, although there was wide variation, the "average" market test: (1) utilized three test areas, (2) lasted about ten months, (3) used both store audits and consumer surveys to document the impact of the marketing mix, (4) tested different levels of one or more marketing mix variables, particularly advertising, and (5) was conducted in a "normal" market environment.[36]

In addition to advertising levels, price and consumer promotions were the most common mix variables that were tested. For example, General Foods tested its *American Recipe* frozen vegetables in Phoenix and Syracuse. Both the price and advertising were higher in Syracuse.[37] This enabled the researchers to compare these two total products with each other as well as with management's objectives.

Disadvantages of Test Markets. All of the comments made earlier concerning after-only designs apply to most test market situations. In addition, it is important to note that in most test marketing programs only two or three versions of the overall marketing mix are tested. Thus, the fact that the tested versions do not prove successful (in terms of management's expectations) may not leave a clear-cut basis for eliminating other versions of the total product. Most marketers approach this problem by extensive consumer testing prior to test marketing. These consumer tests are often in the form of laboratory experiments. As a result of these preliminary tests, the researcher can often identify two to six versions of the total product that appear most likely to succeed. These are then subjected to test marketing.

One of the goals for most test marketing programs is to project the sales of the test product from the test area to the entire market. To increase "projectability" the researcher must increase the representativeness of his test areas. This generally requires more and larger test cities. However, the more and the larger the areas tested, the greater is the cost of the test.

---

[34] A. A. Achenbaum, "The Purpose of Test Marketing," in R. M. Kaplan, ed., *The Marketing Concept in Action* (Chicago: American Marketing Association, 1964), 582.

[35] S. Scanlon, "Test Markets/Is the Chemistry Changing?", *Sales Management,* **110** (April 16, 1973), 33.

[36] V. B. Churchill, Jr., "New Product Test Marketing—An Overview of the Current Scene," an address to the Midwest Conference on Successful New Marketing Research Techniques, March 3, 1971.

[37] Scanlon, op. cit., 32.

Therefore, the researcher, as usual, must trade off accuracy for cost. The Bayesian approach to determining the value of information can be useful in making this decision.

Selecting cities for a test marketing program is obviously a critical aspect. Random techniques are seldom utilized. Test market cities must generally meet at least five criteria:[38] (1) *they must be large enough to produce meaningful data but not so large as to be prohibitive in cost;* (2) *they should be self-contained from a media standpoint;* (3) *they should be demographically similar to the larger market area (generally the entire United States);* (4) *the buying of television time should be relatively efficient in the area,* and (5) *the area should be a self-contained trading area to avoid transshipments into and out of the area.*

As these criteria suggest, the selection of test market areas often involves a judgment approach to sampling. Test area selection is a particularly acute issue when more than one version of the product is to be tested. Not only must the areas meet criteria similar to those described but they must also be similar to each other to allow comparison of the various versions of the product.

A number of techniques, particularly cluster analysis, recently have been developed which can be used to assist the researcher in selecting both representative and equivalent test areas.[39] However, most decisions as to which market to test in are based primarily on tradition and the researcher's judgment.

In addition to the normal types of problems associated with experimental designs, and particularly after-only designs, test marketing faces two unique problems. First, firms routinely take direct actions such as lowering their price or increasing their advertising to disrupt a competitor's test marketing program.[40] For example, it is reported that Vick Chemical distorted test results for a new Colgate cough preparation by distributing 25,000 Nyquil samples into Colgate's two test markets.[41]

Another problem occurs when competitors successfully "read" a firm's test. Any market test is likely to alert competitors to the existence of the new product and its planned promotion. This allows competitors to begin to prepare their own versions of the product or to prepare other strategies. In addition, it is often possible for competitors to gain as much informa-

---

[38] T. Angelus, "Expert's Choice: Top Test Markets," *Marketing/Communications,* **298** (May 1970), 29, 32. The article contains a list of 34 cities selected using these criteria.

[39] See for example P. E. Green, R. E. Frank, P. J. Robinson, "Cluster Analysis in Test Market Selection," *Management Science,* 13 (April 1967), B-387–400; D. G. Morrison, "Measurement Problems in Cluster Analysis," *Management Science,* 13 (August 1967), B-775–780; and J. B. Kernan and G. D. Bruce, "The Socioeconomic Structure of an Urban Area," *Journal of Marketing Research,* IX (February 1972), 15–18.

[40] Angelus, op. čit., 29.

[41] Ibid., 36–37.

tion from the test as the sponsoring firm because most major cities are included in various store auditing programs to which many firms subscribe. An accurate reading of a competitor's test market may allow a firm to match or beat it to the national market.

This is reported to have happened when Lever Brothers test marketed an ammoniated household cleaner and were subsequently beaten to the national market. The same firm also lost some advantage when General Foods (*Log Cabin* pancake syrup) audited Lever's year-long test marketing of *Mrs. Butterworth* and managed to go national with a buttered syrup at the same time as Lever.[42]

Controlled Test Markets.   To overcome these problems, some firms have turned to an approach known as *control store tests*. In a normal or traditional test market situation, the product is distributed to the stores through the firm's regular distribution channels. In a control store test, a market research firm handles all the warehousing, distribution, pricing, shelving, and stocking. The research firm typically pays a limited number of outlets to let it place the product in their stores. These tests frequently take place in smaller cities rather than major markets. This reduces the likelihood of competitors' becoming aware of the test.

Exhibit 12–1 provides a promotional description of one research firm's control store test program. The speed, security from competitors, and relatively low cost of this approach offer some important advantages. Although it is unlikely that this approach will eliminate traditional test marketing, it will probably emerge as a substantial supplement to it.[43]

Conclusions on Test Marketing

Test marketing represents a common, final step in the go-no decision concerning the introduction of a new product. It is a version of the after-only experimental design and is subject to the weaknesses associated with this design.[44] In addition, the cost of test marketing, seldom less than $200,000 for a full test, and the need to project the results to a national market place a large burden on the sampling process. For these reasons, a small judgmental sample is generally selected.

Despite problems and flaws, test marketing is widely used. And, as the costs of a nationwide product failure continue to increase, the use of test

[42] "Product Tryouts: Sales Tests in Selected Cities Help Trim Risks of National Marketing," *Wall Street Journal,* (August 10, 1962), 1.

[43] Churchill, Jr., op. cit.

[44] For an excellent description of a more complex experimental design used in an actual test marketing situation see J. C. Becknell, Jr., and R. W. McIsaac, "Test Marketing Cookware Coated with 'Teflon,'" *Journal of Advertising Research,* **3** (September 1963), 2–8.

Exhibit 12–1   A Description of a Commercial Control Test Store Service*

This is what the *Purchase* system does:
  (a) Warehouses and distributes products.
  (b) Maintains distribution and shelf facings by weekly visits to stores.
  (c) Handles arrangements for displays, point-of-purchase, or direct mail advertising.
  (d) Audits and reports product category movement in stores each four-week period.
  (e) Maintains, processes, and reports the behavior of mail panelists every four weeks.
  (f) Can make available auxiliary panels for attitude and usage tracking, and other direct consumer surveys.

Here is the *Purchase* basis of operation stated quite briefly:

This system is operated in three geographically dispersed markets: Binghamton, New York, Peoria, Illinois, Tucson, Arizona. However, it can be set up in any other markets that are deemed desirable.

Within each market at least six large food stores are selected for controlled testing (18 stores in total).

A mail purchase diary panel is built around each store. Panel households are screened and selected on the basis of at least 75 per cent of purchasing done among these specified stores. These households report their purchases on a number of product categories every two weeks. Panelists are never aware of the store test relationship. Approximately 350 households per market are members of the panel.

Consumers can be made aware of the product through the normal channels of print advertising, direct-mail advertising, couponing, point-of-purchase advertising, and sampling.

The *Purchase* system makes these reports:
  (a) Every four weeks it reports:
    —sales movement and market summaries of the product category (audits and diary panels)
    —per cent of consumers trying product
    —per cent repeat and subsequent repeats
  (b) Special analyses present:
    —characteristics of buyers/repeaters
    —purchase patterns
    —interaction with other brands (source of business)
    —volume projection model

As for the time required, at least one four-week *base period* is needed; more if the source of business, particularly cannibalization, is an issue. This should be followed by a minimum of 20 weeks *product exposure*, which we deem necessary for repeat stabilization as an input for the volume projection model. The household panel of 1,000 to 1,100 households representing those who do at least 75 per cent of their shopping among the 18 stores is generally large enough to split for the testing of alternatives or for a test/control situation. The panel can be "beefed up" if necessary.

* *Source: The Purchase System* (New York: The Lloyd H. Hall Co., undated), 1–2. Reprinted by permission.

marketing will expand. At one time, it was believed that simulation would drastically reduce the need for test marketing. Although this may yet happen, it is not likely to occur in the immediate future.[45]

Computer Simulation

"The computer is destined to become a marketing laboratory."[46] When simulation models are adequately developed, they "can be used at a reasonable cost as test markets for elaborate experimentation with various marketing strategies."[47] It is no exaggeration to suggest that computer simulations will one day represent the third primary environment for marketing experiments. Indeed, existing simulations are currently serving as experimental environments and numerous others are under development. Unfortunately, much of the current work in market simulation is proprietary and confidential in nature. However, a number of nonclassified simulations have been reported in the literature.[48]

Simulation may be described as *"the act of creating a complex model to resemble a real process or system, and running and experimenting with the model in the hope of learning something about the real system."*[49] Given the general complexity of the marketing environment, simulations of all or even parts of this environment generally require the use of computer models to manipulate mathematical and probabilistic descriptions of this environment.

A description of each of the numerous approaches to simulation is beyond the scope of this section.[50] Instead, we describe one existing simulation of a consumer environment. This description should indicate the tremendous potential that simulations have as an environment for marketing experiments.

The simulation to be described was developed by Amstutz.[51] Basically the simulation is a computer program with four sets of capacities.[52] First,

---

[45] See H. Weitz, "The Promise of Simulation in Marketing," *Journal of Marketing,* **31** (July 1967), 28–33.

[46] M. K. Starr, "Computers: The Marketing Laboratory," in P. Langhoff, ed., *Models, Measurement and Marketing* (Englewood Cliffs, N.J.: Prentice-Hall, Inc., 1965), 58.

[47] Ibid.

[48] For an excellent description of a number of these see P. Kotler and R. L. Schultz, "Marketing Simulations: Review and Prospects," *Journal of Business,* **43** (July 1970), 237–295.

[49] Ibid., 238.

[50] A brief description of the various types of simulations is provided by P. E. Green and D. S. Tull, *Research for Marketing Decisions,* 3rd ed. (Englewood Cliffs, N.J.: Prentice-Hall, Inc., 1974), 94–98.

[51] A. E. Amstutz, *Computer Simulation of Competitive Market Response* (Cambridge, Mass.: The M.I.T. Press, 1967).

[52] The following description is based on Kotler and Schultz, op. cit., 249–254.

the program can generate a consumer population of any required size. This population can be "representative" of any particular region or market segment in terms of demographic characteristics. The selection of consumers can be based on a probability selection from census type data or on actual consumers selected in an initial survey.

The second stage involves assigning product ownership, usage rates, and attitudes to the consumers. Again the computer can use actual consumer data from current surveys, frequency distributions derived from older surveys, or managerial judgment.

In the third stage, each "consumer" is "subjected" to a series of experiences based on mathematical functions and/or probability distributions. Thus, a given consumer *might* be exposed to certain media, *might* note any product relevant advertisements contained in the media, or be subjected to other influences that will affect purchasing behavior. Attitude and behavior can change according to initial attitude, product need, exposure to advertisements, exposure to word-of-mouth communications, and as the result of other variables. Finally, the computer predicts the resulting behavior of all the "consumers" and issues weekly brand share reports.

This abbreviated and simplified description of an operational computer simulation should indicate the potential that such an approach offers. Varying prices, advertising levels, and product designs could be tested by means of experiments with the simulation model and none of the error inherent in real world experiment would cloud the results.

Why then aren't computer simulations more prevalent? First, they are expensive to design. However, this is not the primary problem. What is lacking is the knowledge necessary to create simulations that realistically reflect the complexities of consumer behavior even on a probabilistic basis. Until we are able to model consumer behavior *accurately,* we will be constrained to conducting our experiments in the laboratory or the field.

Experimentation and Decision Making

A reason that experiments, particularly field experiments, are not more widely used in marketing is a failure of marketing executives to "think experiment" in terms of everyday decisions. Most marketing executives have had little or no training in experimental designs and do not recognize that many marketing variables can be manipulated in an experimental manner at a low cost. For example, a relatively large national firm was recently concerned with determining the appropriate number of sales calls per year per account. The firm had a large number of territories, each with a sales manager and separate reporting system. This situation was ideal for a field experiment. The number of salesmen, and thus sales calls per year, could be varied and the effect on contribution margin measured over a period of several years. The economic risk was low and the time delay, although substantial, was bearable. Yet such simple experimentation had not occurred to management.

Situations such as the one described are not atypical. If a firm operates with a number of divisions, stores, sales territories, or products, low cost experiments on sales compensation plans, packages, price elasticity, advertising elasticity, and other variables are often practical. In the section on questionnaire design, we recommended the use of the split-ballot technique whenever possible. This was, in fact, a recommendation for experiments on questionnaire designs.

A truly innovative management could well view the firm as a series of ongoing experiments. This approach to management will not only result in the development of sound current practices, it will also produce the knowledge and information necessary to design superior programs for the future.

Summary

Experimentation is a common activity for both individuals and firms. The purpose of this chapter was to encourage more useful experimentation by describing the principles of experimental design as they relate to applied marketing experiments.

Experimentation involves the manipulation of one or more variables by the experimenter in such a way that their effect upon a second variable can be determined. The variable(s) being manipulated is called the *independent variable(s)*. The variable(s) being measured is called the *dependent variable(s)*. Any other variables operating in the situation are termed *extraneous variables*. A measure taken prior to the manipulation of the independent variable is called a *premeasurement* whereas one taken after the manipulation is a *postmeasurement*.

The timing of the measurements and the manipulations of the independent variable in various groups are altered to form various experimental designs. These designs have varying abilities to control for experimental errors that reduce the accuracy of the resulting data.

The setting of the experiment, *laboratory, field,* or *simulation,* also affects the accuracy and meaning of the final results. The results of laboratory experiments, although often replicable in a laboratory setting, frequently fail to predict behavior outside the laboratory. Field experiments, on the other hand, are subject to substantial impact from extraneous variables. This is particularly true for test markets since competitors often attempt to distort the results. Simulation has not yet developed to the point of being widely used as a research environment.

Field experiments are underutilized in marketing. Marketing executives should "think experiment" in terms of everyday decisions. The firm can in fact be viewed as a series of ongoing experiments. Unfortunately, there is a tendency to structure these as after-only or before-after with no control group studies. As this chapter indicates, often other designs will provide more useful information.

Questions and Problems

12.1. The data in the following table were collected in a study involving 900 housewives in Chicago. Suppose you were marketing manager of Brand D scouring cleanser and received these data.

Brand of Scouring Cleanser	% of Housewives Who Know the Brand	% of Users Who Give Brand Top Rating	% of Housewives Now Using Brand
A	95.1	45.7	41.2
B	62.8	44.9	16.3
C	43.6	29.4	11.0
D	36.0	46.7	10.0
E	65.8	24.6	6.1

(a) What element of the marketing mix would you consider likely to need corrective action. Why?

(b) Design a field experiment to give information for making final decisions concerning specific corrective actions you might take. Assume that the product is distributed nationally.

12.2. How would you decide whether or not to conduct the experiment described in problem 12.1b? Give a specific, step-by-step answer.

12.3. The *Times* research department was requested to run a split-run test for the purpose of testing advertising appeals.

(a) Evaluate the split-run technique as a device for testing advertising appeals. In your evaluation, state the assumptions on which the split-run technique is based and how realistic you believe them to be.

(b) Of which type of experimental design is the split-run technique an example? Explain.

12.4. Assume a firm wants to run a sales test on its prepared baby foods with the present salt content versus the same baby foods with a lower salt content. Further assume that you were called in as a consultant to advise the firm concerning the proper experimental design. You were told that (a) the firm subscribes to a national consumer panel providing data on a weekly basis on purchases of prepared baby foods by brand by 105 market areas; (b) inventory in the distributive "pipeline" was equal to about four weeks of sales; (c) the firm required an answer within four months; (d) the average user buys a two-week supply of baby foods at each purchase; (e) the firm was only interested in obtaining data on the effect of salt content on sales—no other variable was to be tested, and (f) the new salt level meets all government standards and poses absolutely no health problem.

What experimental design would you have recommended and why?

12.5. A meat packer had enjoyed a substantial share (22 per cent) of the market for a particular canned meat. The can used by the packer and the entire industry was tall and square. Periodic surveys of purchasing housewives consistently found dissatisfaction with the can. The meat was not the proper size for bread, the can was difficult to open, and it was hard to get the meat out in one piece for slicing. After four years of intensive research, the packer developed an easy opening, flatter can that appeared to management to overcome all of the problems associated with the old can. The firm decided that it would take the competition between 10 and 18 months to duplicate the new can.

Despite the advantages of the new can, management was nervous about putting it on the market. Past innovations in package designs had frequently failed. Management believed that the new design had a 60 per cent chance of success. A successful introduction would produce a net benefit to the firm of $1 million; a failure would produce a net cost of $500,000.

Describe how you would develop additional data prior to introducing the new can.

12.6. Industrial Supplies, Inc., distributes a line of industrial supplies throughout the United States. It is divided into 75 geographic sales divisions. Each sales division is headed by a division manager who supervises ten salesmen. The divisions produce roughly equivalent sales levels. All salesmen are paid a straight salary. The firm's management would like to determine the impact on sales of shifting to either a straight commission plan or a base salary plus a commission.
(a) Design an experiment that would allow you to test the impact of the two proposed plans.
(b) How would your experiment change, if at all, if 10 per cent of the territories generated 40 per cent of the total sales, 30 per cent generated another 30 per cent of the sales, and 60 per cent of the territories generated only 30 per cent of the total sales?

12.7. Mary Enis, manager of William's Fashions, is considering advertising in the newspaper of the local university. Enis thinks that about 30 per cent of her business currently comes from university students. However, this is no more than a guess as she has no way of knowing for sure. William's Fashions has never advertised in the student newspaper before. Enis would like to run an experiment to determine the impact of full-page advertisement on the university students.

(a) Develop an experiment that will allow Enis to evaluate the impact of the proposed advertising.

12.8. What problems are encountered in experiments with human subjects that are not encountered in experiments with inanimate objects such as those a chemist might conduct?

Selected Bibliography

BANKS, S. *Experimentation in Marketing.* New York: McGraw-Hill Book Co., 1965. A detailed discussion of the utilization of experiments in marketing.

CAMPBELL, D. T., and J. C. STANLEY. *Experimental and Quasi-Experimental Designs for Research.* Chicago: Rand McNally College Publishing Company, 1963. An outstanding treatment of experimental errors and the nature of experimental designs.

COX, K. K., and B. M. ENIS. *Experimentation for Marketing Decisions.* Scranton, Pa.: International Textbook Co., 1969. An excellent discussion of experimental designs and the ways they can be used to assist in marketing decision making.

HOLLAND, C. W., and D. W. CRAVENS. "Fractional Factorial Experimentation Designs in Marketing Research." *Journal of Marketing Research,* **10** (August 1973), 270–276. A brief but good discussion of this important type of experimental design.

ROSENTHAL, R. *Experimenter Effects in Behavioral Research.* New York: Appleton-Century-Crofts, 1966. A thorough treatment of this critical and often overlooked aspect of experimental research.

Case 12–1

Del Monte Instant Mashed Potato Sales Performance Test*

Del Monte retained the services of Elrick and Lavidge, Inc., to work with Del Monte's internal marketing research department in an effort to provide information on whether or not to market a new instant mashed potato (IMP) developed by Del Monte. A 20-week sales performance test was designed and conducted.

Procedure

Elrick and Lavidge made arrangements with 32 supermarkets (16 in Philadelphia and 16 in Cincinnati) to sell Del Monte IMP for 20 weeks (5 4-week periods) between September 26, 1966, and February 13, 1967. In addition, a 4-week base period sales audit (prior to the sale of Del Monte IMP) was made between June 20 and July 17, 1966.

In each city half of the stores stocked Del Monte IMP in the instant section and the other half stocked Del Monte IMP in the canned vege-

---

* Used with permission of Del Monte Corporation and Elrick and Lavidge, Inc.

tables section. In all stores, the 10-servings size had three facings (two rows high) and the 24-servings size had two facings.

The Del Monte IMP sales were not supported by advertising. (This would have been impractical since only 16 stores in each city were handling the product.) However, once every 4 weeks product displays were erected during Wednesday through Saturday. No displays were in effect during the fifth 4-week audit period.

During mid-September (prior to audit Period I) coupons good for a discount of $.13 on the purchase of a 10-serving can of Del Monte IMP were offered to shoppers in each of the 32 stores. The primary purpose of the coupon was to identify homemakers who purchased Del Monte IMP at least once so that their repurchase rates could be determined. Within 10 days after these coupons were redeemed, a panel of 400 homemakers in each city was established. The homemakers were not told they were being recruited into the panel because they had purchased Del Monte IMP.

In each city, 250 of the 400 panel members were infrequent users of IMP (had not purchased any IMP except Del Monte in the previous three months) and 150 were frequent users of IMP (in addition to the Del Monte they had purchased IMP at least once in the previous three months). Within each group of frequent and infrequent users, half were recruited using coupons from stores stocking Del Monte IMP in the instant section and the other half had purchased Del Monte IMP in stores stocking it in the canned vegetables section. Homemakers reported (using a diary) the purchases of all types of potatoes.

In interpreting the findings, it is well to recognize that the data were obtained from a sales performance *experiment* rather than from normal market place conditions. In the experiment, Del Monte had 100 per cent distribution (that is, all 32 stores that were audited stocked both sizes of Del Monte IMP). It is possible, but not likely, that 100 per cent distribution could be achieved under normal marketplace conditions. On the other hand, Del Monte IMP was not supported by advertising during the experiment. The only promotion was an "in-store" display erected for each week in each store during each of the first four four-week sales periods. No displays were used in the fifth period to test their effect.

Results

Exhibit A illustrates the market share trend of Del Monte IMP during the 20-week test period. Market share is calculated on a "servings" basis. Thus, one 24-servings box contributes 2.4 times more to the market share than a 10-servings package. Total unit sales per period are shown in Table A.

Exhibit A Sales Trend of Del Monte Instant Mashed Potatoes.

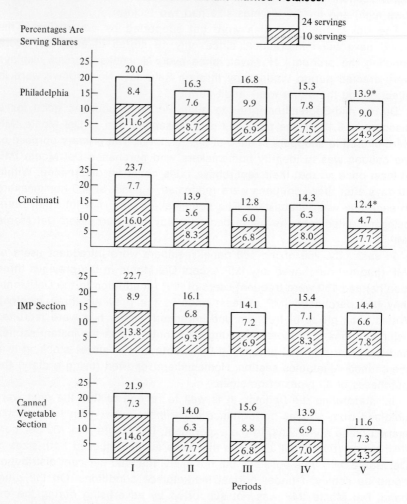

*For Period V the average share for both cities combined is 13.2% (10 serving—6.3% and 24 serving—6.9%).

Table A Total Unit Sales Per Period

Size	Period				
	I	*II*	*III*	*IV*	*V*
10 serving	2075	1202	987	1259	965
24 serving	498	388	476	476	444

Exhibit B   Highlights of Del Monte Repurchase Rate

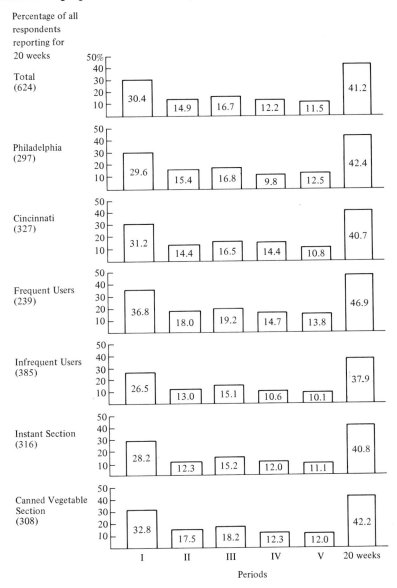

Percentage of all
respondents
reporting for
20 weeks

Total (624)

Philadelphia (297)

Cincinnati (327)

Frequent Users (239)

Infrequent Users (385)

Instant Section (316)

Canned Vegetable Section (308)

Periods

Exhibit B provides an illustration of the repurchase rate for Del Monte IMP. The percentage figures represent the per cent of panel families that purchase the product during a given time period. Since the families were recruited based on a previous purchase of IMP, any subsequent purchase automatically qualifies them as a repeat purchaser.

The major findings of the study are presented as follows.

Retail Sales

1. After 20 weeks of sales, Del Monte's average share of servings (both cities combined) is about 13 per cent. The 10-serving size has about 6 per cent and the 24-serving size has almost 7 per cent. The market shares in servings and dollars by city and by stocking condition are shown in Exhibit A.

2. It can be noted that serving shares in both Philadelphia and Cincinnati for Period V are down slightly over Period IV. This may have been the result of eliminating the in-store displays or it may have been the result of normal fluctuations of sales in the marketplace.

3. In all of the sales periods, except Period III, Del Monte's share in servings was slightly greater in the IMP section than in the canned vegetable section. The differences between the serving shares in each section are small, however, and should be considered as being about equal, indicating that the location in the store where Del Monte IMP is shopped is not likely to have a substantial effect on sales volume.

   However, it will probably be much easier to secure distribution if chain and independent stores are allowed to stock Del Monte where they choose and it is likely that this will be with competitive products in the instant section.

4. The total number of units sold (all brands and all sizes) remained relatively stable throughout the first three sales periods. However, in Period IV total unit sales in both Philadelphia and Cincinnati increased substantially. Virtually all of this increase resulted from increased volumes of Blue Label sales in Philadelphia and Butterfield sales in Cincinnati.

   In Period V total unit sales increased again in Philadelphia and again this increase resulted almost entirely from the volume of sales secured by Blue Label. However, the volume in Cincinnati in Period V dropped back to the approximate level of Periods I, II, and III.

   During part of sales Period IV, Blue Label was sold at a special price of 2/$.19 in most stores in Philadelphia but during Period V prices were increased to their previous level of 2/$.23. No specific information is available about whether Butterfield was on a special price during Period IV.

5. The Del Monte 24-serving container has a substantially greater share in Philadelphia than it did in Cincinnati (9.0 per cent compared with 4.7 per cent). Conversely, Del Monte's share of the

10-serving size is only 4.9 per cent in Philadelphia compared with 7.7 per cent in Cincinnati.

Betty Crocker's 40-serving size in Cincinnati may be taking business from Del Monte's 24-serving size, and Del Monte's 10-serving size is not under heavy competitive pressure from a strong brand such as Blue Label in Philadelphia.

In Philadelphia, Betty Crocker is not selling its 40-serving size. On the other hand, the Blue Label 5-serving size is an exceptionally strong brand in Philadelphia (24 per cent of the servings in Period V), and this may be depressing the sales of Del Monte's 10-serving size.

Repurchase Rates

6. About 41 per cent of those homemakers who purchased Del Monte IMP using the coupon purchased it again at least once (Exhibit B). The repurchase rate is slightly higher in Philadelphia than in Cincinnati (12.5 per cent vs. 10.8 per cent) and as might be expected higher among frequent users than infrequent users (46.9 per cent vs. 37.9 per cent). The repurchase rate in Period V increased over Period IV in Philadelphia but decreased in Cincinnati. However, the repurchase rates in the previous periods in both cities have shown some variability from period to period.

7. In any one period (four weeks) a majority of both frequent and infrequent users of IMP buy Del Monte only rather than along with other brands. However, during the entire 20-week sales period fewer frequent than infrequent users bought Del Monte exclusively. Half of the infrequent users (18.7 per cent) bought *only* Del Monte whereas the remaining half (19.2 per cent) bought Del Monte and other brands.

8. Of the households that repurchased Del Monte (41 per cent), 38 per cent bought the 10-serving size and 11 per cent bought the 24-serving size (some families bought both sizes).

9. Among the homemakers who repurchased Del Monte (41 per cent), 52 per cent of these purchased more than one package. Another way of stating these data is to say that about 22 per cent of all panel households (41.5 per cent × 52.5 per cent) rebought Del Monte more than once during the 20 weeks of sales. Almost 26 per cent of those who repurchased Del Monte made 4 or more purchases during the 20 weeks of sales (or, about 11 per cent of all homemakers who repurchased Del Monte made 4 or more purchases during the 20 weeks.)

10. An analysis of the demographic characteristics of repurchasers shows that Del Monte is being purchased by the same types of homemakers or households that purchase any brand of instant mashed potatoes, except that Del Monte appears to be somewhat weaker among upper income families and those with professional or managerial occupations (these factors are likely related.)

11. A comparison of the repurchase rates for Del Monte, Betty Crocker, and French's indicates that the repurchase rate of Del Monte is substantially higher than the purchase and repurchase of Betty Crocker or French's. (When interpreting these data keep in mind that all of the panel members purchased Del Monte at least once prior to being recruited into the panel but all homemakers did not have similar experience with Betty Crocker or French's.)

However, after 20 weeks of sales, Del Monte had been purchased 3 or more times by 14 per cent of the homemakers whereas Betty Crocker had been repurchased 3 or more times by only 7 per cent and French's by less than 4 per cent.

1. What are the strengths and weaknesses of the sales performance test as it is now designed?

2. What changes, if any, would you recommend?

3. What action would you take based on the results of this study?

Case 12–2
Fritch Laboratories

Fritch Laboratories, a manufacturer of several nationally advertised non-ethical drug products (a headache remedy, a nasal spray, cough drops, a decongestant, and antacid mints) was planning to market test a new antacid powder. The powder was mint flavored and, in addition to the antacid ingredient, contained a mild analgesic and a carbonating agent that caused the mixture to fizz when water was added.

During a discussion of the market test, Dixon Guthrie, the marketing vice-president, had asked the marketing research manager, Katie Lynn, how many market areas she thought should be included in the test. Lynn had replied that the conventional answer to this question was to use four. She explained further that the usual practice was to stratify the four test market areas geographically so that one was chosen from each quadrant of the marketing area. She stated that as far as she knew, the use of four cities rather than some other number was not based on any theoretical calculation. Rather, it appeared to be a rule-of-thumb choice to balance the increased precision against the increased costs resulting from the addition of each area.

In thinking about the problem later, however, Lynn concluded that there might be a better solution than to rely solely on convention. It seemed to her that the number of test areas chosen depended on the variation in per capita sales among the test areas. If the test areas were no different at all in the sales they would produce on a per-capita basis, only one test area would be needed. If, however the test areas were greatly different in this respect, several areas might be needed.

For a number of years Fritch had subscribed to a syndicated data service that provided data on purchases by each of 50 market areas. It occurred to Lynn that she could get an estimate of the variation in test market sales of the antacid powder by using the variation in actual sales of the similar Fritch product already on the market. If she found the standard deviation for sales of the antacid mints among the 50 market areas for last month, for example, that should be a reasonably good estimate of the standard deviation of test market sales of the antacid powder in the same 50 market areas.

From that point on, Lynn concluded, determining the number of test areas to use could be done using either traditional or Bayesian methods.

Evaluate this proposed procedure.

Case 12–3
Television Advertising of Fresh Strawberries*

From mid-April to mid-May, a television advertising campaign for fresh California strawberries was conducted by the California Strawberry Advisory Board (CSAB) in a number of major metropolitan areas. The television campaign was part of an overall merchandising program designed to increase sales of fresh strawberries by stimulating retailers to increase or improve their marketing activities for strawberries. Several weeks in advance of the television campaign, the board's staff held meetings with many major food chains and wholesalers to inform them about the forthcoming television program.

Elrick and Lavidge, Inc., a marketing consulting firm, was retained to assess the effectiveness of the television campaign in meeting these

* Used with permission of the California Strawberry Advisory Board and Elrick and Lavidge, Inc.

goals. *Part* of the methodology used by Elrick and Lavidge is reported in the following paragraphs.

Study Procedure

The study consisted of two basic parts. One part of the study was concerned with evaluating the effect of the television advertising and merchandising program on grocery chain store newspaper advertisements for fresh strawberries. The other part concerned the effect of the television advertising and merchandising program on store level merchandising.

CSAB collected, measured, and tabulated all store sponsored newspaper advertisements for fresh strawberries appearing in the major newspapers of eight test and eight control markets. These measurements began two weeks before the television advertising campaign commenced, continued through the four weeks of the television advertising campaign, and continued two weeks after the television campaign had ended. The eight metropolitan areas identified as "test markets" are those in which the television campaign was undertaken, and the eight markets identified as "control markets" are markets in which there was no television advertising for fresh strawberries. Comparisons have been made between the measurements of newspaper advertisements in the test cities with the measurements in the control cities in order to isolate the effects of the television advertising-merchandising program.

The tabulation of the newspaper advertisements has been analyzed by Elrick and Lavidge to determine whether the TV advertising program had any effect on the number of advertisements, the size of the advertisements, the use of illustrated advertisements, and advertised prices.

In order to determine the effect of the television advertising/merchandising program on store-level merchandising activity, a panel of 16 stores was selected in the test markets in which there was television advertising and another panel of 16 stores was selected in the control markets in which there was no television advertising.

In both the test and control markets, suburban stores in middle-income areas were selected to represent the major chains in the markets. In each of the four geographical regions, one test city was matched with one control city. For each pair of cities, the sample of chains selected was restricted to chains that appeared to be a factor in only one of the markets. (The reason for this is that if a chain appeared in both markets in a pair, it would be conceivable that the chain would react to the television advertising campaign in such a way as to affect the entire region rather than just the test market.)

Observations and measurements were taken beginning two weeks before the television advertising, for the four weeks of the advertising campaign, and continuing two weeks after the television campaign.

The observations and measurements were made on Fridays, which were judged to be the most typical period for peak merchandising activity in the stores. These observations and measurements included an opinion rating by trained observers of the displays, the presence of point-of-purchase material, the physical size of the displays, and retail prices in the individual stores.

On either the seventh or eighth week of the observations (which was after the end of the television advertising campaign), brief interviews were conducted with the produce managers in the panel of stores to determine their awareness and opinions of the television advertising campaign. The major purpose of these interviews was to secure information that would aid in evaluating any changes, or lack of changes, that occurred in the in-store merchandising activity in the test markets as compared with the control markets.

1. Evaluate the experimental procedure used.

2. What specific changes, if any, would you recommend?

Case 12–4
Scents, Incorporated: New Product Testing

Scents, Incorporated, is a major manufacturer of men's and women's toiletries. The firm's technical research department recently developed a new aftershave lotion scent that had passed initial consumer acceptance screening tests. However, in this industry the brand name and product image are at least as important to a new product's success as are its physical properties. Therefore, a product development team was assigned the task of determining an appropriate target market and brand image for the new scent.

An examination of studies of company and industry sales figures by demographic groupings convinced the team that the high school market was both large and relatively undeveloped. The general lack of concern by high school students for products of this nature that existed throughout much of the 1960s was now being replaced by more of an interest. Therefore, the product team decided to tailor the product and the product image to the high school market.

A representative from the firm's advertising agency reported that recent surveys of this market revealed a large and growing interest in astrology.

She stated that a large percentage of high school students were knowledgeable in this area and were familiar with the various signs of the Zodiac. In light of this, she suggested naming the product after one of these signs. If the initial product were successful, additional products could be introduced until each of the 12 signs were represented by a distinct aftershave lotion and cologne.

Additional investigation by the product team convinced them of the virtue of this approach. The team was concerned, however, that the first version be widely accepted in the market. At this point, Mary Beth Kerrigan, director of marketing research, was asked to conduct a "quick study" to find the signs most likely to gain widespread acceptance among the market. In response, she retained a nationwide consulting firm to conduct 50 open-ended interviews in each of six cities scattered throughout the United States. The firm's trained interviewers were instructed to find the most preferred signs regardless of the respondents' own signs.

Three signs were found to be popular with the male high school students. *Taurus,* the Bull, has an easygoing nature. A Taurus is tolerant of others but brooks no interference. He has a warm, friendly attitude and a love of beauty and luxury. *Scorpio,* the Scorpion, is ruled by Mars. A Scorpio is passionate, energetic, proud, and obstinate. He goes into everything with gusto and energy. *Leo,* the Lion, has the Sun as the dominant heavenly body. It is the sign of people born to rule. The Leonine is dominating, high-minded, and tireless. He has a sense of responsibility and superior ability; but he is also generous, dramatic, and demonstrative.

The product team was pleased with these findings, as each seemed to have rich potential for image development. However, Kerrigan warned that these preferences had been expressed as abstractions and had not been tied to a product category such as aftershave lotion. She made the following proposal to the team.

We need to find out how the target market will react to an aftershave lotion with a given scent and these particular names. We can take four random samples of 250 male high school students each and develop this information. One group will try the product from an unlabeled bottle. They will be asked to rate the product on a scale of 1 to 25 and will be given an adjective checklist to use in describing the product. Finally, they will complete a description of a "typical" purchaser of this product by means of a set of semantic differential scales. Each of the remaining three samples of 250 students will complete the same activities. However, they will each be evaluating a sample of the product selected from a point-of-purchase display and labeled with one of the three potential brand names. The point-of-purchase display and labels will approximate those to be used in the actual product introduction.

1. What are the strengths and weaknesses of this proposal?

2. Will it provide the data required?

3. Should the proposal be implemented?

CHAPTER 13

Analysis of Data: Data Reduction

Data become useful only after they are analyzed. Data analysis involves converting a series of recorded observations (data) into descriptive statements and/or inferences about relationships. With the advent of the digital computer this process has become both easier and more complex; easier because the computer does most of the tedious and time-consuming tabulation and calculations required, and more complex because it has made possible large numbers of new analytic techniques that were unavailable before.

Both this chapter and the next are concerned with data analyses. In this chapter, we deal with *data reduction,* which refers to *the process of getting the data ready for analysis and the calculation of summarizing or descriptive statistics.* Data reduction, by and large, is a tiresome, time-consuming, tedious—but highly important—part of analysis. The phrase "garbage in, garbage out" has become a cliché regarding data analysis because, like many clichés, it is a graphic way of making a true statement. The analysis that comes out can be no better than the data that go in.

To illustrate the analytic process and the specific techniques discussed in this and the following chapter, an actual survey is used. The case study described should be read carefully (including the questionnaire) before going on to the sections of the chapter that follow.

Following the case study, the steps involved in data reduction—*field controls, editing, coding, generating new variables, tabulation,* and *calculation of summarizing statistics* are discussed. Each step is illustrated with examples from the case study.

A Survey of Bread Purchase and Consumption Patterns

Far West Research Associates, a marketing research and consulting firm, was approached by Willamette Bakeries concerning a survey of purchase and consumption patterns for bread in its market area. Willamette is a small, independent bakery that, like most independents, had been losing market share for several years to the private brand breads of the food chains. The purpose of the survey was to obtain information about the market to help the bakery in taking action to reverse a declining trend in sales.

After some discussion it was agreed that Far West Research would conduct a survey as a part of an overall consulting project. The objectives of the survey were "to determine if there are viable market segments for bread based upon (1) characteristics of purchasing families and amounts of purchase, (2) communication media and appeals, and (3) distribution outlets."

Willamette had been advertising using "wholesomeness," "goodness," and "quick energy" themes. The budget had been allocated primarily to 30-second spot commercials on television in the afternoon. A limited amount of daytime radio advertising was also being done using the same appeals.

After a preliminary investigation by Far West researchers, a discussion was held with Willamette management. Those attending were in general agreement on the following statements concerning the market area served by Willamette:

1. The decline in the position of independent bakeries in Willamette's market area is indicated by the fact that, since 1964, about 20 per cent of all bakeries have gone out of business. All of these bakeries were independent.
2. Most brands of standard white bread do not have identifiable differences in taste, texture, freshness, or other characteristics. Some

whole wheat and most specialty breads can be differentiated by these characteristics.

3. The prices of most brands of standard white bread are highly competitive. There is a greater price spread among brands of whole wheat and specialty breads.

4. Repeated purchases of the same brand of standard white bread is likely the result of store loyalty, availability, and/or habit rather than preferences based on brand characteristics or price.

5. About half of the families in Willamette's market area are blue-collar families (craftsmen, foremen, operators, transport equipment drivers, laborers, farmers and farm laborers, and service workers). White-collar families (clerical, sales, technicians, and teachers) comprise about 40 per cent of the market and managerial-professional families (managers, administrators, physicians, lawyers, dentists, engineers, and others) amount to about 10 per cent. (These estimates were based on Census of Population data.)

6. Blue-collar families probably eat greater amounts of white and whole wheat bread per person than either white-collar or managerial-professional families.

7. White-collar and managerial-professional families eat greater amounts of specialty breads (rye, pumpernickel, and the like) per person than blue-collar families.

8. Blue-collar families very likely have a different consumption pattern for white and whole wheat bread than managerial-professional and white-collar families. (Blue-collar families tend to look upon bread as a staple food to be served at all meals whereas white-collar and managerial-professional families do not view it this way. Blue-collar families are more inclined to have large breakfasts and lunches whereas the major meal of the day for white-collar and managerial-professional families is the evening meal. Blue-collar wage earners are more likely to be taking their lunch to work and to have sandwiches than are white collar and managerial-professional wage earners.)

9. Blue-collar, white-collar, and managerial-professional families differ in their attitudes toward bread and bread characteristics. (Managerial-professional housewives are more likely to like bread that has texture (is "chewier"), are more diet conscious, and are more likely to think that whole wheat and other dark breads are healthier than white breads. White-collar housewives are more concerned about nutrition and the right brand. Blue-collar housewives are more concerned about bread being soft (softness is equated with freshness) and being sliced right.

10. Media exposure differs among blue-collar, white-collar, and managerial-professional families. (Blue-collar and white-collar

families will view television more than managerial-professional families. Blue-collar families will read newspapers less, on the average, than white-collar or managerial-professional families. The programs listened to on radio and viewed on television will also differ among the three occupational groups.)

11. Bread consumption per person will be higher for the "young single," "young married without children," "married with youngest child under 6," "married with youngest child 6 to 12," and "married with youngest child over 13" stages of the life cycle than it will for the "empty nest" and "solitary survivor" stages of the life cycle.

12. It is doubtful if there are any distinguishable differences among people who buy bread at supermarkets and those who buy it at neighborhood markets, retail bakeries, and bake their own bread.

Following this discussion it was decided that a pilot survey would be done that could be expanded later as needed. The basic purpose of the survey was to help ascertain the accuracy of, and to refine further these propositions. The survey was to be a quota sample of approximately 180 households in the Eugene-Springfield, Oregon area. The strata to which quotas were assigned were "blue-collar," "white-collar," and "managerial-professional" occupations and the various stages of the life cycle.

It was decided that rather than have the interviewer read the questions to the respondent, he would go to the respondent's home, determine in which cell of the sample the family fell, and, for those families in cells where respondents were still needed, he would leave a questionnaire with an agreed upon time to return and pick it up. This would permit the use of less skilled interviewers and save interviewing time.

A questionnaire was prepared and pretested. After a reworking of some questions and a change of order in others, the questionnaire was discussed with Willamette executives. Further changes were made and another pretest was conducted. The final questionnaire (reproduced as Exhibit 13–1) was agreed upon after some minor changes following the second pretest.

Data Reduction

The steps involved in the reduction of data are (*1*) *field controls,* (*2*) *editing,* (*3*) *coding,* (*4*) *generating new variables,* (*5*) *tabulating, and* (*6*) *calculating summarizing statistics.* The first five of these steps are concerned with developing a basic data array that is as complete and as error free as possible. The last step involves calculations made from the array.

A *basic data array* is a table comprised of the value of each variable for each sample unit. In the bread study just described, data were collected on 219 variables and two additional variables were generated from them. There were 176 respondents. Thus, the basic data array for the bread study consists of a table of values for 221 variables for 176 respondents. This means that there are $221 \times 176 = 38{,}896$ measurements. The initial task of the data reduction process was to ensure that these measurements were transcribed from the questionnaires into the form of basic array in as complete and error free a manner as possible. The first step in this process is establishing and maintaining *field controls*.

Field Controls

Every selected sample unit in a well-designed and competently conducted field study involving a probability sample will be accounted for. The units should be identified by serial number and identifying characteristics (name, address, or sampling plan procedure for respondents) in a *sample book*. If the field study is a survey, the date(s) the interview is attempted should be recorded along with a notation as to whether it was a completed interview, a noncontact, or a refusal. A notation should also be made for completed interviews to indicate whether they were accepted by the editor or returned to the interviewer for clarification or added information.

Exhibit 13–1 Far West Research Associates Survey of Bread Purchase and Usage Patterns

We appreciate your help in the study of how consumers buy and use bread.

For Editor's Use Only

Please answer all questions that apply to you (or your family). If the meaning of a question is not clear, ask the interviewer to explain it when she returns.

_____ Sequence Number

Far West Research Associates

1. Do you usually do the shopping for food?   Yes __ No __   _____ 1
2. (Do you) (Does your family) eat white bread?
   Yes __ No __   _____ 2
3. (a) About how often would you say you buy white bread?   _____ 3
   Three times a week   __
   Twice a week   __
   Once a week   __
   Once a month   __
   Twice every three months __
   Once every three months __

Exhibit 13–1 *(Continued)*

For Editor's Use Only

(b) About how many loaves of white bread do you buy each time? _____ 4
    One loaf   __
    Two loaves __
    Three loaves __
    Four loaves __
    More than four loaves (list number) __

(c) What size of loaves of white bread do you buy each time? _____ 5
    (please check one)
    Extra large (Approx. 32 oz.) __
    Large (Approx. 22 oz.)   __
    Medium (Approx. 15 oz.)   __
    Small (less than 15 oz.)   __

(d) Where do you usually buy white bread?
    Supermarket   __ _____ 6
    Neighborhood grocery __ _____ 7
    Bakery   __ _____ 8
    Bake my own bread   __ _____ 9
    Other (please specify) _____ _____ 10

(e) At what meals at home is white bread usually served?
    Breakfast __ Noon Meal __ Evening Meal__ _____ 11, 12, 13

(f) Is white bread used for sandwiches to be eaten away from home, such as at school or at work?
    Yes __ No __ _____ 14

(g) Is white bread used for between-meal snacks at home, such as sandwiches or with spreads like butter and jam or peanut butter and jelly?
    Yes __ No __ _____ 15

(h) When you have friends over for a meal or other special occasion when food is prepared, is white bread usually served?
    Yes __ No __ _____ 16

4. (Do you) (Does your family) eat whole wheat bread?
   Yes __ No __ _____ 17
   If yes, please answer the questions below.
   If no, skip to question 6.

5. (a) About how often would you say you buy whole wheat bread? _____ 18
       Three times a week   __
       Twice a week   __
       Once a week   __
       Once every two weeks   __
       Once a month   __
       Twice every three months __
       Once every three months __

Exhibit 13–1   *(Continued)*

(b) About how many loaves of whole wheat bread do you
   buy each time?   _____ 19
   One loaf   —
   Two loaves —
   Three loaves __
   Four loaves __
   More than four loaves (list number) __
(c) What size of loaves of whole wheat bread do you buy
   each time?   _____ 20
      (please check one)
   Extra large (approx. 32 oz.) __
   Large (approx. 22 oz.)   —
   Medium (approx. 15 oz.)   —
   Small (less than 15 oz.)   —
(d) Where do you usually buy whole wheat bread?
   Supermarket   —   _____ 21
   Neighborhood grocery __   _____ 22
   Bakery   —   _____ 23
   Bake my own bread   —   _____ 24
   Other (please specify) _____   _____ 25
(e) At what meals at home is whole wheat bread usually
   served?
   Breakfast __ Noon meal __ Evening meal __   _____ 26, 27, 28
(f) Is whole wheat bread used for sandwiches to be eaten
   away from home, such as at school or at work?
   Yes __ No __   _____ 29
(g) Is whole wheat bread used for between-meal snacks at
   home, such as sandwiches or with spreads like butter
   and jam or peanut butter and jelly?
   Yes __ No __   _____ 30
(h) When you have friends over for a meal or other special occasion when food is prepared, is whole wheat
   bread usually served?
   Yes __ No __   _____ 31
6. (Do you) (Does your family) eat specialty bread, like rye,
   pumpernickel, etc.?
   Yes __ No __   _____ 32
   If yes, please answer questions below.
   If no, skip to question 8.
7. (a) What type(s) of specialty bread (do you) (does your
      family) eat?
      1. _____ *(Type I)*   _____ 33
      2. _____ *(Type II)*   _____ 34
      3. _____ *(Type III)*   _____ 35
   Please answer the following questions for the type I
   specialty bread you indicated above. Mark your response in the column with the heading "type I."
(b) About how often would you say you buy this type of
   specialty bread?

Exhibit 13–1   *(Continued)*

	Type I	*Type II*	*Type III*
Three times a week	—	—	—
Twice a week	—	—	—
Once a week	—	—	—
Once every two weeks	—	—	—
Once a month	—	—	—
Twice every three months	—	—	—

———— 36
(Type I)

———— 37
(Type II)

———— 38
(Type III)

(c) About how many loaves of this type of specialty bread
do you buy each time?

	Type I	*Type II*	*Type III*
One loaf	—	—	—
Two loaves	—	—	—
Three loaves	—	—	—
Four loaves	—	—	—
More than four loaves (list number)	—	—	—

———— 39
(Type I)

———— 40
(Type II)

———— 41
(Type III)

(d) What size of loaves of specialty bread do you buy
each time? (Please check one)

	Type I	*Type II*	*Type III*
Large (approx. 22 oz.)	—	—	—
Medium (approx. 15 oz.)	—	—	—
Small (less than 15 oz.)	—	—	—
Fancy	—	—	—

———— 42
(Type I)

———— 43
(Type II)

———— 44
(Type III)

(e) Where do you usually buy this type of specialty
bread?

	Type I	*Type II*	*Type III*
Supermarket	—	—	—
Neighborhood grocery	—	—	—
Bakery	—	—	—
Bake my own bread	—	—	—
Other (please specify)	———————————————————

———— 45–49
(Type I)

———— 50–54
(Type II)

———— 55–59
(Type III)

(f) At what meals at home is this type of specialty bread
usually served?

Exhibit 13–1   *(Continued)*

*For Editor's
Use Only*

	Type I	Type II	Type III	
				_____ 60–62 *(Type I)*
Breakfast	—	—	—	_____ 63–65
Noon meal	—	—	—	*(Type II)*
Evening meal	—	—	—	_____ 66–68 *(Type III)*

(g) Is this type of specialty bread used for sandwiches to
be eaten away from home, such as at school or at
work?

	Type I	Type II	Type III	
				_____ 69 *(Type I)*
Yes	—	—	—	_____ 70
No	—	—	—	*(Type II)*
				_____ 71 *(Type III)*

(h) Is this type of specialty bread used for between-meal
snacks at home, such as sandwiches or with spreads
like butter and jam or peanut butter and jelly?

	Type I	Type II	Type III	
				_____ 1 *(Type I)*
Yes	—	—	—	_____ 2
No	—	—	—	*(Type II)*
				_____ 3 *(Type III)*

(i) When you have friends over for a meal or other special occasion when food is prepared, is this type of
specialty bread usually served?

	Type I	Type II	Type III	
				_____ 4 *(Type I)*
Yes	—	—	—	_____ 5
No	—	—	—	*(Type II)*
				_____ 6 *(Type III)*

If you (or your family) eat(s) more than one type of
specialty bread, as indicated under question 7a, please
go back to question 7b. This time answer questions 7b

Exhibit 13–1 *(Continued)*

through i for type II and type III specialty bread respectively. (Your answer under question 7 indicates which type of bread types II and III are). Mark your responses in the appropriate columns ("Type II," "Type III").

8. What brand or brands of bread are you using now?

Northridge	—	Albertsons	—
Williams	—	Home (Bakery)	—
Franciscan	—	Mackenzie Farms	—
Mayfair	—	Oroweat	—
Franz	—	Stoneground	—
Hi-Gluten	—	Amrit (Bakery)	—
Willamette	—	Safeway	—
Wonder	—	Sheepherder	—
Christensons (Bakery)	—		

_____ 7–15
(Northridge-
Christenson)
_____ 16–23
(Albertsons-
Sheepherder)

9. Now, please take the stack of *white* cards in front of you. Each of these cards has a characteristic of bread printed on them. We would like you to sort the cards into three piles—those you think are *very important* for a bread to have, those that are *somewhat important* for a bread to have, and those that are *not important* for a bread to have. There are no right or wrong numbers of cards for any pile. You should also feel free to move the cards from one pile to another until you feel that they are in the right one.

10. Now, we would like you to arrange the cards in each pile by putting the most important one on top, the next most important one under it, and so on until you have arranged all the cards in each of the piles.

Please record below for each of the piles the order in which you arranged the cards. (Record letters printed on cards.)

Very Important	*Somewhat Important*	*Not Important*
1. __	1. __	1. __
2. __	2. __	2. __
3. __	3. __	3. __
4. __	4. __	4. __
5. __	5. __	5. __
6. __	6. __	6. __
7. __	7. __	7. __
8. __	8. __	8. __
9. __	9. __	9. __
10. __	10. __	10. __

_____ 24–33
(Very Important)
_____ 34–43
(Somewhat
Important)
_____ 44–53
(Not Important)

11. Below you will find some statements about which we would like your opinion. We ask you to indicate how much you agree or disagree with these statements. The phrases indicating how much you agree or disagree with the statements are listed on top of question *a* and on top of each page. Please choose the phrase that best describes

Exhibit 13-1 *(Continued)*

your feelings about the statements printed on the left. There are no right or wrong answers and we would like you to be completely frank in your answers.

	Strongly Agree	Agree	Agree Somewhat	Neither Agree or Disagree	Disagree Somewhat	Disagree	Strongly Disagree	Don't Know	
a. Foods ought to be made only of natural ingredients rather than have additives.	—	—	—	—	—	—	—	—	_____ 54
b. I usually buy the same brand once I find one that I like.	—	—	—	—	—	—	—	—	_____ 55
c. All white breads are pretty much alike.	—	—	—	—	—	—	—	—	_____ 56
d. I am considered to be a good cook.	—	—	—	—	—	—	—	—	_____ 57
e. "Stocky" people are naturally overweight and there isn't much they can do about it.	—	—	—	—	—	—	—	—	_____ 58
f. Brands are important because you know what quality of product you're buying.	—	—	—	—	—	—	—	—	_____ 59
g. Having bread at most meals is necessary for a balanced diet.	—	—	—	—	—	—	—	—	_____ 60
h. It doesn't matter whether you're buying bread or anything else, you only get what you pay for.	—	—	—	—	—	—	—	—	_____ 61
i. If you eat white bread, answer the following question: I am willing to pay 10 or 15 cents extra									_____

Exhibit 13–1   (*Continued*)

for a loaf of white
bread to get the
kind I want. — — — — — — — — — — ———— 62

j. If you eat whole
wheat bread, an-
swer the following
question:
I am willing to pay
10 or 15 cents extra
for a loaf of whole
wheat bread to get
the kind I want. — — — — — — — — — — ———— 63

k. If you eat specialty
bread, answer the
following question:
I am willing to pay
10 or 15 cents extra
for a loaf of spe-
cialty bread to get
the kind I want. — — — — — — — — — — ———— 64

l. A man needs a
hearty breakfast to
start the day right. — — — — — — — — — — ———— 65

m. Bread bought at a
bakery is better
than that you buy
off the counter at
the store. — — — — — — — — — — ———— 66

n. Whole wheat and
other dark breads are
more healthful than
white bread. — — — — — — — — — — ———— 67

o. I like to try new
brands to see if they
are better. — — — — — — — — — — ———— 68

p. Soft white bread is
bad for the teeth. — — — — — — — — — — ———— 69

q. Crust on bread should
be thick and chewy — — — — — — — — — — ———— 70

r. Bread for sandwiches
should be softer than
that used on the table. — — — — — — — — — — ———— 71

s. If there ever was a
shortage of bread it
would cause quite a
change in (my) (our)
eating habits. — — — — — — — — — — ———— 72

12. Now, please take the stack of *pink* cards in front of you.
Each of these cards has a brand name of bread on them.

Exhibit 13–1 *(Continued)*

We would like for you to sort them into two piles. In the first pile put those you *have heard of* and in the second pile those you have *never heard of*. There is no necessary reason you should have heard of any particular brand. After you have sorted the cards, please record below which cards are in the *Never Heard* of pile using the letter printed on top of each card.

"Never Heard Of" Brands _____ 1–12

— —
— —
— —
— —
— —
— —

13. Now, we would like you to sort the brands *you have heard of* into two piles. In the first pile place the cards with the names of those you *have used in the last year* and in the second pile put those you *have not used in the last year*.
Record below the brands you have not used in the last year. Again, use the letters printed on top of each card.

Brands Heard of But Not Used in Last Year _____ 13–24

— — —
— — —
— — —
— — —

14. Now one more sort. Arrange the cards with the brands *you have used in the last year* by their quality. That is, put the card with the name of the brand you judge to have the highest quality on top, the brand with the next highest quality second, and so on until you have arranged all the cards.
Record below the order of the cards using the letter on top of the card.

Quality of Brands Used _____ 25–31

__ (Highest)
—
—
—
—
__ (Lowest)

Now we want to ask you some questions about watching television, reading the newspaper, and listening to the radio.

Exhibit 13–1 *(Continued)*

For Editor's
Use Only

15. About how many hours of television would you say you
watch at different times of the day?
(If you don't watch television at all, check here __)   _____ 32

	Week- days	Week- ends	
Morning (7 A.M.–12 A.M.)	—	—	_____ 33–38
Early Afternoon (12 A.M.–4 P.M.)	—	—	(Weekdays)
Late Afternoon (4 P.M.–6 P.M.)	—	—	
News (6 P.M.–7 P.M.)	—	—	
Evening (7 P.M.–11 P.M.)	—	—	_____ 39–44
Night (after 11 P.M.)	—	—	(Weekends)

(a) How often do you read a newspaper?
Every day   —   _____ 45
Almost every day   —
Several times a week __
Once or twice a week __
Seldom or never   —

(b) Which newspaper (is it) (are they)?
Register Guard __   _____ 46
Oregonian   —   _____ 47
Home town newspaper (specify)_____   _____ 48
Other (specify)_____ _____ 49

16. (a) About how many hours would you say you listen to
the radio at different times during the day?

	Week- days	Week- ends	
Morning (7 A.M.–12 A.M.)	—	—	_____ 50–53
Afternoon (12 A.M.–5 P.M.)	—	—	(Weekdays)
Early Evening (5 P.M.–9 P.M.)	—	—	
Late Evening (from 9 P.M. on)	—	—	_____ 54–57
			(Weekends)

(b) Do you listen to AM, FM, or both?
AM __   FM __   Both __   _____ 58

(c) What are your favorite kinds of programs?

Music:		*Other:*		
Country	—	News	—	_____ 59–62
Contemporary (pop)	—	Sports	—	(Music)
Easy listening	—	Talk Shows	—	
Classical	—	Other (specify)	—	_____ 63–66
		_____		(Other)

Now we need to ask you some questions about you (and
your family).

17. How long have you lived in the Eugene-Springfield area?   _____ 1

18. Do you live alone or with your family?
Alone __   Family __   _____ 2

Exhibit 13–1 *(Continued)*

(a) If you live alone, please indicate which age group you
are in:
    Below 35 __
    35–55   __
    Over 55 __   (Skip to question 19)   _____ 3

(b) If part of family, how many people are there in the
family who live in your home?
    1 __   4 __   7 __
    2 __   5 __   8 __
    3 __   6 __   9 or more __   _____ 4

(c) Are there children who live with you?
    Yes __   No __   _____ 5
    If yes,

(d) How old is the youngest child?
    Under 6 __   13–18   __
    6–12   __   Over 18 __   _____ 6

19. What is the occupation of the chief wage earner? (Please
give type of job, not company) _____   _____ 7

20. Which of the following categories comes closest to (your)
(the family's) total income per year before taxes?
    Less than $5,000 __ $10,001–$15,000 __
    $5,001–$7,000   __ $15,001–$20,000 __
    $7,001–$10,000 __   Over $20,000   __

21. What was the last grade of school you completed?   _____ 9
    Some high school   __   Some collete   __
    Completed high school __   Completed college __

Please check to see that you did not miss any items.
The interviewer will be back at the time agreed to answer any questions.
Our sincere thanks for your assistance.
    Far West Research Associates

Respondent, Interviewer, and Editor Identification

Sequence Number
_____

To be completed by interviewer when completed questionnaire picked up.
Respondent Name _____   Time questionnaire left _____
Address (Street)_____   Time completed
    questionnaire picked up _____

    (City) _____(State) _____
Interviewer Name _____
Date of Interview _____
My impression is that the responses are
    generally valid _____
    may be invalid with respect to

_____

_____

_____

Exhibit 13–1   *(Concluded)*

To be completed by editor
  Date received _____
  Disposition:
    a) accepted _____
    b) Returned to interviewer _____
    c) If (b), date returned _____
  Date edited _____
  Editor _____

Addendum

(Not a part of questionnaire)

Bread characteristics appearing on *white cards* used in answering questions 9 and 10:
  G—Bread that is soft
  H—Bread that is low in calories
  I—Bread that is not too dry
  J—Bread that "sticks to the ribs"
  K—Bread that is nutritious
  L—Bread that tastes good
  M—Bread that has the right crust
  N—Bread that is sliced right
  O—Bread that has the right preservatives added
  P—Bread that provides quick energy
  Q—Bread that is fresh
  R—Bread that has the right texture
  S—Bread that comes in the right-sized loaf
  T—Bread that has the right vitamins added
  U—Bread that smells good
Brands of bread appearing on *pink cards* used in questions 12, 13, and 14

G—Northridge	O—Christensons (Bakery)
H—Williams	P—Albertsons
I—Franciscan	Q—Home (Bakery)
J—Mayfair	R—Mackenzie Farms
K—Franz	S—Oroweat
L—Hi-Gluten	T—Stoneground
M—Williamette	U—Amrit (Bakery)
N—Wonder	V—Safeway
	W—Sheepherder

A method of checking to ensure that the interviews were actually made should also be a part of the control procedure. (See Chapter 11 for details.) If the sample is large, it is usually worthwhile to assign a *sequence number* to the interviews. This serves to identify the sequence in which the interviews were received and is used for purposes of grouping the interviews into batches for editing and coding, and for checking to ensure that each interviewer is maintaining his schedule.

It is not necessary to keep a sample book on nonprobability samples since selection of the sample is done by the interviewer rather than being prespecified. Assigning sequence numbers to interviews as they are received is useful, however, as the sequence number can serve as an identification number. Sequence numbers were assigned for the Willamette Bakeries interviews.

Editing

The responsibility of the editor is to ensure that the data requested are *present, readable, and accurate*. These requirements, several examples of editing problems encountered in the Willamette study, and some procedural rules for editing are discussed in this section.

Obtaining Missing Data, Making Data Readable, and Ensuring Accuracy

Almost every questionnaire will have some items not responded to as well as no responses at all from some of the sample respondents. Some items, and sometimes entire pages, will be overlooked by the interviewer or the respondent if the questionnaire is self-administered. In other cases there is a direct refusal to respond to specific items or to the overall questionnaire.

The editor has several options in the way he deals with item non-response. The item can be left unanswered, the editor can enter estimated data, a telephone call can be made to the respondent requesting the data, the questionnaire can be returned to the interviewer with a request that another call be made on the respondent to obtain the missing data, the item can be treated as having a "don't know" response, or the questionnaire can be discarded and treated as a complete nonresponse.

The editor is also called upon to decipher ambiguous and illegible data. Check marks are sometimes placed between the "yes" and "no" boxes; which was the intended answer? Answers are sometimes written in an illegible form and the intended meaning somehow has to be determined. The editor can resolve some of these questions directly and must refer others back to the interviewer.

The accuracy of the data is a continuing concern to the editor. He must watch both for *internal inconsistencies* and an *undue amount of consistency* in the interviews. An interview that shows a brand as "never heard of" and also as "currently used" clearly contains an error. A similarity of responses in all of the interviews of the same interviewer is cause for concern as well. This may be an indication of interviewer bias or cheating.

Here, as in all other phases of the gathering of information to help make the decisions, the cost versus the value of the added accuracy must be evaluated. One investigator has conducted an experiment in which a sample of questionnaires was edited carefully whereas another sample of questionnaires from the same survey was edited only superficially.[1] He concluded that the careful (and expensive) editing contributed little in the way of added accuracy.

Some Examples of Editing Problems—Willamette Bakeries Study

Lack of Data Required for Life Cycle Classification. While editing the first set of completed questionnaires it was discovered that the data necessary for distinguishing between the "young married without children" and the "empty nest" stages of the life cycle were not provided by the questionnaire. Question 18(a) asks "If you live *alone* (italics added), please indicate which age group you are in: below 35____, 35–55____, over 55____." This question was intended to separate the "young single" from the "solitary survivor" respondents. Questions 18(b), (c), and (d) were concerned with whether children lived with the family and, if so, how many and the age of the youngest, but no age was determined for married respondents whose household did not include children.

In some cases the editor could infer the probable correct life cycle stage from the response to the question, *"How long have you lived in the Eugene-Springfield area?"* (Question 17). If the response was 35 years or more, it was assumed that "empty nest" rather than "young married without children" was the correct assignment. When the response to this question was less than 35 years, the interviewer had to be contacted and asked the approximate age of the respondent.

Interviewers were instructed to obtain a response to the question on age for all respondents (not just those who lived alone) thereafter.

Missing Income Information. The largest single item for which responses were not obtained was income. Since the income classes that had been established were fairly wide (Question 20) and information on the occupation of the chief wage earner and age was available (Questions 18(a) and 19), reasonably good estimates of the income of the *chief wage earner* could be made. In those cases where the respondent lived alone, this estimate was used. It was also used for those families with a child under six, as it was *assumed* that the chief wage earner was the *only* wage earner. In other cases an attempt was made to find a matching family in terms of general nature of occupation and age and the same income class was assigned. Failing that, the assumption that the chief wage earner was the only wage earner was made and an estimate of his or her income was

---

[1] S. Nordbotten, "The Efficiency of Automatic Detection and Course of Errors in Individual Observations as Compared with Other Means for Improving the Quality of Statistics," *Proceedings of the 35th Session of the International Statistical Institute,* Belgrade, Yugoslavia, September 1965, 417–441.

used. Note that some fairly tenuous assumptions were made in this area. Fortunately, income was not a major variable in the analyses.

Some Procedural Rules in Editing

Several rules have evolved out of the accumulated experience of editors that are worth noting.

1. *Interviews should be turned in and edited promptly.* With prompt receipt and editing, missing, illegible, and ambiguous data can be identified quickly and referred to the interviewer while the interview is still recent. It may enable instructions to be given to the interviewers to obtain additional information that the editing process discloses is needed. This was the case with regard to age in the Willamette study.

2. *Editors should be assigned interviews by interviewer.* The better an editor knows the recording style and the handwriting of an interviewer, the better he is able to interpret the data on the questionnaire. It is also easier to discover instances of interviewer bias or cheating if this procedure is followed.

3. *Editors should make changes by crossing out or transferring data rather than by erasing.* The original data should be preserved for future reference if required. Changes made in the data on the questionnaire should be in colored pencil so that they are easily identifiable as editorial entries.

4. *When more than one editor is used, editing instructions should be prepared.* Editing requires extensive use of judgment. Whenever possible, however, instructions should be developed to reduce the amount of editorial judgment required. Agreement among editors on the general procedures to be used for such editorial problems as supplying missing data, checking for internal inconsistency, and treating ambiguous responses will provide for greater consistency in the editing of the data when more than one editor is involved.

Coding

Although coding may also be done by the editor, it is a separate step. It involves *establishing categories* and *assigning data to them.*

Establishing Categories

Categories for the answers to multiple-choice or dichotomous questions are established at the time the question is formulated. In the Willamette study, for example, the question on the frequency of purchase of white bread (Question 3(a)) has six different possible response categories ranging from "three times a week" to "once every three months."

Response categories to open-end (free answer) questions have to be established after the interviews are made. If a question has been asked in the Willamette study such as "What is there about a really good white bread that makes it good?", it would have been necessary for the coder to read the responses and then establish categories. Such categories as "good taste," "freshness," and others suggested by the responses would be selected.

Assigning Data to Categories

Structured questionnaires using multiple-choice or dichotomous questions allow *precording.* That is, the code may be put directly on the questionnaire so that the responses are automatically coded as they are recorded. This approach was not used in the Willamette study. Instead, *postcoding,* the assignment of code values to the responses after the responses are received, was utilized.

Postcoding of data to categories for open-end questions is much more difficult than it is for either multiple-choice or dichotomous questions. Consider the following (hypothetical) answer to the question shown:

Question: What is there about a really good white bread that makes it good?
Answer: I like bread that is soft and fresh and not too crumbly and doesn't let the tomato juice drip out when I'm eating a sandwich. For dinner I like a bread that is chewy and tastes good.

Should the coder code the response to show that "softness" or that "chewiness" was one of the characteristics desired? The response involves two different ways of eating bread, which adds further complications to the coding problem.

Assuming the data are to be tabulated by machine, they will need to be arrayed in a form that is easily readable and conducive to few errors by the keypunch operator. If the data are to be keypunched, they sometimes can be punched satisfactorily from the questionnaire, particularly if they are located in a coding strip on the margin of each page. (This was the procedure used in the Willamette study.) Otherwise, they should be transferred to a standard coding form of the type used to prepare data of other kinds for keypunching.[2]

Tabulation

For all but the simplest kinds of studies, it is worthwhile to tabulate the data by machine. This eliminates the tedium of hand tabulation, reduces

[2] For an extensive discussion of all aspects of coding see P. S. Sidel, "Coding," in R. S. Ferber, ed., *Handbook of Marketing Research* (New York: McGraw-Hill Book Company, 1974), 2–178 to 2–199.

errors, and leaves the data in a form suitable for direct input to a computer for analysis. It also permits a check by the computer on the internal consistency of the data thus the identification of some recording, editing, coding and/or transcription errors that have not been detected to that point. New variables can be generated by the computer as well.

Transcription of Data

By far the most common type of transcription process to get the data into machine readable form is keypunching into tab cards (that is, computer or IBM cards). Other methods that are available and are sometimes used include *mark sensed questionnaires* and *optical scanning*. Mark sensing requires that the answer be recorded by marking it with a special pencil in an area that is coded for that answer and a machine "reads" it by sensing the area in which it is recorded. An elaborate system named FOSDIC (Foto-Electric Sensing Device for Input to Computers) using this principle was designed for and is used by the Bureau of the Census for transcription of census data. Optical scanning involves direct machine "reading" of alphanumeric codes and transcription onto cards, magnetic tape, or disk. These methods are usually too expensive and awkward to use, however, except for very large or repeated studies in which the same collection form is used. Consumer panels, buyer intention surveys, and the Census of Population are examples of field studies in which automated transcription processes are used.

Keypunching will normally be used in a sample survey. It is relatively fast (about 100 cards per hour) and a competent operator does not make many errors. A verifier, a machine that gives an error signal if a duplicate card that is being punched does not match the first, is available. Verifying doubles the cost of keypunching. Since a good operator will not make many errors, verification is often skipped if the operator is experienced and the data are not difficult to punch accurately, particularly when the data are to be machine "cleaned."

Although a competent keypunch operator was used for the Willamette study data, the cards were verified. The punching was done from the coding strip on the questionnaire rather than code sheets and the data were not to be checked by the computer.

Computer Editing of Data

Computer editing, or "cleaning," of data consists of a computerized check for errors. Using either a specially written or a general-purpose program, the computer is programmed to check for logical errors and inconsistencies in the punched data. The major error types[3] that can be identified by computer are:

1. *Wild code check.* If the respondent can only answer "yes" or "no" to a question, and the card is punched to indicate a third response, an error is indicated.

2. *"Not applicable" inconsistencies.* If the respondent indicates that the family does not eat whole wheat bread, the questions on frequency, amounts, and place of purchase of whole wheat bread should be coded "not applicable." If this is not the case, an error is indicated.

3. *Internal inconsistencies.* An example is when the occupation of the chief wage earner is shown as "physician" and the level of education is coded as "one year of college."

4. *Reliability question inconsistencies.* Sometimes the same question is asked the respondent in two different ways as a check on the reliability of responses. An example is "When did you complete high school?" and "How old are you?" If the punched responses are inconsistent, an error or an unreliable response is indicated.

5. *Checks on items for known or suspected coding errors.*

The errors that are discovered can either be listed for correction after review by the coder or, in some cases, automatically corrected by the computer.

Generating New Variables

It is often necessary to create new variables as a part of the analysis procedure. Although several kinds of such variables are possible, only the three most commonly used are discussed here.[4]

First, *new variables are often generated from combinations of other variables in the data.* In the Willamette study two such variables were generated, "amount of (white) (whole wheat) (specialty) bread purchased per person per week" and "stage of life cycle" of the respondent. The first of these variables was created by programming the computer to make the necessary calculations and the second by programming it with the logical rules necessary to assign cases.

Second, *it may be desirable to collect intervally scaled data as such and later assign them to classes.* Family income is often collected in dollars, for example, and later classified by a convenient number of income brackets or deciles. The coder can classify by brackets but would have to examine the entire income array to code by decile. A new variable generated by the computer, income decile, is the usual way this is done.

---

[3] This listing of errors follows that given in Sidel, op. cit.

[4] For a detailed discussion of new variable generation, see J. B. Lansing and J. N. Morgan, *Economic Survey Methods* (Ann Arbor: Institute for Social Research, 1971), 238–243.

Third, *new variables may be added from secondary data*. It may be desirable to add such information as the median level of income, education, and employment in the county of residence of the respondent to be used in the analysis.

Tabulation of Frequency Distributions and Calculation of Summarizing Statistics for Each Variable

Although it is necessary to get the data into a form such that the basic data array described at the beginning of the chapter (an array showing the value of each variable for each sample unit) could be produced if desired, the total array is seldom reproduced as such. Rather, the data for each variable are tabulated as a separate, one-way frequency distribution. The data reduction process is completed by calculating measures of central tendency (mean, median, mode) and measures of dispersion (standard deviation, variance, range). Although the tabulation of frequency distributions and calculation of the summarizing statistics are two separate steps, they are discussed jointly here because the computer programs that do the tabulating typically calculate the summarizing statistics as well.

One-Way Frequency Distributions

The frequency distribution of the hours spent watching television during weekday evenings (Question 15) is shown in Table 13–1 in three different forms: an *absolute frequency* (the count of respondents falling in each time class), a *relative frequency* (the percentage of respondence in each class), and a *cumulative frequency* (the percentage of respondents who report watching as much or less than the time of that class.)

Table 13–1   Time Television Watched During Weekday Evenings (7 p.m.–11 p.m.)

Time Watched	*Absolute Frequency*	*Relative Frequency (per cent)*	*Cumulative Frequency (per cent)*
Less than 0.1 hours	42	23.9	23.9
0.1 to 1.0 hours	60	34.1	58.0
1.1 to 2.0 hours	41	23.3	81.2
2.1 to 3.0	23	13.1	94.3
3.1 to 4.0 hours	10	5.7	100.0
Total	176	100.0	100.0

Mean 0.98	Standard Deviation 1.15
Mode 0.1 to 1.0 hours	Variance 1.33
Median 0.82	Range 4.0

A *one-way* frequency distribution is a frequency distribution for a single variable. It is also called a *simple tabulation* and is to be distinguished from a *two-way* or *n-way* frequency distribution (two variables, *n* variables). These *n*-way frequency distributions are also known as *cross tabulations* and are described in the next chapter.

Summary Statistics

There are two major kinds of summarizing statistics. The first provides measures of the midpoint of the distribution and is known as *measures of central tendency*. The second gives an indication of the amount of variation in the data comprising the distribution and is known as *measures of dispersion*.

Measures of Central Tendency. The three primary measures of central tendency are the *arithmetic mean,* the *median,* and the *mode*.

The *arithmetic mean* can be computed only from intervally scaled data. It is obtained by adding all the observations and dividing the sum by the number of observations. When the exact value of each observation is known, this is a simple process. Often, however, arithmetic means must be calculated from absolute frequency distributions. In these cases, the midpoint of each category is multiplied by the number of observations in that category, the resultant category values are summed, and the total is divided by the total number of observations, or:

$$\bar{x} = \frac{\sum_{i=1}^{h} f_i x_i}{n}$$

where

f_i = the frequency of the *i*th class
x_i = the midpoint of that class
h = the number of classes, and
n = the total number of observations.

The mean amount of time that television was watched by the 176 respondents in the Willamette Bakeries study was 0.98 hours.

The *median,* which requires only ordinal data, is obtained by finding the value below which 50 per cent of the observations lie. If cumulative frequencies were calculated for the data array, it would be the value for which the cumulative frequency was 50 per cent. The median amount of time spent watching television on weekday evenings, as reported by the sample in the bread study, was 0.82 hours.

The *mode,* requiring only nominal data, is found by determining the value that appears most frequently. In a relative frequency distribution, it is the class that has the highest frequency. In the bread study the modal amount of time spent watching television in the evening on weekdays was 0.1 to 1.0 hours (34.1 per cent of the respondents reported watching this amount.)

The three measures will *not* be the same for distributions of values that are not symmetrical, but they are useful for different purposes. For obtaining an *estimate of a total amount,* the sample *arithmetic mean* times the number of population units provides the best estimate. One could estimate the total weekday evening television viewing time in the bread study sample area, for example, if one wanted an estimate of energy consumed by television sets, number of commercials aired while sets were on, and so on. If one wants an *estimate of the most representative amount,* then the *mode* should be used. In the bread study the mode would provide the best basis for estimating the most representative number of commercials seen by viewers, for example. If one wants an average that is *unaffected by extremes,* the *median* is the best estimator. The median is a better measure of average income than either the mean or the mode, for example, since the distribution is asymmetrical and a few large incomes distort the mean. Weekday evening television viewing time in the bread study has a similar distribution (also skewed toward the higher values). The median would, therefore, provide the best estimate of the average number of commercials aired while sets were on in the sample area.

Measures of Dispersion. The *standard deviation, variance,* and *range* were described in the chapter dealing with the determination of sample size (Chapter 6). All three are measures of how "spread out" the data are. The smaller these three values are the more compact are the data.

The formula for the standard deviation of a sample calculated from an array of the sample data is[5]

$$s = \sqrt{\frac{\sum_{i=1}^{n}(x_i - \bar{x})^2}{n}}$$

where

[5] The formula for the sample standard deviation calculated from data in a frequency distribution is

$$s = \sqrt{\frac{\sum_{i=1}^{n} f_i(x_i - \bar{x})^2}{h}}$$

where f_i = the frequency of the ith class, x_i = the midpoint of the ith class, h = the number of classes, and all of the other symbols are the same as the formula for arrayed data.

$$s = \text{sample standard deviation}$$
$$x_i = \text{the value of the } i\text{th observation}$$
$$\bar{x} = \text{the sample mean, and}$$
$$n = \text{the sample size}$$

The *variance,* the square of the standard deviation, is found by the same formulas with the square root sign removed. The *range* is equal to the maximum minus the minimum value in the data array.

In the bread study the standard deviation of the amount of weekday evening television viewing time was 1.15 hours, the variance was 1.33 hours, and the range 4.0 hours.

Computer Programs for Data Reduction

A large number of packaged statistical programs for computers will tabulate one-way frequency distributions and calculate summary measures. Most of them will tabulate 2-way and/or n-way frequency distributions as well and provide measures of association between the variables (chi square, correlation coefficient, t value, or F value). These package programs include BASIC, BMD, DATATEXT, STAT PACK, and SPSS.[6]

The choice among programs will be governed in part by the capabilities of the computer that is available. The smaller computers do not have the capacity to handle the BMD, DATATEXT, and SPSS programs, for example. The choice of program will also depend on the desired output of summary measures and on such features as easy to use, ability to deal with missing data, and maintenance of accuracy when dealing with large numbers.

The *SPSS (Statistical Package for the Social Sciences)* is a widely used package program and was used in the Willamette study. It provides one-way absolute, relative, and cumulative frequency distributions and mean, median, mode, standard deviation, standard error, variance, range, and other summarizing measures[7] for each variable. It also can be used to provide tabulations for two or more variables for which it computes and prints chi square and other measures of association and can do bivariate

[6] For descriptions of these programs see the following: W. J. Dixon, ed., *Bio-medical Computer Programs* (Los Angeles: University of California Press, 1968); A. Couch, *DATATEXT Manual,* rev. ed. (Cambridge, Mass.: Harvard University Laboratory of Social Relations, 1971); *Stat Pack Statistical Package* (Kalamazoo, Mich.: Western Michigan University, undated); *Time Shared Basic Program Library Handbook* (Cupertino, Calif.: Hewlett-Packard Software Center, 1971); and N. Nie, D. H. Bent, and C. H. Hull, *SPSS-Statistical Package for the Social Sciences* (New York: The McGraw-Hill Book Co., 1970).

[7] The other measures provided include a coefficient of skewness (a measure of the asymmetry of the distribution) and a coefficient of kurtosis (a measure of the peakedness of the distribution).

and multivariate regressions and factor analyses. Techniques such as these for statistical inference are covered in the next chapter.

Summary

Data reduction is an important, if unglamorous, part of data analysis. It consists of all the *steps necessary to get the data ready for analysis and the calculation of summarizing statistics.*

The data are ready for analysis when a *basic data array* that is as complete and as error free as possible is prepared. This is a table comprised of the recorded values for each variable for each sample unit. Even a small scale survey will have several thousand recorded values in a basic data array; the study of bread purchasing and consumption patterns reported here involved over 38,000 values in the array.

The steps involved in developing the basic data array are (1) establishing *field controls,* (2) *editing,* (3) *coding,* (4) *tabulating,* and (5) *generating new variables.* The basic array is typically reproduced in the form of a series of tables, each table presenting a one-way frequency distribution for a variable.

The data for most studies are tabulated by machine. This procedure has the advantages of permitting computer editing ("cleaning" of the data), generating new variables by computer, and having the data accessible to the computer for analysis. A number of "package" computer programs are available for preparing tabulations and running analyses of data.

Summarizing statistics enable the analyst to understand the data array better. They may also be used for some purposes in lieu of the data from which they were calculated, including *measures of central tendency* (the mean, median, and mode are the most commonly used) and *measures of dispersion* (standard deviation, variance, and range).

Questions and Problems

13.1. Coding instructions were not prepared in the Willamette Bakeries Study since there were only 176 questionnaires and one person did all of the coding. However, assume there was a larger sample, more than one coder was to be used, and coding instructions were needed.
   (a) Develop instructions for coding the response to Question 19 (*What is the occupation of the chief wage earner?*) by whether the response is (1) *blue-collar,* (2) *white-collar,* or (3) *managerial-professional.*
   (b) Using your instructions, how should the following occupations be coded?
      elementary schoolteacher, surgical nurse, lumber mill foreman, supervision of highway maintenance, owner of neighborhood grocery store, owner-driver of truck and trailer—hauls on contract.

(c) How should "unemployed" responses be coded?

(d) How should "retired" responses be coded?

13.2. Prepare instructions for the computer programmer for generating the new variable, "quantity of white bread purchased per family member per week," in the tabulation of the Willamette Bakeries study data.

13.3. A consumer survey conducted by the Institute for Social Research* contained the questions,

C19 *Do you (or your family) do any of your own repair work on cars?*
— Yes   — No (go to Section D)
(If yes)

C20 *What kind of work have you done on your cars in the last year?*
_____
_____

The Codebook for question C20 gave the following codes and examples for each:

Code	Example of Answer for Code
5	*Yes, complex repairs that usually take a skilled mechanic (rebuilt engine or transmission).*
4	*Yes, extensive repairs taking much skill (rings, valves, bearings), install factory rebuilt engine, king pins, ball joints, transmission work, motor work, or "I do anything that needs doing."*
3	*Yes, some skill required (brakes, wheel bearings, exhaust system, starter).*
2	*Yes, some skill (tune-up, points, plugs, adjust carburetor, fuel pump).*
1	*Yes, little or no skill, mostly maintenance (oil change, greasing, tire switching, touch-up painting).*
0	*Inappropriate, family does not have car, does no repair work.*
9	*Answer not given whether repairs were done or what kind of repairs.*
7	*Yes, but not in the last year.*

How should the following replies have been coded? Justify your decisions.
(a) "I owned different cars, and so did lots—first one overhauled engine four times—always grease car; tune it up"
(b) "Installed new alternator"
(c) "Did minor motor tune-up"
(d) "Put in new speedometer cable and installed stereo system"
(e) "Put in new head gasket"
(f) "Haven't had to do anything on my car other than change the oil and put in new plugs but I helped my neighbor install a new transmission"
(g) "I haven't worked on my car but I put a new inboard engine in my boat"

* J. B. Lansing and J. N. Morgan, *Economic Survey Methods* (Ann Arbor: Institute for Social Research, 1971), 247. Copyright © 1971 by the University of Michigan; reprinted by permission of the publisher, the Survey Research Center of the Institute for Social Research.

13.4. An open-end question that was considered for use in the Willamette
Bakeries Study was

"What is there about a really good white bread that makes it good?"
It was decided to use questions 9 and 10 instead with bread characteristics
listed on cards. (The characteristics used are given in the addendum to
the questionnaire.)

(a) What effect(s), if any, do you think this decision had on
    (i) the nature of responses received?
    (ii) the *editing* of the interviews?
    (iii) the *coding* of the interviews?
    (iv) the *tabulation* of the interviews?

(b) Prepare the coding instructions for this question that would have
been needed if the question was used.

(c) All things considered, do you think that the question, or Questions
9 and 10 of the questionnaire, was the better choice? Explain.

13.5. Three alternative codes for the age of family members are given as follows. Which code would you choose? Why?

1		*2*		*3*	
Code	*Age*	*Code*	*Age*	*Code*	*Age*
0	1–10	0	0–9	0	Under 1 year
1	10–20	1	10–19	1	1–10
2	20–30	2	20–29	2	11–20
3	30–40	3	30–39	3	21–30
4	40–50	4	40–49	4	31–40
5	50–60	5	50–59	5	41–50
6	60 or over	6	60 or over	6	51–60
9	no information	9	no information	7	60 or over
				9	no information

13.6. In designing a birth control campaign for a developing country, a consulting firm found that the length and complexity of its messages must be
based on the education level of the population. Messages that are effective
with individuals with limited educations were not effective with those
with more education, and vice versa. This relationship held even with
only one year's difference in education. Research found that the mean
education level was 10 years, the median 8 years, and the mode 7 years.
In order to reach the most people, what education level should the message be aimed at? Why?

13.7. A multinational firm has developed a new product that is particularly
appropriate for developing countries. In order to meet the firm's sales
potential requirements, the product will be introduced only in those countries with 1 million or more households with an annual income of $800
or more. Initial research uncovers the following data. In which country
or countries, if any, should the product be introduced? In which countries
should the product *not* be introduced?

Annual Household Income

Country	Mean	Median	Mode	Variance	Number of Households
A	$1,000	$274	$250	$1250	5,000,000
B	870	318	294	968	3,500,000
C	806	804	796	200	2,700,000
D	830	780	720	800	2,000,000
E	834	820	816	648	1,900,000

Selected Bibliography

LANSING, J. B., and J. N. MORGAN. *Economic Survey Methods*. Ann Arbor: Institute for Social Research, 1971. A book that reflects the extensive experience of the authors and of the Institute for Social Research in conducting surveys on economic (and social) problems.

NIE, N. H., D. H. BENT, and C. H. HULL. *SPSS–Statistical Package for the Social Sciences*. New York: McGraw-Hill Book Company, 1970. A description of one of the more widely used package programs for tabulating and running (selected) analyses of data from field investigations.

SIDEL, P. S. "Coding," chapter in Robert Ferber, ed. *Handbook of Marketing Research*. New York: McGraw-Hill Book Co., 1974, 2–178 to 2–199. An authoritative discussion of the problems of developing and assigning codes to survey data.

STONE, P. J., D. C. DUNPHY, M. S. SMITH, and D. M. OGILVIE. *The General Inquirer: A Computer Approach to Content Analysis*. Cambridge: Mass.; The M.I.T. Press, 1966. A description of one of the better generalized programs for computer editing of data.

STUART, W. J., "Computer Editing of Survey Data—Five Years of Experience in BLS Manpower Surveys." *Journal of the American Statistical Association*, **61** (June 1966). A discussion of an application of computer editing of survey data.

CHAPTER 14

Analysis of Data: Statistical Techniques

In decisional research the analysis of data is done to provide information to help solve the problem at hand. It is an important, sometimes difficult, and always interesting part of the research process. Without a sound analysis the best that can happen is that part of the information that could have been provided will not be available. The worst possibility is that misleading "information" will be supplied that will contribute to a bad decision.

In this chapter we discuss the analysis of data once it has been edited, coded, tabulated, and the basic summarizing statistics have been calculated. Our concern here is with the *estimation* of population values, *hypothesis testing,* and the use of techniques for analyzing relationships between two variables—*bivariate techniques*—and more than two variables—*multivariate techniques*.

These analytic techniques are illustrated where appropriate by application of data from the Willamette Bakeries study. Our approach is nontechnical and descriptive in nature. Most of the more sophisticated techniques, particularly the multivariate analyses, are practical only with the assistance of a computer. Fortunately, there are "canned" computer programs available for all of the common techniques.[1] In order to use them properly, however, one must know *when to use* them and *how to interpret* the results.

This chapter can only serve as an introduction to the *whens* and *hows* of applying inferential statistical techniques. The reader should consult more comprehensive descriptions of the techniques in which he is interested.[2]

Findings of Bread Purchase and Consumption Patterns Study

The analysis of the data of the Willamette Bakeries study resulted in some findings that were supportive of the judgments expressed in the early stages of the study by the Willamette management and reported earlier (pages 478–480). Some of the findings were at variance with management's prior opinions, however, and others concerned topic areas in which management had not expressed opinions.

A number of the findings that relate directly to the prior judgments of the Willamette management are reported as follows (the Willamette management's prior judgments are stated again wherever that is appropriate).

1. Consumption of white and whole wheat bread by occupational segments of market.

    Management's prior judgment. "Blue-collar families probably eat greater amounts of white and whole wheat bread per person than either white-collar or managerial-professional families."

    Findings of study. Blue-collar families eat greater amounts of white bread per person than either white-collar or managerial-professional families. The point estimates (in terms of pounds per person per

---

[1] For descriptions of these programs see the following: W. J. Dixon, ed., *Biomedical Computer Programs* (Los Angeles: University of California Press, 1968); A. Couch, *DATATEXT Manual*, rev. ed. (Cambridge, Mass.: Harvard University Laboratory of Social Relations, 1971); *Stat Pack Statistical Package* (Kalamazoo, Mich.: Western Michigan University, undated); *Time Shared Basic Program Library Handbook* (Cupertino, Calif.: Hewlett-Packard Software Center, 1971); and N. Nie, D. H. Bent, and C. H. Hull, *SPSS-Statistical Package for the Social Sciences* (New York: The McGraw-Hill Book Co., 1970).

[2] A good place to begin is the chapters in "Part D: Statistical Inference" and "Part E: Statistical Analysis of Relationships" in R. Ferber, ed., *Handbook of Marketing Research* (New York: McGraw-Hill Book Company, 1974).

week) are 1.59 lbs. for blue-collar families, 0.58 lbs. for white-collar families, and 0.66 for managerial-professional families.

The findings of the study do not support the judgment that blue-collar families eat more whole wheat bread than those of the other occupational groups, however. The point estimates are 0.43 lbs. for blue-collar families, 0.48 lbs. for white-collar families, and 0.56 lbs. for managerial-professional families.

2. Consumption of specialty breads by occupational segments of market.

   Management's prior judgment. "White-collar and managerial-professional families eat greater amounts of specialty breads (rye, pumpernickel, and the like) per person than blue-collar families."

   Findings of study. The findings are in agreement with this opinion. The combined mean amounts of three types of specialty breads eaten per person per week as estimated from the survey was 0.15 lbs. for blue-collar families, 0.29 lbs. for white-collar families, and 0.36 lbs. for managerial-professional families.

3. Attitudes toward bread and bread characteristics.

   Management's prior opinions. "All families are concerned about nutrition and taste in bread."

   "Managerial-professional housewives are more likely to like bread that has texture (is "chewier"), are more diet conscious, and are more likely to think that whole wheat and other dark breads are healthier than white breads. White-collar housewives are more concerned about nutrition and the right brand. Blue-collar housewives are more concerned about bread being soft (softness is equated with freshness) and being sliced right.

   Families with young children are concerned about the energy-giving characteristics of bread."

   Findings of study. The occupational groups showed marked differences with respect to only a few attitudes toward bread and bread characteristics.

   The bread characteristics considered to be the most important were nutrition, taste, and freshness. These were the three most important characteristics for each of the occupational groups.

   Managerial-professional respondents attached a higher degree of importance to texture and to bread having a thick, chewy crust than did the white-collar and blue-collar respondents. A higher proportion of managerial-professional respondents also thought that whole wheat and other dark breads were healthier than white breads than did their white-collar and blue-collar counterparts. All of the occupational groups placed the bread attribute "low in calories" as being unimportant. White-collar respondents gave no indications of being more brand conscious than blue-collar or managerial-professional respondents.

"Bread that is soft" and "bread that is sliced right" were among those bread attribute statements considered to be the least important. The blue-collar respondents joined those of the other two occupational groups in this opinion. (Other attributes considered to be unimportant were "bread that is low in calories," "bread that sticks to the ribs," "bread that has the right preservatives added," and "bread that comes in the right-sized loaf.")

Respondents generally ranked the attribute statement, "bread that provides quick energy," as being relatively unimportant. Families with young children were no exception to this practice.

4. Consumption pattern of bread among occupational groups.

Management's prior opinions. "Blue-collar families very likely have a different consumption pattern for white and whole wheat bread than managerial-professional and white-collar families. Blue-collar families tend to look upon bread as a staple food to be served at all meals whereas white-collar and managerial-professional families do not view it this way. . . . Blue-collar wage earners are more likely to be taking their lunch to work and to have sandwiches than are white-collar and managerial-professional wage earners."

Findings of study. Parts of this hypothesis were confirmed. Blue-collar families report more consumption of white bread at all meals, for sandwiches, and for special occasions. The pattern is reversed for specialty breads. Blue-collar families report less consumption of whole wheat bread in general but the only specific time this is reflected is for special occasions. However, no differences were found in the way the occupational groups viewed bread as a necessary staple food (based on responses to Questions 11g and 11s).

5. Amount of bread consumed per person at each life cycle stage.

Management's prior judgment. "Bread consumption per person will generally decrease with the stage of the life cycle of the family. Consumption will be highest for the 'young single' and lowest for the 'empty nest' and 'solitary survivor' stages."

Findings of study. This is the general pattern of consumption for white bread, except that average consumption drops sharply after marriage before children are born, increases again with the coming of children, and then declines over the remaining stages of the cycle. With whole wheat and specialty bread, the highest consumption appears to be at the two end stages of the life cycle, the 'young single' and the 'solitary survivors.'

6. Perceived differences in breads.

Management's prior judgments. Most brands of standard white bread do not have identifiable differences in taste, texture, freshness, or other characteristics. Some whole wheat and most specialty breads can be differentiated by these characteristics.

Findings of study. The respondents perceive that there are marked differences in brands of all types of breads.

7. Media exposure of occupational groups.

Management's prior opinions. Media exposure differs among blue-collar, white-collar, and managerial-professional families. Blue-collar and white-collar families will spend more time watching television than managerial-professional families. Blue-collar families will read newspapers less on the average than white-collar or managerial-professional families. The programs listened to on radio and viewed on television will also differ among the three occupational groups.

Findings of study. These opinions turned out to be generally valid, although the differences were not marked. Managerial-professional respondents reported watching less television during the week than white-and-blue-collar respondents (an average of 2.6 hours versus 3.0 hours per day). Weekend television watching was roughly comparable among the three groups (an average of 2.5 hours per day).

Managerial-professional and white-collar respondents reported listening to radio on weekdays more than blue-collar respondents (2.5 hours versus 2.0 hours per day). About the same amount of time as on weekdays was spent by white- and blue-collar respondents but the amount of listening time of managerial-professional respondents dropped appreciably.

The program preferences were generally in line with (stereotypical) expectations. News was reported as a favorite by all occupational groups. Blue-collar respondents tended to favor country, contemporary, and "easy listening" music; white-collar and managerial-professional respondents preferred "easy listening" music. A reported preference for classical music was highest among managerial-professional respondents.

Subscription rates to newspapers were roughly comparable among the three groups. The managerial-professional respondents reported reading newspapers more regularly, however, followed by white-collar and blue-collar respondents in that order.

8. Distributional segments.

Management's prior judgment. It is doubtful if there are any distinguishable differences among people who buy bread at supermarkets, those who buy it at neighborhood markets, and retail bakeries, and those who bake their own bread.

Findings of study. The study basically confirmed this expectation. However, there were several important exceptions. The higher the education or social class of the respondent, the more likely she is to bake at least some bread. This holds for all three bread types.

The other major finding is that those in the younger stages of the life cycle buy more of their white bread at supermarkets than do those in the later stages of the life cycle.

9. Characteristics of Willamette users.

The sample data indicated that Willamette was receiving a disproportionately high share of the market for bread in the two older life cycle stage segments and a correspondingly lower share in the younger segments. Willamette users were found to be roughly the same in income and slightly higher in educational level than non-users. There were no discernible differences in rankings of importance of bread attributes and in attitudes toward bread. Media exposure also appeared to be roughly comparable between users and nonusers as did type-of-store purchase patterns.

Statistical Estimation

Most of the findings just reported were based upon estimates. Statistical estimation involves the estimation of a *population value we do not know* from *a sample value we do know*. Estimates of the mean amount of a product bought per person per time period, the market share of a brand, or the proportion of outlets that carry the brand are common estimates used in making marketing decisions about a product.

As was pointed out in Chapter 6, there are two kinds of estimation procedures, *point estimation* and *interval estimation*. A brief review and illustration of each of these procedures are useful here.

Point Estimation

A *point estimate* is a single number, or point, that is used to estimate a population value of interest. A point estimate may be made for any population value but the estimates most commonly made are for the *mean* and the *proportion* of the population.

Point Estimates of Population Means

The mean amount of white bread consumed per person per week, as determined from the sample of respondents in the Willamette Bakeries study, was 0.83 pounds. Had the sample for this study been a simple random sample, an unstratified nonprobability sample in which there was no reason to expect bias, or a proportional stratified sample, this would be the best single estimate of the population mean.

The mean of the sample actually taken will be biased if it is not corrected because it was a nonproportional stratified quota sample. The strata were "blue-collar," "white-collar," and "managerial-professional" occupations. The proportions of each occupation as represented in the sample and the population, and the sample mean amounts of white bread consumed per person per week for each occupational group were as follows:

	Blue-Collar	White-Collar	Managerial-Professional
Sample proportion of respondents	$w_1 = \dfrac{n_1}{n} = .249$	$w_2 = \dfrac{n_2}{n} = 0.370$	$w_3 = \dfrac{n_3}{n} = 0.381$
Population proportion of respondents	$W_1 = \dfrac{N_1}{N} = 0.516$	$W_2 = \dfrac{N_2}{N} = 0.290$	$W_3 = \dfrac{N_3}{N} = 0.194$
Sample mean	$\bar{x}_1 = 1.59$ lbs.	$\bar{x}_2 = .57$ lbs.	$\bar{x}_3 = .56$ lbs.

It may be seen that there is an underrepresentation of the "blue-collar" group and an overrepresentation of the "white-collar" and "managerial-professional" groups in the sample. Since the blue-collar group is by far the heaviest consumer of white bread, the use of the uncorrected sample mean as an estimate of average consumption will result in a substantial underestimation.

The sample mean can be corrected by finding the *weighted average* of the sample means of the occupational groups, or

$$\bar{X} = W_1\bar{x}_1 + W_2\bar{x}_2 + W_3\bar{x}_3 \qquad (14\text{--}1)$$
$$= .516(1.59) + .290(.57) + .194(.56)$$
$$= .82 + .16 + .11$$
$$= 1.09 \text{ lbs. per person per week.}$$

If there were reason to expect other biases in the sample or biases arising from nonsampling errors, it would be necessary to make adjustments for them as well. Since no such reasons were discovered, the weighted average sample mean of 1.09 pounds is taken as the best single estimate of the population mean amount of white bread consumed per person per week.

Point Estimates of Population Proportions

The sample proportion of families that report using Willamette bread is .096. Had the sample been a simple random sample, an unstratified non-probability sample in which there was no reason to expect bias, or a proportional stratified sample, this would be the best estimate of the proportion of Willamette users in the population.

This sample proportion, like the sample mean, has to be corrected, however, because the sample was a nonproportional stratified quota sample. The corrected sample proportion can be found by the following formula using the same weights derived to correct the sample mean:

$$p = W_1p_1 + W_2p_2 + W_3p_3 \qquad (14\text{--}2)$$
$$= .516(.093) + .290(.125) + .194(.091)$$
$$= .048 + .036 + .017$$
$$= .101$$

If there were reasons to expect other biases in the data, adjustments should be made for them.[3] No such reasons were found.

Interval Estimation

An *interval estimate* consists of *two points between which the population value is estimated to lie with some stated level of confidence.* An

[3] For a discussion of a method of adjusting data for biases, see D. S. Tull and G. S. Albaum, *Survey Research: A Decisional Approach* (New York: Intext Publishing Co., 1973), Chap. 4.

interval estimate of the mean amount of white bread consumed per person per week in the Eugene-Springfield area, for example, is 0.96 pounds to 1.22 pounds with a 68 per cent level of confidence. An interval estimate of the proportion of families using Willamette bread in its market area is .074 to .128 with a 68 per cent level of confidence.

Interval Estimate of the Mean—$n = 30$ or Larger

How is an interval estimate of the mean made? Recall from the discussion in Chapter 6 that an interval estimate with a specified level of confidence is obtained from an interval formed by the two points,

$\bar{x} - Z\sigma_{\bar{x}} =$ lower point and
$\bar{x} + Z\sigma_{\bar{x}} =$ upper point
where Z represents the number of standard errors for the desired confidence level and $\sigma_{\bar{x}}$ is the size of the standard error.

A confidence level of 68 per cent is obtained when $Z = 1.0$, 90 per cent when $Z = 1.64$, and 95 per cent when $Z = 1.96$ (see Appendix B). Each Z value gives the indicated level of confidence because that percentage of all samples that could be taken (of that size from that population) would have means falling between the lower and upper points formed using that Z value.

A basic assumption of the mathematical model used to calculate interval estimates is that the sampling process produces a random selection of elements to be included in the sample. In the Willamette Bakeries study the sample of persons was taken on a *non*random basis. Is it reasonable to apply this approach to nonrandom sample data?

The answer to this question is conditional upon the specific situation and always dependent upon the *judgment of the analyst.* It is reasonable to apply these formulas to nonrandom sample data when (1) *in the judgment of the analyst,* the nonrandom sampling process is a sufficiently close approximation of its random counterpart that any error introduced by differences will be within an acceptable range for the problem, or (2) *in the judgment of the analyst,* adjustments that he has made to the data allow this standard to be met.

In the Willamette study the plan was to exercise sufficient care in the taking of the nonprobability sample that the results would approximate those of a random sample. A review of the location and the demographic characteristics of the respondents within each of the strata gave no apparent reason to expect the presence of bias or variable errors arising from the nonrandom sampling process that would introduce an unacceptable amount of error. Therefore, analytical techniques that require responses from a random sample were applied to the data.

The sample means, standard deviations, sample sizes and weights (proportions) of each of the strata were as follows:

blue-collar stratum: $\bar{x}_1 = 1.59, s_1 = 1.573$ lbs., $n_1 = 43,$

$$W_1 = \frac{N_1}{N} = .516$$

white-collar stratum: $\bar{x}_2 = .57, s_2 = 0.873$ lbs., $n_2 = 64,$

$$W_2 = \frac{N_2}{N} = .290$$

managerial-professional stratum: $x_3 = .56, s_3 = 1.060$ lbs., $n_3 = 66,$

$$W_3 = \frac{N_3}{N} = .194$$

The estimated *standard error* of the mean is

$$\hat{\sigma}_{\bar{x}_{st}} = \sqrt{\sum_{h=1}^{k} W_h^2 \frac{s_h^2}{n_h}} \tag{14-3}$$

$$= \sqrt{.516^2 \left(\frac{1.573^2}{43}\right) + .290^2 \left(\frac{0.873^2}{64}\right) + .194^2 \left(\frac{1.060^2}{66}\right)}$$

$$= \sqrt{.015 + .001 + .001}$$

$$= .130$$

With a 68.3 per cent level of confidence (the mean plus or minus 1.0 standard error), the interval estimate for the mean amount of white bread consumed is

1.09 lbs. − 1.0(0.130) to 1.09 lbs. + 1.0(0.130),
or 0.96 lbs. to 1.22 lbs.

For a 95.4 per cent level of confidence (the mean plus or minus 2.0 standard errors), the interval estimate is

1.09 lbs. − 2.0(0.130) to 1.09 lbs. + 2.0(0.130),
or .83 lbs. to 1.35 lbs.

Interval Estimate of the Mean—*n* less than 30

For an interval estimate in which the sample size is less than 30 and for which the sample standard deviation, *s,* was used to estimate the population standard deviation, $\hat{\sigma}$, the sampling distribution is no longer normal. Since the distribution of the Z statistic is assumed to be normal, it is not applicable in these small sample situations.

The Student t distribution is used instead of the Z distribution when the sample size is less than 30. The t statistic is calculated and used in the same way as the Z statistic, except that the values for areas of the sampling distribution are looked up in a different table (Table of Appendix F).

Interval Estimate of a Proportion

Interval estimation for proportions is a very similar procedure to that for means. The estimated standard error of the proportion, $\hat{\sigma}_p$, must be determined and then the interval is formed around the sample proportion such that

$$p - Z\hat{\sigma}_p = \text{lower point, and}$$
$$p + Z\hat{\sigma}_p = \text{upper point}$$

where Z = the number of standard errors for the desired confidence level.

When the sample is an *srs* and the population proportion is known, the formula for the standard error of the proportion is

$$\sigma_p = \sqrt{\frac{P(1 - P)}{n}} \qquad (14\text{--}4)$$

If the population proportion is not known, it can be estimated from the sample proportion p and the estimated standard error, $\hat{\sigma}_p$, found from the formula

$$\hat{\sigma}_p = \sqrt{\frac{p(1 - p)}{n}} \qquad (14\text{--}5)$$

If the sample is a stratified random sample, the estimated standard error is the weighted average of the estimated stratum standard errors, or

$$\hat{\sigma}_{p_{st}} = \sqrt{\sum_{h=1}^{k} W_h^2 \frac{\hat{p}_h(1.0 - \hat{p}_h)}{n_h}} \qquad (14\text{--}6)$$

Using this formula to estimate the standard error of the proportion of Willamette bread users, we can calculate it as

$$\hat{\sigma}_{P_{st}} = \sqrt{.516^2 \; \frac{(.093(1.0 - .093)}{43} + .290^2 \; \frac{(.125(1.0 - .125)}{64}}$$

$$+ .194^2 \; \frac{(.091(1.0 - .091)}{66}$$

$$= \sqrt{\frac{.0225}{43} + \frac{.0092}{64} + \frac{.0030}{66}}$$

$$= .027$$

The interval estimate of the proportion of Willamette bread users with a 68.3 per cent level of confidence is

$$p - Z\hat{\sigma}_{P_{st}} \text{ to } p + Z\hat{\sigma}_{P_{st}} = .101 - 1.0(.027) \text{ to } .101 + 1.0(.027), \text{ or}$$
$$0.074 \text{ to } 0.128.$$

Essentially the same logic that underlies interval estimation procedures is used in hypothesis tests, the subject of the next section.

Hypothesis Tests

The procedure for conducting hypothesis tests and the rules of evidence used for evaluating them were discussed in Chapter 2. In this section we conduct hypothesis tests involving both means and proportions for data obtained in the Willamette Bakeries study. In addition, we conduct a test for differences in central tendency of two distributions when the data are ordinally scaled and means cannot be used.

Test Involving One Mean or One Proportion

Hypothesis Test of a Mean—$n = 30$ or Larger

Suppose the analyst in the Willamette Bakeries study had wanted to test the hypothesis that the mean amount of white bread consumed per person per week was greater than 1.0 pounds per week. If the usage were found to be this high, the firm would intensify its marketing efforts related to white bread. Otherwise, no action would be taken. Further suppose that he only wanted to run a risk of 5 per cent of taking this action when in fact the mean usage was 1.0 pound or less (alpha error = .05). How should such a test have been run?

As discussed in Chapter 6, three specifications are necessary in hypothesis tests of the mean. As they apply to this problem, these specifications are

1. *the hypothesis to be tested*
     The null hypothesis is
     H_0: $M \leq 1.0$ lbs. of white bread per person per week
2. *the level of sampling error permitted in the test*
     An α error of .05 is specified, $Z_\alpha = 1.64$
3. *the standard deviation of the population/standard error of the mean*
     The estimated standard error of the mean, as determined earlier, is .130.

The level of α specified results in a *rejection region* for H_0. The boundary of this region nearest the mean is the *critical* value in the test. Any sample value lower than the critical value means that H_0 will be accepted. The test is illustrated in Figure 14–1.

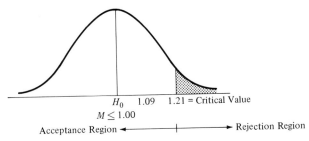

H_0 1.09   1.21 = Critical Value
$M \leq 1.00$
Acceptance Region ← | → Rejection Region

Figure 14–1   Test of hypothesis H_0: $M \leq 1.00$ lbs.

The distance to the critical value from the mean of the sampling distribution ($M = 1.00$) is

$$Z_\alpha \hat{\sigma}_{\bar{x}_{st}} = 1.64(0.130) = .213$$

The critical value is then

$$1.00 + .213 = 1.213 \text{ lbs.}$$

This critical value is greater than the sample value of 1.09 lbs. and so *the null hypothesis is accepted.*

Had the test been run for a basic research project, this would be all the information that would be required. For a decisional research project, however, the *probability* that the hypothesis is correct should be reported.

This probability is determined by finding the shaded area of the sampling distribution shown in Figure 14–2. To find it, the Z value for the distance of the sample mean from the hypothesized mean is calculated and the area of the sampling distribution determined from Appendix B.

The probability corresponding to this Z value is .25. Thus, *there is a 25 per cent chance that the true mean population consumption of white bread is 1.00 pounds or less per person per week.*

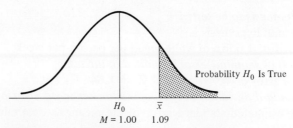

Figure 14–2   Probability that H_0 is true.

In a decisional context, there may be a substantially different interpretation given to the conclusion, "there is only a 25 per cent chance of the null hypothesis being correct" than to the conclusion, "the null hypothesis is accepted." For this reason, the probability of the hypothesis being correct should always be reported in decisional research projects.

Hypothesis Test of a Proportion

The test of a hypothesis concerning a proportion is run in a similar manner. A test of the proportion of Willamette bread users was conducted with the following specifications

1. *The hypothesis to be tested:* the proportion of the population using Willamette bread is no more than .05; H_0: $P \leq .05$.
2. *The level of sampling error permitted in the test:* $\alpha = .10$, $Z_\alpha = 1.28$.
3. *The standard error of the proportion* was calculated earlier as 0.027.

As calculated earlier, the adjusted sample proportion is .101. The test was run and the null hypothesis was rejected. The probability of the null hypothesis being correct was found to be .03. You should verify these results by making the calculations involved in the test using the same approach illustrated earlier for a test of a single mean.

Tests Involving Two Means, Medians, or Proportions

Hypothesis Test of Difference in Two Means

Oroweat was the leading brand of bread in the Willamette marketing area. The analyst decided to run a test to see if Oroweat users were the same as Willamette users in the amount of white bread eaten, or if there were differences between the two in this respect.

A hypothesis test of the difference in two sample means is similar to that for testing whether a sample mean differs from a hypothesized mean value. The specifications required in general for such a test and the ones used for this test are as follows:

1. *The hypothesis to be tested:* the null hypothesis was that the mean amount of white bread consumed by Willamette users, M_A, was the same as that by Oroweat users, M_B, or H_0: $M_A - M_B = 0$.
2. *The level of sampling error permitted in the test* was set at .10; $\alpha = .10$, $Z_\alpha = 1.64$.
3. *The estimated standard error of the differences in means is given by the formula*

$$\hat{\sigma}_{\bar{x}_{A-B}} = \sqrt{\frac{\hat{\sigma}_A^2}{n_A} + \frac{\hat{\sigma}_B^2}{n_B}} \tag{14-7}$$

The sample values were

$$s_A^2 = .497 \qquad s_B^2 = .442$$
$$n_A = 19 \qquad n_B = 74$$
$$\bar{x}_A = .416 \qquad \bar{x}_B = .529$$

Substituting $\dfrac{n_A}{n_A - 1}\, s^2$ and $\dfrac{n_B}{n_B - 1}\, s^2$ for $\hat{\sigma}_A^2$ and $\hat{\sigma}_B^2$, respectively, the value for the estimated standard error is calculated to be .184.

Since either a positive or negative difference is of interest to the researcher and he is not able to predict in advance which type of difference will occur, two critical values must be calculated. (This is commonly called a nondirectional or two-tailed test.) The *critical values* for the difference in the two sample means was found to be

$$(M_A - M_B) - Z_\alpha \hat{\sigma}_{\bar{x}_{A-B}} =$$
$$0 - 1.64(.184) = -.302$$

and

$$(M_A - M_B) + Z_\alpha \hat{\sigma}_{\bar{x}_{A-B}} =$$
$$0 + 1.64(.184) = +.302$$

The actual difference in the two sample means was

$$\bar{x}_A - \bar{x}_B =$$
$$.416 - .529 = -.113$$

The difference in the sample means is within the critical values. The null hypothesis of no difference is therefore accepted. The test is illustrated in Figure 14–3.

The probability that the hypothesis of no difference is correct can be calculated by finding the area corresponding to the Z value.

$$Z = \frac{(\bar{x}_A - \bar{x}_B) - (M_A - M_B)}{\hat{\sigma}_{\bar{x}_{A-B}}} \tag{14-8}$$
$$= \frac{-.113 - 0}{.184}$$
$$= .614$$

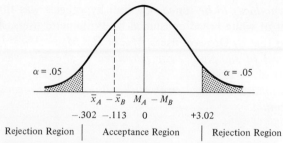

Figure 14–3 Hypothesis test of difference in mean amounts of white bread consumed by Willamette and Oroweat users.

The probability associated with a Z value of .614 in a two-tailed test is .46. Thus, differences as large as those observed could be expected to occur because of sampling variations in almost half the samples of this size taken from these populations.

Hypothesis Test of Difference in Two Medians

As was discussed in Chapter 13, the mean is a measure of central tendency that is appropriate for intervally scaled and ratio scaled data. When the data are not at least intervally scaled, tests of central tendency utilizing the mean are not appropriate. Ordinally scaled data are commonly encountered in marketing research, and there are tests that can be used to test for differences in central tendency between two distributions with ordinal data.

The analyst wanted to test to see if there were differences in the responses on the bread attitude statements (Question 11 of the questionnaire) between "committed" Willamette and Oroweat users. (A "committed" user was defined as an individual who both used the brand and selected it as first in terms of quality of brands used during the past year.) Since Oroweat was the most popular brand, he believed that an analysis of any differences in attitudes of users might provide information of value for choosing promotional themes.

Although the analyst felt fairly confident that the seven gradations from *strongly agree* to *strongly disagree* used in obtaining responses to each statement comprised an interval scale, he decided to treat the data as if they were ordinal in nature for at least this part of the analysis. He had no question that a *strongly agree* response was always of the same rank with respect to an *agree* response, an *agree* response was always of the same rank with respect to an *agree somewhat* response, and so forth.

The test he chose to use was the *Mann-Whitney U* test, which is designed to determine if there is a difference between the distribution of

Table 14–1   Results of Mann-Whitney U Tests of Attitude Statements*—
Willamette vs. Oroweat Users

	Significant (S) or nonsignificant (NS). α = .10	Probability that Willamette users more agreeable to statement than Oroweat users
b. I usually buy the same brand once I find one that I like.	S	.93
c. All white breads are pretty much alike.	S	.93
g. Having bread at most meals is necessary for a balanced diet.	NS	.85
h. It doesn't matter whether you're buying bread or anything else, you only get what you pay for.	NS	.88
k. I am willing to pay $.10 or $.15 extra for a loaf of specialty bread to get the kind I want.	S	.98
l. A man needs a hearty breakfast to start the day off right.	S	.94
m. Bread bought at a bakery is better than that you buy off the counter at the store.	S	.98
n. Whole wheat and other dark breads are more healthful than white bread.	NS	.86

* The attitude statements are those in the Willamette Bakeries questionnaire, see pp. 487–488

rankings of items in the populations from which the two samples were taken. It retains much of the efficiency of the Z test without necessitating the assumption of having intervally scaled data in circumstances in which this is questionable.

The mechanics of the test are not described here.[4] However, the analyst ran a Mann-Whitney U test for each of the 19 attitude statements. He found that as a group, the sample of 11 committed users of Willamette bread were more favorably disposed toward each of the attitude statements than were the 43 committed Oroweat users. The results of the tests for the attitude statements in which the differences were most pronounced are given in Table 14–1.

Hypothesis Test of the Difference in Two Proportions

The analyst in the Willamette Bakeries study was interested in determining whether the proportion of blue-collar families in the population

[4] For a description of this test see S. Siegel, *Non-Parametric Statistics for the Behavioral Sciences* (New York: McGraw-Hill Book Co., 1956), 116–126.

who eat white bread was greater than that for all other families (white collar and managerial-professional). A hypothesis test of the difference in these two proportions was, therefore, run with the following specifications:

1. *The hypothesis to be tested:* the null hypothesis was that the proportion of blue-collar families who eat white bread, P_A, was equal to or less than that for all other families, P_B.

$$H_0: P_A - P_B \leq 0$$

2. *The level of sampling error permitted in the test* was set at .10; $\alpha = .10$, $Z_\alpha = 1.28$.

3. *The estimated standard error of the differences in proportions*

The estimated standard error is given by the formula

$$\hat{\sigma}_{p_{A-B}} = \sqrt{\frac{\hat{\sigma}_{p_A}^2}{n_A} + \frac{\hat{\sigma}_{p_B}^2}{n_B}} \qquad (14\text{--}9)$$

where

$$\hat{\sigma}_{p_A}^2 = \frac{p_A(1 - p_A)}{n_A}$$

The sample values were

$$p_A = .814 \qquad p_B = .715$$
$$n_A = 43 \qquad n_B = 130$$

The calculated value for the standard error if the differences in proportions is calculated to be .072.

The critical value for the difference in the two sample proportions was found to be

$$(P_A - P_B) + Z_\alpha \hat{\sigma}_{p_{A-B}} =$$
$$0 - 1.28(.072) = .092.$$

The actual difference in the two sample proportions was

$$p_A - p_B = .814 - .715 = .099$$

Since the actual difference was greater than the critical value, the conclusion was drawn that a greater proportion of blue-collar families eat white bread than do all other families.

The probability that the hypothesis of no difference was true was calculated by finding the area corresponding to the Z value.

$$Z = \frac{(p_A - p_B) - (P_A - P_B)}{\hat{\sigma}_{p_{A-B}}}$$
$$= \frac{.099 - 0}{.072}$$
$$= 1.37 \qquad (14\text{--}10)$$

This corresponding probability was found to be .085. Thus, there is a .085 probability that the proportion of blue-collar families who eat white bread is no greater than that for white-collar and managerial-professional families.

Analyzing Association of Two or More Variables

In addition to estimation and hypothesis tests (of the kind just described), an important part of the analysis of the data in most marketing research projects is to determine the degree of *association* between variables. Depending upon the purpose for which the data were obtained, one may be interested in examining the degree of association of such variables as price, amount of advertising, perceived quality, life cycle stage, social class, income, and education to variables such as purchaser—nonpurchaser of brand, attitudes toward brands, brand preference, sales, and market share.

In analyzing associative relationships two types of variables are used, *predictor* variables and *criterion* variables. Predictor variables are used to help predict, or "explain," the level of criterion variables. Market share is an example of a criterion variable that such predictor variables as relative price, amount of advertising, and number of outlets are often used to explain.

Several factors must be considered in choosing a method of analyzing an associative relationship. Included among these are the considerations of (1) *number of criterion and predictor variables,* (2) *the scale(s) used for the measurements* and (3) *whether the data meet the assumptions on which the analytic method is based.* A few remarks on each of these factors may be helpful before we proceed.

(1) *Number of Criterion and Prediction Variables.* The minimum number of criterion and predictor variables is one each, since at least two variables are necessary to have association. The techniques appropriate for analysis of two variable association are known as *bivariate techniques.* When more than two variables are involved in the analysis, the techniques employed are known as *multivariate techniques.* The next two sections of this chapter are concerned with these two types of technique.

(2) *The Scale(s) Used for the Measurement.* As discussed in Chapter 7, measurements may be made using a *nominal, ordinal, interval,* or a *ratio* scale. As one might expect, association techniques that are appropriate for analyzing the degree of association between intervally scaled vari-

Table 14–2 Statistical Methods for Analyzing Association of Two or More Variables

Criterion Variables		Predictor Variables		Methods (p) = parametric (np) = nonparametric	Examples of Applications
Scale	Number	Scale	Number		
nominal	1	nominal	1	Cross-tabulation Chi square (np) Contingency coefficient (np)	numbers of purchasers—nonpurchasers of brand of bread by life-style.
nominal	1	nominal	more than 1	Cross-tabulation AID (np)	numbers of purchasers—nonpurchasers of brand by life-style and stage of life cycle.
nominal	more than 1	nominal	more than 1	Cross-tabulation Canonical correlation with dummy variables (p)	numbers of purchasers—nonpurchasers of brand by type of bread (white, whole wheat, or specialty) by life-style and stage of life cycle.
nominal	1	ordinal	1	Coefficient of differentiation (np)	number of purchasers—nonpurchasers of brand by ranking as to quality.
nominal	1	ordinal	more than 1	Kendall's nonparametric discriminant analysis (np)	number of purchasers—nonpurchasers of brand by ranking as to quality and perceived price.
nominal	more than 1	ordinal	more than 1	Transform ordinal scales followed by canonical correlation with dummy variables (p)	number of purchasers—nonpurchasers of brand and type of bread (white, whole wheat, or specialty) by ranking as to price and healthfulness.
nominal	1	interval-ratio	1	Correlation ratio Point biserial coefficient (p)	number of purchasers—nonpurchasers of brand by income level of respondent.
nominal	1	interval-ratio	more than 1	Discriminant analysis (p)	number of purchasers—nonpurchasers by income level of respondent and price of brand.

nominal	more than 1	interval-ratio	more than 1	Multiple discriminant analysis, canonical correlation with dummy variable (p)	number of purchasers—nonpurchasers of brand and type of bread by income level of respondent and price of bread.
ordinal	1	nominal	1	Coefficient of differentiation	preference with respect to type of bread (white, whole wheat, or specialty) by life-style.
ordinal	1	nominal	more than 1	Kruskal's monotone ANOVA	preference with respect to type of bread by life-style and stage of life cycle.
ordinal	more than 1	nominal	more than 1	Transform ordinal scales followed by multivariate analysis of variance	preference with respect to type of bread and type of store patronized by life-style and stage of life cycle.
ordinal	1	ordinal	1	Spearman's rank correlation (np), Kendall's tau (np)	preference for brand of bread ranking with respect to freshness.
ordinal	1	ordinal	more than 1	Guttman-Lingoes CM-2 regression	preference for brand by ranking with respect to freshness and price.
ordinal	more than 1	ordinal	more than 1	Transform ordinal scales followed by canonical correlation (p)	preference for brand and relative frequency of purchase by ranking with respect to freshness and price.
ordinal	1	interval-ratio	1	Coefficient of point multiserial correlation (p)	preference for brand by income level.
ordinal	1	interval-ratio	more than 1	Carroll's Monotone regression (np)	preference for brand by income level and price of brand.
ordinal	more than 1	interval-ratio	more than 1	Transform ordinal scales followed by canonical correlation (p)	preference for brand and relative frequency of purchase by income level of respondent and price of brand.
interval-ratio	1	nominal	1	Correlation ratio (np) Point biserial coefficient (np)	amount of bread purchased by life-style.

Table 14-2 (Continued)

Criterion Variables		Predictor Variables		Methods (p) = parametric (np) = nonparametric	Examples of Applications
Scale	*Number*	*Scale*	*Number*		
interval-ratio	1	nominal	more than 1	ANOVA (p) AID (np)	amount of bread purchased by life-style and stages of life cycle.
interval-ratio	more than 1	nominal	more than 1	Multivariate analysis of variance (p)	amount of white bread, whole wheat, and specialty bread purchased by life-style and stage of life cycle.
interval-ratio	1	ordinal	1	Coefficient of point (np) multiserial correlation	amount of bread purchased by ranking with respect to quality
interval-ratio	1	ordinal	more than 1	Transform ordinal scales of predictor variables to interval scales followed by multiple regression (p)	amount of brand purchased by rankings with respect to quality and price.
interval-ratio	more than 1	ordinal	more than 1	Transform ordinal scale followed by canonical correlation (p)	amount of white, whole wheat, and specialty bread purchased by rankings with respect to price and healthfulness.
interval-ratio	1	interval-ratio	1	bivariate regression (p)	amount of brand purchased by income level
interval-ratio	1	interval-ratio	more than 1	multiple regression (p)	amount of brand purchased by income level and amount of advertising.
interval-ratio	more than 1	interval-ratio	more than 1	canonical correlation (p)	amount of white, whole wheat, and specialty bread purchased of each brand by income level and amount of advertising.

ables may be entirely inappropriate for use with variables measured in other scales.

(3) *The Assumptions on Which the Analytic Technique Is Based.* All analytic techniques are developed from assumptions on the nature of the data that they will be used to analyze. An assumption common to all analytic techniques involving inferences drawn from samples, for example, is that the sample is random in nature.

Analytic techniques can be classified into two different categories, depending upon the nature of the assumptions that underlie them. Those that require assumptions about the population distribution, mean, variance, or other population values (parameters) are called *parametric* techniques. Those that do not require such assumptions are called *nonparametric* techniques.

Table 14–2 contains a listing of selected techniques that are applicable for analyzing associations classified by number and scale of criterion and predictor variables. Examples of applications to the data in the Willamette Bakeries study are also given. It will be helpful to scan this table now to observe how each technique fits into the overall scheme of analysis of associative variation.

Analysis of Bivariate Associative Data

Many analytic methods can be used for analyzing bivariate data. The most commonly used ones are *cross tabulation, chi-square, Spearman's rank correlation, bivariate correlation,* and *bivariate regression.*

Cross Tabulation

The simplest way to analyze relationships between two variables is to tabulate the data by categories of both variables at the same time. This is known as a *two-way* cross tabulation.

An example of such a tabulation is given in Table 14–3. An examination of the table suggests that a higher percentage of blue-collar families buy white bread than do either white-collar or managerial-professional families. More than 80 per cent of the blue-collar families are buyers and less than 70 per cent of the white-collar and managerial-professional families are buyers.

Cross tabulation is a valuable first step in the analysis of association between variables. It enables one to see the data arrayed with respect to the variables used and to form a judgment about the degree of association present. In those cases where the presence, or absence, of a relationship is important to the problem solution and where the visual examination of the

Table 14–3 Observed Number of Buyers and Nonbuyers of White Bread by Occupation of Chief Wage Earner

	Occupation of Chief Wage Earner			
Buyer Status	*Blue-Collar*	*White-Collar*	*Managerial-Professional*	*Total*
Buyer	35 (81.4%)	44 (68.7%)	46 (69.7%)	125
Nonbuyer	8 (18.6%)	20 (31.3%)	20 (30.3%)	48
Total	43	64	66	173

data does not provide the necessary degree of assurance, additional analytic techniques can be used.

Both variables in the cross tabulation of white bread users—nonusers and occupation of chief wage earner—are nominally scaled. If the data are not nominal in nature, categories for each variable have to be established if cross tabulations are to be used. In cross tabulating income data that were collected to the nearest $100, for example, it would be necessary to set up income brackets. (As an example, "less than $5,000, $5,000–$6,999, $7,000–$9,999, $10,000–$14,999, $15,000–$24,999, and $25,000 or more" is one set of income brackets used by the Bureau of the Census.) The responses would then be sorted simultaneously into these brackets and the categories of the other variable.

Cross-tabulations are not limited to two variable analyses; *n-way* cross tabulations can also be prepared. When more than three variables are involved, however, the analysis becomes cumbersome.

Chi-Square—χ^2

One formal analytic method used for determining the degree of association in cross-tabulated data is *chi-square*. *Chi-square* is a nonparametric technique that *can be used for determining the probability that differences in the expected and observed number of cases falling in each cell of the cross tabulation table occurred because of sampling variation.*[5]

The value of chi square is computed by the formula

$$\chi^2 = \sum_{i=1}^{c} \left[\frac{(O_i - E_i)^2}{E_i} \right] \tag{14–19}$$

In this formula, i denotes the ith cell, c is the total number of cells, O_i is the observed value for cell i, and E_i is the expected value for cell i. The

[5] For a detailed discussion of chi-square see ibid., 104–111.

χ^2 value is used to determine the probability of the differences in the observed and expected values having occurred because of sampling variation rather than as a result of association of the variables.

The probability of association between white bread buyer status and occupation can be determined using this approach. If there were *no* association between buyer status and occupation, the number of *expected* respondents (E) in the upper left-hand cell of Table 14–3 would be found by solving the proportion

$$\frac{E}{43} = \frac{125}{173}, \text{ or}$$

$$E = \frac{43 \times 125}{173} = 31.07$$

The expected number was determined by multiplying the total for row 1 (125) by the total for column 1 (43), and dividing by the total number of cases (173). This follows the general rule that *the expected number for any cell will always be equal to the product of the row and column totals common to the cell divided by the total number of cases.*

The expected number for each cell is shown in Table 14–4.

Table 14–4   Expected Number of Buyers and Nonbuyers of White Bread by Occupation of Chief Wage Earner

		Occupation of Chief Wage Earner		
Buyer Status	*Blue-Collar*	*White-Collar*	*Managerial-Professional*	*Total*
Buyer	$\dfrac{43 \times 125}{173} = 31.1$	$\dfrac{64 \times 125}{173} = 46.2$	$\dfrac{66 \times 125}{173} = 47.7$	125
Nonbuyer	$\dfrac{43 \times 48}{173} = 11.9$	$\dfrac{64 \times 48}{173} = 17.8$	$\dfrac{66 \times 48}{173} = 18.3$	48
Total	43.0	64.0	66.0	173

The value of χ^2 for this problem is calculated using the observed values in Table 14–3 and the expected values in Table 14–4. The calculated value is

$$\chi^2 = \frac{(35 - 31.1)^2}{31.1} + \frac{(44 - 46.2)^2}{46.2} + \frac{(46 - 47.7)^2}{47.7} + \frac{(8 - 11.9)^2}{11.9}$$

$$+ \frac{(20 - 17.8)^2}{17.8} + \frac{(20 - 18.3)^2}{18.3}$$

$$= .49 + .10 + .06 + 1.28 + .27 + .16$$

$$= 2.46$$

The probability of this value of chi square for a cross tabulation table with this number of rows and columns is found from the χ^2 table in Appendix D (p. 717). The probability that the differences of observed and expected values occurred by chance is slightly less than .30. (Refer to the table to verify this probability.) Although this would not be significant at any of the usual significance levels ($\alpha = .01$, $\alpha = .05$, or $\alpha = .10$), it indicates that there is a probability of $1.0 - .30 = .70$ (approximately) that white bread buyer status is associated with occupation.

Usually it is not necessary to calculate the χ^2 value and look up the corresponding probability when an actual analysis is being done. If the data are tabulated by machine and a general purpose computer program used for obtaining cross tabulations, χ^2 will usually be computed and both it and the corresponding probability will be provided on the printout. Some programs, however, do not incorporate safeguards against computing χ^2 when it is not appropriate to use. One should always be sure that the sample size is 20 or more, and that the smallest *expected* frequency for any cell will be at least 5. If either of these conditions are not met, the Fisher Exact Probability Test should be used instead of chi-square.[6]

Spearman Rank Correlation Coefficient

As we have just seen, a commonly used method of measuring the degree of association between two *nominally* scaled variables is chi-square. A commonly used method of measuring the degree of association between two *ordinally* scaled variables is *Spearman's rank correlation coefficient*.

One of the advertising themes being considered by Willamette was "freshness." An examination of the data on bread attributes (Question 10 of the questionnaire) indicated that freshness was perceived as being one of the three most important bread attributes (the other two were "taste" and "nutrition"). If most consumers believed that the softness of bread was associated with freshness, Willamette might build this into a television advertising campaign stressing freshness by showing consumers squeezing the bread before buying it.

As an indication of whether there was a close association of the two attributes, the analyst decided to examine the rankings of each in terms of importance. He decided to use Spearman's rank correlation coefficient to determine the degree of association between the two sets of rankings.

This method provides a rank order correlation coefficient, r_s, which is a measurement of how closely the two sets of rankings correspond. A coefficient of $+ 1.0$ indicates perfect correspondence of the rankings, a coefficient of $- 1.0$ indicates an inverse relation of the rankings, and a coefficient of 0 indicates no association at all between them.

---

[6] For a discussion of the conditions of use of chi-square and a description of the Fisher test, see Siegel, op. cit., 96–104.

The test was run by computer using a standard program to determine r_s[7]. The value was found to be -0.192. The relatively weak inverse relationship indicates that softness is *not* used by consumers as an indicator of freshness of bread.

A complete description of this method of determining degree of association between two variables may be found in Siegel.[8]

Bivariate Correlation Analysis

A method of finding the degree of association between two variables that are *intervally* scaled is *correlation analysis.* Two intervally scaled variables that are associated will have a relationship that can either be plotted with a straight line (a linear relationship) or with a curved line (a nonlinear relationship). We consider only linear relationships here.

Correlation analyses are used in marketing research to determine the degree of relationship between company sales and such variables as price, competitive price, advertising, competitive advertising, number of outlets carrying the product, purchasing behavior, and income, and others. In many applications a correlation analysis is done using more than two variables. This is called *multiple correlation analysis* and is discussed later in this chapter.

The linear correlation coefficient, *r,* is the measure of the degree of association between the two variables in a bivariate correlation analysis. It has a value ranging from -1.0 to $+1.0$. A value of $+1.0$ indicates that each time one of the variables changes in value the other changes by a proportionate amount and in the same direction. A value of -1.0 indicates that the amount of the change in the two variables is proportionate but the direction is different. A value of 0 indicates no pattern of relationship at all. The value of *r* is determined by the formula

$$r = \frac{\Sigma\, x_i y_i}{\sqrt{\Sigma\, x_i^2 \Sigma y_i^2}} \qquad (14\text{--}10)$$

where x_i and y_i are the individual values of the two variables.

A more commonly used measure of association is *r* squared (r^2). This measure indicates *the per cent of variation in the criterion variable that is accounted for or explained by variation in the predictor variable.*

There were no purely intervally scaled variables in the Willamette study on which the analyst was interested in running a correlation analysis. He was interested in determining the relationship between the responses to

---

[7] See N. H. Nie, D. H. Bent, and C. H. Hull, *SPSS: Statistical Package for the Social Sciences* (New York: McGraw-Hill Book Company, 1970), 174–195.

[8] Siegel, op. cit., 42–47.

attitude statements (in Question 11) and white bread usage, however. Seven responses were possible ranging from "strongly agree" to "strongly disagree," coded from 1 to 7. For this purpose he assumed that these responses were intervally scaled.

A correlation analysis was run between each of the 19 attitude statements and the amount of white bread consumed per person per week. The highest correlation was between the responses to the statement, "Foods ought to be made only of natural ingredients rather than have additives." The r was .22, a relatively low correlation. The value of r^2 was .048. Thus, less than 5 per cent of the variation in white bread consumption could be explained by variations on this attitude. He concluded that, although the response to this statement might be closely associated with the sales of brands of white bread that were advertised as having no additives, it was not closely related to the level of sales of white bread in general.

A large number of statistical programs are available for running correlation analyses on the computer. The r values are computed and indicate the *degree* of the relationship between the two (or more) variables. *Regression analysis,* typically run in conjunction with correlation analysis, is concerned with the *nature of the association* between the two variables and is discussed shortly.

Although one may calculate correlation coefficients relatively easily, especially if it is done by computer, one should use this method of establishing the degree of relationship between variables only after a check has been made to ensure that the data being analyzed meet the assumptions of the correlation model. Least squares correlation analysis is a parametric method and, therefore, involves assumptions about the nature of the population from which the sample is drawn. These assumptions are:

1. For each value of the X variable, the distribution of the Y variable is normal. For each value of the Y variable, the distribution of the X variable is normal.
2. The variances of these normal distributions of the Y variable are all the same.
3. The means of the normal distributions of the Y variable are all the same.

If there is any reason to believe that there are any substantial departures from any of these assumptions in the data being used, care should be exercised in the interpretation of the correlation coefficients that result.[9]

---

[9] For an example of the effect of a violation of the equal variance assumption in one study, see D. S. Tull, "The Relationship of Actual and Predicted Sales and Profits in New Product Introductions," *Journal of Business,* **40** (July 1967), 233–250, and the later correcting note by D. S. Tull and H. C. Rutemiller, *Journal of Business,* **41** (July 1968), 385–387.

Bivariate Regression Analysis

Bivariate least squares *regression analysis* involves the fitting of a line to measurements of the two variables such that the algebraic sum of deviations of the measurements from the line are zero and the sum of the squares of the deviations are less than they would be for any other line. The equation describing this line is, in effect, a mathematical statement of the nature of the relationship between the two variables. It can be used to help us understand this relationship or to predict the values of one of the variables given a value for the second variable.

The general equation for a regression line fitted to two variables is

$$Y = a + bX \tag{14-11}$$

where Y is the criterion variable, X the predictor variable, a a constant, and b the amount Y changes for each unit of change in X. Both a and b are unknown and are determined by the regression analysis. Values for a and b were obtained from a regression analysis on the relationship between the amount of white bread bought per person per week (Y) and the response to the statement on the importance of natural ingredients in bread (X). The resulting equation, $Y = 0.504 + .241X$ indicates that (1) 0.504 pounds of white bread are bought per week when the response to the attitude statement is set at zero and (2) for every increase of 1.0 in the response to the attitude statement, there tends to be an increase of .241 pounds in the amount of bread purchased.

Many programs are available for regression analysis; the one used in this case was SPPS.[10] Since a description of the regression program is usually given in the program manual, and complete descriptions of the formulas and procedures for running regression analyses by hand are available in other sources,[11] we do not discuss the mathematics of fitting least squares regression lines here.

Approximations to the a and b values obtainable from a least squares regression analysis can be arrived at quickly by graphic analysis. A line can be fitted visually to a plot of the values of the two variables such as shown in Figure 14–4. A plot such as this is called a *scatter diagram*. The line is fitted in such a way as to attempt to make the sum of all the distances of points above the line equal the sum of all those below the line. (The number of points above and below the line need not be equal, however.) The estimate of the a value is the intercept of the Y axis. The estimate of the b value may be determined by solving the question, $\bar{Y} = a + b\bar{X}$, after substituting in the numerical values of $\bar{Y}$, a, and $\bar{X}$.

For many purposes the accuracy of the measurements, the required ac-

---

[10] Nie, Bent, and Hull, op. cit.

[11] See J. Johnston, *Econometric Methods* (New York: McGraw-Hill Book Co., 1963) for a more complete discussion of regression analysis.

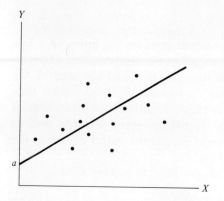

Figure 14–4 Scatter diagram and visually fitted regression line for two variables (hypothetical data).

curacy of the regression line values, and/or the degree of instability of the relationship between the two variables is such that a visually fitted line is fully as satisfactory as a mathematically fitted one.

If the line is fitted mathematically, care should be taken to ensure that the assumptions of the model are met by the data. Least squares regression analysis is a parametric method that requires the same set of assumptions as required for least squares correlation analysis with one exception. The exception is that it is not necessary to assume that the population of the X variable is normally distributed for each value of the Y variable.

Multivariate Methods

Marketing is a field in which the relationships of interest typically involve several variables. Sales, market share, brand preference, and market potential are all examples of variables of interest to the marketing manager that are usually determined by several predictor variables. It is therefore not difficult to understand why multivariate methods—methods of analysis involving three or more variables—have become so widely used in marketing research.

In this section we describe *multiple correlation* and *regression analysis, multiple classification analysis* (MCA), *canonical analysis, analysis of variance* (ANOVA), *automatic interaction detection* (AID), *cluster analysis, multiple discriminant analysis,* and *factor analysis.* Examples of the use of these methods in the Willamette study are given where appropriate.

Multiple Correlation and Regression Analysis

Multiple correlation and regression methods are extensions of the two variable correlation and regression methods we have discussed. Multiple correlation and regression methods are used in situations where it is desired to analyze the associative relationship among three or more variables.

These techniques have wide application in marketing research. Multiple regression analysis uses include the following.

1. *To measure the determinants of demand and market share.* An example is the analysis of demand in terms of passenger flights between cities, both overall and in terms of market share for one airline. Estimates of profit maximizing levels were found for both numbers of flights and dollars of advertising.[12]

2. *Sales forecasting.* An example is a furniture manufacturer who developed a forecasting equation in which sales for the coming year were forecast as a function of sales during the current year, housing starts during the current year, estimated disposable income during the coming year, and a time trend factor.[13]

3. *To determine the relationship between the criterion variable and one predictor variable while the effect of other predictor variables are held constant.* An example is the estimate of the reliance on price as an indicator of quality of furniture while other factors such as brand of product and stores in which it is available were held constant.[14]

4. *To determine if predictor variables other than those now being considered are related to the criterion variable.* An example is the finding that the inclusion of a variable to allow for the effect of past advertising by American Airlines in a multiple regression equation to forecast revenues gives a better forecast than if it were excluded.[15]

5. *To adjust data obtained from experiments for factors not controlled for and believed not to be randomly distributed.* An example is adjusting the data obtained from an experiment on the effects of height of shelf placement on sales of a product to allow for the effects of differences in store traffic.[16]

Multivariate correlation analysis uses.

1. *To determine which of a set of predictor variables is most related to the criterion variable.* An example is the finding in the Willamette study of a multiple correlation analysis of the responses to the atti-

[12] L. Schultz, "Market Measurement and Planning with a Simultaneous Equation Model," *Journal of Marketing Research,* **8** (May 1971), 153–164.

[13] G. G. C. Parker and E. C. Segura, "How to Get a Better Forecast," *Harvard Business Review,* **49** (March–April 1971), 101.

[14] B. P. Shapiro, "Price Reliance: Existence and Sources," *Journal of Marketing Research,* **10** (August 1973), 286–289.

[15] D. S. Tull, J. J. Bisschop, and M. G. Nelson, "Advertising-Revenue Relationships of Airline Companies: Multicollinearity and Lagged Models," Working Paper, University of Oregon, 1972.

[16] P. E. Green and D. S. Tull, "Covariance Analysis in Marketing Experimentation," *Journal of Advertising Research,* **6** (June 1966), 45–53.

tude statements and their relationship to white bread consumption that agreement with the statement "Foods ought to be made only of natural ingredients rather than have additives" was the best single predictor of the amount of white bread consumed among white bread users.

2. *To determine the overall degree of the relationship between the predictor variables and the criterion variable.* The multiple coefficient of correlation of the responses to all 17 relevant attitude statements was only +.38. Clearly, other variables (quality, price, advertising, and availability) affect sales of white bread as well as attitudes. In addition, the computer printout showed that three variables would produce an r of +.33. The remaining 14 variables add little to the overall relationship.

The model on which multiple regression and correlation analysis is based involves the assumption that both predictor and criterion variables measurements be of an interval or ratio scale. If care is exercised in use and interpretation, however, some of the predictor variables and the criterion variable can be nominally or ordinally scaled. These variables are called *dummy variables.*[17]

For nonforecasting applications of multiple regression analysis, care must be exercised to ensure that two or more of the predictor variables are not themselves closely associated. The coefficients for such variables obtained from a multiple regression analysis of the data are of questionable validity and must be used with care.[18] This is not a problem for forecasting applications, however, since the interest there is in the predicted value of the forecast variable and not the coefficients of the predicted variables.

Multiple Classification Analysis

Multiple classification analysis (MCA) is a form of multiple regression analysis that can be used with predictor variables that are *nominally* scaled. The criterion variable can be *interval, ordinal,* or *nominal* so long as it is reasonably symmetrically distributed.[19] A multiple correlation coefficient is obtained from an MCA analysis that is not unlike that obtained from a multiple regression. The range of values is -1.0 to $+1.0$ and the

---

[17] See D. B. Suits, "Use of Dummy Variables in Regression Equations," *Journal of the American Statistical Association,* 52 (December 1957), 548–551 for a discussion of the use of such variables.

[18] For a discussion of this problem, including steps that can be taken to identify and to cope with it, see J. Johnston, *Econometric Methods,* 2nd ed. (New York: McGraw-Hill Book Company, 1972).

[19] A detailed description of MCA is given in F. M. Andrews, J. N. Morgan, J. A. Sonquist, and L. Klem, *Multiple Classification Analysis,* 2nd ed. (Ann Arbor: Institute for Social Research, 1973).

interpretation is similar. This provides a considerable amount of needed flexibility in marketing problems because both the predictor and the criterion variables in which one is interested are often nominal in nature. Some examples of nominal predictor variables are *sex, occupation, stage of life cycle,* and *home owner or renter. Purchaser* or *nonpurchaser, brand loyal* or *not brand loyal,* and *"aware of"* or *"not aware of"* are examples of nominal criterion variables of common interest.[20]

Canonical Analysis

Canonical analysis is a method that *allows the association between two or more criterion variables and two or more predictor variables to be determined.*[21] A canonical correlation coefficient is obtained that has a range of -1.0 to $+1.0$ and is interpreted in a manner similar to that for r from a regression analysis.

A canonical analysis was run on the amounts of white, whole wheat, and specialty breads bought per person per week (three criterion variables) and the responses to the attitude statements of Question 11 in the Willamette study questionnaire (19 predictor variables). The resulting canonical correlation coefficient was .57. This indicates that certain clusters of these attitudes could explain some of the variation in overall bread purchasing patterns. However, the correlation is relatively low. Variables other than these attitudes are important in explaining overall bread purchasing behavior.

Analysis of Variance—ANOVA

Analysis of variance (ANOVA) is a method of analysis that is important in analyzing data from experiments. *ANOVA is a method of determining what the probability is that the observed differences of the mean responses of groups receiving different experimental treatments are the result of sampling variation.*

ANOVA is a parametric method that involves the following assumptions:

---

[20] For an example of a study using MCA see J. W. Newman and R. A. Werbel, "Multivariate Analysis of Brand Loyalty for Major Household Appliances," *Journal of Marketing Research,* **10** (November 1973), 404–409.

[21] For a more complete discussion of canonical analysis see P. E. Green, M. H. Halbert, and P. J. Robinson, "Canonical Analysis: An Exposition and Illustrative Application," *Journal of Marketing Research,* **3** (February 1966), 32–39, and M. I. Alpert and R. A. Peterson, "On the Interpretation of Canonical Analysis," *Journal of Marketing Research,* **9** (May 1972), 187–192.

1. Treatments are assigned at random to test units.
2. Measurements are intervally scaled and are taken from a population that is normally distributed.
3. The variances in the test groups are equal.
4. The effects of treatments on response are additive.[22]

Although one of the assumptions of the ANOVA model is that treatments are assigned at random to test units, this is often overlooked in practice by using *pseudotreatments* such as occupation, stage of life cycle, or urban or rural residency and analyzing to see what effect they have on the mean amounts of a particular product purchased. This use of nonrandomly assigned pseudotreatments greatly increases the possibility that other variables associated with them will affect responses and these effects will be attributed to the pseudotreatment.

An analysis of white bread consumption by occupation (blue-collar, white-collar, and managerial-professional) was made on the Willamette data using ANOVA. The assumptions of the ANOVA model other than the random assignment of treatment were met reasonably well. The probability that the observed differences in means of white bread consumed by the three occupational groups occurred as a result of sampling variation was less than .01.

Discriminant Analysis

The objective of *discriminant analysis* is *to classify persons or objects into two or more categories using a set of predictor variables.* Examples of the use of discriminant analysis in marketing include an attempt to classify Ford and Chevrolet owners by demographic and psychological variables,[23] classification of buyers versus nonbuyers of new products,[24] a determination of audience characteristics of radio stations,[25] and an examination of differences of persons saving money at commercial banks and those saving at savings and loan associations.[26]

[22] For a discussion of ANOVA and its applications in marketing, see S. Banks, *Experimentation in Marketing* (New York: McGraw-Hill Book Co., 1965).

[23] F. B. Evans, "Psychological and Objective Factors in the Prediction of Brand Choice: Ford versus Chevrolet," *Journal of Business,* 32 (October 1959), 340–369.

[24] E. A. Pessemier, P. C. Burger, and D. J. Tigert, "Can New Product Buyers Be Identified?" *Journal of Marketing Research,* 41 (November 1967), 349–354.

[25] W. F. Massy, "On Methods: Discriminant Analysis of Audience Characteristics," *Journal of Marketing Research,* 5 (March 1965), 39–48.

[26] H. J. Claycamp, "Characteristics of Owners of Thrift Deposits in Commercial Banks and Savings and Loan Associations," *Journal of Marketing Research,* 2 (May 1965), 163–170.

When a discriminant analysis is run, the goal is to develop a model that will result in a large proportion of the cases being correctly classified. The discriminant equation can then be used to predict which class a new case will belong to or, more importantly, to demonstrate which variables are most important in distinguishing between the classes. For example, a discriminant analysis of attitudes toward a department store found that the perceived price level of the store was the major discriminating factor between shoppers and nonshoppers.[27]

A discriminant analysis was run on the Willamette data (attitudes and media habits) to determine which were the best predictor variables to discriminate between nonusers and users of whole wheat bread. The best discriminators were found to be a strong concern for quality brands (Questions 11i and 11j), a concern for natural ingredients (Question 11a) and morning television viewing (Question 15).

Linear discriminant analysis was used in this study. Like linear multiple regression, linear discriminant analysis is a much simpler technique than its nonlinear counterpart. The assumptions of the linear discriminant model that must be met for the procedure to be valid are as follows:

1. The variances of the predictor variables for the persons or objects classified into each category are equal.
2. The predictor variables are normally distributed.[28]

Automatic Interaction Detection (AID)

Automatic Interaction Detection (AID), still another technique for analyzing association between a single criterion variable and two or more predictor variables,[29] was developed primarily for use in analyzing the results of surveys. Survey data are often nominal or ordinal rather than interval in nature. AID can be used to analyze data for association with no restriction as to the scale of the data.

To use AID effectively, data from large samples—1,000 cases or more —are required. The mathematical procedures employed are iterative in

[27] G. Albaum, R. Best, and D. I. Hawkins, unpublished, proprietary research report, 1973.

[28] For a more complete discussion of linear discriminant analysis, see D. F. Morrison, "Discriminant Analysis," in R. Ferber, ed., *Handbook of Marketing Research* (New York: McGraw-Hill Book Company, 1974), 2-442-2-457. For a full mathematical development of the topic see T. W. Anderson, *Introduction to Multivariate Statistical Analysis* (New York: John Wiley & Sons, Inc., 1958).

[29] J. A. Sonquist, E. L. Baker, and J. N. Morgan, *Searching for Structure* (Ann Arbor: Survey Research Center, University of Michigan, 1971).

nature, involving successive divisions of the sample into two subsamples based on the largest amount of variance in the criterion variable explained by one of the predictor variables. Both the large sample size and the iterative procedures make the amount of computations so large that the use of a computer is essential.

A complete description of AID is available in Sonquist, et al.[30]

Factor Analysis

The objective of *factor analysis* is to summarize a large number of original variables into a small number of synthetic variables, called *factors*. Determining the factors that are inherent in a data array has a number of applications in marketing. These applications, and an example of each, are as follows:

1. *Determine Underlying Dimensions of the Data.*

A factor analysis of a set of semantic differential data on coffee attributes revealed four latent dimensions of coffee preference—flavor, heartiness, genuineness, and freshness.[31]

2. *Determining Relationships Among Variables.*

Factor analysis of the frequency and pattern of purchase of products has been used as one means of measuring brand loyalty.[32]

3. *Clustering of People or Objects.*

A factor analysis of data on benefits sought in toothpaste suggests that the market consists of four segments: those consumers that are primarily concerned with (1) flavor and product appearance, (2) brightness of teeth, (3) decay prevention, and (4) price.[33]

4. *Condensing and Simplifying Data.*

Studies using AIO (activity, interest, and opinion) inventories often involve data from as many as 300 statements from large samples of respondents. Factor analysis is one method employed to condense the AIO data, both by finding groupings of related statements and by finding respondents with related response patterns.[34] The factors can in turn be used as "predictor" variables for a multiple regression analysis.

---

[30] Ibid.

[31] B. N. Mukherjee, "A Factor Analysis of Some Qualitative Attributes of Coffee," *Journal of Advertising Research,* **5** (March 1968), 35–38.

[32] J. N. Sheth, "A Factor Analytic Method of Brand Loyalty," *Journal of Marketing Research,* **5** (November 1968), 395–404.

[33] R. I. Haley, "Benefit Segmentation: A Decision Oriented Research Tool," *Journal of Marketing,* **32** (July 1968), 30–35.

[34] For a discussion of one such study see W. D. Wells and D. J. Tigert, "Activities, Interests, and Opinions," *Journal of Advertising Research,* **11** (August 1971), 27–35.

A number of factor analysis techniques are possible.[35] A *principal components* analysis followed by a *varimax rotation* was run on the attitude data in the Willamette study to determine if there were identifiable sets of attitudes about bread that would be helpful in preparing advertising copy. Of the seven factors that were isolated, among the more interesting were factors that could be labeled concern for health (items *a, n,* and *p*), taste (items *m* and *q*), and brand importance (items *f* and *h*).

Cluster Analysis

The purpose of *cluster analysis* is to separate objects into groups such that the groups are relatively homogeneous. Cluster analysis has been used in marketing research for test market selection,[36] to construct market segments by groups of consumers,[37] to examine similarities among markets in different countries,[38] and to group magazine readers for media selection purposes.[39]

Several techniques are available for conducting cluster analyses.[40] Depending upon the choice of method, the data used may be nominal, ordinal, interval, or ratio in nature.[41]

Summary

Once data are collected, they must be analyzed to provide information relevant to the problem at hand. This chapter has been concerned with the

---

[35] For a definitive discussion of the various types of factor analytic techniques and the assumptions of each see H. H. Harman, *Modern Factor Analysis* (Chicago: University of Chicago Press, 1967).

[36] P. E. Green, R. E. Frank, and P. J. Robinson, "Cluster Analysis in Test Market Selection," *Management Science,* **13** (April 1967), 387–400.

[37] J. B. Kernan, "Choice Criteria, Decision Behavior and Personality," *Journal of Marketing Research,* **5** (May 1968), 155–164; V. P. Lessig and J. O. Tollefson, "Market Segmentation Through Numerical Taxonomy," *Journal of Marketing Research,* **8** (November 1971), 480–487; and D. B. Montgomery and A. J. Silk, "Clusters of Consumer Interests and Opinion Leaders' Sphere of Influence," *Journal of Marketing Research,* **8** (August 1971), 317–321.

[38] S. P. Sethi, "Comparative Cluster Analysis for World Markets," *Journal of Marketing Research,* **8** (August 1971), 348–354.

[39] F. M. Bass, E. A. Pessemier, and D. J. Tigert, "A Taxonomy of Magazine Readership Applied to Problems in Marketing Strategy and Media Selection," *Journal of Business,* **42** (July 1969), 337–363.

[40] For a general description of techniques and applications to marketing problems see P. E. Green and D. S. Tull, *Research for Marketing Decisions,* 3rd ed. (Englewood Cliffs, N.J.: Prentice-Hall, Inc., 1974), Chap. 15.

[41] For a technical discussion of the various clustering techniques see R. R. Sokal and P. H. A. Sneath, *Principles of Numerical Taxonomy* (San Francisco: W. H. Freeman and Company, 1963), and N. Jardine and R. Sibson, *Mathematical Taxonomy* (New York: John Wiley & Sons, Inc., 1971).

estimation of population values, hypothesis testing, and techniques for analyzing the association between two or more variables. Data from the Willamette study were used to illustrate the techniques wherever appropriate.

The estimation of population can involve either *point* or *interval estimates*. When a *srs* is taken, the sample value obtained serves as the point estimate of the population value. When a nonproportional stratified sample (or any other sample likely to produce a biased estimate) is used, the sample values must be adjusted to accurately reflect the characteristics of the population of interest.

An *interval estimate of a population value requires the determination of two points between which the population value is estimated to lie with some stated level of confidence.* Interval estimates are based on the characteristics of the sampling distribution as described in Chapter 6.

Hypothesis tests were first described in Chapter 2 and later in Chapter 6. In this chapter, the logic underlying hypothesis tests is developed more fully and examples of several kinds of hypothesis tests are given.

A wide variety of specific techniques are available for determining the degree and nature of the association between two or more variables. Table 14–2 provides a description and classification of these techniques based on the number and scale level of both the criterion and predictor variables. A close examination of this table should serve as an adequate review of these important techniques.

Questions and Problems

14. 1. Are there any differences in testing hypotheses in basic research and in decisional research? Explain.

14. 2. (a) Prepare a point estimate from the following data from the Willamette study. Assume that a simple random sample was taken.
    (b) Prepare an interval estimate from the data using a 90 per cent confidence interval. Assume that a simple random sample was taken.

Sample mean number of loaves of white bread bought at each purchase	2.13
Sample standard deviation	1.93
Sample size	176

14. 3. (a) Prepare a point estimate of the mean amount of whole wheat bread consumed per person per week from the data given from the Willamette study.
    (b) Prepare an interval estimate using a 95 per cent confidence interval from the following data. Assume that a simple random sample was taken in each stratum.

	Blue-Collar Families	White-Collar Families	Managerial-Professional Families
Sample mean amount of whole wheat bread consumed per person per week	0.43 lbs.	0.57 lbs.	0.29 lbs.
Sample standard deviation	0.93 lbs.	0.87 lbs.	0.38 lbs.
Proportion in population	0.52	0.29	0.19
Sample size	43	64	66

14. 4. (a) Prepare a point estimate of the proportion of families that have white bread for the noon meal using the following data from the Willamette study. Assume that a simple random sample was taken.

   (b) Prepare an interval estimate with a 99 per cent confidence interval using the data. Assume that a simple random sample was taken.

Proportion of families that have white bread for noon meal	.483
Sample size	176

14. 5. (a) Prepare a point estimate of the proportion of families who eat one or more kinds of specialty bread using the following data from the Willamette study.

   (b) Prepare an interval estimate with a 75 per cent confidence interval using the data. Assume that a simple random sample was taken in each stratum.

	Blue-Collar Families	White-Collar Families	Managerial-Professional Families
Sample proportion of families who eat one or more kinds of specialty bread	.59	.74	.82
Proportion in population	0.52	0.29	0.19
Sample size	39	62	66

14. 6. Using the data in the table in Problem 14.2, find the probability that the mean number of loaves of white bread bought at each purchase is 2.0 or less.

14. 7. Using the data in the table in Problem 14.3, find the probability that the mean amount of whole wheat bread consumed per person per week is 0.50 pounds or more.

14. 8. Using the data in the table in Problem 14.4, find the probability that the proportion of families who have white bread at their noon meals is 0.50 or more.

14. 9. Using the data in the table in Problem 14.5, find the probability that the proportion of families who eat one or more kinds of specialty bread is .60 or less.

14.10. Run an analysis of the data given in the following table.

Occupation	Eat White Bread	Do Not Eat White Bread	Total
Blue-collar	35	8	43
White-collar	47	17	64
Managerial-professional	46	20	66
Total	128	45	173

What conclusion do you draw?

14.11. Run an analysis of the data given in the following table.

Occupation	Eat Whole Wheat Bread	Do Not Eat Whole Wheat Bread	Total
Blue-collar	29	14	43
White-collar	51	9	60
Managerial-professional	54	11	65
Total	134	34	168

What conclusion do you draw?

14.12. Run an analysis of the data in the following table.

Occupation	Eat Specialty Bread	Do Not Eat Specialty Bread	Total
Blue-collar	23	16	31
White-collar	46	16	62
Managerial-professional	54	12	66
Total	123	44	167

What conclusion do you draw?

14.13. (a) From an inspection of the following table, what tentative conclusions do you draw?

Mean Pounds Per Person Per Week of White Bread Eaten by Occupation and Stage of Life Cycle

			Stage of Life Cycle				
Occupation	Young Single	Young Married— No Children	Married— Youngest Child Under Six	Married— Youngest Child Over Six	Empty Nest	Solitary Survivor
Blue-collar	$\bar{x} = 3.60$ $s^2 = 5.33$ $n = 5$	$\bar{x} = 0.70$ $s^2 = 0.67$ $n = 5$	$\bar{x} = 1.58$ $s^2 = 1.88$ $n = 9$	$\bar{x} = 1.27$ $s^2 = 1.61$ $n = 14$	$\bar{x} = 1.25$ $s^2 = 1.61$ $n = 8$	$n = 0$
White-collar	$\bar{x} = 1.03$ $s^2 = 3.07$ $n = 9$	$\bar{x} = 0.43$ $s^2 = 0.31$ $n = 7$	$\bar{x} = 0.57$ $s^2 = 0.14$ $n = 11$	$\bar{x} = 0.45$ $s^2 = 0.36$ $n = 15$	$\bar{x} = 0.09$ $s^2 = 0.07$ $n = 8$	$\bar{x} = 0.63$ $s^2 = 0.43$ $n = 8$
Managerial– Professional	$\bar{x} = 0.42$ $s^2 = 0.28$ $n = 9$	$\bar{x} = 0.52$ $s^2 = 0.32$ $n = 12$	$\bar{x} = 0.88$ $s^2 = 3.57$ $n = 16$	$\bar{x} = 0.50$ $s^2 = 0.41$ $n = 20$	$\bar{x} = 0.40$ $s^2 = 0.80$ $n = 5$	$\bar{x} = 0.09$ $s^2 = 0.02$ $n = 3$

(b) What analytic technique(s), if any, would be appropriate for making a formal analysis of the data?

Selected Bibliography

AAKER, D. *Multivariate Analysis in Marketing.* San Francisco: Scott, Foresman and Co., Inc., 1971. An anthology of articles dealing with multivariate techniques and their applications in marketing.

FERBER, R. *Handbook of Marketing Research.* New York: McGraw-Hill Book Company, 1974. Parts D—Statistical Inference and E—Statistical Analysis of Relationships comprise a total of 13 chapters devoted to the analysis of marketing research data.

GREEN, P. E., and D. S. TULL. *Research for Marketing Decisions,* 3rd ed. Englewood Cliffs, N.J.: Prentice-Hall, Inc., 1974. A book that is more strongly oriented toward analysis than most texts in marketing research. The last nine chapters are concerned with analysis and the description of analytical techniques.

MENDENHALL, W., and J. E. REINMUTH. *Statistics for Management and Economics.* Belmont, Calif.: Duxbury Press, 1971. An elementary statistics text that deals with statistical inference and the less complex methods for analyzing relationships among variables. It is an unusually well-written book that contains large numbers of illustrative examples.

MORRISON, D. F. *Multivariate Statistical Methods.* New York: McGraw-Hill Book Company, 1967. A well-written book that covers the major multivariate statistical techniques.

SHETH, J. "The Multivariate Revolution in Marketing Research," *Journal of Marketing Research,* **8** (January 1971), 13–19. An overview of applications of multivariate methods to marketing. An especially valuable feature is the classificatory scheme he uses for multivariate methods.

Case 14–1

Willamette Bakeries (A)

A necessary step in analyzing the Williamette Bakeries study data was to specify which cross tabulations should be run. If the objectives of the survey were "to determine if there are viable market segments for bread based upon (1) characteristics of purchasing families and amounts of purchase, (2) communication media and appeals, and (3) distribution outlets," what cross tabulations do you think should have been requested by the Far West Research analyst? Why?

Case 14–2

Willamette Bakeries (B)

One of the bases for segmenting the market for bread that the management of Willamette Bakeries thought might be useful was the occupation of the chief wage earner. Management believed that blue-collar families might have different bread purchase and consumption patterns than white-collar families and that the buying patterns of managerial-professional families might be different than either of the others.

1. What questions bear on this issue? What cross tabulations do you think should be run?

2. What kind(s) of analyses can be run to determine if there is a relationship between occupation and type of store at which bread is purchased?

Case 14–3

Willamette Bakeries (C)

The answer to Questions 9 and 10 on bread characteristics have some obvious marketing implications. How would you analyze the answers to these questions to determine if

1. there is a relationship between *brands of bread* now used and importance of bread characteristics to respondents?

2. there is a relationship between *kinds of bread* now used and importance of bread characteristics to respondents?

3. there is a relationship between *amounts of bread* now used and importance of bread characteristics to respondents?

Case 14–4
Willamette Bakeries (D)

How would you analyze the data to determine which variables are the best predictors of mean amounts of white bread purchased?

Case 14–5
Del Monte Instant Mashed Potato Price Level Test*

At the conclusion of the Del Monte Instant Mashed Potato (IMP) sales performance test (Case 12–1), it was decided to extend the study for two additional four-week periods in order to test the impact of price level on sales. Half (eight) of the stores in each city raised the price to a level $.02 higher than the price charged at the remaining stores.

Exhibits A and B provide sales and brand share data for each price level for the two additional periods. Brand share for Del Monte IMP declined in both period VI and period VII. Elrick and Lavidge isolated three confounding factors that might be responsible for this decline:*

a. For the third period in a row, there has been no in-store promotional activities for the Del Monte product.
b. For the second consecutive period, French's is offering a $.25 refund coupon, printed on the backs of its packages.
c. In each market, a new product has been introduced. (Philadelphia: Idaho Supreme—12 servings, 8.3% serving share.) (Cincinnati: French's "Country-Style"—24 servings, 5.9% share.)

1. Would the data obtained in periods VI and VII alter the conclusions reached during the first five periods (Case 12–1)?

2. Is this an effective approach to determining the impact of price level? Explain.

* Used with permission of Del Monte Corporation and Elrick and Lavidge, Inc.

Exhibit A Period VI—Total Movement by Price (February 13–March 12)

Brand & No. of Servings in Package	High Price				Percentage Brand Share		Low Price				Percentage Brand Share	
	Total Units	No. of Stores Stock.	Units/ Store/ Week	Aver. Price (cents)	Serv.	$	Total Units	No. of Stores Stock.	Units/ Store/ Week	Aver. Price (cents)	Serv.	$
Del Monte												
10	396	16	6.2	35	6.5	7.7	446	16	7.0	33	5.8	6.5
24	156	16	2.5	70	6.1	6.1	185	16	2.9	68	5.8	5.6
Betty Crocker												
8	451	15	7.5	30	5.9	7.5	789	16	12.3	30	8.2	10.5
24	387	15	6.5	68	15.1	14.5	541	16	8.5	68	16.9	16.3
40	149	6	2.7	115	9.7	9.5	192	6	3.4	115	10.0	9.8
French's												
10	698	16	10.9	33	11.4	12.7	889	16	13.9	33	11.6	13.0
21	391	16	6.2	63	13.4	13.6	519	16	8.1	63	14.2	14.4
Idahoan												
10	193	6	8.0	29	3.1	3.1	194	6	8.0	29	2.5	2.5
16	271	10	6.8	30	7.0	4.5	338	10	8.5	31	7.0	4.6
Borden's												
6–8	13	1	4.3	25	0.1	0.5	7	2	0.9	25	0.1	0.1
12–16	168	7	6.0	39	3.8	3.6	199	8	6.2	39	3.6	3.4
Pillsbury												
8	172	10	4.3	32	2.2	2.9	163	10	4.1	32	1.7	2.3
24	131	10	3.3	69	5.1	4.9	137	10	3.4	69	4.3	4.2
Blue Label												
5	589	8	18.4	11.5	4.8	3.7	735	8	23.0	11.5	4.8	3.7
Butterfield												
4–6	536	8	16.7	12.5	4.4	3.7	440	8	13.8	12.5	2.9	2.4
Ore-Ida												
12	72	2	9.0	39	1.4	1.5	38	2	4.8	39	0.6	0.7
Totals	4773				100%	100%	5812				100%	100%

Exhibit B Period VII—Total Movement by Price (March 13–April 9)

Brand & No. of Servings in Package	High Price						Low Price					
	Total Units	No. of Stores Stock.	Units/ Store/ Week	Aver. Price (cents)	Percentage Brand Share Serv.	$	Total Units	No. of Stores Stock.	Units/ Store/ Week	Aver. Price (cents)	Percentage Brand Share Serv.	$
Del Monte												
10	257	16	4.0	35	4.2	5.2	309	16	4.3	33	3.9	5.0
24	139	16	2.2	70	5.5	5.1	209	16	3.2	68	6.3	6.9
Betty Crocker												
8	557	15	9.3	30	7.4	9.6	763	16	11.9	30	7.7	11.2
24	402	16	6.3	68.5	15.9	15.8	636	15	10.6	69	19.3	12.3
40	87	5	4.4	115	5.7	5.8	97	6	4.0	115	4.9	5.5
French's												
10	631	16	9.8	33	10.4	12.0	655	16	10.2	33	8.3	10.6
21	383	16	6.0	63	13.3	13.9	455	16	7.1	63	12.1	14.1
24	108	7	3.9	69	4.3	4.3	63	8	2.0	69	1.9	2.1
Idahoan												
10	221	6	9.2	29	3.5	3.7	287	6	12.0	29	3.6	4.1
16	256	9	7.1	29	6.8	4.2	457	10	11.4	25	9.3	5.6
Borden's												
6–8	11	1	2.8	25	0.1	0.2	6	2	1.3	25	—	—
12–16	146	7	5.2	37	3.4	3.1	173	8	5.4	39	3.1	3.3
Pillsbury												
8	109	10	2.7	31	1.4	1.9	151	10	3.8	31	1.5	2.3
24	102	10	2.6	69	4.0	4.1	182	10	4.6	69	5.6	6.1
Blue Label												
5	496	8	15.5	11.5	4.1	3.3	835	8	26.1	11.5	5.3	4.7
Butterfield												
4–6	380	8	11.9	12.5	3.1	2.7	531	8	16.6	12.5	3.4	3.2
Ore-Ida												
12	58	2	7.3	39	1.1	1.3	34	2	4.3	39	0.5	0.6
86	—	—	—	—	—	—	3	1	0.8	119	0.3	0.2
Idaho Supreme												
12	291	8	9.1	23	5.8	3.8	197	8	6.2	23	3.0	2.2
Totals	4634				100%	100%	6043				100%	100%

CHAPTER 15

Demand Analysis

The analysis of demand is a necessary step in translating marketing *objectives* into marketing *programs*. It is a continuing activity to determine where and to what extent markets for the company's products and services exist, and how they can best be served. It involves analyses to help determine market segments, market potential and share of market in each segment, sales analyses, investigation of the effects of changes in products, prices, promotion and distribution, and considerations of introducing new products and entering new markets. A continuing surveillance of competitors and their marketing programs is also a part of demand analysis. The role of demand analysis in marketing is shown schematically in Figure 15–1.

A marketing manager is called upon to make some kind of demand analysis every time he makes a decision about the marketing program. In those cases where he is so uncertain about his own analysis that he is reluctant to rely upon it, he may turn to the marketing research department (or an outside research agency) for a formal analysis of the situation. In

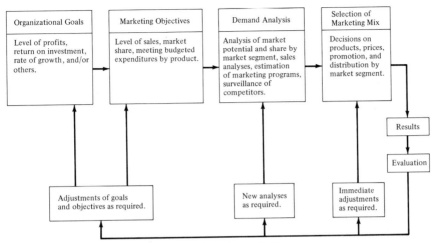

Figure 15–1 The role of demand analysis in marketing.

this chapter we deal with the methods used by marketing researchers in conducting such analyses of demand.

Market Segmentation Research

Effective marketing programs are rooted in a sound understanding of the consumer. The marketer needs to know consumer attitudes and motivations, buying behavior, and use behavior. These characteristics form a consumption system. There is usually more than one type of consumption system for a product class, and when there is, different segments of the market are the result.

The existence of differing consumption systems and resulting market segments for bread was illustrated by the Willamette Bakeries study described earlier (Chapters 13 and 14).

Bases for Segmenting Markets

To be useful for marketing purposes, a segment must consist of a group of consumers (or industrial users) that can be *identified as a group,* is *accessible* as a group, and is of *sufficient size* to make it worthwhile to develop a different marketing program for it. The many possible bases for segmenting markets include (1) *geographic location,* (2) *demographic characteristics,* (3) *socioeconomic characteristics,* (4) *psychological characteristics,* and (5) *product related characteristics.*

Geographic Location

Division of a market by geographic area is the oldest and still the most widely practiced basis for market segmentation. Appropriate geographic areas are relatively easy to identify, are accessible to the application of differing marketing programs, and can be defined to have a sufficient number of buyers to make establishing the segment worthwhile. A summary description of the use of geographic location as a segmenting variable is given in Table 15–1.

The demand for a given product will vary by geographic area as a result of variations in income, climate, custom, and other factors. For example, cordial liquor sales in 1970 ranged from a low of 3.6 fifths per hundred persons in Alabama to over 200 fifths per hundred persons in the District of Columbia.[1] As compared with the national average, families in the South spend more for such food products as cereals, sugar, sweets, beverages, and fats and oils; families in the Northeast spend more for fish and meat; those in the North Central region spend more for dairy products and potatoes; and those in the West spend more for fruits and vegetables.[2] Some 60 per cent of rural families have freezers whereas only 24 per cent of urban families have them.[3] The demand for such products as skis, air conditioners, lobster pots, and cotton gins clearly will vary substantially by geographic location as well.

Aggregate demand for product classes is not the only aspect to vary by geographic area. Preferences for flavors, colors, and advertising themes also vary. For example, Anisette (a liqueur) is sold in most of the United States as a clear liquid. However, in one major market area, Louisiana, it must be colored red to obtain consumer acceptance.

The usual way of establishing geographic segments is to use politically defined units such as cities, counties, or states. This is true, in part, because the secondary data on which demand analyses are often based are usually available only for these geographic areas. Cities are also often used as geographic segments for the obvious reason that they provide a concentrated, high-volume market for many consumer and industrial products.

The use of *Zip Code areas* as geographic segments has become common for firms that solicit orders by mail. A mail order insurance company that

[1] *The Liquor Handbook* (New York: Gavin-Johnson Associates, Inc., 1970), p. 232.

[2] U.S. Department of Agriculture, *National Food Situation,* Washington, D.C.: (U.S. Government Printing Office, 1967).

[3] National Rural Electric Cooperative Association, as reported in C. G. Walters and G. W. Paul, *Consumer Behavior: An Integrated Framework* (Homewood, Ill.: Richard D. Irwin, Inc., 1970).

was already using selected states and counties as segments, reports that an analysis by Zip Code area revealed a variation in past sales of more than 300 per cent.[4] There are 561 section areas (first three digits of Zip Code) that contain some 46,000 Zip Code areas. Data on population, number of households, total retail sales, shopping good sales, passenger car regis- trations, and total square miles of land area are given for each section area in the *Commercial Atlas and Marketing Guide* published annually by Rand, McNally & Company.

Demographic Characteristics

The demographic characteristics used for market segmentation include *age, position in the life cycle, sex, race, national origin, religion,* and *family size.* A summary description of the use of these characteristics as segmenting variables is given in Table 15–1.

Age and Position in the Life Cycle.   Age and the position in the life cycle are so closely interrelated as segmenting variables that it is useful to consider them jointly.

The stages in the life cycle are usually defined in relation to marital status and the presence and ages of children. A commonly used definition of life stages and a description of typical consumption patterns in each is given in Table 15–2.

One study,[5] covering a wide range of consumer products, shows that purchases for about 50 per cent of the products were equally responsive to age and life-cycle variables, 10 per cent were more sensitive to age, and 40 per cent were sensitive to life cycle. According to this study, therefore, choosing to segment by stage of life cycle rather than age would be ap- propriate for about 90 per cent of the consumer products covered in the study.

Age is used as a basis for charging different prices for some products such as health and life insurance, tickets to movies (children's and senior citizens'), public transportation fares, and (children's) meals in restau- rants.

Sex.   Sex is used as a basis for segmentation both because of differing physical characteristics and differing subcultures of the sexes. Some prod- ucts are used by only one of the sexes as a result of differences in physical characteristics that necessarily limit the market to that sex; maternity clothing is an example. There are also products that are used by both

[4] M. Baier, "Zip Code—New Tool for Marketers," *Harvard Business Review,* **45** (January–February 1967), 136–140.
[5] W. D. Wells and G. Gubar, "Life Cycle Concept in Marketing Research," *Journal of Marketing Research,* **3** (November 1966), 360.

Table 15–1 Market Segmentation—Summary Description of Geographic Location and Demographic Characteristics as Segmenting Variables

Description	Geographic Location	Age, Stage of Life Cycle	Sex	Race, National Origin, Religion	Family Size
Segmenting proposition	Similarities of demand characteristics within geographic areas and differences among them make it worthwhile to offer different products, use different advertising, set different prices, and/or distribute products differently in two or more areas.	Similarities of demand characteristics within age groups (or stages in life cycle) and differences among such groups may make it worthwhile to offer different advertising, set different prices, and/or distribute products differently to two or more such groups.	Similarities of demand characteristics among members of the same sex and differences between the sexes may make it worthwhile to offer different products, use different prices, and/or distribute products differently to women and to men.	Similarities of demand characteristics by race (or national origin, or religion) and differences among them may make it worthwhile to offer different products, use different advertising, set different prices, and/or distribute by racial group (or national origin or religious group).	Similarities of demand characteristics by size of family and differences among them may make it worthwhile to offer different products, use different advertising, set different prices, and/or distribute products differently by family size.
Segmenting variables	Cities, counties, states, Zip Code areas or other areas.	Age groups and specific life cycle stages used depend on the product category.	Physical and/or subcultural attributes of sex of consumer.	Racial groups, groups with common behavior based on a common national origin, and religious groups.	Number of children.
Data required	Data on potential and actual sales by area	Purchase data by brand by age group (stage of life cycle).	Purchase and use data by sex.	Purchase data by race (or national origin, or religion).	Purchase data by family size.

Method(s) of obtaining data	Primarily secondary data from government and trade sources and analysis of own company sales.	Survey of consumers, consumer panel data, credit card data, Public Use Sample of Bureau of Census, and warranty card information.	Survey of consumers, consumer panel data, and credit card data.	Survey of consumers, consumer panel data.	Survey of consumers, consumer panel data, Public Use Sample of Bureau of Census and warranty card information.
Application	Oldest and most widely practiced form of market segmentation.	Used for both consumer durables and nondurables. Life cycle stage appears to be better than age as segmenting variable for most products.	Used for consumer nondurables and personal services.	Segmentation by race and national origin more widely used than by religion. Used primarily for consumer nondurables.	Used primarily for size determination in consumer durables. (No. of bedrooms in housing, size of refrigerators.)
Used by	Consumer goods manufacturers. Industrial goods manufacturers, wholesalers, retailers.	Consumer goods manufacturers. Banks, savings and loan institutions. Retailers.	Consumer goods manufacturers. Retailers.	Consumer goods manufacturers. Retailers.	Consumer goods manufacturers. Retailers.
Reference	R. E. Frank, W. F. Massy, and Y. Wind, *Market Segmentation* (Englewood Cliffs, N.J.: Prentice-Hall, Inc., 1972), Chap. 2.	W. D. Wells and G. Gubar, "Life Cycle Concept in Market Research," *Journal of Marketing Research,* 3 (November 1966).	Frank, Massy, and Wind, op. cit., Chap. 2.	V. P. Lessig and J. O. Tolletson, "Market Segment Identification Through Consumer Buying Behavior and Personal Characteristics" in J. F. Engel, et al., *Market Segmentation: Concepts and Applications* (New York: Holt, Rinehart and Winston, Inc., 1972), 435–455.	

Table 15–2 An Overview of the Life Cycle

Bachelor Stage; Young Single People Not Living at Home	Newly Married Couples; Young, No Children	Full Nest I; Youngest Child Under Six	Full Nest II; Youngest Child Six or Over Six	Full Nest III; Older Married Couples with Dependent Children	Empty Nest I; Older Married Couples, No Children Living with Them, Head in Labor Force	Empty Nest II; Older Married Couples, No Children Living at Home, Head Retired	Solitary Survivor in Labor Force	Solitary Survivor Retired
Few financial burdens. Fashion opinion leaders. Recreation oriented. Buy: Basic kitchen equipment, basic furniture, cars, equipment for the mating game, vacations.	Better off financially than they will be in near future. Highest purchase rate and highest average purchase of durables. Buy: Cars, refrigerators, stoves, sensible and durable furniture, vacations.	Home purchasing at peak. Liquid assets low. Dissatisfied with financial position and amount of money saved. Interested in new products. Like advertised products. Buy: Washers, dryers, TV, baby food, chest rubs and cough medicine, vitamins, dolls, wagons, sleds, skates.	Financial position better. Some wives work. Less influenced by advertising. Buy larger sized packages, multiple-unit deals. Buy: Many foods, cleaning materials, bicycles, music lessons, pianos.	Financial position still better. More wives work. Some children get jobs. Hard to influence with advertising. High average purchase of durables. Buy: New, more tasteful furniture, auto travel, nonnecessary appliances, boats, dental services, magazines.	Home ownership at peak. Most satisfied with financial position and money saved. Interested in travel, recreation, self-education. Make gifts and contributions. Not interested in new products. Buy: Vacations, luxuries, home improvements.	Drastic cut in income. Keep home. Buy: Medical appliances, medical care, products which aid health, sleep, and digestion.	Income still good but likely to sell home.	Same medical and product needs as other retired group; drastic cut in income. Special need for attention, affection, and security.

Source: W. D. Wells and G. Gubar, "Life Cycle Concept in Marketing Research," *Journal of Marketing Research,* **3** (November 1966), 362. Reprinted with permission of the author and the American Marketing Association.

sexes and are designed to allow for physical differences; clothing, bicycles, and golf clubs are examples.

Most of the segmentation based on sex is a product of the different subcultures of the sexes. A *subculture* refers to a manner of behaving peculiar to a group that is a part of some larger group.[6] A subgroup shares many of the roles and values and much of the status of the main group, but it also exhibits differences in these respects. Although the traditional stereotypes of the roles and values of the sexes in our society have tended to become somewhat blurred over the past several years, one still has no difficulty in recognizing distinctions. Consider the following list of polar traits: weak-strong, soft-hard, homemaker-breadwinner, practical-impractical, active-passive, yielding-unyielding, emotional-emotionless. Each of these (and many other) traits still has a masculine or feminine connotation in our society.

These sex-related traits are widely used for market segmentation. Some examples of their use are *Better Homes and Gardens* and *Business Week* magazines, *Chanel No. 5* and *English Leather* cologne, *Dove* and *Lifebuoy* bath soaps, and *Virginia Slims* and *Marlboro* cigarettes. However, segmentation based on sex-role cultures will become increasingly difficult in the future as traditional stereotypes continue to lose ground.

Race, National Origin, and Religion.   Race, national origin, and religion are also bases for subcultures in our society and can be used to form market segments.

A *race* consists of a group of people who share distinctive physical features stemming from a common biological heritage. The principal racial groups in the United States are the Caucasian, the Negro, the Oriental, and the American Indian.

Blacks are the largest racial minority in the United States, constituting 11.1 per cent of the population in 1970. They are followed by the Orientals (0.5 per cent) and the American Indian (.04 per cent). A large number of studies have been conducted concerning the black population as a market for products. Some major conclusions are that blacks are more brand conscious than whites,[7] Blacks spend a higher percentage of increases in aftertax income on education, medical care, and consumer durables than do whites,[8] black men spend over 40 per cent more for clothing than do white males, and black families tend to own larger

---

[6] B. Berelson and G. Steiner, *Human Behavior: An Inventory of Scientific Findings* (New York: Harcourt Brace, Jovanovich, Inc., 1964), 645.

[7] "The Negro Consumer—What Broadcasters Have Learned," *Sponsor Magazine,* **18** (September 14, 1964), 36–40.

[8] Andrew F. Brimmer, "Economic Program in Black and White," Department of Commerce, 1966.

Table 15–3 Estimated Brand-Share Studies for Selected Products*

Product	Anglo	Latin
Soaps (powdered or flakes)		
Tide	30.6	15.3
Cheer	15.0	42.3
Lipstick		
Revlon	26.5	21.0
Avon	23.9	50.7
Indigestion remedies		
Alka Seltzer	31.6	7.7
Pepto-Bismol	31.3	65.4
Cold remedies		
Contac	54.1	45.5
Coricidin	20.3	9.1
Coldens	2.7	13.6
Dristan	10.8	0.0
Soft drinks		
Pepsi-Cola	25.0	52.4
Coca-Cola	25.0	33.0
7-Up	9.0	5.1
Cigarettes		
Winston	31.1	7.0
Marlboro	7.3	21.6
Viceroy	2.2	12.5

* *Source:* R. P. Jones, "Spanish Ethnic Market Second Largest in U.S.," *Marketing Insights* (November 27, 1967), 11.

automobiles than do white families in the same income class.[9] There is also a substantial amount of evidence concerning differences in food buying habits and consumption between blacks and whites.[10]

National origin is a segmenting variable that is similar to race in terms of its application. National minority groups in the United States include the Polish, Irish, Italians, Puerto Ricans, Chinese, and Mexicans. Depending upon their degree of assimilation, these groups retain food preferences, customs, and mores that form the basis for segmentation.

The difference in brand shares that can exist among consumers of differing national origins is illustrated by Table 15–3. The brand shares of products purchased by Spanish-speaking consumers ranges from less than one-fourth to several times those of Anglo-Americans.

Religion is the basis for another set of subcultural groups in our society. The principal religious groups in the United States are the Protestants, Catholics, Mormons, and Jews.

[9] F. C. Akers, "Negro and White Automobile Buying Behavior: New Evidence," *Journal of Marketing Research,* **V** (August 1968), 283–292.
[10] See "Negro Food Buying Differs," *Marketing Insights* (January 29, 1968).

Religions affect buying behavior in both a positive and a negative way. The celebration of some religious holidays (Christmas, Easter, Hanukkah) are occasions for giving gifts and are preceded by a high level of purchases of suitable items. Some religions (in the United States, notably that of the Orthodox Jew) require that specially prepared foods be eaten. In such cases market segments are the natural result.

Most religions have taboos about the use of certain products and religions in the United States are no exception. The use of alcohol, tobacco and other products with nicotine, and contraceptives are examples of products that are forbidden by one or more religions in this country.

Family Size. Products that are intended for family use often have to be designed with a particular size of family in mind. The size of the apartments in a new apartment building, the size of a refrigerator, and the number of seats and "moving around" room in a family car are examples of factors that may be considered.

Socioeconomic Characteristics

The characteristics of *income, occupation, education,* and *social* class are the segmenting variables that fall within this classification. They are closely interrelated concepts: income is associated with education, education is one of the determinants of occupation, and social class, to a considerable extent, is a product of all of the other three factors. There can be little question that socioeconomic characteristics of families play a powerful role in determining spending and usage patterns. As is evident from the discussion that follows, however, the closeness of the interrelationships between the individual characteristics has sometimes made it difficult to sort out the individual effects of each. A summary description of socioeconomic characteristics as segmenting variables is given in Table 15–4.

Income. Broad expenditure patterns for American families were studied extensively in two studies sponsored by *Life* magazine in the mid-1960s.[11] The studies show that, as income rises the *proportion* spent on food, housing and household operations, medical and dental care, and tobacco decreased. With the exception of tobacco, these necessities must be provided regardless of income level. As incomes rise, better food and better housing is provided, and preventive as well as curative medical and dental care is bought. However, the amounts spent do not increase in the same proportion as income.

The proportion of income spent for home furnishings and equipment,

[11] F. Linden, ed., *Expenditure Patterns of the American Family* (New York: National Industrial Conference Board, 1965), and F. Linden, ed., *Market Profiles of Consumers* (New York: National Industrial Conference Board, 1967).

Table 15–4 Market Segmentation—Summary Description of Socioeconomic Characteristics as Segmenting Variables

Description	Income	Occupation	Education	Social Class
Segmenting proposition	Similarities of demand characteristics by size of income and differences among consumers with different income levels may make it worthwhile to offer different products, use different advertising, set different prices, and/or distribute products differently to consumers with different income levels.	Similarities of demand, characteristics by occupational group and differences among groups may make it worthwhile to offer different products, use different advertising, set different prices, and/or distribute products differently to different occupational groups.	Similarities of demand characteristics of consumers with similar educational backgrounds, and differences among those with different educational backgrounds may make it worthwhile to offer different products, use different prices, and/or distribute products differently to the different groups.	Similarities of demand characteristics of consumers of the same "social class," and differences among classes may make it worthwhile to offer different products, use different advertising, set different prices, and/or distribute products differently to consumers in different social classes.
Segmenting variables	Usual brackets are those used by *Census of Population*.	Usual occupational classification is "blue-collar," "white-collar," and "managerial-professional."	Usual educational classification is number of years of formal schooling completed.	Most widely known classification scheme is Warner's "upper-upper," "upper-lower," "upper-middle," "lower-middle," "upper-lower," and "lower-lower."
Data required	Purchase data by income level.	Purchase data by occupational group.	Purchase data by number of years of formal schooling of purchaser.	Purchase data by social class.

Method(s) of obtaining data	Survey of consumers, consumer panel data, credit card data, Public Use Sample of Bureau of Census, and warranty card information.	Survey of consumers, consumer panel data, credit card data, and Public Use Sample of Bureau of Census.	Survey of consumers, consumer panel data, credit card data and Public Use Sample of Bureau of Census.
Application	Used for consumer non-durables and durables, recreation and personal service, often used for media selection.	Perhaps used more for media selection than any other purpose. Used for consumer nondurables.	Used for consumer non-durables and durables, personal services.
Used by	Consumer goods manufacturers. Personal service firms (banks, recreation, etc.). Retailers.	Consumer goods manufacturers. Retailers.	Consumer goods manufacturers. Retailers.
References	V. P. Lessig and J. O. Tollefson, "Market Segment Identification Through Consumer Buying Behavior and Personal Characteristics," in J. F. Engel, et al., *Market Segmentation: Concepts and Applications* (New York: Holt, Rinehart and Winston, Inc., 1972), 435–455. Frank, Massy, and Wind, op. cit., Chap. 2.		J. M. Carman, *The Application of Social Class in Market Segmentation*, (Berkeley, Calif.: I.B.E.R. Special Publications, University of Calif., 1965).

clothing and accessories, recreation and equipment, reading and education, and alcoholic beverages was found to *increase* as income increased. With increased income and the addition to discretionary purchasing power in which it results, there is an increase by more than a proportional amount in expenditures on amenities and the enjoyment of leisure time.

As reflected in part by these findings, income level has a considerably greater effect on the purchase of durable goods than it does on the purchase of nondurable goods. A number of studies indicate very clearly that income is an important determinant of the purchase of durable consumer goods, and especially those such as automobiles and higher priced appliances.[12]

The effects of income on the purchase of consumer nondurables are not so clear. One study relating income and whether or not a brand of the product class was on hand at the time of the interview shows a significant association (at the .05 level) in 88 of 91 products. The products involved in the study included toiletries, drugs, cosmetics, soaps, plastic items, paper items, soft drinks, liquors, frozen foods, nonfrozen foods, and pet foods.[13] The purchase of higher priced foods has been found to vary directly with income.[14] However, another investigator concluded from a review of segmentation research that income "appears to have at best a relatively low degree of association with household purchases."[15]

Occupation.   Occupation has seldom been used alone as a segmenting variable. It is frequently used as one of the indicators of social class, however, which, in turn, is used for segmentation.

In the study of bread purchase and usage patterns reported in Chapters 13 and 14, substantial differences were found between the "blue-collar," "white-collar," and "managerial-professional" occupational groups in the types of breads bought and the way they were consumed.

Education.   The effects of education are closely associated with, but not limited to, those of income and occupation. Educational levels have con-

---

[12] See R. Ferber, "Factors Influencing Durable Goods Purchases" in L. H. Clark, ed., *The Life Cycle and Consumer Behavior* (New York: New York University Press, 1955); R. Ferber, "Research on Household Behavior," *American Economic Review,* **12** (March 1962), 19–63; G. Katona and E. Mueller, *Consumer Response to Income Increases* (Washington, D.C.: The Brookings Institution, 1968), and L. R. Klein and J. B. Lansing, "Decision to Purchase Consumer Durable Goods," *Journal of Marketing,* **20** (October 1955), 109–132.

[13] J. H. Myers, R. Stanton, and A. F. Haug, "Correlates of Buying Behavior: Social Class versus Income," *Journal of Marketing,* **35** (October 1971), 8–15.

[14] H. H. Harp and M. Miller, "Convenience Foods: The Relationship Between Sales Volume and Factors Influencing Demand," Agricultural Economic Report No. 81, U.S. Department of Commerce, 1965.

[15] R. E. Frank, "Market Segmentation Research: Findings and Implications," in Frank Bass, et al., *Application of the Sciences in Marketing Management* (New York: John Wiley & Sons, Inc., 1968).

tinued to rise such that the average adult (25 years of age or older) in the United States in 1972 had completed 12.2 years of schooling.[16] Men with college degrees had an average yearly income of $16,200 in 1971, whereas men who were only high school graduates earned, on the average, $10,430.[17]

Exposure to specific media is associated with level of education. Persons with less than a high school education are much more likely to read movie and scandal magazines than are, say, college graduates. People who have more education are, in turn, more likely to read magazines such as *Time, Fortune, Saturday Review, Scientific American,* and *Harper's Magazine.* There are similar differences in television programs watched; *Roller Derby* viewers have a considerably lower average number of years of formal education than do the viewers of a *Boston Pops* concert, for instance.

Social Class. Social classes are groups of people in a society with similar interests, attitudes, values, and behavior patterns. Several systems for classifying people by social class are possible. The two that are most widely used in market investigations are those of Warner and Carman.[18]

Warner identifies six classes: upper-upper, lower-upper, upper-middle, lower-middle, upper-lower, and lower-lower. The determinants of class standing in his system are occupation, source of income, residential area, and type of dwelling, with occupation receiving the heaviest weighting. Carman uses weighted factors of occupation, education, and property value (or rent paid) to develop a social class "score." The number of classes can vary depending upon the requirements of the investigation.

A substantial number of studies document the different interests, attitudes, values, and behavior patterns of the different social classes. These differences between social classes are reflected in the assortment and the styles of consumer durables that are purchased by members of the different classes. Consider the following listings of living room furnishings and recreational equipment:

Living Room Furnishings

(1)	(2)
Overstuffed furniture	Danish modern furniture
TV set	No TV set (located elsewhere)
Curtains and drapes on windows	Drapes only on windows
No bookshelves or books	Bookshelves and books
"Pretty" pictures	Reproductions of paintings by well-known artists

[16] U.S. Department of Commerce, Bureau of the Census, *Statistical Abstract of the United States* (Washington, D.C.: U.S. Government Printing Office, 1973), 114.

[17] Ibid., p. 331.

[18] Described in W. L. Warner, et al., *Social Class in America* (New York: Harper & Row, Publishers, Inc., 1960), and J. M. Carman, *The Application of Social Class in Market Segmentation* (Berkeley, Calif.: I.B.E.R. Special Publications, University of California, 1965).

Recreational Equipment

(3)	(4)
Pickup with camper	Tent
Motorboat	Golf clubs
Hunting equipment	Tennis rackets
Fishing gear	Fishing gear

No one familiar with contemporary American society is likely to have difficulty in deciding which assortments probably belong to an upper-lower class family and which belong to an upper-middle class family.

The effect of the differences in values and interests on the purchase and usage patterns of consumer nondurables is not as pronounced, however. In a study of household products referred to earlier,[19] income was found to have a higher degree of association with whether or not the product was on hand for 78 of 91 products than did social class. After reviewing various studies of frequently purchased household products, another investigator has concluded that "socioeconomic characteristics (including social class) are not particularly effective bases for segmentation either in terms of their association with household differences in average purchase rate or in response to promotion."[20]

One study suggests that a matrix consisting of life-cycle stages stratified by social classes is a useful way of segmenting markets.[21]

Psychological Characteristics

The principal psychological variables that have received attention as segmenting variables are (1) personality, (2) attitudes, and (3) activities, interests, opinions, and life-styles. A summary description of these attributes and their use as segmenting variables is given in Table 15–5.

Personality. Many of the findings with respect to personality as a predictor of consumer buying and behavior are negative and others are contradictory. An early study of the personalities of Ford and Chevrolet owners showed no significant differences between the two,[22] a finding that was later confirmed by another study.[23] The acceptance of new fashions by

[19] J. H. Myers, R. R. Stanton, and A. F. Haug, "Correlates of Buying Behavior: Social Class versus Income," *Journal of Marketing,* **35** (October 1971), 8–15.

[20] R. E. Frank, "Market Segmentation Research: Findings and Implications," in F. Bass, et al., eds., *Applications of the Sciences in Marketing Management* (New York: John Wiley & Sons, Inc., 1968), 53. For conflicting findings see S. U. Rich and S. C. Jain, "Social Class and Life Cycle as Predictors of Shopping Behavior," *Journal of Marketing Research,* **5** (February 1968), 41–49.

[21] R. H. Evans and N. R. Smith, "A Selected Paradigm of Family Behavior," *Journal of Marriage and the Family,* **31** (August 1969), 512–517.

[22] F. B. Evans, "Psychological and Objective Factors in the Prediction of Brand Choice: Ford versus Chevrolet," *Journal of Business,* **32** (October 1959), 340–369.

[23] R. Westfall, "Psychological Factors in Predicting Product Choice," *Journal of Marketing,* **24** (October 1960), 11–17.

Table 15–5 Market Segmentation—Summary Description of Psychological Characteristics as Segmenting Variables

Description	*Personality*	*Attitudes*	*"Life-Style"*
Segmenting proposition	Similarities of demand characteristics of consumers of the same personality type, and differences in demand among consumers with different personality types may make it worthwhile to offer different products, use different prices, and/or distribute products differently to consumers with different types of personality.	Similarities of demand characteristics by attitudinal sets of consumers, and differences in demand among consumers with different attitudinal sets may make it worthwhile to offer different products, use different prices, and/or distribute products differently to consumers with differing sets of attitudes.	Similarities of demand characteristics by "life-style" and differences in demand among "life-style" groups may make it worthwhile to offer different advertising, set different prices, and/or distribute products differently to consumers with differing life-styles.
Segmenting variables	No one method of classification in use.	No one method of classification in use.	Responds to statements concerning activities, interests, and opinions (AIO inventory).
Data required	Purchase data by personality type.	Purchase data by sets of attitudes.	Purchase data by AIO inventory responses. Usually used with demographic and socioeconomic data as well.
Method(s) of obtaining data	Survey of consumers.	Survey of consumers.	Survey of consumers.
Application	Very limited use. Consumer nondurables and durables.	Consumer nondurables and durables, retail store patronage.	Consumer nondurables primarily, some personal services.
Used by	Primarily used only in basic research to date.	Consumer goods manufacturers. Retailers.	Consumer goods manufacturers. Banks.
Reference	H. H. Kassarjian, "Personality and Consumer Behavior: A Review," *Journal of Marketing Research*, **8** (November 1971).	Frank, Massy, and Wind, op. cit., Chap. 3.	W. D. Wells and D. J. Tigert, "Activities, Interests, and Opinions," *Journal of Advertising Research*, **11** (August 1971).

males was found to be positively related to the personality traits of ascendancy and sociability.[24] The use of antacids and analgesics was found to be higher among compulsive than noncompulsive persons in one study,[25] negatively related to ascendancy and emotional stability in another study involving the use of headache remedies (an analgesic),[26] and unrelated to degree of compliance, aggression, or detachment in a third study.[27] The use of cigarettes was found to be unrelated to any of the personality traits measured in two studies[28] and was positively related to needs for sex, aggression, achievement, and dominance in another.[29]

Not only are the findings linking personality traits and product purchase and use behavior limited and tenuous but they are also difficult to apply. It seems reasonable to conclude on the basis of research results to date that the use of personality traits as segmenting variables is not of much practical value.[30]

Attitudes. The findings concerning the relationship of attitudes and product usage confirm what one would expect, namely,

1. Persons with a more favorable attitude toward a product tend to have have a higher incidence of usage of it, and
2. Persons with a more unfavorable attitude toward a product are more likely to stop using it.

Findings of the same study also indicate that

3. Measurements of attitudes of persons who have not tried a product tend to be normally distributed around the mean.[31]

Attitudes have been found to be useful in both explaining variation in brand shares and in predicting future behavior.[32] A detailed discussion of

[24] W. T. Tucker and J. J. Painter, "Personality and Product Use," *Journal of Applied Psychology,* **45** (October 1961), 325–393.

[25] Ibid.

[26] M. J. Gottlieb, "Segmentation by Personality Types," in L. H. Stockman ed., *Proceedings of the American Marketing Association* (1959), 148–158.

[27] J. B. Cohen, "The Role of Personality in Consumer Decisions," in Harold H. Kassarjian and T. S. Robertson, eds., *Perspectives in Consumer Behavior* (Glenview, Ill.: Scott, Foresman and Co., 1968), 220–233.

[28] Tucker and Painter, op. cit. and Cohen, op. cit.

[29] A. Koponen, "Personality Characteristics of Purchasers," *Journal of Advertising Research,* **1** (September 1960), 6–12.

[30] See H. H. Kassarjian, "Personality and Consumer Behavior: A Review," *Journal of Marketing Research,* **8** (November 1971), 409–419 for a thorough review of this area.

[31] A. A. Aachenbaum, "Knowledge Is a Thing Called Measurement," in L. Ader and I. Crespi, eds., *Attitude Research at Sea* (Chicago: American Marketing Association, 1966), 111–126.

[32] H. Assael and G. S. Day, "Attitudes and Awareness as Predictors of Market Share, *Journal of Advertising Research,* **8** (December 1968), 3–10. See also J. H. Myers and M. I. Alpert, "Determinant Buying Attitudes: Meaning and Measurement," *Journal of Marketing,* **32** (October 1968), 13–20.

the measurement and utilization of attitudes in marketing is provided in Chapter 10.

Activities, Interests, Opinions (AIO), and Life-Style. The concept of *life-style,* introduced in 1963, has been described as follows:

Life-style . . . refers to the distinctive or characteristic mode of living, in its aggregate and broadest sense, of a whole society or segment thereof. It is concerned with those unique ingredients or qualities which describe the style of life of some culture or group, and distinguish it from others.[33]

Research in life-style patterns and their relationships to consumer behavior since 1963 has been conducted using a variety of techniques. The most widely used approach, however, is based upon the reasoning that an individual's (1) use of time, (2) interests, (3) opinions, and (4) demographic characteristics are the primary characteristics that determine his style of life.

AIO inventories have been developed to measure the first three of these characteristics. The letters AIO stand for *activities, interests,* and *opinions.* The basic inventory used consists of 300 statements on the topics listed in Table 15–6. The respondent is asked to rate each of the statements on a scale, indicating degree of agreement or disagreement.[34]

An example of the use of an AIO inventory is shown in Table 15–7. The study was conducted to determine differences in life-styles between

Table 15–6   Life-Style Characteristics*

Activities	Interests	Opinions
Work	Family	Themselves
Hobbies	Home	Social Issues
Social Events	Job	Politics
Vacation	Community	Business
Entertainment	Recreation	Economics
Club Membership	Fashion	Education
Community	Food	Products
Shopping	Media	Future
Sports	Achievements	Culture

* *Source:* Adapted from J. T. Plummer, "The Concept and Application of Life-Style Segmentation," *Journal of Marketing,* **38** (January 1974), 33–37.

[33] W. Lazer, "Life-Style Concepts and Marketing," in *Toward Scientific Marketing,* S. A. Greyser, ed. (Chicago: American Marketing Association, 1964), 130.

[34] See W. D. Wells and D. J. Tigert, "Activities, Interests, and Opinions," *Journal of Advertising Research,* **11** (August 1971), 27–35, for a description of the basic inventory.

Table 15–7 Cross-Tabulation Results of AIO Agreement With Male Bank Charge Card Usage*

Number	Statement	Card Users Definite and General Agreement	Noncard Users Definite and General Agreement
8.	I enjoy going to concerts.	25%	17%
10.	A woman's place is in the home.	27	41
17.	In my job I tell people what to do.	53	21
18.	I am a good cook.	36	26
23.	My greatest achievements are ahead of me.	56	42
24.	I buy many things with a charge or credit card.	39	22
29.	We will probably move once in the next five years.	46	37
39.	Five years from now the family income will probably be a lot higher than it is now.	71	60
42.	Good grooming is a sign of self-respect.	52	71
53.	There is too much advertising on TV today.	59	70
70.	Women wear too much make-up today.	43	51
74.	My job requires a lot of selling ability.	51	37
77.	I like to pay cash for everything I buy.	26	67
86.	Television is a primary source of our entertainment.	25	40
94.	Investing in the stock market is too risky for most families.	47	56
109.	To buy anything other than a house or car on credit is unwise.	29	47
117.	Young people have too many privileges today.	52	64
112.	I love the outdoors.	54	76
126.	There is too much emphasis on sex today.	52	64
130.	There are day people and there are night people; I am a day person.	58	69
135.	I expect to be a top executive in the next ten years.	44	27
152.	I am or have been president of a society or club.	51	36
174.	I would like to have my boss' job.	42	33
175.	A party wouldn't be a party without liquor.	29	17
177.	I would rather live in or near a big city than in or near a small town.	46	34
183.	I often bet money at the races.	18	8
184.	I like to think I'm a bit of a swinger.	38	26
194.	I stay home most evenings.	62	71
198.	Advertising can't sell me anything I don't want.	55	68
200.	I often have a cocktail before dinner.	36	20
202.	I like ballet.	26	16
209.	When I must choose between the two, I usually dress for fashion, not comfort.	19	10
214.	Liquor is a curse on American life.	34	49
217.	Movies should be censored.	41	57
218.	I read one or more business magazines regularly.	34	18
230.	I am active in two or more service organizations.	28	17
248.	I do more things socially than most of my friends.	19	10
269.	We often serve wine with dinner.	30	16
272.	I buy at least three suits a year.	25	11
273.	*Playboy* is one of my favorite magazines.	25	16
275.	I spend too much time talking on the telephone.	31	17
282.	It is good to have charge accounts.	33	21

Table 15–7 (*Continued*)

Number	Statement	Card Users Definite and General Agreement	Noncard Users Definite and General Agreement
283.	Hippies should be drafted.	48	61
286.	When I think of bad health, I think of doctor bills.	31	46
290.	My days seem to follow a definite routine.	47	58

Note: All differences are significant above the .05 level based on Chi-square tests of significance.
* *Source:* Joseph T. Plummer, "Life-Style Patterns and Commercial Bank Credit Card Usage," *Journal of Marketing*, **35** (April 1971), 38. Reproduced with permission of the author and the American Marketing Association.

users and nonusers of commercial bank charge cards.[35] From the responses shown in the table one could conclude that male users of credit cards, as compared to nonusers, are more "social" (responses to Questions 8, 86, 130, 175, 184, 194, 209, 248, 275), "open-minded" (responses to Questions 10, 70, 117, 126, 217, 283), "self-confident" (responses to Questions 17, 18, 23, 74, 94, 198), "ambitious" (responses to Questions 39, 135, 174, 218), "urban oriented" (responses to Questions 112, 177), and "community minded" (responses to Questions 152, 230).

When differing life-style segments are identified, the results can be combined with demographic and product usage data in selection of advertising and promotional campaigns, or in changing product configurations. The life-style profile of the commercial bank credit card user that emerges from the study just described has obvious application for such a purpose. This approach may also provide a basis for an analysis of competitor advertising to determine the target segments of other brands and whether worthwhile segments are being ignored. Insights may also be provided as to the difficulty of converting nonusers to users of the product.

Life-style research using AIO inventories and related methods frequently has been referred to as *psychographics*. This term is avoided here, however, as it has been used in so many ways that its meaning is not always clear.

Product-Related Characteristics

The principal variables associated directly with the product that have been used as segmenting variables are (1) *product benefits,* (2) *product-space configuration,* (3) *brand loyalty,* (4) *time of purchase,* and (5) *patronage patterns.* An overview of the use of these characteristics as segmenting variables is given in Table 15–8.

[35] J. T. Plummer, "Life-Style Patterns and Commercial Bank Credit Card Usage," *Journal of Marketing,* **35** (April 1971), 35–42.

Table 15–8 Market Segmentation—Summary Description of Product Related Characteristics as Segmenting Variables

Description	Product Benefits	Product-Space Configuration	Brand Loyalty	Time of Purchase	Patronage Patterns
Segmenting proposition	Similarities of demand characteristics of groups of users who perceive the product providing similar benefits and differences in demand among groups with differing perceptions of benefits, make it worthwhile to offer different products, use different advertising, set different prices, and/or distribute products differently to the different groups.	Similarities of demand characteristics of groups of users whose ratings of product attributes are similar, and differences in demand among groups with differing ratings, may make it worthwhile to offer different products, use different advertising, set different prices, and/or distribute products differently to two or more such groups.	Similarities of demand characteristics of users who are "loyal" to a brand, and differences in demand among groups with lower degrees of loyalty, may make it worthwhile to offer different products, use different advertising, set different prices, and/or distribute products differently to two or more such groups.	Similarities of demand characteristics of consumers who make initial purchase early in the product life cycle; and differences with those who buy at later stages, may make it worthwhile to offer different products, use different advertising, set different prices, and/or distribute products differently to two or more such groups.	Differences in the level of demand among consumers grouped by degree of patronage may make it worthwhile to offer different product characteristics, use different advertising, set different prices, and/or distribute products differently to two or more such groups.
Segmenting variables	Benefits are related to specific products.	Ratings are related to attributes of specific products.	No one method of classification of "loyalty" in general use.	Time of such groups purchase relative to product life cycle stage.	Proportion of purchases from a retail store or wholesale establishment.

Data required	Purchase data by perceived product benefits, usually used with demographic and socioeconomic data as well.	Purchase data by attribute ratings, usually used with demographic and socioeconomic data as well.	Purchase data by degree of loyalty to brand.	Purchase data by product life cycle stage, usually used with demographic and socioeconomic data as well.	Purchase data by retailer, wholesaler, usually used with demographic and socioeconomic data as well.
Method(s) of obtaining data	Survey of consumers, industrial uses.	Survey of consumers, industrial users.	Consumer panel data, surveys of industrial users.	Consumer panel data, consumer surveys.	Consumer panel data, credit card data.
Application	Consumer nondurables. Industrial nondurables. Used in selection of advertising appeals.	Consumer nondurables. Industrial nondurables.	Consumer nondurables. Industrial nondurables.	Consumer nondurables and durables.	Consumer nondurables, industrial nondurables.
Used by	Consumer goods manufacturers. Industrial goods manufacturers.	Consumer goods manufacturers. Industrial goods manufacturers.	Consumer goods manufacturers. Industrial goods manufacturers.	Consumer goods manufacturers. Retailers.	Retailers, some wholesalers.
Reference	R. I. Haley, "Benefit Segmentation, A Decision Oriented Research Tool," *Journal of Marketing*, **32** (July 1968).	R. M. Johnson, "Market Segmentation, A Strategic Management Tool," *Journal of Marketing Research*, **8** (February 1971).	Frank, Massy, and Wind, op. cit., Chap. 3.	Frank Massy, and Wind, op. cit., Chap. 3.	Frank, Massy, and Wind, op. cit., Chap. 3.

Product Benefits. Benefit segmentation, as the name implies, is segmenting on the basis of the perceived benefits of the product or service. For example, the following segments of toothpaste users were found in one study: (1) flavor, product appearance—children, (2) brightness of teeth—smokers, (3) decay prevention—large families, and (4) price—heavy users.[36]

The use of benefit segmentation data is largely in the selection of advertising appeals, although it may also be used for positioning new products so that they complement rather than compete with existing ones. It has been observed, for example, that the *Falcon* cut heavily into the market for the *Ford* whereas the *Mustang* did not. This has been attributed to the fact that the *Mustang* was designed specifically for the 18–24 age segment and the benefits of *Mustang* ownership shown in the advertising were selected for that target segment.[37]

Product-Space Configuration. Figure 15–2 shows the perceptions of voters on the position of presidential hopefuls in the 1968 primary election with respect to their perceived degree of liberalism-conservatism and positions on amount of government involvement. It also shows clusters of voters—voter segments—in terms of their positions on the same dimensions.

Although this representation of candidate and voter positions deals only with issues (not with personalities), it is not surprising that (ex) President Nixon won the election over Senator Humphrey by a sizable margin. Nixon's perceived position is much closer to most of the voter segments than is Humphrey's. Other things being equal, one would expect voters to vote for the candidate whose views they perceive as being closest to their own—the action they apparently chose in this election.

This approach to segmentation involves locating the *actual products* (political candidates in this case) and the *ideal products of each consumer* in the same geometric space. The dimensions of the space represent product attributes that are important to consumers in differentiating among the products. Clusters of the ideal product locations (ideal points) then indicate market segments.

Several approaches have been used in making the measurements and analyzing the data necessary to construct the space and locate actual and ideal products within it. These include direct scaling of attribute data, discriminant analysis of scaled attribute data, factor analysis of scaled attribute data, and nonmetric multidimensional scaling. Although it is be-

[36] R. I. Haley, "Benefit Segmentation, A Decision-Oriented Research Tool," *Journal of Marketing*, **32** (July 1968), 30–5.

[37] G. D. Hughes, *Demand Analysis for Marketing Decisions* (Homewood, Ill.: Richard D. Irwin, Inc., 1973), pp. 28–32.

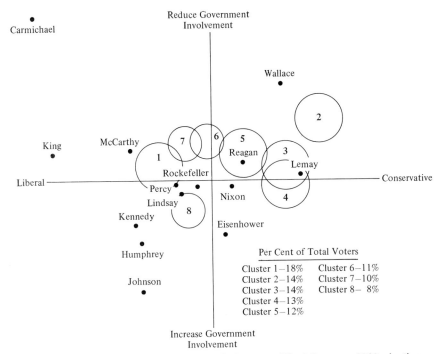

Figure 15-2 Voter segment positions relative to political figures—1968 elections. [R. M. Johnson, "Market Segmentation: A Strategic Management Tool," *Journal of Marketing Research,* **8** (February 1971), 16. Reproduced with permission.]

yond our purpose to describe these methods as they apply to segmentation studies, collectively these techniques show substantial promise for this application. Examples of their use have been reported concerning beer,[38] coffee,[39] ethical drugs,[40] liquor,[41] bakery products,[42] building materials,[43] automobiles,[44] and computers.[45] Dupont reports having used a multi-

[38] R. M. Johnson, "Market Segmentation: A Strategic Management Tool," *Journal of Marketing Research,* **8** (February 1971), 13–18.

[39] B. W. Mukherjee, "A Factor Analysis of Some Qualitative Attributes of Coffee," *Journal of Advertising Research,* **5** (March 1965), 35–38.

[40] L. A. Neidell, "The Use of Nonmetric Multidimensional Scaling in Marketing Analysis," *Journal of Marketing,* **33** (October 1969), 37–43.

[41] J. Stoltzel, "A Factor Analysis of the Liquor Preferences of French Consumers," *Journal of Advertising Research,* **1** (December 1960), 7–11.

[42] P. E. Green and D. S. Tull, *Research for Marketing Decisions,* 3rd ed. (Englewood Cliffs, N.J.: Prentice-Hall, Inc., 1975), Chap. 16.

[43] C. M. Lillis, *An Investigation of the Use of Non-metric Multidimensional Scaling in Identification and Analysis of Market Segments,* unpublished Doctoral Dissertation, Eugene, Oregon, 1972.

[44] Green and Tull, op. cit., Chap. 16.

[45] G. T. Ford, "Patterns of Competition in the Computer Industry: A Cluster Analytic Approach," unpublished Ph.D. dissertation, S.U.N.Y. of Buffalo, 1973.

dimensional scaling approach to investigate market segments for 45 different products between 1963 and 1968.[46]

Brand Loyalty. Brand loyalty has been variously defined as (1) sequence of brand choices,[47] (2) proportion of purchases,[48] (3) repeat purchase probabilities,[49] and (4) brand preference.[50] However defined, it will be useful to the marketer if viable segments can be established based on brand loyalty. The marketing problem with loyal customers is to maintain (and perhaps extend) their loyalty; the problem with nonloyal consumers is to induce trial and to develop loyalty. The kinds of appeal, price promotion, distribution of samples of the product, and other efforts appropriate to loyal and nonloyal segments obviously will vary greatly.

The research to date has focused on grocery products because of the availability of data from consumer panels. No strong associations have been shown between loyalty to the products studied and socioeconomic, demographic, and personality characteristics of consumers.[51] Some evidence, however, suggests that brand loyalty is related to attitudes[52] and to psychological characteristics of buyers.[53]

Time of Purchase. There is evidence that buyers who adopt products early in the product life cycle differ in several respects from those who are late adopters. For a number of products, those who adopt early tend to have higher income, be somewhat better educated, be younger on the average, read more print media, and use more of the class of products concerned.[54] Substantial differences have been found between the buyers

---

[46] D. H. Doehlert, "Similarity and Preference Mapping: A Color Example," in Robert L. King, ed., *Marketing and the New Science of Planning* (Chicago: American Marketing Association, 1968), 250–258.

[47] G. H. Brown, "Brand Loyalty—Fact or Fiction," *Advertising Age,* **33** (June 19, 1952), 53–55.

[48] R. Cunningham, "Brand Loyalty—What, Where, How Much," *Harvard Business Review,* **34** (January–February 1956), 116–128.

[49] A. A. Kuehn, "Consumer Brand Choice as a Learning Process," *Journal of Advertising Research,* **2** (1962), 10–17.

[50] L. Guest, "A Study of Brand Loyalty," *Journal of Applied Psychology,* **38** (1944), 16–27.

[51] See, for example, W. F. Massy, R. E. Frank, and T. M. Lodahl, *Purchasing Behavior and Personal Attributes* (Philadelphia: University of Pennsylvania Press, 1968).

[52] R. Ito, "Differential Attitudes of New Car Buyers," *Journal of Advertising Research,* **7** (March 1967), 38–42, and G. S. Day, *Buyer Attitudes and Brand Choice Behavior* (New York: The Free Press, 1970).

[53] Y. Wind, "Enduring vs. Situation Dependent Customer Characteristics as Bases for Market Segmentation," in D. L. Sparks, *Broadening the Concept of Marketing* (Chicago: American Marketing Association, 1970), 58.

[54] A review of the literature on this subject is given in T. S. Robertson, *Innovative Behavior and Communications* (New York: Holt, Rinehart and Winston, Inc., 1971).

of automobiles at the beginning and the end of the model years, for example.[55]

Patronage Patterns.   The evidence from studies of store patronage tend to confirm what everyday observation suggests—patrons of different types of stores tend to have different socioeconomic and demographic characteristics. This is true for department, specialty, and chain (versus independent) stores.[56]

The retailer, who is the principal user of segmentation studies based on patronage, can apply the findings both to designing in-store promotions and to communications with customers on mailing lists.

Methodology of Segmentation Research

The Data Base

In order to conduct a segmentation study, information on purchase and/or use behavior and on the segmenting characteristics have to be collected.[57] The usual way of obtaining the information used in segmentation studies is by conducting a survey. The survey data may be from a survey conducted at a single point in time, a single period's observations from a consumer panel, or successive period observations from a consumer panel.

Other sources of data are used for segmentation studies as well. The Census of Population provides information on ownership of many consumer durables (automobiles, washing machines, and so on) and many demographic and socioeconomic variables. These data are available at the household level in Public Use Samples available from the Bureau of the Census.

Manufacturers often use warranty cards as a source of segmentation data. A typical card for an electric appliance, for example, will ask for information on where and what type of store the purchase was made, and whether it was purchased for the purchaser's use or as a gift.

Retail stores, oil companies, and other organizations that have credit

[55] F. Wiseman, "A Segmentation Analysis of Automobile Buyers During the Model Year Transition Period," *Journal of Marketing,* **35** (April 1971), 42–49.

[56] P. Martineau, "The Personality of the Retail Store," *Harvard Business Review,* **36** (January–February 1958), 47–55; S. Banks, "Some Correlates of Coffee and Cleanser Brand Shares," *Journal of Advertising Research,* **1** (June 1961), 22–28; A. C. Samli, "Segmentation and Carving a Niche in the Market Place," *Journal of Retailing,* **44** (September 1968), 35–49.

[57] For a discussion of methods of conducting segmentation studies see R. C. Frank, "The Design of Market Segmentation Studies," in R. Ferber, ed., *Handbook of Marketing Research* (New York: McGraw-Hill Book Co., 1974), B4-99–B4-111.

cards have access both to information in purchases and to the demographic and socioeconomic data required on the application for the card.

Research Designs

The two general types of research design in segmentation studies are *cross-sectional* and *time-series—cross sectional.*

The *cross-sectional* design results from using information from either a one-time survey or from a single period's observations of a consumer panel. The purpose of a segmentation study employing such a design is to determine the relationship of the characteristics of interest (income, social class, and life-cycle stage) with purchase and-or usage behavior as of the particular period in time covered by the survey. Cross-sectional designs are used in the majority of segmentation studies conducted.

The *time-series-cross sectional* combination design utilizes information from successive periods of operation of a consumer panel. The purpose of using data that cover several time periods is to determine any differences in purchase responses among segments to changes in price, advertising, product, or other marketing actions. Such segmentation studies are necessarily more complex than the usual cross-sectional study.[58]

Methods of Analysis

The methods that may be used for analyzing the data in a segmentation study are the same as those available for analysis of data in any multiple variable study. They include *cross-tabulation, multiple regression, factor analysis, automatic interaction detection (AID), multiple classification analysis (MCA), multiple discriminant analysis,* and *canonical analysis.*

Each of these techniques was described in Chapter 14.

Estimation of Market Potential

All companies are concerned with (1) defining sales territories, (2) allocating marketing budgets, (3) setting sales targets, and (4) evaluating performance. Sound market potential estimates are needed as the basis for each of these aspects of managing the marketing of products and services. The terms *market potential* and *industry sales forecast* are not neces-

[58] See R. E. Frank and W. F. Massy, "Market Segmentation and the Effectiveness of a Brand's Price and Dealing Policies," *Journal of Business,* **37** (April 1965), 186–200.

sarily the same, although they are often used in that way. The word *potential* implies existing in possibility or capable of being developed although not existing at the moment. For some purposes it is useful to define market potential as the industry sales that would result from the optimum development of the market. This is the case when one is investigating a potential new product that has no well-defined product class. The electronic computer in the late 1940s is an example. It is also true when new markets and/or new uses for existing products suddenly open up so that present industry sales are not a valid measure of the potential that exists. The use of Teflon in cooking ware—it had previously been used as an insulating material in electrical equipment—is an example of a new market for a product that resulted in large increases in industry sales.

To avoid confusion, whenever we refer to market potential it is in the sense of the potential sales for the product class with optimum market development. Industry sales, or an industry forecast, is referred to as such.

Four major methods are available for estimating marketing potential: (1) *adjusted industry sales,* (2) *purchase proportion,* (3) *correlative indexes,* and (4) *surveys of users.*

(1) *Adjusted Industry Sales Method.* Industry sales data are compiled for many industries by trade associations and by governmental agencies. The National Electrical Manufacturers Association, for example, collects and reports data on shipments of television sets to retailers by area. The Air Transport Association provides detailed data on passenger and cargo traffic for domestic airplanes. The Bureau of the Census publishes the *Survey of Manufacturers* annually and the *Census of Manufacturers* every five years. Each work contains sales data for more than 500 industries.

Market potential is a measure of what *could be* rather than what *is.* Therefore, when industry sales data are available, estimates of market potential can be made using the industry sales figure as a base and making suitable adjustments. If one were interested in estimating the market potential for margarine, for example, one might reasonably view it as being the sum of margarine and butter sales for the preceding period adjusted for expected growth (or decline) in the coming period. Similarly, an estimate of the potential for ton-miles of freight in an area served by a trucking concern could be prepared by aggregating data on all area intercity freight traffic by the various types of carriers (rail, air, truck, and water) and adjusting the aggregate for growth.

(2) *Purchase Proportion.* Industry sales data are not always available for the territories of interest. In such cases it becomes necessary to estimate industry sales before adjusting them to obtain the market potential estimate.

Data from the *Census of Manufacturers* permits estimates of sales of industrial products to be made by Standard Industrial Classification (SIC) code by using industry by county and by Standard Metropolitan Statistical Area (SMSA). It involves calculating and applying a purchase proportion. The method is illustrated in the example of determining industry sales of printing inks by using industry in the San Francisco–Oakland SMSA.

The *Census of Manufacturers* gives data on materials consumed by each using industry for the United States as a whole. For the industries using printing inks, the total value of materials and supplies consumed and the dollar amounts of printing inks used are shown in columns (1) and (2) of Table 15–9. For newspapers $1,438,200,000 was spent for all materials and supplies of which $25,600,000 was for printing inks. The proportion of all materials and supplies purchased by newspapers comprised by printing inks was then $25,600,000/$1,438,200,000, or .018 (column 3).

The value of all materials and supplies consumed is also provided by consuming industry by county and SMSA for newspapers in the San Francisco–Oakland SMSA; this amounted to $35,900,000 (column 5 of Table 15–9). Estimated sales of printing inks to newspapers in this area were then as follows:

Industry Sales of Printing Inks to Newspapers in San Francisco–Oakland SMSA	=	Value of all materials and supplies purchased by newspapers in San Francisco–Oakland SMSA	×	Proportion of printing inks to all materials and supplies purchased by newspapers in the United States
	=	$35,900,000	×	.018
	=	$646,200		

This procedure, when repeated for each using industry, results in the estimates of sales to each of the industries using printing inks shown in column 6 of Table 15–9. The estimated total for the San Francisco–Oakland SMSA will need to be adjusted for growth from the year the census was taken to the year for which the estimate of potential is required.

Another example of the use of a purchase proportion in estimating market potential is for this book. There are approximately 300,000 undergraduate students in business schools in the United States.[59] Based upon the experience at a (small) sample of these business schools, 12 to 14 per cent of undergraduate students take a course in marketing research each year, and of these, about 75 per cent buy a new book for this class. The estimated potential market for a new market research text for the undergraduate market in the United States is, therefore,

$$300,000 \times (.12 \times .75) \text{ to } (300,000 \times (.14 \times .75)$$
$$= 27,000 \text{ to } 31,500 \text{ copies per year.}$$

[59] *Digest of Educational Statistics*, 1971, U.S. Office of Education, Division of Education Statistics. The number has been extrapolated to 1975 and is thus an estimate for that year.

Table 15–9 Estimate of Sales of Printing Inks by Using Industry in San Francisco–Oakland Standard Metropolitan Statistical Area*

		Materials Consumed, U.S.			San Francisco–Oakland SMSA		
Industry	SIC Code	All Materials and Supplies ($000,000) (1)	Printing Inks ($000,000) (2)	Proportion Printing Inks of all Materials and Supplies (3)	Number of Establishments (4)	All Materials and Supplies ($000,000) (5)	Estimate of Sales to Consuming Industries (6)
Newspapers	2711	$1,438.2	$ 25.6	.018	89	$35.9	$ 646,200
Periodicals	2721	510.3	18.2	.035	45	7.6	266,000
Book Publishing	2731	252.4	3.5	.014	26	3.8	43,200
Book Printing	2732	224.4	11.5	.051	15	2.6	132,600
Commercial Printing	275	2,112.3	139.3	.066	419	67.0	–422,000
Manifold Business Forms	2761	348.9	4.4	.013	11	13.0	169,000
Total							$5,679,000

* *Source: 1967 Census of Manufacturers,* **1,** *Summary and Subject Statistics and* **III,** *Part 1, Area Statistics.*

This does not include sales to libraries, use in graduate classes, or sales in Canada or other foreign countries.

(3) *Correlative Indexes.* Indexes are useful primarily as indicators of the *relative* market potential between geographic territories. The principle underlying their use is that when one series is highly correlated with another one, the first series may be used to predict the second. The number of births during the past three years in an area is highly correlated with sales of baby foods, for example. Thus, an index of births by geographic area of the type

$$MP_i = (b_i/b_t)100$$

where

$$MP_i = \text{measure of relative market potential for baby}$$
$$\text{foods in territory } i$$
$$b_i = \text{number of births in area}$$
$$b_t = \text{total number of births in all geographic areas}$$

is a good indicator of the relative market potential for baby foods by area.

An index may be *single* or *multiple fator* in nature. The example cited is of a single factor index. As is evident from inspection of the formula, single factor index numbers are simply the percentages of each of a set of variates to some quantity selected as a base. The relative market potential for baby food in area i is the proportion represented by the percentage of births in area i of the total of all births in the marketing areas of the company.

For most products a single factor is not a satisfactory indicator of market potential. For consumer products other than low priced staples, some measure of *number* of consumers and of *income* are usually necessary for making estimates of potential of the accuracy required. Other factors may be required as well; a furniture manufacturer may find it necessary to add a measure of marriages by area, for example, and an ethical drug manufacturer may need to add the number of pharmacists by area to obtain the accuracy desired.

Multiple factor indexes usually take the form

$$RMP_i = \frac{f_{1,i}W_1}{f_{1,t}} + \frac{f_{2,i}W_2}{f_{2,t}} + \cdots\cdots + \frac{f_{n,i}W_n}{f_{n,t}}$$

where RMP_i is the market potential in area i relative to that for the total marketing area of the company

$f_{1,i}$ is a measure of factor 1 in area i
$f_{1,t}$ is a measure of factor 1 for the total marketing
    area of the company, and
W_1 is the weight assigned factor 1

An analyst for a furniture manufacturer, for example, might conclude that a multiple factor index by area using income (I), population (N) and number of marriages (M) is needed as an indicator of relative market potential. He might further conclude that the factor weights should be such that income and population should be weighted equally and each have one-half the weight assigned to the number of marriages. This would result in relative weights of $W_I = .25$, $W_N = .25$, and $W_M = .50$. The index number for each area would then be determined as

$$RMP_i = \frac{.25 I_i}{I_t} + \frac{.25 N_i}{N_t} + \frac{.50 M_i}{M_t}$$

This may seem like a highly subjective procedure for deciding which factors to include in the index and the weights to be assigned to each. When unaided judgment is the sole basis for drawing such conclusions, it is in fact a highly subjective process. Statistical procedures are available to aid in constructing the index, however, and should generally be used whenever the data available permit it.

The critical data requirement for applying the statistical procedures for determining the factors to use and the weight to assign to each is a satisfactory substitute for industry sales for the individual marketing areas for which an index of market potential is desired. Direct data on industry sales by such a territorial breakdown will not be available: if they were there would be no need to resort to a correlative index as an indicator of market potential. Data for each of the factors to be considered for inclusion in the index have to be available for each of the territories or else they are of no value for the index.

If a satisfactory substitute for industry sales data by the territorial breakdown desired is available, a *principal components analysis* can be run on the candidate factors to help select those factors that should be included in the index. Recall that principal components analysis permits one to choose the best predictor variables from a contending set, the exact kind of problem involved in selecting of factors to include in an index.

Once the factors are selected, one may run a multiple regression analysis on the substitute industry sales data. The coefficients for the factors in the resulting regression equation can then be used to determine the factor weights.

The question that remains is "What kinds of data are available to be used as substitutes for industry sales data?" The answer is that generally they are data series for a *related industry,* a *different time,* or a *different set of geographic areas* than desired. In the case of the furniture manufacturer, for example, monthly data on department store sales are available by region and selected SMSAs. These data could be used in lieu of furniture industry sales in selecting the factors and determining the weights for the index. An alternative would be to use the sales data on "furniture, home furnishings, and equipment" by county that are collected and published every five years in the *Census of Business*. Still another alternative would be to use the annual estimate of retail sales of "furniture and home furnishings" by state published by *Sales Management* in the annual *Survey of Buying Power* issue.

Perhaps the best known general index used for setting market potentials is the annual *Sales Management Buying Power Index*. The factors used in this index are population, net income, and retail sales. The weights assigned to each are, respectively, .2, .5 and .3.[60] This index is best suited for estimating potentials for low priced products that are mass marketed, and is given by county and city for each state.

(4) *Surveys of Users*. One of the major producers of coal chemicals (chemicals that are produced as a by-product of the coking of coal) conducts an annual survey of all known present and potential users of the chemicals the company produces. The purpose of the survey is to obtain an estimate from the responding companies of how much of each chemical they will use during the coming year. The market potential for each of their products by geographic area is then determined as the sum of the requirements of the individual firms in that area for that chemical. Potentials can also be determined by end use (the amount of benzene required for automobile and truck tires, solvent for paint, and the like) from survey data.

In the example just cited, a *census* was taken of all known present and potential users of a group of industrial products. In this case, a census was used instead of a sample because the total population of users was reasonably small and the purposes of the survey included generating sales leads as well as developing estimates of potentials. If the population of users is large, however, a census may be too costly. In that case a sample may be warranted.

The sample results will, of course, have to be inflated to obtain overall estimates of potential. The usual method of projecting sampling totals to population totals requires that information on both S.I.C. industry and number of employees, as well as the anticipated amount of the product to be purchased, be obtained from each of the firms in the sample. An estimate of expected usage per employee per S.I.C. industry represented in the sample can then be developed. These estimates can be projected to S.I.C. industry totals by geographic area by multiplying by the number of employees in that industry in that area (obtained from the latest *Census of Manufacturers* or the current *Annual Survey of Manufacturers,* whichever is appropriate). Summing the using industry totals by an area then gives the estimate of overall market potential for that area.

---

[60] *1973 Survey of Buying Power* issue of *Sales Management,* **III,** no. 2 (July 23, 1973), CS–11.

A similar procedure is employed to obtain overall estimates of potential for a consumer good from a survey of a sample of consumers. Data on the usage of the product and on the income of the responding family can be obtained in the survey. Estimates of average usage amounts by income level can then be developed. Since family income data are available at the county (and SMSA) level, estimates of potential by income level can be obtained by county by multiplying the average usage per family for each income level by the number of families in that income level in each county. The overall potential for each county is then found by summing the potentials across income levels.

Estimation of Market Share

Market share, the proportion of total industry sales made by one of the firms in the industry, may be computed on either a unit or a dollar basis. That is

$$\text{market share} = \frac{\text{company sales in units}}{\text{industry sales in units}}$$

or, alternatively,

$$\text{market share} = \frac{\text{company sales in dollars}}{\text{industry sales in dollars}}$$

The share in dollars reflects the effect of price differences as well as units sold.

The estimation of market share by either formula requires determining the appropriate industry figure for the time period involved as well as the sales of the company. Although it might be assumed that company sales are known, this is true in only an approximate sense if middlemen are used and the share of sales to the consumer is the market share of interest.

Market share data are used primarily for evaluation of performance. An absolute increase (or decrease) in sales is meaningful only in terms of industry experience; if company sales increased 5 per cent and industry sales were up 10 per cent, performance for the period involved was not up to par. Changes in share measured at the consumer level during periods of special promotions by either the company or its competitors are also used for evaluative purposes.

Sales Analysis

The usual sales invoice has a sizable amount of information on it, which generally includes *name of customer, location of customer, items ordered, quantities ordered, quantities shipped, dollar extensions, back orders, discounts allowed, date of shipment, and method of shipment.* In addition, the invoice often contains information on sales territory, salesmen, and warehouse of shipment.

This information, when supplemented by data on costs and industry and product classification, as well as from sales calls, provides the basis for a comprehensive analysis of sales by product, customer, industry, geographic area, sales territory, and salesman as well as the profitability of each sales category.

Analysis of sales is a necessary part of performance research. If sales targets are to be set for territories and quotas established for salesmen, measurement of actual sales must be made to determine how well these standards were met. But the use of sales analysis extends far beyond the routine compilation and comparison of figures. It can identify serious problems in the marketing program that are not recognizable by other means. As has been observed:

In most enterprises a small proportion of the territories, customers, orders or products are responsible for the overwhelming bulk of the profits. By the same token, a very large proportion of the money spent on marketing effort is wasted. One manufacturer, for example, found that 78 per cent of his customers yielded only slightly more than 2 per cent of his volume. In another concern, 48 per cent of the number of orders produced only 5 per cent of sales. In yet another firm, 46 per cent of the number of products manufactured accounted for only 3 per cent of income. And in a fourth business, 59 per cent of the salesmen's calls were made on customers from whom only 12 per cent of the sales were obtained.[61]

Evaluating Sales Effects of Changes in Marketing Variables

The principal responsibility of the marketing manager is the making and implementing of decisions dealing with the products, prices, promotion, and distribution channels of the firm. To make intelligent decisions he

[61] C. H. Sevin, "Analyzing Your Cost of Marketing," *Management Aids for Small Manufacturers,* Annual no. 5 (1959), 39–40.

must have information dealing with the sales effects of potential changes in these variables. Questions such as "Should we increase our advertising budget next year and, if so, by how much?", "Should we meet the price cut that our major competitor just announced?", and "The Cincinnati territory manager has just asked for four more salesmen. Should we give them to him?" are continually being asked. The answers to these questions require an evaluation of the effect on sales of the change in the variable in question.

Six general methods can be used for estimating the effect on sales of changes in marketing mix variables. These are (1) *judgment based on experience*, (2) *statistical analysis of past sales data*, (3) *surveys*, (4) *laboratory experiments*, (5) *simulation*, and (6) *market tests*. Each of these methods has been discussed in previous chapters. For purposes of review, however, a brief description, a listing of typical applications, a statement of data and time required, an assessment of accuracies, and reference to the chapter in which each method is discussed is given in Table 15–10.

Surveillance of Competitors

Finally, every marketing manager needs current information on his competitors as a part of the analysis of demand for his own products. The story of Macy's shopping Gimbels, and Gimbels shopping Macy's is an old one but it illustrates the need for the continuing collection of competitor price information. Automobile manufacturers buy and test each other's products at the beginning of each model year. Detergent manufacturers run chemical tests on competitive detergents at regular intervals to see if there is a formula change even when none has been advertised. Advertising agencies maintain a continuing surveillance of the level and content of advertising of their clients' competitors. When changes in the marketing mix of competitors are found, their effects can be assessed and appropriate retaliatory actions can then be taken.

Summary

This chapter has been concerned with the various elements of demand analysis: market segmentation; estimation of market potential; determination of market share; sales analysis; measurement of effects of changes in the price, promotion, product, and distribution variables; and surveillance of competitors.

Table 15–10 Basic Methods of Evaluating Sales Effects of Changes in Marketing Variables (product, price, distribution, advertising, personal selling, and sales support effort)

	Judgmental	Statistical Analysis of Sales Data	Surveys	Laboratory Experiment	Simulation	Market Test
Description	Judgmental evaluations based on experience.	An analysis of past sales data using econometric techniques (primarily multiple regression analysis).	A survey of customers to determine exposure and reaction to past changes, reaction to proposed changes.	An experiment to determine effect of proposed changes in marketing variables that is conducted in simulated actual purchase conditions in a laboratory.	An "experiment" conducted by changing the level of the variables in a mathematical model used to simulate the actual situation.	A field experiment conducted by actually making the proposed change in a selected number of test areas.
Typical applications	Decisions on levels of line item marketing budgets.	Determination of sales effects of price changes, advertising budget changes, and number of sales calls.	Determination of sales effects of changes in price, advertising, personal selling, and sales support effort.	Determining reaction to product changes, determining simulated purchase levels at varying prices, finding attitude and opinion changes with differing advertising messages.	Pricing in competitive bidding situations, allocating advertising among media, determining advertising budget, routing salesmen and optimum number of sales calls by customer location of warehouses, determination of inventory levels.	New products, changes in existing products, advertising level, numbers of sales calls, promotions, and sales support effort (catalogs, handbooks, engineering support for customers).

Data required	Accounting reports, salesmen reports and information from informal sources generated as a part of the standard operations of the company.	Same as for judgmental evaluations with some adjusting of the data required. The greater the differences in level of the variables by region and over time the better the analysis will be.	That developed through the survey (a sample or census) of customers.	The data developed in the experiment.	The data required to determine the variables and their parameters for the model appropriate.	Sales results in the test versus the control market areas.
Assessment of Accuracy	Poor to excellent.	Fair to excellent for advertising and personal selling changes. Fair to good for price changes.	Fair to good for product changes. Fair for advertising, personal selling and sales support changes. Poor for price changes.	Fair to good for product changes. Fair for advertising changes. Poor for price changes.	Good to excellent for decisions involving distribution of product and routing of salesmen. Good for competitive bid pricing. Fair to good for advertising decisions.	Good to excellent for all uses except price changes. Fair to excellent for price changes (depending upon competitor reaction).
Time required	Varies by executive.	1–3 months initially. 1–3 days thereafter.	1–3 months	1–2 months	2–3 months for developing each model and running the simulation.	3 months–1½ years.
Chapter(s) in which discussed	—	Chapter 14, pp. 536–537 Chapter 15, pp. 577–578	Chapter 11, pp. 372–404 Chapter 13, pp. 477–503	Chapter 12, pp. 453–456	Chapter 12, pp. 461–462	Chapter 12, pp. 456–461

1. *Market segmentation* should be practiced whenever there are differing segments that can be identified, are accessible to differing marketing actions, and are substantial enough to make such differential treatment profitable.

2. A sizable number of variables are potentially useful for segmentation purposes. These include *geographic, demographic, socioeconomic, psychological,* and *product related* characteristics. A summary description of each of these variables was given in Tables 15–1, 15–4, 15–5, and 15–7. None of these variables has proven to be universally useful for segmentation but each has been shown to be of value for segmenting the market for some products. The trick in segmentation research is to find the variables that are useful in the product being studied.

3. *Market potential* is the potential sales for the product class under conditions of optimum market development. Estimates of market potential are used for such purposes as defining sales territories, allocating marketing budgets, setting sales targets, and evaluating performance. Of the several different ways of making market potential estimates, the four major ones are (1) *adjusted industry sales,* (2) *purchase proportions,* (3) *correlative indexes,* and (4) *surveys of users.*

4. *Market share* is the proportion of total industry sales made by one of the firms in the industry. It involves the determination of industry sales and, in those cases in which share is being measured at the consumer level and sales are made through middlemen, of sales of the firm as well. Market share estimates are used primarily for performance evaluation. For example, if total sales increased but market share decreased, action may be necessary.

5. *Sales analysis* is conducted using the basic document of the sales transaction, the invoice. When supplemented with information on costs, it can provide data on profitability by customer, industry, amount of sales, frequency of sales calls, sales territories, and salesman.

6. The *measurement of effects of changes in the marketing variables* of product, price, promotion, and methods of distribution were covered in earlier chapters but were reviewed in this chapter. Six methods of making such measurements are available: (1) judgmental, (2) statistical analysis of sales data, (3) surveys, (4) laboratory experiment, (5) simulation, and (6) market test. A summary description of each method is given in Table 15–10.

Finally, the need for *surveillance of competitors* was considered as a part of demand analysis. The marketing manager must know what actions his counterparts in competitive companies are taking in order to make sound decisions concerning his own company.

Questions and Problems

15.1. What are the characteristics that a potential segment of the market must have in order for it to be viable from a marketing management standpoint?

15.2. What segmentation bases would you investigate if you were doing a study on market segments of (a) vacation trailers, (b) wine, (c) bicycles, (d) furniture?

15.3 Suppose you are responsible for mail order sales for Sears, Roebuck & Co.
(a) How might Zip Codes be of use to you?
(b) What information would you want kept by Zip Code area?
(c) How would you want it analyzed?

Carstairs Furniture Company
190 E. Calmus Street
Grand Rapids, Michigan

Sold to
(Name) _____   Date Sold: _____
(Address) _____   Date Shipped: _____
_____   Shipped: _____

Shipment No. _____

Items Shipped:	Number	Unit Price	Extension

Salesman: _____   Total _____

Shipping Clerk: _____   Less allowances _____

Payment Received: ____   Net amount owed _____

15.4. Describe how you would construct an index of market potential for (a) automobile tires, (b) outboard motors, (c) enchilada sauce, (d) women's double knit suits?

Be specific about (a) the form of the index, (b) the source(s) of the data, and (c) the techniques of data analysis you would use in constructing the index.

15.5 Describe how you would construct an index of market potential by country for a furniture manufacturer whose market area includes the states of Michigan, Ohio, Indiana, Illinois, and Wisconsin. Be specific about (a) the form of the index (b) the source(s) of data, and (c) the techniques of data analysis you would use.

15.6. Estimate the market potential in the United States for an undergraduate textbook in *Money and Banking*.

15.7. Suppose you are the marketing manager for the Carstairs Furniture Company, a manufacturer of dining room furniture. A current sales invoice form of the company is reproduced on page 591.

(a) What additional information, if any, would you want recorded on the invoice if it were to be revised?

(b) What analyses would you want conducted using the data on the revised invoice?

(c) How would you use each analysis?

Selected Bibliography

CARMAN, JAMES M. *The Application of Social Class in Market Segmentation,* I.B.E.R. Special Publications. Berkeley, Calif.: *University of California,* 1965. A carefully researched and well-written monograph on social class as a segmenting variable.

FRANK, RONALD E., WILLIAM F. MASSY, and YORAM WIND. *Market Segmentation.* Englewood Cliffs, N.J.: Prentice-Hall, Inc., 1972. The major book that has been written on market segmentation. Contains both a review of the literature (through 1970) and a description of the use of multivariate techniques in segmentation research.

HUGHES, G. DAVID. *Demand Analysis for Marketing Decisions.* Homewood, Ill.: Richard D. Irwin, Inc., 1973. Models and empirical studies with economic, sociological, and psychological orientations are emphasized. An especially good chapter deals with demographics and population projection and their use in market planning.

JOHNSON, RICHARD M. "Market Segmentation, A Strategic Management Tool." *Journal of Marketing Research* (February 1971). This article is primarily concerned with product-space configuration as a means of segmenting markets. It is a comprehensive article and serves as a good means of reviewing the early developments with respect to this promising segmentation technique.

KASSARJIAN, HAROLD H. "Personality and Consumer Behavior: A Review," *Journal of Marketing Research,* **8** (November 1971). A definitive review article on personality theory and empirical findings relating personality and the behavior of consumers.

Case 15–1

Tipton's Shoe Stores: Core Market, Trade Area, and Image Study*

Tipton's Shoe Stores are two large shoe stores in a medium-sized city. One store is located in the downtown area, and another is located in the city's major shopping center. The management of Tipton's is in the process of evaluating the results of a recently completed research study. The research was conducted at the management's request to assist it in three basic tasks: (1) determining the sociodemographic characteristics of its basic core market; (2) determining the image that customers have of Tipton's; and (3) determining the trade area from which it currently draws customers.

Research Procedure and Results

The first step in the research procedure was the administration of subjective interviews to a limited number of shoe purchasers. Since the purpose of this procedure was to provide insights into what type of people shop at different shoe stores and why they do so, a nonrandom sampling procedure was used. Ten people who had just purchased shoes from Tipton's downtown store and ten people from the shopping center store were interviewed. In addition, five purchasers from each of four competitive outlets were interviewed. The subjects were interviewed as they left the retail outlet with their purchases. Four basic areas were covered in each interview: (1) demographic data (occupation, number of children); (2) general shopping habits (what area of town and what type of store they preferred); (3) shoe purchasing patterns (important attributes, who initiates the purchase); and (4) media exposure (what are the preferred media, preferred television programs). The results of the subjective interviews are summarized in Table A. As can be seen, only a few clear-cut distinctions between Tipton's customers and their competitors appeared.

In addition to the subjective portion of the interviews, each respondent was handed a form and asked to rate each of six attributes on a six-point scale ranging from "Very Important" to "Not Important" according to the role that that attribute played in the selection of a specific shoe or shoe

* Originally prepared by D. I. Hawkins and C. M. Lillis. Used with permission of the authors.

Table A Results of the Subjective Interviews

	Tipton's (SC)	Tipton's (DT)	Store A[1] (DT)	Store B[2] (DT)	Store C[3] (SC)	Store D[4] (SC)
Prefers shopping at SC	8 of 10	3 of 10	3 of 5	3 of 5	4 of 5	5 of 5
Prefers shopping at DT	1 of 10	4 of 10	2 of 5	1 of 5	1 of 5	None
Prefers small specialty shoe stores	10 of 10	10 of 10	1 of 5	3 of 5	5 of 5	4 of 5
Prefers buying shoes at large department stores	None	None	4 of 5	1 of 5	None	None
Looks at related shoe accessories	1 of 10	6 of 10	3 of 5	None	4 of 5	2 of 5
Service plays a role in preference	10 of 10	8 of 10	5 of 5	5 of 5	5 of 5	4 of 5
Location is not important in shoe store preference	10 of 10	6 of 10	2 of 5	3 of 5	5 of 5	None
Believes price relates to quality	5 of 10	8 of 10	4 of 5	5 of 5	5 of 5	5 of 5
Rather pay cash for shoes	9 of 10	9 of 10	4 of 5	4 of 5	5 of 5	2 of 5
Was not aware of any shoe advertising done by the store	1 of 10	10 of 10	4 of 5	2 of 5	5 of 5	5 of 5
Husband is the initiator of the purchase	1 of 10	None	4 of 5	None	2 of 5	None

[1] "Medium-priced" chain department store
[2] "Expensive" local women's clothing store
[3] Discount chain shoe store
[4] "Expensive" regional department store

Table B Shoe Store Selection Determinants*

Name of Store Shopped at	Location	Service	Quality of the Product	Variety	Pleasantness of the Store	Prices Charged	Number of Respondents
Tipton's (SC)	4.8	3.3	1.2	2.8	4.2	4.7	10
Tipton's (DT)	4.9	2.9	1.5	3.4	5.6	2.7	10
Store A[1] (DT)	3.2	3.8	2.6	4.2	5.6	1.6	5
Store B[2] (DT)	1.4	5.0	5.0	3.4	3.2	3.0	5
Store C[3] (SC)	5.8	2.2	3.4	3.6	4.2	1.8	5
Store D[4] (SC)	3.8	4.0	2.4	2.6	5.8	2.4	5
Overall	4.2	3.4	2.4	3.3	4.8	3.0	40

[1] Medium-priced chain department store
[2] Expensive local women's clothing store
[3] Discount chain shoe store
[4] Expensive regional department store
* The lower the score, the more important the attribute is to the consumer

Table C Shoe Store Selection Determinants*

Name of Store Shopped at	Quality of Construction	Comfort	Fit	Support	Style	Price of the Shoe	Number of Respondents
Tipton's (SC)	2.5	2.7	1.9	4.0	4.6	5.3	10
Tipton's (DT)	3.0	4.9	3.1	3.7	3.5	2.6	10
Store A[1] (DT)	4.4	3.0	2.8	4.0	4.4	2.4	5
Store B[2] (DT)	5.0	2.6	2.6	4.4	3.2	3.0	5
Store C[3] (SC)	3.4	2.4	4.4	4.8	4.4	1.8	5
Store D[4] (SC)	4.0	3.0	1.4	5.8	2.4	4.4	5
Overall	3.5	3.3	3.6	4.3	3.4	3.4	40

* The lower the score, the more important the attribute is to the consumer
[1] Medium-priced chain department store
[2] Expensive local women's clothing store
[3] Discount chain shoe store
[4] Expensive regional department store

store. The results of these ratings are presented in Tables B and C. The scores presented in the tables represent the average ratings with a lower score indicating greater importance.

Following completion of the subjective interviews, a telephone questionnaire was developed and administered to a sample of approximately 500 respondents. The respondents were selected randomly from the telephone directory that was four months old at the time the sample was drawn. The major analytical technique was to cross-tabulate the responses given by Tipton's customers and noncustomers. The results of this procedure are presented in Table D.

Table D Cross-Tabulation Analysis

	Non-Tipton's Customers n = 305	Tipton's Customers n = 188
1. *Sex*		
Female	64%	65%
Male	36	35
2. *Do you find it convenient to shop for shoes?*		
Inconvenient	42	42
Convenient	58	58
3. *Number of drivers in household*		
None	2	1
1	21	23
2	52	49
3	15	17
4	10	10
4. *Number of cars in household*		
None	0	0
1	5	3
2	36	42
3	42	42
4	14	11
5	3	2
5. *Where would a construction or mill worker buy:*		
Dress shoes?		
Would buy at Tipton's	10	20
Would buy elsewhere or no response	90	80
Casual shoes?		
Would buy at Tipton's	5	7
Would buy elsewhere or no response	95	93
6. *Where would a bank teller or draftsman buy:*		
Dress shoes?		
Would buy at Tipton's	39	59
Would buy elsewhere or no response	61	41

Table D *(continued)*

	Non-Tipton's Customers n = 305	*Tipton's Customers n = 188*
Casual shoes?		
Would buy at Tipton's	39%	50%
Would buy elsewhere or no response	61	50
7. *Where would a doctor or lawyer buy:*		
Dress shoes?		
Would buy at Tipton's	50	65
Would buy elsewhere or no response	50	35
Casual shoes?		
Would buy at Tipton's	47	66
Would buy elsewhere or no response	53	34
8. *Newspaper reading*		
Never	11	6
1–4 times/week	17	16
Daily	72	78
9. *What was the last shoe advertisement you remember seeing in the newspaper?*		
Total recalling a specific ad	42	44
Total recalling none	58	56
Total recalling a Tipton's ad	17	26
10. *Do you own a television set?*		
Yes	95	96
No	5	4
11. *Hours spent watching TV per day*		
0–2	50	50
2–6	44	46
6+	6	4
12. *Shoe purchases/year*		
Respondent		
1–2	65	49
3–5	29	42
6+	6	9
Spouse		
1–2	75	71
3–5	22	19
6+	3	10
13. *Do you usually shop for shoes and clothes on the same trip?*		
Yes	32	36
No	68	64
14. *Do you charge shoes?*		
Rarely	90	90
Sometimes	3	2
Frequently	7	8
15. *How long as an area resident?*		
0–2 years	21	24
2–6 years	21	27
7 + years	58	49

Table E Family Life-Style Matrix (Per Cent of Each Cell Classified As Tipton's Customers)

	Student	Blue-Collar	White-Collar	Managerial-Professional	Retired
Old Married No Children Home	0%	29%	65%	14%	36%
Old Married with Children	0	0	18	50	0
Young Married with Children	46	41	59	38	0
Young Married	30	46	58	0	0
Young Single	45	40	61	0	0

Table F Family Life-Style Matrix (Number of Adults and Families in the Area)

	Student	Blue-Collar	White-Collar	Managerial-Professional	Retired
Old Married No Children Home	0	7.5	3.7	1.5	5.5[a]
		4,964	2,449	993	3,640[b]
		8,156	4,024	1,631	5,981[c]
		2,670	1,317	534	1,958[d]
		4,293	2,118	858	3,148[e]
Old Married with Children	0	1.3	2.4	1.3	.2[a]
		860	1,588	860	1,132[b]
		1,413	2,610	1,413	217[c]
		463	854	463	71[d]
		744	1,374	744	114[e]
Young Married with Children	2.8	15.1	10.1	4.6	0[a]
	1,853	9,994	6,684	3,044	0[b]
	3,045	16,421	10,983	5,002	0[c]
	997	5,375	3,595	1,637	0[d]
	1,603	8,644	5,781	2,633	0[e]
Young Married	2.2	5.3	7.2	0	0[a]
	1,456	3,058	4,765	0	0[b]
	2,392	5,764	7,830	0	0[c]
	783	1,886	2,563	0	0[d]
	1,259	3,034	4,122	0	0[e]
Young Single	20.6	3.3	5.0	.2	0[a]
	13,634	2,184	3,309	132	0[b]
	N.A.	3,589	5,437	217	0[c]
	7,332	1,175	1,780	71	0[d]
	N.A.	1,889	2,862	114	0[e]

[a] % Sample Population, [b] No. Adults—City, [c] No. Adults—10-Mile Area, [d] No. Families—City, [e] No. Families—10-Mile Area.

In order to define Tipton's core market, the telephone survey gathered information that would allow each respondent to be placed in a "Family Life Style Matrix." This matrix is a cross-classification scheme that utilizes occupational categories along one axis and stage in the family life cycle on the other. Table E shows the percentage of respondents in each cell who purchased their last pair of shoes at Tipton's. Table F provides the percentage of the telephone sample that fell in each cell. This percentage was then applied to population statistics to provide estimates of the total number of adults and families per cell in the city and within a ten-mile radius of the city. These estimates are also shown in Table F.

In order to determine the market area from which Tipton's customers come, the sales personnel were to request the Zip Code of each customer who made a purchase during a one-week period. However, because of resistance on the part of the sales personnel to ask for this information and reluctance or inability on the part of many customers to supply it, Zip Codes were obtained from only a small percentage of the purchasers. The information on Zip Codes that was obtained was not used.

1. Evaluate the overall research procedure.

2. How would you define Tipton's "core" market? What additional information, if any, would you like to have?

Case 15–2
Packer's Tar Soap: Special Deal Decision

Packer's Tar Soap was one of the first soaps to be promoted exclusively as a shampoo. It was a bar of good quality soap with a generous amount of pine tar added. It was advertised heavily in the magazines of the day and, by 1920, was one of the best known and most widely used shampoos on the market.

By the early 1930s, however, sales of Packer's Tar Soap had fallen substantially. Several liquid shampoos were introduced by competitors during the 1920s and became popular. Packer's had been forced to introduce a liquid shampoo of its own and to divert part of its advertising budget to it. Both the reduced level of advertising and the increased amount of competition had cut tar soap sales considerably. The Depression that had begun in 1929 had resulted in consumers' sharply reducing expenditures for such nonessential items as shampoos and sales had declined further.

In November of 1934, Edward A. Olds, the president of Packer's, had a meeting in his New York offices with members of the Blackman Company, the advertising agency for Packer's. He stated that the company had thus far held the wholesale price of the tar soap to $1.20 per dozen but was beginning to get some serious pressures to reduce it. Sales were down to 93,000 cakes per month, the lowest they had been in more than 30 years. Production costs had fallen somewhat but the average cost per bar was still about $.05. After allowing for advertising costs and overhead, it appeared that the company would be fortunate to break even on the tar soap in 1934. Unless some positive actions were taken, it looked as if sales would decline even more in 1935 and Packer's would incur a loss on the tar soap.

Tom Markham, the Packer's account executive at Blackman, suggested that Packer's consider a "deal" for the tar soap to try and get new retail customers and forestall any general price cut. He said that he would prepare a report and come to the Packer's plant to present it to the Packer's management in about two weeks.

The report prepared by Markham is given as follows.

Market Calculation for Packer's Manufacturing Company

The Blackman Company   November 21, 1934

Client:	Packer's Manufacturing Company
Product:	Packer's Tar Soap
Subject:	Estimate of the market for a special deal on Packer's Tar Soap
Description of Deal:	Deal consists of one dozen cakes of Packer's Tar Soap, each cake having an attached free sample cake.
	The deals are to be sold to the trade at the regular price of ten cakes. The deal, as described, is equivalent to an additional discount of 16⅔ per cent without taking into account the free sample cakes.
	Each deal will be packed in a special display carton.
Objectives:	Since the deal is aimed at securing new customers, our objective is to obtain as wide a retail distribution of the deal as possible, but without loading the wholesale and retail trade too heavily at a special low price.
	In the retail store the deal will probably be most effective during the first two or three months. Therefore, we feel we should not supply retailers with more than a six months' normal supply of Packer's Tar Soap—for even if the special display trebled the usual movement of Packer's, the six months' normal supply would still last the store two months.
Calculation:	

Based on Nielsen reports for August and September, 1934, Packer's Tar Soap business divides approximately as follows:

Drugstores	90%
Department Stores	10%
	100%

From sales figures, Packer's Tar Soap volume is 93,000 dozen cakes per year, or 93,000 cakes per month.

Drugstores

Sales through drugstores equal 90 per cent of total—or 83,700 cakes per month.

There are 58,000 drugstores in the United States.

The average sale of Packer's Tar Soap per drugstore = 83,700 ÷ 58,000 = 1.44 cakes per month.

Obviously some drugstores do more business than others. The following breakdown is from the U.S. Census of Distribution:

Class of Stores	Number of Stores	Sales per Store	Normal Movement Packer's Tar Soap Cakes per Month
A	7,000	325% of average store	4.7
B	12,000	126% of average store	1.8
C	39,000	52% of average store	.75

Department Stores

There are approximately 4,200 department stores (U.S. Census of Distribution).

Nielsen estimates that about 60 per cent of department stores have drug departments.

60 per cent of 4,200 equals approximately 2,500 department stores with drug departments.

Department stores sell 10 per cent of Packer's Tar Soap volume, or 9,300 cakes per month.

9,300 + 2,500 = 3.7 cakes per month per store.

*   *   *

Deals That Probably Could Be Moved to Retail Stores Under Ideal Conditions

	Class of Store	Normal Movement Packer's Tar Soap	Time One Deal Would Last	Number of Deals to Last Six Months	Number of Stores	Number of Deals
Drugstore	"A"	4.7	2.55 months	2.36	7,000	16,500
	"B"	1.8	6.66 "	.91	12,000	11,000
	"C"	.75	16 "	Recommend no Deals		
Department Stores		3.7	3.22 "	1.86	2,500	4,600
					Total Deals	32,100

1) analyze case w/ respect with what they did.
2) If we were going to do this
what changes would we make

602   Marketing Research

* * *

These figures are based on 100 per cent distribution in worthwhile outlets. Obviously, operating through jobbers over whom we have no control, we cannot hope to attain 100 per cent distribution in worthwhole outlets. The following table shows the number of deals required for 55 per cent, 60 per cent, and 65 per cent distribution:

> 55%—17,600 deals
> 60%—19,300 deals
> 65%—20,900 deals

1. What other information might Olds have wanted before making a decision about the proposed deal? How might it have been obtained?

2. Based on the information available, what decision should Olds have made?

Look at Ch 17

✗ Case 15–3

Marson's Marine Hardware

Carl Marson had operated a marine hardware store at Newport Beach for 28 years. The business had grown each year with the increase in the number of boats using Newport Bay. The growth had been especially rapid during the 1960s and early 1970s.

In 1974 a new marina was opened just south of Los Angeles. It was named the Marina De La Bahia, and had an initial capacity of 2,000 slips for mooring boats. This capacity was to be increased to 6,000 slips by 1978. Four marine hardware stores had already opened there the first ten months of 1974.

Marson was interested in the possibility of adding a branch there but was not sure that the market potential was yet high enough to warrant adding a fifth store. He decided to hire a consultant to provide him with estimates of the present and future market potentials. He also wanted to get advice regarding potential sites and operating costs for a store and to obtain estimates of sales for the first few years if a branch were opened there.

Frank Cordiner, the owner of a small local consulting firm, came to the store in Newport and the men discussed the project Marson had in mind. An agreement was reached that Cordiner would conduct a study to obtain answers to the following questions:

1. Is there sufficient present and future market potential in the Marina De La Bahia area to support an additional marine hardware store?

2. What are the operating costs for a retail store in the area?

3. What is the extent of the present competition in the area?

4. What are the generally desirable site locations for a marine hardware store in the area?

5. What are forecasts of sales for each of the next three and one-half years for a marine hardware store opened on the best available site in July of this year?

It was then November 27 and Cordiner wasted no time. The most difficult problem in the study as he saw it was to obtain reliable estimates of the market potential for marine hardware in the area. He began to collect data to help him make estimates by arranging to talk to the harbor master of the bay in which the Marina was located. There he learned that 1,965 boats were presently moored in slips at the Marina and that the projection was that this number would increase to 5,500 by the end of 1978. Cordiner obtained estimates of the average number of boats that would be moored at the marina each year through that time. He learned that two boat ramps were currently operating at the marina for the launching of transient boats. The ramps had a combined capacity of 250 launchings per day and, during the first 11 months of 1974, 9,410 launchings had been made. A new 10-lane ramp with a capacity of launching 500 boats per day was to be opened in May, 1976.

Obtaining information on average expenditures for marine hardware by boat owners proved to be more of a problem. After a fruitless search of the secondary data sources, Cordiner reluctantly concluded that the only way he could obtain estimates of such expenditures was to conduct a survey. He prepared questionnaires and made arrangements with interviewers to do a telephone survey of the owners of boats permanently moored at the marina and to conduct personal interviews of the owners of transient boats launched there.

Cordiner decided to take samples of 100 of the boat owners in each of the groups. He was able to get access to a list of all owners of permanently moored boats prepared by the harbor master's office. He took a simple random sample of 100 owners by recording the first 100 nonduplicated numbers between 0000 and 1,965 from a table of random numbers and matching them with names on the list. He recorded name, address, telephone numbers, and type and size of boat from the list.

There was no listing of transient boat owners. Cordiner decided that the only feasible way to get a sample of these owners was to select it at the launch sites in the Marina. He stationed interviewers at each of the two launch sites and instructed them to interview the driver of every vehicle launching a boat until they had each obtained 50 interviews. Two weekends were required to complete these interviews.

When the tabulated results of the interviews were completed, Cordiner began the estimates of market potential for marine hardware at the marina. The first draft of the section of the report he was preparing for Marson dealing with the potential estimates is reproduced below.

1. Evaluate the procedures Cordiner used to estimate market potential.

2. What changes, if any, need to be made in the estimated potentials before the report is submitted?

Market Potential Projections

What is the Market Potential for Marine Hardware Supplies in the Marina De La Bahia Area? (Based on data collected and calculation presented in the supporting exhibits as noted in this section.)

Step 1	Average expenditure by boat owners whose boats are permanently moored in the marina for a 6-month period (Exhibit A)	$ 173.50	$ 173.50	$ 173.50	$ 173.50
Step 2	Multiply by estimated average population of permanently moored boats for each of the next 3½ years (Exhibit B)	2,650.	3,350.	4,250.	5,100.
	Market potential for permanently moored boats for 6 months	$459,775	$ 581,225.	$ 737,375.	$ 884,850.
Step 3	Multiply years 1976–1978 by two (2) to obtain market potential for the year for the same permanently moored population		× 2 $1,162,450	× 2 $1,474,750	× 2 $1,769,700
Step 4	Average expenditure by transient boat owners for a 6-month period (Exhibit A)	78.00	78.00	78.00	78.00
Step 5	Multiply by estimated transient boat population for each year for the next 3½ years (Exhibit C)	1,000	1,800	1,900	2,000
	Market potential transient boat owners for 6 months	78,000	140,400	148,200	156,000
Step 6	Multiply years 1976–1978 by two (2) to obtain market potential for the year for the transient boat owners	78,000	× 2 280,800	× 2 296,400	× 2 312,000

Data

Step 7   Add totals obtained from Step 3 to totals obtained in Step 6

| + 459,775 | + 1,162,450 | + 1,474,750 | + 1,769,700 |

Sum represents total market potential for boating supplies and Marina De La Bahia

| $537,775 | $1,443,250 | $1,771,150 | $2,081,700 |

Exhibit A   Calculation to Obtain Average Expenditures for Six-Month Period July 1–Dec. 31, 1974 for Two Groups of Boat Owners Interviewed

The following table uses the information obtained from a cross-tabulation of the questions in the questionnaire:

1. Is your boat an outboard, inboard, or sailboat?
2. What size is it?
3. About how much have you spent on boating supplies in the last six months?

	Owners of Permanently Moored Boats			Owners of Transient Boats
	Mean Expenditure per Class	Sample Weight	Total	Total*
Inboard (less than 20 feet)	$ 87.25	.03 × 100	261.75	$ 754.50
Inboard (equal to or greater than 20 feet)	207.90	.40 × 100	8,316.00	104.50
Outboard (all sizes)	306.50	.02 × 100	613.00	5,027.00
Sailboat (less than 24 feet)	90.30	.25 × 100	2,257.50	1,817.50
Sailboat (equal to or greater than 24 feet)	196.71	.30 × 100	5,901.30	58.00
			$17,349.55	$7,761.50

$\frac{17,344.55}{100(=n)}$ 173.50 = average expenditure for permanently moored boats

how do we know?

$\frac{$7,761.50}{100(=n)}$ = $77.62, or $78.00 = average expenditure for transient boats

* Self-weighting so average expenditures per class not calculated.

Exhibit B Information on Present and Projected Boat Population at Marina De La Bahia

Telephone Interview of Stan Shull, Harbor Master
    December 3, 1974
Shull supplied the following information:
1. The boat population at Marina De La Bahia during 1974 was as follows:

January	1,391
February	1,427
March	1,449
April	1,533
May	1,592
June	1,671
July	1,841
August	1,927
September	1,950
October	1,977
November	1,975
December	1,965

Mean boat population
for 1974 was 1,725

(as of December 1)

2. Current boat slip capacity is 2,000 boats.
3. The numbers of boat by type and size that are now moored at the marina are as follows:

	Number	Proportion
Inboards (less than 20 feet)	59	.03
Inboards (equal to or larger than 20 feet)	789	.40
Outboards (all sizes)	39	.02
Sailboats (less than 24 feet)	488	.25
Sailboats (equal to or larger than 24 feet)	590	.30
Total	1965	1.00

4. Boat slip capacity will reach 6,000 by the end of 1978. Shull believes this will be a steady growth; he does not anticipate any major delays in building and he expects capacity to develop fairly evenly over time.
5. Shull does not expect that the marina will have a boat population of more than 5,500 by the end of 1978. He believes that it has already drawn most of the present boat owners from San Pedro, Long Beach, and Newport that it is likely to draw. He expects the bulk of the boats coming into the marina over the next 3–4 years to be new ones.
6. Estimates by the harbormaster's office of the average number of boats that will be moored each year for the next 3½ years are as follows:

1975	2,650	(July 1–December 31)
1976	3,350	
1977	4,250	
1978	5,100	

7. Currently 2 launching ramps are located in the marina and one is located at a public beach nearby. The two ramps in the marina have a combined capacity of 250 launches per day. The ramp at the public beach has a capacity of 100 launches per day. A 10-lane boat ramp to be completed in the marina in May, 1976 will have a capacity of launching 500 boats per day.

Exhibit C   Estimation of Number of Transient Boats Launched at or near
Marina De La Bahia

1. The transient boat owners were asked the questions
    #6 About how many times did you launch your boat from Marina De La
        Bahia each month last summer—from May through September?
    #8 About how many times have you launched your boat from Marina De La
        Bahia each month so far this winter—from October until now?
    The tabulated totals for the 100 boat owners were
        Summer months—202 total launches/month
        Winter months—121 total launches/month
    Estimated total summer launches $= 202 \times 4 =$ 808
    Estimated total winter launches $= 121 \times 8 =$ 969
    Estimated total launches for year for
        sample of 100 transient boat owners $= \overline{1,776}$
2. According to the harbor master's office, there were 9,410 total launches at transient boat sites within the first 11 months of 1974.
3. $\dfrac{100 \text{ (sample)}}{1,776 \text{ (estimated total launches)}} \qquad \dfrac{X \text{ (unknown total transient population)}}{9,410 \text{ (total)}}$
        $X = 529 =$ approximate transient boat population for first 11
                        months of 1974
4. Since the sample of 100 boat owners did not include any owners using the public launching area adjacent to the marina, and the estimate is for only the first 11 months of the year, the estimate of 529 transient boat owners has been adjusted upward to 750 for the year ending December 31, 1974.
    Estimates of the number of transient boats that will be launched for each of the next $3\frac{1}{2}$ years are as follows
        1975   1,000   (July 1–December 31)
        1976   1,800
        1977   1,900
        1978   2,000

CHAPTER 16

Forecasting

Forecasting is a necessary part of every decision. A purposive choice among alternative actions in a problem situation requires that an outcome for each action be predicted. We can no more avoid forecasting than we can avoid making decisions.

Forecasting sales of both present and potential products, an integral part of most marketing decisions, is usually the responsibility of the marketing research department. A study sponsored by the American Marketing Association in 1973 shows that 43 per cent of the marketing research departments in responding companies do short-term forecasting and 42 per cent do long-term forecasting.[1]

To be useful, a forecast must *provide a specified level of accuracy over a specified future time period*. Both the required level of accuracy and the time period are functions of the decision at hand. The accuracy of the

[1] D. W. Twedt, *1973 Survey of Marketing Research* (Chicago: American Marketing Association, 1973), 41.

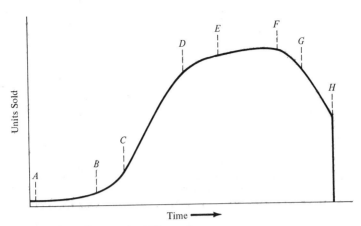

Figure 16–1 The product life cycle.

forecast and the time period of the forecast are *not* independent. In general, short-run forecasts are more accurate than long-run forecasts.

One special aspect of accuracy involves *turning points*. A turning point occurs when there is a relatively abrupt change in the direction or rate of growth of the forecast variable. Consider the standard product life-cycle chart shown in Figure 16–1. Most forecasting techniques will do a reasonably good job of predicting sales between *A–B, C–D, E–F,* and *G–H.* However, the most critical marketing decisions generally involve predicting the turning points shown in the areas *B–C, D–E,* and *F–G.*

In this chapter, we are concerned with several aspects of forecasting. Our first concern is with the various *methods of forecasting* and *their ability to satisfy the requirements of a forecast.* We then consider the *cost versus value of forecasting,* the economics of acquiring forecast information. The *choice of forecasting method(s)* is then examined, followed by the important consideration of the *evaluation of forecasts.*

Methods of Forecasting

Aside from astrology and other forms of the occult, there are three major methods of forecasting: (1) *judgmental* methods, (2) *time series analysis* and *projection,* and (3) *causal methods.* Several specific techniques may be used for each of these general methods.

Judgmental Methods of Forecasting

Some element of judgment is, of course, involved in all methods of forecasting. A method is classified as *judgmental,* however, when the forecasting procedure used cannot be described well enough to allow more than one forecaster to use it and arrive at substantially the same result. Three methods of making judgmental forecasts of sales are (1) *aggregate of individual salesman forecasts,* (2) *expert consensus,* and (3) the *Delphi* method. A brief description of each method, its applications, the data and time required to use it, and an assessment of its accuracy and ability to identify turning points is provided in Table 16–1.

Aggregate of Individual Salesman Forecasts

One of the oldest methods of sales forecasting is to ask each salesman to estimate his sales by product for the forecast period. The overall forecast is then arrived at by summing the individual salesmen forecasts.

This technique is widely used, especially by manufacturers of industrial products. It has the virtues of being relatively accurate over the short term (the next one or two quarters), of being inexpensive to use, and, for industrial products forecasting, of providing a record on a customer-by-customer basis of the sales that the salesman expects to make during the forecast period. These customer forecasts often are used for monitoring and evaluating performance during the forecast period as well as for making the sales forecast itself.

There are problems in using this method, however. One of them is in motivating the salesman to do a conscientious job in forecasting each customer's requirements rather than to look upon the entire procedure as being only more "paperwork" from the home office. Another problem is to adjust the data provided by each salesman for any consistent optimistic or pessimistic biases he may display. In addition to individual biases, at times the entire sales force may tend to over- or underpredict sales. In cases where the salesmen's estimates by customers are to be used for establishing sales quotas, there may be an understandable tendency for them to be intentionally conservative. An opposite bias may be introduced when a product is in short supply; the salesman may believe that his customers will get larger allocations if he forecasts them as having larger requirements than they actually have. Allowance for such biases must be made if they exist. This requires a continuing comparison of each salesman's estimates with the actual sales made for each period.

Although salesmen are usually aware of and sensitive to any changes anticipated in purchase levels by their customers during the next few months, they are often unaware of broad economic movements or trends

Table 16–1 Judgmental Methods of Forecasting

	Aggregate of Individual Salesman Forecasts	"Expert" Consensus	Delphi Method
Description	Salesmen are asked to make estimates of sales by product to each customer and potential customer for the forecast period. These are aggregated (after adjustment for any biases observed in past forecasts) to obtain an overall sales forecast by product.	A panel of "experts" (company executives, economists, and/or consultants) make individual forecasts from which a consensus is reached through discussion. Social factors (dominance due to personality, rank, and the like) may play an important role in the weighting of individual forecasts in the consensus reached.	A panel of "experts" respond individually to questionnaires that ask for a forecast and a series of questions about the assumptions that underlie it. The responses are kept anonymous and provided to all forecasters. Successive questionnaires are sent out and responses exchanged until a working consensus is reached.
Accuracy			
Short term (0–6 months)	Good	Poor to fair	Fair to very good
Medium term (6 months to 2 years)	Fair to good	Poor to fair	Fair to very good
Long term (2 years or more)	Poor	Poor	Fair to very good
Identification of turning points	Poor	Poor to fair	Fair to good
Typical applications	Next-quarter and annual sales forecast by product.	Next-quarter, annual, and long-range sales forecasts of existing and new products, forecasts of margins.	Annual and long range only, forecasts of existing and new products, forecasts of margins.
Data required	Data on past sales for the appropriate period for each customer of the salesman are provided.	No data are provided other than (a) those requested by the individual forecasters as they prepare the initial forecast and (b) any additional data requested during the meeting(s) held to reach consensus.	A coordinator edits, consolidates, and distributes the responses to each round of questionnaires.
Time required	3–4 weeks	2–3 weeks	1–2½ months

and their likely effects on the industries of the customers on which they call. For this reason, aggregating their individual forecasts produces overall forecasts of questionable accuracy beyond, say, the next two quarters. This technique is weak in identifying turning points for the same reasons.

Companies utilizing this method of forecasting generally use several means to help improve accuracy. These include (1) supplying each salesman with his past performance record in forecasting, (2) providing a forecast on the business outlook for the forecast period, and (3) having the regional manager discuss the forecast with each salesman before it is submitted. Cross checks are sometimes made by those companies that have a product manager type of organization by obtaining independent forecasts from the product managers and comparing them with the aggregated forecasts made by the salesmen.

Average or Consensus of "Expert" Forecasts

An expert is anyone whom we judge has "acquired special skill in or knowledge of a particular subject." In weather forecasting this role is reserved almost exclusively for the meteorologist and in insurance the expert forecaster is the actuary. No generally recognized equivalent professional training is available for sales forecasters. Thus, the role of "expert" is accordingly less well defined. As used here, it includes executives of the company, consultants, trade association officials, trade journal editors, and, in some cases, officials in governmental agencies. The expertise of company executives and consultants can be used for forecasts of either company sales or industry sales, whereas that of the other categories of experts normally applies only to forecasts of industry sales.

Sales forecasts can be obtained from experts in one of three forms. In ascending order of the amount of information provided (and the difficulty of obtaining it), these are (1) *point* forecasts, (2) *interval* forecasts, and (3) *probability distribution* forecasts.

A *point forecast* of sales, as the name implies, is a sales forecast of a specific amount. A forecast by an executive of the Winchester Bay Company, a builder of boats, might be that "sales will be $11,604,000 during the coming fiscal year." Point forecasts are the simplest forecasts to make because they give the least information. They are almost certain to be wrong but there is no indication of how much or with what probability. Although sales forecasts eventually must be stated as point estimates for production scheduling and inventory management purposes, information on the likely range and probability of errors is useful to help set the specific number. For this reason, it is desirable to obtain forecasts in either an interval or a probability distribution form.

An *interval sales* forecast is a forecast that sales will fall within a stated range with a given level of confidence. An example is the statement that

"I am 80 per cent confident that Winchester Bay Company sales during the coming year will be between $11,000,000 and $12,200,000." An interval forecast is directly analogous to an interval estimate except that the probability attached is subjective in nature.

A *probability distribution* forecast is one in which probabilities are assigned to two or more possible sales intervals. An example is the following forecast for the Winchester Bay Company:

Sales of Winchester Bay Co.	Probability
$10,500,000 to $11,300,000	.25
$11,300,000 to $11,900,000	.50
$11,900,000 to $12,700,000	.25

Although the executive would no doubt concede that there is some chance of sales being less than $10,500,000 or more than $12,700,000, he believes that the probability of sales being beyond either of these extremes is so remote that it can be ignored for planning purposes.

The intervals used represent low, medium, and high sales levels, also designated as *pessimistic, most probable,* and *optimistic* levels. Although the distribution can be broken down into as many intervals as desired, a distribution with three intervals is a useful one and easier for executives to use than one with four or more intervals.

Two questions logically arise at this point. They are, (1) *"What procedures should be used to obtain forecasts from 'experts'?"* and, (2) *"How do we obtain a joint forecast from several 'experts'?".* The answers to both these questions are important in determining how useful forecasts by experts will be in any forecasting situation.

(1) *"What procedures should be used to obtain forecasts from 'experts'?"* Philip Kotler reports a dialogue between an executive and a marketing research analyst concerning a sales forecast for a new sales territory:[2]

Analyst: What do you think annual sales will be?
Executive: I don't have the foggiest idea. I just think it will be a good territory.
Analyst: Do you think sales will go over $10 million a year?
Executive: No, that's very unlikely.
Analyst: Do you think sales will go over $8 million a year?
Executive: That's possible.
Analyst: Could sales be as low as $4 million a year?
Executive: Absolutely not. We wouldn't open the territory if we thought they were going to be that low.

[2] P. Kotler, "A Guide to Gathering Expert Estimates," *Business Horizons* (October 1970).

Analyst: Would it be more likely that sales will be around $6 million?
Executive: That's quite possible. In fact, I would say that's a little on the low side.
Analyst: Where would you place sales?
Executive: Around $7 million.

Three aspects of this example are worth noting. First, an executive who began the conversation by saying he had no idea of what sales would be concluded by giving a point forecast. This was not just the selection of a figure to satisfy the analyst; he specifically stated that sales of $6 million were likely to be "a little on the low side" and gave a point forecast of "around $7 million."

A second aspect of interest is the analyst's technique. The analyst's questions were designed successively to narrow the forecast range by asking for opinions on specific forecast levels. He bracketed the estimate with sales levels of $10 million and $4 million by questions involving increments (or decrements) from those levels. The principle involved here is, whenever possible, to *allow the forecaster to state his opinion about someone else's forecast rather than try to force him to make one of his own.*

A third characteristic of interest in the dialogue is the implicit probability estimates stated by the executive. He stated that it was "very unlikely" that sales would exceed $10 million, "possible" that they would go over $8 million, "quite possible" that they would be around $6 million, and that they "absolutely" would not be as low as $4 million. Judgments as to the probability of sales level intervals are there; the trick is to get them verbalized.

Interval forecasts can best be obtained by beginning with a point forecast. This (1) establishes the fact that a forecast can be given and (2) gives a reference point for the interval forecast. If the analyst in the conversation reported earlier had wanted an 80 per cent confidence interval, for example, he might have proceeded as follows:

Analyst: You've just given me your best estimate of sales. Now give me an estimate of sales high enough that you believe there is only a 10 per cent chance we will sell more.
Executive: Well, I don't have any good idea of what that would be.
Analyst: Would you say there is a 10 per cent chance we will have sales of $9 million or more?
Executive: No, I don't think so. It wouldn't be that high.
Analyst: About how much lower would it be?
Executive: I would say about $8.5 million.
Analyst: Now I need a low estimate of sales such that you believe there is only a 10 per cent chance that we will do worse.

Executive: Well, that wouldn't be as low as $4 million or even $5 million and it wouldn't be as high as $6 million. I would say it would be about $5.5 million.

The procedure we have discussed thus far has been concerned with getting forecasts from a single executive. We now need to consider the second question raised earlier, namely,

(2) *"How do we obtain a joint forecast from several 'experts'?"* One approach is to obtain individual forecasts from each "expert" and to combine them using some method of weighting. Four methods are possible:

a. Use equal weights if degree of expertise is believed to be the same.
b. Use weights that are proportional to a subjective assessment of expertise.
c. Use weights that are proportional to a self-assessment of expertise.
d. Use weights that are proportional to the relative accuracy of past forecasts.[3]

The choice among these methods must rest with the judgment of the analyst in each specific situation. None are demonstrably superior for all situations.

An obvious alternative to combining differing forecasts into a joint forecast is to have the executives make a joint forecast initially. If this is done in a group meeting, however, level of rank and strength of personality become biasing factors in reaching a consensus from individual forecasts that differ. This is to be avoided if possible, since there is no evidence to suggest that ability to forecast is highly correlated with position held or ability to present one's views in a forceful manner.

The Delphi Method

A method of avoiding both the problems of weighting individual forecasts of experts and the biases introduced by rank and personality in the consensus method is provided by the *Delphi* method. The method consists of (1) *having the participants make separate forecasts* (point, interval, probability distribution, or some combination of the three), (2) *returning them to the analyst who combines them using one of the weighting systems described previously,* (3) *returning the combined forecast to the forecasters,* (4) *who make a new round of forecasts with this information.*

---

[3] See R. L. Winkler, "The Consensus of Subjective Probability Distributions," *Management Science* (October 1968), B 61–75.

This process is continued until it appears that further rounds will not result in an added degree of consensus.[4]

The underlying premises on which the Delphi method is based are: (1) that successive estimates will tend to show loss dispersion, and (2) that the median of the group response will tend to move toward the true answer. Convergence of the group estimates is almost invariably observed. The critical issue is, of course, whether the movement is toward the true value.

The method has been applied in sales forecasting to medium- and long-term forecasting for existing products and to forecasting demand for new products during their introductory period. A comparison of final round joint forecasts with initial round individual forecasts indicates that forecasting accuracy is improved by using the method.[5] This is consistent with other research that has shown that a consensus reached by a group of five or more judges is superior to individual decision making, majority votes, decision by the leader, and an average of individual decisions.[6]

Forecasting by Time Series Analysis and Projection

A *time series* is a set of observations on a variable, such as sales, such that the observations are arranged in relation to time. Table 16–2 provides the time series for the consumption of malt beverages in the United States from 1966 through 1972. The sales data in this table are presented for both months and years. Quarterly, weekly, and occasionally daily sales figures are also subject to time series analysis.

Forecasting using time series analysis is based on the assumption that patterns observed in the changes in levels of past periods' sales can be used to predict sales in future periods. A time series such as that shown in Table 16–2 is usually considered to be comprised of four separate types of movements of variations—*trend, cycle, seasonal,* and *random* variations.

---

[4] See N. Dalkey and O. Helmer, "An Experimental Application of the Delphi Method to the Use of Experts," *Management Science* (April 1963), 458–467. Examples of applications are given in H. Q. North and D. L. Pyke, "Probes of the Technological Future," *Harvard Business Review* (May–June 1969), 68–76; M. A. Jolson and G. L. Rossow, "The Delphi Process in Marketing Decision Making," *Journal of Marketing Research,* **8** (November 1971), 443–448, and R. Best, "An Experiment in Delphi Estimation in Marketing Decision Making," *Journal of Marketing Research,* **11** (November 1974), 448–452.

[5] See, for example, Jolson and Rossow, op. cit., Mikonick, et al., op. cit.; and Best, op. cit.

[6] A. Van de Ver and A. Delberg, "Nominal Versus Interacting Group Processes for Committee Decision-Making Effectiveness," *Academy of Management Journal,* **14** (June 1971), 203–212; and C. Halloman and H. Hendrick, "Adequacy of Group Decisions as a Function of the Decision-Making Process," *Academy of Management Journal,* **15** (June 1972), 175–184.

Table 16–2 Consumption of Malt Beverages by Months 1966–1972 (in barrels, 000 omitted)*

Month	1966	1967	1968	1969	1970	1971	1972
January	6,702	7,206	7,722	7,925	8,401	8,485	8,848
February	6,631	6,934	7,287	7,374	7,797	8,382	8,753
March	8,457	9,099	8,744	8,940	10,238	10,563	11,155
April	8,456	9,110	9,334	9,769	10,406	10,937	10,898
May	9,100	10,038	10,162	10,126	11,217	10,998	11,917
June	10,586	10,491	10,270	9,772	11,891	12,587	12,955
July	10,593	9,830	11,482	11,371	11,971	12,557	12,131
August	10,479	10,392	10,987	11,896	11,057	11,976	12,752
September	9,044	8,947	9,313	10,511	10,490	10,906	11,016
October	7,837	8,312	9,171	9,944	9,701	9,720	10,493
November	7,855	8,096	8,264	8,853	8,794	9,560	9,832
December	8,115	8,331	8,312	9,312	9,638	9,745	9,355
Total	103,853	106,786	111,049	115,793	121,601	126,416	130,106

* *Source:* United States Brewers Association, Inc., *Brewers Almanac, 1973*, Table 54, 83. Used with permission of the United States Brewers Association, Inc.

Trend is the basic, long-term underlying pattern of growth, stability, or decline in the series. The plot of annual consumption of malt beverages for the period 1966–1972 shown in Figure 16–2 indicates that consumption increased by a fairly constant amount each year during that period. The *trend* in consumption was, therefore, one of relatively steady growth over the period.

The level of sales of most companies shows considerably greater fluctuations over time than the data plotted in Figure 16–2. Sales rise and fall depending upon the general state of business, the level of demand for the products the company produces, the activities of competitors, and other factors. When a fluctuation is of more than a year's duration, it is said to be a *cyclical variation.* These variations usually do not occur on a regular basis and predicting their occurrence, or even isolating their past effects, is thus difficult.

Seasonal variations are regular, recurring fluctuations with a duration of one year or less. An examination of the monthly data in Table 16–2 reveals that malt beverage consumption peaks sharply during the summer months. Sales of children's shoes tend to increase markedly prior to the start of the school year and to have smaller peaks prior to Christmas and Easter. Periodic effects on retail sales are reflected in the sales for particular days of the week or week of the month; the custom of concentrating retail newspaper advertising in the Wednesday or Thursday editions and of holding end-of-the-month sales is based on these patterns.

The final group of forces affecting time series sales data is *random variation.* Random variation, sometimes called *residual variation* or *statistical noise,* is the effect of such unexplained (statistically) occur-

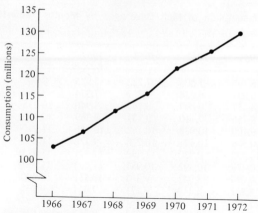

Figure 16–2 Annual consumption of malt beverages, 1966–1972.

rences as unusual weather, strikes, nonrecurring political events, and so forth. It is that part of the time series data that cannot be explained as trend, cycle, or seasonal variation.

A number of forecasting methods are in use that consist of formal, explicit models for analyzing time series data and forecasting by projecting on the basis of an identified or assumed pattern. These methods vary in complexity from those that involve only some simple form of trend projection up through sophisticated, computerized models in which trend, cyclical, and seasonal variations are analyzed and projected.

Isolating Seasonal Fluctuations

Seasonal fluctuations are generally large enough to be taken into account in monthly and quarterly sales forecasts (the same general principles apply to daily and weekly forecasts). This is typically done by computing a *seasonal index number* and using it to adjust the values obtained by forecasting trend alone.

In its simplest form, a seasonal index number for a period is the value for that period divided by the average value for all periods for a year. The resulting ratio is usually multiplied by 100, so that 100 represents an average value, an index number of less than 100 a lower than average value, and one of more than 100 a higher than average value.

The many known methods of computing seasonal indexes differ with respect to the number of past periods of data required, technical considerations with respect to the "centering" of the period for which the index number is to be calculated, whether trend and cyclical influences in the data are removed before the calculation is made, and other considerations. The more complex methods require the use of a computer.

Centered Moving Average. A relatively simple method of calculating a seasonal index number is the *centered moving average* method. To illustrate its use, suppose in early 1972 we had wanted to calculate a seasonal index number for malt beverage consumption for the month of June. Using the centered moving average method we would have gone through the following steps:

1. *Decide how many years of data are to be included in the calculation.* Although an index number can be calculated using only one year's data, data for at least two years are necessary to determine seasonal variation with reasonable accuracy. If seasonal effects seem to fluctuate very much, a longer period may be required. We use two years in this example.

2. *Calculate a weighted average of monthly sales for the 13 months in which June, 1970, is the middle month.* The use of 13 months of data allows the index to be "centered" on the month for which it is being calculated. In the example, the average is calculated using data for the months December, 1969, through December, 1970. In order that December sales are not overweighted in the average, a weight of "1" is assigned them, a weight of "2" is assigned the sales of the other 11 months, and the sum of the weighted sales values is divided by 24.

In the example this weighted average is calculated as follows:

$$\frac{\begin{array}{l}(\text{Dec. '69 sales} \times 1) + (\text{Jan. '70 sales} \times 2) + (\text{Feb. '70 sales} \times 2) \\ + (\text{March '70 sales} \times 2) + (\text{April '70 sales} \times 2) + (\text{May '70 sales} \times 2) \\ + (\text{June '70 sales} \times 2) + (\text{July '70 sales} \times 2) + (\text{Aug. '70 sales} \times 2) \\ + (\text{Sept. '70 sales} \times 2) + (\text{Oct. '70 sales} \times 2) + (\text{Nov. '70 sales} \times 2) \\ + (\text{Dec. '70 sales} \times 1)\end{array}}{24}$$

$$= \frac{\begin{array}{l}(9,312 \times 1) + (8,401 \times 2) + (7,797 \times 2) + (10,238 \times 2) + (10,406 \times 2) \\ + (11,217 \times 2) + (11,891 \times 2) + (11,971 \times 2) + (11,057 \times 2) \\ + (10,490 \times 2) + (9,701 \times 2) + (8,794 \times 2) + (9,638 \times 1)\end{array}}{24}$$

$$= \frac{242,976}{24} = 10,120$$

3. *Calculate an index number for June, 1970, by dividing the weighted average monthly sales into the sales for June, 1970, and multiply by 100.*

The resulting index number is

$$\frac{11,891}{10,120} \times 100 = 117.5$$

4. *Repeat steps (2) and (3) for the 13 months in which June, 1971, is the middle month.*

The resulting index number is 119.5

5. *Average the single year index numbers obtained in steps (3) and (4).*

The average is $\dfrac{117.5 + 119.5}{2} = 118.5$. This is the unadjusted seasonal index for June.

6. *Add the unadjusted monthly index numbers for each month of the year and divide by 12. If the average obtained is not equal to 100.0, divide each unadjusted monthly index number by the average and multiply by 100 to obtain an adjusted monthly index number.* Analogous procedures are used for calculating seasonal index numbers for quarters, weeks, or days when using the centered moving average approach.[7]

The seasonal index for each month, as it would have been calculated using data up to mid-1972 using this method, is shown in Table 16–3.

Table 16–3 Seasonal Indexes for Malt Beverage Consumption, 1971

	Seasonal Index Computed by		
Month	*Centered Moving Average*	*Census Method II*	*Regression*
January	82.6	83.3	82
February	78.9	77.4	81
March	101.4	97.1	103
April	103.9	102.4	103
May	108.2	108.6	108
June	118.8	109.7	120
July	118.9	118.8	116
August	111.1	116.7	116
September	102.9	105.5	102
October	93.1	98.8	93
November	87.7	88.1	89
December	92.5	93.5	87

Census Method II. The Census Method II approach is an advanced form of the moving average approach. A computer program eliminates the trend and cycle component from the data utilizing complex moving averages. In addition, irregular or random fluctuations are removed by averaging seasonal indexes over the time period covered by the data with periods containing extreme fluctuations controlled for. Finally, the program provides a forecast of seasonal indexes for one year in advance.[8]

[7] See S. B. Richmond, *Statistical Analysis* (New York: The Ronald Press Company, 1964).

[8] See R. L. McLaughlin, *Time Series Forecasting* (Chicago: American Marketing Association, 1962), for details.

Such a forecast of season indexes is provided for the 1971 malt beverage consumption in Table 16–3. These indexes are based on 1966 through 1970 data.

Regression: The most commonly included technique in the software programs of the major computer manufacturers utilizes a regression model as the basis for computing the seasonal indexes. This approach requires at least two years sales data and involves five steps:

1. *Calculate the slope of the regression line formed by the sales data.*
2. *Detrend the sales figures by the formula $DS_i = S_i - b(i - 1)$ where:* DS_i = detrended sales for the ith month; S_i = sales for the ith month; b = slope of the regression line.
3. *Average the detrended sales for each specific month.* For example, using two years sales data would require that the detrended sales for each month of year one be added to the detrended sales for each month in year two and each resulting sum be divided by two.
4. *Average the detrended sales for all the months being utilized.* Two years data would require that all 24 months detrended sales values be summed and divided by 24.
5. *Compute the seasonal indexes by dividing each specific month's average detrended sales* (step 3) *by the overall average detrended monthly sales* (step 4) *and multiplying the resulting values by 100.*

An examination of Table 16–3 clearly reveals the seasonal nature of malt beverage consumption, high in summer and low in winter. Although this same seasonal pattern is shown for the index numbers produced by each of the methods, the values for the individual months vary, in some cases by substantial amounts. Good descriptions of other methods of calculating seasonal index numbers are available elsewhere and should be consulted before a choice of methods is made in an actual forecasting situation.[9]

Obtaining a seasonal index is generally only the first step in making a short-term forecast. We must also estimate the trend and, on occasion, the cyclical patterns in the data. The trend values can then be adjusted if necessary by the seasonal index to provide final forecasts of monthly or quarterly sales.

[9] See, for example, R. E. Croxton and D. J. Cowden, *Applied General Statistics,* 2nd ed. (Englewood Cliffs, N.J.: Prentice-Hall, Inc., 1955), 320–363; S. J. Richmond, *Statistical Analysis,* 2nd ed. (New York: The Ronald Press Company, 1964), Chap. 16, and L. Salzmon, "Time Series Analysis," in R. Ferber, ed., *Handbook of Marketing Research* (New York: McGraw-Hill Book Company, 1974), 2–323 to 2–365.

Table 16–4 Forecasting by Use of Time Series Analysis and Projection

	"Naïve" Model	Moving Average	Exponential Smoothing	Statistical Trend Analysis	Box-Jenkins	X-11
Description	Forecasts made using a deliberately naïve model such as "next period sales will be the same as this period sales," or next period sales will be the same as this period sales adjusted for the change from last period sales."	The forecast consists of an average of the sales for the last X periods, where X is chosen so that the effects of seasonal factors on sales is eliminated.	Similar to a moving average except that the more recent period sales have a greater weight.	Uses of regression analysis to determine the underlying pattern of growth, stability, or decline in the data.	A technique for selecting the optimal model in terms of "fit" to the time series.	A technique for breaking a time series into seasonal, cyclical, trend, and random components.
Assessment of accuracy						
Short term (0–3 months)	Poor to good	Poor to good	Fair to very good	Fair to very good	Very good to excellent	Very good to excellent
Medium term (6 mos.–2 years)	Poor	Poor	Poor to good	Poor to good	Poor to good	Good
Long term (2 years or more)	Very poor	Very poor	Very poor	Very poor	Very poor	Very poor

					Fair	Good
Prediction of turning points	Never forecasts turning points; incorporates them after they occur.	Never forecasts turning points; incorporates them after they occur.	Never forecasts turning points; incorporates them faster than moving average after they occur.	Never forecasts turning points; late in incorporating them after they occur.		
Typical applications	A standard for judging accuracy of other techniques. Short-term sales forecasts.	Inventory control for standard items. Short-term sales forecasts.	Inventory control for standard items. Short-term sales forecasts.	Inventory control for standard items. Short-term sales forecasts.	Inventory control, forecasts of fund flows. Short-term sales forecasts.	Forecasting sales.
Data required	Data for the preceding periods.	A minimum of 8 quarters or 24 months if seasonals are present, otherwise less data	Same as for a moving average.	Same as for a moving average.	Same as for a moving average.	12 quarters or 36 months of data.
Time required	1 day	1 day	1 day	1 day	1–2 days	1 day

Time Series Forecasting Models

In this section, we examine six formal approaches to making extrapolative forecasts from time series data. These approaches are (1) *naïve model forecasts*, (2) *moving average*, (3) *exponential smoothing*, (4) *statistical trend analysis*, (5) *the Box-Jenkins model*, and (6) *the X-11 model*. Summary comments on each of these methods are given in Table 16–4.

Naïve Model Forecasts.   Naïve model forecasts are characterized by reliance on the last period's sales as a forecast of the next period's sales. The simplest possible model is "next period's sales will be the same as the present period's sales." This model provides accurate sales forecasts only to the extent that the trend in sales is "flat," rather than increasing or decreasing, and when random, cyclical, and seasonal effects are negligible.

A similar but somewhat more sophisticated model is, "next period's sales will be equal to last period's sales adjusted for the change from the sales for the period before that." One approach to the adjustment is to add or subtract the difference between the last two period's sales to present period sales, or $Y_{t+1} = Y_t + (Y_t - Y_{t-1})$. As long as the trend in sales consists of a relatively fixed amount of increase or decrease each period, and any cyclical or seasonal effects are negligible, this model will work well.

The forecasts that would have resulted from using this method of forecasting for malt beverage consumption for the years 1968–1972 are shown in Table 16–5. As is indicated by the low error percentages, this method would have provided very accurate annual forecasts for that period.

Moving Average Forecasts.   A moving average is an average of the values for the last X periods. The average is updated—"moves"—each period. As the value for the new period becomes available it is added and the value for the $X + 1$ period is dropped. For example, if the moving average is for 8 quarters, the value for the most recent quarter is added when it becomes available and the value for the ninth quarter back is dropped.

Moving averages are most commonly used for forecasting sales for short periods: a week, a month, or a quarter is the usual time period involved. A moving average is typically computed for 8 quarters, 24 months, or 104 weeks. In situations with little or no seasonal variations, moving averages can be used as computed as a forecast for the next period's sales. As such, the model involved is "sales for the next period will be equal to the average sales for the last X periods."

Table 16–5 Forecasts of Annual Malt Beverage Consumption
Using the Forecasting Model $Y_{t+1} = Y_t + (Y_t - Y_{t-1})$, 1968–1972
(000's of Barrels)

	Actual Consumption	*Forecast Consumption*	*Per Cent Error*
1966	103,853	—	—
1967	106,786	—	—
1968	111,049	109,719	−1.2
1969	115,793	115,312	−0.4
1970	121,601	120,537	−0.9
1971	126,416	127,409	+0.8
1972	130,106	131,231	+0.9

The usual situation is that the seasonal effects on sales are large enough so that the forecast should be adjusted by the appropriate *seasonal index number*. The forecasting model then becomes "sales for the next period will be equal to the average sales for the last X periods adjusted by the seasonal index for the next period."

The adjustment for seasonal variation is made by multiplying the value to be adjusted by the appropriate seasonal index number and dividing by 100. For example, suppose a forecast was to be made for malt beverage sales for June, 1972, using the adjusted moving average method of forecasting. The moving average value of malt beverage consumption from June, 1970, through May, 1972, was 10,480,000 barrels and the seasonal index for June (Census Method II) was 109.7. The forecast for June, 1972, would then have been $(10,480,000 \times 109.7)/100 = 11,497,000$ barrels.

The results of applying a seasonally adjusted, two-year moving average forecasting method to the malt beverage data are shown in Table 16–6. As can be seen, the forecast values are generally less than the actual values. This occurred because the moving average method assumes an underlying trend of no growth whereas the malt beverage data show a growth pattern. However, since the growth is not dramatic, most of the forecasts are within acceptable limits of error.

The moving average forecasts shown in the table are for only one period in advance. Longer term forecasts tend to lose accuracy rapidly. In addition, the moving average never forecasts turning points. It only incorporates changes in sales in the average after they occur. The length of the lag before sales are incorporated depends upon the length of the data period; a moving average of quarterly data will have a longer lag than one of monthly data, for example.

The primary use of moving average forecasts (as for exponentially smoothed forecasts, the next method discussed) is in inventory control systems for standard items. A company producing and selling many items must develop systematic methods of forecasting inventory requirements as the cost of nonsystematic individual forecasts would be prohibitive. The Crane Company, for example, manufactures and sells thousands of valves, fittings, meters, pumps, and other items. To attempt to forecast sales of each product by any of the judgmental methods discussed earlier would be very cumbersome and costly. Computer programs are available from each of the major computer manufacturers for inventory control systems that provide both perpetual inventory data and an updated moving average (or exponentially smoothed) forecast at the desired intervals.

Exponential Smoothing. Exponential smoothing is a technique for obtaining a *weighted moving average* such that the more recent the observation the heavier is the weight assigned. The logic of such a weighting pattern in sales forecasting is that the more recent periods' sales are more likely to be better predictors of next period's sales than are those for earlier periods.[10]

In its simplest form, the exponential smoothing forecasting equation is

$$Y_{t+1} = \alpha Y_t + (1 - \alpha)\bar{Y}_t$$

where

Y_{t+1} = forecast sales for next period
α = the weight for the present period actual sales
Y_t = present period sales, and
$\bar{Y}_t$ = present period smoothed sales.

The initial level of smoothed sales $(\bar{Y}_t)$ can be an average of sales for the last few periods. After the first exponentially smoothed forecast is made, the present period smoothed sales are then used for $\bar{Y}_t$.

Although the logic underlying exponential smoothing is simple, the computational process is rather burdensome and is generally performed by means of a computer.[11] The computer is particularly useful since it is often helpful to try several different weighting factors (called *smoothing constants*) and to select the one that provides the best "forecast" of known data.

Because of the heavier weighting of the recent observations, the accuracy of exponentially smoothed forecasts is generally somewhat better

---

[10] For an authoritative discussion of exponential smoothing as a forecasting method see R. G. Brown, *Smoothing, Forecasting and Prediction of Discrete Time Series* (Englewood-Cliffs, N.J.: Prentice-Hall, Inc., 1963).

[11] M. D. Geurts and K. Luke, "FORECAST: Exponential Smoothing Simulation and Alpha Analyzer Program with Options," *Journal of Marketing Research,* **11** (May 1974), 195.

than that for moving average forecasts. The seasonally adjusted forecasts obtained by exponential smoothing for malt beverage consumption for 1972 were better, but only slightly better, than those arrived at by the seasonally adjusted moving average method. As shown in Table 16–6, the average per cent of error for the exponentially smoothed ($\alpha = .2$) forecasts (4.6 per cent) is slightly lower than that for the 24 month moving average forecasts (4.9 per cent).

Statistical Trend Analysis. Statistical trend analysis involves a determination of the underlying trend or pattern of growth, stability, or decline in the series. A *regression analysis* is run using time as one variable and the variable to be forecast (sales in this case) as the other. For a simple linear regression (other regression models can be used) the equation obtained from the analysis is

$$Y_{t+1} = a + b(t + 1)$$

where

Y_{t+1} = a forecast of next period sales,
a = a constant
b = the slope of the trend line (the relative amount of change per period)
$t + 1$ = the number of periods plus 1 of data in the time series used for deriving the value of the slope.

If necessary, the value forecast by the regression equation is adjusted by the relevant seasonal index number to produce the final forecast. Table 16–6 contains seasonally adjusted forecasts of sales for each month in 1972 using the monthly data from 1970 and 1971 to derive the regression formula. As can be seen, the linear regression model also does a reasonably good job of forecasting this particular set of data.

Other Forecasting Models. The Census Bureau has developed a comprehensive computerized model for analyzing time series known as the *X-11 technique.* It provides information on seasonals, trends, trend-cycles, and measures of how closely they fit the data. It also provides a measure of growth rate that can be used to help identify turning points.[12]

The *Box-Jenkins* method is a mathematical technique that enables the computer to select the statistical model of the time series that gives the

---

[12] See U.S. Bureau of the Census, "X-11 Information for the User," *Papers Prepared for the Seminar on Seasonal Adjustments of the National Association of Business Economists,* U.S. Department of Commerce, March 10, 1969; and J. C. Chambers, S. K. Mullick, and D. D. Smith, "How to Choose the Right Forecasting Technique," *Harvard Business Review,* **49** (July–August, 1971), 71–72.

Table 16–6 Predictions of Monthly Malt Beverage Consumption for 1972

Month	Actual Consumption	Adjusted Last Period Estimate	Per Cent Error	24 Month Moving Average*	Per Cent Error	Exponential Smoothing*	Per Cent Error	Linear Regression*	Per Cent Error
Jan.	8,848	9,930	12.2	8,608	− 2.7	8,653	−2.2	9,051	7.4
Feb.	8,753	7,951	− 9.2	8,012	− 8.5	8,064	−7.9	8,443	− 3.5
March	11,155	8,658	−22.4	10,092	− 9.5	10,332	−7.4	10,633	− 4.7
April	10,898	13,557	−24.4	10,680	− 2.0	11,037	1.3	11,206	2.8
May	11,917	10,641	−10.7	11,350	− 4.8	11,765	−1.3	11,986	0.6
June	12,955	12,936	− 0.2	11,497	−11.2	11,904	−8.1	12,154	− 6.2
July	12,131	13,993	15.4	12,504	3.1	13,105	8.0	13,213	8.9
Aug.	12,752	11,307	−11.3	12,290	− 3.6	12,693	−0.5	13,202	3.5
Sept.	11,016	13,373	21.4	11,185	1.5	11,510	4.5	11,823	7.3
Oct.	10,493	9,280	−11.6	10,497	—	10,658	1.6	11,114	5.9
Nov.	9,832	9,970	1.4	9,389	4.5	9,444	−3.9	9,948	1.2
Dec.	9,354	9,171	2.0	10,005	7.0	10,171	8.7	10,598	13.3
Average Per Cent Error			11.9	—	4.9	—	4.6	—	5.4

* Seasonally adjusted using Census Method II weights.

best fit.[13] If the assumption of stability of the process generating the time series is a reasonably correct one, this model will also provide the best forecast.

Using this method the computer "tries," as it were, naïve models, moving averages of various numbers of periods, exponential smoothing over a range of smoothing constants, and various trend, trend-and-cycle, and trend-cycle-and-seasonal models to determine which one most closely fits the data. Its accuracy is, therefore, equal to the best of the forecasting models from which it selects.

Problems in Using Time Series Analysis. The researcher using time series analysis as a sales forecasting technique must keep in mind that this approach is based on the assumption that *patterns observed in the past will continue in the future.* This often is not true for industry sales and frequently does not hold for individual firm sales. Thus, any time series forecast should be carefully evaluated in light of management's knowledge of changing future events. For example, a firm planning a major price decrease should not naïvely rely on forecasts based on sales at the old price. Formal, as well as informal, techniques are available for incorporating anticipated atypical events into time series forecasts.[14]

Causal Methods of Forecasting

A *causal* method of sales forecasting involves the development and use of a forecasting model in which changes in the level of sales are the result of changes in one or more other variables.

Causal methods of forecasting require the identification of causal (predictor) variables, measuring or estimating the change in them, and establishing the functional relationship between them and sales. A local utility supplying water to an Arizona community, for example, may have found that water usage is a function of the number of residential meters, income, the rate charges, and the amount of rainfall. By forecasting any changes in the level of these variables, and knowing the functional relationship between them and residential usage of water, a forecast can be made.

The illustration just given involves a *causal regression model* in the forecast. Of the many other kinds of causal methods of forecasting, the most commonly used, in addition to regression models, include *leading indicators, survey of buyer intentions, input-output,* and *econometric models.* These methods are each discussed, and a brief description of them and their salient characteristics is given in Table 16–7.

[13] G. E. P. Box and G. M. Jenkins, *Time Series Analysis, Forecasting and Control* (San Francisco: Holden-Day, Inc., 1970).

[14] J. E. Reinmuth and M. D. Geurts, "A Bayesian Approach to Forecasting Effects of Atypical Situations," *Journal of Marketing Research* **9** (August 1972), 292–297.

Table 16–7 Causal Methods of Forecasting

	Regression Model	Econometric Model	Surveys of Buyer Intentions	Input-Output Model	Barometric Forecasting
Description	An equation relating sales to predictor variables (disposable income, relative price, level of promotion) is derived using multiple regression analysis.	A system of interrelated regression equations used to forecast sales (or profits).	Surveys that measure buyer intentions for selected durable goods.	A method employing data on the flow of goods between industries in the economy. Useful only for forecast-sales of industrial products and services.	A time series whose movements precede those of the series to be predicted.
Accuracy					
Short term (0–3 months)	Good to very good	Good to very good	Poor to good	Not applicable	Poor to good
Medium term (6 months–2 years)	Good to very good	Very good	Poor to good	Good to very good	Poor to good
Long term (2 years or more)	Poor	Good	Very poor	Good to very good	Very poor
Identification of turning points	Fair to good	Good to excellent	Fair to good	Poor to fair	Tend to identify most turning points that occur. The problem is that they also signal some that do not.

631

	Forecasting of product line sales.	Forecasting of product line sales.	Forecasting of product line sales.	Forecasts of industrial product line sales by using industry.	Forecasts of product line sales.
Typical applications					
Data required	Data can be sales (and values of predictor variables) by region as well as over time. Need 20 or more observations for acceptable results.	Similar to data required for regression model.	Several periods of data are required to determine relationship of intentions to company sales.	Basic data developed by U.S. Department of Commerce and updated each 5 years.	The indicators most widely used are published monthly by U.S. government agencies.
Time required	1 day once variables are identified and data available.	2–3 months	2–3 months	6–8 months	2 weeks–1 month

Adapted from J. C. Chambers, S. K. Mullick, and D. D. Smith "How to Choose the Right Forecasting Technique," *Harvard Business Review* (July–August 1971), 45–74.

Barometric Forecasting—Leading Indicators

It has been found that decreases in the money supply in the United States tend to lead declines in the price of stocks by about 15 months and increases in the money supply lead stock price increases by about two months.[15] Since stock sales by brokers increase during rising prices and decrease in periods of falling prices, data on money supply provides a leading indicator for sales of stocks.

A baby food manufacturer has found that the number of births in each area for the past three years, lagged by six months, is a good leading indicator of nonmilk baby food sales. The marketing research department of a manufacturer of industrial packaging materials has found that changes in the Federal Reserve Board *Index of Industrial Production* tend to lead change in company sales by about three months.[16]

These are examples for which one would intuitively expect lead-lag relationships to exist between the indicator and company sales. The company that has products with such dependent relationships on variables whose changes precede changes in the firm's sales can make profitable use of leading indicators as a forecasting technique.

Most companies are not in this fortunate position. As a consequence, leading indicators have been used more widely in forecasting changes in overall business conditions than for directly forecasting sales for individual companies. The level of sales of most companies is at least partially dependent upon general business conditions. In those cases, some forecast of the overall level of economic activity is necessary before a company sales forecast can be made.

The Department of Commerce collects and publishes data each month on 40 different time series that tend to lead the overall economy.[17] Among these leading indicators are series on the *average workweek in manufacturing, new business formation, new orders in durable goods industries, contracts and orders in plant and equipment, new building permits, industrial materials prices,* and *stock prices of 500 common stocks.*

The use of individual leading indicators presents two interpretive problems to the forecaster. The first arises from *mixed* signals. The direction of movement signaled (that is, an indication that the economy is rising or falling) by each of a group of indicators is rarely the same for all indicators. In such a case it is difficult to know which direction to accept as

[15] B. W. Sprinkel, *Money and Stock Prices* (Homewood, Ill.: Richard D. Irwin, Inc., 1964), pp. 3–4.

[16] As reported by R. P. Welch in "Corporate Sales Forecasting at Bemis" at the ninth Annual Marketing Conference, National Industrial Conference Board, 1961.

[17] These series are published in *Business Conditions Digest,* U.S. Department of Commerce, Social and Economics Statistics Administration, Washington, D.C.

the correct one. The second problem is one of *false* signals. Most leading indicators have a reasonably good record of predicting turning points that actually occur. The problem is that they also predict many turning points that do *not* occur.

A *diffusion index* is one means of dealing with the mixed signals problem. The index number for a given group of indicators during a specified time period is the percentage of the indicators that have risen (shown an increase in economic activity) during the period. An index number of 100 indicates that all the series have risen whereas one of 0 indicates that they have all fallen. Series that are unchanged are counted as one-half having risen and one-half having fallen.

The use of a diffusion index may help solve the false signal problem as well, depending upon the series used and the skill of the analyst. A succession of low index numbers over a number of months in an expansionary period should precede a downturn. A high index number in a recessionary period generally signals an upturn. Interpretation of the movements of the index is something similar to that for movements of a barometer; data on other variables and forecasting skills are required to predict accurately the nature of the coming (economic) weather.

Surveys of Buyer Intentions

One might reasonably conclude that a good way of forecasting sales is to ask customers to forecast their purchases. After all, customers know more about their prospective purchases than anyone else.

This reasoning has led many companies and a number of agencies to conduct periodic surveys of buyer intentions. A major steel company conducts a survey each quarter among companies in each of 13 steel-using industries to determine their expected purchases during the next quarter and the next 12 months. A company that manufactures bearings for railroad cars conducts a similar survey among railroad car builders each quarter. Several surveys of planned business plant and equipment expenditures are conducted in the United States, including those taken by the Securities and Exchange Commission, McGraw-Hill Publishing Company, the National Industrial Conference Board, and *Fortune* magazine.[18]

These are all surveys of industrial products. Many private surveys of consumer durables are conducted as are a number that are publicly available. The General Electric Company has used a panel to obtain purchase

[18] The results of the Securities and Exchange Commission Survey are published quarterly in the *Survey of Current Business.* The McGraw-Hill survey results are published twice a year in *Business Week.* The National Industrial Conference Board survey results are published in the *Survey of Current Business* and the board's own publications. The *Fortune* survey results are, of course, published there.

intention information on appliances on a continuing basis.[19] Published surveys are conducted regularly by the Survey Research Center, the University of Michigan, *Consumers Union,* and others.[20]

The forecasting record of these surveys has been an uneven one. Although no data on private surveys are available, it appears safe to conclude that the forecasts of industrial products provided by such surveys have been substantially better than that of consumer products. The Department of Commerce survey of new plant and equipment expenditures for the period 1948 through 1969, for example, had an average error of less than 3 per cent.[21] The Bureau of the Census discontinued the Consumer Buying Expectations Survey after April, 1973, because a "large number of data users and subject analysts representing universities, private firms, nonprofit research organizations, and other government agencies" invited to review the results of the operation of the survey concluded the data it provided were "only marginally useful."[22] The experience with the Canadian Buying Intentions Survey, conducted quarterly since 1960, has been a similar one. The conclusion of one analyst concerning the continuing results of that survey is that "Buying intentions, when used alone, have limited predictive ability for sales of (consumer) durable goods over time."[23]

At the present stage of development, at least, it appears that forecasts of consumer goods are best made by means other than the collection and use of buying intentions data. However, the forecasting of industrial goods using intentions data appears to be a reasonable approach for at least some industries.

Input-Output Models

Every company keeps a ledger in some form or another in which sales to other companies are recorded. If the sales ledgers of all companies for a year were collected, the sales data classified by the industries of the seller and the buyer, and total sales from each selling industry to each buying

[19] See, for example, R. W. Pratt, Jr., "Understanding the Decision Process for Consumer Durable Goods: An Example of the Application of Longitudinal Analysis," in P. D. Bennett, ed., *Marketing and Economic Development, Proceedings of the Fall Conference of the American Marketing Association, 1965* (Chicago: The American Marketing Association, 1966).

[20] The results of the Survey Research Center survey are published in the center's own publications and the Consumer Union survey in *Consumer Reports.* A private survey done by the Albert Sindlinger Co. is published in the *Business Record,* a publication of the National Industrial Conference Board.

[21] As reported in G. B. Nimsatt and J. T. Woodward, "Revised Estimates of New Plant and Equipment in the United States, 1947–1969: Part II," *Survey of Current Business,* 50 (February 1970), 23.

[22] "Consumer Buying Indicators," *Current Population Reports,* Series P-65, No. 46, U.S. Department of Commerce, Bureau of the Census, April 1973, 5.

[23] J. Murray, "Canadian Consumer Expectational Data: An Evaluation," *Journal of Marketing Research,* VI (February 1969), 60.

industry determined, an interindustry sales ledger would result. This has been done (although not directly by this method) for some 370 industries in the United States. The result is known as an *input-output table,* which is a 370 × 370 matrix that shows sales from each industry to itself and to each of the other industries. The table in which the data appear in this form is called a *transactions* table.[24]

The application of the input-output tables for forecasting has been more at the overall economy than at the individual firm level. These tables are particularly useful in evaluating the effects of a demand change in one industry upon other industries. As an illustration, suppose that a gasoline shortage is expected to result in a 10 per cent decrease in the number of automobiles produced in the coming year. This will result in less steel production, which in turn will require less iron ore, limestone, coal, and electricity. The automobile manufacturers will require less rubber, plastics, and synthetic fibers, which will lead to a reduction in the demand for chemicals and other raw materials used in their manufacture. By using input-output analysis one can trace the effects of the reduction through the entire industrial chain reaction it brings about.

Forecasting at the individual firm level using input-output tables is possible and done by some companies. It is limited to forecasts for industrial products and, as a practical matter, to fairly broad groupings of products. From the illustration given, one can see how a firm that manufactures and sells, for example, a broad line of industrial plastics might use input-output analysis to evaluate the effects of an anticipated drop in final demand of a major industry such as automobiles.

We have several problems with input-output tables for forecasting at the present stage of development. The data in the tables are not recent; it was not until 1969 that data for the 370 industries collected in 1963 were available. Although comparison with the 1958 and 1947 tables indicates that the interindustry transaction pattern changes slowly, one would feel more comfortable with more recent data. Another problem is the level of aggregation. Most of the companies using the tables have found that the industry designations are too broad to be useful. This, in turn, has forced them to develop additional data at their own expense. The result has sometimes been expenditures in the hundreds of thousands of dollars and long periods of delay.

For these and other reasons, input-output analysis has been used sparingly for forecasting and planning purposes. When it has been used, the using companies have almost invariably been large ones.

[24] The tables resulting from the 1963 input-output study are given in *Input-Output Structure of the U.S. Economy: 1963;* Vol. I, *Transactions Data for Detailed Industries;* Vol. 2, *Direct Requirements for Detailed Industries;* and Vol. 3, *Total Requirements for Detailed Industries,* Office of Business Economics, U.S. Department of the Census, 1969. They are described there and in "Input-Output Structure of the U.S. Economy: 1963," *Survey of Current Business,* **49** (November 1969), 16–47.

Causal Regression Models

A regresison model is perhaps the most widely used causal model for forecasting sales. A causal regression model is an equation relating sales to predictor variables such as disposable income, price relative to competitive products, level of advertising, and others. The equation is derived using multiple regression analysis (see Chapter 14).

The steps involved in developing a regression model for forecasting consists of the following:

1. *Select the predictor variables that are believed to be the major determinants of sales.* These variables are selected on the basis of judgment. In order to be useful they should be variables that can either be measured (the number of color television sets now in use as a predictor variable of next period color television set sales, for example) or can be forecast more easily than can sales (price of own product relative to that of competitive products, for example).

2. *Collect time series and/or cross sectional data for each predictor variable.* In general, 20 or more observations for each predictor variable are necessary for acceptable results.

3. *Decide whether the relationship between each predictor variable and sales is likely to be linear or curvilinear.* Many demand functions are more nearly logarithmic than linear. When this is believed to be the case, the data should be converted to a logarithmic form.

4. *Run the regression analysis to obtain the coefficients and determine goodness of fit.*

5. *Repeat steps (1) through (4) until a satisfactory model is obtained.* A "satisfactory" model is one that forecasts historical sales data with an acceptable degree of accuracy.

Regression models are used for forecasts of both consumer and industrial products. The American Can Company, for example, forecasts the demand for beer cans with a regression equation of the form

$$Y_{t+1} = a + b_1 \hat{I}_{t+1} + b_2 D_t + b_3 A_t$$

where

Y_{t+i} = forecast sales for the coming year,
    a is a constant derived from the regression analysis,
$\hat{I}_{t+1}$ = estimated disposable income for the coming year,
  D_t = number of drinking establishments in the current year,
  A_t = age distribution of the current year, and
    b_i, b_2, b_3 are the coefficients or weights derived from the regression analysis.[25]

[25] G. E. S. Parker and E. C. Segura, "How to Get a Better Forecast," *Harvard Business Review,* **49** (March–April 1971), 101.

A furniture manufacturer has found that the forecasting equation

$$Y_{t+1} = a + 0.373Y_t + 0.033H_t + 0.672\hat{I}_{t+1} - 11.03T$$

where

Y_{t+1} = forecast sales for the coming year,
  a is a constant,
  Y_t = sales during the current year,
  H_t = housing starts during the current year,
  $\hat{I}_{t+1}$ = estimated disposable income during the coming year,
  T = time trend (first year = 1, second year = 2, and so on)

yields a satisfactory forecast.[26]

A forecast of revenues of American Airlines over a number of quarters using the equation

$$Y_{t+1} = a + 25.225A_t + .856Y_t$$

where

Y_{t+1} = forecast revenues for the coming quarter,
  a is a constant,
  A_t = advertising in the current quarter, and
  Y_t = revenues in the current quarter

gave a median error of less than 3 per cent.[27]

A manufacturer of industrial containers has found that an equation of the form

$$Y_{t+1} = a + b_1 FRB_{t-1} + b_2 P_t$$

where

Y_{t+1} = forecast of company sales in the coming quarter,
  a is a constant,
  FRB_{t-1} = Index of Industrial Production lagged one quarter,
  P_t = current quarter average of raw materials price index,
    and b_1, b_2 are coefficients,

produces a forecast that is well within the company's requirements for accuracy.[28]

Recall from the discussion of the use of multiple regression in the analysis of data that the use of predictor variables that are intercorrelated

[26] Ibid.

[27] D. S. Tull, J. J. Bisschop, and M. G. Nelson, "Advertising-Revenue Relationships of Airline Companies: Multicollinearity and Lagged Models," "Unpublished working paper, University of Oregon, 1972.

[28] R. P. Welch, "Corporate Sales Forecasting at Bemis," Ninth Annual Marketing Conference, National Industrial Conference Board.

produces unstable regression coefficients and is thus to be avoided whenever possible (Chapter 14, pp. 537–538). This warning is not applicable to forecasting, however. Here we are interested only in the forecast and not in size or stability of the regression coefficients.

Econometric Models

The amount of water resistance a new design for a sailboat hull will have can be determined by two methods. The first is to build a scale model of the hull, instrument it as needed, and test it in a boat tank. This method employs a model that is a physical analog of the hull. The second method is to simulate the hull with a series of mathematical equations and to calculate the water resistance it will have. This method uses a model that is a mathematical analog of the hull. If the two methods are competently carried out, they will produce comparable results and excellent predictions of the actual resistance of the hull when the boat is built.

Physical analogs of economic processes are rarely built. However, a conspicuous part of the economic literature in recent years has been devoted to the development and description of mathematical analogs, called *econometric* models.

A promising start in the use of econometric models for forecasting has been made at the overall economy level. An appraisal of the forecasting accuracy of four econometric models vis-à-vis that of 36 professional economic forecasters using judgmental methods concludes that "the median judgmental forecast is about as accurate as the median econometric forecast."[29] Since explicit models are much more susceptible to systematic evaluation and improvement than implicit ones, one would expect that econometric forecasts will begin to outperform judgmental forecasts of the overall economy in the not-too-distant future.

The use of econometric models in sales forecasting has been limited. They are expensive to develop and to maintain, and the statistical problems of estimating appropriate values of predictor variables are magnified in the highly dynamic economic environment of the individual firm. Despite their problems, a recent review of forecasting techniques concluded that "Econometric models will be utilized more extensively in the next five years, with most large companies developing and refining econometric models of their major business."[30]

Forecasting by Experiment

Another causal method of forecasting that has not been described here is the use of experiments for forecasting. As discussed in Chapter 12,

[29] S. K. McNees, "The Predictive Accuracy of Econometric Forecasts," *New England Economic Review* (September–October 1973), 23.
[30] Chambers, Mullick, and Smith, op. cit., 73.

both laboratory and field experiments are used for evaluating new products and the sales effects of the other mix variables.[31] Market tests, a widely used form of field experiment, are particularly useful in forecasting sales during the introductory period of prospective new products.[32]

Error Costs and the Value of Forecasts

Errors in forecasts results in costs that are either *outlay* or *opportunity* in nature. In general, a forecast that is too high results in outlay costs and one that is too low in results in opportunity costs.

Forecasts that are too high result in prospective new products being introduced when they shouldn't be and in excess inventories for existing products. The extra costs incurred as a result of sales being less than they were forecast to be are actual dollar and cents outlays that appear in the appropriate cost accounts in the income statement.

The new product failures that occur as a result of overly optimistic forecasting are the most visible and dramatic evidences of forecast error. The Gourmet Foods line of General Foods, Hunt's Flavored Ketchups, and the Ford Edsel are examples of costly product misfires.[33] The costs of carrying excess inventory for a successful product as a result of a forecast that was too high are just as real, if not as apparent, as those incurred from product failures.

The costs incurred from lost opportunities as a result of overly conservative forecasts do not appear in the cost section of the income statement. The fact that current accounting practice does not permit these "costs" to be entered in a set of accounts does not make them any less real, however. A missed opportunity for a profitable new product or the sales lost on existing products because of inventory outages result in lower revenues and profits than would have been the case with more accurate forecasting.

The lost opportunities for new products are sometimes as dramatic, although seldom as well publicized, as product failures. Sperry-Rand developed and marketed the first commercial electronic computer, the Univac I, in the early 1950s. A point forecast of the potential market in the United States for computers of that size (very small by today's standards) was a total of 20. This forecast was made before IBM had

---

[31] J. R. Nevin, "Laboratory Experiments for Estimating Consumer Demand: A Validation Study," *Journal of Marketing Research,* **11** (August 1974), 261–268.

[32] See also J. E. Reinmuth, "Forecasting the Impact of a New Product Introduction," *Journal of the Academy of Marketing Science,* **2** (Spring 1974), 391–400.

[33] See T. L. Berg, *Mismarketing: Case Histories of Marketing Missfires* (Garden City, N.Y.; Doubleday & Company, Inc., 1970) and "New Products: The Push Is on Marketing," *Business Week* (March 4, 1972), 72–77, for other new product failures.

placed its first computer on the market and undoubtedly contributed to Sperry-Rand's loss of position in the field. Lever Brothers did not introduce a detergent until Proctor and Gamble's Tide was successfully marketed because of a forecast that detergents would not get an appreciable share of the soap market. Hiram-Walker underestimated the initial demand for a new chocolate-mint liqueur.

The costs of forecasting errors are usually asymmetrical. That is, the cost of errors of high forecasts will usually not be the same as the cost of errors of low forecasts. This suggests that one will ordinarily want to make the forecast such that *the risk of incurring the higher cost error is less than that for the lower cost error.*[34]

The Choice of Forecasting Model

More than a dozen different forecasting methods have been presented in this chapter and variations of most of them exist that have not been discussed. Since such a variety of methods exist, the question may legitimately be raised, "How does one go about selecting a forecasting method?"

In selecting a method in a specific forecasting situation, one should first compare the requirements of the forecast with the capabilities of the method. In general, forecast requirements consist of (1) *accuracy* specification, (2) *data* requirement, and (3) *time* availability. If accuracy to within ±5 per cent is required, methods that are judged to yield forecasts of no better than ±10 per cent accuracy need no longer be considered (unless, of course, no other method is expected to give better accuracy than that). If the *data* required by the method are not available (as, for example, time series data in forecasting sales of new products), then some other method must be found. A similar situation exists with respect to *time;* if a method cannot reasonably be expected to produce a forecast within the time available, it logically cannot be considered further for use.

The application of these screening criteria will usually eliminate a sizable number of potential forecasting methods. The choice among those remaining methods is essentially a cost/benefit type of decision where greater accuracy is weighed against added costs. This decision can be made using an appropriate decision rule, as discussed in Chapter 2.

As a final comment, the option of using more than one forecasting method for the same sales forecast should always be considered. In the authors' experience most companies do, in fact, use at least two methods of forecasting sales.

[34] See E. C. Bratt, *Business Forecasting* (New York: McGraw-Hill Book Co., Inc., 1970), p. 317 for an elaboration of this point.

Evaluation of Forecasts

The results of a study of the accuracy of forecasts of sales and profits of 338 companies made in 1972 are shown in Table 16–8. As indicated there, about one-third of division sales forecasts for the coming year are within 5 per cent and about three-quarters of such forecasts are within 10 per cent of the actual sales. As would be expected, the accuracy of earnings forecasts is lower; only about one of five division annual forecasts of profits is within 5 per cent and three of five are within 10 per cent. The quarterly and corporate forecasts are more accurate for both sales and earnings.

Table 16–8 Comparison of Forecasting and Actual Sales and Earnings—
338 Companies*

Forecast Variable and Time Period	Cumulative Percentage of Responding Companies— Variation of Forecast from Actual Less Than			
	±5%	±10%	±15%	±20%
Sales				
Quarterly				
Corporate	72%	94%	96%	98%
Division	55	87	95	98
Annual				
Corporate	53	84	93	95
Division	36	74	88	94
Earnings				
Quarterly				
Corporate	58	85	90	93
Division	43	76	87	92
Annual				
Corporate	37	70	80	87
Division	22	58	73	82

*Source: Study commissioned by the Financial Executive Foundation and reported in "How Accurate Are Forecasts?" *Financial Executive*, **61** (March 1973), 25–28.

Forecasts for new products are substantially less accurate than for existing products. A study of forecasts of sales for 63 new products and of earnings for 53 of the same products indicates that only about one in four of the sales forecasts and one in six of the earning forecasts for the first year were within 10 per cent of the actual. The performance for the full planning period—an average of three years—did not improve appreciably.

The median error for the planning period for sales forecasts was 26 per cent and for earnings forecasts was 46 per cent.[35]

Although the data given on forecasting results give some general indications of the level of accuracies that may be expected, they cannot necessarily be used as a benchmark for evaluation of an individual company's forecasts. They represent, at best, an average of forecast performance for a number of companies. A wide range of products and market situations are included. An individual company may be in a forecasting situation that is substantially more or less difficult than the average reflected in the tables.

Evaluation of sales forecasts is best done using two measures: (1) *a*

Table 16–9 Actual and Forecast Sales of New Cars in the United States, 1968–1972 (In millions of units. Seasonally adjusted; moving two-quarter totals at annual rates)*

			Forecasts			
			Intentions Data		$Y_{t+1} = Y_t$	
		Actual Sales	*Forecast*	*Error*	*Forecast*	*Error*
Two Quarter Period		(1)	(2)	(1)–(2)	(3)	(1)–(3)
1968:	1st & 2nd	7.7	7.4	.3	—	—
	2nd & 3rd	8.3	7.6	.7	7.7	.6
	3rd & 4th	8.3	7.6	.7	8.3	0
	4th & 1st	7.9	7.8	.1	8.3	.4
1969:	1st & 2nd	8.3	7.1	.7	7.9	.4
	2nd & 3rd	8.2	7.9	.3	8.3	.1
	3rd & 4th	7.9	8.3	.4	8.2	.3
	4th & 1st	7.4	8.0	.6	7.9	.5
1970:	1st & 2nd	7.1	7.9	.8	7.4	.3
	2nd & 3rd	7.4	7.5	.1	7.1	.3
	3rd & 4th	7.0	7.8	.8	7.4	.4
	4th & 1st	6.9	7.7	.8	7.0	.1
1971:	1st & 2nd	7.8	8.0	.2	6.9	.9
	2nd & 3rd	8.2	7.6	.6	7.8	.4
	3rd & 4th	8.4	7.6	.8	8.2	.2
	4th & 1st	8.5	8.4	.1	8.4	.1
1972:	1st & 2nd	8.6	8.0	.6	8.5	.1
	2nd & 3rd	8.8	8.6	.2	8.6	.2
	3rd & 4th	8.4	8.6	.2	8.8	.4

* *Source:* Adapted from data given in "Consumer Buying Indicators," *Current Population Series* P-65, No. 45, U.S. Department of Commerce, Bureau of the Census (March 1973), 5.

[35] D. S. Tull, "The Relationship of Predicted to Actual Sales and Profits of New Product Introductions," *The Journal of Business,* **40** (July 1967), 249.

forecast of sales should be made each forecasting period using a naïve model and the accuracies compared over time with those of the primary forecasting method(s), and (2) *a review of forecasting accuracy over time should be made periodically.* If the accuracy of the primary method(s) forecasts is not better than that of the naïve model, on the average, a serious forecasting problem may be indicated. (Of course, in some cases, the naïve method may provide such accurate forecasts that no improvement is required.) If the accuracy of the primary method forecasts does not improve over time, a forecasting problem may also be indicated.

An example of the use of a naïve model in evaluating forecasts made by another method is the evaluation and resulting decision made by the Bureau of the Census concerning forecasts made from surveys of consumers to determine their intentions with respect to buying automobiles during the next six months. The decision, made in early 1973, was to stop publishing data on anticipated levels of purchases of automobiles because the accuracy of the forecasts obtained was not an improvement upon the accuracy of the forecasts "which would be obtained under the naïve assumption that the level of purchases during any six-month period would be equal to the level during the previous six months."[36]

The actual sales and the sales forecast from the intentions data and the naïve model are shown in Table 16–9.

Summary

This chapter has dealt with an important and pervasive problem of marketing management, namely sales forecasting. The three general methods of sales forecasting (*judgmental methods, time series analysis* and *projection,* and *causal methods*) were discussed. Each of several forecasting techniques that can be used in each of these methods was described, typical applications given, the data and time required listed, and accuracy and ability to identify turning points assessed. A discussion of *error costs* and *the value of information in forecasts* was then given. The chapter concluded by considering *the evaluation of forecasts.*

Questions and Problems

16.1. The Bayshore Company has been producing an automatic dishwasher detergent for several years. Until the last two years it has advertised at a monthly rate of $100,000 and has had a case price to the trade of $19.

---

[36] "Consumer Buying Indicators," *Current Population Reports,* Series P-65, No. 45, U.S. Department of Commerce, Bureau of the Census (March 1973), 5.

During the last 21 months it has changed prices and amounts of advertising as shown. The seasonal sales index for each of the months is as shown in the table.

Month	Sales ($000)	Advertising ($000)	Bayshore Price/Case	Average of Competitors Price/Case	Seasonal Index
Last year					
J	$1,404	$105	$19.00	$20.00	1.05
F	1,399	115	19.00	20.00	1.03
M	1,404	115	18.50	20.00	1.01
A	1,347	125	18.50	19.00	1.00
M	1,391	140	18.50	19.00	.97
J	1,337	140	18.00	18.50	.96
J	1,287	130	18.00	18.50	.94
A	1,274	125	18.00	18.50	.94
S	1,380	120	17.50	18.50	1.00
O	1,398	140	17.50	18.00	1.01
N	1,430	135	18.00	18.50	1.04
D	1,457	130	18.00	19.00	1.05
Present year					
J	1,470	130	18.50	19.50	1.05
F	1,474	130	18.50	20.00	1.03
M	1,407	130	19.00	20.00	1.01
A	1,371	120	19.00	20.00	1.00
M	1,383	135	19.50	21.00	.97
J	1,360	140	20.00	21.00	.96
J	1,343	145	20.00	21.00	.94
A	1,305	140	20.00	20.50	.94
S	1,418	140	20.00	21.00	1.00

(a) Consideration is being given by Bayshore management to raising price to $21. per case beginning October 1. Management does not believe that the competitors will change their prices during the month. Assuming this to be the case, what reply should the marketing research department give to a request by management for an estimate of the effect that such a price change by Bayshore would have on sales in October?

(b) In July, a proposal to raise the October, November, and December advertising budgets to $150,000 was being considered. A request was made to the marketing research department to estimate the effect that such an increase would have on sales. What estimate should the research department have given?

(c) Advertising and price for the Bayshore detergent for October, November, and December have been set at the levels shown. The average price of competitive products has been forecast for each of the months and is also shown. Prepare a sales forecast for each of the months for the Bayshore product.

Month	Sales ($000)	Adver- tising ($000)	Bayshore Price/Case	Average of Competitor Price/Case	Seasonal Index
October		$140	$20.50	$21.00	1.01
November		145	21.00	21.50	1.04
December		150	21.00	21.50	1.05

16.2. The sales and the seasonal sales index for a standard food item over the two-year period just concluded were as follows:

	Sales (Seasonally Unadjusted, in Units)		Seasonal Sales Index*
	Year Before Last	Last Year	
J	174,980	195,497	1.23
F	137,615	162,229	1.24
M	117,325	143,651	1.21
A	154,865	192,453	1.10
M	120,749	133,087	.89
J	96,160	113,597	.63
J	153,454	114,603	.93
A	109,833	115,795	.74
S	122,374	131,700	.90
O	175,995	187,486	1.23
N	145,077	130,709	.95
D	140,765	149,143	.95

* Calculated from sales data for past 4 years.

(a) Prepare a forecast for January for the present year using your judgment after having inspected the data.

(b) Prepare a forecast for January for the present year using the naïve model (i) $Y_{t+1} = Y_t + (Y_t - Y_{t-1})$ and (ii) $Y_{t+1} = \dfrac{Y_t}{Y_{t-1}} Y_t$.

(c) Prepare a forecast for January using a 24-month moving average.

(d) Prepare a forecast for January using a 12-month moving average.

(e) Prepare a forecast for January using exponential smoothing with $\alpha = .2$.

16.3. Wholesale sales of beer and personal income in the United States by month during 1972–1973 were as follows:

	Wholesale Sales of Beer in the United States, 1972–73 (Seasonally Unadjusted, Millions of Dollars at Current Prices)		Personal Income (Annual Rate Billions of Dollars)	
	1972	*1973*	*1972*	*1973*
J	$432	$493	901.5	989.1
F	461	469	912.8	997.4
M	536	543	918.0	1,003.3
A	499	545	923.6	1,011.6
M	646	676	927.7	1,018.7
J	668	686	927.0	1,026.6
J	629	685	935.0	1,035.6
A	678	699	944.4	1,047.3
S	574	565	951.3	1,058.5
O	547	620	969.0	1,068.5
N	540	566	977.6	1,079.4
D	530	558	983.6	1,089.0

Make a forecast for wholesale sales of beer for January, 1974. (The seasonal index for January is .80.)

(a) using your judgment after inspecting the data.

(b) using the naïve model (i) $Y_{t+1} = \dfrac{Y_t}{Y_{t-1}} \cdot Y_t$ and (ii) $Y_{t+1} = Y_t + (Y_t - Y_{t-1})$.

(c) using a 12-month moving average.

(d) using a 6-month moving average.

(e) using exponential smoothing with $\alpha = .2$.

(f) using statistical trend analysis (simple linear regression).

(g) using a regression model with personal income as a predictor variable. (Note: personal income for January, 1974, will have to be estimated in order to make the forecast.)

(h) How would you compute a seasonal index for June from these data?

16.4. Department store sales in Scranton, Pennsylvania, by month for 1972–1973 were as follows:

Department Store Sales in Scranton, Pa., 1972–1973 (Seasonally unadjusted, $000 at current prices)

	1972	*1973*
J	$2,827	$3,216
F	2,674	3,162
M	4,115	4,435
A	3,827	4,767
M	4,501	4,792
J	3,985	4,587

Department Store Sales in Scranton, Pa., 1972–1973
(Seasonally unadjusted, $000 at current prices)

	1972	1973
J	4,393	4,223
A	4,603	5,062
S	4,727	5,030
O	5,106	5,270
N	5,892	7,021
D	8,380	9,181

Make a forecast for January, 1974 (The seasonal index for January is .63.)

(a) using your judgment after inspecting the data.

(b) using the naïve model (i) $Y_{t+1} = \dfrac{Y_t}{Y_{t-1}} \cdot Y_t$ and (ii) $Y_t = Y_t + (Y_t - Y_{t-1})$.

(c) using a 12-month moving average.

(d) using exponential smoothing with $\alpha = .10$.

(e) using a regression model with personal income as a predictor variable. (Note: personal income in the United States for this period is given in Problem 16.3. An estimate for January, 1974, must be made in order to make the forecast).

16.5. Sales of lumber and construction materials by merchant wholesalers, an index of industrial materials prices, an index of construction contracts, and an index of new private housing unit building permits by month for 1972–1973 are as follows:

	Sales of Lumber and Construction Materials by Merchant Wholesalers (Seasonally Unadjusted, Millions of Dollars at Current Prices)	Index of Industrial Material Prices (1967–100)	Index of Construction Contracts Total Value (Seasonally Adjusted 1967–100)	Index of New Private Housing Units Authorized by Local Building Permits (Seasonally Adjusted, 1967–100)
1972				
J	1.051	110.7	160	195.2
F	1.026	113.0	155	185.8
M	1.211	117.2	159	185.5
A	1.208	119.5	167	184.9
M	1.383	124.3	165	176.2
J	1.434	123.8	154	189.7
J	1.305	123.7	155	189.2
A	1.542	124.6	180	196.6

	Sales of Lumber and Construction Materials by Merchant Wholesalers (Seasonally Unadjusted, Millions of Dollars at Current Prices)	Index of Industrial Material Prices (1967–100)	Index of Construction Contracts Total Value (Seasonally Adjusted 1967–100)	Index of New Private Housing Units Authorized by Local Building Permits (Seasonally Adjusted, 1967–100)
S	1.427	124.8	187	203.9
O	1.532	128.1	171	199.8
N	1.486	131.6	177	191.8
D	1.231	134.8	163	206.7
1973				
J	1.339	139.3	181	192.4
F	1.293	147.5	191	190.4
M	1.594	155.3	193	183.5
A	1.675	158.2	177	167.1
M	1.759	162.9	173	158.4
J	1.729	170.1	183	174.9
J	1.608	178.1	175	153.4
A	1.755	189.8	199	150.8
S	1.544	186.3	182	137.5
O	1.630	188.1	191	113.4
N	1.538	192.4	194	113.2
D	1.349	208.9	161	106.6

(a) Do either the index of construction contracts or index of new private housing unit building permits appear to lead sales of lumber and construction materials of merchant wholesalers? If so, by how many months? (Note: It will be necessary to deseasonalize and deflate the time series on sales.)

(b) Make a forecast for January, 1974, for lumber and construction material sales by

    i. using your judgment after inspecting the data.

    ii. using the naïve model (1) $Y_{t+1} = \dfrac{Y_t}{Y_{t-1}} \cdot Y_t$ and (2) $Y_{t+1} = Y_t + (Y_t - Y_{t-1})$.

    iii. using a 12-month moving average.

    iv. using exponential smoothing with $\alpha = .2$.

    v. using statistical trend analysis.

    vi. using a regression model with the index of construction contracts and index of new private housing unit building permits lagged by the number of months that appears to be appropriate.

16.6 Monthly whiskey production for the years 1969 through 1972 was as shown.

1969*	1970*	1971*	1972*
17,007,814	15,298,200	12,686,714	12,865,426
16,095,067	14,955,686	12,957,953	12,280,062
17,103,444	15,608,291	13,418,074	13,372,218
17,253,981	15,210,767	10,473,359	11,308,730
14,369,113	12,846,089	8,540,448	12,107,558
12,074,002	10,148,179	6,850,735	9,889,771
10,646,109	9,120,832	6,578,899	4,716,770
7,711,356	7,155,924	5,858,591	3,625,706
12,224,358	10,373,164	8,556,804	6,616,937
16,032,923	12,198,024	10,791,203	9,319,127
13,998,832	11,154,360	11,410,252	10,514,738
15,357,945	12,290,856	11,254,274	9,943,736

* *Source:* Distilled Spirits Institute, *1972 Annual Statistical Review.*
Reprinted with permission.

    (a) Prepare a seasonal index for all 12 months using the
       i. centered moving average method
      ii. Census Method II approach (requires a computer program)
    (b) Using the index for January produced in (a), compute a forecast for
        January, 1973 using
       i. 24-month moving average
      ii. exponential smoothing with $\alpha = .2$
     iii. statistical trend analysis

16.7. Obtain a (a) point (b) interval (c) probability distribution forecast from a friend of the average of his final grades for courses being taken during the current term.

Selected Bibliography

Box, G. E. P., and G. M. Jenkins. *Time Series Analysis—Forecasting and Control* (San Francisco: Holden-Day, 1970). An excellent treatment of the analysis of time series and their applications to forecasting.

Brown, R. G., *Smoothing, Forecasting, and Prediction of Discrete Time Series.* Englewood-Cliffs, N.J.: Prentice-Hall, Inc., 1963. Despite its age, perhaps still the best book available on exponential smoothing.

Chisholm, R. K., and G. R. Whitaker, Jr. *Forecasting Methods.* Homewood, Ill.: Richard D. Irwin, Inc., 1971. A concise and clearly written book that deals with all the major methods of forecasting discussed in this chapter.

Daniels, L. M., *Business Forecasting for the 1970's: A Selected Annotated Bibliography.* Boston, Mass.; Baker Library, Harvard University, 1970. Although now somewhat dated, this bibliography is still a useful reference work for materials on forecasting methods and data sources.

Elliot-Jones, M. F., *Input-Output Analysis: A Nontechnical Description.* New York: The Conference Board, 1971. A well-written treatment of input-output analysis with application to an industry.

MOORE, G. H., and J. SHISHIN. *Indicators of Business Expansion and Contraction,* National Bureau of Economic Research, 1967. A definitive book by two of the leading investigators of economic indicators.

NELSON, C. R., *Applied Time Series Analysis for Managerial Forecasting.* San Francisco; Holden-Day, Inc., 1973. Still another good book on time series analysis, although written at a level that requires some background in statistics in order to be read easily.

EVANS, M. K., *Macro-Economic Activity: Theory, Forecasting and Control.* New York: Harper & Row Publishers, Inc., 1969. A good reference work on econometric models and forecasting.

SILK, S., and M. C. CURLEY. *A Primer on Business Forecasting.* New York: Random House, Inc.: 1970. A simply written book that deals with both methods and sources of data for business forecasting.

Case 16–1

Tipton's Downtown Store: Relocation Analysis*

Tipton's currently operates two shoe stores (See Case 15–1). The downtown store must soon be either closed permanently, moved into another downtown location, or moved outside the downtown area because of an urban renewal program. Since the firm already has an outlet in the area's only major shopping center, moving outside the downtown area is not considered to be a feasible alternative at this time.

The urban renewal program that is forcing an immediate decision on management has been in progress for three years and is scheduled to last two more years. Most of the previously deteriorating downtown area has been or will be completely rebuilt or remodeled. Portions of the area will be made into pedestrian malls, and the area will be ringed by free parking lots.

During the past three years, construction on buildings, roads, and parking lots has undoubtedly kept many customers away from the downtown area. These problems will continue to exist for two more years, although they should not be as severe. In addition, numerous stores have closed their downtown outlets and moved into the major shopping center or one of the smaller centers. However, the city planners are confident that new retail outlets will move in as the modern buildings become available. In addition, they have commitments for much of the extensive professional and office space being constructed.

Tipton's can acquire either of two spaces in the downtown area. Both are as desirable as the existing outlet as far as location is concerned. The first is the same size as the current outlet and would cost the same.

---

* Originally prepared by D. I. Hawkins and C. M. Lillis. Used with permission of the authors.

Maximum monthly sales possible in the current outlet are $120,000. The outlet is operating right at the break-even level.

The second available outlet is 15 per cent larger than the existing store and would require a 4 per cent increase over current annual sales to reach the break-even point.

Sales data for the past two years (since the shopping center outlet was opened) are provided as follows.

Monthly Sales Figures for Tipton's Downtown Store			
Date	Sales	Date	Sales
April	$ 70,715	April	$ 70,856
May	71,877	May	71,554
June	80,461	June	86,261
July	61,906	July	85,522
August	105,521	August	113,703
September	109,314	September	105,583
October	86,125	October	100,327
November	71,072	November	75,743
December	111,876	December	110,479
January	74,131	January	77,204
February	57,333	February	55,522
March	61,050	March	58,601

What should Tipton's do with the downtown store?

Case 16–2
Tipton's Shopping Center Store: Expansion Analysis*

Tipton's shopping center store has, after only two year's operation, exceeded the capacity of its current location. Management believes that the maximum capacity of the current store is $120,000 in sales in any month. Anytime sales are above that level, as it was three times in the past eight months, management believes that potential sales and customer goodwill are lost because of slow service and overcrowding.

Tipton's was located in the shopping center when it opened. The entire center has experienced growth similar to Tipton's although not as dramatic. The shopping center has decided to add a new wing, and Tipton's has an option to lease as much space in the new wing as it desires. Although the management of Tipton's is fairly convinced that a larger outlet is required, it is undecided as to how large it should be.

* Originally prepared by D. I. Hawkins and C. M. Lillis. Used with permission of the authors.

As can be seen in the following figures, sales have shown steady growth over the past two years. However, management is not certain how long this trend will continue. It is aware that the downtown area has lost business to the center in part because of the ongoing urban renewal program. (See Case 16–1 for background information.) This program ends in two years and may result in a shift of business back to the downtown area.

Should the outlet be expanded? By how much?

Monthly Sales Figures for Tipton's Shopping Center Store			
Date	Sales	Date	Sales
April	$ 53,702	April	$ 71,615
May	67,695	May	74,104
June	65,400	June	83,149
July	54,197	July	64,602
August	110,029	August	134,104
September	101,990	September	120,109
October	82,871	October	107,038
November	81,956	November	98,611
December	114,610	December	129,856
January	73,305	January	80,900
February	52,177	February	64,108
March	76,553	March	92,508

Case 16–3

Acacia Cement Company

The management of the Acacia Cement Company located in Los Angeles County, California, had been looking for an improved method of forecasting sales. The company's market area included Imperial, Inyo, Kern, Los Angeles, Orange, Santa Barbara, San Bernardino, San Luis Obispo, San Diego, Riverside, and Ventura counties. Forecast errors had averaged almost 10 per cent during 1969 and 1970, and the error in the first quarter of 1971 had been almost 13 per cent.

Sales forecasts were made for two quarters ahead, with a new forecast made each quarter. The forecasting was done by the president and the marketing manager using what they referred to as their "wet finger in the wind" method. Once each quarter they met in the president's office with data on orders, construction contract awards for the market area, salesman call reports, and other information. After reviewing these data, they each wrote their forecasts for the next two quarters on a piece of paper.

Differences were discussed and a final sales forecast (usually a compromise that was close to the average of their individual forecasts) was made for each quarter.

As a result of their inability to forecast accurately, the company had been forced to keep large inventories on hand to avoid losing sales when demand was unexpectedly high. Both labor and interest costs were rising in 1971, adding to the already high costs of carrying excess inventory. The president decided that some means had to be found to make better forecasts so they could reduce inventories and operating costs.

A consultant was called in to work on the problem. He found that a trade association of cement manufacturers and importers and exporters provided data on cement sales each month to contractors in each of the counties of Acacia's market area. He ran an analysis of past sales data for the industry and for Acacia and found that Acacia's market share had remained close to 9.2 per cent for some time. In discussions with the president and marketing manager, they stated that it was reasonable to expect that the company's share would continue to be at about this same level unless some major change took place in the industry.

The consultant recognized that if this were the case, the major problem was to forecast industry sales. If Acacia's share stayed relatively constant (or it changed slowly over time), finding a method of forecasting industry sales with the required degree of accuracy would permit Acacia's sales to be forecast with the accuracy needed. Acacia would only have to multiply the industry sales forecast by its estimated market share to obtain a company sales forecast.

Acacia's sales force called on contractors engaged in three different kinds of construction. Residential contractors were called on who specialized in houses and apartment buildings as were nonresidential contractors who built commercial, industrial, and military buildings. The largest contractors were those involved in construction of such projects as highways, dams, flood control, bridges, and miscellaneous other civil and military engineering projects. The consultant was aware that there was a lag time of several months between the awarding of a contract for a construction project and the use of cement in the actual construction. Although the lag was shortest for residential construction and longest for the larger engineering projects (highways and dams), the company officials believed that the average lag time was about six months.

Contract award data were made available each month for each of these types of construction projects from one or more governmental agencies. Data on residential construction contracts were available from the county and city agencies responsible for issuing permits and inspecting the buildings, the California Division of Highways announced awards for constructing highways and bridges, and the other state and federal agencies involved in construction activity in Southern California made similar announcements. The dollar amounts for residential and non-residential construction contracts in each county were compiled and published each month by the research department of a bank in Los Angeles. A trade publication, the *Engineering News Record,* published information every month on awards for engineering projects. Acacia's marketing department had been collecting this information since 1966 for the salesmen to use in planning their sales calls.

The consultant decided to run some regression analyses for the period from 1966 to early 1971 to see if dollar contract awards for a given month could be used to forecast industry cement sales several months later. He planned to try lead times of five, six, and seven months for the contract awards to see which one gave the regression equation that forecast cement sales most accurately. Before he could run the regressions, however, he knew that he would have to make several adjustments to the contract award data.

One necessary adjustment was for changes in construction costs since 1966. Costs had risen an average of 3 per cent per year since then, and so a dollar of contract award in 1971 represented substantially less actual construction (and less cement to be used in it) than a dollar in 1966.

Another adjustment was required for the different number of working days each month. After allowing for calendar variation and union holidays, the number of working days varied from as few as 18 to as many as 23 per month. Other things being equal, cement sales in an 18-workday month could be over 20 per cent less than those in a 23-workday month for this reason alone. The contract awards and industry cement sales were both converted to averages per working day in each month to allow for this factor.

An adjustment was also needed for seasonal variation in construction activity. In Southern California this was mainly the result of rain since there was no freezing weather. The months with the heaviest rain were in the winter and this was when the amount of construction was lowest.

The consultant also decided that he needed to adjust the construction award data for the effects of large engineering awards. The award for a dam, for example, was so large that it might amount to as much as one-half of all other engineering awards. The effect would be to distort the relationship between contract awards and cement sales since all the cement to be used in the dam would not be used in one month.

After obtaining daily averages of the adjusted data for each of the three sectors of construction activity, the values were summed for each month to obtain average daily contract awards for all construction. The resulting data, along with data on industry sales of cement in Acacia's market area, are given for the period from July, 1966, through March, 1971, in the following table.

Average Daily Construction Activity (*X*) and Cement Consumption (*Y*) in Southern California

Year	Month	X Seasonally adjusted, 1964 dollars (000)	Y Barrels of cement (000)	Year	Month	X Seasonally adjusted, 1964 dollars (000)	Y Barrels of cement (000)
1966	August	99.8	83.7	1969	January	108.3	89.3
	September	96.5	82.3		February	110.0	89.3
	October	99.2	80.9		March	108.3	86.9
	November	94.9	79.5		April	11.2	94.5
	December	97.6	73.5		May	109.3	94.5
1967	January	93.3	75.1		June	106.9	96.2
	February	93.3	75.9		July	107.5	96.3
	March	91.7	81.3		August	105.4	93.5
	April	94.1	78.7		September	106.2	88.1
	May	91.6	77.0		October	103.6	84.6
	June	87.1	75.9		November	107.0	84.9
	July	84.7	76.3		December	106.5	86.0
	August	84.8	78.2	1970	January	105.8	85.3
	September	89.2	78.2		February	102.2	86.2
	October	92.0	78.6		March	102.8	88.0
	November	90.0	75.4		April	98.3	90.2
	December	90.4	79.9		May	99.5	87.9
1968	January	88.4	74.1		June	99.8	87.9
	February	93.2	70.3		July	101.7	87.0
	March	91.0	62.7		August	106.2	85.4
	April	88.9	70.3		September	106.5	84.2
	May	94.0	77.7		October	108.1	80.5
	June	103.7	83.6		November	110.5	83.4
	July	109.2	83.9		December	113.4	84.6
	August	109.0	85.0	1971	January	115.0	92.1
	September	103.6	86.3		February	105.8	93.0
	October	105.0	89.4		March	102.6	93.6
	November	103.8	92.7				
	December	108.1	96.9				

The consultant planned to run simple linear regression analyses with the contract awards lagged by five, six, and seven months to see which gave the best "fit." He then planned to use the regression equation for the lag period with the best fit to forecast daily average values for industry cement sales for each month for the number of months (five, six, or seven) that the equation permitted. These forecasts could then be converted from daily averages to monthly totals by multiplying by the number of workdays in that month. He would also have to deseasonalize the forecast by multiplying each monthly total forecast by the index for that month.

He had already calculated the number of workdays in each of the next seven months and had the monthly indexes available from his earlier adjustments. These values were

	April	May	June	July	August	September	October
Number of working days in month	20.50	22.00	22.00	20.50	22.75	20.25	22.25
Monthly index of constrution activity	100.3	104.3	106.0	106.0	106.3	106.3	105.0

1. Should the consultant have used a lag period of five, six, or seven months for the construction awards for forecasting industry cement sales? Why?
2. Prepare a forecast of industry cement sales in Acacia's market area for each month for the number of months consistent with your answer to Question 1.
3. The actual cement consumption (000 barrels) for each of the next seven months was as listed. What was the per cent error of the forecast for each month? For the next quarter? Was this an improvement?

April	1,885	July	1,948
May	2,079	August	2,220
June	2,019	September	1,969

CHAPTER 17

The Control, Evaluation, and Reporting of Marketing Research

Marketing research, like all other activities in a business firm, must be subject to control and evaluation by the firm's top executives. Typically, control of the day-to-day research operations are delegated to the director of the research department. However, ultimately top management is responsible for both the control and evaluation of the research function.

Evaluation of the contribution of marketing research is a difficult process. Part of the reason for this difficulty is that its contribution depends not only on the technical competence with which it is conducted but also on the extent to which it is utilized by the marketing managers. Marketing research is generally a staff function, and the research director cannot order the various marketing managers to utilize his output. Therefore, effective communication is a particularly important aspect of the research function. This chapter is concerned with all three of these areas—*control, evaluation,* and *communication.*

Control and Evaluation

The control and evaluation of marketing research must take place on two distinct levels: the *aggregate* level of the firm's total research effort and the *individual project level*.[1] Systematic efforts to control and formally evaluate the performance of the marketing research department or specific projects have been rather uncommon. However, as marketing research continues to increase in importance in decision making and in share of the total budget, formal control procedures will become more widely adopted.

Individual Projects

Control of individual projects can be achieved in a number of ways. The simplest technique, yet an extremely useful one, is the *checklist*. It is possible to develop specific checklists for standard research studies such as product tests, package tests, and evaluations of advertising copy. Such a list helps ensure that the researcher (or the research proposal) has not overlooked any serious area of concern.

PERT networks provide an excellent means for controlling individual research projects (see Chapter 4). Actual time and direct cost figures can be compared with projected time and cost figures *while the project is in progress*. Unfavorable deviations from projection can be investigated rapidly and corrective action initiated before permanent damage is done. Using PERT for a day by day or weekly control mechanism does require substantial supervision effort. However, this effort mainly involves frequent reports from the various field groups and clerical compilation and comparison of actual against planned performance.

After each project is completed, various members of the project team should be interviewed to uncover any problems or potential errors that might not be reflected in the final report. The ultimate use (or nonuse) of the resultant data should also be determined. This will indicate how accurately the management problem is being translated into a research problem, how timely the research is, and how effective the researchers are at communicating with management. Finally, as time passes and actions are taken based on the research project, an attempt should be made to assess the accuracy and usefulness of the data. If the research data proves to be inadequate, steps should be taken to determine why. The long-run result of such investigations is improved research.

[1] This section is based on J. H. Myers and R. R. Mead, *The Management of Marketing Research* (Scranton, Pa.: International Textbook Company, 1969), Chap. 7; and J. H. Myers and A. C. Samli, "Management Control of Marketing Research," *Journal of Marketing Research,* **6** (August 1969), 267–277.

The Total Research Effort

Each individual research project can be well done and have a higher expected value than cost and yet the total research effort may not be as effective as it should be. This can occur when too many individual projects are of the "fire fighting" nature and are not focused on the long-range information needs of the firm. For example, a series of studies that select the "best" advertisement from a set of competing advertisements without generating information on what constitutes a good advertisement is not as effective as it might be.

The Advisory Committee. A *marketing research advisory* committee represents an effective means of providing guidance for the firm's total research effort. Such a committee consists of representatives from all of the major functions served by research such as advertising, sales, product planning, long-rang planning, and so forth. The committee should be chaired by the chief marketing executive. Naturally, the director of marketing research is also a member of the committee.

The committee's function is to provide *"the overall direction of the marketing research program, channeling efforts toward problem areas and projects of the greatest importance to the marketing system."*[2] The committee should establish a running "annual research plan" that is updated every three to six months. In companies where research is extensively utilized, a more general five- and even ten-year plan may also be maintained. Such plans are stated in terms of general information needs, *not* specific research projects.

Each committee meeting should begin with a review of projects completed since the last meeting. The review should focus on the use being made of the resultant information and how this information relates to the annual research plan. Limited output or projects not closely related to the firm's long-run information needs can be quickly identified.

After the review session, the committee should examine future needs for information. Since representatives from all the primary users of marketing research will be present, a relatively accurate appraisal or short-term future needs should be possible. However, the committee must also keep in mind the longer run information requirements of the firm that may utilize scarce resources without short-term returns. In addition, the research department should not be "overcommitted." Approximately 25 per cent of its total time should be left free for unexpected requirements.[3] For example, the test marketing of a new competing product may force the research department into a rapid analysis of the new product's sales potential.

[2] Myers and Mead, op. cit., 116.
[3] Ibid., 118.

The research department should also be allowed 5 to 10 per cent of its time to do as it desires. It should have the freedom and resources to engage in some pure or applied research of its own choosing. Such a practice helps a research department stay fresh and enthusiastic. And important practical findings are often obtained from such "spare time" research.

Two major benefits are derived from the use of a marketing research advisory committee. The first is a well-developed guide that focuses research efforts on the information needs of the firm. Even more important is the fact that everyone directly concerned with the marketing research department helps define its goals. This requires communication with and understanding of the research department. The result tends to be a more effective working relationship between the research department and the users of marketing research.

Auditing Marketing Research. A periodic audit, every two to five years, of a firm's research department is an excellent supplementary control and evaluation technique. Such an audit can generally be done with maximum effectiveness by an outside consulting firm. An outsider has no personal or departmental position to protect and, if wisely selected, has had research experience with a variety of industries and research methodologies. This experience provides a broader perspective than most "in-house" audit teams can provide.

The audit should follow the general format used by the advisory committee. The audit should, at a minimum, complete the following activities:

1. An examination of several specific research projects to ensure that sound methodologies are being used.
2. An analysis of the utilization of the information generated by the research department.
3. A determination of future information needs of the firm.
4. An examination of the organizational position of the research department in the firm and the internal organization of the department.
5. An analysis of the level of resources allocated to the department in light of its actual and potential contributions to the firm.
6. An analysis of the training and competencies of the staff in light of the future goals of the department.

An audit of the marketing research department by an outside specialist can, if properly conducted, help revitalize the research function. It can introduce new methodologies, change organization structures, and identify new information needs. However, if not properly handled, the outside auditor can be viewed as a threat and the final result will be negative instead of positive. Therefore, it is essential that the research department itself recognize the need for periodic audits and play an active role in the auditing process.

Reporting Research Results

The results of a research project may be reported in written or oral format or both. The importance of *effective* reporting cannot be overemphasized. Regardless of the quality of the research process and the accuracy and usefulness of the resulting data, the data will not be utilized if it is not effectively communicated to the appropriate decision makers.

Written Research Report[4]

Good research reports begin with *clear* thinking on the part of the researcher. The researcher should carefully analyze his readers' needs and organize a detailed outline *prior* to writing the first draft. The first draft should be considered just that—a *first* draft. Few of us write well enough to produce a polished draft the first time. The writer should plan on at least one major rewrite.

Concern for the Audience. The only reason for writing a research report is to communicate something to someone. The someone is the most important aspect of the communications process.[5] The entire research project was performed to generate information that will aid one or more decision makers. The research report must convey that information to these decision makers.

Several facts must be kept in mind. First, most managers are busy. Second, they are generally much less interested in the technical and logical aspects of a research problem than the researcher is. Third, they are seldom well versed in research techniques and terminology. Fourth, if there is more than one reader, and there usually is, they are likely to be different in terms of interests, training, and reasons for reading the report. Finally, managers, like everyone else, prefer interesting reports over dull ones. With these facts in mind, a number of general guides to writing can be offered.

(1) *Focus on the objectives of the study.* The research was initiated to help make a decision. The report should be built around the decision and how the resultant information is relevant to the decision. This is what the manager is interested in. Researchers are often more interested in the research problem and the methodology used to solve it. Unfortunately, many research reports reflect the interest of the researcher rather than the

[4] This section is based on S. H. Britt, "The Writing of Readable Research Reports," *Journal of Marketing Research,* **8** (May 1971), 262–266.

[5] For a theoretical discussion of this aspect of the communications process see W. Schram, "How Communication Works" in W. Schram, ed., *The Process and Effects of Mass Communication* (Urbana, Ill.: University of Illinois Press, 1949).

manager. This can result in unread (and perhaps unreadable) reports, an "ivory tower" image of the research department, and the slow erosion of the research department.

(2) *Minimize the reporting of the technical aspects of the project.* Researchers have an unfortunate, if natural, tendency to attempt to convince management of their expertise and thoroughness in the research report. This leads to detailed discussions of the sampling plan, why it is superior to alternative sampling plans, and so on. Yet few executives are interested in this level of detail. However, the research department might keep such a detailed report *internally* to serve as a guide for future studies and to answer any questions that might arise concerning the methodology of the study.

(3) *Use terminology that matches the vocabulary of the readers.* As Britt expresses it: "Few (managers) can balance a research report, a cup of coffee, and a dictionary at the same time."[6] Terms such as *skewed distribution, correlation coefficient,* or even *significance level* are not necessarily familiar to all marketing managers. It is, of course, often necessary to utilize the concepts that underlie these terms in many research reports. Three strategies are available for dealing with this problem. First, the term can be used, followed by a brief description or explanation. Or, the explanation may be provided first followed by the term. Finally, the technical terms may be omitted altogether and only the underlying concept used. Which approach, or combination of approaches, is best depends on the nature of the audience and the message.

(4) *Develop an interesting writing style.* Research reports should be as interesting to read as possible. There is no inherent reason for a research report to be dull, tedious, or boring. Consider the following statement made by a well-known research executive:

> The use of the analytical techniques of the behavioral sciences will gradually revolutionize the communication arts by predicating their practice upon a body of demonstrably general principles which will be readily available to creative people for increasing their knowledge of consumer response to advertising communication.[7]

Can you imagine reading a report composed of such statements? Unfortunately most researchers have not been trained in effective writing. However, it is never too late to learn. The researcher can consult numerous books and articles on expository writing for sound guidance.

In general, the researcher should strive for simplicity and conciseness. Simplicity does not mean that the audience is talked down to, nor does conciseness mean that the report necessarily be short. However, unnecessary complexity in sentence structure and long-windedness in reporting should be avoided.

---

[6] Britt, op. cit., 265.
[7] This example was provided by Britt, op. cit., 265. It is *not* his statement.

(5) *Use visual aids whenever practical.* Consider the following statement: *Monthly sales by department were: (1) appliances, $453,268; (2) hardware, $362,179; (3) drugs and cosmetics, $198,415; (4) household supplies, $169,327; (5) sporting goods, $69,462; and (6) toys, $38,917.* Data presented in this format are difficult to read and, even more important, seldom leave the reader with a clear impression of the meaning of the data. One way to make the data more meaningful is to present them in a table such as Table 17–1 showing both the absolute amounts and the relative (percentage) amount associated with each department. Each table should be explained in the body of the text.

Table 17–1   Monthly Sales by Department

Department	Sales	Per Cent of Total
Appliances	$ 453,268	35.1%
Hardware	362,197	28.0
Drugs and Cosmetics	198,415	15.4
Household Supplies	169,327	13.1
Sporting Goods	69,462	5.1
Toys	38,917	3.0
Total	$1,291,586	100.0%

Although the table is a definite improvement over presenting the data solely in the text, a *pie chart* is an even more effective manner of conveying the meaning of the data. A pie chart is a circle divided into sections such that each section represents the percentage of the total circle associated with one variable. For example, 35.1 per cent of the firm's monthly sales were appliances. Therefore, 35.1 per cent of the area of the circle should be assigned to appliances. Since there are 360 degrees to a circle, 3.6 degress are 1 per cent of the circle. The section of the circle representing appliance sales should have a central angle of $3.6 \times 35.1 = 126.4$ degrees. Figure 17–1 demonstrates a pie chart based on the data in Table 17–1. Notice how quickly and effectively this figure conveys the relative sales levels of the various departments.

Another useful visual aid is the *bar chart,* which may be either vertical or horizontal. Since the same principles apply in either case, we limit our discussions to the vertical bar chart. A vertical bar chart is constructed by placing rectangles or bars over each value or interval of the variable of interest. The height of the bar represents the level of the variable on the vertical axis. Vertical bar charts are often used to represent changes in a variable over time. Figure 17–2 shows changes in the per-capita consumption of beer in the United States between 1963 and 1972.

The data shown in the bar chart in Figure 17–2 could also be shown in

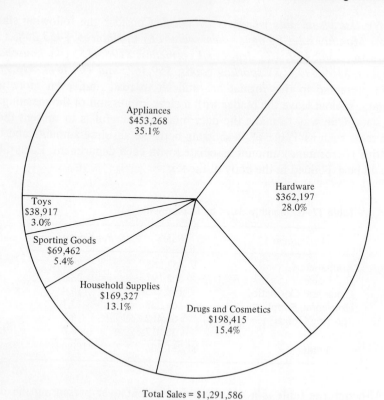

Total Sales = $1,291,586

Figure 17-1   Pie chart of monthly sales by department.

the form of a *line chart* as in Figure 17–3. The bar chart is somewhat less complex appearing and may be more suited to those unaccustomed to dealing with figures.[8] However, line charts are generally superior under the following conditions: (1) *When the data involve a long time period,* (2) *when several series are compared on the same chart,* (3) *when the emphasis is on the movement rather than the actual amount,* (4) *when trends of frequency distribution are presented,* (5) *when a multiple-amount scale is used,* (6) *when estimates, forecasts, interpolation, or extrapolation are to be shown.*[9]

A *histogram* is a vertical bar chart in which the height of the bars represents the relative or cumulative frequency of occurrence of the variable of interest. For example, assume that 730 respondents rate the service provided by a restaurant on a six-point semantic differential scale bounded

[8] M. E. Spear, *Practical Charting Techniques* (New York: McGraw-Hill Book Co., 1969), 163.

[9] Ibid., 74.

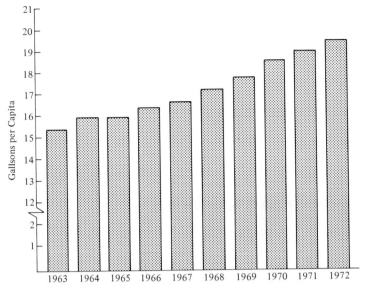

Figure 17–2 Bar chart of per capita consumption of beer in the United States, 1963–1972. [Constructed from material in *Brewers Almanac 1973* (Washington, D.C.: United States Brewers Association, Inc., 1973), p. 82.]

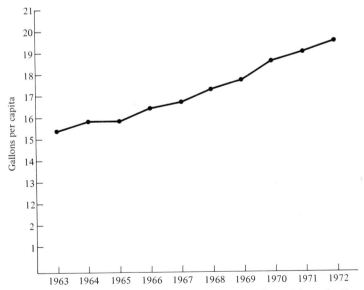

Figure 17–3 Line chart of per capita consumption of beer in the United States, 1963–1972.

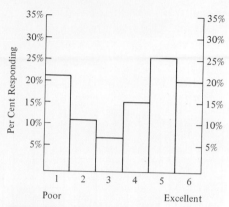

Figure 17–4 Relative frequency histogram of the poor service–excellent service semantic differential item.

by *poor* on the left and *excellent* on the right. The number marking each response from left to right is 154, 79, 50, 112, 198, and 146. Stated in percentages, the responses from left to right would be 21.2, 10.8, 6.8, 15.3, 25.9, and 20.0. Figure 17–4 demonstrates the advantages of presenting this type of data in the form of a histogram.

The histogram makes clear at a glance the bimodal nature of the response (that is, the fact that responses are clustered in two groups). A text presentation of the raw data and/or a comment on the fact that the responses were bimodal would not have the same impact on many readers as the histogram.

In addition to utilizing appropriate visual aids, the report should be as physically attractive as possible. Clear typing, the use of subdivisions, quality paper, and so forth enhance the appearance and, indirectly, the effectiveness of the report.

All of the comments offered are of a general nature. As a researcher becomes familiar with a group of managers, his report style should be adapted to fit their particular needs and preferences.

The Organization of the Report

There is no one format that is best for all occasions. The nature of the audience and the topic of the report combine to determine the most desirable format. However, a general format is suggested in Exhibit 17–1 that can be altered to meet the requirements of most situations. (The minimum content of a research report from an ethical standpoint is presented in Chapter 18.)

Exhibit 17–1   Generalized Format for a
Research Report

I. Title Page
II. Table of Contents
III. Summary
IV. Background
V. Objectives
VI. Research Design
VII. Findings
VIII. Limitations
IX. Conclusions and Recommendations
X. Appendixes

Title Page.   The title page should identify the date of the report, the researcher(s), the topic, and for whom the report is prepared. If the report is for limited distribution, this fact should also be noted on the title page. The title of the report should indicate the nature of the research project as precisely as possible.

Table of Contents.   Unless the report is exceptionally brief, it should contain a table of contents, including the page numbers of major sections and subdivisions within the sections, and a list of all appendixes. If numerous tables or charts are utilized, they should also be listed on a separate page immediately following the table of contents.

Summary.   Not all reports require a summary. Those reports to be read in depth by only a few individuals need not have an initial summary. However, such a summary allows the busy executive to get a "feel of the report" in a short time. He can then decide whether to read the more detailed report, to pass it on to others, or to take other relevant actions.

Generally, the initial summary will emphasize the objectives, findings, conclusions, and recommendations—presented in abbreviated form. The background and research design will be outlined or omitted entirely.

The summary may be sent to some individuals in lieu of the actual report. In an era of increasing shortages and a need to minimize costs, maintaining a limited number of complete reports in the firm's library or research office and sending summaries to most readers makes substantial sense.

Background.   The first section of the report should contain a detailed description of the management problem and the factors that influence it. The researcher cannot assume that everyone who will read the report is familiar with the underlying problem. Often this section can be "lifted" intact from the research proposal.

Objectives.   This section of the report should be a concise statement of the objectives, which involves the management problem and its translation into a research problem. The objectives arise out of the background data but are so critical that they should be explicitly stated in a separate section of the report.

Research Design.   This section summarizes the methodology used to meet the objectives of the research project. Technical details should be minimized. Where necessary, such details should be placed in appendixes. The researcher must remember that, although he is deeply interested in research design, most managers are not. This should *not* be the major section of the report.

Findings.   The major portion of the report should be devoted to the findings, which should be organized around the objectives of the study. The findings should not consist of an endless series of statistical tables. Instead it should discuss, in meaningful terms, what the research found. Summary tables and visual aids (charts, graphs, and the like) should be used to clarify the discussion.

Limitations.   The researcher should not overlook or hide any problems in the research. Furthermore, he should take care to point out limitations that are apparent to skilled researchers but that a manager might overlook. For example, the danger in generalizing to the national market from local studies or the potential problems of nonresponse error are often overlooked by executives. The limitations section should, without unduly degrading the overall quality of the work, indicate the nature of any potential limitations.

Conclusion and Recommendations.   The researcher should draw conclusions from the findings in light of the objectives of the study. A good way to organize this section is to state each objective and then present the specific conclusions relevant to that objective.

Recommendations may or may not be made. An argument against having the researcher recommend courses of action is that he may not have "the big picture." However, the researcher can make recommendations based on his knowledge. Management can reject these recommendations if it has knowledge unavailable to the researcher that renders his recommendations impractical. Having the researcher recommend specific courses of action can have two beneficial effects. First, it forces the researcher to "lay it on the line." Second, it keeps the researcher closely attuned to the management process. Both of these effects should ultimately lead to better, more usable research. Even more important, however, is the fact that the researcher's recommendations may help solve the problem.

Appendixes.   Items that will appeal to only a few readers or that may be needed only for occasional reference should be confined to an appendix. Such things as details of the sampling plan, detailed statistical tables, interview verification procedures, copies of questionnaires and interviewer instruction, and so on generally belong in an appendix.

Oral Presentations

Oral presentations range from informal telephone calls to major formal presentations to large groups. The various suggestions for written reports are equally applicable for oral presentations, particularly the use of visual aids. As one successful researcher states: "After working six months or more on a project, the researcher may get 30 to 60 minutes of top management's time. The oral report had better be effective!"

The first step in ensuring that the oral report is effective is the same as for a written report—an analysis of the audience. The next step is the development of a detailed report outline or, preferably, a written *script* for the report. Once the oral presentation is prepared, it should be rehearsed. Even highly trained actors and speakers typically rehearse material prior to making a formal presentation. Researchers, generally with limited training in oral presentations, should plan on several "dry runs" before making a presentation to management.

The use of visual aids is essential for most oral presentations of research results. The oral presentation of a list of several numbers or percentages simply will not register on many listeners. Even the visual presentation of the numbers in a table will often not have the necessary impact. Many people have to "study" a table to understand it. Therefore, oral presentations should make extensive use of the various charting techniques referred to earlier as well as any other appropriate visual aids.[10]

A number of kinds of equipment are available to assist in the presentation of visual materials. *Chalkboards* allow the researcher to write out and manipulate numbers as he progresses. They are particularly useful when technical questions concerning the findings are anticipated. *Magnetic boards* and *felt boards* offer some of the same advantages but are not as flexible. They do, however, allow the rapid presentation of previously prepared materials.

A *flip chart* is a large pad of blank paper mounted on an easel. Visual aids are drawn on the pages in advance, and the speaker flips to the appropriate chart as he progresses through his talk. The use of colored felt-tip pens can effectively increase the impact of the flip chart. Blank pages can be left at appropriate intervals and the speaker can create new exhibits as the need arises.

[10] See ibid. for additional techniques.

Overhead projectors are widely used to show previously prepared images against a screen or wall. The materials presented in this manner can range from simple charts to complex overlays. An overlay is produced by the successive additions of new images to the screen without removing the previous images. In addition, the speaker can write on the transparency (the acetate sheet on which the image is carried) and the writing will appear on the screen as he writes.

Transparent slides of anything that can be photographed can be projected onto a screen. Although these slides are not as flexible as those used on overhead projectors (that is, they cannot be written on while in use), the existence of remote-control, magazine-loaded projectors allows an extremely smooth presentation using this technique. Other techniques such as *16 mm. film* and *videotape* can be used in specific situations but are not widely applicable.

Summary

The marketing research function, like all other aspects of the firm, is the final responsibility of top management. The *control* and *evaluation* of the day-to-day operations of the research department *are typically delegated to the research director*. The research director can use checklists or PERT charts to control specific research projects. In addition, each project should be evaluated after completion for accuracy and usefulness.

A *marketing research advisory committee* is a useful approach to the control and evaluation of the overall research effort. Such a committee consists of the chief marketing officer, the director of marketing research, and representatives from all the major functions served by the research department. The basic purpose of the committee is to ensure that the research effort is directed in an effective manner toward the most critical information needs of the firm. A *periodic audit* by an outside consultant is an excellent supplementary control and evaluation technique.

The effectiveness of the research department is closely related to its ability to communicate with the users of research data. Therefore, preparing the research report is a critical part of the overall research process.

The research report should be prepared with the needs and capabilities of the intended audience in mind. It should (1) *focus on the needs of the audience,* (2) *minimize the reporting of the technical aspects of the project,* (3) *use terminology appropriate for the audience,* (4) *be as interesting as possible,* and (5) *utilize visual aids whenever practical*. Rehearsals and visual aids are particularly important for oral presentations.

Questions and Problems

17.1. Develop one or more visual aids for the presentation of the following data showing the relationship between store sales and profits and department A's sales and profits.

	Sales		Profits	
Year	Store	Department A	Store	Department A
1968	5,500,000	775,000	595,000	80,900
1969	5,770,000	843,000	620,000	88,700
1970	6,056,000	917,000	646,000	97,400
1971	6,360,000	998,000	673,000	106,700
1972	6,681,000	1,088,000	702,000	117,600
1973	7,022,000	1,187,000	732,000	129,500
1974	7,383,000	1,296,000	763,000	142,600
1975	7,766,000	1,415,000	797,000	156,200

17.2. As a new marketing researcher for a medium-sized department store, you have been asked to prepare a report showing "what happens to sales revenue" after it is received. The report will be presented in the local newspaper in an "in depth" examination of the store. Investigation reveals the following figures. Prepare a visual aid for use in the newspaper article.

Net Sales (Revenue)	$4,000,000
Cost of goods sold	1,600,000
Sales force compensation	400,000
Administrative salaries	600,000
Overhead (rent, insurance, etc.)	600,000
Inventory shrinkage (spoilage, theft, etc.)	200,000
Advertising	75,000
Taxes (local, state, and federal)	375,000
Aftertax profit	150,000

17.3. Average daily sales for a grocery store were found to be Monday, $100,000; Tuesday, $120,000; Wednesday, $125,000; Thursday, $175,000; Friday, $190,000; Saturday, $200,000. Prepare a visual aid to show this information.

17.4. The survey on bread usage in Chapter 13 produced the following data on television viewing during weekday evenings. Prepare one or more visual aids for presentation of this data.

	Absolute Frequency	Relative Frequency	Cumulative Frequency
Less than 0.1 hours	42	23.9	23.9
0.1–1.0 hours	60	34.1	58.0
1.1–2.0 hours	41	23.3	81.2
2.1–3.0 hours	23	13.1	94.3
3.1–4.0 hours	10	5.7	100.0
	176	100.0	

17.5. Prepare a visual aid for presentation of the following annual sales data (in thousands).

1952	$1,220	1958	1,515	1964	2,100	1970	2,400
1953	1,460	1959	1,570	1965	2,050	1971	2,350
1954	1,800	1960	1,770	1966	2,400	1972	2,100
1955	1,815	1961	1,950	1967	2,450	1973	2,400
1956	1,920	1962	2,125	1968	2,500	1974	2,515
1957	1,850	1963	2,230	1969	2,475	1975	2,620

Selected Bibliography

CASEY, R. S. *Oral Communication of Technical Information.* New York: Reinhold Book Division, 1958. A good treatment of this critical topic.

DAWE, J., and W. J. LORD, JR. *Functional Business Communications,* Englewood Cliffs, N.J.: Prentice-Hall, Inc., 1968. A thorough treatment of all aspects of business communications. Chapters 3, 7, 8, 9, 10, 11, and 12 are particularly appropriate for presenting research results.

MYERS, J. H., and R. R. MEAD. *The Management of Marketing Research.* Scranton, Pa.: International Textbook Co., 1969, Chap. 7. A brief but good treatment of the process of control and evaluation of marketing research.

SPEAR, M. E. *Practical Charting Techniques.* New York: McGraw-Hill Book Co., 1969. An outstanding, extremely thorough treatment of the various forms of visual aids. An invaluable reference for the report writer.

Case 17–1

Research Details Reported in *Who Buys What in Chicago Now**

The following paragraphs describe the research methodology utilized in a product usage survey by the Chicago *Sun-Times*/Chicago *Daily News*.

* Reprinted with permission of the Chicago *Sun-Times*/Chicago *Daily News*.

Rank of Products

In the grocery and toiletry categories, items reported are those found physically on hand in a periodic audit of sample households by professionally trained interviewers. The rank of each brand shown is based on its ratio to all brands reported. No attempt is made to determine sales volume, purchase frequencies, or quantities consumed.

The ready-to-wear, home furnishings, and small appliance categories are based on purchases reported to have been made in the last 12 months. Major appliance categories report on current ownership and purchases made in the last three years.

Area Studied

The area covered in this survey is the Chicago Standard Metropolitan Statistical Area as defined by the U.S. Bureau of the Census. This area consists of six Illinois counties in their entirety: Cook, DuPage, Kane, Lake, McHenry, and Will.

Sample Design

The sample used in this study is a two-stage area-probability sample of all dwelling units in the survey area. The principal characteristics of this sample are: (1) every dwelling unit in the survey area had an equal chance of being selected as a sample household, (2) selection of 300 interviewing areas was by mathematical random procedure and sample dwelling units were predesignated to eliminate any interviewer preference, and (3) no household was interviewed more than once and no substitution of households was allowed.

Two callbacks plus the original call were made at dwelling units where no respondent was found at home. The original sample is drawn to contain 2,700 dwelling units per six-month period. Due to respondents' not at home and those refusing to be interviewed, this total yields 2,000 to 2,200 completed interviews per six-month period.

Interviewing

The interviewing for this study starts on the first Tuesday in January and June and continues for a period of 20 weeks.

Fieldwork is conducted on Tuesday through Friday between 3 P.M. and 9 P.M. and from 10 A.M. to 4 P.M. on Saturdays. These hours were selected to ensure including the correct proportion of employed housewives.

Tabulation

All data obtained from each interview are transferred to magnetic computer tapes. Additional analyses, special cross-tabulations, and technical information can be requested from the market research department of the Chicago *Sun-Times* and the Chicago *Daily News*.

What other information, if any, should be reported?

Case 17–2

American Marketing Association— Report on a Survey of Marketing Research

In 1973 a report was published by the American Marketing Association on the findings of a survey of American firms with regard to their use of marketing research. The types of research used, the place of the research department in the organization, expenditures on research, and the extent to which the services of outside research firms are used were among the areas investigated in the study. A similar study was the subject of a report published by the American Marketing Association in 1963.

1. Evaluate the 1973 report as a report of the findings (not on the basis of its substantive content). (The report was done by D. W. Twedt and its title is *A Survey of Marketing Research*. Its library call number is HF 5415.2 .A46 1973).
2. Evaluate the 1973 report in terms of the methods used and the probable extent and direction of the errors present.
3. What conclusions can be drawn from a comparison of the 1963 and 1973 reports with respect to trends in the usage of marketing research by American firms? (The 1963 report has the same author and title. Its library call number is HF 5415.2 .A46 1963).

Case 17–3

Packer's Tar Soap: Report Analysis

In November, 1934, a report on a proposed "deal" for Packer's Tar Soap was prepared by the New York office of The Blackman Company, an advertising agency. (The report is contained in Case 15–2). Packer's Tar Soap was a well-known bar shampoo at that time, but was experiencing substantial and continuing losses of sales. The "deal" was proposed as a means of getting new retail customers and to relieve some of the pressures that had been brought by wholesalers and chains to reduce price.

Evaluate the report as a report (not on substantive content) on the basis of the criteria you believe to be applicable.

CHAPTER 18

Ethical Issues in Marketing Research

In Chapter 9, both observational and projective techniques were described as means of gathering data that respondents are unable or *unwilling* to provide in response to direct questioning. Is it ethical to secure information from individuals that they are unwilling to provide? Should opinions be elicited that the respondent does not want to give? Questions such as these—*ethical questions*—are often ignored in marketing research. Yet, many ethical questions are involved in the marketing research process.

It is essential that we, as marketing research students, practitioners, and professors, develop an awereness of and concern for the ethical issues of our profession. The process of studying and practicing a profession can apparently alter an individual's perceptions of the rights and prerogatives of that profession. For example, in one empirical study evidence was found that suggests that the pursuit of a business education leads to more tolerant attitudes toward "questionable" business practices than those held by students with other majors.[1]

If these findings are correct, the person engaging in marketing research may use techniques and practices that, unknown to him, the general public considers unethical. Therefore, we should examine our field for activities that may be questionable in the view of the general public. Such an examination should lead to research practices in line with the general ethical expectations of society. This approach is not only "good" in some absolute sense but it is also self-serving. Most of us would prefer to maintain high standards of conduct voluntarily rather than have standards set and enforced by governmental action. We should recognize that the government (national, state, or local) seldom regulates areas where there is no evidence of malpractice.

A final benefit from a highly ethical approach to the marketing research process is improved public acceptance. The essential nature of public acceptance is made clear by Carlson:

Let's face it, we are able to collect our research data only because the general public continues to be willing to submit to our interviews. This acceptance of us by the public is the basic natural resource on which our industry is built. Without it, we would be out of business tomorrow.[2]

Unfortunately, we do not have a list of ethical and unethical marketing practices that covers all the situations the marketing researcher may face. Several issues are controversial within the profession.[3] Some widely accepted social values, such as the individual's right to privacy, support one position, whereas equally accepted values, such as the individual's right to seek knowledge, may support an opposing position.

This chapter begins with an examination of the nature of *ethics* in marketing research and then discusses specific ethical issues. The concept of *privacy* is so crucial to ethical conduct in marketing research that a major section is devoted to it. Finally a brief treatment of *corporate espionage* is provided.

[1] D. I. Hawkins and A. B. Cocanougher, "Student Evaluations of the Ethics of Marketing Practices: The Role of Marketing Education," *Journal of Marketing,* **36** (April 1972), 61–64. See also B. D. Gelb and R. H. Brien, "Survival and Social Responsibility: Themes for Marketing Education and Management," *Journal of Marketing,* **35** (April 1971), 3–9.

[2] R. O. Carlson, "The Issue of Privacy in Public Opinion Research," *Public Opinion Quarterly,* **31** (Spring 1967), 5.

[3] C. M. Crawford, "Attitudes of Marketing Executives Toward Ethics in Marketing Research," *Journal of Marketing,* **34** (April 1970), 46–52; and E. E. Furash, "Industrial Espionage," *Harvard Business Review,* **37** (November–December 1959) 6–12+.

The Nature of Ethical Issues in Marketing Research

Where does one turn for guidance in ethical conduct when engaged in marketing research? Models for ethics in the general field of marketing have been proposed by a number of writers.[4] Each of these models provides useful insights and a general guide for action. However, none of these models are specific enough to provide an unambiguous guide to behavior in specific marketing research situations.

The American Marketing Association (AMA) provides a Marketing Research Code of Ethics that is reproduced in Exhibit 18–1. This code is an excellent starting point, but it leaves some of the more crucial issues untouched.

Exhibit 18–1   Marketing Research Code of Ethics*

The American Marketing Association, in furtherance of its central objective of the advancement of science in marketing and in recognition of its obligation to the public, has established these principles of ethical practice of marketing research for the guidance of its members. In an increasingly complex society, marketing management is more and more dependent upon marketing information intelligently and systematically obtained. The consumer is the source of much of this information. Seeking the cooperation of the consumer in the development of information, marketing management must acknowledge its obligation to protect the public from misrepresentation and exploitation under the guise of research.

Similarly the research practitioner has an obligation to the discipline he practices and to those who provide support for his practice—an obligation to adhere to basic and commonly accepted standards of scientific investigation as they apply to the domain of marketing research.

It is the intent of this code to define ethical standards required of marketing research in satisfying these obligations.

Adherence to this code will assure the users of marketing research that the research was done in accordance with acceptable ethical practices. Those engaged in research will find in this code an affirmation of sound and honest basic principles which have developed over the years as the profession has grown. The field interviewers who are the point of contact between the profession and the consumer will also find guidance in fulfilling their vitally important role.

For Research Users, Practitioners and Interviewers

1. No individual or organization will undertake any activity which is directly or indirectly represented to be marketing research, but which has as its real

* Reprinted with permission from the American Marketing Association.

[4] Four of these are summarized in T. F. McMahon, "A Look at Marketing Ethics," *Atlanta Economic Review*, **18** (March 1968), 5–8+. Also see H. O. Pruden, "Which Ethic for Marketers?" in J. R. Wish and S. H. Gamble, eds., *Marketing and Social Issues* (New York, John Wiley & Sons, Inc., 1971), 98–104.

purpose the attempted sale of merchandise or services to some or all of the respondents interviewed in the course of the research.

2. If a respondent has been led to believe, directly or indirectly, that he is participating in a marketing research survey and that his anonymity will be protected, his name shall not be made known to anyone outside the research organization or research department, or used for other than research purposes.

For Research Practitioners

1. There will be no intentional or deliberate misrepresentation of research methods or results. An adequate description of methods employed will be made available upon request to the sponsor of the research. Evidence that fieldwork has been completed according to specifications will, upon request, be made available to buyers of research.

2. The identity of the survey sponsor and/or the ultimate client for whom a survey is being done will be held in confidence at all times, unless this identity is to be revealed as part of the research design. Research information shall be held in confidence by the research organization or department and not used for personal gain or made available to any outside party unless the client specifically authorizes such release.

3. A research organization shall not undertake marketing studies for competitive clients when such studies would jeopardize the confidential nature of client-agency relationships.

For Users of Marketing Research

1. A user of research shall not knowingly disseminate conclusions from a given research project or service that are inconsistent with or not warranted by the data.

2. To the extent that there is involved in a research project a unique design involving techniques, approaches or concepts not commonly available to research practitioners, the prospective user of research shall not solicit such a design from one practitioner and deliver it to another for execution without the approval of the design originator.

For Field Interviewers

1. Research assignments and materials received, as well as information obtained from respondents, shall be held in confidence by the interviewer and revealed to no one except the research organization conducting the marketing study.

2. No information gained through a marketing research activity shall be used directly or indirectly, for the personal gain or advantage of the interviewer.

3. Interviews shall be conducted in strict accordance with specifications and instructions received.

4. An interviewer shall not carry out two or more interviewing assignments simultaneously unless authorized by all contractors or employers concerned.

Members of the American Marketing Association will be expected to conduct themselves in accordance with the provisions of this Code in all of their marketing research activities.

In the following pages, a number of issues that the marketing research profession faces are presented. The presentation is *not* neutral. The authors' position, which is stated explicitly on most of the issues, views marketing research as evolving into a full-fledged profession that will eventually call for certain types of training, certification of competence, and a well-developed and enforced code of ethics. Such a professional code will be based on a concern for the general public and respondents first, the client second, and the researcher, last. The code will bind both practitioners and users of research. Finally, it will be more comprehensive than the existing American Marketing Association code.

Ethical Issues Involving Protection of the Public

A true profession focuses first on the needs of the general public or innocent third parties. A falsified research report used to justify funding for the client by a bank would be unethical (and illegal) despite the fact that it might be economically advantageous to *both* the researcher and the client. Two major areas of concern arise in this context (both can also influence the client-researcher relationship): *incomplete reporting* and *nonobjective research*. These two areas are closely interrelated in their effects.

Incomplete Reporting

A client requesting that information that could be harmful to the sale of a product not be included in a research report to be released to the public is analogous to a seller of a product not disclosing potentially damaging information about his product in a sales presentation to the buyer. Both are attempts to mislead the potential buyer by leaving him uninformed about undesirable features or characteristics of the product.

In response to growing demand for protection of consumers, the earlier legal doctrine of *caveat emptor,* "let the buyer beware," has been changing to one of *caveat venditor,* "let the seller beware."[5] This is true with respect to disclosure in some reports released to the public as well. For example, the Securities and Exchange Commission requires full disclosure of potentially negative information in securities prospectuses. Tobacco companies are required to add a warning concerning the hazards of smoking in their advertisements and on their packages.

There are no legal requirements per se about failure to disclose negative information in research reports to be released to the public. There are

---

[5] For a discussion of this change see R. N. Corley and W. J. Robert, *Principles of Business Law,* 9th ed. (Englewood Cliffs, N.J.: Prentice-Hall, Inc., 1971), 11–12.

clear ethical requirements to do so, however, and the reputable researcher will ensure that such information is included.

Nonobjective Research

The researcher, the client, or both will often benefit if certain research findings were obtained. There is no doubt that "intentional or deliberate misrepresentation of research methods or results" is unethical as specified in the American Marketing Association code. However, research techniques can be selected that will maximize the likelihood of obtaining a given finding.

The ease of using relatively standard techniques in a nonobjective way can be seen in the following example. A small community wishes to attract retail outlets from several chain stores. A researcher is hired to develop a presentation to the managements of the chains. The researcher realizes that the chain stores weigh per capita income very heavily in their location decisions. He also realizes that the community is quite poor except for a very few people who are quite wealthy. He takes a census of the population and computes an average income figure. He has done nothing incorrect from a technical point of view. However, a median rather than an average income figure would give a more realistic picture of the community's income as it relates to the decision at hand. For marketing research to be a profession, such practices, if done intentionally, would have to be considered unethical.

Ethical Issues Involving Protection of Respondents

Two ethical issues confront the researcher in his relationship with respondents; namely, the use of the guise of conducting a survey to sell products and the invasion of the privacy of the respondent.

Use of "Marketing Research" Guise to Sell Products

The use of the statement "I am conducting a survey" as a guise for sales presentations or to obtain information for sales leads to a major concern of legitimate researchers.[6] Both telephone and personal "interviews" have

[6] A. Biel, "Abuses of the Survey Research Technique: The Phony Interview," *Public Opinion Quarterly,* **31** (Summer 1967), 298. See also W. D. Rugg, "Interviewer Opinion on the 'Salesman as Interviewer' Problem," *Public Opinion Quarterly,* **35** (Winter, 1971–72), 625–626; R. Baxter, "The Harassed Respondent: I. Sales Solicitation in the Guise of Consumer Research," in C. Berenson and H. Eilbirt, eds., *The Social Dynamics of Marketing* (New York: Random House, Inc., 1973), pp. 339–345.

been used as an opportunity for sales solicitation. Some mail "surveys" may have served to generate sales leads or mailing lists. One survey found that 60 per cent of those responding had been approached with a request for an interview that turned into a sales presentation. Although the public still appears to support legitimate surveys, the widespread incidence of phony interviewing could change this essential acceptance.[7]

The practice is, of course, prohibited by the American Marketing Association code of ethics and by many state and community laws. It would seem in the research profession's best interest to encourage laws against this practice and to cooperate to the fullest extent in their enforcement.

Invasion of Privacy of Respondents

Two aspects of privacy should concern the marketing researcher. The *law of privacy* refers to an individual's legal right "to be left alone." The *right to privacy* refers to the public's general feeling or perception of their ability to restrict the amount of personal data they will make available to outsiders. However, the law of privacy and the right to privacy are not necessarily congruent. Both have important implications for the marketing research profession.

The Law of Privacy[8]

Privacy is neither a constitutionally guaranteed right nor a part of our heritage of Common Law, although it is considered by some to be implicit in the First Amendment to the Constitution with its emphasis on freedom of speech and, presumably, the concomitant liberty of silence. Others consider the Fourth Amendment's safeguards against search and the Fifth Amendment's concern for due process and self-incrimination to be constitutional guarantees of privacy as well.[9]

The law of privacy gained its initial legal momentum from an article by Warren and Brandeis in 1890.[10] Other legal scholars began to write on the topic and judges began to refer to these writings in decisions relevant to

---

[7] I. L. Allen and J. D. Colfax, "Respondents" Attitudes toward Legitimate Surveys in Four Cities," *Journal of Marketing Research,* **5** (November 1968), 431–433, E. L. Hartmann, H. L. Isaacson, and C. M. Jurgell, "Public Reaction to Public Opinion Surveying," *Public Opinion Quarterly,* **32** (Summer 1968), 295–298.

[8] This section is based on C. S. Mayer and C. H. White, Jr., "The Law of Privacy and Marketing Research," *Journal of Marketing,* **33** (April 1969), 1–4.

[9] U.S. Executive Office of the President, Office of Science and Technology, *Privacy and Behavioral Research* (Washington, D.C.: U.S. Government Printing Office, 1967), 9.

[10] S. D. Warren and L. D. Brandeis, "The Right to Privacy," *Harvard Law Review,* **4** (December 1890), 193–220.

the area. Thus, the law of privacy has evolved on a decision-by-decision basis and, as a result tends to differ among the states.

Privacy falls under *tort* law—a civil wrong that will support an action for damages. The four different kinds of tort action representing breaches of four different types of privacy right can be defined in general terms as follows:

1. *Disclosure:* the act of making public embarrassing private facts about an individual.
2. *False Light:* the act of placing an individual in a false light in the public eye—of publicizing misrepresentative statements concerning him.
3. *Appropriation:* the act of appropriating an individual's name or likeness for the appropriator's advantage.
4. *Intrusion:* the act of intruding upon an individual's private affairs, his solitude, or his seclusion.[11]

Disclosure, False Light, and Appropriation. Disclosure, false light, and appropriation generally require the publication or dissemination of information. Since the right to privacy is strictly an individual right, the researcher who does not release *individual* data appears to be immune from these three torts. In fact, the profession's general reluctance to reveal even aggregate data serves as an even greater protective shield. These particular torts are of more concern to the general public opinion researcher whose findings are frequently made public than they are to the decision-oriented marketing researcher

As stated previously, the refusal to publicize individual data is apparently a sound defensive against these three torts. However, the release of group data can, at least on a probabilistic basis, reveal facts about individuals. In an extreme case, to reveal that a census of some population found that 100 per cent of the group held a given attitude is the same as revealing each individual member's attitude. It is an interesting, and untested, legal question as to whether or not releasing a finding that 99 per cent (or 95 or 51 per cent) of a population holds a given attitude is the same as revealing an individual's attitude.

Intrusion. Intrusion, unlike disclosure, false light, or appropriation, *does not* require publication. The act of intrusion itself gives rise to the tort. The tort of intrusion is firmly established for *physical* intrusion, *visual* intrusion, and *auditory* intrusion. The case against *psychological* intrusion, namely, invading an individual's psychological privacy through such things as projective techniques, is a logical extension and seems to be developing.

[11] Quoted from Mayer and White, Jr., op. cit., 2, based on W. L. Prosser, "Privacy," *California Law Review,* **48** (August 1960), 383–424.

The legal right to privacy and the more specific right to be free from intrusion can be waived by either an explicit or an implied consent. Thus, consenting to be interviewed or to take part in a marketing experiment releases the researcher from intrusion *as long as the questioning or activities coincide with what an "average" respondent would expect given the request for cooperation.* However, it is doubtful if consent to be interviewed automatically allows the researcher to utilize projective or other disguised techniques. As Mayer and White state:

> The respondent's consent is to answer these surface level questions; it is unlikely that he would willingly consent to have his psyche plumbed by an interviewer. A defensive argument based on the theory of implied consent would be difficult to sustain. The respondent and the interviewer/agency are by definition on different communication levels when disguised questioning techniques are used. It is unlikely that there has been a suffecent meeting of the minds to support an implied consent agreement.[12]

However, the legal basis for such an conclusion has never been established in court. Torts are neither self-assertive nor self-initiating. The injured party must set the corrective action in motion by suing for damages. Thus, it seems fairly unlikely that a marketing researcher will face legal action based on an intrusion of an individual's psychological privacy.

A more realistic legal concern is that legislative action, either at the state or national level, may prohibit or restrict the utilization of disguised techniques based on the same arguments presented earlier. The claim, made in this book as well as most others on the topic, that disguised technique can produce information that respondents would be unable *or unwilling* to give in response to direct techniques would seem an adequate basis for some to propose restrictive legislation.

The defense that the techniques really do not work all that well is not adequate. A more defensible position would seem to be that, as long as the individual's anonymity is maintained, no harm is done to the individual. That is, a person may agree to spend 30 minutes in an interview situation responding to picture response projective tests. If these techniques reveal that he views the ownership of a certain product being more important for status reasons than functional reasons, he is not harmed unless his individual responses are publicized.

A final strategy would be to acquire explicit consent to measure underlying attitudes using disguised techniques. A great deal of work would be necessary to develop requests that would adequately inform the respondent of the nature of the procedure without biasing the results or seriously affecting the response rate. However, it does not seem an impossible task and is preferable to restrictive legislation.

[12] Mayer and White, Jr., op. cit., 3.

The Right to Privacy[13]

In contrast to the relatively vague and uncertain status of the law of privacy is the widely shared if inarticulated concept of an individual's *right to privacy*. The three important elements involved in this "right" are the *concept of privacy* itself, the concept of *informed consent* by which an individual can waive his right to privacy, and that *anonymity and confidentiality* can help protect those whose privacy has, to some extent, been invaded.

The Nature of Privacy.   The right to privacy is the right of the individual to decide for himself how much he will share with others his thoughts, his feelings, and the facts of his personal life. It is the right to live one's life in one's own way, to formulate and hold one's own beliefs, and to express thoughts and share feelings without fear of observation or publicity beyond that which one seeks or acquiesces in.

What is private varies between individuals and within individuals from day to day and setting to setting. The essence of the concept is the right of *each individual to decide for himself in each particular setting or compartment of his life how much of himself he will reveal.*

Given this concept of privacy, any ethical code or law that focuses on the *area* being examined completely misses the point. Such a prohibition would protect some people from what they would consider an invasion of privacy. However, unless virtually all areas of inquiry were closed, it would fail to protect other individuals from an invasion of their privacy. More importantly, it would "protect" some individuals who are quite willing or even eager to reveal the prohibited information. When an individual *consents* freely and fully to reveal aspects of himself to others, no invasion of privacy takes place regardless of the nature of the information revealed.

Free and Informed Consent.   Since the essence of the right of privacy is the individual's ability to *choose* what he will reveal, the marketing researcher must not abrogate the respondent's ability to choose. This requires the researcher to obtain the free and informed consent of the potential respondents. *Free consent* implies that the potential respondent is not encumbered by any real or imagined pressure to participate in the study other than his own desire to cooperate or contribute.

Free consent is not as simple a concept as this definition makes it appear. For example, suppose the researcher offers the potential respondent a monetary inducement to encourage participation in a study. Does this place at least some potential respondents under external pressure to par-

[13] This section is based on U.S. Executive Office of the President, Office of Science and Technology, *Privacy and Behavioral Research* (Washington, D.C.: U.S. Government Printing Office, 1967).

ticipate in a study that they would otherwise avoid? This is a generally accepted practice in our society. However, some of its extensions are somewhat more suspect. Releasing prison inmates, soldiers, or students from unpleasant assignments in return for participation in a study is somewhat more questionable. Some individuals can be intimidated by an aggressive interviewer. Is their consent truly free?

Informed consent is an equally troublesome point. It is generally impossible to bring each respondent up to the researcher's level of knowledge on the research methods and implications. In practice, *informed* means providing the potential respondent with sufficient information for him to determine whether or not his participation is worthwhile and desirable *from his point of view*. This would, in general, involve a description of the types of questions to be asked or task required, the subject areas covered, the time and physical effort involved, and the ultimate use of which the resultant data will be put.

Few requests for cooperation for marketing research studies convey all of this information. Yet there are, in the authors' opinion, relatively few studies where either the response rate or accuracy would be adversely affected by this approach. However, no empirical studies have focused on this point.

Some marketing studies and techniques are less able to withstand full disclosure. Disguised techniques are based on the premise that more accurate or meaningful answers can be obtained if the respondent is not aware of the purpose of the questions. As Bogart stated: "Must we really explain, when we ask the respondent to agree or disagree with the statement, 'Prison is too good for sex criminals; they should be publicly whipped or worse,' that it is really the authoritarianism of his personality we are investigating, and not public opinion on crime and punishment."[14]

Informed consent does not seem to require the level of detail suggested in this quote. However, it does require that the respondent be told that some of the questions during the interview will be used to measure certain aspects of his personality. Likewise, when projective techniques are being used, the respondent can be told that some of his responses will be analyzed to reveal his underlying attitudes on certain topics. Such information seems sufficient to allow the respondent to decide if he wishes to participate. Again, we have no research to indicate what effects, if any, this type of information will have on the responses.

Regardless of how much preliminary information is provided, the respondent's right to discontinue participation at any point in the study should be stipulated in clear terms. Again, few marketing studies are explicit on this point. Most researchers assume that the respondents are

---

[14] L. Bogart, "The Researcher's Dilemma," *Journal of Marketing*, **26** (January 1962), 9.

aware of the fact that they can terminate an experiment or interview at their pleasure. To remind them of this right might increase suspicion and result in more refusals than would normally occur. However, some individuals or groups of individuals are not aware of this right or are psychologically not prepared to exercise it unless it is explicitly stated.

In some situations the respondent cannot be told of the nature of the research without distorting his response. In these cases, he can be asked to cooperate based on trust in the researcher. Such trust obligates the researcher to ensure the respondent that no physical or psychological harm will ensue from the research and that any temporary discomfort or loss of privacy will be remedied in an appropriate way during the course of the research or at its completion.

Anonymity and Confidentiality. To the extent that fully informed consent cannot be obtained, anonymity and confidentiality are important. *Anonymity* means that the identity of the subject is never known to anyone. *Confidentiality* means that the respondent's identity is known at one point in time to only a limited number of investigators but is otherwise protected from dissemination.

Any time that nonconsenting respondents are utilized, full anonymity should be maintained. There are relatively few occasions when consent at some level of information cannot be obtained. Observational studies are sometimes in this class. Observations taken without the consent of the respondent should be limited to behaviors in public places normally subject to observation.

The Right to Seek Knowledge

In the above paragraphs emphasis was given to the right of privacy of the respondent. On the other hand, the right to learn or to seek knowledge is also highly valued in our society. The right of the researcher to learn about human behavior and its causes is definitely restricted by the preceding view of the right of privacy. An alternative view that focuses more on the rights of the researcher can be labeled the "no harm, no foul" approach. The view of privacy that has been presented is based on the proposition that the researcher must refrain from engaging in any activity to which the respondent *might* object *if* he knew its exact nature even though he does not object to it with current knowledge.

A competing view is that the researcher should feel free to conduct any study that does not harm the respondents physically or psychologically. Thus, the fact that a respondent would object to revealing his real reasons for purchasing a certain product should not deter the researcher from using projective techniques to uncover these reasons. The respondent reacts to a series of vague stimuli and leaves feeling he has helped in a research project and perhaps feeling that researchers are a little weird for showing such strange pictures. The researcher has data that allow him to understand "subconscious" purchase motives. If the research is competently done, the final result is a better product, more meaningful advertising, more efficient distribution, or a more appropriate price.

This approach requires strict attention to anonymity and confidentiality but does not require informed consent. It does not suggest that respondents be abused, deceived unnecessarily, or pressured into cooperating. It does maintain the position that no physical or psychological harm occur to the respondent. Basically, it says that a person's privacy cannot be invaded if he is unaware of the invasion and the invasion in no way harms him.

There is no doubt that many marketing researchers lean toward the latter point of view rather than the former. This approach appears to offer the researcher the maximum freedom and capacity to generate needed data while still protecting the respondent from harm.

However, we have little doubt that the respondent's right to privacy as expressed in the preceding section is becoming the predominant mode of thought outside research circles. It underlies the basis of grants and contracts that involve human subjects that are supported by the Department of Health, Education, and Welfare.[15] This general approach can be expected to play an increasingly important role in codes of ethics, court cases, and legislation concerning the research process. It would behoove us as marketing researchers to begin to adapt our techniques to the requirements of this type of ethical and legal standard.

Ethical Issues Involving the Protection of the Client

Every professional has the obligation to protect his client in matters relating to their professional relationship. The marketing researcher is no exception. The issues concerning matters in which the client may expect protection when he authorizes a marketing research project include his protection against (1) *abuse of position arising from specialized knowledge*, (2) *unnecessary research*, (3) *unqualified researcher*, (4) *disclosure of client identity*, (5) *treating data as nonconfidential and/or nonproprietary*, (6) *misleading presentation of data*, and (7) *incomplete reporting*.

Protection Against Abuse of Position

The marketing manager is generally at a substantial disadvantage in discussing a research project. Most researchers have specialized knowledge

---

[15] U.S. Department of Health, Education, and Welfare, *The Institutional Guide to DHEW Policy on Protection of Human Subjects* (Washington, D.C.: U.S. Government Printing Office, 1971).

and experience that the marketing manager cannot match. He is frequently forced to accept the researcher's suggestions at face value just as we often accept the advice of medical doctors or lawyers. Like other professionals, the marketing researcher often has the opportunity to take advantage of his specialized knowledge to the detriment of his client.

Of particular concern in this area is the opportunity for, and the temptation to, use faulty research designs and/or methodological shortcuts to meet time or cost constraints. The concern in this area is with such practices as applying pressure, financial or otherwise, on the interviewers to obtain a high response rate in short time periods and then not using a verification procedure to ensure that the interviews were actually done. Another example would be using a new questionnaire without adequate pretesting.

The issue is not a simple one. Both of these practices would be ethical *if* the client were informed beforehand of the practice and the risks involved. An even more complex issue is the level of expertise involved. A relatively unskilled researcher might engage in these practices not knowing that they are suspect. Is he then unethical or simply not fully competent? All researchers, like other professionals, make mistakes, although this does not necessarily mean that they are unethical. However, this issue does point out the need for some form of certification for professional researchers. As it is, any one can declare himself a marketing researcher. The CPA in accounting offers a reasonable certification model that the marketing research profession could follow.

Protection Against Unnecessary Research

Researchers are frequently requested to engage in a specific research project that is unrelated to the underlying problem, has been done before, or is economically unjustified. The researcher can often benefit from such an activity. This gain will frequently exceed whatever goodwill might be generated by refusing to conduct unwarranted research. Should the researcher accept such assignments?

A salesman may not feel obligated to assure himself that the customer really needs the product (although a careful application of the marketing concept would require that he should). Yet a doctor or lawyer is ethically prohibited from prescribing unwarranted medicine or legal action. This issue is not addressed in the American Marketing Association code of ethics. However, it seems to the authors that the researcher has a professional obligation to indicate to the client that, in his judgment, the research expenditure is not warranted. If, after this judgment has been *clearly* stated, the client still desires the research, the researcher should feel free to conduct the study. The reason for this is that the researcher can never know for certain the risk preferences and strategies that are guiding the client's behavior. Therefore, he should feel an obligation to indicate his evaluation of the merits of conducting the study but, in the end, should yield to the client's wish on this point.

Protection Against Unqualified Researchers

Another area of concern involves the request for research that is beyond the capabilities or technical expertise of the individual researcher or research organization. The cost, both psychological and economic, from saying "I cannot do this as well as some other individual" can be quite high. However, accepting a project beyond the researcher's capacities typically results in time delays, higher costs, and decreased accuracy.

Again, professional ethics should compel the researcher to indicate to the potential client the fact that the research requires the application of techniques that are outside his area of expertise. If the researcher feels capable of completing the project, he has every right to attempt to convince the client of this. However, if the task is not one that the researcher can reasonably expect to perform well, a more suitable researcher should be suggested.

Protection of Anonymity of Client

The client will have authorized a marketing research project either to help identify or to help solve marketing problems. In either case, it may well be to the advantage of competitors to know that the study is being done. The researcher is therefore obligated ethically to preserve the anonymity of the client. The fact that a particular firm is sponsoring a study should not be revealed to *any* outside party unless the client so agrees. This includes respondents and other existing and potential clients.

Protection of Confidential and Proprietory Information

The data generated for a particular client and the conclusions and interpretations from those data are the exclusive property of the client. It is obvious that a researcher should not turn over a client's study to one of the client's competitors. However, what if the researcher gathers basic demographic material on a geographic area for one client and the same information is required for a study by a noncompeting client? The American Marketing Association code is not clear on this point but it seems to suggest that such data cannot be used twice without the explicit consent of the original client. Reuse of the data, assuming that permission is granted, should result in the two clients sharing the cost of this aspect of the research rather than the research organization charging twice.

A research agency should not conduct studies for competitive clients if there is a possibility that this would jeopardize the confidential nature of the client-agency relationship.

Protection Against Misleading Presentations of Data

Reports that are presented orally or are written in such a way as to give deliberately the impression of greater accuracy than the data warrant are obviously not in the best interest of the client. Such an impression can be left by reports by a number of means. These include the use of *overly technical jargon, failure to round numbers properly, unnecessary use of complex analytic procedures,* and *incomplete reporting.*

Overly Technical Jargon. All specialties tend to develop a unique terminology. By and large, this is useful as it allows those familiar with the field to communicate in a more concise and precise way. However, technical jargon and extensive mathematical notation can also convey a false aura of complexity and precision. The research report's primary function is to convey *to the client* the results of the research. It is not the proper place to demonstrate the complexity of sampling formulas or the range of terms that are unique to the research process.

Failure to Round Numbers Properly. An impression of greater precision than the data warrant can also be created through the failure to round numbers properly. For example, a statement that the average annual expenditure by some group for furniture is $261.17 implies more precision than is generally warranted. If the researcher believes that the data are accurate to the nearest $10, the average should be rounded to $260. If the data were developed from a sample, the use of a confidence interval may be appropriate as well.

Unnecessary Use of Complex Analytic Procedures. The transformation of the data into logarithms when they could just as well be analyzed in arithmetic form, the use of a least squares regression analysis when a trend line fitted visually would serve the needs of the analysis, or the normalizing of data when it would be better left in its nonnormalized state are examples of needlessly complex analytic procedures. When unnecessary, the use of such procedures is confusing at best and misleading at worst.

Incomplete Reporting. Incomplete reporting renders an objective appraisal of the research report impossible. It can create false impressions of the accuracy of the research or even of the meaning of the resultant data. Both the initial client and any concerned third party have a right to expect a report that will allow them to make a reasonable assessment of the accuracy of the data.

An example should make this point clear. Assume that a sample is drawn from a population of 10,000 individuals and the final report shows an obtained sample size of 750. On the surface this may appear to be a very reasonable sample size. However, unless other descriptive data are given, there is no way to estimate the potential impact of nonresponse error. An evaluation of the probable effects of this source of error requires a knowledge of the response rate. The 750 respondents could represent a response rate as low as 10 or 20 per cent and as high as 100 per cent. One's confidence in the resulting data (depending, of course, on the nature of the data) would vary considerably between these two extremes.

One guide to what should be presented in a research report, from an ethical standpoint, is presented in Exhibit 18–2. This represents a portion

Exhibit 18–2   Information to Be Included in the Research Firm's Report*

Every research project differs from all others. So will every research report. All reports should nonetheless contain specific reference to the following items:

1. The objectives of the study (including statement of hypotheses);
2. The name of the organization for which the study is made and the name of the organization that conducted it;
3. Dates the survey was in the field and date of submission of final report;
4. A copy of the full interview questionnaire, including all cards and visual aids, used in the interview; alternatively, exact question wording, sequence of questions, etc.;
5. Description of the universe(s) studied;
6. Description of the number and types of people studied:
   a. Number of people (or other units),
   b. Means of their selection,
   c. If sample, method of sample selection,
   d. Adequacy of sample representativeness and size,
   e. Percentage of original sample contacted (number and type of callbacks),
   f. Range of tolerance,
   g. Number of cases for category breakouts,
   h. Weighting and estimating procedures used.

Where trend data are being reported and the methodology or question wording has been changed, these changes should be so noted.

On request—clients and other parties with legitimate interests may request and should expect to receive from the research firm the following:

   a. Statistical and/or field methods of interview verification (and percentage of interviews verified);
   b. Available data *re* validation of interview techniques;
   c. Interviewing instructions;
   d. Explanation of scoring or index number devices.

* *Source:* Paper developed by The Market Research Council's Ethics Committee. Reprinted with permission from Leo Bogart, ed., *Current Controversies in Marketing Research* (Chicago: Rand McNally College Publishing Company, 1969), 156. Copyright © 1969 by Markham Publishing Company, Chicago, p. 156. Reprinted by permission of Rand McNally College Publishing Company.

of a "position paper" on ethical issues and problems adopted in 1968 by the Market Research Council.

Ethical Issues Involving Protection of the Research Firm

Several issues can arise in the research firm-client relationship in which the research organization needs protection. These include protection against *improper solicitation of proposals, disclosure of proprietary information on techniques,* and *misrepresentation of findings.*

Protection Against Improper Solicitation of Proposals

Research proposals should be requested *only* as an aid in deciding whether or not to conduct the research and/or which research firm to use. Similarly, proposals should be evaluated solely on their merit unless the other criteria (size and/or special capabilities of the research firm) are made known in advance. Proposals from one research firm should not be given to a second firm or an in-house research department for implementation.

Protection Against Disclosure of Proprietary Information on Techniques

Research firms often develop special techniques for dealing with certain types of problems. Examples are models for predicting the success of new products, models for allocation of advertising expenditures among media, and simulation techniques for predicting effects of changes in the mix variables. They properly regard these techniques as being proprietary. The client should not make these techniques known to other research firms nor appropriate them for its own use without the explicit consent of the developer.

Protection Against Misrepresentation of Findings

Suppose the *Honest and Ethical Research Firm* is commissioned to do a study of analgesics by the manufacturer of *Brand A* aspirin. In its report of the finding the statement is made that, *"Brand A* aspirin was reported to be the aspirin most preferred by two of three respondents using only aspirin as an analgesic for headaches." In its advertising on television to consumers, however, the firm makes the statement, "According to a study conducted by the *Honest and Ethical Research Firm,* two of three consumers preferred *Brand A* aspirin to all other products for treatment of headaches."

This is a clear distortion of the findings. It not only misleads the viewer but is potentially damaging to the research firm as well. Other manufacturers of analgesics will recognize that this is not a true statement and may conclude that the research firm is guilty either of a careless piece of research or of dishonesty in reporting the results.

Corporate Espionage

In the section of Chapter 9 that dealt with observation techniques, it was suggested that observation techniques were widely used to monitor shifts in competitors' prices, advertising, products, and the like. No ethical issue is involved in observing the *public* behavior of competitors. Corporate espionage is not concerned with this type of observation, however. Rather, it refers to observations of activities or products that the competitor is taking reasonable care to conceal from public view. Activities of this nature pose both ethical and legal questions. In the words of Judge Irving L. Goldberg of the U.S. Fifth Circuit Court of Appeals:

> our devotion to free-wheeling industrial competition must not force us into accepting the law of the jungle as the standard of morality expected in our commercial relations. . . . One may use his competitor's secret process if he discovers it by his own independent research; but one may not avoid these labors by taking the process from the discoverer without his permission at a time when he is taking reasonable precautions to maintain its secrecy.[16]

Judge Goldberg was speaking in reference to the use of aerial photography in an attempt to discover the nature of a secret but unpatented production process during the construction of a new plant. Espionage techniques include such activities as electronic eavesdropping, bribing competitor's employees, planting "spies" in a competitor's organization, sifting through garbage, eavesdropping at bars frequented by competitor's employees, and hiring away competitor's employees to learn of their future plans, secret processes, and so on.

The threat, real or imagined, of espionage by competitors has led many firms to engage in elaborate security systems. These systems may be internal or external. It is a sad comment that the industrial counter-espionage business is apparently flourishing.

We have at least some evidence to suggest that the threat of industrial espionage is somewhat more imagined than it is real. A mail questionnaire to a "cross section of *Harvard Business Review* readers" (21 per cent response rate) produced the data shown in Tables 18–1 and 18–2.

[16] "The Great Game of Corporate Espionage," *Dun's Review,* **96** (October 1970), 30.

Table 18-1* Extent to Which Executives Think Companies in Their Industry Use Specified Practices to Gather Information about Competitors (as per cent of all respondents)

	Extent of Use						
	Never	Rarely	Occasionally	Frequently	Regularly	Do Not Know	Total
Comparison shopping	24.8%	13.4%	19.4%	13.8%	15.6%	13.0%	100.0%
Indirectly pumping competitors	7.3	14.6	39.3	21.7	7.2	9.9	100.0
Surveillance of competitor's activities	11.8	13.7	22.5	20.0	20.4	11.5	100.0
Hiring employee of competitor	16.6	32.7	27.3	8.8	1.7	12.9	100.0
Rewarding competitor's employee for information	67.4	14.3	1.1	0.3	0.1	16.8	100.0
Wiretapping or other electronic eavesdropping	78.8	3.7	0.7	0.0	0.2	16.6	100.0
Misrepresentation so as to enter plants	65.0	15.0	3.7	i2	0.1	16.0	100.0
Posing as buyer or supplier	54.7	17.0	10.6	2.0	0.2	15.5	100.0
Planting confederate in competitor's company	66.1	12.4	1.8	0.2	0.2	19.3	100.0

* Reprinted from E. E. Furash, "Industrial Espionage," *Harvard Business Review*, 37 (November–December 1959). Reproduced by permission of *Harvard Business Review*.

Table 18–2* Executive Opinions of Various Situations That Have Occurred in Industry, by Position Level (as per cent of executives in each position category)

Situation	Top Management		Upper Middle Management		Lower Middle Management	
	Approve	Disapprove	Approve	Disapprove	Approve	Disapprove
A retailer sends someone out to "shop" in a competitor's store to get product and pricing information	95.7%	4.3%	96.3%	3.7%	96.4%	3.6%
An oil company establishes a scout department to watch the drilling activities of competitors	71.2	28.8	76.6	23.4	75.0	25.0
A company, learning of a competitor's test market, quickly puts on a special sale in the same location	64.1	35.9	68.7	31.3	58.9	41.1
A key employee is hired away from a competitor	59.0	41.0	68.1	31.9	69.6	30.4
Sales manager wines and dines his competitive counterpart, pumping him for information	47.5	52.5	52.0	48.0	44.6	55.4
Company representative poses as a prospective customer to get information from a competitor	32.5	67.5	32.6	67.4	39.3	60.7
A vice-president hires a detective agency to watch the proving grounds of a competitor	16.3	83.7	18.8	81.2	32.1	67.9
Design engineer steals the plans of a competitor's new model	4.2	95.8	6.9	93.1	9.9	90.1
Company president instructs his aide to secretly record conversations in a competitor's office	4.1	95.9	2.9	97.1	7.1	92.9
Production manager rewards a competitor's employee for certain process information	2.9	97.1	1.5	98.5	1.8	98.2
District manager wiretaps the phone of his local competitor, without his vice-president's knowledge	1.2	98.8	0.9	99.1	0.0	100.0
A company plants confederates in a competitor's organization	1.6	98.4	2.5	97.5	7.1	92.9

* Reprinted from E. E. Furash, "Industrial Espionage," *Harvard Business Review*, 37 (November–December 1959). Reproduced by permission of *Harvard Business Review*.

Although these tables indicate a relatively low incidence of corporate spying, the reader should be aware of potential nonresponse error and measurement error. Indeed, others have concluded that "corporate espionage, always a more thriving business than most executives care to admit, is today bigger and probably better than ever."[17]

Techniques of corporate espionage have not been described in any detail in this text. The authors do not consider such activities even to be a legitimate part of the business world, much less an acceptable part of the marketing research function. Many of these practices are illegal and virtually all are unethical. They are referred to in this section of the text only to prevent the student from naïvely thinking that they do not exist.

One issue that is not clear-cut is the hiring of a competitor's employees. On a free labor market, each firm has a right to bid for the talents of the various members of the work force. The issue would seem to hinge on the motive behind the hiring. Was the person hired because of his competencies or was he hired to take advantage of specific knowledge directly related to a competitor's activities? The first case is obviously ethical; the authors consider the second case unethical. Of course, some situations fall in between these two extremes and no generalized statement can be made covering all cases.

Summary

The most meaningful guide for professional ethics in marketing research is a genuine concern for those affected by the research process. This includes the general public, the respondents, and the clients. Hewever, before the practice of marketing research can truly become a profession, a more comprehensive and enforceable code of ethics will be required.

In this chapter a number of issues that a research code of ethics would have to consider have been examined. The public should be protected from *incomplete* and *biased research reports*. Respondents should be protected from *sales presentations made under the guise of interviews*. In addition, the researcher must respect the *respondent's right to privacy*. The right to privacy is both legal and personal. To the extent possible, the researcher should obtain the *free and informed consent* of the respondent and should maintain the *confidentiality* of all individual responses.

The *client's anonymity* should be maintained. In addition, he should not be subjected to *unnecessary research, research by unqualified researchers, disclosure of proprietary data,* or *incomplete or inaccurate research reports*. In turn, the *client should not misuse research proposals, disclose proprietary research techniques,* or *misrepresent research findings*.

[17] Ibid.

Corporate espionage—seeking data that a competitor is taking reasonable care to conceal from public view—is not a part of the research function. Researchers should resist any efforts to make it so.

Questions and Problems

18.1. Discuss the ethical implications of the following situations.*

(a) A project director recently came in to request permission to use ultraviolet ink in precoding questionnaires on a mail survey. He pointed out that the letter referred to an anonymous survey, but he said he needed respondent identification to permit adequate cross tabulations of the data. The M. R. Director gave his approval.

(b) One product of the X Company is brassieres, and the firm has recently been having difficulty making some decisions on a new line. Information was critically needed concerning the manner in which women put on their brassieres. So the M. R. Director designed a study in which two local stores cooperated in putting one-way mirrors in their foundations dressing rooms. Observers behind these mirrors successfully gathered the necessary information.

(c) In a study intended to probe rather deeply into the buying motivations of a group of wholesale customers by use of a semistructured personal interview form, the M. R. Director authorized the use of the department's special attaché cases equipped with hidden tape recorders.

(d) Some of X Company's customers are busy executives, hard to reach by normal interviewing methods. Accordingly, the market research department recently conducted a study in which interviewers called 'long distance' from near-by cities. They were successful in getting through to busy executives in almost every instance.

(e) In another study, this one concerning magazine reading habits, the M. R. Director decided to contact a sample of consumers under the name of Media Research Institute. This fictitious company name successfully camouflaged the identity of the sponsor of the study.

(f) In the trial run of a major presentation to the Board of Directors, the marketing vice-president deliberately distorted some recent research findings. After some thought, the M. R. Director decided to ignore the matter since the marketing head obviously knew what he was doing.

18.2. Is it ethical to utilize projective techniques to determine an individual's attitudes about a product without telling him the reason? Justify your answer.

18.3. What, if any, are the ethical issues involved in publishing the following *hypothetical* results from confidential surveys?

(a) The median per capita consumption of Scotch among blacks is significantly (statistically) higher than among non-blacks.

* Used with permission from C. M. Crawford, "Attitudes of Marketing Executives Toward Ethics in Marketing Research," *Journal of Marketing,* **34** (April 1970), 46–52. Reprinted with permission of the American Marketing Association.

(b) The median educational level of Jews is significantly higher than that of non-Jews.

(c) Eighty-five per cent of all doctors responding to the survey admitted taking action that was detrimental to their patients on at least one occasion in the past year because of carelessness.

(d) The median consumption of beer among male blue-collar workers is 14 bottles per day.

(e) The incidence of alcoholism is higher among the wives of professional men than in any other single group.

18.4. Mercy Drug Producer, Inc., has a minor share of the national prescription drug market for several major drugs. However, within a 100-mile radius of their headquarters they enjoy a market share of over 80 per cent. They recently conducted a survey of the doctors living within this 100-mile radius. Eight of every 10 doctors that responded indicated that *Mercy* was the brand name he preferred for a specific drug compound. The findings were placed in a national advertisement as follows: "Eight out of every 10 doctors contacted in a recent survey prefers *Mercy* brand over all competitors for relief of. . . ." Comment on this use of the research data.

18.5. Should the response rate always be reported when reporting the results of survey research? Why?

Selected Bibliography

Ethical Principles in the Conduct of Research with Human Participants, Washington, D.C.: American Psychological Association, 1973. A thorough treatment of this critical area. It includes numerous incidents with a discussion of the ethical issues involved in each incident.

MAYER, C. S., and C. H. WHITE, JR. "The Law of Privacy and Marketing Research," *Journal of Marketing, 33* (April 1969), 1–4. A detailed discussion of the law of privacy and its implications for the marketing researcher.

U.S. Department of Health, Education, and Welfare, *The Institutional Guide to DHEW Policy on Protection of Human Subject.* Washington: D.C.: U.S. Government Printing Office, 1971. The official position of the DHEW on the researcher's obligation to human subjects is presented in this brief publication.

U.S. Executive Offices of the President, Office of Science and Technology, *Privacy and Behavioral Research*, Washington, D.C.: U.S. Government Printing Office, 1971. Prepared by a distinguished panel of social scientists, this short publication discusses the major issues of privacy in behavioral research.

Case 18–1

CompuMap, Inc.

In early 1974 a group of students in a class in marketing research at the University of Oregon agreed to conduct a research project for CompuMap,

Inc., a local firm producing computer associated hardware for use in mapping. The students who were to conduct the project had elected to do so in lieu of writing a term paper for the course. CompuMap was to pay all expenses and compensate the students for the extra time they spent on the project. The professor in the marketing research course was not to be compensated for the extra time he spent on the project. However, the department of which he was a member was to receive $300 for use in supporting basic research projects and travel to professional meetings by faculty members.

CompuMap had developed an electronic graphics terminal that, when connected with a computer, permits the user to call for geographic data stored in the computer and to have it displayed almost instantly on a television type screen. CompuMap was interested in obtaining an estimate of the market for this device for displaying of geocoded information.

Geocoding is the term used to describe the conversion and manipulation of street address information to geographic coordinates or areal codes. Geocoded information is used regularly in a number of applications. Law enforcement agencies use it in planning police patrol coverage and in identifying dangerous street intersections. Educational agencies use geocoded information for school desegregation and bussing studies. Environmental planners convert future growth estimates by households and commercial and industrial plants into areal codes for the planning of sewage lines and treatment facilities.

Telephone companies use geocoded customer locations for determining mileage assignments for pricing telephone services. Electrical utilities use geocoded locational data for transformers and types of lines for maintenance and repair services.

An agreement was reached with CompuMap that the project would focus on determining the demand for the graphics terminal for applications in city and regional government agencies. It was agreed that a questionnaire would be prepared and mailed to a sample of 300 such government agencies. Three follow-up mailings were to be conducted.

Bill Hamilton, the student director of the research project, prepared the cover letter for the mailing. It, along with the questionnaire, was sent to the sample of 300 respondents. This cover letter and a letter from Cihoski, an addressee who chose not to complete the questionnaire, are reproduced as follows.

In your opinion, is it ethical for a university to allow students to engage in decisional research projects of this type?

March 25, 1974

Mr. Richard Cihoski
Executive Secretary
Head of the Lakes Council of Governments
409 City Hall
Duluth, Minnesota 55802

Dear Mr. Cihoski:

We are writing to ask your help with regard to a study we are conducting on geocoding. The purpose of this study is to determine the potential and the major application areas for geocoding techniques in urban planning.

Enclosed is a questionnaire. We would like you to participate in our project by answering the questions and returning the questionnaire to us. This study is being done for a firm in the Northwest. The responses will be available to them. The data received will be aggregated for statistical analysis, the results will be interpreted, and conclusions will be drawn. If you are interested in receiving a summary of the findings, please enclose your name and address or write to us at the above address.

You will note that on a separate sheet we have defined a few terms associated with geocoding in a seemingly simplistic manner. We have done this in order to reduce the ambiguity of the questions for respondents possessing various technical backgrounds. Although the questionnaire is addressed to you, please feel free to refer it to other members of your staff or other local government units or agencies in your area who you feel may be able to respond.

For your convenience, we enclose a self-addressed prestamped envelope. We would greatly appreciate your returning the completed questionnaire to us at your earliest convenience within the next two weeks.

If you have any questions regarding the questionnaire or the study, please do not hesitate to contact us.

We thank you very much for your help.

Sincerely,

/s/ BILL HAMILTON

Bill Hamilton
Director, Research Team
(503) 686–4162

BH:aw
Enclosure

April 16, 1974

Mr. Bill Hamilton
Geocoding Research Survey
College of Business Administration
Commonwealth Box 412
University of Oregon
Eugene, Oregon 97403

Dear Mr. Hamilton:

I recently received your survey questionnaire package of March 25th.

First, I must congratulate you on your cover letter and instructions. It is the best I have seen in the past several years, being both complete and concise.

Second, as we began to complete the forms, we began to realize that this is simply a marketing survey for a private company! You were straightforward about it in your cover letter, but as the questions were answered, it was apparent that it would result in some sort of proposal by that company (and probably a sales push). If this is the case, I feel it is unfortunate that the University of Oregon should lend its aegis to such a *private,* nonscholarly survey. Even if your area is experiencing unemployment and you would like to help, this format is inappropriate.

The cover letter states: "results will be interpreted, and conclusions will be drawn." It would have been more honest to describe what *private* actions will flow from those *private* conclusions.

Respectfully,

/s/ RICHARD CIHOSKI

Richard Cihoski
Executive Secretary

RC:ej

cc: President, University of Oregon, Eugene

Case 18–2

Florida Food Products

For years Florida Food Products (FFP) had been known in the trade as "50 cents off a case" marketers. It marketed a complete line of canned vegetables and fruits under its own brand. The firm had never engaged in extensive advertising, as its approach to the business was to pack as large a quantity of good quality products as it could and to sell them at a price necessary to move the inventory.

After a new marketing manager was hired, these policies began to change. The new manager, Martin Holmes, initiated an advertising program on television and in women's magazines that stressed quality and freshness of the FFP brand. An attractive, well-groomed home economist in her early thirties was brought into the company to begin a program of public relations with housewives. Known as "Marge Bradford," she appeared in the company's ads, spoke to women's groups, and visited state and county fairs with a traveling FFP exhibit. A program of developing recipes was begun from the "FFP kitchens."

The district sales managers had always had discretionary authority to reduce price, up to a maximum of 15 per cent per case, any time they thought that local competitive conditions warranted it. Within a few months after the advertising and public relations program had been started, Holmes decided that too much reliance was being placed on price to move FFP products. He wrote a letter to the district managers stating his belief and withdrawing discretionary pricing authority at the district level.

The response was immediate. Every district manager wrote a letter expressing his disagreement with the decision and explaining why some discretion in pricing was needed in his district. Several of them predicted that substantial losses of sales would result in their districts unless this decision were reversed.

The letters did not change Holmes' opinion that the district managers were making unnecessary price cuts. Rather, the letters seemed to him to be evidence that the district managers needed to be educated to the effectiveness of a good advertising program. He began to consider ways in which this might be done.

A sales meeting was to be held in the home office in about a month. All of the district managers would be there. The agenda had been planned to include a discussion of district sales quotas for the coming quarter, a briefing and discussion on the new advertising program, and the playing of a computerized business game. The business game would take all of the last day and would be played by teams of four district managers. Each member of the team would take turns representing the marketing, production, and financial vice-presidents, and the president of the company. Tom Jensen, the manager of the marketing research department, had been asked to make the necessary arrangements for the business game.

Holmes called Jensen to inquire if he could make the determination of sales in the play of the game more responsive to advertising and less responsive to price than the way it was now programmed. Jensen replied that the sales effects of price and advertising changes could be set at any level desired over a wide range. Holmes then asked him to double the effect of advertising changes and to halve the effect of price changes from the levels then programmed for the game.

1. Was the change requested in the program for the business game ethical?
2. Should Jensen have made the change as requested?

Appendix A
Sample Size Determination: Two Additional Methods

References were made in Chapter 6 to determining sample sizes (1) for non-*srs* random samples and (2) by using the Bayesian approach. The first section below deals with the determination of the sample size for a single stage stratified random sample in problems requiring the estimation of a mean or a proportion. There are many other kinds of non-*srs* random samples, but a discussion of determining sample size for them is beyond the scope of this book. The reader will find the necessary formulas to determine the sample size of other commonly used non-*srs* random sampling methods in either of the following books, as well as in other more advanced texts dealing with sampling theory.

William G. Cochran, *Sampling Techniques,* 2nd ed. New York: John Wiley & Sons, Inc., 1963.

Leslie Kish, *Survey Sampling.* New York: John Wiley & Sons, Inc., 1965.

The second section of this appendix is concerned with the Bayesian method of determining sample size.

Sample Size for Single Stage Stratified Random Samples

A *stratified random sample* is one in which the population is first divided into strata and a probability sample is then taken from each stratum. The strata are ideally selected in such a way as to provide the maximum variance *between* them and minimum variance *within* them. In practice, this ideal can rarely be met as stratification is limited to those characteristics of the population that can be identified—age, sex, income, education, and the like. These demographics often do not correlate highly with the measure of the attitude, actual behavior, or planned behavior being studied. However, to the extent that they do, stratification provides a gain in sample efficiency over a *srs*.

In this section we assume that the sample from each stratum is selected as a *srs*. This is an unrealistic assumption for most stratified samples taken from human populations because of the lack of adequate sampling frames. However, the simplification is warranted here, as one of our purposes is to illustrate the application of *srs* principles to other kinds of probability samples.

There are two kinds of single stage stratified samples, *proportional* and *nonproportional*. It is useful to discuss these separately.

Sample Size for Proportional Single Stage Stratified Random Samples

Suppose that the invoices that we examined in Chapter 6 are for sales to companies in two industries. Further suppose that 750 of these invoices were to companies in industry 1 and 500 to companies in industry 2. Finally, suppose that there is reason to believe that the variances of the two strata are different; the standard deviation of industry 1 is estimated to be $20.00 ($\hat{\sigma}_1 = \$20.00$) and for industry 2 is $30.00 ($\hat{\sigma}_2 = \$30.00$). Given the same allowable error ($\bar{x} - M = \$10.00$) and confidence coefficient (90 per cent, $Z = 1.64$) as used before, what size single stage, stratified random sample should be taken?

In order to answer this question, it is first necessary to specify whether the sample is to be a *proportional* or a *nonproportional* stratified random sample. A proportional sample is one in which the proportion of the sample assigned to each stratum is the same as it is in the population. That is, if we let

$n_1 =$ the sample size for industry 1
$n_2 =$ the sample size for industry 2
$N_1 =$ the population size of industry 1, and
$N_2 =$ the population size of industry 2

then a proportional sample is one in which

$$\frac{n_1}{n} = \frac{N_1}{N} = \frac{750}{1250} = .60, \text{ and}$$

$$\frac{n_2}{n} = \frac{N_2}{N} = \frac{500}{1250} = .40.$$

A *nonproportional* sample is, of course, one in which the strata proportions in the sample and the population are not equal. We discuss nonproportional samples shortly.

The formula for the sample size of a *srs* in an estimation of the mean problem was given in equation 6–6 (in Chapter 6) as

$$n = \frac{Z^2 \hat{\sigma}^2}{(\bar{x} - M)^2} \tag{6-6}$$

The formula for the sample size of a stratified sample is of the same general form, the only difference being that the formula for the variance of a stratified sample is substituted. For a proportional stratified sample the estimated variance about the mean is

$$\hat{\sigma}_{st}^2 = \sum_{h=1}^{k} W_h \frac{\hat{\sigma}_h^2}{n} \tag{A-1}$$

where

$$W_h = \text{weight of stratum } h = \frac{N_h}{N},$$

$\acute{\sigma}_h^2$ = estimated variance of stratum h, and
k = total number of strata.

Substituting this variance formula for the one in equation 6–6 gives the comparable formula for sample size for a proportional stratified sample, namely

$$n = \frac{Z^2}{(\bar{x} - M)^2} \sum_{h=1}^{k} W_h \acute{\sigma}_h^2 \qquad \text{(A–2)}$$

We can now answer the question concerning sample size in the example. Substituting the appropriate values in equation A–2 we get

$$n = \frac{1.64^2(.60 \times \$20.00^2 + .40 \times \$30.00^2)}{(\$10.00)^2}$$

$$= \frac{2.69(.60 \times 400 + .40 \times 900)}{100}$$

$$= 17 \text{ (rounded to the next larger number)}$$

The sample sizes for each stratum are determined as

$$n_1 = W_1 n = .60 \times 17 = 10 \text{ (rounded to nearest number)}$$
$$n_2 = W_2 n = .40 \times 17 = 7$$

Recall that the sample size calculated for a simple random sample with the same specifications was 23. This reduction illustrates the principle that *stratification permits a smaller sample size with the same error specification* or *a smaller error specification with the same sample size*. This, of course, assumes that the stratification is done with stratifying characteristics that are related to the variance and that variances differ among strata.

The formula for the sample size for a single stage stratified proportional random sample for estimation of proportions is derived similarly to that for the mean. It is

$$n = \frac{Z^2}{(p - P)^2} \sum_{h=1}^{k} W_h P_h (1.0 - P_h) \qquad \text{(A–3)}$$

where P_h = population percentage in stratum h, and

$$W_h = \frac{N_h}{N}.$$

Sample Size for Nonproportional Single Stage Stratified Random Samples

In the ideal situation one would almost always choose to take a nonproportional rather than a proportional stratified sample. The reason for this can be seen by examining an extreme situation. Suppose industry 1 has *no* standard deviation (all of the invoices are for the same amount.) All of the standard deviation would then necessarily be in industry 2. We would then want a sample size of only 1 ($n_1 = 1$) in industry 1 and the rest of the sample in industry 2. This would clearly be a nonproportional sample.

This suggests that stratum sample size should be proportional to stratum standard deviation. This inference is correct but not complete; optimum stratum sample size is proportional to both the proportion of the population contained in the stratum and the stratum standard deviation. The formula for the optimum allocation of a sample of size n to stratum h is

$$n_h = n \frac{N_h \hat{\sigma}_h}{\sum\limits_{n=1}^{k} N_h \hat{\sigma}_h} \tag{A-4}$$

Thus, it would only be in those cases in which the strata have equal variances that we would want a proportional sample, at least insofar as sampling theory is concerned.

The formula for the sample size of a single stage nonproportional stratified sample for an estimation problem concerned with a mean is

$$n = \frac{Z^2}{(\bar{x} - M)^2} \left(\sum_{h=1}^{k} W_h \hat{\sigma}_h \right)^2 \tag{A-5}$$

If our previous statements concerning the optimum allocation of a sample among strata are correct, it should also follow that a nonproportional stratified sample should require a smaller sample for the same error specification so long as strata variances are unequal. We may test this inference by working through our example again.

Substituting values and solving for overall sample size gives

$$n = \frac{Z^2}{(\bar{x} - M)^2} \left(\sum_{n=1}^{k} W_h \hat{\sigma}_h \right)^2$$

$$= \frac{1.64^2}{\$10.00^2} (.60 \times \$20.00 + .40 \times \$30.00)^2$$

$$= 16 \text{ (rounded to next larger number)}$$

This compares with a sample size of 17 ($n = 17$) for the proportional sample. The difference is small insofar as the example is concerned, but the point is illustrated.

The nonproportional sample is allocated among strata (using equation A-4) as

$$n_1 = \frac{16(750 \times \$20.00)}{(750 \times \$20.00) + (500 \times \$30.00)}$$

$$= 8$$

and

$$n_2 = 8.$$

The corresponding formula for the sample size for a nonproportional sample involving estimation of a proportion is

$$n = \frac{Z^2}{(p - P)^2} \left(\sum_{h=1}^{k} W_h \sqrt{P_h(1.0 - P_h)} \right)^2 \qquad \text{(A–6)}$$

The sample size for each stratum is found by the formula

$$n_h = \frac{W_h \sqrt{P_h(1.0 - P_h)}}{\sum_{h=1}^{k} W_h \sqrt{P_h(1.0 - P_h)}} \qquad \text{(A–7)}$$

The Bayesian Method of Determining Sample Size

A presentation of the Bayesian approach to determining sample size is presented in this section. The reader should have a clear understanding of the material presented in Chapter 3 of the text before studying the concepts that follow. The Bayesian approach is illustrated using the oil company direct-mail merchandising program described in Chapter 6. This allows a direct comparison of the traditional and Bayesian approaches to sample size determination.

The analyst for the oil company assigned to investigate the direct-mail merchandising program actually ran a Bayesian analysis to determine sample size. Based upon information obtained from other companies with similar programs, cost estimates supplied by the purchasing and accounting departments, and the combined judgments of management and the analyst, a conditional payoff table for order rates at intervals of 1 per cent from 0 to 9.0 per cent was prepared. This table showed that there was a .60 prior probability of the venture being profitable. Conditional on a profitable outcome, the expectation was that an average 5.0 per cent order rate would result with a net return of $60,000 for the three mailings. There was a .40 prior probability of a loss with a conditional expected order rate of 3.50 per cent. The conditional loss for the three mailings was $30,000. The two state payoff table incorporating these estimates is shown in Table A–1.

It was estimated that there would be a fixed cost of $1,000 for sampling and a variable cost of $2.50 per credit card holder included in the sample. The total estimated cost for a given sample size n is then

$$CS = \$1,000 + \$2.50n$$

Given these specifications, what size sample should have been taken?

Table A–1   Conditional Payoff Table for Three Mailings

	S_1 Order rate of 5.0%		S_2 Order rate of 3.5%	
	$P(S_1)$	Payoff	$P(S_2)$	Payoff
A_1—Start Program	.6	$60,000	.4	<$30,000>
A_2—Stop Consideration of Program	.6	0	.4	0

Principles, Method, and Specification Required for Bayesian Sample Size Determination

The principle involved in determining sample size using a Bayesian approach is to *choose the sample size that results in the greatest positive difference in the expected monetary value of the information to be obtained from the sample minus the cost of taking it*. This difference is called the expected net gain of sampling (*ENGS*). The principle is then to choose the sample size with the greatest *ENGS*.

How is *ENGS* for a given sample size determined? From the statement,

$$\text{expected net gain} = \text{expected monetary} - \text{cost of}$$
$$\text{of sampling} \qquad \text{value of information} \qquad \text{sampling}$$

or

$$ENGS = EMVII - CS$$

where *EMVII* is determined in the same way as developed in Chapter 3 and the cost of sampling (*CS*) is an estimate of sampling cost. In Chapter 3 it was shown that, for venture analysis problems,

$$EMVII = EVPI - \alpha|P(S_2)V_2| - \beta P(S_1)V_1 \text{ (equation 3–1)}.$$

Thus,

$$ENGS = [EVPI - \alpha|P(S_2)V_2| - \beta P(S_1)V_1] - CS \qquad (A–8)$$

where

$$EVPI = \text{expected value of perfect information} = |P(S_2)V_2|$$
$$\alpha = \text{probability of Type I error} = P(T_1|S_2)$$
$$\beta = \text{probability of Type II error} = P(T_2|S_1)$$

$V_2 =$ loss incurred if "go" action chosen and S_2 is actual market situation

$V_1 =$ profit realized if "go" action chosen and S_1 is actual market situation, and $P(S_2)$ and $P(S_1)$ are the prior probabilities of the states.

The terms in this equation represent the values that must be specified or otherwise determined. Inspection indicates that the terms in the bracketed portion of the equation are provided in a *conditional payoff table*, with the exception of α and β. Values for α and β must be provided from another source along with the estimate of the cost of sampling (CS).

In the example in Chapter 3 the conditional error probabilities α and β were assessed judgmentally and *specified*. Here they may be *determined* for each sample size. The method by which they may be determined becomes evident from Figure A–1. One need only determine the Z value for the distance from P_o to the break-even point to find Z_α. That is

$$Z_\alpha = \frac{P_0 - \text{Break-even Value}}{\sigma_{p_0}}$$

$$= \frac{P_0 - \text{Break-even Value}}{\sqrt{\dfrac{P_0(1.0 - P_0)}{n}}}$$

Similarly, Z_β may be found as

$$Z_\beta = \frac{\text{Break-even Value} - P_1}{\sigma_{p1}}$$

$$= \frac{\text{Break-even Value} - P_1}{\sqrt{\dfrac{P_1(1.0 - P_1)}{n}}}$$

The error probabilities α and β may then be found from their Z values by reference to Appendix B on page 713.

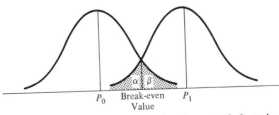

Figure A-1 Areas corresponding to α and β probabilities for sample size *n*.

The specifications required for the Bayesian approach to sample size determination for this kind of problem is then

(1) *the two state, two action conditional payoff table,* (2) *the values of* P_0, *and* P_1, *and* (3) *the estimated cost of sampling.*
The values for α and β do not have to be specified.

Determination of Sample Size

Before proceeding with the calculations required to determine sample size, it will be helpful to give the specified values so that reference will not have to be made.

The specified values were

$$V_1 = 3 \times \$20{,}000 = \$60{,}000$$
$$V_2 = 3 \times <\$10{,}000> = <\$30{,}000>$$
$$P(S_1) = .60$$
$$P(S_2) = .40$$
$$CS = \$1{,}000 + \$2.50n.$$

It makes no difference with what sample size we start. Suppose we begin with $n = 1{,}600$. When $n = 1{,}600$,

$$Z_\alpha = \frac{P_0 - \text{Break-even Value}}{\sqrt{\dfrac{P_0(1.0 - P_0)}{n}}}$$

$$= \frac{.035 - .040}{\sqrt{\dfrac{.035(1.00 - .035)}{1600}}}$$

$$= 1.09$$

Similarly,

$$Z_\beta = \frac{\text{Break-even Value} - P_1}{\sqrt{\dfrac{P_1(1.0 - P_1)}{n}}}$$

$$= \frac{.040 - .050}{\sqrt{\dfrac{.050(1.00 - .050)}{1600}}}$$

$$= -1.84$$

The probabilities for $Z_\alpha = 1.09$ and $Z_\beta = 1.84$ are, respectively (Appendix B)

$$\alpha = .138, \beta = .033$$

As developed in Chapter 3, *EMPVI* in this type of problem (two state, two action, with one action having zero payoffs) is

$$EMPVI = |P(S_0)V_0|$$

Substituting this and the other necessary values in equation A–1 we obtain

$$
\begin{aligned}
ENGS(n = 1,600) = {}& [EMVPI - \alpha|P(S_2)V_2| - \beta P(S_1)V_1] - CS \\
& |.4 \times <\$30,000>| - .138|.4 \times <\$30,000>| \\
& - .033(.6 \times \$60,000) - (\$1,000 + \$2.50 \times 1600) \\
= {}& \$4,156
\end{aligned}
$$

Suppose we now find *ENGS* for a value on either side of 1,600, say $n = 900$ and $n = 2,500$. Making the same calculations with 900 instead of 1,600 used for n gives $\alpha = .208$ and $\beta = .004$ and

$$ENGS \ (n = 900) = \$3,230$$

For $n = 2,500$ we obtain $\alpha = .087$, $\beta = .011$ and $ENGS \ (n = 2,500) = \$3,310$. Since $ENGS \ (n = 900)$ and $ENGS \ (n = 2,500)$ are both less than $ENGS \ (n = 1,600)$, the sample size must be greater than 900 and less than 2,500.

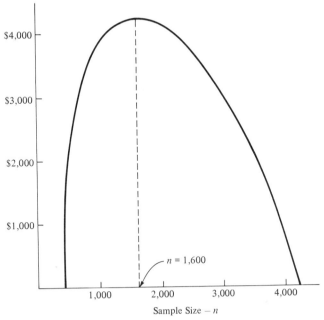

Figure A-2 Expected net gain from sampling—direct mail merchandising program.

By calculating *ENGS* for various sample sizes and plotting them, we obtain the curve shown in Figure A–2. As is evident from inspection of it, *ENGS* is maximized at about $n = 1,600$. This compares with a sample size of 1,932 arrived at by the traditional method in which α and β were specified (at the .05 level).

Note that the Bayesian method involves *calculating the expected cost of errors* $(\alpha P(S_2)|V_2|$ and $\beta P(S_1)V_1)$, *estimating sampling costs,* and subtracting both from the *expected value of perfect information.* None of these considerations were present in the traditional model.

A computer program for calculating the optimal sample size for problems of this kind is described in *Computer Programs for Elementary Decision Analysis,* a book by Robert Schlaifer.[1]

[1] Division of Research, Graduate School of Business Administration, Harvard University, 1971.

Appendix B
Area Under Normal Curve*

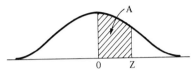

Z	A	Z	A	Z	A	Z	A
0.00	.0000	0.82	.2939	1.62	.4474	2.44	.4927
0.02	.0080	0.84	.2995	1.64	.4495	2.46	.4931
0.04	.0160	0.86	.3051	1.66	.4515	2.48	.4934
0.06	.0239	0.88	.3106	1.68	.4535	2.50	.4938
0.08	.0319	0.90	.3159	1.70	.4554	2.52	.4941
0.10	.0398	0.92	.3212	1.72	.4573	2.54	.4945
0.12	.0478	0.94	.3264	1.74	.4591	2.56	.4948
0.14	.0557	0.96	.3315	1.76	.4608	2.58	.4951
0.16	.0636	0.98	.3365	1.78	.4625	2.60	.4953
0.18	.0714	1.00	.3413	1.80	.4641	2.62	.4956
0.20	.0793	1.02	.3461	1.82	.4656	2.64	.4959
0.22	.0871	1.04	.3508	1.84	.4671	2.66	.4961
0.24	.0948	1.06	.3554	1.86	.4686	2.68	.4963
0.26	.1026	1.08	.3599	1.88	.4699	2.70	.4965
0.28	.1103	1.10	.3643	1.90	.4713	2.72	.4967
0.30	.1179	1.12	.3686	1.92	.4726	2.74	.4969
0.32	.1255	1.14	.3729	1.94	.4738	2.76	.4971
0.34	.1331	1.16	.3770	1.96	.4750	2.78	.4973
0.36	.1406	1.18	.3810	1.98	.4761	2.80	.4974
0.38	.1480	1.20	.3849	2.00	.4772	2.82	.4976
0.40	.1554	1.22	.3888	2.02	.4783	2.84	.4977
0.42	.1628	1.24	.3925	2.04	.4793	2.86	.4979
0.44	.1700	1.26	.3962	2.06	.4803	2.88	.4980
0.46	.1772	1.28	.3997	2.08	.4812	2.90	.4981
0.48	.1844	1.30	.4032	2.10	.4821	2.92	.4982
0.50	.1915	1.32	.4066	2.12	.4830	2.94	.4984
0.52	.1985	1.34	.4099	2.14	.4838	2.96	.4985
0.54	.2054	1.36	.4131	2.16	.4846	2.98	.4986
0.56	.2123	1.38	.4162	2.18	.4854	3.00	.4987
0.58	.2190	1.40	.4192	2.20	.4861	3.05	.4989
0.60	.2257	1.42	.4222	2.22	.4868	3.10	.4990
0.62	.2324	1.44	.4251	2.24	.4875	3.15	.4992
0.64	.2389	1.46	.4279	2.26	.4881	3.20	.4993
0.66	.2454	1.48	.4306	2.28	.4887	3.25	.4994
0.68	.2517	1.50	.4332	2.30	.4893	3.30	.4995
0.70	.2580	1.52	.4357	2.32	.4898	3.35	.4996
0.72	.2642	1.54	.4382	2.34	.4904	3.40	.4997
0.74	.2704	1.56	.4406	2.36	.4909	3.45	.4997
0.76	.2764	1.58	.4429	2.38	.4913	3.50	.4998
0.78	.2823			2.40	.4918	3.55	.4998
0.80	.2881	1.60	.4452	2.42	.4922	3.60	.4998

*Source: Adapted from *Handbook of Mathematical Functions With Formulas, Graphs, and Mathematical Tables*, U.S. Department of Commerce, National Bureau of Standards, Applied Mathematics Series 55, June 1964, pp. 966–972.

Appendix C
Table of Present Values

Present Value of $1 Received at the End of Period: $PV = (1 + r)^{-t}$

Years Hence	1%	2%	4%	6%	8%	10%	12%	14%	15%	16%	18%	20%
1	0.990	0.980	0.962	0.943	0.926	0.909	0.893	0.877	0.870	0.862	0.847	0.833
2	0.980	0.961	0.925	0.890	0.857	0.826	0.797	0.769	0.756	0.743	0.718	0.694
3	0.971	0.942	0.889	0.840	0.794	0.751	0.712	0.675	0.658	0.641	0.609	0.579
4	0.961	0.924	0.855	0.792	0.735	0.683	0.636	0.592	0.572	0.552	0.516	0.482
5	0.951	0.906	0.822	0.747	0.681	0.621	0.567	0.519	0.497	0.476	0.437	0.402
6	0.942	0.888	0.790	0.705	0.630	0.564	0.507	0.456	0.432	0.410	0.370	0.335
7	0.933	0.871	0.760	0.665	0.583	0.513	0.452	0.400	0.376	0.354	0.314	0.279
8	0.923	0.853	0.731	0.627	0.540	0.467	0.404	0.351	0.327	0.305	0.266	0.233
9	0.914	0.837	0.703	0.592	0.500	0.424	0.361	0.308	0.284	0.263	0.225	0.194
10	0.905	0.820	0.676	0.558	0.463	0.386	0.322	0.270	0.247	0.227	0.191	0.162
11	0.896	0.804	0.650	0.527	0.429	0.350	0.287	0.237	0.215	0.195	0.162	0.135
12	0.887	0.788	0.625	0.497	0.397	0.319	0.257	0.208	0.187	0.168	0.137	0.112
13	0.879	0.773	0.601	0.469	0.368	0.290	0.229	0.182	0.163	0.145	0.116	0.093
14	0.870	0.758	0.577	0.442	0.340	0.263	0.205	0.160	0.141	0.125	0.090	0.078
15	0.861	0.743	0.555	0.417	0.315	0.239	0.183	0.140	0.123	0.108	0.084	0.065
16	0.853	0.728	0.534	0.394	0.292	0.218	0.163	0.123	0.107	0.093	0.071	0.054
17	0.844	0.714	0.513	0.371	0.270	0.198	0.146	0.108	0.093	0.080	0.060	0.045
18	0.836	0.700	0.494	0.350	0.250	0.180	0.130	0.095	0.081	0.069	0.051	0.038
19	0.828	0.686	0.475	0.331	0.232	0.164	0.116	0.083	0.070	0.050	0.043	0.031
20	0.820	0.673	0.456	0.312	0.215	0.149	0.104	0.073	0.061	0.051	0.037	0.026
21	0.811	0.660	0.439	0.294	0.199	0.135	0.093	0.064	0.053	0.044	0.031	0.022
22	0.803	0.647	0.422	0.278	0.184	0.123	0.083	0.056	0.046	0.038	0.026	0.018
23	0.795	0.634	0.406	0.262	0.170	0.112	0.074	0.049	0.040	0.033	0.022	0.015
24	0.788	0.622	0.390	0.247	0.158	0.102	0.066	0.043	0.035	0.028	0.019	0.013
25	0.780	0.610	0.375	0.233	0.146	0.092	0.059	0.038	0.030	0.024	0.016	0.010
26	0.772	0.598	0.361	0.220	0.135	0.084	0.053	0.033	0.026	0.021	0.014	0.009
27	0.764	0.586	0.347	0.207	0.125	0.076	0.047	0.029	0.023	0.018	0.011	0.007
28	0.757	0.574	0.333	0.196	0.116	0.069	0.042	0.026	0.020	0.016	0.010	0.006
29	0.749	0.563	0.321	0.185	0.107	0.063	0.037	0.022	0.017	0.014	0.008	0.005
30	0.742	0.552	0.308	0.174	0.099	0.057	0.033	0.020	0.015	0.012	0.007	0.004

Appendix D
Table of Values of Chi Square

Probability of χ^2 occurring because of sampling variation

df	.99	.98	.95	.90	.80	.70	.50	.30	.20	.10	.05	.02	.01	.001
1	.00016	.00063	.0039	.016	.064	.15	.46	1.07	1.64	2.71	3.84	5.41	6.64	10.83
2	.02	.04	.10	.21	.45	.71	1.39	2.41	3.22	4.60	5.99	7.82	9.21	13.82
3	.12	.18	.35	.58	1.00	1.42	2.37	3.66	4.64	6.25	7.82	9.84	11.34	16.27
4	.30	.43	.71	1.06	1.65	2.20	3.36	4.88	5.99	7.78	9.49	11.67	13.28	18.46
5	.55	.75	1.14	1.61	2.34	3.00	4.35	6.06	7.29	9.24	11.07	13.39	15.09	20.52
6	.87	1.13	1.64	2.20	3.07	3.83	5.35	7.23	8.56	10.64	12.59	15.03	16.81	22.46
7	1.24	1.56	2.17	2.83	3.82	4.67	6.35	8.38	9.80	12.02	14.07	16.62	18.48	24.32
8	1.65	2.03	2.73	3.49	4.59	5.53	7.34	9.52	11.03	13.36	15.51	18.17	20.09	26.12
9	2.09	2.53	3.32	4.17	5.38	6.39	8.34	10.66	12.24	14.68	16.92	19.68	21.67	27.88
10	2.56	3.06	3.94	4.86	6.18	7.27	9.34	11.78	13.44	15.99	18.31	21.16	23.21	29.59
11	3.05	3.61	4.58	5.53	6.99	8.15	10.34	12.90	14.63	17.28	19.68	22.62	24.72	31.26
12	3.57	4.18	5.23	6.30	7.81	9.03	11.34	14.01	15.81	18.55	21.03	24.05	26.22	32.91
13	4.11	4.76	5.89	7.04	8.63	9.93	12.34	15.12	16.98	19.81	22.36	25.47	27.69	34.53
14	4.66	5.37	6.57	7.79	9.47	10.82	13.34	16.22	18.15	21.06	23.68	26.87	29.14	36.12
15	5.23	5.98	7.26	8.55	10.31	11.72	14.34	17.32	19.31	22.31	25.00	28.26	30.58	37.70
16	5.81	6.61	7.96	9.31	11.15	12.62	15.34	18.42	20.46	23.54	26.30	29.63	32.00	39.29
17	6.41	7.26	8.67	10.08	12.00	13.53	16.34	19.51	21.62	24.77	27.59	31.00	33.41	40.75
18	7.02	7.91	9.39	10.86	12.86	14.44	17.34	20.60	22.76	25.99	28.87	32.35	34.80	42.31
19	7.63	8.57	10.12	11.65	13.72	15.35	18.34	21.69	23.90	27.20	30.14	33.69	36.19	43.82
20	8.26	9.24	10.85	12.44	14.58	16.27	19.34	22.78	25.04	28.41	31.41	35.02	37.57	45.32
21	8.90	9.92	11.59	13.24	15.44	17.18	20.34	23.86	26.17	29.62	32.67	36.34	38.93	46.80
22	9.54	10.60	12.34	14.04	16.31	18.10	21.24	24.94	27.30	30.81	33.92	37.66	40.29	48.27
23	10.20	11.29	13.09	14.85	17.19	19.02	22.34	26.02	28.43	32.01	35.17	38.97	41.64	49.73
24	10.86	11.99	13.85	15.66	18.06	19.94	23.34	27.10	29.55	33.20	36.42	40.27	42.98	51.18
25	11.52	12.70	14.61	16.47	18.94	20.87	24.34	28.17	30.68	34.38	37.65	41.57	44.31	52.62
26	12.20	13.41	15.38	17.29	19.82	21.79	25.34	29.25	31.80	35.56	38.88	42.86	45.64	54.05
27	12.88	14.12	16.15	18.11	20.70	22.72	26.34	30.32	32.91	36.74	40.11	44.14	46.96	55.48
28	13.56	14.85	16.93	18.94	21.59	23.65	27.34	31.39	34.03	37.92	41.34	45.42	48.28	56.89
29	14.26	15.57	17.71	19.77	22.48	24.58	28.34	32.46	35.14	39.09	42.56	46.69	49.59	58.30
30	14.95	16.31	18.49	20.00	23.36	25.51	29.34	33.53	36.25	40.26	43.77	47.96	50.89	59.70

Source: R. A. Fisher, *Statistical Methods for Research Workers*, 14th ed. (Copyright © 1972 by Hafner Press, a Division of Macmillan Publishing Co., Inc.)

How to use the table and interpret the probability found:

1. Find the *degrees of freedom* (df) of the contingency table for the problem by multiplying the number of rows minus one $(r - 1)$ times the number of columns minus one $(k - 1)$:

$$df = (r - 1)(k - 1)$$

2. Look up the probability for the number of degrees of freedom and the calculated value of χ^2, approximating if necessary. This will be the *probability that the differences between the observed and the expected values occurred because of sampling variation.*

Appendix E
Table of Random Numbers

```
69 47 26 60 28 33 65 51 63 91 41 07 85 54 48 47 89 89 28 16 53 63 25 95 88
36 14 60 08 90 71 30 34 43 18 96 70 86 34 51 06 51 11 14 03 33 67 85 71 90
62 16 07 76 94 09 32 30 74 76 86 78 75 52 70 37 57 13 08 29 32 23 91 70 56
75 46 96 99 49 03 54 14 38 20 58 77 01 14 85 16 66 99 28 95 46 57 76 48 08
32 53 72 54 45 60 27 95 50 61 94 74 24 19 78 12 00 75 85 97 32 75 62 45 62
66 09 42 47 16 57 33 42 44 67 41 75 32 43 09 79 78 39 01 27 21 30 48 49 20
12 56 30 19 62 47 50 43 45 05 13 13 79 58 36 73 10 71 17 77 56 92 66 44 72
93 63 44 66 76 44 76 82 75 38 09 46 79 96 66 80 57 46 23 99 32 05 27 34 43
99 96 86 08 57 19 62 73 25 37 61 76 95 17 07 61 40 57 34 44 54 85 84 40 08
92 95 55 56 71 43 33 26 00 73 43 15 01 66 82 74 35 10 28 92 17 90 92 95 63
88 77 70 08 13 16 60 87 60 67 80 97 39 58 27 90 59 22 75 49 43 63 83 03 90
71 43 59 44 65 08 48 18 95 88 73 16 98 95 53 70 49 86 71 25 87 37 88 73 79
81 71 50 68 32 00 95 95 39 17 83 77 07 95 65 90 61 10 52 48 74 48 32 49 54
85 35 17 54 65 57 99 07 07 65 21 93 79 91 42 77 75 10 96 19 13 78 19 34 56
97 98 88 17 00 58 81 12 61 35 25 42 21 18 68 84 37 73 30 88 85 19 59 16 47
40 50 04 89 66 51 21 91 82 71 15 80 17 88 38 27 49 65 30 34 49 28 22 14 67
22 73 51 48 82 14 87 85 46 89 19 46 67 54 20 61 33 11 68 14 55 25 25 25 92
21 29 99 31 69 64 45 42 00 84 18 46 43 44 30 16 40 07 95 26 63 24 69 37 48
18 09 80 67 79 82 33 35 05 92 31 34 64 39 62 35 51 99 31 87 41 61 85 97 94
26 72 96 60 46 44 75 28 54 62 38 92 97 05 53 34 53 64 56 43 93 64 05 68 42
66 28 80 86 71 43 11 46 59 63 17 27 36 56 92 37 11 11 86 57 44 98 34 87 82
62 99 58 99 85 78 25 10 31 75 63 00 87 08 78 22 12 12 52 85 49 86 18 07 70
55 60 57 69 48 19 41 83 50 67 59 12 99 19 02 00 28 19 08 11 96 28 36 61 43
76 62 89 95 48 58 09 12 03 61 59 06 54 85 46 84 63 96 51 96 65 12 98 54 11
94 66 26 20 23 40 59 39 40 32 15 16 54 81 79 63 12 78 47 16 58 70 58 97 02
50 73 51 48 98 54 66 93 14 37 81 30 87 07 65 99 55 12 72 94 81 51 49 09 37
94 11 04 04 22 92 49 83 08 57 01 85 53 53 23 75 41 14 29 11 66 15 93 94 90
97 87 81 59 36 66 29 96 73 78 67 53 01 98 78 74 15 70 42 62 68 10 52 98 34
46 50 73 23 03 04 37 49 13 66 97 24 11 63 83 18 23 87 99 66 21 91 79 12 63
43 85 00 91 54 39 67 34 53 17 21 10 43 16 80 81 09 79 08 82 51 07 40 95 83
18 20 00 87 87 11 61 72 26 45 62 83 74 27 48 29 35 71 96 66 24 78 91 94 06
68 94 94 68 84 27 04 78 14 17 14 84 79 82 01 96 90 62 31 73 19 12 96 97 05
04 19 46 04 41 94 03 09 64 84 26 45 84 77 37 82 23 36 75 78 06 25 19 44 15
18 58 79 01 03 59 56 25 50 68 29 21 93 72 00 20 31 12 49 91 03 44 85 01 90
26 87 32 08 99 64 30 36 58 90 58 70 80 67 30 42 75 00 20 65 26 58 88 47 67
90 20 49 76 36 22 43 33 57 79 13 28 77 43 95 15 19 29 43 38 90 92 24 43 00
68 93 78 50 75 23 01 32 08 15 82 88 68 41 71 56 17 53 39 40 70 98 59 39 46
23 61 67 72 61 78 97 23 52 21 04 28 70 85 52 07 48 39 83 91 49 36 55 45 83
36 81 30 45 20 87 66 57 46 10 63 90 44 51 16 34 99 76 34 99 29 73 43 68 75
64 82 04 03 25 82 97 21 68 67 47 59 76 41 65 23 03 25 96 48 23 25 04 85 76
67 92 73 22 99 94 89 62 03 72 78 24 18 67 17 97 70 95 77 12 27 85 69 67 31
05 45 92 49 35 00 70 97 89 69 11 90 73 09 40 37 10 16 23 31 67 28 57 94 01
33 29 57 36 32 45 53 75 40 28 99 21 70 95 70 42 17 58 80 35 02 21 44 63 12
91 42 82 67 44 48 86 50 23 86 56 80 70 72 60 20 71 43 46 05 08 23 02 87 65
24 98 47 67 18 87 74 90 59 94 35 56 47 21 76 38 48 64 71 93 50 38 79 12 10
62 91 99 52 60 90 70 65 91 82 81 09 39 55 97 31 79 48 61 18 48 33 50 08 00
74 58 79 34 74 09 90 75 69 72 05 17 86 75 39 43 84 44 89 66 61 55 09 08 27
76 88 26 52 23 09 90 35 96 91 04 09 24 83 47 12 27 77 65 87 07 99 92 92 70
40 32 79 41 51 66 56 78 85 99 92 43 96 55 24 50 07 25 50 35 77 62 65 21 17
15 32 70 90 68 94 21 44 85 64 37 87 37 68 64 14 45 65 33 14 33 99 83 60 23
14 03 62 04 19 90 20 87 62 99 75 87 38 39 63 70 30 92 95 93 65 23 13 78 10
10 16 42 17 06 50 75 65 87 66 47 88 93 43 63 18 79 80 71 72 36 69 63 64 76
76 10 61 42 98 08 79 97 47 21 36 73 41 15 98 69 51 74 85 37 84 64 20 56 78
```

Appendix F
Percentile of the t distribution
(one- and two-tailed tests)*

d.f.	P = .90 (.45)	.80 (.40)	.70 (.35)	.60 (.30)	.50 (.12)	.40 (.20)
1	.158	.325	.510	.727	1.000	1.376
2	.142	.289	.445	.617	.816	1.061
3	.137	.277	.424	.584	.765	.978
4	.134	.271	.414	.569	.741	.941
5	.132	.267	.408	.559	.727	.920
6	.131	.265	.404	.553	.718	.906
7	.130	.263	.402	.549	.711	.896
8	.130	.262	.399	.546	.706	.889
9	.129	.261	.398	.543	.703	.883
10	.129	.260	.397	.542	.700	.879
11	.129	.260	.396	.540	.697	.876
12	.128	.259	.395	.539	.695	.873
13	.128	.259	.394	.538	.694	.870
14	.128	.258	.393	.537	.692	.868
15	.128	.258	.393	.536	.691	.866
16	.128	.258	.392	.535	.690	.865
17	.128	.257	.392	.534	.689	.863
18	.127	.257	.392	.534	.688	.862
19	.127	.257	.391	.533	.688	.861
20	.127	.257	.391	.533	.687	.860
21	.127	.257	.391	.532	.686	.859
22	.127	.256	.390	.532	.686	.858
23	.127	.256	.390	.532	.685	.858
24	.127	.256	.390	.531	.685	.857
25	.127	.256	.390	.531	.684	.856
26	.127	.256	.390	.531	.684	.856
27	.127	.256	.389	.531	.684	.855
28	.127	.256	.389	.530	.683	.855
29	.127	.256	.389	.530	.683	.854
30	.127	.256	.389	.530	.683	.854

Source: R. A. Fisher, *Statistical Methods for Research Workers*, 14th ed. (Copyright © 1972 by Hafner Press, a Division of Macmillan Publishing Co., Inc.)

* The p in parentheses is for a one-tailed test.

.30 (.15)	.20 (.10)	.10 (.05)	.050 (.025)	.02 (.01)	.01 (.005)
1.963	3.078	6.314	12.706	31.821	63.657
1.386	1.886	2.920	4.303	6.965	9.925
1.250	1.638	2.353	3.182	4.541	5.841
1.190	1.533	2.132	2.776	3.747	4.604
1.156	1.476	2.015	2.571	3.365	4.032
1.134	1.440	1.943	2.447	3.143	3.707
1.119	1.415	1.895	2.365	2.998	3.499
1.108	1.397	1.860	2.306	2.896	3.355
1.100	1.383	1.833	2.262	2.821	3.250
1.093	1.372	1.812	2.228	2.764	3.169
1.088	1.363	1.796	2.201	2.718	3.106
1.083	1.356	1.782	2.179	2.681	3.055
1.079	1.350	1.771	2.160	2.650	3.012
1.076	1.345	1.761	2.145	2.624	2.977
1.074	1.341	1.753	2.131	2.602	2.947
1.071	1.337	1.746	2.120	2.583	2.921
1.069	1.333	1.740	2.110	2.567	2.898
1.067	1.330	1.734	2.101	2.552	2.878
1.066	1.328	1.729	2.093	2.539	2.861
1.064	1.325	1.725	2.086	2.528	2.845
1.063	1.323	1.721	2.080	2.518	2.831
1.061	1.321	1.717	2.074	2.508	2.819
1.060	1.319	1.714	2.069	2.500	2.807
1.059	1.318	1.711	2.064	2.492	2.797
1.058	1.316	1.708	2.060	2.485	2.787
1.058	1.315	1.706	2.056	2.479	2.779
1.057	1.314	1.703	2.052	2.473	2.771
1.056	1.313	1.701	2.048	2.467	2.763
1.055	1.311	1.699	2.045	2.462	2.756
1.055	1.310	1.697	2.042	2.457	2.750

Index

I. Intro
II. Analysis
    A) Prob Def
    B) Design
    c) Implementation
    D Analysis & Interpretation

III. Alternatives
IV. Summary